Mastering iOS 11 Programming

Second Edition

Build professional-grade iOS applications with Swift 4 and Xcode 9

Donny Wals

BIRMINGHAM - MUMBAI

Mastering iOS 11 Programming

Second Edition

First published: December 2016

Second edition: October 2017

Production reference: 1251017

Published by Packt Publishing Ltd.
Livery Place
35 Livery Street
Birmingham
B3 2PB, UK.
ISBN 978-1-78839-823-7

www.packtpub.com

Credits

Author
Donny Wals

Reviewer
Alexandre Freire García

Acquisition Editor
Nitin Dasan

Contente Development Editor
Sreeja Nair

Technical **Editor**
Surabhi Kulkarni

Copy Editor
Safis Editing

Project Coordinator
Sheejal Shah

Proofreader
Safis Editing

Indexer
Rekha Nair

Graphics
Jason Monteiro

Production Coordinator
Melwyn D'sa

About the Author

Donny Wals is a passionate, curious, developer from The Netherlands. Ever since he started his communications and multimedia design studies in Amsterdam, he knew that he didn't just want to build great websites and apps, but also transfer knowledge to his peers and newcomers. He got involved with coaching, mentoring, and assisting in his freshman year.

During his final two years at college, he's been a teacher in web development and spent most of his free time exploring iOS and Objective-C. When Swift was first announced, it didn't take long for him to start playing around with it, and after just a few months of learning and experimenting Donny became the lead iOS developer for the start-up where he'd been working at the time.

As an active member of the iOS-developers Slack community, Donny is always up for helping out people with their code and sharing his own knowledge with his peers.

First and foremost, I would like to thank Dorien for putting up with me while writing this book. She has not only accepted that I spent many hours working on this book instead of spending time with her, even during a much-deserved holiday to the Belgian Ardennes, but she actively supported and encouraged me constantly.
Also, I want to thank my parents, friends and everybody that has given me advice, feedback, tips and sometimes some much-needed distraction while writing this book. I wouldn't have been able to finish this book without all the wonderful people around me supporting me.
A big thank you goes out to Smeet Thakkar for reaching out to me about writing this book. In addition to Smeet, I also want to thank Sreeja Nair for all the hard work and guidance while working on this book.
Lastly, I want to thank you. If you're reading this, you are one of the people that make it possible for me have the amazing adventure of writing this book for you.

About the Reviewer

Alexandre Freire is the reviewer of this book. He is a Spanish iOS developer and the author of several software development courses. At the young age of 26, Alexandre sold his own startup (Apparcar). When he is not coding, you can usually find him supporting Deportivo de A Coruña--his favourite football team--or exploring the most beautiful landscapes of Galicia with his family. You can connect to Alexandre on Twitter at `@xandrefreire`.

www.PacktPub.com

For support files and downloads related to your book, please visit `www.PacktPub.com`.

Did you know that Packt offers eBook versions of every book published, with PDF and ePub files available? You can upgrade to the eBook version at `www.PacktPub.com` and as a print book customer, you are entitled to a discount on the eBook copy. Get in touch with us at `service@packtpub.com` for more details.

At `www.PacktPub.com`, you can also read a collection of free technical articles, sign up for a range of free newsletters and receive exclusive discounts and offers on Packt books and eBooks.

`https://www.packtpub.com/mapt`

Get the most in-demand software skills with Mapt. Mapt gives you full access to all Packt books and video courses, as well as industry-leading tools to help you plan your personal development and advance your career.

Why subscribe?

- Fully searchable across every book published by Packt
- Copy and paste, print, and bookmark content
- On demand and accessible via a web browser

Customer Feedback

Thanks for purchasing this Packt book. At Packt, quality is at the heart of our editorial process. To help us improve, please leave us an honest review on this book's Amazon page at `https://www.amazon.com/dp/1788398238`.

If you'd like to join our team of regular reviewers, you can email us at `customerreviews@packtpub.com`. We award our regular reviewers with free eBooks and videos in exchange for their valuable feedback. Help us be relentless in improving our products!

Table of Contents

Preface

When Apple launched Swift in 2014, the iOS ecosystem became more accessible than it had ever been for developers. Being able to write apps with Swift's beautiful, readable, and straightforward syntax instead of having to write clunky Objective-C code suddenly enabled a lot of people to play around with iOS development. For me, Swift sparked a renewed interest in developing iOS applications, and the new passion has remained ever since.

This book will hopefully transfer some of that passion to you. This book is written to match my personal preferred way of learning, which is learning by doing. In this book, you'll find examples of applications that you might actually want to build some day. The problems that are tackled in this book are real and practical. This book doesn't cover every single framework that you can use in your apps; there are simply way too many. Instead, the focus is on understanding how you can navigate Apple's documentation, how you can refactor your code, and how you can solve real-world development problems.

If you have tried to build something for iOS before but never really managed to make a full blown app, or if you're looking to expand your knowledge with some iOS-11 specific topics, this book is perfect for you. We'll step beyond the basics and learn everything you need to know to build high-quality applications.

What this book covers

`Chapter 1`, *UITableView Touch Up*, is all about table views. Most iOS developers will hVE already seen a table view in their attempts at learning iOS. This chapter is intended as a warm-up for what's to come in the next chapters.

`Chapter 2`, *A Better Layout with UICollectionView*, informs that the table view's superpowered sibling is the collection view. This chapter will cover implementing a collection view and writing a custom layout object for it.

`Chapter 3`, *Creating a Contact Details Page*, says that if you're building apps, you'll need to make them work on many different screen sizes. This chapter will show you how to use auto layout in order to create beautiful, adaptive layouts.

`Chapter 4`, *Immersing Your Users with Animation*, informs that the best apps set themselves apart with beautiful and subtle animations. You'll learn multiple animation techniques, and to top it off, you'll learn how to create custom transitions between view controllers.

`Chapter 5`, *Improving Your Code with Value Types*, explains the difference between reference and value types. You'll learn why it's a good idea to use value types as much as possible.

`Chapter 6`, *Making Your Code More Flexible with Protocols and Generics*, explains that once you've learned about value types, their possibilities and their limitations, it's only logical to learn about protocol-oriented programming. This style of programming was introduced by Apple and serves as a way to avoid complex inheritance hierarchies and to make code clearer and more testable.

`Chapter 7`, *Refactoring the HelloContacts Application*, teaches you to apply the lessons learned from the previous two chapters to improve an app you've already worked on.

`Chapter 8`, *Adding Core Data to Your App*, says that many apps have a need to store data into a database. This chapter introduces Apple's CoreData framework as a way to include a database for user data in your app.

`Chapter 9`, *Storing and Querying Data in Core Data*, covers how to store data in the database you set up in the previous chapter. We'll also cover querying this data using fetch requests and predicates.

`Chapter 10`, *Fetching and Displaying Data from the Network*, showcases how to make use of web APIs to fetch and display data.

`Chapter 11`, *Being Proactive with Background Fetch*, teaches that iOS allows apps to refresh and load data in the background. This chapter covers how to do this, and briefly introduces you to dispatch groups.

`Chapter 12`, *Enriching Apps with the Camera, Motion, and Location*, shows how to build a login screen for an art app that uses several sensors in the iPhone to create a more immersive experience.

`Chapter 13`, *Extending the World with ARKit*, demonstrates how you can use Apple's groundbreaking ARKit framework to build an augmented reality experience.

`Chapter 14`, *Exchanging Data with Drag and Drop*, takes you through how to augment an app to allow users to drag contents from your app to other apps and vice versa.

`Chapter 15`, *Making Smarter Apps with CoreML*, teaches everything you should know about the CoreML framework. You'll implement a machine learning model that recognizes dominant objects in a scene.

`Chapter 16`, *Increasing Your App's Discoverability with Spotlight and Universal Links*, explores how you can make an iOS index for your app's contents to make it available through the powerful Spotlight search index.

`Chapter 17`, *Instant Information with a Notification Center Widget*, says that developers can add widgets to the Notification Center to disclose quick information to users; this chapter will teach you how.

`Chapter 18`, *Implementing Rich Notifications*, is a walk through everything you need to know about providing a great notification experience for your users. We'll cover both the UI extension and content extension.

`Chapter 19`, *Extending iMessage*, shows how to build a sticker app for iMessage or something more complex.

`Chapter 20`, *Integrating Your App with Siri*, covers how to integrate the SiriKit APIs in your own applications. This enables you to integrate your app deeply into the iOS platform.

`Chapter 21`, *Ensuring App Quality with Tests*, focuses on testing an often overlooked aspect of developing an app. This chapter will teach you how to set up tests for your application.

`Chapter 22`, *Discovering Bottlenecks with Instruments*, takes you through how to profile your app's performance with instruments.

`Chapter 23`, *Offloading Tasks with Operations and GCD*, informs that apps perform increasingly complex tasks. This chapter teaches you how to ensure that complex or slow tasks don't freeze your user interface.

`Chapter 24`, *Wrapping Up the Development Cycle and Submitting to the App Store*, teaches how to distribute your app to beta testers through TestFlight and how to submit your app for review in order to publish it to the App Store.

What you need for this book

All the code samples are written in Swift 4.0 with Xcode 9; you'll need a Mac that can run Xcode 9. In order to test all of the code samples in this book, you'll need an iOS device that runs iOS 11 and a payed subscription to Apple's developer program.

Who this book is for

This book is for developers who have some experience with iOS and want to take their skills to the next level by unlocking the full potential of the latest version of iOS with Swift for building impressive applications. It is assumed that you have some knowledge of iOS development throughout the book.

Conventions

In this book, you will find a number of text styles that distinguish between different kinds of information. Here are some examples of these styles and an explanation of their meaning.

Code words in text, database table names, folder names, filenames, file extensions, pathnames, dummy URLs, user input, and Twitter handles are shown as follows: "Once you have your app configured, open the `Main.storyboard` file. This is where you will create your `UITableView` and create its layout."

A block of code is set as follows:

```
func doSomething(completionHandler: Int -> Void) {
    // perform some actions
    var resultingValue = theResultOfSomeAction()
    completionHandler(resultingValue)
}
```

When we wish to draw your attention to a particular part of a code block, the relevant lines or items are set in bold:

```
func tableView(_ tableView: UITableView, cellForRowAt indexPath: IndexPath)
->
  UITableViewCell {
    let cell = tableView.dequeueReusableCell(withIdentifier: "contactCell")
as!
      ContactTableViewCell
    let contact = contacts[indexPath.row]

    cell.nameLabel.text = "(contact.givenName) (contact.familyName)"
    if let imageData = contact.imageData where contact.imageDataAvailable {
        cell.contactImage.image = UIImage(data: imageData)
    }

    return cell
}
```

New terms and **important words** are shown in bold. Words that you see on the screen, for example, in menus or dialog boxes, appear in the text like this: "You can inspect these constraints in detail in the **Document Outline** on the right."

Warnings or important notes appear in a box like this.

Tips and tricks appear like this.

Reader feedback

Feedback from our readers is always welcome. Let us know what you think about this book-what you liked or disliked. Reader feedback is important for us as it helps us develop titles that you will really get the most out of. To send us general feedback, simply e-mail `feedback@packtpub.com`, and mention the book's title in the subject of your message. If there is a topic that you have expertise in and you are interested in either writing or contributing to a book, see our author guide at `www.packtpub.com/authors`.

Customer support

Now that you are the proud owner of a Packt book, we have a number of things to help you to get the most from your purchase.

Downloading the example code

You can download the example code files for this book from your account at `http://www.packtpub.com`. If you purchased this book elsewhere, you can visit `http://www.packtpub.com/support` and register to have the files e-mailed directly to you. You can download the code files by following these steps:

1. Log in or register to our website using your e-mail address and password.
2. Hover the mouse pointer on the **SUPPORT** tab at the top.
3. Click on **Code Downloads & Errata**.
4. Enter the name of the book in the **Search** box.

5. Select the book for which you're looking to download the code files.
6. Choose from the drop-down menu where you purchased this book from.
7. Click on **Code Download**.

Once the file is downloaded, please make sure that you unzip or extract the folder using the latest version of:

- WinRAR / 7-Zip for Windows
- Zipeg / iZip / UnRarX for Mac
- 7-Zip / PeaZip for Linux

The code bundle for the book is also hosted on GitHub at `https://github.com/PacktPublishing/Mastering-iOS-11-Programming`. We also have other code bundles from our rich catalog of books and videos available at `https://github.com/PacktPublishing/`. Check them out!

Downloading the color images of this book

We also provide you with a PDF file that has color images of the screenshots/diagrams used in this book. The color images will help you better understand the changes in the output. You can download this file from `https://www.packtpub.com/sites/default/files/downloads/MasteringiOS11Programming_ColorImages.pdf`.

Errata

Although we have taken every care to ensure the accuracy of our content, mistakes do happen. If you find a mistake in one of our books-maybe a mistake in the text or the code-we would be grateful if you could report this to us. By doing so, you can save other readers from frustration and help us improve subsequent versions of this book. If you find any errata, please report them by visiting `http://www.packtpub.com/submit-errata`, selecting your book, clicking on the **Errata Submission Form** link, and entering the details of your errata. Once your errata are verified, your submission will be accepted and the errata will be uploaded to our website or added to any list of existing errata under the Errata section of that title. To view the previously submitted errata, go to `https://www.packtpub.com/books/content/support` and enter the name of the book in the search field. The required information will appear under the **Errata** section.

Piracy

Piracy of copyrighted material on the Internet is an ongoing problem across all media. At Packt, we take the protection of our copyright and licenses very seriously. If you come across any illegal copies of our works in any form on the Internet, please provide us with the location address or website name immediately so that we can pursue a remedy. Please contact us at `copyright@packtpub.com` with a link to the suspected pirated material. We appreciate your help in protecting our authors and our ability to bring you valuable content.

Questions

If you have a problem with any aspect of this book, you can contact us at `questions@packtpub.com`, and we will do our best to address the problem.

1

UITableView Touch Up

Chances are that you have built a simple app before, or maybe you tried but didn't quite succeed. If you have, there's a good probability that you have used `UITableView`. The `UITableView` is a core component in many applications on the iOS platform. Virtually all applications that display a list of some sort make use of `UITableView`.

Because `UITableView` is such an important component in the world of iOS, I want you to dive in to it straightaway. You may or may not have looked at `UITableView` before, but that's OK. You'll be up to speed in no time and you'll learn how this component achieves that smooth 60 **frames per second** scrolling that users know and love. If your app can maintain a steady 60 fps, your app will feel more responsive and scrolling will feel perfectly smooth to users, which is exactly what you want.

In addition to covering the basics of `UITableView`, like how a `UITableView` uses a pattern called delegation to obtain information about the contents it should display, you'll learn how to make use of `Contacts.framework` to build an application that shows a list of your users' contacts. Much like the native Contacts app does on iOS.

`UITableView` makes use of cells to display its contents. In this chapter, you will create a cell with a custom layout to display the user's contacts. You will learn to do so using Auto Layout. Auto Layout is a technique that will be used throughout this book because it's an important part of every iOS developer's tool belt. If you haven't used Auto Layout before, that's OK. We will start with the basics in this chapter and we'll cover more complex uses of Auto Layout as we go.

To sum it all up, this chapter covers:

- Configuring and displaying a `UITableView`
- Fetching a user's contacts through `Contacts.framework`
- `UITableView` delegate and data source
- Creating a custom `UITableViewCell`
- `UITableView` performance characteristics

Setting up the user interface (UI)

Every time you start a new project in Xcode, you must pick a template for your application. Each template that Xcode offers provides you with some boilerplate code or sometimes they will configure a very basic layout for you. Throughout this book, the starting point will always be the **Single View Application** template. This template provides you with a bare minimum of boilerplate code. This enables you to start from scratch every time, and it will boost your knowledge of how the provided templates work internally.

In this chapter, you'll create an app called *HelloContacts*. This is the app that will render your user's contacts in a `UITableView`. Create a new project by selecting **File -> New -> Project**. Select the **Single View Application** template, give your project a name (*HelloContacts*), and make sure you select **Swift** as the language for your project. You can uncheck all Core Data- and testing-related checkboxes; they aren't of any use to this project. Your configuration should resemble the following screenshot:

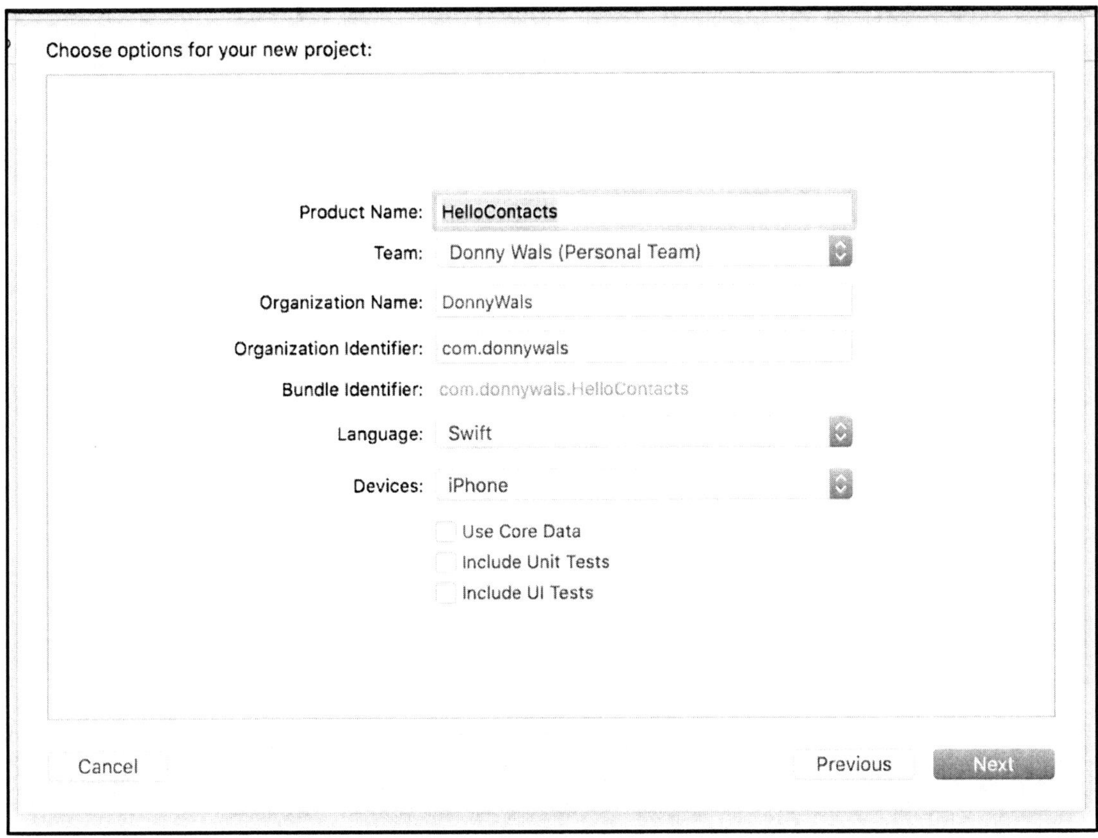

Once you have your app configured, open the `Main.storyboard` file. This is where you will create your `UITableView` and create its layout. Storyboards are a great way for you to work on an app and have all the screens in your app visualized at once.

If you have worked with `UITableView` before, you may have used `UITableViewController`. This is a subclass of `UIViewController` that has a `UITableView` set as its view. It also abstracts away some of the more complex concepts of `UITableView` that are key to understand for any experienced iOS developer. So, for now, you will be working with the `UIViewController` subclass that holds `UITableView` and is configured manually.

On the right-hand side of the window, you'll find the **Object Library**. The **Object Library** is opened by clicking on the circular icon that contains a square in the bottom half of the sidebar. In the **Object Library**, look for a `UITableView`. The following screenshot shows the **Object Library**:

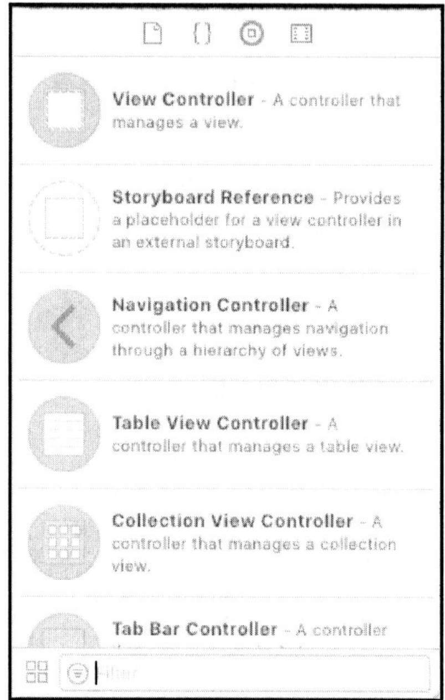

If you begin typing the name of the component you're looking for in the search box, it should automatically be filtered out for you. After you locate it, drag it into your app's view. Then, with `UITableView` selected, drag the white squares to all corners of the screen so that it covers your entire viewport.

If you go to the dynamic viewport inspector at the bottom of the screen by clicking on the current device name as shown in the following figure and select a larger device such as an iPad or a smaller device such as the iPhone SE, you will notice that `UITableView` doesn't cover the viewport as nicely. On smaller screens, the `UITableView` will be larger than the viewport. On larger screens, `UITableView` simply doesn't stretch.

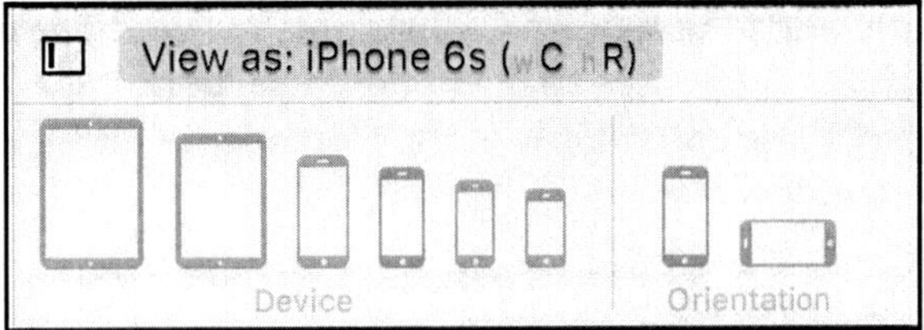

To achieve a more flexible layout that does scale, we must use Auto Layout. Auto Layout enables you to create layouts that will adapt to different viewports to make sure it looks good on all devices that are currently out there. For `UITableView`, you can pin the edges of the table to the edges of the superview, which is the view controller's main view. This will make sure the table stretches or shrinks to always fill the screen.

Auto Layout uses constraints to describe layouts. `UITableView` should get some constraints that describe its relation to the edges of your view controller. The easiest way to add these constraints is to let Xcode handle it for you. To do this, switch the dynamic viewport inspector back to the view you initially selected.

First, ensure that your `UITableView` properly covers the entire viewport, and then click on the **Resolve Auto Layout Issues** button at the bottom-right corner of the screen and select **Reset to Suggested Constraints**.

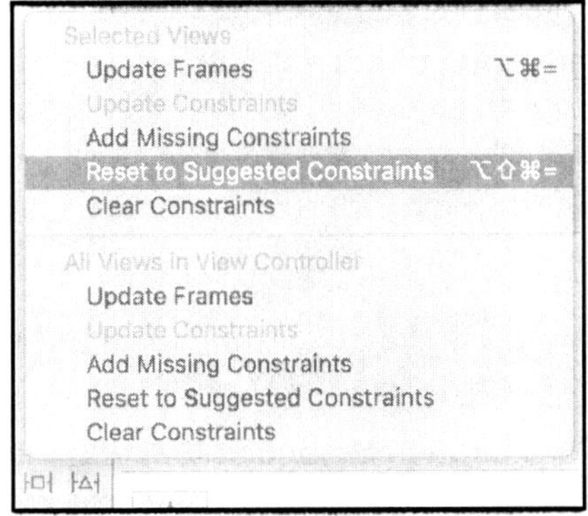

This button automatically adds the required constraints for you. The added constraints will ensure that each edge of `UITableView` sticks to the corresponding edge of its superview. You can manually inspect these constraints in the Document Outline on the left-hand side of the Interface Builder window.

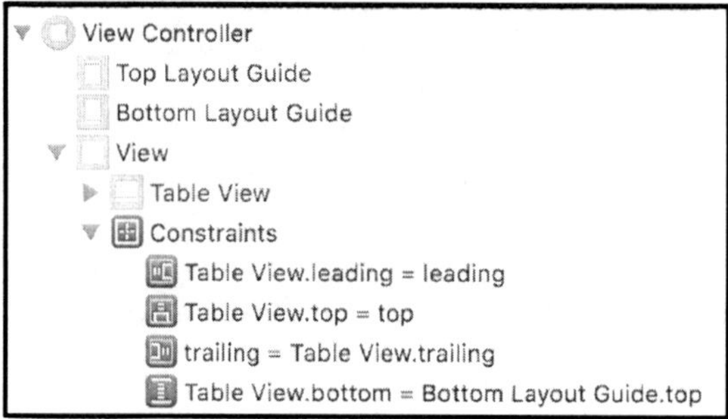

Each constraint describes how the table view should behave in relation to other views on the screen. The added constraints in this case describe how each edge of the table should be equal to each edge of its super view, which covers the entire screen.

Make sure that everything works by changing the preview device in the dynamic viewport inspector again. You should be able to verify that no matter which device you choose now, the table will stretch or shrink to always cover the entire view.

Now that you have set up your project with a `UITableView` added to the view and the constraints required to make the `UITableView` cover the entire screen have been added, it's time to start writing some code. The next step is to use `Contacts.framework` to fetch some contacts from your user's address book.

Fetching a user's contacts

The introductory section of this chapter mentioned that you would use `Contacts.framework` to fetch a user's contacts list and display it in a `UITableView`.

Before we can display such a list, we must be sure we have access to the user's address book. Apple is very restrictive about the privacy of their users, if your app needs access to a user's contacts, camera, location, and more, you need to specify this in your application's `Info.plist` file. If you fail to specify the correct keys for the data your application uses, it will crash without warning. So, before attempting to load your user's contacts, you should take care of adding the correct key to `Info.plist`.

To add the key to access a user's contacts, open `Info.plist` from the list of files in the **Project Navigator** on the left and hover over **Information Property List** at the top of the file. A plus icon should appear, which will add an empty key with a search box when you click it. If you start typing Privacy – contacts, Xcode will filter options until there is just one option left. This option is the correct key for contact access. In the value column for this new key, fill in a short description about what you are going to use this access for. In the *HelloContacts* app, something like read contacts to display them in a list should be sufficient.

Whenever you need access to photos, Bluetooth, camera, microphone, and more, make sure you check whether your app needs to specify this in its `Info.plist`. If you fail to specify a key that's required, your app crashes and will not make it past Apple's review process.

Now that you have configured your app to specify that it wants to access contact data, let's get down to writing some code. Before reading the contacts, you'll need to make sure the user has given permission to access contacts. Your code will need to check the required permissions first. Once the current permissions have been determined, the code should either fetch contacts or it should ask the user for permission to access the contacts. Add the following code to `ViewController.swift`. After doing so, we'll go over what this code does and how it works:

```
class ViewController: UIViewController {
    override func viewDidLoad() {
        super.viewDidLoad()

        let store = CNContactStore()
        let authorizationStatus = CNContactStore.authorizationStatus(for:
.contacts)

        if authorizationStatus == .notDetermined {
            store.requestAccess(for: .contacts, completionHandler: {[weak
self] authorized, error in
                if authorized {
                    self?.retrieveContacts(fromStore: store)
                }
            })
        } else if authorizationStatus == .authorized {
            retrieveContacts(fromStore: store)
        }
    }

    func retrieveContacts(fromStore store: CNContactStore) {
        let containerId = store.defaultContainerIdentifier()
        let predicate =
```

```
CNContact.predicateForContactsInContainer(withIdentifier:
 containerId)

        let keysToFetch =
            [CNContactGivenNameKey as CNKeyDescriptor,
             CNContactFamilyNameKey as CNKeyDescriptor,
             CNContactImageDataKey as CNKeyDescriptor,
             CNContactImageDataAvailableKey as CNKeyDescriptor]

        let contacts = try! store.unifiedContacts(matching: predicate,
          keysToFetch: keysToFetch)

        print(contacts)
    }
}
```

In the `viewDidLoad` method, we create an instance of `CNContactStore`. This is the object that will access the user's contacts database to fetch the results you're looking for. Before you can access the contacts, you need to make sure that the user has given your app permission to do so. First, check whether the current `authorizationStatus` is equal to `.notDetermined`. This means that we haven't asked permission yet and it's a great time to do so. When asking for permission, we make use of a `completionHandler`. This handler is called a **closure**. It's basically a function without a name that gets called when the user has responded to the permission request. If your app is properly authorized after asking permission, the `retrieveContacts` method is called from within the callback handler to actually perform the retrieval. If the app already has permission, the code calls `retrieveContacts` right away.

Completion handlers are found throughout the `Foundation` and `UIKit` frameworks. You typically pass them to methods that perform a task that could take a while and is performed parallel to the rest of your application, so the user interface can continue running without waiting for the result. A simplified implementation of a function that receives a callback looks like the following:

```
func doSomething(completionHandler: Int -> Void) {
    // perform some actions
    var resultingValue = theResultOfSomeAction()
    completionHandler(resultingValue)
}
```

You'll notice that the part of the code calling `completionHandler` looks identical to calling any ordinary function or method. The idea of such a completion handler is that we can specify a block of code, a closure, that is supposed to be executed at a later time. For example, after performing a task that is potentially slow.

You'll find plenty of other examples of callback handlers and closures throughout this book as it's a pretty common pattern in iOS and programming in general.

The `retrieveContacts` method in `ViewController.swift` is responsible for fetching the contacts and is called with a parameter named `store`. It's set up like this so we don't have to create a new store instance as we already created one in `viewDidLoad`. When fetching a list of contacts, you use a predicate. We won't go into too much detail on predicates and how they work yet because that's covered more in depth in `Chapter 9`, *Storing and Querying Data in Core Data*. The main purpose of a predicate is to set up a filter for the `contacts` database.

In addition to a predicate, you also provide a list of keys you want to fetch. These keys represent properties that a contact object can have. Each property represents a piece of data. For instance there are keys that you can specify for retrieving the contact's e-mail address, phone numbers, names, and more. In this example, you only need to fetch a contact's given name, family name, and contact image. To make sure the contact image is available at all, there's a key for that as well.

When everything is configured, a call is made to `unifiedContacts(matching: keysToFetch:)`. This method call can throw an error, and since we're currently not interested in the error, `try!` is used to tell the compiler that we want to pretend the call can't fail and if it does, the application should crash.

When you're writing real production code, you'll want to wrap this call in `do {} catch {}` block to make sure that your app doesn't crash if errors occur. The following is a very simple example of this:

```
do {
    let contacts = try store.unifiedContacts(matching: predicate,
keysToFetch: keysToFetch)
    print(contacts)
} catch {
    // fetching contacts failed
}
```

If you run your app now, you'll see that you're immediately asked for permission to access contacts. If you allow this, you will see a list of contacts printed in the console. Next, let's display some of this fetched information in the contacts table instead of printing it to the console!

Creating a custom UITableViewCell for our contacts

To display contacts in your `UITableView`, you will must set up a few more things. First and foremost, you'll need to create a `UITableViewCell` that displays contact information. To do this, you'll create a custom cell by creating a subclass of `UITableViewCell`. The design for this cell will be created in Interface Builder. To make the views added to the cell in Interface Builder available to our code, `@IBOutlets` are added to the `UITableViewCell` subclass. These `@IBOutlets` are the connections between the visual layout in Interface Builder and your code.

Designing the contact cell

The first thing you need to do is drag a `UITableViewCell` out from the **Object Library** and drop it on top of the `UITableView`. This will add the cell as a prototype cell. The design you create in this cell will be replicated in all other cells that are added to the `UITableView` through code.

Next, drag out a `UILabel` and a `UIImageView` from the **Object Library** to the newly added `UITableViewCell`, and arrange them as they are arranged in the following screenshot. After you've done this, select both the `UILabel` and `UIImage` and use the **Reset to Suggested Constraints** option you used earlier to lay out the `UITableView`. If you have both the views selected, you should see the same blue lines that are visible in the following screenshot:

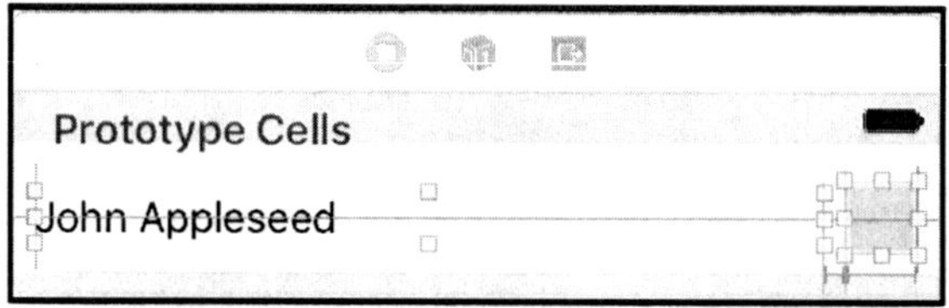

These blue lines represent the constraints that were added to lay out your label and image. You can see a constraint that offsets the label from the left side of the cell. Between the label and the image, a constraint is shown that spaces these two views. The horizontal line through the middle of the cell is a constraint that vertically centers the label and image inside of the cell. You can inspect these constraints in detail in the **Document Outline** on the right. Now that our cell is designed, it's time to create a custom subclass for it and hook up `@IBOutlets`.

Creating the cell subclass

To get started, create a new file (**File | New | File...**) and select a Cocoa Touch file. Name the file `ContactTableViewCell` and make sure it subclasses `UITableViewCell`, as shown in the following screenshot:

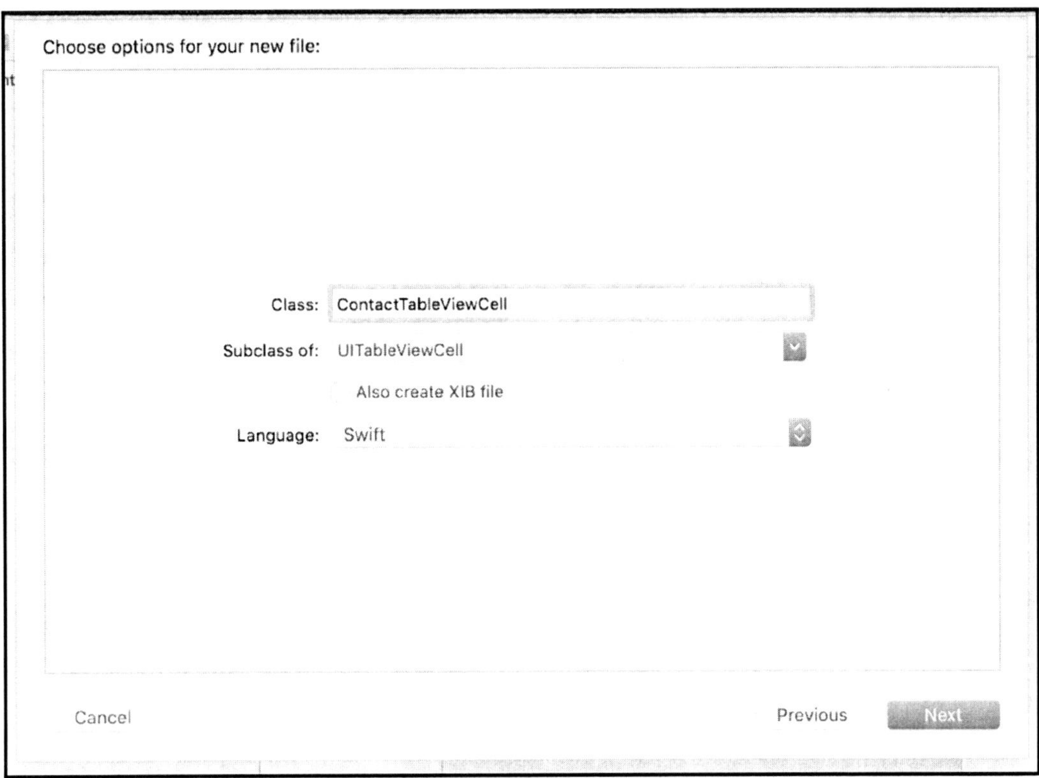

When you open the newly created file, you'll see two methods already added to the template for `ContactTableViewCell.swift`. These methods are `awakeFromNib` and `setSelected(_:animated:)`. The `awakeFromNib` method is called the very first time this cell is created; you can use this method to do some initial setup that's required to be executed only once for your cell.

The other method is used to customize your cell when a user taps on it. You could, for instance, change the background color or text color or even perform an animation. For now, you can delete both of these methods and replace the contents of this class with the following code:

```
@IBOutlet var nameLabel: UILabel!
@IBOutlet var contactImage: UIImageView!
```

The preceding code should be the entire body of the `ContactTableViewCell` class. It creates two `@IBOutlets` that will allow you to connect your prototype cell with them so that you can use them in your code to display the contact's name and image later.

In the `Main.storyboard` file, you should select your cell, and in the **Identity Inspector** on the right, set its class to `ContactTableViewCell` (as shown in the following screenshot). This will make sure that the Interface Builder knows which class it should use for this cell, and it will make the `@IBOutlets` visible to Interface Builder.

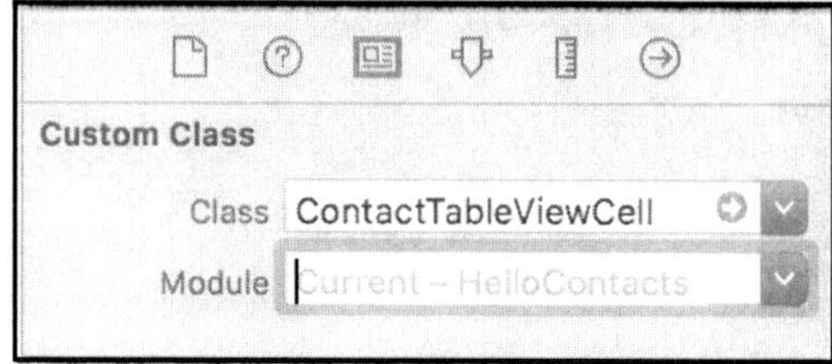

Now that the prototype cell has the correct class, select the label that will hold the contact's name in your prototype cell and click on **Connections Inspector**. Then, drag a new referencing outlet from the **Connections Inspector** to your cell and select **nameLabel** to connect the `UILabel` in the prototype cell to the `@IBOutlet` that was added to the `UITableViewCell` subclass earlier (refer to the following screenshot). Perform the same steps for the `UIImageView` and select the **contactImage** option instead of **nameLabel**.

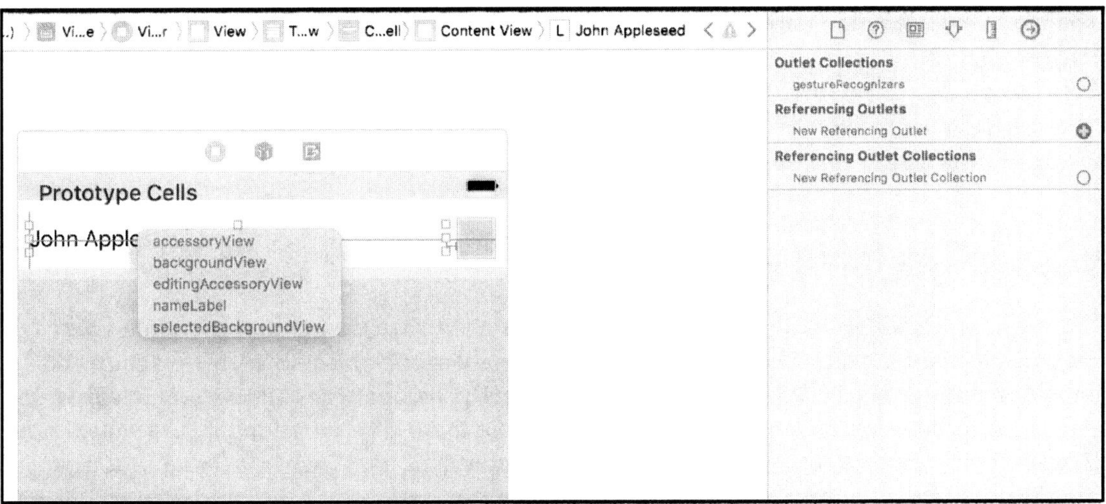

The last thing you will need to do is to provide a reuse identifier for the cell. The reuse identifier is the identifier that is used to inform the `UITableView` about which cell it should create or reuse when needed. Cell reuse is an optimization feature that will be covered more in depth later in this chapter.

To set the reuse identifier you must open the **Attributes Inspector** after selecting your cell. In the **Attributes Inspector**, you will find an input field for the **Identifier**. Set this input field to **ContactTableViewCell**.

Now that the custom `UITableViewCell` is all set up, you need to make sure that the `UITableView` is aware of the fact that our `ViewController` class will provide it with the required data and cells by setting the delegate and data source properties.

Displaying the list of contacts

One easily overlooked fact about `UITableView` is that no matter how simple it might seem to use in your apps it's a pretty complex component. By not using a `UITableViewController`, we expose some of this complexity. You already had to manually set up Auto Layout constraints so the list always covers the full view. Then, you had to manually create and configure a prototype cell that's used to display data.

The next step in implementing the list of contacts is to provide the `UITableView` with information about the contents we want it to display. In order to do so, you'll implement the data source and delegate for your `UITableView`. These properties make use of some advanced concepts that you're likely to have seen before, but you have probably never been aware of what they are and how they work. Let's change that right now.

Protocols and delegation

Throughout the iOS SDK and the `Foundation` framework, a design pattern named *the delegation pattern* is used. The delegation pattern enables one object to perform actions on behalf of another object. When implemented correctly, this patterns allows you to separate the concerns between different objects and decouple them. The following figure shows how the delegation pattern for a `UITableView` component and its `UITableViewDataSource` works:

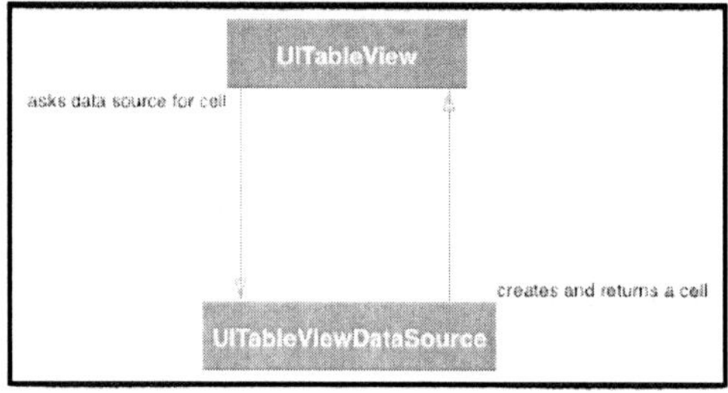

The `UITableView` makes use of two delegates in order to render a list. One is called the delegate, the other is called the data source. Whenever you use a `UITableView`, you must explicitly configure the data source and delegate properties. At runtime, the `UITableView` will call methods on its delegate and data source in order to obtain information about cells, handle interactions, and more.

If you look at the documentation for the `UITableView`'s `delegate` property you'll find out that its type is `UITableViewDelegate?`. There are two things that we learn from this type. First, it tells you that any object that wants to act as the `UITableView`'s delegate must conform to the `UITableViewDelegate` protocol. Second, the question mark tells you that the delegate is an `Optional` property. The question mark after the type is what gives this away. An `Optional` property can either have a value of the specified type (`UITableViewDelegate` in this case) or `nil`. The `UITableView`'s delegate must be `Optional` because it's not strictly required to set it; you can create an instance of `UITableView` without ever setting the `delegate` property.

A protocol, like `UITableViewDelegate`, provides a set of properties and/or methods that any object that conforms to (or adopts) this protocol must implement. In some cases all of these properties and methods are required; the compiler will throw an error if a method specified by the protocol is not implemented. In other cases, there might be methods that are optional; you don't have to implement these in order to conform to the protocol. An example of a protocol with optional methods is `UITableViewDelegate`. You can conform to this protocol without implementing any extra methods.

When implementing a `UITableView`'s data source, you'll find that the `UITableViewDataSource` protocol has a couple of mandatory methods to ensure that a data source is able to provide `UITableView` with the minimum amount of information needed in order to render the cells you want to display.

If you've never heard of delegation and protocols before, you might feel like this is all a bit foreign and complex. That's OK; throughout this book you'll gain a deeper understanding of protocols and how they work. You'll even learn a thing or two about a special programming paradigm called protocol-oriented programming. For now, it's important to be aware that a `UITableView` always asks another object for data through the `UITableViewDataSource` protocol and that interactions are handled though the `UITableViewDelegate`.

When you take a closer look at `UITableView` and the steps involved in displaying a list of contents you'd find the following steps:

1. `UITableView` needs to reload the data.
2. `UITableView` checks whether it has a `dataSource` and asks it for the number of sections in the list.
3. Once the `dataSource` responds with the number of sections, the table view will figure out how many cells are required for each section. This is done by asking the `dataSource` for the number of cells in each section.
4. Now that the cell knows the amount of content it needs to render, it will ask its `dataSource` for the cells that it should display.
5. Once the `dataSource` provides the required cells based on the number of contacts, the `UITableView` will request that it displays the cells one by one.

This process is a good example of how `UITableView` uses other objects to provide data on its behalf. Now that you have a good understanding of how delegation works for `UITableView`, it's about time you start implementing this in your own app.

Conforming to the UITableViewDataSource and UITableViewDelegate protocol

In order to specify the `UITableView`'s delegate and data source, the first thing you need to do is to create an `@IBOutlet` for your `UITableView` in `ViewController.swift`. Add the following line to your `ViewController`, before the `viewDidLoad` method:

```
@IBOutlet var tableView: UITableView!
```

Now, using the same technique as before when designing `UITableViewCell`, select the `UITableView` in your `Main.storyboard` file and use the **Connections Inspector** to drag a new outlet reference to the `UITableView`. Make sure you select the `tableView` property and that's it. You've now hooked up your `UITableView` to the `ViewController` code.

To make the `ViewController` code both the data source and the delegate for `UITableView`; it will have to conform to the `UITableViewDataSource` and `UITableViewDelegate` protocols. To do this, we should create a new extension for `ViewController` to make it conform to each protocol. It is good practice to add conformance for each protocol in its own extension as it helps to keep your code clean and organized. In the `ViewController.swift` file, add the following two extensions:

```
extension ViewController: UITableViewDataSource {
    // extension implementation
}

extension ViewController: UITableViewDelegate {
    // extension implementation
}
```

Once you have done this, you have introduced an error in your code. That's because even though your class definition claims to implement these protocols, you haven't actually implemented the required functionality yet. If you look at the errors Xcode is giving you, it becomes clear that there are two methods you must implement. These methods are `tableView(_:numberOfRowsInSection:)` and `tableView(_:cellForRowAt:)`.

So let's fix the errors by adjusting our code a little bit in order to conform to the protocols. This is also a great time to refactor the contact fetching a little bit. You'll want to access the contacts in multiple places so that the list should become an instance variable. Also, if you're going to create cells anyway, you might as well configure them to display the correct information. To do so, add the following code to `ViewController.swift`:

```
class ViewController: UIViewController {
    var contacts = [CNContact]()
```

```
    // ... viewDidLoad
    // ... retrieveContacts
}

extension ViewController: UITableViewDataSource {
    func tableView(_ tableView: UITableView, numberOfRowsInSection section:
Int) ->
  Int {
        return contacts.count
    }

    func tableView(_ tableView: UITableView, cellForRowAt indexPath:
IndexPath) -> UITableViewCell {
        let cell = tableView.dequeueReusableCell(withIdentifier:
"contactCell") as!
      ContactTableViewCell
        let contact = contacts[indexPath.row]

        cell.nameLabel.text = "(contact.givenName) (contact.familyName)"
        if let imageData = contact.imageData where
contact.imageDataAvailable {
            cell.contactImage.image = UIImage(data: imageData)
        }

        return cell
    }
}
```

The preceding code is what's needed to conform to the `UITableViewDataSource` protocol. Right next to the `@IBOutlet` of your `UITableView`, a variable is declared that will hold the list of contacts. The following code snippet was also added to the `ViewController`:

```
func tableView(_ tableView: UITableView, numberOfRowsInSection section:
Int) ->
  Int {
    return contacts.count
}
```

This method is called by the `UITableView` to determine how many cells it should render. This method just returns the total number of contacts that's in the contacts list. You'll notice that there's a section parameter passed to this method. That's because a `UITableView` can contain multiple sections. The contacts list only has a single section; if you have data that contains multiple sections, you should also implement the `numberOfSections(in:)` method.

The following screenshot shows an example of a table view with multiple sections:

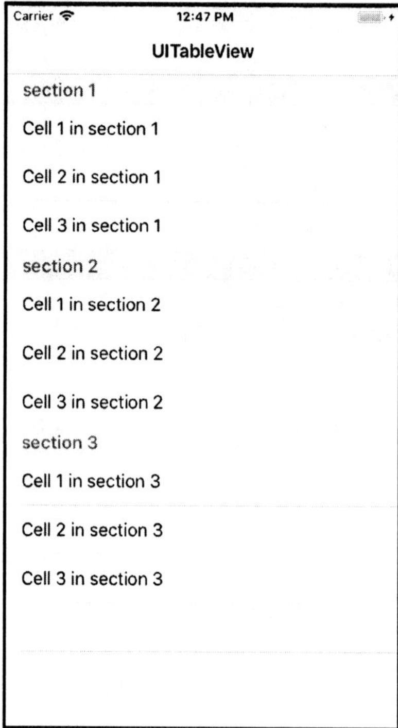

The second method we added was the following:

```
func tableView(_ tableView: UITableView, cellForRowAt indexPath: IndexPath)
->
  UITableViewCell {
    let cell = tableView.dequeueReusableCell(withIdentifier: "contactCell")
as!
      ContactTableViewCell
    let contact = contacts[indexPath.row]

    cell.nameLabel.text = "(contact.givenName) (contact.familyName)"
    if let imageData = contact.imageData where contact.imageDataAvailable {
        cell.contactImage.image = UIImage(data: imageData)
    }

    return cell
}
```

This method is used to get an appropriate cell for our `UITableView` to display. This is done by calling `dequeueReusableCell(withIdentifier:)` on the `UITableView` instance that's passed to this method. This is because `UITableView` can reuse cells that are currently off screen. This is a performance optimization that allows `UITableView` to display vast amounts of data without becoming slow or consuming big chunks of memory. The return type of `dequeueReusableCell(withIdentifier:)` is `UITableViewCell`, and our custom outlets are not available on this class. This is why we force cast the result from that method to `ContactTableViewCell`. Force casting to your own subclass will make sure that the rest of your code has access to your `nameLabel` and `contactImage`.

Casting an object converts it from one type to another. This usually only works correctly when you're casting from a superclass to a subclass like we're doing in our example. Casting can fail, so force casting is dangerous and should only be done if you want your app to crash or consider it a programming error in case the cast fails.

We also grab a contact from the contacts array that corresponds to the current `row` of `indexPath`. This contact is then used to assign all the correct values to the cell and then the cell is returned. This is all the setup needed to make your `UITableView` display the cells. Yet, if we build and run our app, it doesn't work! A few more changes will have to be made for it to do so.

Currently, the `retrieveContacts` method does fetch contacts for your user, but it doesn't update the `contacts` variable in `ViewController`. Also, the `UITableView` won't know that it needs to reload its data unless it's told to. Currently, the last few lines of `retrieveContacts` look like the following:

```
let contacts = try! store.unifiedContacts(matching: predicate, keysToFetch:
  keysToFetch)
print(contacts)
```

Let's update these lines to the following code:

```
contacts = try! store.unifiedContacts(matching: predicate, keysToFetch:
  keysToFetch)

DispatchQueue.main.async { [weak self] in
    self?.tableView.reloadData()
}
```

Now, the result of fetching contacts is assigned to the instance variable that's declared at the top of your `ViewController`. After doing that, we tell the `tableView` to reload its data, so it will go through the delegate methods that provide the cell count and cells. It's important to wrap the reload call the way we did. This makes sure that the table view is reloaded on the main thread; the thread that is responsible for the UI. If you want to learn more about threads, I recommend that you have a look at `chapter 23`, *Offloading Tasks with Operations and GCD*.

Lastly, the `UITableView` doesn't know that the `ViewControler` instance will act as both the `dataSource` and the `delegate`. So, you should update the `viewDidLoad` method to assign the `UITableView's` delegate and `dataSource` properties. Add the following lines to the end of the `viewDidLoad` method:

```
tableView.dataSource = self
tableView.delegate = self
```

If you build and run your project now, your app works! If you're running it in the simulator or you haven't assigned images to your contacts, you won't see any images. If you'd like to assign some images to the contacts in the simulator, you can drag your images into the simulator to add them to the simulator's photo library. From there, you can add pictures to contacts just as you would on a real device. If you have assigned images to some of your contacts you will see their images appear in the list. You can now scroll through all of your contacts, but there seems to be an issue. When you're scrolling down your contacts list, you might suddenly see somebody else's photo next to the name of a contact that has no picture! This is actually a performance optimization. Let's have a look at what's going on and how you can fix this.

Under the hood of UITableView performance

Earlier in this chapter you briefly read about the cell reuse in `UITableView`. You had to assign a reuse identifier to your `UITableViewCell` so the `UITableView` knows which cell you want to use. This is done so `UITableView` can reuse existing cells. This means that `UITableView` only needs to hold the visible cells and a few offscreen cells in memory instead of all of the cells you might want to show, even if the cell is off screen. Refer to the following figure for a visualization of what this looks like:

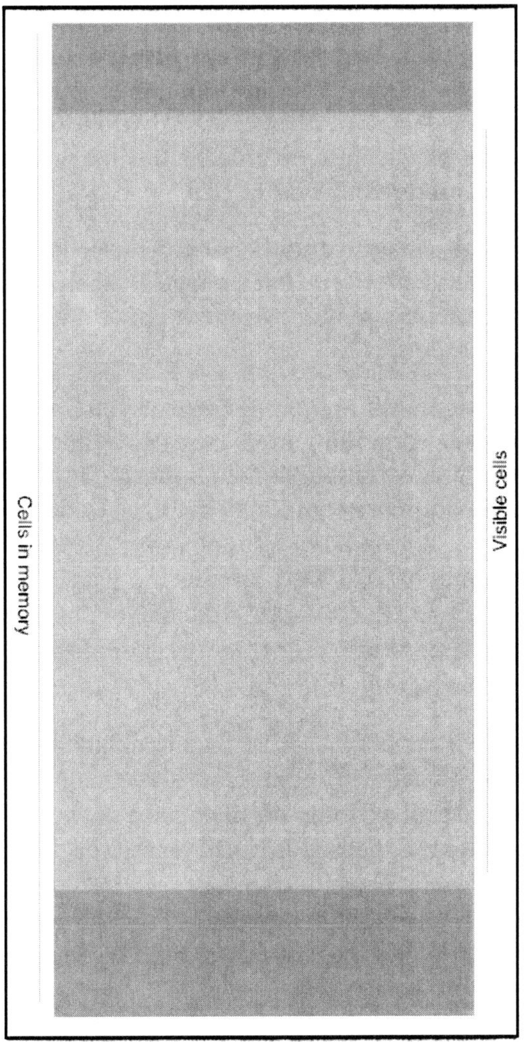

You can see that there are only a couple more cells in memory, or rendered, than there are visible cells. The `UITableView` does that so it can display huge amounts of data without rendering the content slower or losing its scroll performance. So no matter how many rows you have in your `UITableView`, it will not use more system resources than needed. This optimization was especially important in the initial days of iOS because the older iPhones were a lot more memory constrained than current devices are. Even though it's not as much of a necessity anymore, it's still one of the reasons users love iOS so much. It has amazing scroll performance.

If you've looked at our table view implementation really closely, you might have spotted an issue that's related to reusing cells. The contacts app displays other people's images for people who don't have images. Because cells are being reused, any property that you don't reset or overwrite in `tableView(_:cellForRowAt:)` will keep its previous value. Also, since not all contacts have an image and you only set the image if a contact does have one, it makes sense that you've encountered this bug.

For example, John, who has no image, could be rendered into Jeff's old cell. Since John doesn't have an image, we don't overwrite Jeff's image at all and Jeff's image remains visible. In order to solve this cell reuse bug, we should have a look at the life cycle of a `UITableViewCell`.

If you haven't seen this bug occur because you don't have a lot of contacts in the table view, try adding more contacts in the contacts app. Alternatively, you could implement a sneaky little workaround to pretend that there are a lot more contacts to display. To do this, update the `tableView(_:numberOfRowsInSection:)` method so it returns `contacts.count * 10`. Also, update `tableView(_:cellForRow:AtIndexPath:)` so the contact is retrieved as follows: `let contact = contacts[indexPath.row % contacts.count]`.

A cell is first created when we ask the `UITableView` to dequeue a cell from the reuse queue. This happens when you call `dequeueReusableCell(withIdentifier:)`. The `UITableView` will either reuse an existing cell or create a new one. When the cell is dequeued, the `prepareForReuse` method is called on the cell. This is the point where a cell should be reset to its default state. Next, `tableView(_:willDisplay:forRowAt:)` is called on `UITableViewDelegate` right before the cell is displayed. Some last minute configurations can be done here, but the majority should be already done while dequeuing the cell. Finally, the cell goes off screen and `tableView(_:didEndDisplaying:forRowAt:)` is called on `UITableViewDelegate`. This signals that a cell was on screen and has been scrolled offscreen now.

The fix for the image reuse bug is to implement `prepareForReuse` on your `UITableViewCell` because you'll want to reset its `imageView` before it is reused. Add the following code to `ContactTableViewCell.swift`:

```
override func prepareForReuse() {
    super.prepareForReuse()

    contactImage.image = nil
}
```

This method is called every time the `UITableView` reuses this cell. Make sure you call the superclass implementation as well by calling `super.prepareForReuse()` first. Then, set the image for the `contactImage` to nil. This will remove any image that is currently set on it and leave behind a clean cell that is reset in a way that prevents wrong images from showing up.

Improving performance with prefetching

Ever since iOS 10 was introduced, `UITableView` gained a performance optimization that can make a huge difference to a lot of apps. This feature is specified in a protocol named `UITableViewDataSourcePrefetching`. This protocol allows a data source to prefetch data before it is required. If your app is performing an expensive operation, such as downloading data from the internet or, as this contacts app does, decoding image data to display, prefetching will make the performance of `UITableView` a lot better.

Let's go ahead and implement prefetching in the *HelloContacts* app because we're currently decoding image data in `tableView(_ tableView: UITableView, cellForRowAt indexPath: IndexPath)`. Decoding image data isn't a very fast operation, and it slows down the scrolling for your users. Kicking off this decoding a bit sooner in the prefetching stage will improve the scrolling performance of your users.

To conform to the `UITableViewDataSourcePrefetching`, you need to implement one method and add an extension for the `UITableViewDataSourcePrefetching` protocol. Update the code in `ViewController.swift`, as shown in the following code snippet:

```
extension ViewController: UITableViewDataSourcePrefetching {
    func tableView(_ tableView: UITableView, prefetchRowsAt indexPaths:
      [IndexPath]) {
        for indexPath in indexPaths {
            // we will implement the actual prefetching in a bit
        }
    }
}
```

The method that's implemented in this snippet receives a `UITableView` and an array on `IndexPaths` that should be prefetched as its arguments. Before you implement the actual prefetching logic, you'll need to think about the strategy you're going to apply to prefetching.

It would be ideal to have to decode each contact image only once. This can be solved by creating a class that holds the fetched `CNContact` instance, as well as the decoded image. This class should be named `HCContact` and should be set up so that you have to change a bare minimum of code in the `ViewController.swift` file.

Let's start by creating a new file (**File** | **New** | **File...**), and select the Swift file template. Name the file `HCContact`. Inside this file you should add the following code:

```
import UIKit
import Contacts

class HCContact {
    private let contact: CNContact
    var contactImage: UIImage?

    var givenName: String {
        return contact.givenName
    }

    var familyName: String {
        return contact.familyName
    }

    init(contact: CNContact) {
        self.contact = contact
    }

    func fetchImageIfNeeded() {
        if let imageData = contact.imageData, contactImage == nil {
            contactImage = UIImage(data: imageData)
        }
    }
}
```

There are two parts of this code that are interesting in particular. The first part is as follows:

```
var givenName: String {
return contact.givenName
}

var familyName: String {
    return contact.familyName
}
```

These lines use computed properties to provide a proxy to the `CNContact` instance that is stored in this class. By doing this, you ensure that you don't have to rewrite the existing code that accesses these contact properties. Also, it prevents you from writing something such as `contact.contact.givenName`. Setting your properties up like this is good practice because you have detailed control over the exposed properties and you could easily swap out the underlying contact storage if needed.

The second part of this snippet that is interesting is:

```
func prefetchImageIfNeeded() {
    if let imageData = contact.imageData, contactImage == nil {
        contactImage = UIImage(data: imageData)
    }
}
```

This method performs the decoding of the image data. It makes sure that the stored contact has image data available and it checks whether the contact image isn't set yet. If this is the case, the image data is decoded and assigned to `contactImage`. The next time this method is called, nothing will happen because `contactImage` won't be nil since the prefetching already did its job.

Now, make a few changes to `ViewController.swift` and you're good to go. The code snippet contains only the code where changes need to be made:

```
class ViewController: UIViewController {

    var contacts = [HCContact]()

    func retrieveContacts(fromStore store: CNContactStore) {
        // ...

        contacts = try! store.unifiedContacts(matching: predicate,
keysToFetch:
          keysToFetch).map { contact in
            return HCContact(contact: contact)
        }
        tableView.reloadData()
    }
}

extension UIViewController: UITableViewDataSource
    func tableView(_ tableView: UITableView, cellForRowAt indexPath:
IndexPath)
      -> UITableViewCell {
        // ...
```

```
        contact.fetchImageIfNeeded()
        if let image = contact.contactImage {
            cell.contactImage.image = image
        }

        return cell
    }
}

extension UIViewController: UITableViewDataSourcePrefetching {
    func tableView(_ tableView: UITableView, prefetchRowsAt indexPaths:
      [IndexPath]) {
        for indexPath in indexPaths {
            let contact = contacts[indexPath.row]
            contact.fetchImageIfNeeded()
        }
    }
}
```

First, we change the type of our contacts array from `CNContact` to `HCContact`, our own `contact` class. When retrieving contacts, we use Swift's powerful map method to convert the retrieved `CNContacts` to `HCContacts`.

Calling `.map` on an array allows you to transform every element in that array into something else. In this case, from `CNContact` to `HCContact`. When configuring the cell, `fetchImageIfNeeded` is called in case the table view did not call the `prefetch` method for this index path.

At this point, it's not guaranteed that the data for this cell has been prefetched. However, since the prefetching you implemented is pretty clever, this method can safely be called to make sure that the image is available. After all, the method does nothing if the image has already been prefetched. Then, we safely unwrap `contactImage` and then we set it on the cell.

In the prefetching method, the code loops over the `IndexPaths` we should prefetch data for. Each `IndexPath` consists of a section and a row. These properties match up with the sections and rows in the table view. When prefetching, a contact is retrieved from the contacts array, and we call fetchImageIfNeeded on it. This will allow the contact to decode the image data it contains before it needs to be displayed. This is all you have to do in order to optimize your UITableView for prefetching. Now let's take a look at some of the UITableView delegate methods.

UITableViewDelegate and interactions

Up until this point, the `ViewController` has conformed to `UITableViewDelegate` according to its declaration, but you haven't actually implemented any interesting delegate methods yet. Whenever certain interactions occur in `UITableView`, such as tapping a cell or swiping a cell, `UITableView` will attempt to notify its delegate about the action that has occurred. There are no required methods in the `UITableViewDelegate` protocol, which is why you could conform to it and act as a delegate without writing any implementation code. However, just implementing a list and doing nothing with it is kind of boring, so let's add some features that will make `UITableView` a little bit more interesting. If you look at the documentation for `UITableViewDelegate` you'll see that there's a large collection of methods you can implement in our app.

You can hold the *Alt* key when clicking on a class, struct, enum, or protocol name to make an information dialog pop up. From this dialog pop up, you can navigate to the documentation for the definition you clicked.

In the documentation, you'll find methods for configuring cell height, content indentation level, cell selection, and more. You can also implement methods so you're notified when a `UITableView` is about to display a cell, or stops displaying it. You can hook into reordering, adding, and deleting cells. You can handle cell selection, highlighting, and more. All of the interactions that are supported by the `UITableView` are part of the `UITableViewDelegate` protocol. The first thing you will implement is row selection. Most apps that implement a `UITableView` will perform some kind of an action when a user taps on an item in the list. Once you've implemented cell selection, you will also implement cell reordering and cell removal.

Responding to cell selection

To respond to cell selection, you should implement the `tableView(_:didSelectRowAt:)` method. Because you've already set the `ViewController` instance as the `UITableView` delegate, declaring and implementing this method on your `ViewController` is all you need to do.

The `UITableView` will automatically call all of the `UITableViewDelegate` methods that its delegate has implemented. This is why we don't need to do anything more than just implementing `tableView(_:didSelectRowAt:)`. The implementation that we'll write for now is very simple. When a user taps a cell, an alert will be displayed. In `Chapter 3`, *Creating a Contact Detail Page*, you will learn how to do something more meaningful like displaying a detail page. The following code should be added to the `UITableViewDelegate` extension in `ViewController.swift`:

```
func tableView(_ tableView: UITableView, didSelectRowAt indexPath:
IndexPath) {
    let contact = contacts[indexPath.row]

    let alertController = UIAlertController(title: "Contact tapped",
message:
      "You tapped (contact.givenName)", preferredStyle: .alert)

    let dismissAction = UIAlertAction(title: "Ok", style: .default,
handler:
      {action in
        tableView.deselectRow(at: indexPath, animated: true)
    })

    alertController.addAction(dismissAction)
    present(alertController, animated: true, completion: nil)
}
```

The preceding code implements the `tableView(_:didSelectRowAt:)` delegate method. This method receives two arguments, the first argument is an instance of the `UITableView` that called this method. The second argument is the `IndexPath` where the selection occurred. Most of the `UITableViewDelegate` methods are passed these two arguments. In most cases, you will need the `indexPath` in order to determine the exact action to perform. In the preceding example, the `indexPath` argument is used to retrieve the contact details that belong to the tapped cell. This information is not read directly from the cell because we don't want to couple the cell's layout directly to the data. If you want to change the cell at a later time, you don't want to have to rewrite a lot of code that is not directly related to the cell itself.

Once the contact data is obtained, a `UIAlertController` is instantiated. This class is used whenever you want to present an alert to the user. Whenever you create an instance of `UIAlertController`, you are expected to pass it a title and a message. The third argument you must pass to the `UIAlertController` initializer is the preferred style. In this case the preferred style is an alert, but you could also use an action sheet as the preferred style.

Once you have created your `UIAlertController` instance, you should associate at least one action with it. This is done through instances of `UIAlertAction`. Each action has a title, style, and a completion handler that is called whenever the user selects the action it's associated with. For the example you have just implemented a single dismiss action should suffice. In the completion handler for the dismiss action, `tableView.deselectRow(at:animated:)` is called. Calling this method makes sure that the selected cell is deselected so it doesn't remain highlighted all the time.

Once the action is configured, it is added to `alertController` and the `alertController` is presented on the current `UIViewController`. If you hit build and run now, you can tap on a cell and you will see the alert modal pop up. Tapping on **Ok** will dismiss the alert and deselect the selected row.

Even though setting this up wasn't very complex, it's really powerful. The delegation pattern makes it really easy to implement handlers for `UITableView`'s actions without a lot of boilerplate code. You could even write a dedicated class or struct that conforms to `UITableViewDelegate` and use that as the delegate for your `UITableView`. This means you are able to split up `ViewController` and `UITableViewDelegate`; doing so allows you to reuse the `UITableViewDelegate` implementations in other view controllers in your app. We won't do that in this chapter, but if you'd like you can try to do it. It will truly help you to gain a deeper understanding of delegation and why it's such a powerful technique.

Try to extract your delegate and/or data source for `UITableView` out to a separate class or struct. This will enable you to reuse your code, and you will gain a deeper understanding of what delegation is and how it works.

Implementing cell deletion

Now that we have covered selecting rows we'll move on to something that's slightly more complex; deleting cells. Deleting data from `UITableView` is a feature that many apps implement. If you have used the mail app on iOS 10 or earlier, you might have noticed how it implemented swipe actions on both the left side and the right side of cells. In iOS 11, Apple has enabled us to implement this too. These swipe actions are a great place to implement a delete action. We won't actually be deleting contacts from the user's address book even though this would be possible.

In this example, you'll be deleting contacts from the array of contacts that we use to populate the `UITableView`. In order to support this deletion, you need to implement another `UITableViewDelegate` method. This time you'll have to implement `tableView(_:trailingSwipeActionsConfigurationForRowAt:) -> UISwipeActionsConfiguration?`. This delegate method, called to obtain the actions, should be displayed whenever the user swipes from right to left over a `UITableViewCell`.

After adding the following code to the `UITableViewDelegate` extension in the `ViewController.swift` file, the **Delete** button will appear if the user performs a swipe gesture on top of a `UITableViewCell`:

```
func tableView(_ tableView: UITableView,
trailingSwipeActionsConfigurationForRowAt indexPath: IndexPath) ->
UISwipeActionsConfiguration? {
    let deleteHandler: UIContextualActionHandler = { [weak self] action,
view, callback in
        self?.contacts.remove(at: indexPath.row)
        callback(true)
    }

    let deleteAction = UIContextualAction(style: .destructive, title:
"Delete", handler: deleteHandler)
    let actions = [deleteAction]
    let config = UISwipeActionsConfiguration(actions: actions)

    return config
}
```

The preceding code configures a single delete action that is added as a trailing action, meaning that it will be visible on the right-hand side of the table view cell. There also is a `tableView(_:leadingSwipeActionsConfigurationForRowAt:) -> UISwipeActionsConfiguration?` method that allows you to configure actions for the lefthand side of the cell. Each action has a handler; this is called whenever the user selects the action it belongs to. The `UIContextualAction` contains all configuration for the action: its style, title, and handler. Lastly, a `UISwipeActionConfiguration` instance is created and it has passed all the actions that you want to be displayed. Even though there is quite a lot of code involved and this isn't easy per se, it's quite straightforward. You might want to study the code a couple of times to make sure that you understand what's going on exactly.

If you build and run the app now and you swipe over a cell, you are able to swipe from right to left on the cell to make a delete button appear. If you tap the delete action, nothing happens to the row. Why is that? Doesn't the preceding snippet remove the contact at the swiped index from the contacts array? Well, it does remove the contact from the array of contacts, but this isn't reflected on `UITableView` automatically. Let's implement this cell removal now. Replace the `deleteHandler` variable with the following code:

```
let deleteHandler: UIContextualActionHandler = { [weak self] action, view,
callback in
    self?.contacts.remove(at: indexPath.row)
    self?.tableView.beginUpdates()
    self?.tableView.deleteRows(at: [indexPath], with: .fade)
    self?.tableView.endUpdates()
    callback(true)
}
```

This snippet removes the contact from the contacts array as it did before. After that, `beginUpdates` is called on the `tableView`. This tells your `UITableView` that you are about to update it by either inserting, removing, or selecting rows. In this case, you don't strictly need to do this because you only have a single deletion to perform. If you're doing a more complex update, such as removing multiple rows or simultaneously adding and removing rows in your `UITableView`, you are required to call `beginUpdates` in order to ensure that the `UITableView` doesn't reload its data in the middle of the update sequence you're performing.

Once you have made all of the required updates to your rows, in this case deleting a single row, you should call `endUpdates`. Calling this method tells `UITableView` that all updates have been processed and it's time to reflect these updates in the user interface. This sequence of `beginUpdates`, performing updates, and `endUpdates` is also used when you're inserting or removing sections in a `UITableView`.

Now that we have properly implemented the removal of cells, let's build and run to test the app. If you swipe over a cell now and press the delete button, the cell will fade out and is removed from the view. Great! Next up, implementing cell reordering.

Allowing the user to reorder cells

In some applications it makes sense for users to reorder the cells shown in a `UITableView`. For example, if you are building a list of a user's favorite contacts or a list that simply doesn't have any logical order where it makes sense for users to reorder it to their own taste. In order to implement reordering in `UITableView`, we will need to do a couple of things.

First of all, you'll need a way to enter editing mode for `UITableView`. The easiest way to achieve this is by wrapping your `ViewController` in a `UINavigationController`. This will provide the app with a nice bar at the top of the screen, which is a perfect place to add an **Edit/Done** button.

`UIViewController` actually has a very nice convenience method to do this, so we'll make use of that. When you tap the **Edit/Done** button, the `setEditing(_:animated:)` method is called on `ViewController`. We'll override this method so the code can call `UITableView`'s `setEditing(_:animated:)` method to enable and disable its edit mode. Finally, you need to make sure that the cells can be reordered and you'll then implement the `tableView(_:moveRowAt:to:)` delegate method to update the contacts array.

So, let's wrap out `ViewController` in a `UINavigationController` first. Open the `Main.storyboard` file and select the `ViewController`. Next, in the top menu, click on **Editor** | **Embed In** | **Navigation Controller**. This will make all the required changes to embed the `ViewController` inside the `UINavigationController`. Now, to add the **Edit/Done** button to the navigation bar, open up `ViewController.swift`, and add the following line of code to the end of the `viewDidLoad` method:

```
navigationItem.rightBarButtonItem = editButtonItem
```

This line adds a `UIBarButtonItem` that automatically toggles itself and calls `setEditing(Bool, animated: Bool)` on the `ViewController`. This button set as the value of your `ViewController`'s `navigationItem.rightBarButton` property so it appears on the right-hand side of the newly added navigation bar.

If you build and run your app now, you should see a top bar and that the top bar contains a button that says **Edit**. Clicking on this button will toggle the text to say **Done**. Great, step one is done.

Now, we need to override the `setEditing(Bool, animated: Bool)` method in the `ViewController` so editing is enabled on `UITableView` when the **Edit** button is clicked. The implementation of this method is added to `ViewController.swift`, as follows:

```
override func setEditing(_ editing: Bool, animated: Bool) {
    super.setEditing(editing, animated: animated)

    tableView.setEditing(editing, animated: animated)
}
```

All that happens in this method is the calling of the super class' implementation of the method, and then we call `setEditing(_:animated:)` on `UITableView`. Doing this updates the state of the `UITableView` so that the user is able to make changes to its rows. Try to run your app now and you'll see that tapping the edit button will make a bunch of red circles appear on the left side of your cells.

Tapping the **Done** button will make these circles disappear. However, reordering isn't enabled yet because you still need to make the cells themselves show a reorder control and you need to implement the delegate method that handles row reordering.

First, open up `Main.storyboard` again and select your `UITableViewCell`. In the Attributes Inspector on the right side, search for the **Shows Re-order Controls** checkbox. Checking this will make the cell display a special control when `UITableView` enters the editing mode. The last step is to update the array of contacts whenever the user has dragged a row from one spot to another. Doing this is very similar to the deletion of cells except you don't have to update `UITableView` because the reordering was already performed internally.

If you build and run your app now, you can already reorder cells. Even though the cells are visually reordered, the underlying array of contacts isn't. This is a problem because reloading the list would undo all the changes your user has made. Add the following code to the `UITableViewDelegate` extension to fix this:

```
func tableView(_ tableView: UITableView, moveRowAt sourceIndexPath:
IndexPath, to destinationIndexPath: IndexPath) {
    let contact = contacts.remove(at: sourceIndexPath.row)
    contacts.insert(contact, at: destinationIndexPath.row)
}
```

This code implements the delegate method that is called whenever a `UITableView` reorders a row. It contains the source `IndexPath` and the destination `IndexPath`. The implementation first removes the reordered contact from the array at the old `IndexPath`'s row value. The remove method returns the removed contact. After removing the contact, we reinsert it at its new index, which is stored in the `destinationIndexPath`.

That's all you need to implement, you can now safely reorder your cells and handle the reordering by implementing the appropriate `UITableViewDelegate` method. For more delegate methods, you should have a look at Apple's documentation. As mentioned earlier, there are many delegate methods that can be implemented and it's a really powerful way to allow other objects to handle certain tasks on behalf of, in this case, `UITableView`.

Summary

The *HelloContacts* app is complete for now. The next few chapters will focus on improving it with a new layout, a detail page, and a couple more changes. You've covered a lot of ground on the way towards iOS mastery. You've used Auto Layout, the `Contacts` framework, you learned about delegation, custom table view cells, and you've implemented several delegate methods to implement several features on your table view.

If you want to learn more about `UITableView`, I don't blame you! The table view is a very powerful and versatile component in the iOS developer's tool belt. Make sure to explore Apple's documentation because there is a lot more to learn and study. One of the most important patterns you learned about is delegation. You'll find implementations of the delegate pattern throughout this book and `UIKit`. Next up? Converting the `UITableView` to its even more powerful and interesting sibling, `UICollectionView`.

2

A Better Layout with UICollectionView

When Apple released iOS 6, they added a new component to UIKit: `UICollectionView`. `UICollectionView` is very similar to `UITableView` in terms of the APIs that are available and the way it handles delegation to other objects. The main difference between the two is that `UICollectionView` is a lot more powerful and flexible. It provides an easy to use grid layout out of the box. However, you're free to create any type of layout that you desire with a `UICollectionView`. You could even create a list that looks like a `UITableView` but has all of the flexibility that `UICollectionView` provides.

In this chapter, you'll build upon the *HelloContacts* app that you built in the previous chapter, `Chapter 1`, *UITableView Touch Up*. First, all `UITableView` code should be replaced with `UICollectionView` code. This will enable you to create a more interesting grid layout to display contacts in.

You'll also create a good-looking custom cell that shows a contact's image and name. To make your layout really stand out, we need to explore the `UICollectionViewFlowLayout`, which will enable us to implement a pretty cool custom layout. Once the app's looks are improved with custom cells and a custom layout, we'll have a look at performance in comparison to `UITableView`. Lastly, we'll implement some of the available delegate methods, just as we did with `UITableView`.

The topics covered in this chapter are as follows:

- Converting from a `UITableView` to a `UICollectionView`
- Creating a custom `UICollectionViewCell`
- Using `UICollectionViewFlowLayout`
- Creating a custom `UICollectionViewLayout`
- `UICollectionView` performance
- User interactions with `UICollectionView`

Converting from a UITableView to UICollectionView

Displaying contacts in a list with `UITableView` is a fine idea. It's functional, looks alright, and people are used to seeing data displayed in a list. However, wouldn't it be nice if you had a more interesting way to display contacts, with bigger images maybe? Alternatively, maybe it would be nice to display contacts in a custom-designed grid?

Interesting and compelling layouts make your users happy. They will notice that you have put some extra effort in your layout to please them. Users enjoy apps that have received some extra attention. With that said, using a grid layout is no silver bullet. When implemented appropriately, it will delight your users. However, different apps and content types require different layouts so make sure that you always pick the right tool for the job.

For the use case of displaying contacts, a grid is a good choice. The goal is to show the user's contacts in an interesting way. We're not really interested in sorting them alphabetically. If we were, we would have used a list; a list is way better at showing a sorted list.

To display contacts in a grid, some of the existing code must be cleaned up first. All of the tableView-related code and layouts should be removed. That's what we'll cover now. When you're done cleaning up, you'll be left with a great starting point for implementing a `UICollectionView`. The steps we'll take for the cleanup process are as follows:

1. Delete all the `UITableView` code.
2. Delete the `UITableView` from the storyboard and replace it with a `UICollectionView`.
3. Add code for the `UICollectionView`.

Let's start off by simply deleting all of the code that relates to `UITableView` in `ViewController.swift`. This means you'll remove protocol conformance, all of the `@IBOutlets`, the `reloadData` call, and all of the delegate and data source methods. When you're done removing all of this code, you should be left with the following contents in your `ViewController.swift` file:

```
import UIKit
import Contacts

class ViewController: UIViewController {
    var contacts = [HCContact]()

    override func viewDidLoad() {
        super.viewDidLoad()

        let store = CNContactStore()

        if CNContactStore.authorizationStatus(for: .contacts) ==
          .notDetermined {
            store.requestAccess(for: .contacts, completionHandler:
             {[weak self] authorized, error in
                if authorized {
                    self?.retrieveContacts(fromStore: store)
                }
            })
        } else if CNContactStore.authorizationStatus(for: .contacts) ==
          .authorized {
            retrieveContacts(fromStore: store)
        }
    }

    func retrieveContacts(fromStore store: CNContactStore) {
        guard let containedId = store.defaultContainerIdentifier()
            else { return }
        let predicate =
CNContact.predicateForContactsInContainer(withIdentifier: containerId)

        let keysToFetch =
            [CNContactGivenNameKey as CNKeyDescriptor,
             CNContactFamilyNameKey as CNKeyDescriptor,
             CNContactImageDataKey as CNKeyDescriptor,
             CNContactImageDataAvailableKey as CNKeyDescriptor]

        contacts = try! store.unifiedContacts(matching: predicate,
keysToFetch:
          keysToFetch).map { contact in
            return HCContact(contact: contact)
```

```
            }
        }
    }
```

You'll probably remember that you created a `ContactTableViewCell` in the previous chapter. Don't remove that for now. You're going to reuse this code later when you implement the `UICollectionViewCell`.

Now that the code is cleaned up, it's time to clean up the user interface. Open the storyboard file and delete the `UITableView`. You're now left with a clean view controller that implements no special views anymore. Time to add a `UICollectionView` so you can start working on displaying the contacts in a grid view!

Drag a `UICollectionView` from the object library to your view controller, just as you did earlier with the `UITableView`. Make sure that it covers the entire viewport, including the navigation bar that's displayed at the top. Then, use the **Reset to Suggested Constraints** option from the **Resolve Auto Layout Issues** menu. This will add the same four constraints you've seen before when you were implementing a `UITableView`: one constraint that pins the `UICollectionView` to the left side of the superview, one to the right side, one to the bottom, and one to the top.

Select the collection view and open the **Attributes Inspector** and search for the background color property. Set this property to white to give the collection view a white background color. `UICollectionView` has a transparent background by default, which means if you build the app without setting a specific background color, it will result in a black background. This is not the behavior we want for this app.

The last step in this phase is to connect the `UICollectionView` to the code. To do this, open up `ViewController.swift`. You need to add a single line of code, above the `viewDidLoad` method. The following line of code creates the `@IBOutlet` for the `UICollectionView`:

```
@IBOutlet var collectionView: UICollectionView!
```

Now, back in the storyboard, you'll need to connect this `@IBOutlet` to the collection view. Do this by selecting the collection view and opening the **Connections Inspector**. Then, drag out a new referencing outlet to the collection view and select the **collectionView** from the list of options.

You have successfully replaced all of the `UITableView` code with some of the `UICollectionView` code that you'll be writing during this chapter. The collection view doesn't display any cells yet because its data source and delegate are not set up yet, but you'll get to that soon. Before you can start displaying cells, you should create a nice custom cell first. Let's do that right now.

Creating and implementing a custom UICollectionViewCell

When you implemented the `UITableViewCell` in the previous chapter, you designed a custom cell. This cell was a view that was reused by the `UITableView` for every contact in the contacts array. `UICollectionView` also uses cells but you can not use `UITableViewCell` in a `UICollectionView`. However, the two different cells do share a lot of functionalities, such as the `prepareForReuse` method and the `awakeFromNib` method, we saw in the previous chapter, `Chapter 1`, *UITableView Touchup*.

When you replaced the table view with a collection view, you might have noticed that the collection view immediately contained a default cell. This cell is a lot more flexible than the table view cell was; you can resize both its width and its height while you could not manually resize the table view cell at all.

If you look at the **Document Outline** on the left-hand side, you can see an object called **Collection View** flow layout. This object is responsible for the layout of `UICollectionView`, and we'll have an in-depth look at it soon. For now, select it and go to the **Size Inspector** in the right panel and set the item size properties for the layout object. The width should be set to 110 and the height to 90. Your cell will resize accordingly.

Now that the cell size is set up, drag a `UILabel` and a `UIImageView` into the cell. Attempt to position these views as they are in the following screenshot:

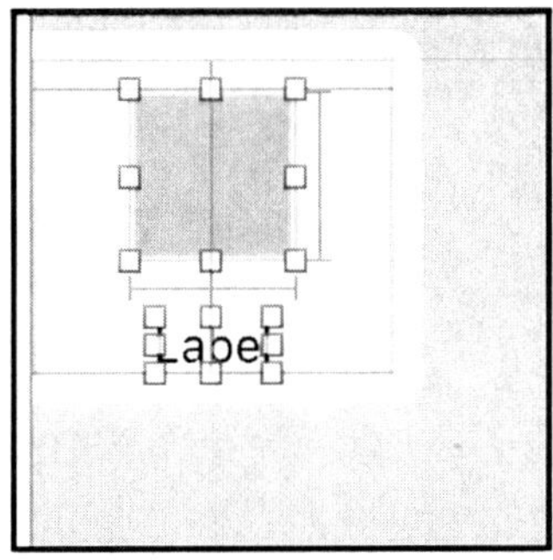

After dragging these views into their respective positions, you'll need to add constraints to them. Try to make Xcode add the constraints for you. You'll notice that, this time, Xcode doesn't do a very great job. Instead of aligning the image in the middle, it gets offset from the left. That might be fine for now; but if you decide to resize your cell later on, the current constraints will misplace the elements. Undo this step by using *cmd* + *z* or by navigating to **Edit | Undo**. This time, you'll need to manually set up the required constraints.

Whenever you add constraints, there are a few rules you should use to make your life easier. In fact, these rules are so important that they deserve to be in their own information box.

When adding constraints, it's important that every view can figure out its *width*, *height*, *x*, and *y* positions based on just the constraints that affect it, and its own intrinsic content size. The intrinsic content size can be calculated by a view dynamically depending on its contents. Labels are a good example of views using an intrinsic content size to determine their size based on the text that should be rendered.

So, applying this to your layout means that the following constraints need to be added to the `UIImageView`:

- Center horizontally in the container (*x* position)
- Stick to the top of the container (*y* position)
- Be 50 points wide (*width*)
- Be 50 points high (*height*)

For the `UILabel`, the constraints are as follows:

- Center horizontally in the container (*x* position)
- Stick to the bottom of the container (y position)

There is no need to set up size constraints for the `UILabel` because it implements the `intrinsicContentSize` method. This method returns the size that fits the text for the label, and the layout engine will use this size instead of constraints in case no size constraints are given.

To add constraints to the `UIImageView`, select it in your **storyboard**. Then, click on the **Align** button in the bottom-right corner. There are a couple of options available here, but the one you need is the **Horizontally in Container** option. Add that constraint with a value of *0*. This means that you want 0 offset from the container's center (refer to the following screenshot). After doing this, go to the **Pin** button that's next to the **Align** button. Select the **Width** and **Height** constraints and set both to *50*. Also, set a value of **0** for the constraint at the top, with **Constrain to margins** checked. This will pin the image to the top of the view with some margin (see the following screenshot):

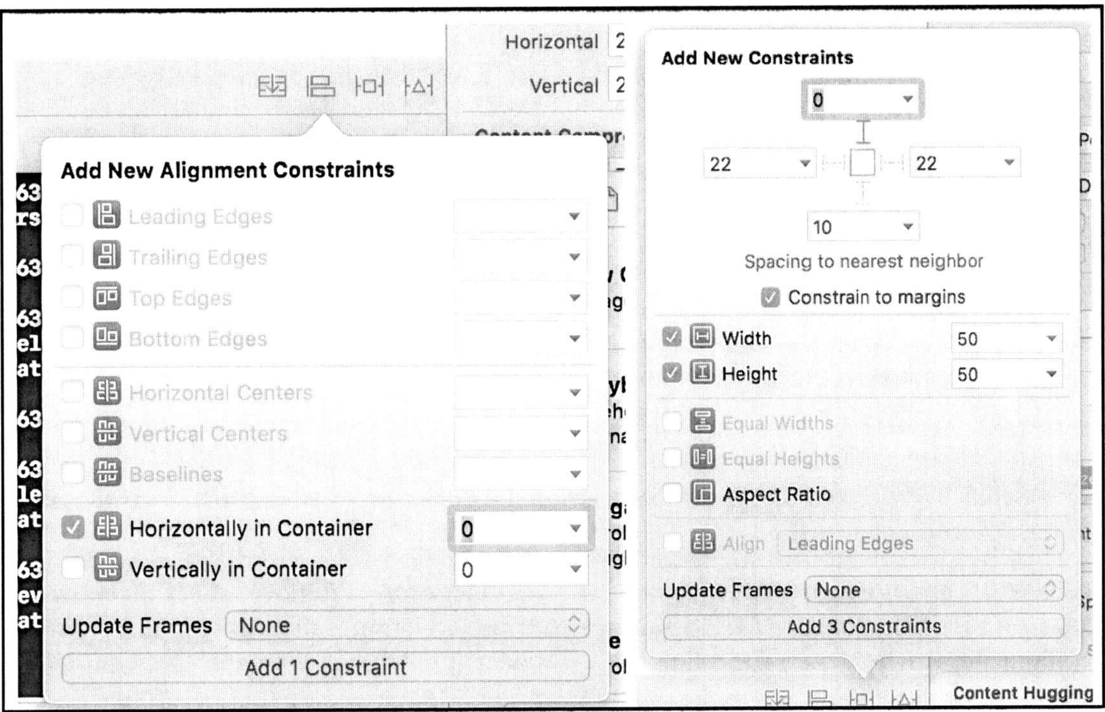

Repeat the centering step for the label. Also, instead of pinning it to the top of the container, pin it to the bottom. This provides **Auto Layout** with enough information to properly render it.

Remember that old `UITableViewCell` class that you didn't have to delete earlier? Now is the time to refactor that into a `UICollectionViewCell`. This new cell displays the same data as the `UITableViewCell` used to do. The `prepareForReuse` method exists on both `UITableViewCell` and `UICollectionViewCell`; this means that all you need to do to refactor `UITableViewCell` into `UICollectionViewCell` is rename it and change its superclass. Technically, you only need to change the superclass, but that would leave you with a `UICollectionViewCell` that calls itself a `ContactTableViewCell`. Not very pretty, is it? Replace the class definition as follows:

```
class ContactCollectionViewCell: UICollectionViewCell
```

Replacing the class definition like this enables you to use this class as the class for the `UICollectionViewCell` you just created in **Interface Builder**. Before connecting the `@IBOutlets` and updating the `UICollectionViewCell` class, you'll want to take a moment to rename the file your `ContactCollectionViewCell` is in to `ContactCollectionViewCell.swift`. If you don't rename the file, you could confuse yourself or others because you wouldn't expect a collection view cell to exist inside a file that says it's a table view cell.

To rename a file, select it in the **File Inspector** on the left-hand side and press *Enter*. You can now rename the file.

Now switch back to your storyboard and assign the `ContactCollectionView` as the class for the collection view cell.

Just like `UITableView`, `UICollectionView` uses delegation to retrieve cells. Currently, you won't see any cells if you build and run your project because there are no data source methods implemented yet. The following is a code snippet that implements the required data source methods; but this would actually be a great exercise for you to do yourself because implementing a `UICollectionViewDataSource` is very similar to implementing a `UITableViewDataSource`.

Go ahead and try to implement the data source methods on your own by using the knowledge you gained in `Chapter 1`, *UITableView Touch Up*. The data source methods are roughly the same so Xcode's autocomplete and Apple's documentation should provide you with plenty of information to figure this out on your own:

```
import UIKit
import Contacts

class ViewController: UIViewController {
```

```
    var contacts = [HCContact]()
    @IBOutlet var collectionView: UICollectionView!

    override func viewDidLoad() {
        super.viewDidLoad()

        collectionView.dataSource = self

        let store = CNContactStore()
        let authorizationStatus = CNContactStore.authorizationStatus(for:
.contacts)

        if authorizationStatus == .notDetermined {
            store.requestAccess(for: .contacts, completionHandler:
              {[weak self] authorized, error in
                if authorized {
                    self?.retrieveContacts(fromStore: store)
                }
            })
        } else if authorizationStatus == .authorized {
            retrieveContacts(fromStore: store)
        }
    }

    func retrieveContacts(fromStore store: CNContactStore) {
        guard let containerId = store.defaultContainerIdentifier()
            else { return }

        let predicate =
CNContact.predicateForContactsInContainer(withIdentifier:
 containerId)

        let keysToFetch =
            [CNContactGivenNameKey as CNKeyDescriptor,
             CNContactFamilyNameKey as CNKeyDescriptor,
             CNContactImageDataKey as CNKeyDescriptor,
             CNContactImageDataAvailableKey as CNKeyDescriptor]

        contacts = try! store.unifiedContacts(matching: predicate,
keysToFetch:
            keysToFetch).map { contact in
             return HCContact(contact: contact)
        }

        DispatchQueue.main.async { [weak self] in
            self?.collectionView.reloadData()
        }
    }
```

```
extension ViewController: UICollectionViewDataSource {
    func collectionView(_ collectionView: UICollectionView,
      numberOfItemsInSection section: Int) -> Int {
        return contacts.count
    }

    func collectionView(_ collectionView: UICollectionView,
      cellForItemAt indexPath: IndexPath) -> UICollectionViewCell {
        let cell = collectionView.dequeueReusableCell(withReuseIdentifier:
          "contactCell", for: indexPath) as! ContactCollectionViewCell
        let contact = contacts[indexPath.row]

        cell.nameLabel.text = "\(contact.givenName) \(contact.familyName)"

        contact.fetchImageIfNeeded()
        if let image = contact.contactImage {
            cell.contactImage.image = image
        }

        return cell
    }
}
```

The details regarding this code are covered in `Chapter 1`, *UITableView Touch Up*. The preceding code implements methods for cell count and cell creation. It also loads the contacts and reloads the collection view when the contacts are fetched.

If you build and run the app now, the cells won't look amazing. Images will seem to be a little distorted, and the fact that we're using plain squares for the images isn't very appealing either. This can be fixed by setting up the `UIImageView` so that the image it holds will stretch to fill while maintaining its aspect ratio instead of stretching (and deforming) to fit. Some rounded corners won't hurt this design either, so let's add those as well. Also, finally, it would be nice to have a background color for the image so that the design doesn't fall apart as much when there's no image available.

Open your storyboard and select the `UIImageView` that's inside your cell. In the **Identity Inspector**, you'll find an option that's called **Content Mode**. This option describes the way images should be rendered inside this image view. The default is set to **Scale to Fill**. A better value would be **Aspect Fill**. This mode allows the image to scale while maintaining its aspect ratio until it covers the available space. You can experiment with the other options if you like; just choose one and build the project to see what happens.

Next, look for the **Background** option on the image. Open up the drop-down menu and pick a color. The light gray one will be perfect for this cell. You might notice that there is no option to set rounded corners in the Identity Inspector or in any other panel, really. Despite this option being unavailable in Interface Builder's Attributes Inspector, we can still implement it with some code. One final thing before we do this: make sure that **Clips to Bounds** is enabled for the `UIImageView`. You can find this option in the Identity Inspector.

In addition to the technique demonstrated below, you can set User Defined Runtime Attributes in a view's Identity Inspector panel. You can use this to manipulate any property that is not exposed through the Attributes Inspector. To set a corner radius, you could set the following User Defined Runtime Attributes: Key Path-layer.cornerRadius, Type-Number - Value-25.

One of the methods that you saw but didn't use in the previous chapter was the `awakeFromNib` method in `UITableViewCell`. This method is executed only once for every cell and is intended for any additional setup you want to run once and only once. A great example of something that should be done only once for every cell is setting its corner radius. The radius will never change, and it will never require an update. To set the corner radius on the image view, add the following code to `ContactCollectionViewCell.swift`:

```
override func awakeFromNib() {
    super.awakeFromNib()

    contactImage.layer.cornerRadius = 25
}
```

All that's done here is changing the `cornerRadius` value of the `contactImage` layer. Every view has a layer. This layer is used for rendering and animation. You can't change the corner radius for a `UIView`, but you can change the corner radius for a `CALayer`. This layer can also be used to add or manipulate drop shadows, borders, and more.

Just assigning a value to the corner radius is everything that's required to give the image rounded corners. If you run your project now, you'll see that the cells look much better. The next step is to explore the layout of the collection view.

Understanding the UICollectionViewFlowLayout and its delegate

In its simplest form, a `UICollectionView` has a grid layout. In this layout, all items are evenly spaced and sized. You can easily see this if you open the storyboard for the *HelloContacts* app. Select the prototype cell in the collection view, give it a background color, and then run the app. Doing this makes the grid layout very visible; it also shows how the constraints you set up earlier nicely center the cell's contents.

The ease of use and performance of `UICollectionView` make implementing grid layouts a breeze. However, the current implementation of the grid is not perfect yet. The grid looks alright on an iPhone 6s but on an iPhone SE, the layout looks like it's falling apart and it doesn't look much better when viewed on an iPhone 6s Plus. Let's see if we can fix this by making the layout a bit more dynamic.

In the storyboard, select the **Collection View Flow Layout** in the **Document Outline**. In the Attributes Inspector, you can change the scroll direction for a `UICollectionView`. This is something that a `UITableView` couldn't do; it only scrolls vertically. If you don't have enough contacts to make the collection view scroll, refer back to `Chapter 1`, *UITableView Touch Up*. The workaround presented there can easily be adapted for the collection view.

When you switch to the Size Inspector, you'll see that there are options available that change the cell's spacing and size. You might know that an iPhone SE is 320 points wide, so let's update the item size for the layout object from 110 to 106. This will make a grid that has cells with just a single pixel of spacing on the iPhone SE. Also, update the minimum spacing properties for cells and lines to a value of 1. These values indicate the minimum spacing that should be taken into account for the cells in the layout. In practice, the spacing could be more if this allows the cells to fit better. However, it will never be less than the value specified.

If you build and run now, your layout will look great on the iPhone SE. However, larger phones have different spacing between the cells, whereas the line spacing is always just 1 point. Luckily, we can dynamically manipulate the layout in the code to make sure the grid looks just right on all screen sizes.

The examples above illustrate that `UICollectionViewFlowLayout` provides a pretty powerful solution for grid layouts, but it's not perfect. Different screen sizes require different cell sizes, and we simply can't set this through Interface Builder. Usually, you'll want your layouts to look perfect on any device, regardless of screen size.

`UICollectionViewFlowLayout` has a delegate protocol called `UICollectionViewDelegateFlowLayout`, which allows you to implement a few customization points for the layout. For instance, you can dynamically calculate cell sizes or manipulate the cell spacing. In this case, we'll leave the minimum cell spacing as it is: we want a space between cells that is as small as possible, but not smaller than 1 pixel.

The line spacing should be the same as the cell spacing (1 pixel or more), and the cell size should be dynamic so it covers as much of the horizontal space as possible. The delegate method that you need to implement in order to provide dynamic cell sizes is `collectionView(_:layout:sizeForItemAt:)`. We'll use this to return a value that's approximately a third or less of the width of the `UICollectionView` and 90 points in height. First, add a new extension to `ViewController`:

```
extension ViewController: UICollectionViewDelegateFlowLayout {

}
```

Then, implement the following `UICollectionViewDelegateFlowLayout` method in the extension:

```
func collectionView(_ collectionView: UICollectionView,
                    layout collectionViewLayout: UICollectionViewLayout,
                    sizeForItemAt indexPath: IndexPath) -> CGSize {
    return CGSize(width: floor((collectionView.bounds.width - 2) / 3),
height: 90)
}
```

This method is called for every cell, and it dynamically calculates cell sizes at the time they are needed. All that this method does is figure out how wide a cell should be, based on the width of the collection view it belongs to. From the collection view width, 2 is subtracted because that's the minimum amount of spacing between items so that space can't be used in this calculation.

If you run the app now, you'll notice that the spacing between cells is always nice and tight. However, the spacing between lines is slightly off. You may have to look real close to notice it but it will be off by a little bit when compared to the spacing between cells. This can be fixed by implementing the `collectionView(_:layout:minimumLineSpacingForSectionAt:)` method. This method is called to figure out the spacing between rows. By using a minimum width of 1, combined with a calculation similar to how the cell width was determined, you can figure out what the correct line spacing should be as follows:

```
func collectionView(_ collectionView: UICollectionView,
                    layout collectionViewLayout: UICollectionViewLayout,
                    minimumLineSpacingForSectionAt section: Int) -> CGFloat
{
    let cellsPerRow: CGFloat = 3
    let widthRemainder = (collectionView.bounds.width -
      (cellsPerRow-1)).truncatingRemainder(dividingBy: cellsPerRow)
      / (cellsPerRow-1)
    return 1 + widthRemainder
}
```

First, a variable with the number of cells per row is set. This is 3 for the current layout. Then, the same calculation is done as before when calculating cell size; this time, the result will be the remainder of this calculation. The remainder is then divided by the number of gutters that will be on screen. The calculation works like this because the remainder is the number of pixels that will be distributed between the gutters. In order to get the spacing between each gutter, you need to divide by the number of gutters. Finally, the return value is `1 + widthRemainder`. The minimum spacing we always want is `1` and `widthRemainder` is the extra spacing that will be added to these gutters. If you check the spacing now, it will be exactly equal between both the cells and the lines.

The combination of what's been provided out of the box and what's been gained by implementing just a couple of delegate methods is extremely powerful. We can create beautiful, tight grids with just a few calculations. However, sometimes you will want more than just a grid. Maybe you're looking for something that looks a bit more playful? A layout where cells are laid out as if they have been scattered across the screen evenly? This is all possible by implementing a custom `UICollectionViewLayout`.

Creating a custom UICollectionViewLayout

Implementing something as big and complex as a custom `UICollectionViewLayout` looks like quite a challenge for most people. Creating a custom layout involves calculating the position for each and every cell that your collection view will display. You will have to make sure that your code does this as fast and efficiently as possible because your layout code will directly influence the performance of the entire collection view. Luckily, the documentation for implementing a custom layout is pretty good.

If you look at the documentation for `UICollectionViewLayout`, you can read about its role in a `UICollectionView`. This information shows that a custom layout requires you to handle layout for cells, supplementary views, and decoration views. Supplementary views are header and footer views. The *HelloContacts* app doesn't use these views so we can skip those for now. Decoration views are views that aren't related to the `UICollectionView` data, but are part of the view hierarchy. The only purpose of these views is decoration, as the name already suggests. The *HelloContacts* app doesn't use these either so we'll skip those as well for the sake of simplicity.

The documentation also outlines methods that any custom layout should implement according to Apple. Not all of these are mandatory. For example, methods that relate to supplementary views or the ones that involve decoration views are completely optional. The methods that we will implement are the ones that affect the cells. The following is a list of all of these methods:

- `collectionViewContentSize()`
- `layoutAttributesForElements(in:)`
- `layoutAttributesForItem(at:)`
- `shouldInvalidateLayout(forBoundsChange:)`
- `prepare()`

When you scroll further down on the documentation page, you'll find some information about updating layout, which we won't worry about for now. One method you can find in the docs is the `prepare` method. This method is the perfect method for a `UICollectionViewLayout` to calculate all of the layout attributes that will be used for all of the cells. Since all cells in the *HelloContacts* app are of the same size and most users won't have millions of contacts, we can calculate the entire layout in the `prepare` method. Precalulating the full layout will work perfectly fine for this layout due to the predictable nature of the cells; they are always the same size.

A custom collection view layout is always a subclass of `UICollectionViewLayout`. The first thing you'll need to do is create a new Cocoa Touch class and name it `ContactsCollectionViewLayout`. Make sure that your new class inherits from `UICollectionViewLayout`.

We're going to implement the design in the following screenshot. This design is very similar to a grid layout that scrolls horizontally; the main difference is that all of the odd-numbered rows (if you start counting at 0 like a true iOS master) are indented a bit:

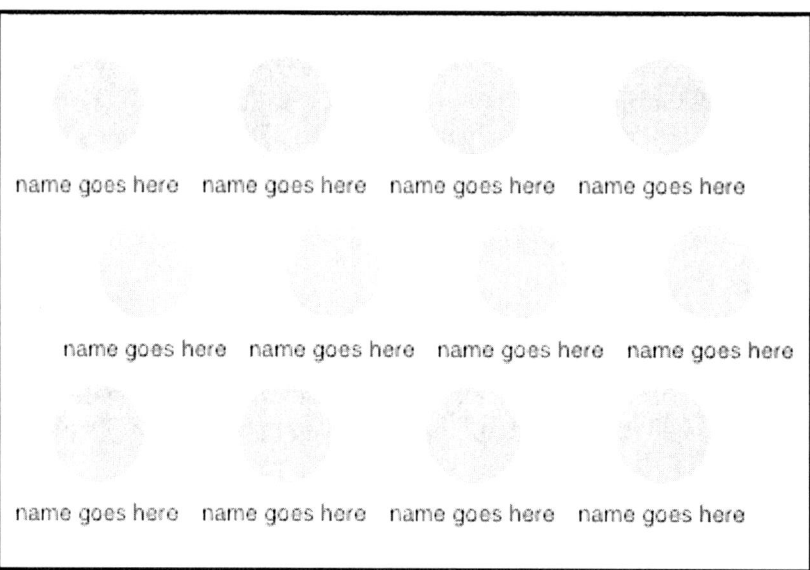

Since all elements in this layout have a predictable size that doesn't depend on any external factors, such as the bounds of the collection view this layout belongs to, all of the heavy lifting will be done in the `prepare` method. This is where all of the layout attributes for every cell will be calculated so they are available right away whenever the collection view needs to lay out its cells.

The steps required to implement the layout are the following:

1. Precalculate the `layout` in the prepare method.
2. Implement `collectionViewContentSize` to provide the collection view with enough information to configure its scrolling.
3. Implement `layoutAttributesForElements(_:)` to provide the layout attributes for all elements in a certain area.

4. Implement ;`layoutAttributesForItem(_:)` to provide the layout attributes for a specific item.
5. Implement `shouldInvalidateLayout(_:)` to determine whether the layout should invalidate for certain changes in the bounds of the collection view.
6. Assign the custom layout to the collection view.

Precalculating the layout

In order to calculate the layout for the collection view, it's nice to use a playground first. A playground enables you to quickly experiment with values, calculations, or other ideas and you don't have to wait for your entire app to build and run every time. You can make quick changes to your code and you'll see the effects of the change almost instantly. You can create a playground by navigating to **File** | **New** | **Playground**.

The approach we'll take to calculating this layout is to assign a row and column to each cell. You don't have to create an actual property that assigns these but you do need a way to map each cell to a position in the grid.

There should be as many contacts on the screen as possible so step 1 is to figure out how many cells fit on the vertical axis of the collection view. The horizontal axis isn't relevant because the layout will scroll horizontally. Imagine the collection view has a height of 667 points. Every cell is 90 points high and they have 10 points of spacing in between them. This means that *(667+10) / 100 = 6.77* cells fit on the vertical axis. You need to add 10 points to the height of the collection view because a margin was added to every cell earlier. In reality, the number of cells that have a margin is one less than the total number of cells, so we need to compensate for the 10 extra points that are involved in the calculation. The number of cells per row can now be calculated as well. If there are 60 cells that need to be divided on 6 rows, the number of cells per row is *60 cells / 6 rows = 10* cells per row.

Now that this information is available, a loop can be written that calculates the frame for every cell. Open the playground you created earlier and add the following code to it:

```
import UIKit

let collectionViewHeight = 667
let itemHeight = 90
let itemWidth = 100
let itemSpacing = 10

let numberOfItems = 60

let numRows = (collectionViewHeight + itemSpacing) / (itemHeight +
itemSpacing)
let numColumns = numberOfItems / numRows
```

The preceding snippet sets up some variables based on the rules that were established earlier. An important thing to note is that `numRows` isn't 6.77 but just 6. The reason for this is that we're not going to display partial cells. Using the variables defined, it's now possible to write a loop that calculates the frame for every cell. To do this, you can create a range from 0 to the total amount of items and iterate over it to calculate the frame based on the row and the column the item would be in, as follows:

```
var allFrames = [CGRect]()

for itemIndex in 0..<numberOfItems {
    let row = itemIndex % numRows
    let column = itemIndex / numRows

    var xPos = column * (itemWidth + itemSpacing)
    if row % 2 == 1 {
        xPos += itemWidth / 2
    }

    var yPos = row * (itemHeight + itemSpacing)

    allFrames.append(CGRect(x: xPos, y: yPos, width: itemWidth, height:
itemHeight))
}
```

The preceding code creates an array. This array is then populated with the frame for every item. Note that the modulus operator(`%`) is used to determine whether an item is in an even row or not. If it isn't, the *x* position is offset by half the `itemWidth`. We must do this because in the design, each odd row is offset from the left a little bit more than its siblings in even rows. If you print the result of this loop, you will see the following output:

```
[(0.0, 0.0, 100.0, 90.0), (50.0, 100.0, 100.0, 90.0), (0.0, 200.0, 100.0,
90.0), (50.0, 300.0, 100.0, 90.0), (0.0, 400.0, 100.0, 90.0), (50.0, 500.0,
100.0, 90.0), (0.0, 600.0, 100.0, 90.0), (50.0, 700.0, 100.0, 90.0), (0.0,
800.0, 100.0, 90.0), (50.0, 900.0, 100.0, 90.0), (110.0, 0.0, 100.0, 90.0),
(160.0, 100.0, 100.0, 90.0), (110.0, 200.0, 100.0, 90.0), (160.0, 300.0,
100.0, 90.0), (110.0, 400.0, 100.0, 90.0), (160.0, 500.0, 100.0, 90.0),
(110.0, 600.0, 100.0, 90.0), (160.0, 700.0, 100.0, 90.0), (110.0, 800.0,
100.0, 90.0), (160.0, 900.0, 100.0, 90.0), (220.0, 0.0, 100.0, 90.0),
(270.0, 100.0, 100.0, 90.0), (220.0, 200.0, 100.0, 90.0), (270.0, 300.0,
100.0, 90.0), (220.0, 400.0, 100.0, 90.0), (270.0, 500.0, 100.0, 90.0),
(220.0, 600.0, 100.0, 90.0), (270.0, 700.0, 100.0, 90.0), (220.0, 800.0,
100.0, 90.0), (270.0, 900.0, 100.0, 90.0), (330.0, 0.0, 100.0, 90.0),
(380.0, 100.0, 100.0, 90.0), (330.0, 200.0, 100.0, 90.0), (380.0, 300.0,
100.0, 90.0), (330.0, 400.0, 100.0, 90.0), (380.0, 500.0, 100.0, 90.0),
(330.0, 600.0, 100.0, 90.0), (380.0, 700.0, 100.0, 90.0), (330.0, 800.0,
100.0, 90.0), (380.0, 900.0, 100.0, 90.0), (440.0, 0.0, 100.0, 90.0),
(490.0, 100.0, 100.0, 90.0), (440.0, 200.0, 100.0, 90.0), (490.0, 300.0,
100.0, 90.0), (440.0, 400.0, 100.0, 90.0), (490.0, 500.0, 100.0, 90.0),
(440.0, 600.0, 100.0, 90.0), (490.0, 700.0, 100.0, 90.0), (440.0, 800.0,
100.0, 90.0), (490.0, 900.0, 100.0, 90.0), (550.0, 0.0, 100.0, 90.0),
(600.0, 100.0, 100.0, 90.0), (550.0, 200.0, 100.0, 90.0), (600.0, 300.0,
100.0, 90.0), (550.0, 400.0, 100.0, 90.0), (600.0, 500.0, 100.0, 90.0),
(550.0, 600.0, 100.0, 90.0), (600.0, 700.0, 100.0, 90.0), (550.0, 800.0,
100.0, 90.0), (600.0, 900.0, 100.0, 90.0)]
```

This output isn't the easiest to read but if you examine it closely, you'll notice that this result is exactly what it is supposed to be. Every cell has the correct width (100) and height (90), and every other row is indented by 50 points. Now that the formula to calculate these frames is complete, let's create the actual implementation. You've already created a placeholder class for the layout, so open `ContactsCollectionViewLayout.swift` and add the following skeleton code to it:

```
import UIKit

class ContactsCollectionViewLayout: UICollectionViewLayout {
    var itemSize = CGSize(width: 110, height: 90)
    var itemSpacing: CGFloat = 10

    var layoutAttributes = [UICollectionViewLayoutAttributes]()

    override var collectionViewContentSize: CGSize {
```

```
        return CGSize.zero
    }

    override func prepare() {

    }

    override func shouldInvalidateLayout(forBoundsChange newBounds: CGRect)
    -> Bool {
        return false
    }

    override func layoutAttributesForElements(in rect: CGRect) ->
[UICollectionViewLayoutAttributes]? {
        return nil
    }

    override func layoutAttributesForItem(at indexPath: IndexPath) ->
      UICollectionViewLayoutAttributes? {
        return nil
    }
}
```

The preceding code implements some placeholders. An important thing to note is that the `itemSize` and `itemSpacing` are mutable variables. This allows external sources to update these values if they'd prefer to do so. The default values are the values that make sense for the *HelloContacts* app so our app won't have to customize these. However, if you reuse this layout, you might want to use different sizes. Also, instead of using an array of `CGRect` instances, this class uses an array of `UICollectionViewLayoutAttributes`. This is the type of object that's used to lay out collection view cells.

The implementation for prepare is the following:

```
private var numberOfItems = 0
private var numRows = 0
private var numColumns = 0

override func prepare() {
    guard let collectionView = collectionView
        else { return }
    let availableHeight = Int(collectionView.bounds.height + itemSpacing)
    let itemHeightForCalculation = Int(itemSize.height + itemSpacing)

    numberOfItems = collectionView.numberOfItems(inSection: 0)
    numRows = availableHeight / itemHeightForCalculation
    numColumns = Int(ceil(CGFloat(numberOfItems) / CGFloat(numRows)))
    layoutAttributes.removeAll()
```

```
    for itemIndex in 0..<numberOfItems {
        let row = itemIndex % numRows
        let column = itemIndex / numRows

        var xPos = column * Int(itemSize.width + itemSpacing)
        if row % 2 == 1 {
            xPos += Int(itemSize.width / 2)
        }

        let yPos = row * Int(itemSize.height + itemSpacing)

       let index = IndexPath(row: itemIndex, section: 0)
       let attributes = UICollectionViewLayoutAttributes(forCellWith:
index)
       attributes.frame = CGRect(x: CGFloat(xPos), y: CGFloat(yPos), width:
itemSize.width, height: itemSize.height)

        layoutAttributes.append(attributes)
    }
}
```

This implementation is very similar to the playground implementation. The most important differences are highlighted. The number of items isn't a fixed number anymore but it's determined by asking the collection view for the number of items in section 0. This works because the collection view in *HelloContacts* only has a single section. If it had more sections, the implementation would have been a bit more complex because it would need to keep track of these sections somehow.

Another difference is the use of `UICollectionViewLayoutAttributes`. This class contains information about the cell's `IndexPath` and its frame. The frame is assigned right after it's created and that line is basically the same as it was already in the playground.

This wraps up *step 1*. The implementation of `prepare` is complete, and the content size can be derived because of it. Let's move on to the next step and implement the skeleton's `collectionViewContentSize` computed property.

Implementing collectionViewContentSize

The `collectionViewContentSize` property is used by the collection view to determine the size of its contents. It's important for the collection view to know the size because this size is used for the scroll indicators that hint to the user how far along they are when scrolling in a list. Another reason this property is important is because it will give the collection view enough information to determine in which direction it should scroll.

The implementation for this property uses the number of rows in the collection view and the number of columns in the collection view. These numbers will be multiplied by the sizing of each item while the spacing between the items is taken into account.

Finally, a `CGSize` is returned that represents the size of the collection view's entire contents. The following snippet shows the implementation:

```
override var collectionViewContentSize: CGSize {
    let width = CGFloat(numColumns) * itemSize.width + CGFloat(numColumns -
1) * itemSpacing
    let height = CGFloat(numRows) * itemSize.height + CGFloat(numRows - 1)
* itemSpacing

    return CGSize(width: width, height: height)
}
```

Because the layout is properly prepared, determining the size for the entire layout isn't very complex. Two simple calculations are enough to figure out the size of the collection view's contents.

Implementing layoutAttributesForElements(_:)

The `layoutAttributesForElements(_:)` method is a more complex method to implement. This method is used by the collection view when it needs the layout for multiple items at once. The collection view will specify the visible section of its contents, and the layout is expected to figure out which layout attributes to return for the items that fall within the specified `CGRect`.

Even though only a certain number of cells is displayed at the same time, the collection view knows about the fact that there's a lot more content outside the viewport that may not be visible. If the collection view needs to suddenly jump to a certain point in the collection view that wasn't visible before, it will use the layout object to ask for the layout attributes for items that will become visible after the jump. Based on these attributes, the collection fetches the required cells and renders them on screen. This is possible because `UICollectionViewLayoutAttributes` doesn't just contain the frames for the cells, it also knows about the `IndexPath` for all cells.

This is all pretty complex and just reading about it won't make it any less complex. The most important takeaway from this is that the collection view layout should be able to figure out which cells, or layout attributes, overlap with any given `CGRect` inside of the collection view. It's probably best that we dive right into an example so you can immediately see what we need to achieve.

To determine which attributes have overlap with a given `CGRect`, the `intersects` method on `CGRect` is used as follows:

```
override func layoutAttributesForElements(in rect: CGRect) ->
[UICollectionViewLayoutAttributes]? {
    return layoutAttributes.filter { attributes in
        attributes.frame.intersects(rect)
    }
}
```

For something that required a couple of paragraphs to explain, the preceding code is pretty simple. To find out which attributes overlap the given `CGRect`, the `filter` method is used on the `layoutAttributes` that were calculated by `prepare`. Filter is a powerful and convenient method, just like the `map` method that was demonstrated previously, to convert fetched `CNContact` objects to `HCContact` objects.

The `filter` method loops over every item in the `layoutAttributes` array and calls the supplied closure (which must return `true` or `false`), once for each attribute instance in the array. If the closure returns true, the attributes instance will be included in the output array; if it returns false, then it will be omitted. Once again, the extensive preparation pays off because we were able to come up with a very simple, concise, and fast implementation for this calculation.

Implementing layoutAttributesForItem(_:)

You're almost ready to make use of your beautiful custom layout. Just a few more methods remain to be tackled. The method you need to implement next is `layoutAttributesForItem(_:)`. This method receives the `IndexPath` for a single item, and the layout is supposed to return the correct layout attributes for it. The following is the implementation:

```
override func layoutAttributesForItem(at indexPath: IndexPath) ->
UICollectionViewLayoutAttributes? {
    return layoutAttributes[indexPath.row]
}
```

This implementation is nice and clean; once again, we can thank the preparation we did earlier. You can simply use the `row` property of the `IndexPath` to retrieve the required layout attributes from the stored array of attributes.

Implementing shouldInvalidateLayout(_:)

The `shouldInvalidateLayout(_:CGRect)` method is pretty important. This method is responsible for determining whether or not the layout for the collection view needs to be recalculated. If this method returns true, the layout will be reset, and if it returns false, the layout will remain the same. We want to carefully implement this method to make sure that we only invalidate the layout if we believe that the attributes for the layout will change. The simplest implementation would check whether the new bounds are different from the old bounds. This would be an okay solution, but for this layout, we can do better! Let's have a look at the following screenshot:

This screenshot illustrates that the layout wouldn't change if the collection view's bounds still allow for the same number of rows to be displayed. So, the best implementation for this layout would check this and only return true if the collection view's new bounds would either have more room, so we can render more rows, or less room, so we need to render fewer rows. Refer to the following code snippet for the implementation:

```
override func shouldInvalidateLayout(forBoundsChange newBounds: CGRect) ->
Bool {
    guard let collectionView = collectionView else { return true }

    let availableHeight = newBounds.height -
collectionView.contentInset.top - collectionView.contentInset.bottom
    let possibleRows = Int(availableHeight + itemSpacing) /
Int(itemSize.height + itemSpacing)

    return possibleRows != numRows
}
```

This snippet uses the same calculation as before, except it uses the height for the new bounds instead of the collection view's height. The return value is the result of comparing the inequality between the possible amount of rows and the current amount of rows. If they are the same, this method returns false. If they are different, true is returned, and the layout will be recalculated.

Assigning the custom layout to the collection view

The final step is to assign this new layout to the collection view. You saw that Interface Builder has the option to assign a custom class to the layout for the `UICollectionView`. However, we can't use this. Setting a custom class on this only works if the custom layout inherits from `UICollectionViewFlowLayout`. Our custom layout inherits from `UICollectionViewLayout`. To assign the layout to the collection view, you'll need to use some code. Open `ViewController.swift` and add the following code; the code that's different than before is highlighted and should be added by you:

```
collectionView.dataSource = self
collectionView.delegate = self
collectionView.collectionViewLayout = ContactsCollectionViewLayout()

let store = CNContactStore()
```

The highlighted line in the preceding snippet assigns the custom layout to the collection view. All that's needed to make this work is to assign an instance of the custom layout to the `collectionViewLayout`. After assigning this layout, the layout delegate methods that you added earlier aren't needed anymore. You can delete those, and you can also remove the conformance to `UICollectionViewDelegateFlowLayout` from the class definition.

Final words on the custom layout

The custom layout that was created in this subsection is a great example of the powers of `UICollectionView`. However, with great power comes great responsibility. The implementation that's provided isn't entirely reusable since it doesn't deal with headers or multiple sections. If you're building your own app, this might be completely fine. If all you'll ever deal with is a single array of items that isn't divided in sections or uses decoration views, you'll be good. However, if you want to create a layout that can be reused and is ready for anything, you should take care of implementing all of the methods that can affect layout.

More importantly, even simple layouts can make an otherwise fast collection view really slow. It's very easy to do a recursive or complex calculation that will run more times than needed, resulting in a collection view that will scroll exponentially slower until it won't scroll at all. These situations are frustrating for users, and instead of praising you and your creative layout, they will be annoyed by it.

If you are able to properly create and implement a beautiful custom layout, you have a very powerful tool in your toolbox. You know now that implementing something different than a standard grid isn't rocket science and the implementation isn't overly complex. With some careful planning and experimenting in playgrounds, you can make amazing layouts for your users.

Reader exercise: The current layout is aligned to the top of the collection view and fills up the view as much as possible. There is space left at the bottom. A great exercise is to adapt the layout to be centered vertically within the collection view. You will need to change the layout preparation method and the layout invalidation method. Good luck!

UICollectionView performance

We've already established how similar `UITableView` is to `UICollectionView` in terms of how you implement each component. In terms of performance, the similarities just don't stop. `UICollectionView` is optimized to display cells on screen as fast as possible with as little memory usage as possible, just like `UITableView` is. For `UICollectionView`, these optimizations are even more important than they are for `UITableView` because `UICollectionView` typically displays a lot more cells at the same time than `UITableView` does.

The fact that `UICollectionView` can show a lot of cells at once makes it a little bit harder to manage its performance behind the scenes. Before iOS 10 came out, cell reuse was managed as depicted in the next screenshot. All of the cells on a single row are requested right before they need to be displayed. Because we're not scrolling one cell into view but multiple cells, the collection view must obtain multiple cells in the same time frame that a table view requests a single cell.

If you have a complex layout in your cells or if you have a somewhat slow operation in one of your cells, a collection view can quickly start to drop frames. The result of this is choppy scrolling in your `UICollectionView`, which is something you should avoid at all costs:

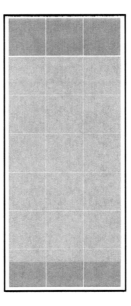

When you're aiming for a 60fps scrolling, you only get about 16 milliseconds to perform the calculations you need for the layout before the system has to render a new frame. So, assuming that the `UICollectionView` works just like `UITableView` and that it requests cells just in time, you are calculating the layout for not just one cell in 16 milliseconds, but potentially you're setting up five cells or maybe even more. This is a significant increase in the calculations that need to be performed, and it's easy to miss that 16-millisecond window. Also, once this expensive operation is finally completed, there is a short period of time with barely any calculations going on. The following diagram displays this uneven distribution of the work that's required with the pre-iOS-10 way of requesting cells:

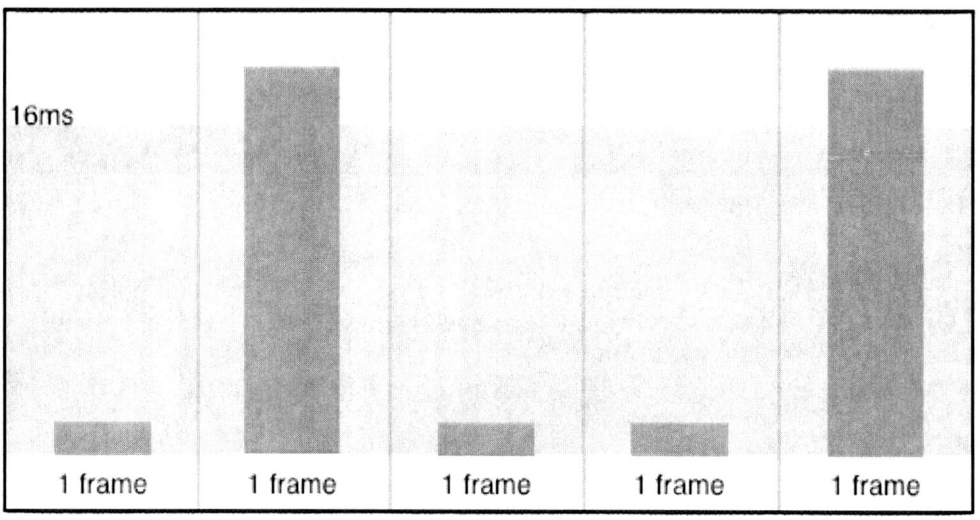

You can see the peaks and drops in the time that's spent for each frame. Ever since iOS 10, the process of requesting cells has become a lot smarter. Cells aren't requested just in time, but they are requested in a more predictive manner. While a user is scrolling in a certain direction, the `UICollectionView` will start asking for cells that aren't just on the next row but also for cells that are one or two rows down or up. It won't request all of them at once but it will request them in small batches. The next figure shows how this looks compared to the old visualization:

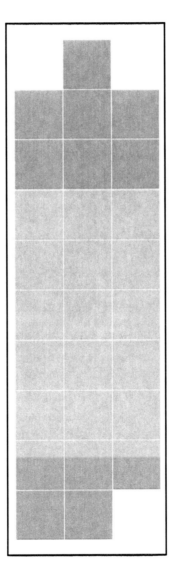

This results in a much more evenly distributed workload for the `UICollectionView`, which means better scrolling performance for your users. The following graph visualizes the new iOS 10 style. You can see that there aren't peaks in the 16ms+ range anymore. This is an awesome improvement for performance that you get entirely for free:

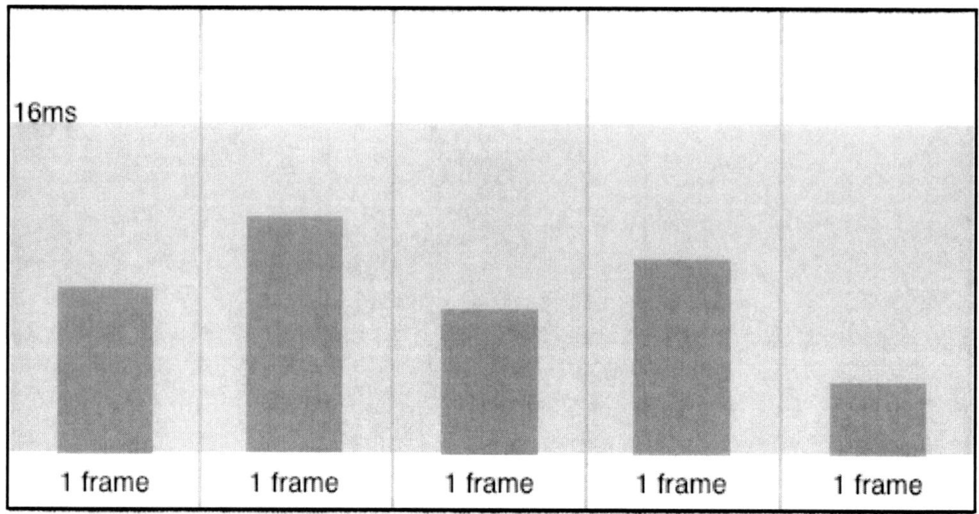

The last performance optimization you should know about is prefetching. This technique is present in `UITableView` as well, and it helps the *HelloContacts* collection view with decoding images, just like it did for the original table. With the knowledge you gained from the previous chapter, you should be able to implement this on your own. If you want to see the implementation for the collection view, you can have a look at this book's code bundle.

Cell prefetching in `UICollectionView` will benefit your application a lot more than it did for `UITableView`. This is mainly because the `UITableView` won't prefetch as many cells at once as the `UICollectionView` has owing to the amount of cells that are displayed at any given time. Typically, a `UICollectionView` displays more cells at a given time so prefetching is more beneficial.

User interactions with UICollectionView

In the previous chapter, you saw how a `UITableView` uses delegation to handle user interactions. If a user interacts with a cell, the delegate can handle that interaction by implementing a method that handles the action performed by the user. `UICollectionView` works exactly the same, except that some of the details may vary from their `UITableView` counterparts. A `UICollectionView` can't be reordered as easily, for example, and it doesn't support swipe gestures for deletion. Because of this, these actions don't have any corresponding delegate methods in `UICollectionViewDelegate`. Similar actions can be implemented regardless, and in this subsection, you'll see how you can do it.

The interactions you'll implement are the following:

- Cell selection
- Cell deletion
- Cell reordering

Cell selection is the easiest to implement; the collection view has a delegate method for this. Cell deletion and reordering are a little bit harder because you'll need to write some custom code for them to work. So, let's start with the easy one: cell selection.

Cell selection

Implementing cell selection for `UICollectionView` works the same for `UICollectionView` as it does for `UITableView`. With the knowledge you gained from `Chapter 1`, *UITableView Touch Up*, you should be able to implement this on your own. However, because the previous chapter just showed a simple alert view, it might be nice to implement something that's more interesting now. If you tap on a cell right now, nothing really happens. However, users like to see some feedback on their actions. So let's implement some of that precious touch feedback.

The feedback that you'll implement is in the form of movement. The tapped cell will slightly shrink and expand its image view with a little bounce effect. In `Chapter 4`, *Immersing Your Users with Animation*, we'll go more in-depth with animation and some of the powerful things you can do with it. `UIKit` provides powerful and straightforward methods to animate views.

Add the following code to the `collectionView(_:didSelectItemAt:)` delegate method to a new extension on `ViewController` that makes it conform to `UICollectionViewDelegate`:

```
func collectionView(_ collectionView: UICollectionView, didSelectItemAt
indexPath: IndexPath) {
    guard let cell = collectionView.cellForItem(at: indexPath) as?
ContactCollectionViewCell
        else { return }

    UIView.animate(withDuration: 0.1, delay: 0, options: [.curveEaseOut],
animations: {
        cell.contactImage.transform = CGAffineTransform(scaleX: 0.9, y:
0.9)
    }, completion: { finished in
        UIView.animate(withDuration: 0.1, delay: 0, options:
[.curveEaseIn], animations: {
            cell.contactImage.transform = CGAffineTransform.identity
        }, completion: nil)
    })
}
```

This first thing to note in the preceding snippet is that you can ask `UICollectionView` for a cell based on an `IndexPath`. The `cellForItem(_:)` method returns an optional `UICollectionViewCell`. There might not be a cell at the requested `IndexPath`; if this is the case, `cellForItem(_:)` returns `nil`. Otherwise, a `UICollectionViewCell` instance is returned. This needs to be cast to `ContactCollectionViewCell`. Using `as?` for this cast makes it safe; it allows the cast to fail. If either the cast fails or there is no cell retrieved, the function gets canceled by returning immediately.

If the cell retrieval succeeds, an animation is started. Animations such as these are created through `UIView` class's static `animate` method. This method has a couple of versions, from basic to really advanced. We're using a version that's somewhere in between. We pass it the animation duration, delay, some easing, and the state that the animation should animate to. Finally, it's passed a completion handler that reverses the animation, removing the transformation from the image.

For now, you don't have to worry about these details and how they can be tweaked. `Chapter 4`, *Immersing Your Users with Animation*, will cover animation in depth, and you'll know everything you need to know afterward. If you test your app now, you can tap on a cell, and as a result, the image view will get a bit smaller and then bigger again. This is the kind of responsive interaction that users love.

Cell deletion

Any good contacts app allows the removal of contacts. The first iteration of *HelloContacts* implemented this through a swipe gesture on the `UITableView`. This presented the user with a delete button that removes the contact when it is tapped. This was done with a `UITableViewDelegate` method.

If you open up the documentation for `UICollectionViewDelegate`, you'll find that there is no method present for cell editing or deleting. This means that it's up to you to implement the delete behavior yourself. A very naive implementation of this could be to double-tap or long-press a cell, remove a contact from the main contacts array, and reload the data on the `UICollectionView`. If you implemented deletion like this, it would work. However, it wouldn't look very good, and you can do way better.

`UICollectionView` provides methods that can be used to update the `UICollectionView` class's content properly. Properly, in this context, means that the resulting layout update isn't to just jump from one state to the other. Instead, the layout transition will be animated, resulting in a very nice and smooth experience for your user. Being a good iOS programmer isn't just about getting the job done, because simply reloading the content would get the job done, but it's also about creating beautiful user experiences.

So, let's find out which method `UICollectionView` has implemented to make these animated layout changes possible. If you open up Apple's documentation for `UICollectionView` and scroll down to the **Symbols** section, you'll see that there's a subsection called **Inserting, Moving and Deleting Items**. This is the section we're interested in for the cell deletion. The `deleteItems(_:)` method looks of particular interest for the feature that must be implemented. The discussion section for this method verifies that this method performs the task at hand; deleting cells at a certain `IndexPath`.

The final interaction pattern and implementation for this functionality will be as follows:

1. The user long-presses on a cell.
2. A confirmation will appear in the form of an action sheet.
3. If the user accepts deletion, the contact will be removed and the layout animates to the new state, and the contact is removed from the contacts array.

To detect certain interactions, such as double-tapping, swiping, pinching, and long-pressing, we use gesture recognizers. A gesture recognizer is an object provided by `UIKit` that specializes in detecting certain gestures and invoking a certain selector (method) on a target. This method will then handle the gesture accordingly.

To implement contact deletion, add a gesture recognizer to the entire collection view. The gesture recognizer is added to the entire view rather than individual cells because we don't need to use multiple recognizers and also because figuring out the tapped cell is easier to do from the collection view than it is when each recognizer for each cell calls the same selector.

In a moment, you'll see how a single recognizer leads to a simple implementation to determine the pressed cell. First, set up the recognizer by adding the following lines at the end of the `viewDidLoad` method:

```
let longPressRecognizer = UILongPressGestureRecognizer(target: self,
action: #selector(self.receivedLongPress(gestureRecognizer:)))

collectionView.addGestureRecognizer(longPressRecognizer)
```

The first line sets up the long-press gesture recognizer. The target for this gesture recognizer is `self`. This means that the current instance of our `ViewController` is the object that is called whenever the long-press is detected. The second argument is an action. The action is passed in the form of a selector. A selector is written like this: `#selector(YOUR_METHOD_HERE)`. Selectors are roughly the same as references to methods. It tells the long-press recognizer that it should call the part between the parentheses on the target that was specified.

The second line adds the gesture recognizer to the collection view. This means that the `collectionView` will be the view that receives and detects the long-press. The `ViewController` will get notified and handles the long-press.

With the recognizer added to the collection view, it's time to implement the `receivedLongPress(_:)` method as follows:

```
@objc func receivedLongPress(gestureRecognizer:
UILongPressGestureRecognizer) {
    let tappedPoint = gestureRecognizer.location(in: collectionView)

    guard let tappedIndexPath = collectionView.indexPathForItem(at:
tappedPoint),
        let tappedCell = collectionView.cellForItem(at: tappedIndexPath)
else { return }

    let confirmDialog = UIAlertController(title: "Delete this contact?",
message: "Are you sure you want to delete this contact?",
preferredStyle: .actionSheet)

    let deleteAction = UIAlertAction(title: "Yes", style: .destructive,
handler: { action in
        self.contacts.remove(at: tappedIndexPath.row)
        self.collectionView.deleteItems(at: [tappedIndexPath])
```

```
        })
    let cancelAction = UIAlertAction(title: "No", style: .cancel, handler:
nil)

    confirmDialog.addAction(deleteAction)
    confirmDialog.addAction(cancelAction)

    if let popOver = confirmDialog.popoverPresentationController {
        popOver.sourceView = tappedCell
    }

    present(confirmDialog, animated: true, completion: nil)
}
```

There is quite a lot going on in this method, so let's break it down into smaller sections and analyze them bit by bit:

```
let tappedPoint = gestureRecognizer.location(in: collectionView)

guard let tappedIndexPath = collectionView.indexPathForItem(at:
tappedPoint),
    let tappedCell = collectionView.cellForItem(at: tappedIndexPath)
    else { return }
```

This first section is the setup part for this method. It extracts the tapped point from the gesture recognizer. This point is then used to ask the collection view for the index path that belongs to this point. The found index path is used to find out which cell was tapped. Note that these last two steps are preceded by the `guard` statement. It's not guaranteed that the user actually long-pressed on a part where there is a cell present in the collection view. `indexPathForItem(_:)` returns an optional value. This also applies to `cellForItem(_:)`. It's not guaranteed that the index path that's passed to that method actually returns a cell. If either of these method calls returns `nil`, we return immediately; no cell can be deleted for the pressed point. If they do succeed, the code moves on to the next part:

```
let confirmDialog = UIAlertController(title: "Delete this contact?",
message: "Are you sure you want to delete this contact?", preferredStyle:
.actionSheet)

let deleteAction = UIAlertAction(title: "Yes", style: .destructive,
handler: { action in
    self.contacts.remove(at: tappedIndexPath.row)
    self.collectionView.deleteItems(at: [tappedIndexPath])
})
let cancelAction = UIAlertAction(title: "No", style: .cancel, handler: nil)
```

```
confirmDialog.addAction(deleteAction)
confirmDialog.addAction(cancelAction)
```

The preceding code should look familiar to you. It's very similar to the code that displayed an alert when a user tapped on a cell in the table view. First, it creates a `UIAlertController`. The main difference here is the preferred style. By using the `.actionSheet` preferred style, we make sure that this alert is presented as an alert sheet that pops up from the bottom of the screen.

The most interesting part of this snippet is the `deleteAction`. The handler for this action is called whenever the user selects it in the action sheet. The order of operations inside of the handler is extremely important. Whenever you update a collection view by adding or removing items, your data source must be updated first. If you don't do this, an internal inconsistency error occurs and your app crashes. If you want to see what this looks like, just reverse the operations.

If you update a `UICollectionView` in a way that updates its actual contents, **always** make sure to update the underlying data **first**. Failing to do so will make your app crash due to an internal inconsistency error.

The last couple of lines in the snippet attach the created actions to `UIAlertController`.

Now for the last part of the snippet:

```
if let popOver = confirmDialog.popoverPresentationController {
    popOver.sourceView = tappedCell
}

present(confirmDialog, animated: true, completion: nil)
```

These last couple of lines implement some defensive programming that's not directly relevant to the *HelloContacts* application. The first three lines check whether the confirm dialog has a `popoverPresentationController` associated with it. For an iPhone-only app, this will always be `nil`. However, devices with regular/regular trait collections (iPads) do set this property automatically. The devices do not display an action sheet on the bottom of the screen but use a popover instead. If you fail to provide the `sourceRect` or `sourceView` for the `popoverPresentationController`, if it exists, your app will crash because it doesn't know where to display the popover. Therefore, it's important to be aware of this and whenever possible to go ahead and set this property, just to be safe. The last line presents the action sheet to the user.

Whenever you display an action sheet, make sure that you add a `sourceRect` or `sourceView` to the `popoverPresentationController`, if it exists. Devices with a larger screen use popovers instead of action sheets, and failing to provide a source for this popover results in crashes.

This is all that's needed to implement cell deletion; go ahead and test it by long-pressing on some cells. The action sheet will pop up and if you remove the cell, the update is nicely animated. Even though `UICollectionView` doesn't provide the same delegate methods `UITableViewDelegate` does, the implementation for cell deletion wasn't too hard to come up with.

Now let's have a look at cell reordering.

Cell reordering

Since `UICollectionView` doesn't support reordering in the same convenient way `UITableView` does, it takes a bit more work to set it up. For `UITableView`, we only had to set a property on the cells and implement a delegate method. This was very simple and worked well straight out of the box.

To reorder cells in `UICollectionView`, it's required to implement a couple of steps. Luckily, Apple's documentation provides great information on reordering; if you have a look at the documentation for `UICollectionView`, you'll see that there are four methods related to reordering. Each of these four methods has its own role in the act of reordering and you are expected to call each of them yourself at the appropriate time.

The `endInteractiveMovement()` and `beginInteractiveMovementForItem(at:)` methods are interesting because after calling these methods, a data source method on `UICollectionView` is called. When ending the interactive movement, the `UICollectionView` asks the data source to update the selected item by moving it to a new index path. When beginning an interactive movement, the `UICollectionViewDataSource` is asked to confirm that it supports reordering of data.

The collection view does not keep track of moving cells around on its own; this needs to be implemented by you. A pan gesture recognizer can be added to achieve this, but the existing long-press gesture recognizer can also keep track of the movements that the user makes.

In order to reuse the existing long-press gesture recognizer without causing conflicts with deletion, an edit button should be added to the collection view. If the edit button is active, reordering is enabled and if it's inactive, the deletion of cells is enabled when long-pressing.

The steps to implement cell reordering are as follows:

1. Refactor the long-press handler so it calls methods based on the editing state to prevent it from becoming a long, confusing method.
2. Implement the sequence of methods for cell reordering based on the long-press gesture state.
3. Implement the required data source methods to allow interactive movement and update the underlying data.
4. Adding the edit button to the navigation item.

Refactoring the long-press handler

Because the long-press handler will now be used differently based on the `isEditing` state of the `ViewController`, it's a wise idea to separate the two different paths to different methods. The gesture recognizer handler will still make sure that a valid cell and index path are used and after that, it will call out to the correct method. Add the following code to make this separation and add a placeholder for the cell reordering sequence:

```
@objc func receivedLongPress(gestureRecognizer:
UILongPressGestureRecognizer) {
    let tappedPoint = gestureRecognizer.location(in: collectionView)
    guard let tappedIndexPath = collectionView.indexPathForItem(at:
tappedPoint),
        let tappedCell = collectionView.cellForItem(at: tappedIndexPath)
else { return }

    if isEditing {
        reorderContact(withCell: tappedCell, atIndexPath: tappedIndexPath,
gesture: gestureRecognizer)
    } else {
        deleteContact(withCell: tappedCell, atIndexPath: tappedIndexPath)
    }
}

func reorderContact(withCell cell: UICollectionViewCell, atIndexPath
indexPath: IndexPath, gesture: UILongPressGestureRecognizer) {

}
```

```
func deleteContact(withCell cell: UICollectionViewCell, atIndexPath
indexPath: IndexPath) {
    // cell deletion implementation from before
}
```

The preceding code demonstrates how there are now two paths with methods that get called based on the edit state. The `deleteContact(withCell:UICollectionViewCell, atIndexPath: IndexPath)` method is unchanged for the most part, there's just a few variables from the code before that would need to be renamed. This is an exercise for you.

Implementing the reorder method calls

Step 2 in the process of implementing cell reordering is to keep the collection view informed of the state it needs to be in. This is done by tracking the long-press gesture recognizer state and calling appropriate methods on the collection view. Any time the long-press gesture recognizer updates, either when the gesture was first recognized, ended, moved around, or got canceled, the handler is called. The handler will detect that the `ViewController` is in edit mode, and the `reorderContact(withCell:atIndexPath)` method is called. Its implementation looks like the following:

```
func reorderContact(withCell cell: UICollectionViewCell, atIndexPath
indexPath: IndexPath, gesture: UILongPressGestureRecognizer) {
    switch(gesture.state) {
    case .began:
        collectionView.beginInteractiveMovementForItem(at: indexPath)
        UIView.animate(withDuration: 0.2, delay: 0, options:
[.curveEaseOut], animations: {
            cell.transform = CGAffineTransform(scaleX: 1.1, y: 1.1)
            }, completion: nil)
        break
    case .changed:
collectionView.updateInteractiveMovementTargetPosition(gesture.location(in:
collectionView))
        break
    case .ended:
        collectionView.endInteractiveMovement()
        break
    default:
        collectionView.cancelInteractiveMovement()
        break
    }

}
```

The gesture's `state` property is used in a switch statement so we can easily cover all possible values. If the gesture just began, the collection view will enter the reordering mode. We also perform an animation on the cell so the users can see that their gesture was properly registered.

If the gesture has changed, because the user dragged the cell around, we tell this to the collection view. The current position of the gesture is passed along so that the cell can be moved to the correct direction. If needed, the entire layout will animate to show the cell in its new location.

If the gesture ended, the collection view is notified of this. The default case in the switch statement is to cancel the interactive movement. Any state that isn't in the states above is invalid for this use case, and the collection view should reset itself as if the editing never even began. The next step is to implement the required data source methods so the collection view can call them to determine whether cell reordering is allowed and to commit the changes made to its data source.

Implementing the data source methods

There are two required methods to implement for `UICollectionViewDataSource`. The first method will tell the collection view whether it's okay for a certain item to be moved around. The second is responsible for updating the underlying data source based on the new cell order. Let's jump to the implementation right away as follows:

```
func collectionView(_ collectionView: UICollectionView, canMoveItemAt
indexPath: IndexPath) -> Bool {
    return true
}

func collectionView(_ collectionView: UICollectionView, moveItemAt
sourceIndexPath: IndexPath, to destinationIndexPath: IndexPath) {
    let movedContact = contacts.remove(at: sourceIndexPath.row)
    contacts.insert(movedContact, at: destinationIndexPath.row)
}
```

These implementations should be fairly straightforward. If asked whether an item can move, the return value is true because in this app all items can move. Also, updating the order in the data is done just the same as it was done in the previous chapter.

Adding the edit button

To tie this all together, the edit button needs to be implemented. This button will toggle the `ViewController` edit mode, and it enables the rest of the code we implemented to do its job. First, add the button to the `navigationItem`, just like before, as follows:

```
navigationItem.rightBarButtonItem = editButtonItem
```

Once you've done this, you can reorder cells all day long. However, it will not be very clear to the user that the collection view is in an editable state. The cells look exactly the same regardless of being in normal mode or in edit mode. In a perfect world, the cells would start shaking, just like they do on the user's **Springboard** when they want to rearrange apps. We won't implement this for now since we haven't covered animations in depth yet, and this animation would be pretty advanced. What we'll do for now is change the cell's background color using the following code. This should give the user some indication that they're in a different mode than before:

```
override func setEditing(_ editing: Bool, animated: Bool) {
    super.setEditing(editing, animated: animated)

    for visibleCell in collectionView.visibleCells {
        guard let cell = visibleCell as? ContactCollectionViewCell
          else { continue }

        if editing {
            UIView.animate(withDuration: 0.2, delay: 0, options:
              [.curveEaseOut], animations: {
                cell.backgroundColor = UIColor(red: 0.9, green: 0.9,
                  blue: 0.9, alpha: 1)
                }, completion: nil)
        } else {
            UIView.animate(withDuration: 0.2, delay: 0, options:
              [.curveEaseOut], animations: {
                cell.backgroundColor = .clear
                }, completion: nil)
        }
    }
}
```

The `setEditing(editing:Bool, animated: Bool)` method is a great place to kick off a quick animation that changes the cell's background color. If the cell is in editing mode, the color is set to a very light gray, and if the cell is in normal mode, the background color is reset to the default clear color.

This is everything we need to do to allow the user to reorder their contacts. Despite the lack of a simple property and delegate method, this wasn't too complex. `UICollectionView` actually has a good support for reordering and implementing; it is very doable. If you're using a `UICollectionViewController` instead of a `UIViewController` to display the contacts, reordering is very easy. You only need to implement the data source methods; all the other work is baked right in to the `UICollectionViewController`. Now you know how.

Summary

In this chapter, you learned how to harness the powers of `UICollectionView` and `UICollectionViewLayout` in your application. You saw that the collection view layout has a very simple grid by default but that you can implement some delegate methods to improve its rendering to make a nice, tight grid. Next, you created a custom layout by implementing your own `UICollectionViewLayout` subclass. Finally, you learned about performance and you implemented several `UICollectionViewDelegate` methods to enable cell deletion and reordering.

The material covered in this chapter is fairly complex, and it implements some pretty advanced interaction mechanisms, such as custom layouts, gesture recognition, and animation to provide feedback to the user. These concepts are very important in the toolbox of any iOS master because they cover a broad range of features that apps use. The next chapter will cover another important concept in iOS: navigation. We'll look at how to navigate from one view to another using the storyboard in Interface Builder. We'll also dive deeper into **Auto Layout** and `UIStackView`.

3
Creating a Contact Details Page

So far, your app is able to display an overview of contacts. While this is already quite an accomplishment, it does lack one essential aspect of building apps; navigation. When a user taps one of their contacts, they will usually expect to be able to see more information about the contact they've tapped. You'll learn how to set up navigation by using storyboards and segues. Then, you'll see how to pass data between view controllers, which will make setting up details pages for contacts a breeze.

Also, the *HelloContacts* app is currently built with just the iPhone in mind. In the real world, iOS runs on two devices: iPhone and iPad. This chapter will explain how to design for all screen sizes. You'll learn how to make use of **Auto Layout** and **Size classes**-two tools Apple offers to create adaptive layouts that work on virtually any device or screen type.

Layouts with many elements that are positioned in relation to each other can be quite complex and tedious to set up with Auto Layout. In this chapter, you'll use `UIStackView` to easily create a layout with many elements in it. Lastly, we'll look at implementing a cool feature called peek and pop. This feature enables users to 3D Touch an item to get a preview of the details page they will see if they tap a contact.

Throughout this chapter, we'll cover the following topics and use them to create a good-looking contact details page that will work on any device:

- Universal applications
- Segues
- Auto Layout
- UIStackView

- Passing data between view controllers
- 3D Touch

Let's dive right into universal applications, shall we?

Universal applications

It is not uncommon for people to own more than a single iOS device. People who own both an iPhone and iPad tend to expect their favorite apps to work on both of their devices. Ever since Apple launched the iPad, it has enabled and encouraged developers to create universal apps. These are apps that run on both the iPhone and the iPad.

Over time, more screen sizes were added, and the available tools to create a universal, adaptive layout got a lot better. Nowadays, we use a single storyboard file in which a layout can be previewed on any screen size currently supported by Apple. You can even reuse most of your layouts and just apply some tweaks based on the available screen's real estate instead of having to design both versions of your app from the ground up.

If your apps are not adaptive at all, you're giving your users a subpar experience in a lot of cases. As mentioned before, your users expect their favorite apps to be available on each iOS device they own, and Apple actually helps your users if you don't provide a universal app. According to Apple, an iPhone app should be capable of running on the iPad at all times. If you don't support the iPad, your users will be presented with a scaled-up, ugly-looking version of your app. This isn't a great experience, and it often takes minimal changes to add support for adaptive layouts that will look good on any device. To do this, you can make use of Size classes.

A Size Class is a property that belongs to a `UITraitCollection`. A `traitCollection` describes the traits for a certain view or view controller. Some of these traits are relevant to the amount of available screen space. Others describe Force Touch capabilities or the color gamut of the screen. For now, we'll focus on Size classes. Currently, there are just two Size classes: **Regular** and **Compact**. The following is a list of devices and their corresponding Size classes:

- iPhone 6(s) Plus:
  - **Portrait orientation**: Compact width x Regular height
  - **Landscape orientation**: Regular width x Compact height
- iPhone 6(s) and previous models:
  - **Portrait orientation**: Compact width x Regular height
  - **Landscape orientation**: Compact width x Compact height

- iPad and iPad Pro (all sizes):
    - **Portrait orientation**: Regular width x Regular height
    - **Landscape orientation**: Regular width x Regular height

The preceding list is not exhaustive. The iPad has supported multitasking since iOS 9, which means that its width Size Class can switch between Regular and Compact, depending on the size available to your application.

Don't use Size classes as an indication of the device a user is holding. The iPad can look a lot like an iPhone if you base your assumptions on which Size Class is set for the width. If you really need to know the type of device the user is holding, you should check the `userInterfaceIdiom` property in `UITraitCollection`.

The *HelloContacts* app you were working on was created for the iPhone; this is the setting you picked when you first created the app. Try running your app on an iPad simulator and see what happens. The layout looks bad because it's just an enlarged iPhone app. Not such a great experience, is it?

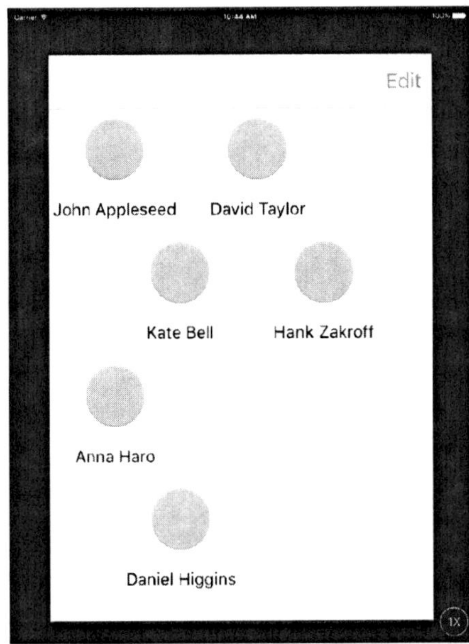

Enabling your app to be universal isn't very complex. All you have to do is go to your project settings and select the **Universal** option in the drop-down menu of your device. Once your app is universal, it will look a lot better already because *HelloContacts* was set up using Auto Layout. However, your app doesn't update when the iPad changes its orientation and it also doesn't support multitasking.

If you want to add multitasking for the iPad (and you do), your app needs to work on all interface orientations. However, on the iPhone, it's recommended that the app should not support the upside down interface orientation. It's possible to specify the device-dependent interface orientation settings in your app's `Info.plist` file. This will make it possible for your app to support all orientations on the iPad and support all orientations except the upside down orientations for the iPhone. To do this, first uncheck all of the supported interface orientations in your project settings. Your settings should look like the following screenshot:

Next, open the `Info.plist` file and search for the **Supported interface orientations** key. Remove this key and add two new keys, **Supported interface orientations (iPad)** and **Supported interface orientations (iPhone)**. Add all of the possible orientations to the `Supported interface orientations (iPad)` key, and add all except for the upside down orientation for the iPhone. You should end up with the settings listed in the following screenshot:

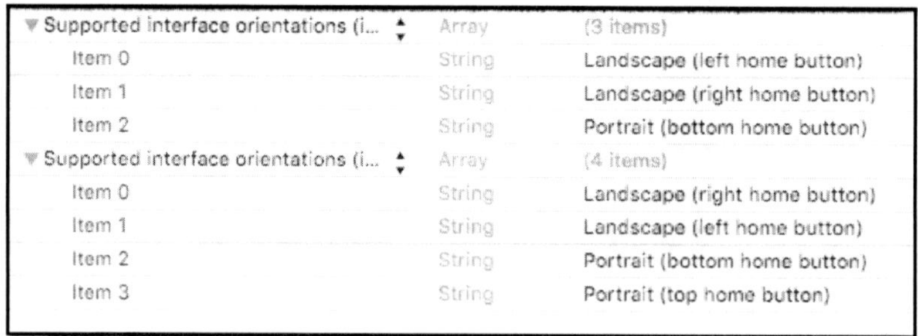

This is all of the work required to set up a universal version of *HelloContacts*. Build and run the app to see what it will look like when it actually adapts to the iPad's layout. It looks much better than before, and you didn't even have to change any code! In the previous chapter, we implemented some special behavior for the cell deletion so the app wouldn't crash if a contact got deleted on an iPad. The iPad doesn't display action sheets in the same fashion the iPhone does; it uses a popover instead. Let's check that out now. Long-press on a contact to see the popover appear, as shown in the following screenshot:

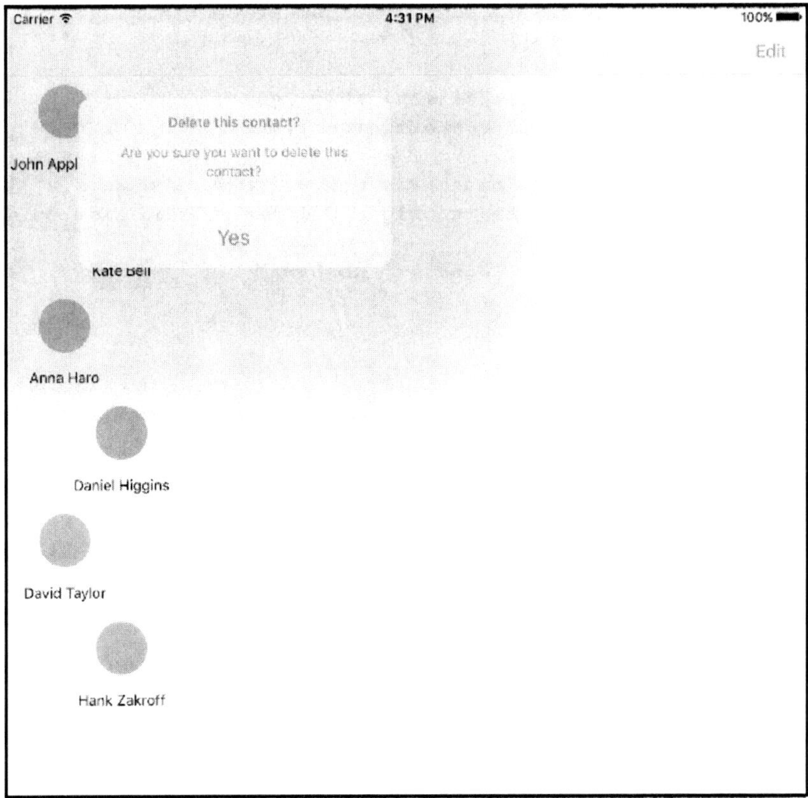

The popover appears, but as shown in the preceding screenshot, its positioning is kind of awkward. Let's take a look at how the popover is positioned and how to fix it. The current implementation to present the popover looks like this:

```
if let popOver = confirmDialog.popoverPresentationController {
    popOver.sourceView = cell
}
```

The preceding code sets the `sourceView` property for the popover. This property tells the popover which view will contain it. In this case, the cell will act as the parent view for the popover view. In addition to the `sourceView` property, there is a property called `sourceRect`. The `sourceRect` property specifies a box in which the popover should be anchored. The coordinates for this box should be relative to the containing view's coordinates. Update the implementation with the following code to position the popover's anchor at the center of the contact image view:

```
if let popOver = confirmDialog.popoverPresentationController {
    popOver.sourceView = cell

if let cell = cell as? ContactCollectionViewCell {
        let imageFrame = cell.contactImage.frame

        let popOverX = imageFrame.origin.x + imageFrame.size.width / 2
        let popOverY = imageFrame.origin.y + imageFrame.size.height / 2

        popOver.sourceRect = CGRect(x: popOverX,  y: popOverY,  width:
        0,  height: 0)
    }
}
```

It might not seem like anything special, but this popover code is actually the first piece of adaptive code that you've written. It checks the current environment by looking for a `popoverPresentationController` property. This property is only available in certain environments, and if it is, you must configure a special part of code that only applies to that specific environment. The beauty in this is that no assumptions are made about the device or screen size; it simply checks the capabilities of the current environment and acts based on them. If Apple were to implement this same popover behavior for the iPhone tomorrow, your code would still work perfectly.

Another important aspect for making your apps adaptive is multitasking. On the iPad, your app can be run alongside another app, meaning that both apps must share the screen. Your app can run in different sizes, so the more flexible your layouts are, the better this will work. Because you've modified the `Info.plist` file in a way that enables multitasking for your app, you can easily see how multitasking works. Run your app on the iPad simulator and swipe left from the right edge of the simulator screen and pick an app to be opened side by side with *HelloContacts*. You can change the available size for *HelloContacts* and change the orientation on the iPad, and the layout will update accordingly.

Congratulations! You just enabled *HelloContacts* to run on any iOS device with any possible screen size. Isn't that amazing? Now, let's take a look at navigation.

Implementing navigation with segues

Most good applications have more than a single screen. I bet that most app ideas you have in your head involve at least a couple of different screens. Maybe you'd display a `UITableView` or `UICollectionView` and a details view, or maybe users will drill down into your app's contents in some other way. Maybe you don't have any real details views but instead you would like to show some modal windows.

Every time your user moves from one screen to another, they're navigating. Navigation is a very important aspect of building an app, and it's absolutely essential that you understand the possibilities and patterns for navigation on the iOS platform. The easiest way to get started with navigation and to explore the way it works is to experiment inside of your `Main.storyboard` file.

Up until now, we've used the storyboard to create the layout for just a single screen. However, as the name implies, your storyboard isn't there for just a single screen. The purpose of the storyboard is to lay out and design the entire flow of your app. Every screen and transition can be designed right inside your storyboard file. We'll use the storyboard to add a new `UIViewController` that will function as a details page for the contacts. The actual contents won't be added right away; a single `UILabel` will have to do for now, so that you can explore different kinds of transitions in your app before implementing a details page.

After opening the `Main.storyboard`, drag a `UIViewController` from the **Object Library** on the right side of your **Interface Builder** screen. Drop it next to the view controller that has the current layout in it. You'll see that you now have two separate screens that you can design. Next, drag a `UILabel` out from the **Object Library** and drop it inside the new view controller. Place the `UILabel` in the center of the view and enter some text in the label so you can easily identify this as your second view controller later. Then, add some constraints to center the `UILabel` in its parent view by clicking on the **Pin** button in the bottom-right corner and selecting the **Horizontal center** and **Vertical center** constraints.

Now that we have a second view controller to display, and some content added to it, let's connect the first and second screens in our app. To do this, we'll create a selection segue. A **segue** is the transition from one screen to the next. This transition does not necessarily have to be animated. Any time you use a storyboard to move from one screen to the next, you're using a segue. Some segues are triggered when a button is tapped. These are called **action** segues. Segues that can only be triggered through code are called manual segues.

You can also connect a cell in a `UITableView` or `UICollectionView` to a screen. This is called a **Selection** segue; it is triggered whenever a cell is selected. A segue that you've already seen is called the relationship segue, which is the connection between `UINavigationController` and `UIViewController` that contains the `UICollectionView` with contacts.

To display the second view controller in the app, we'll use the selection segue; we want the second view controller to display when the user taps on a contact in the collection view. In the `Main.storyboard`, select the **contact collection** view cell. Now, press the *Ctrl* key while you drag from the cell to the second view controller. After doing this, a list of options will pop up where you can pick how to present this new view controller. For example, try the present modally segue. This will animate the new view controller up from the bottom of the screen.

This isn't really the style we're looking for in this app. A new contact should be pushed onto the current navigation stack so users can naturally move back to the contacts overview when they desire; it shouldn't create a new navigation context like present modally does. Ideally, we want a back button to appear in the top-left corner so users can go back to the contacts overview very easily.

The **Show** segue will do this for you. Whenever the presenting view controller is embedded inside a navigation controller, the **Show** segue will push the presented view controller on-to the current navigation stack. This means that the back button is automatically displayed, which is exactly what we're looking for. Go ahead and try it out.

Even though this behavior is perfect for *HelloContacts*, the transition from the overview to the next screen just isn't quite what it should be. If you look closely, the bounce animation on the collection view cell doesn't get a chance to finish before the new view controller is pushed. This looks sloppy, and it's a shame our animation doesn't get enough time to shine. This is a perfect time to use a manual segue; a segue we'll trigger from the code whenever we want to. By using a manual segue, we can take full control over when the next view controller is presented to the user. This is perfect for us because we can allow the animation to finish and show the next view controller afterwards.

In the `Main.storyboard`, select the connection between the overview and the second view controller and press the *Backspace* key to delete it. Create a new, manual segue by dragging from the yellow circle in the top section of your overview view controller to the details view controller. When the modal comes up, select the **Manual** segue. Now, select the segue you just created and set `detailViewSegue` as the value for the identifier field in the **Attributes Inspector**.

To trigger the segue at the right time, open `ViewController.swift` and update the following code in the `collectionView(_:didSelectItemAt:)` method; the updated code is highlighted:

```
func collectionView(_ collectionView: UICollectionView,
  didSelectItemAt indexPath: IndexPath) {

    guard let cell = collectionView.cellForItem(at: indexPath) as?
      ContactCollectionViewCell else { return }

    UIView.animate(withDuration: 0.1,
        delay: 0,
        options: [.curveEaseOut],
        animations: {
            cell.contactImage.transform = CGAffineTransform(scaleX:
            0.9, y: 0.9)
        }, completion: { finished in
            UIView.animate(withDuration: 0.1,
                delay: 0,
                options: [.curveEaseIn],
                animations: {
                    cell.contactImage.transform =
CGAffineTransform.identity
                },
                completion: { [weak self] finished in
                    self?.performSegue(withIdentifier:
                    "detailViewSegue",
                      sender: self)
}
            )
        })
}
```

By adding a completion handler to the animation that resets the contact image back to its original size, you can trigger the manual segue after the entire animation is complete. A manual segue is triggered by calling the `performSegue(withIdentifier:sender:)` method.

The `performSegue(withIdentifier:sender:)` method is implemented in `UIViewController` and is used to programmatically trigger segues. If you build and run the app now, you'll see that the entire animation on the contact image will complete and only after the animation is done is the segue performed.

Now that you know how to use a storyboard for designing multiple screens and visually connecting them with segues, it's time to learn more about Auto Layout. Let's add some actual details to the contact details screen

Creating adaptive layouts with Auto Layout

At the beginning of the chapter, you learned what adaptive layouts are and why they are important. You learned a little bit about Size classes and `traitCollection`. In this section, we'll take a deep dive into these topics by implementing an adaptive contact details page. You'll learn some best practices to implement a layout that is tweaked for different Size classes. Finally, you'll learn how to make use of Auto Layout and Size classes in code because it is not always possible to define your entire layout in a storyboard. The layout you are going to build is shown as follows:

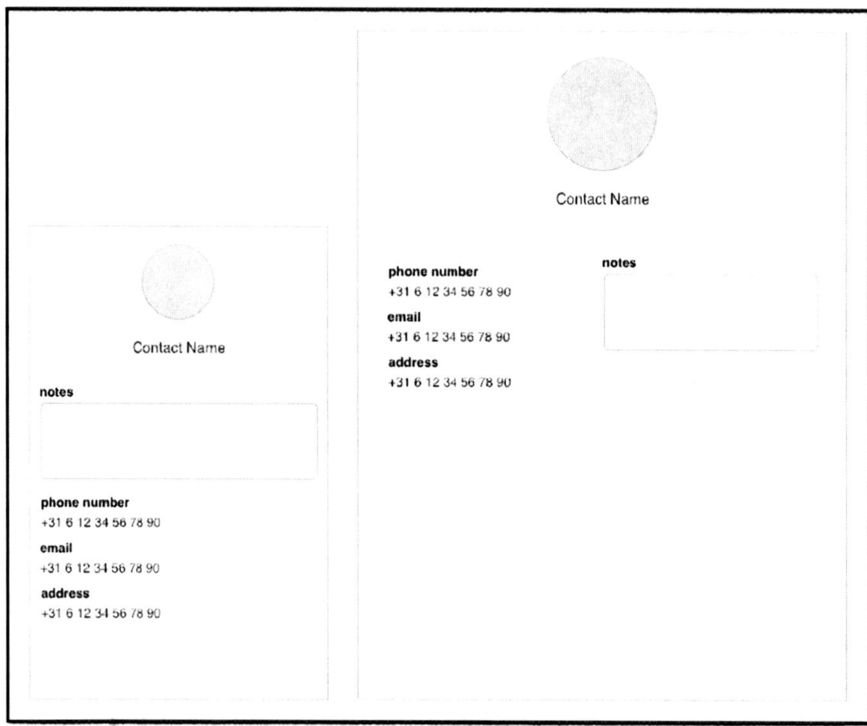

The **Contact details** page contains some of the contact's information, and the user can add notes to a contact. On small screens, the layout is just a single column: the notes fields is at the top, and the rest follows. On larger screens, the layout will be split across two columns to make good use of the available space. Let's see how we can implement both layouts using a **Storyboard**.

Auto Layout with Interface Builder

A good strategy to implement a layout like this is to add constraints that apply to all versions of the design first. These constraints will be active for any Size Class. By doing this, you can implement a general layout first and then apply tweaks for Size Class specific changes. When you implement your layout like this, you'll have a minimum amount of constraints in your design. Having fewer constraints often means that it's easier to maintain and tweak your layout later.

By default, Interface Builder is configured to apply constraints to all Size classes. This means that the width Size Class can be any and the height Size Class can be any as well. If you want to add constraints that only apply to a specific Size Class variation, you can use the **Vary for Traits** button in the bottom-right corner of the device preview section. Before you press this button, you should select the type of device that has the specific traits that you want to add a variation for. Try to click around a little bit to get a feel for how this works. Make sure you exit the **Vary for Traits** mode before you continue. Also, remove the `UILabel` that you added to the details page earlier; we don't need it anymore.

When a user taps on the notes text input, a keyboard will appear. If this happens on a phone in landscape mode, we can be pretty certain that the notes input field will be covered by the keyboard. This behavior is not great because users like to be able to see what they're typing in a text field. To fix this, we can contain the entire contact details page in a scroll view. By doing this, the user can still scroll around to see everything they've typed.

Implementing a scroll view like this has proven to be non-trivial in Auto Layout. So let's get that out of the way first. After that, we can immediately begin implementing the scrollable layout for the contact details page. The following steps outline the process of implementing the full contact details page:

1. Add a scroll view that will contain the entire layout.
2. Lay out the image and label.
3. Lay out the contact's image size for large screens.
4. Lay out the bottom section of the contact details page.
5. Lay out the bottom section of the contact details page for small screens.

Adding a scroll view to make the layout scrollable

A scroll view is a very convenient tool to prevent a keyboard from obscuring contents in your app. Using a scroll view, the user can easily decide which part of the UI they want to see when the keyboard overlays a part of the view. However, a scroll view needs to know how large its child content is in order to enable scrolling. Doing this in Auto Layout isn't very straightforward, but it's a great exercise to learn more about Auto Layout.

The most important aspect is that you need to make sure that the scroll view is pinned to the superview's edges, and it must have only one content view. This content view will have an equal width to the main view. Finally, the content view needs to be pinned to all the edges of the scroll view. Let's add these constraints step by step, as follows:

1. Make sure that you uncheck **Adjust Scroll View Insets** in the **Attributes Inspector** for the entire view controller.
2. Drag a scroll view out from the **Object Library** and add it to the view. Resize it so it covers the view; don't make it cover the navigation bar. Add constraints through the **Pin menu**, as shown in the following screenshot:

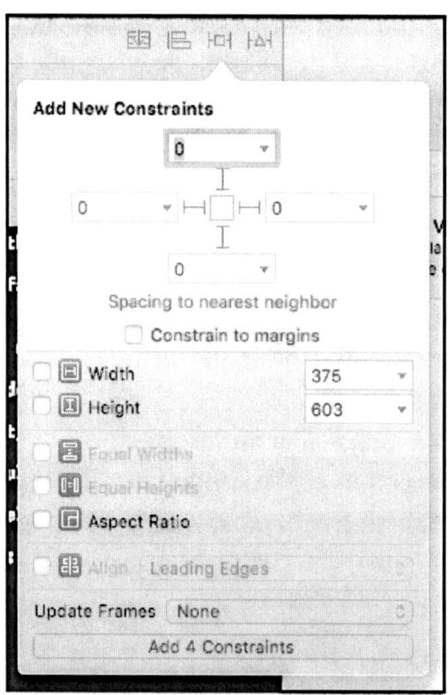

3. Now, drag a regular `UIView` out to the view and make sure that it's a subview of the scroll view. Manually size it so that it covers the entire scroll view. Add the same constraints you added to the scroll view so all the edges are pinned to the superview edges. The content view also needs to be constrained to have an equal width to the main view. Select the content view you just added and press *Ctrl*. Now, drag it to the scroll view's parent: the main view. You can now select **Equal Width** to set an equal width between the content view and the main view. This is done so the scroll view knows how wide its contents will be.

A scroll view that's used in combination with Auto Layout uses its single-child view to determine the scroll width and height. Our app needs a width that's equal to the screen and a dynamic height based on its content. When you implemented step 3, an Auto Layout issue appeared that still needs to be resolved, because the scroll view's child view (the content container view) cannot determine its height. This means that the scroll view has an ambiguous scroll height.

Once we add some child views to this container view, this problem will resolve itself. The container can calculate its height based on its child views. The scroll view will then in turn use this height to determine its scroll height.

Laying out the image and name label

The next step is to add the contact's image and its name label to the content container view. To do this, first drag out `UIImageView` and `UILabel` from the **Object Library**. Position them so that they both are horizontally centered in the view. Also, position them so they have about 10 points of spacing on the vertical axis. Don't forget to apply a nice light gray background color to the image.

You've already seen the following two ways to add constraints:

- Have Xcode add constraints for you
- Add constraints through the menu in the bottom-right corner

We'll add a third technique to that list: *Ctrl* + dragging. You already used *Ctrl* + dragging while setting up the scroll view, but it also works when dragging from one view to another in your design preview.

If you select the `UIImageView` and drag it upward while pressing *Ctrl*, you can add constraints that relate to the view you started dragging it from, the view you let go in, and the direction you were dragging in. Try this now; a menu such as the one in the following screenshot should appear. Press *Shift* and select **Vertical Spacing to Top Layout Guide** and **Center Horizontally in Container**. An **Add Constraints** option should have appeared at the bottom of the list.

Click on that to add the selected constraints. Moving forward, this will be the preferred way to add constraints:

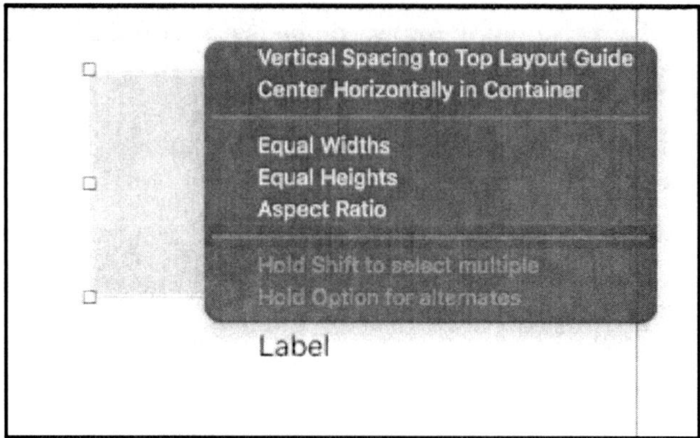

To set an appropriate width and height for the `UIImageView`, press *Ctrl* and drag on the image itself. If you drag and release in a horizontal direction, you can add a width constraint, and dragging vertically allows you to add a height constraint. You can't set the value though; the value will be set to whatever the current size is.

If you want to change the value of a constraint, go to the **Size Inspector** on the right-hand side of the screen and double-click on a constraint. This allows you to change the **Constant** for a constraint. When you're setting a size constraint, the constant will refer to that size. When setting spacing, the constant will refer to the current amount of spacing. Click on the image and correct the width and height constraints so the image will be 60x60 points. Update the preview by clicking on the **Update Frames** option in the **Resolve Auto Layout Issues** menu you've used before. It's located in the bottom-right section of the window.

Now, let's add some constraints to lay out the `UILabel`. Position the `UILabel` approximately ten points beneath the image and make sure that it's centered. Now, press *Ctrl* and drag the `UILabel` to the `UIImageView`. Press *Shift* and add **Vertical Spacing** and **Center Horizontally** constraints. This will set up constraints that horizontally center the `UILabel` relative to the `UIImageView`. It also adds a constraint that vertically spaces the `UILabel` from the `UIImageView`. Finally, drag downward from the `UILabel` to set its vertical spacing to the container view. Modify this constraint so the `UILabel` has a spacing of eight to its container's bottom. This will make sure that the content view has a height, and this resolves the Auto Layout issue we had before.

Change the preview to a couple of different devices and the image and label should always appear nicely centered on every layout. The designs we saw earlier had a larger image on the iPad. This means that we need to add separate sizing constraints for this device. This is what the next step is about.

Adjusting the image and name label for large screens

When you click on the **Vary for Traits** button, you are given three options to base your variation on. You can vary either for the width, height, or both. If you select width, any new constraints you add will apply to all viewports that match the horizontal Size Class that's currently active. So, for example, if you have the iPad view selected and you vary for width, you can see that there are eight possible viewports for your app. These are the landscape and portrait iPad and iPad Pro, and also the 2/3 width multitasking views and the landscape plus sized iPhone. You can see each possible variation that you're currently designing for in the device preview list:

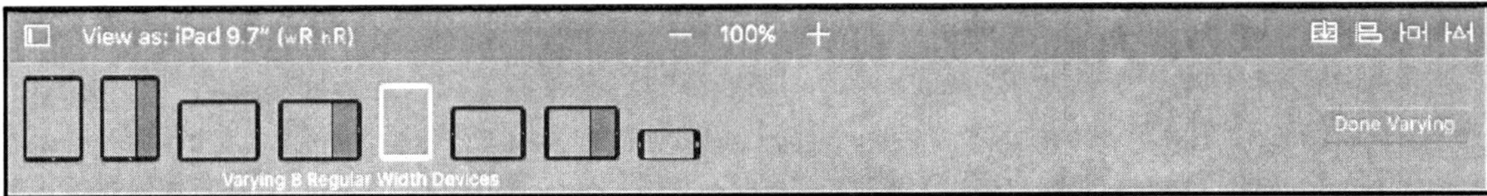

To make the larger image look good, you should vary both the width and height. If the larger image appears on an iPhone 6 Plus in landscape mode, it will cover too much of the viewport, so the bigger image should only be shown on devices that can accommodate it on both the horizontal and vertical axe.

Click on **Vary for Traits** again, and this time check the width and height boxes. You'll notice that the iPhone isn't in the list of devices anymore because a landscape iPhone 6 plus has a regular width and a compact height. On the left-hand side of the Interface Builder window, you can find the document outline. In this outline, look for your image view. You can see the constraints listed under the image view. Expand the constraints and select the width constraint. At the bottom of **Attributes Inspector** on the right-hand side of the screen, you'll find a plus icon and a checkbox labeled **Installed**. Click on the plus symbol and navigate to the **Regular width** | **Regular height** | **Any gamut (current)** option. After doing this, an extra checkbox will appear. Uncheck it so the width constraint is not installed for the current variation. Do the same for the image's height constraint. After doing this, the image might not be visible anymore because Auto Layout doesn't know its dimensions.

With the image view selected, go to the Size Inspector and set the image's size to 120x120. This will make the image reappear. Now, use the *Ctrl* + drag technique to add width and height constraints, as you did before. If you inspect these constraints, you'll see that they have a similar setup to their installation checkboxes, except that the general one is unchecked and the specific one is checked. Great! This means you've successfully set up the constraint variations for your app. Go ahead and exit the variation mode by clicking on the **Done Varying** button and check out your layout on several screens. If the image size doesn't update automatically, select the entire view and update the frames from the **Resolve Auto Layout Issues** menu.

Laying out the bottom section

The bottom section for this page looks simple, but we need to think very carefully about the way it's set up. On small screens, all of the elements should be displayed in a single column. Larger screens have two columns. The simplest way to do this is to wrap both of these sections in a container view as shown in the following figure:

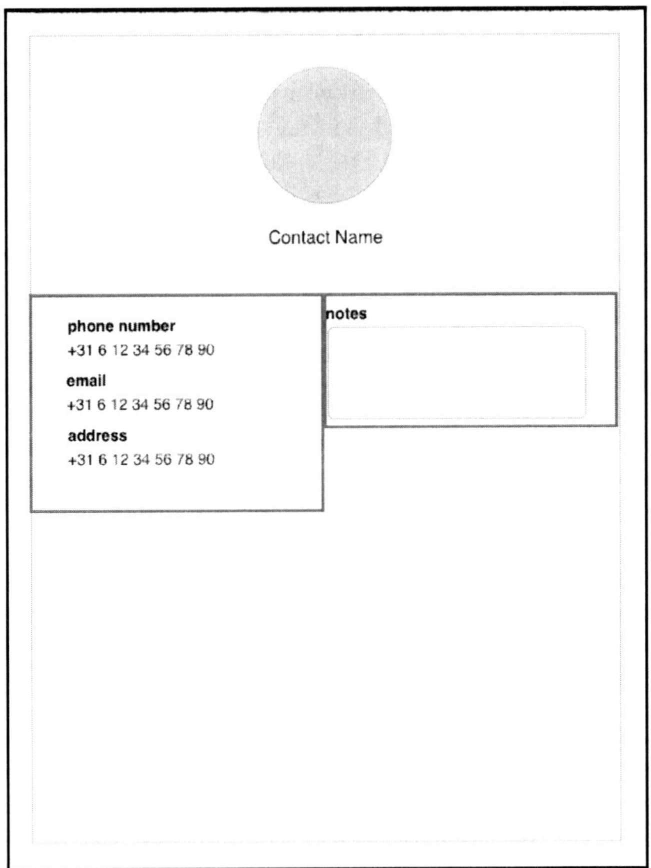

The biggest challenge is to figure out how to make sure that the container view we created earlier is able to calculate the height. Previously, we added a constraint that pinned the bottom of the contact name label to the bottom of the content view. Now, we'll add this constraint to the left view since it's the tallest view we're adding to the details page.

Drag two `UIViews` into the content view. It will be easier to work with the views if you have some more room. In the **Document Outline**, find the constraint that looks like `bottom = Label.bottom`. This constraint currently pins the label's bottom edge to the content view's bottom edge. Select it and delete it by pressing the *Delete* key or Command + *Backspace*. This will give you some more place to work with your views.

Now, size the two `UIViews` so they meet approximately in the middle. They shouldn't overlap but there should be no horizontal space between them. Drag the left edge of the left view to the left side of the content view until you see the blue helper lines. Then, do the same for the right side. Position them both so they are `±40` points beneath the contact name label.

Select the left view, press *Ctrl*, and drag it to the contact name label to add a vertical spacing constraint. Then, drag it to the left side to pin this view's left side to the content view's leading edge. Now, select the right view and do the same, except instead of dragging left, drag right to pin the right side to the content view's trailing edge. Finally, *Ctrl* + drag from the left view to the right view and select the equal width constraint and vertical spacing constraint. This should leave you with two equally sized views that don't have a height yet.

Drag six `UILabels` into the left view. Align them as they are in the design. Use the blue lines as guides for the margins, and make the labels wide enough to cover the view. Stop at the blue lines again; they help you by providing some natural margins. Press *Ctrl* and drag the first label upward to pin it to the top side of the view. Press *Ctrl* and drag left to pin it to the left side, and press *Ctrl* and drag right to pin it to the right side. Then, select the second label and drag it toward the first label. While holding the *Shift* key, select the leading, trailing, and vertical spacing constraints. Repeat this for all other labels. The final label should be pinned to the bottom of the view.

Now, drag a label and the text field to the right side's view. Align the elements by using the blue lines again. Pin the label to the top, right, and left sides of its containing view. Drag the text field to the label and select the leading, trailing, and vertical spacing constraints. Finally, drag upward inside the text field to add a height constraint. Modify this constraint so the text field has a height of `80`. Finally, press *Ctrl* and drag downward to pin the bottom of the text field to the bottom of the view.

The final layout step is to press *Ctrl* and drag the left view down into the content view. Select the vertical spacing constraint and modify the constant so the final spacing is eight. Now use the Attributes Inspector to make the header labels bold font and provide the appropriate text values for them.

Well, that was a lot of instructions, but you should have successfully completed the layout for Regular x Regular devices. Try to run your app on an iPad; looks pretty good, right?

Adjust the bottom section for small screens

The layout we have so far looks pretty good on the iPad. However, it's just too cramped on the iPhone in the portrait mode. Let's create some room by changing it to a single column layout. First, select iPhone view and click on the **Vary for Traits** button. This time, make sure that you only vary for the width.

The easiest way to pull off a change this big is to rearrange the view first without modifying the constraints yet. Rearrange the views so they look as shown in the following screenshot:

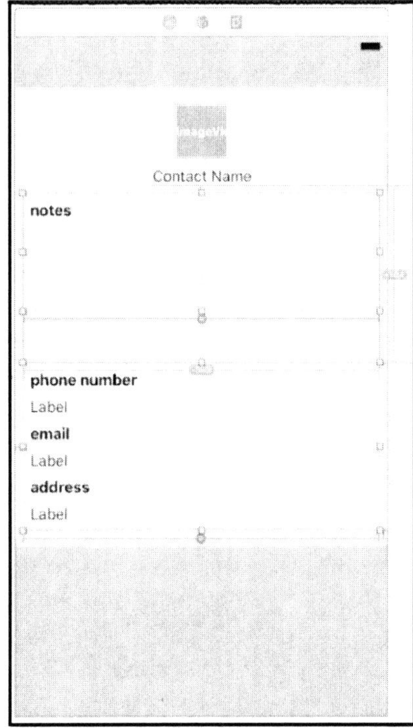

Then, it's a good idea to add constraints that you know are missing. This isn't always straightforward but with some practice, you should get the hang of this pretty soon. Make sure that each view can figure out its x and y position and its width and height.

In this case, the following constraints are missing:

- Top view with notes to the left side of the content view
- Vertical spacing between the top and bottom view
- Bottom view to the right side of the content view

Add the constraints by pressing *Ctrl* and dragging as we did before. You'll end up with a lot of errors and red lines. This is because we haven't disabled the constraints that were created for the two-column layout. In order to fix the errors, the following constraints that only apply to the two-column layout must be removed:

- Vertical spacing between the former left view and the contact name label
- Horizontal spacing between the former left and right view
- Equal with constraint

Select the top view and look for the **Leading Space to: View** constraint. Double click on it and use the plus at the bottom to add an exception. Use the drop-down menu and navigate to **Compact Width** | **Any Height** | **Any Gamut**. This will configure the constraint for a device that has a compact width form factor, regardless of its height. Make sure that you uncheck the installation box for this variation. Do the same for the other two constraints. You can find these constraints by selecting either of the views related to the constraint you're looking for.

Finally, select the vertical spacing constraint for the top and bottom view and modify the constant to `8`; this will provide nice spacing between the two sections. You're done modifying the constraints now; no conflicts should remain and your layout should now look good on all devices. Check out the plus-sized iPhone in particular; it will switch between the single and two column layouts! Pretty cool, isn't it? If you run this in landscape on other devices, you'll notice that you can nicely scroll through the contents as well.

Before we deep dive into Auto Layout on the code side, there's one last thing that needs to be fixed. Whenever the keyboard appears, we want to resize the scroll view so a user can still see the entire page. To do this, we will need to create an `@IBOutlet` for the bottom constraint of the scroll view and then we will need to programmatically set the constant for the bottom constraint to the height of the keyboard. To get started, create a new `UIViewController` subclass (navigate to **File** | **New** | **File...**) and name it `ContactDetailViewController`. Assign this class to the contact details screen's view controller in the Interface Builder. Define the following `@IBOutlet` in `ContactDetailViewController.swift` and connect it by dragging it from the Connections Inspector to the scroll view's bottom constraint in the Document Outline:

```
@IBOutlet var scrollViewBottomConstraint: NSLayoutConstraint!
```

Then, add the following lines to `ContactDetailViewController.swift`:

```
override func viewWillAppear(_ animated: Bool) {
    super.viewWillAppear(animated)

    NotificationCenter.default.addObserver(self,
```

```
            selector: #selector(self.onKeyboardAppear(notification:)),
            name: .UIKeyboardWillShow,
            object: nil)

        NotificationCenter.default.addObserver(self,
            selector: #selector(self.onKeyboardHide(notification:)),
            name: .UIKeyboardWillHide,
            object: nil)
    }

    override func viewWillDisappear(_ animated: Bool) {
        super.viewWillDisappear(animated)

        NotificationCenter.default.removeObserver(self)
    }
```

The preceding code subscribes the details page to keyboard notifications. Whenever the keyboard appears, the system posts a notification that any object can listen to. Whenever the notifications are fired, a selector is performed on the view controller. This selector points to a function in the view controller. We're adding and removing ourselves as observers when the view shows and hides to make sure that we clean up after ourselves like we should. Now, let's implement the actual handling of this notification, which is as follows:

```
    @objc func onKeyboardAppear(notification: NSNotification) {
        guard let userInfo = notification.userInfo,
            let keyboardFrameValue = userInfo[UIKeyboardFrameEndUserInfoKey]
    as?
              NSValue,
            let animationDuration =
    userInfo[UIKeyboardAnimationDurationUserInfoKey]
              as? Double else {
                return
        }

        scrollViewBottomConstraint.constant =
          keyboardFrameValue.cgRectValue.size.height
          UIView.animate(withDuration: TimeInterval(animationDuration),
    animations: {
              [weak self] in self?.view.layoutIfNeeded()
        })
    }

    @objc func onKeyboardHide(notification: NSNotification) {
        guard let userInfo = notification.userInfo,
            let animationDuration =
    userInfo[UIKeyboardAnimationDurationUserInfoKey]
              as? Double else {
```

```
                return
        }

        scrollViewBottomConstraint.constant = 0
        UIView.animate(withDuration: TimeInterval(animationDuration),
    animations: {
            [weak self] in
              self?.view.layoutIfNeeded()
        })
    }
```

The preceding methods read the `userInfo` dictionary of the notification and extract the keyboard's end frame and the time it takes for the keyboard to appear. After doing that, this information is used to animate the scroll view's bottom up or down view so it adjusts its size to the visible portion of the screen.

Auto Layout in code

Auto Layout is a technique that is present throughout iOS, both in Interface Builder and in code. We've created the contacts page entirely in Interface Builder and that's very convenient. However, there are times when you might not be able to create the layout before the app runs. Let's call the moment of designing in the Interface Builder the design time. At design time, it's possible that not all variables in your design are known. This means that you will need to dynamically add, remove, or update constraints when the app is running at runtime.

Setting up a layout with Auto Layout is very well supported and Interface Builder even has some tools that make setting constraints programmatically fairly straightforward. If you have a very dynamic layout, you don't always know every constraint in advance. Especially if you are dealing with unpredictable data from external sources, a layout might need to change dynamically based on the available contents.

To help you with this, Interface Builder allows you to mark constraints as placeholder constraints in the Attributes Inspector. Marking a constraint as a placeholder means that it was used to create a valid layout for Interface Builder at design time, but you'll replace that constraint at runtime.

When you use Auto Layout in code, you can dynamically update constraints by changing the constant for a constraint at runtime. It's also possible to activate or deactivate certain constraints and to add or remove them. It doesn't matter if you created the constraints you're modifying in code or Interface Builder. Any constraints that affect a view are accessible through code.

The best way to explore this is to get started with some coding. For the sake of this exercise, we'll recreate the top part of the contact details page in code. This means we'll set the constraints affecting the contact image and the contact name label as placeholder constraints in the Interface Builder. The constraints for these views will then be added into the view controller, and we'll toggle some constraints' active states based on the current size class. We'll also watch for changes in the size class and update the constraints accordingly.

Now open `ContactDetailViewController.swift` and add two `@IBOutlets`: one for the contact image and one for the contact label. While you're at it, remove the unused code, except for `viewDidLoad`. You should end up with the following implementation for `ContactDetailViewController`:

```
class ContactDetailViewController: UIViewController {

    @IBOutlet var contactImage: UIImageView!
    @IBOutlet var contactNameLabel: UILabel!

    override func viewDidLoad() {
        super.viewDidLoad()

        // Do any additional setup after loading the view.
    }

}
```

The preceding code shouldn't contain any surprises. Now, open the `Main.storyboard` file, select your view controller, and connect the outlets in the Connections Inspector to the correct views. Now we'll change the existing constraints that position these two views to be placeholder constraints. The constraints that need to be changed are as follows:

- Width constraints for the image (both Regular and Compact)
- Height constraints for the image (both Regular and Compact)
- Top spacing constraint for the image
- Horizontal center constraint for the image
- Spacing constraint between the label and the image
- Horizontal center constraint for the label

The vertical spacing constraint between the label and the bottom views should remain intact. To change a constraint to a placeholder, you must select it and check the placeholder checkbox in the **Attributes Inspector**. If you build and run your app after doing this, you'll end up with a completely white view. That's okay; we just remove some essential constraints that need to be re-added in code.

To get everything up and running again, we'll write some code to implement the eight constraints that were removed. One of the tools available to us is **Visual Format Language (VFL)**. This language is an expressive, declarative way to describe Auto Layout constraints. You can describe multiple constraints that affect multiple views at once, which makes this language very powerful.

A visual format string contains the following information:

- **Information regarding its orientation**: This is either horizontal (**H**), vertical (**V**), or not specified. The default is horizontal.
- **Leading space to superview**: This is optional.
- **Affected view**: This is required.
- **Connection to another view**: This is optional.
- **Trailing space to superview**: This is optional.

An example of a visual format string looks like this:

```
V:|-[contactImageView(60)]-[contactNameLabel]
```

Let's take this string apart piece by piece to see what it does:

- `V:`: This specifies that this format string applies to the vertical axis.
- `|`: This represents the superview.
- `-`: This applies a standard spacing of `±8` points. This is equivalent to spacing a view in the Interface Builder using the blue guidelines.
- `[contactImageView(60)]`: This places the `contactImageView` and gives it a height of 60 points. The placement will be `±8` points from the top of the superview.
- `-`: This applies another standard spacing.
- `[contactNameLabel]`: This places `contactNameLabel` with `±8` points of spacing from `contactImageView`.

This way of describing layouts takes some getting used to, but it's a really powerful way to describe layouts. Once you get the hang of all definitions and possibilities, you'll find that a visual format string is a very descriptive representation of the layout you're trying to create.

Let's dive right in and take a look at how to implement the entire layout for the top section of the contact details page. We'll only create the constraints for the Compact Size Class for now and we'll add the Regular constraints later.

Implementing the compact size layout

To implement the compact size layout, we'll use VFL and anchors. Anchors are fairly straightforward, so let's have a look at the implementation right away and discuss them later.

First, add the following two variables that will be used later to activate and deactivate the compact size constraints:

```
var compactWidthConstraint: NSLayoutConstraint!
var compactHeightConstraint: NSLayoutConstraint!
```

These variables will be set in `viewDidLoad`, and we're using implicitly unwrapped optionals for them. This means that we must set these variables before attempting to use them, otherwise the app will crash due to an unexpected `nil` value.

You often want to avoid implicitly unwrapping `optionals`. Using `optionals` without implicit unwrapping enforces safety because you need to unwrap these values before attempting to use them. However, in some cases, you want your program to crash if a value isn't set; for instance, when there's no sensible way to recover such a missing value. Scenarios like these are very rare, and you should use implicit unwrapping with great caution. In this example, it's used for brevity.

The following code should be added to the `viewDidLoad` method:

```
let views: [String: Any] = ["contactImage": contactImage,
                            "contactNameLabel": contactNameLabel]
var allConstraints = [NSLayoutConstraint]()

compactWidthConstraint =
contactImage.widthAnchor.constraint(equalToConstant: 60)

compactHeightConstraint =
contactImage.heightAnchor.constraint(equalToConstant: 60)

let verticalPositioningConstraints = NSLayoutConstraint.constraints(
    withVisualFormat: "V:|-[contactImage]-[contactNameLabel]",
    options: [NSLayoutFormatOptions.alignAllCenterX],
    metrics: nil,
    views: views)

allConstraints += verticalPositioningConstraints

let centerXConstraint = contactImage.centerXAnchor.constraint(
    equalTo: self.view.centerXAnchor)
```

```
allConstraints.append(centerXConstraint)
allConstraints.append(compactWidthConstraint)
allConstraints.append(compactHeightConstraint)
NSLayoutConstraint.activate(allConstraints)
```

In the preceding code snippet, we created a dictionary of views, which is used later in VFL. We will also instantiate an empty array of constraints. This array will be used to activate all the constraints at once. The following lines assign values to the variables you added before adding this code snippet. These lines make use of the anchor technique to add constraints. You'll notice that the syntax is fairly straightforward. The `constraint` method is called on the anchor we wish to use, and the desired value is passed as an argument.

The vertical positioning is defined in VFL. A string is passed that vertically aligns the views with standard spacing. There's also an option passed to align all views involved on the `x` axis so they're centered, and finally the `views` dictionary is passed in. This dictionary is used to map the string values in the format string to the views we want to lay out. The resulting constraints are then merged with the `allConstraints` array.

Next, the contact image is aligned to the main view's `x` axis by using the anchor technique again. Finally, the three constraints that were created using anchors are added to the list of constraints and all of the constraints get activated at once. If you test your app on an iPhone now, everything should work out as expected.

Implementing the regular size layout

In order to implement the layout for regular-sized devices, the `traitCollection` property of the details view controller is used. As mentioned earlier, this collection contains information about the current environment your app is running in. All `UIViews`, `UIViewControllers`, `UIWindows`, `UIPresentationConrollers`, and `UIScreens` conform to the `UITraitEnvironment` protocol. This means all these classes have a `traitCollection` attribute. They also have a `traitCollectionDidChange(_:)` method. This method is called whenever the `traitCollection` changes. This could happen if a user rotates their device (iPhone 6+) or when a multitasking window on the iPad changes its size. We'll use the `traitCollection` and `traitCollectionDidChange(_:)` to correctly adapt the layout.

First, we'll update `viewDidLoad` so it applies the correct layout right off the bat. Then, we'll watch for changes in the `traitCollection` and update the constraints accordingly. Let's start by adding the following two variables into `ContactDetailController.swift`:

```
var regularWidthConstraint: NSLayoutConstraint!
var regularHeightConstraint: NSLayoutConstraint!
```

These variables will hold the larger width and height constraints for the `contactImage`. Now, update `viewDidLoad` as follows; the code you will need to add or modify is highlighted:

```
// unchanged implementation

compactWidthConstraint = contactImage.widthAnchor.constraint(
    equalToConstant: 60)

compactHeightConstraint = contactImage.heightAnchor.constraint(
    equalToConstant: 60)

regularWidthConstraint =
contactImage.widthAnchor.constraint(equalToConstant: 120)
regularHeightConstraint =
contactImage.heightAnchor.constraint(equalToConstant: 120)

// unchanged implementation

allConstraints.append(centerXConstraint)

if traitCollection.horizontalSizeClass == .regular &&
traitCollection.verticalSizeClass == .regular {
    allConstraints.append(regularWidthConstraint)
    allConstraints.append(regularHeightConstraint)
} else {
    allConstraints.append(compactWidthConstraint)
    allConstraints.append(compactHeightConstraint)
}

NSLayoutConstraint.activate(allConstraints)
```

The first modification is to create two new anchor-based constraints. The second is to check the current traits and make sure that both the horizontal and the vertical Size classes are regular. Size classes in code work the same as they do in the Interface Builder. Previously, we only wanted to target devices that were of regular width and regular height, so this still applies. By selectively appending these constraints to all the constraints' arrays, we can immediately apply the correct layout.

When a user is using an iPad, your app can suddenly change from a Regular x Regular environment to a Compact x Regular environment when multitasking is used. To adapt to the layout accordingly, you need to implement the `traitCollectionDidChange(_:)` method. By implementing this method, you can check the new and old traits and decide whether to activate or deactivate certain constraints.

This is exactly what we need to do to make the contact details page adapt to the changing environment. Add the following code to `ContactDetailController.swift`:

```
override func traitCollectionDidChange(_ previousTraitCollection:
UITraitCollection?) {
    super.traitCollectionDidChange(previousTraitCollection)

    guard let previousTraits = previousTraitCollection,
        previousTraits.horizontalSizeClass !=
traitCollection.horizontalSizeClass || previousTraits.verticalSizeClass !=
traitCollection.verticalSizeClass
    else { return }

    if traitCollection.horizontalSizeClass == .regular &&
        traitCollection.verticalSizeClass == .regular {

        NSLayoutConstraint.deactivate([compactHeightConstraint,
compactWidthConstraint])
        NSLayoutConstraint.activate([regularHeightConstraint,
regularWidthConstraint])
    } else {
        NSLayoutConstraint.deactivate([regularHeightConstraint,
regularWidthConstraint])
        NSLayoutConstraint.activate([compactHeightConstraint,
compactWidthConstraint])
    }
}
```

The preceding code first calls the superclass implementation. This makes sure that any default work implemented in the superclass gets executed. Then, we will make sure that there is a previous `traitCollection` and that at least one size class has changed. If this isn't the case, we will return early because there is no work to be done. This check prevents the constraints from being updated when the Size classes haven't changed at all.

If there's a change in Size Class and the current Size classes are checked, based on these new values, we will `deactivate` and `activate` the relevant constraints.

Implementing an adaptive layout in code requires more work than in the Interface Builder. However, the tools make it fairly straightforward. Most of the time, you'll find that the Interface Builder works perfectly fine, but whenever you need more control you can drop down to the code level and take it from there.

Easier layouts with UIStackView

With iOS 9, Apple added an iOS version of macOS's `NSStackView` to `UIKit`. It's called `UIStackView`. This was a huge improvement because this view makes stacked layouts, such as the stack of labels and values the contact details page contains, a whole lot easier to create and maintain. The most common use case for a `UIStackView` is when you have a couple of views that are laid out relative to each other with equal spacing in between the items.

The layout we created earlier for the contact details page can definitely benefit from using `UIStackView`. The list of labels that displays a user's details in a list can be converted to a `UIStackView`. Currently, every label has a constraint to the label beneath it. This means that adding or removing a label right in the middle would involve removing constraints, reordering labels, and then adding new constraints.

With `UIStackView`, you can simply drag in all the labels you want displayed, configure the `UIStackView` class's layout, and reorder the labels by dragging them around. Constraints will be added and maintained by `UIStackView` automatically. You just have to configure its properties. Let's see how.

Containing labels in a UIStackView

Open the `Main.storyboard` and select a compact width device, iPhone 6, for instance. Start by removing the entire view that contains the six contact information labels. Then, look for `UIStackView` in the **Object Library**. You'll notice that you can either select a vertical or a horizontal stack. We'll need a vertical stack; drag it out to the storyboard.

Next, drag a `UILabel` out from the **Object Inspector**. Drag it right to the **Document Outline** on the left side and drop it in the stack view. This is easier than dropping it in the view and trying to get it on the stack view because there are all kinds of layout errors right now.

Once you've added the `UILabel`, rearrange the views so they are positioned roughly the same as before. Manually resize the scroll view's content view if it will make your job easier. Once you've done this, constrain the stack view eight points from the left, bottom, and right of the superview. Also, constrain the vertical space between the notes container view and the stack view to eight points.

If you update the frames now, you should end up with a result similar to the following screenshot:

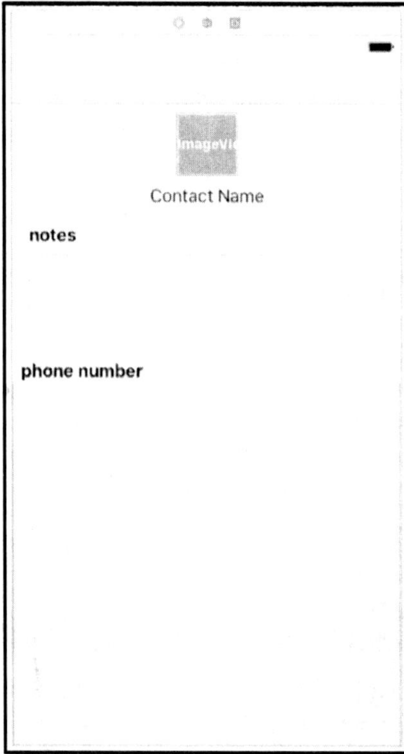

Now, switch to a regular-width device and vary this width trait. Select the **vertical** constraint between the stack view and the notes section and deactivate it for the **Regular Width**, **Any Height**, and **Any Gamut** configurations. Similar to how we deactivated constraints earlier, deactivate the constraint that places the right edge of the stack view eight points from the superview.

Manually rearrange the views so that they look as they did before for **Regular Width,** and add the required constraints. You will need an equal-width constraint between the left and the right, a horizontal spacing constraint of eight points between the left and the right, and finally, a vertical spacing constraint between the contact name and the stack view.

After adding these constraints, drag five more labels to the stack view. You'll see that the layout changes without you having to add any constraints. Neat, isn't it? Let's explore some of the available settings for the stack view. Select the stack view and look at the **Attributes Inspector**.

You'll notice that you can change the stack axis. Currently, it's set to vertical so the views are placed one above the other. Setting them as horizontal will position them next to each other. The **alignment** determines how the views inside of the stack view are aligned. This doesn't change the text alignment at all. It only changes the alignment of the views. Change this value to see what happens (the value you should end up using for this layout is **Fill**).

Changing the distribution doesn't do anything for this stack view. That's because the height is dynamically set based on the contents. If you had a stack view with a fixed height, this would determine how the labels were distributed over the entire available height. The Spacing setting determines how much room there should be between the views inside of the stack view. Set this value to `4` so we have some room for the labels to breathe.

To show you how powerful `UIStackView` really is, we'll refactor the two container views that contain the notes and the contact details.

Varying columns and layouts for traits in UIStackView

Before we add a new stack view for the columns, remove the following constraints in the compact width display mode:

- Vertical spacing between notes and contact name
- Leading space to superview for notes and contact details
- Trailing space to superview for notes and contact details
- Vertical spacing between notes and contact details
- Bottom space to superview for contact details

In the regular width display mode, delete the following constraints:

- Vertical spacing between contact name and contact details
- Horizontal spacing between notes and contact details
- Equal-width constraint between notes and contact details

With all of these constraints removed, it's time to rebuild. Let's stick with the regular-width device. Select the **Stack View**, the view that contains the notes label, and the text view. Refer to the following screenshot to make sure that you have the correct views selected:

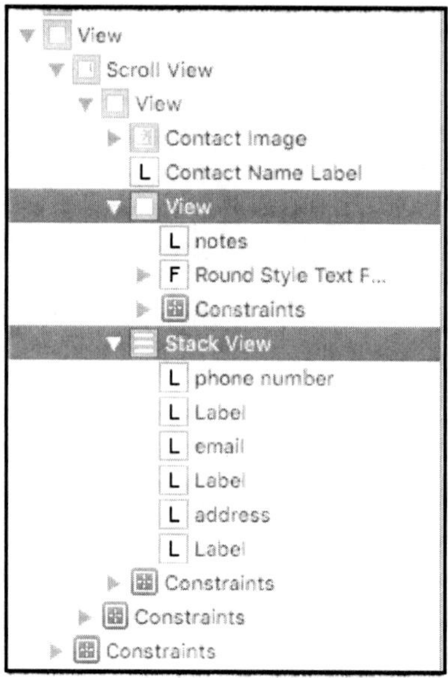

In the top bar, navigate to **Editor** | **Embed in...** | **Stack View**. This will wrap the selected view in a `UIStackView`. Now add some constraints to this stack view. We want the container stack view to be positioned eight points from the superview's leading edge, eight points from the trailing edge, and eight points from the bottom. The spacing between the contact name and the stack view should also be eight points.

Now, select the container stack view and go to the **Attributes Inspector**. Because the stack view now has a predetermined width and we're stacking on the horizontal axis, we can change the distribution. If you set this to **Fill Equally**, set the alignment to **Fill**, and set a spacing of eight points, the result will look identical to the previous version that did not use `UIStackView`, except that this layout involves less constraints, which means less maintenance for you.

Finally, click on the **+** symbol next to the **Axis** property. This enables you to add Size Class variations for this property. Select a **Compact Width**, **Any Height**, **Any Gamut** variation and set the **Axis** to **Vertical**. If you switch to a compact width device now, the layout will update, back to the single column variation we had before. No extra constraints are needed. This is just one example of the power of `UIStackView`; there are many more ways in which `UIStackView` can make your layout work a lot simpler, so make sure you use this component whenever appropriate.

Now let's finish the contacts page by displaying some real data.

Passing data between view controllers

The final bridge to cross for the *HelloContacts* app is to display some actual information about a selected contact. In order to do this, we'll need to add some new outlets to the `ContactDetailViewController`. The data that's loaded for contacts also needs to be expanded a little bit so a contact's phone number, email address, and postal address are fetched. Finally, the contact data needs to be passed from the overview to the details page so the detail page is able to actually display the data. The steps we'll take are as follows:

1. Update the data loading and model.
2. Pass the model to the details page.
3. Implement new outlets and display data.

Updating the data loading and model

Currently, the code in `ViewController.swift` specifies that just the given name, family name, image data, and image availability should be fetched. We need to expand this so the email address, postal address, and phone number are fetched as well. Update the `retrieveContacts(store:)` method with the following code:

```
let keysToFetch = [CNContactGivenNameKey as CNKeyDescriptor,
                   CNContactFamilyNameKey as CNKeyDescriptor,
                   CNContactImageDataKey as CNKeyDescriptor,
                   CNContactImageDataAvailableKey as CNKeyDescriptor,
                  CNContactEmailAddressesKey as CNKeyDescriptor,
                  CNContactPhoneNumbersKey as CNKeyDescriptor,
                  CNContactPostalAddressesKey as CNKeyDescriptor]
```

The new keys are highlighted so you can easily see what has changed.

Previously, you added some computed variables to the `HCContact` class so you could easily access certain properties of the `CNContact` class. We'll do the same for the new keys. Add the following code in `HCContact.swift`:

```
var emailAddress: String {
    return String(contact.emailAddresses.first?.value ?? "--")
}

var phoneNumber: String {
    return String(contact.phoneNumbers.first?.value.stringValue ?? "--
    ")
}

var address: String {
    let street = contact.postalAddresses.first?.value.street ?? "--"
    let city = contact.postalAddresses.first?.value.city ?? "--"
    return "\(street), \(city)"
}
```

If you examine this code closely, you'll notice that the `phoneNumber` and `address` variables aren't as straightforward as the others. That's because the corresponding properties on `CNContact` are arrays of `NSValue` objects. Since we're only interested in the first item available, we use the `first` property that's defined on the array. When available, it returns the first element in the array. Then, the `value` property is used to extract the actual string value. The nil coalescing operator (`??`) is then used to return either the retrieved value or a placeholder string. If the retrieved value doesn't exist, the placeholder is used instead.

For the postal address, the code is more complex. A postal address has multiple fields, so we extract `street` and `city` with the same technique that's used for the phone number. Then, a string is returned with both values separated with a comma.

Now that we have exposed the new properties to users of the `HCContact` class, it's time to pass them on to the details page.

Passing the model to the detail page

The transition from the overview page to the details page is implemented with a segue. The segue is triggered whenever a user has selected a contact, and it takes care of getting the details page on screen. As we're using a segue, there is a dedicated point that we can use to pass data from the overview to the details page. This point is a method called `prepare(for:sender:)`. This method is called whenever a segue is about to happen and provides access to a `destination` variable. The `destination` variable is used to configure data on the view controller that is about to be presented. Let's implement this right now to see how it enables you to pass the selected contact to the details page:

```
override func prepare(for segue: UIStoryboardSegue, sender: Any?) {
    if let contactDetailVC = segue.destination as?
ContactDetailViewController, segue.identifier == "detailViewSegue", let
selectedIndex = collectionView.indexPathsForSelectedItems?.first {

        contactDetailVC.contact = contacts[selectedIndex.row]
    }
}
```

This implementation first verifies that the `destination` is of the correct type. Then, it also makes sure that the segue's `identifier` matches the identifier we set up for this segue. Finally, the first (and only) selected index path is read from the collection view. This information is then used to assign the contact from the contacts array to a `contact` property on the instance of `ContactDetailViewController` we're transitioning to. This property does not exist yet, but we'll implement it momentarily. This method does everything required to pass data from the overview to the detail page.

Implementing new outlets and display data

Using the data that's received on the detail page is pretty straightforward. We need to add some `@IBOutlets` and a contact property. Then, we will use the information available in the contact at an appropriate time to show it to the user. Finally, the created outlets should be hooked up through the Interface Builder.

Let's take a look at the following required code first:

```
@IBOutlet var contactPhoneLabel: UILabel!
@IBOutlet var contactEmailLabel: UILabel!
@IBOutlet var contactAddressLabel: UILabel!

var contact: HCContact?
```

```
override func viewDidLoad() {
    // current implementation...

    if let contact = self.contact {
        contact.fetchImageIfNeeded()
        contactImage.image = contact.contactImage
        contactNameLabel.text = "\(contact.givenName)
\(contact.familyName)"
        contactPhoneLabel.text = contact.phoneNumber
        contactEmailLabel.text = contact.emailAddress
        contactAddressLabel.text = contact.address
    }
}
```

This code should be added to the `ContactDetailViewController.swift` file. The first part declares the outlets and the contact property. The additions to `viewDidLoad` first check that the `contact` is actually set and then assign the values to the user interface elements.

The final step is to go to the storyboard, select the detail view controller, and connect the outlets in the **Connections Inspector** to the user interface elements. After doing this, build and run your app to see the detail page in its full glory. Now, let's add some icing to this cake by implementing peek and pop using 3D Touch!

Previewing content using 3D Touch

One of iOS's lesser-used features is 3D Touch. 3D Touch allows users to make their intent clear by either tapping the screen or by pressing it a little more firmly. The iPhone 6s and newer devices have implemented this functionality and it allows for some pretty neat interactions. One of these is called peek and pop. With peek and pop, a user can Force Touch an element on the screen and they'll see a preview of the detail page they'd see if they had performed a regular tap on the UI element. The following screenshot shows an example of such a preview:

If the user presses a little bit more firmly than when they saw the preview appear, they commit to the preview, meaning they will navigate to the detail page. To implement this, we only need to perform a small amount of work. First of all, the overview view controller must register its desire to provide preview capabilities for its collection view. Second, the overview view controller should implement the `UIViewControllerPreviewingDelegate` protocol so it can provide the preview with the correct view controller and commit to the preview if needed.

Before we get to the code, we should make one minor change to the storyboard. Because the `UIViewControllerPreviewingDelegate` must be able to provide a view controller to preview, we need to make sure that we can create instances of the detail view controller from code.

To do so, open the storyboard file and select the detail view controller. Then, on the right-hand side of the screen, set the view controller's **Storyboard ID** to `ContactDetailViewController`, shown as follows:

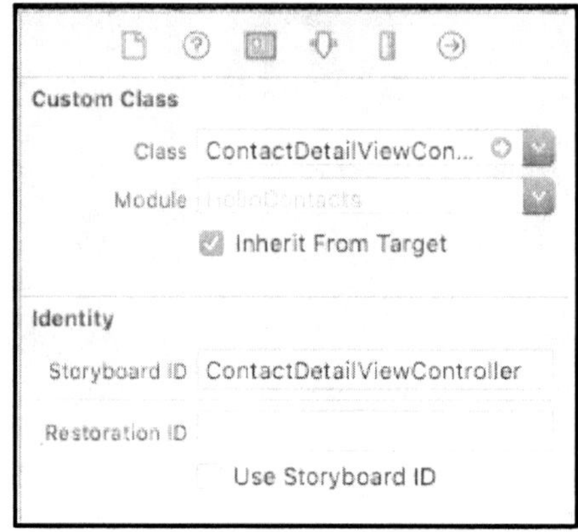

This allows you to create an instance of this view controller from code. You'll learn exactly how in a second. First, we must adjust the `ViewController`'s `viewDidLoad()` method by adding the following lines of code to it:

```
if traitCollection.forceTouchCapability == .available {
    registerForPreviewing(with: self, sourceView: collectionView)
}
```

These lines check the current `traitCollection` to make sure that the environment supports 3D Touch, and if it does, the view controller registers itself as a previewing delegate for the `collectionView`. The final step is to implement `UIViewControllerPreviewingDelegate` for `ViewController`. We're going to implement conformance for this protocol though an extension. Implementing protocol conformance through extensions can be really helpful when your files start to get larger because they provide a nice way to group related methods together. At the bottom of `ViewController.swift`, add the following code:

```
extension ViewController: UIViewControllerPreviewingDelegate {
    func previewingContext(_ previewingContext: UIViewControllerPreviewing,
viewControllerForLocation location: CGPoint) -> UIViewController? {

        guard let tappedIndexPath = collectionView.indexPathForItem(at:
location)
            else { return nil }

        let contact = contacts[tappedIndexPath.row]
```

```
        guard let viewController =
storyboard?.instantiateViewController(withIdentifier:
"ContactDetailViewController") as? ContactDetailViewController
            else { return nil }

        viewController.contact = contact

        return viewController
    }

    func previewingContext(_ previewingContext: UIViewControllerPreviewing,
commit viewControllerToCommit: UIViewController) {
        navigationController?.show(viewControllerToCommit, sender: self)
    }
}
```

This extension implements two methods:
`previewingContext(_:viewControllerForLocation)` and
`previewingContext(_:commit)`. The first method is responsible for providing the previewed view controller. This is done by figuring out the tapped item in the collection view. Next, a view controller is obtained through the storyboard by using the identifier you configured earlier. Finally, the view controller is assigned a contact and returned for previewing.

The second method simply tells the navigation controller to present the view controller that was previewed. When you implement different preview view controllers for your detail pages, you can use the commit method to configure a real detail view controller instead of the preview.

If you run the project on a device that supports 3D Touch, you should be able to apply some force while tapping on a contact to see their preview.

Summary

Congratulations, you have successfully created an application that runs on all iOS devices and screen sizes. You took an application that had just a single page that worked on an iPhone and turned it into a simple contacts application that works on any device. To achieve this, you made use of Auto Layout and `traitCollections`. You learned about Size classes and what they tell you about the available screen's real estate for your application. You also learned how to make use of Auto Layout through code and how to respond to changes in your app's environment in real time. Finally, you learned how to simplify a lot of the Auto Layout work you've done by implementing `UIStackView`. To top it all off, you saw how `prepare(for:sender)` allows you to pass data from an overview page to a details page.

The lessons you've learned in this chapter are extremely valuable. The increase in possible screen sizes over the past few years has made Auto Layout an invaluable tool for developers, and not using it will make your job much harder. If Auto Layout is still a bit hard for you, or it doesn't fully make sense, don't worry. We'll keep using Auto Layout in this book so you will get the hang of it. Going over this chapter again if you feel lost should help you as well; it's a lot to take in, so there's no shame in reading it again. In the next chapter, we'll make some finishing touches to the *HelloContacts* application. The best applications feature clever and useful animations. In the previous chapters, we used little bits of animation. In the next chapter, we will take a deep dive into more complex animations and custom transitions between view controllers.

4
Immersing Your Users with Animation

The *HelloContacts* app is shaping up quite nicely already. We've covered a lot of ground by implementing a custom overview page and a contact detail page that work great on any screen size that exists today. However, there is one more aspect that we can improve to make our app stand out; animation. You have already implemented some animations but we haven't covered how they work yet.

The `UIKit` framework provides some very powerful APIs that you can utilize in your apps to make them look and feel great and natural. Most of these APIs are not even very difficult to use; you can create cool animations without bending over backward.

In this chapter you will learn about `UIViewPropertyAnimator`, a powerful object that was introduced in iOS 10 and can be used to replace the existing animations in the *HelloContacts* app. Next, you'll learn about UIKit dynamics. UIKit dynamics can be used to make objects react to their surroundings by applying physics. Finally, you'll learn how to implement a custom transition from one view to the next.

To sum everything up, this chapter covers the following topics:

- UIViewPropertyAnimator
- Vibrant animations using springs
- UIKit dynamics
- Customizing view controller transitions

Refactoring existing animations with UIViewPropertyAnimator

So far, you have seen animations that were implemented using the `UIView.animate` method. These animations are quite simple to implement and mostly follow the following format:

```
UIView.animate(withDuration: 1.5, animations:
{
    myView.backgroundColor = UIColor.red()
})
```

You have also seen this method implemented in other forms, including one that used a closure that was executed upon completion of the animation. For instance, when a user taps on one of the contacts in the *HelloContacts* app, the following code is used to animate a bounce effect:

```
UIView.animate(withDuration: 0.1, delay: 0, options: [.curveEaseOut],
animations:
{
    cell.contactImage.transform = CGAffineTransform(scaleX: 0.9, y:
    0.9)
}, completion: { finished in
    UIView.animate(withDuration: 0.1, delay: 0, options:
    [.curveEaseIn], animations:
{
        cell.contactImage.transform = CGAffineTransform.identity
    }, completion: { [weak self] finished in
        self?.performSegue(withIdentifier: "detailViewSegue", sender: self)
    })
})
```

When you first saw the code used to implement this animation, you probably weren't too pleased with the way it looks. If you dissect this code, you will find that, in reality, the entire animation is implemented in a single method call. While this might be convenient for small animations, it's not very readable, especially if the animation is more complex.

One reason to favor `UIViewPropertyAnimator` over the implementation you just saw is readability. Let's see what the exact same animation looks like when it's refactored to use `UIViewPropertyAnimator`:

```
let downAnimator = UIViewPropertyAnimator(duration: 0.1, curve: .easeOut) {
    cell.contactImage.transform = CGAffineTransform(scaleX: 0.9, y: 0.9)
}

let upAnimator = UIViewPropertyAnimator(duration: 0.1, curve: .easeIn) {
    cell.contactImage.transform = CGAffineTransform.identity
}

downAnimator.addCompletion { _ in
    upAnimator.startAnimation()
}

upAnimator.addCompletion { [weak self] _ in
    self?.performSegue(withIdentifier: "detailViewSegue", sender: self)
}

downAnimator.startAnimation()
```

The first thing you should notice is how much longer this code is. We went from a 9-line implementation to a 17-line implementation if you count all the blank lines. The second thing you'll notice is how much more readable the code has become. Code readability is something you should never underestimate. You could write great code but if you come back to it a week later and find yourself struggling with that great piece of code due to bad readability, your code suddenly isn't as great as it was when you first wrote it.

It's great that we were able to improve readability, but that still doesn't teach you much about animations. Let's dissect the implementation above to see what's happening under the hood.

The very first lines are all about creating instances of `UIViewPropertyAnimator`. This class has several initializers. The simplest initializer takes no arguments; we can set the duration property and add animations by calling the `addAnimation` method and supplying the animations we want to add as an argument. However, this version would be too basic for *HelloContacts*.

The implementation we need to replace the existing `UIView.animate` code requires us to supply a timing function. There is one initializer that fits this requirement and it takes three arguments. The first argument is the duration of the animation in seconds. The second argument controls the animation curve. An animation curve describes how an animation should progress over time. For instance, the `easeIn` option dictates that an animation starts off slow and speeds up over time. The following figure describes some of the most commonly used timing functions:

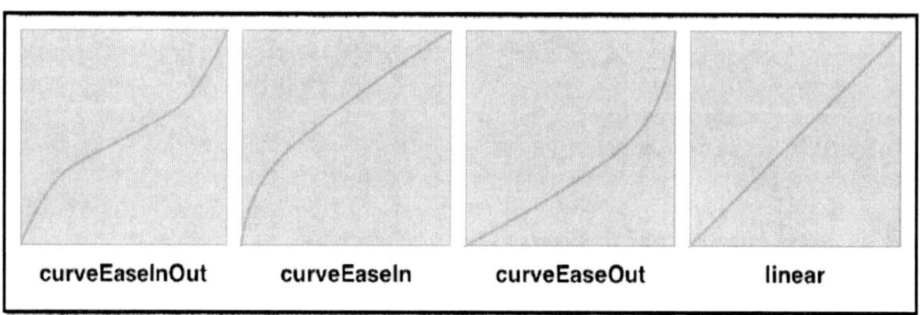

In these graphs, the *horizontal* axis represents the animation's progress. For each graph, the animation timeline is described from left to right on the *x*-axis. The animation's progress is visualized on the *y*-axis from bottom to top. At the bottom-left point, the animation hasn't started yet. At the right of the graph, the animation is completely done. The vertical axis represents time.

The final argument that we pass to the `UIViewPropertyAnimator` initializer is an optional argument for the animation we wish to execute. This is really quite similar to the `UIView.animate` way of doing things; the biggest difference is that we can add more animations after creating the animator, meaning that `nil` can be passed as the argument for the animations and you can add animations you wish to execute at a later time.

Once the animator is set up, a completion closure can be added to the animator. This completion closure receives a single argument. The received argument describes at what point in the animation the completion closure was called. Most typically, this property will be set to `.end`, which indicates that the animation ended at the end position. However, this isn't always true because you can finish animations halfway through the animation if you desire. You could also reverse an animation, meaning that the completion position would be `.start`.

Once the completion closure is added, all you need to do is start the animation by calling `startAnimation()` on your animator object. Once the `startAnimation()` method is called, the animation will begin executing immediately. You could also delay this by calling `startAnimation(afterDelay:)`.

After replacing the animation in `collectionView(_:didSelectItemAt:)` with the `UIViewPropertyAnimator` version of the tap animation, you should be able to replace the remaining `UIView.animate` animations in the project. There are two animations in `ViewController.swift` that are used to animate the changing background color for the collection view cell when you enter or exit edit mode.

There are also two animations in `ContactDetailViewController.swift` that you could replace. However, this animation is so short and simple that creating an instance of `UIViewPropertyAnimator` like we did before might be a bit much. However, as an exercise, it might be nice to try and find the simplest and easiest implementation that you can use to replace the `UIView.animate` calls in the `ContactDetailViewController` class.

Understanding and controlling animation progress

One of `UIViewPropertyAnimator`'s great features is that you can use it to create interactive and reversible animations. Many of the animations you see in iOS are interactive animations. For instance, swiping on a page to go back to the previous page is an interactive transition. Swiping between pages on the home screen, opening the control center, or pulling down the notification center are all examples of animations that you manipulate by interacting with them.

While the concept of interactive animations might seem complex, `UIViewPropertyAnimator` makes it quite simple to implement them. As an example, we'll implement a drawer on the contact detail page in the *HelloContacts* app. First, we'll set up the view so the drawer is partially visible in the app. Once the view is all set up, we'll implement the code to perform an interactive show-and-hide animation for the drawer.

Open **Main.storyboard** and add a plain view to the contact detail view controller's view. Make sure that you do not add the drawer view to the scroll view. It should be added on top of the scroll view. Set up Auto Layout constraints so the drawer view's width is equal to the main view's width. Also align the view to the horizontal center of its container. Next, make the drawer 350 points in height. The last constraint that you must add is a bottom space to view constraint. Set the constant for this constraint to `-305` so most of the drawer view is hidden out of sight.

Next, add a button to the drawer. Align it horizontally and space it 8 points from the top of the drawer. Set the button's label to **Toggle Drawer**. You also might want to add a background color to the drawer so you can easily see it sliding over your contents. The following screenshot shows the desired end result:

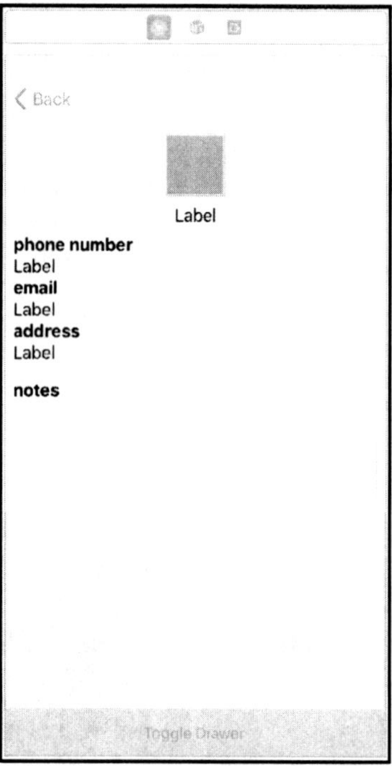

In order to implement the desired effect, the code must be able to do the following:

1. Toggle the drawer by tapping on the toggle button.
2. Toggle the drawer interactively when swiping on the drawer.
3. Allow the user to tap on the toggle button and then swipe the drawer to manipulate or even reverse the animation.

Behavior like this is not straightforward; without `UIViewPropertyAnimator`, you would have to write a lot of complex code and you'd still be pretty far from your desired results. Let's see what `UIViewPropertyAnimator` does to make this effect manageable.

To prepare for the implementation of the drawer, add the following two properties to `ContactDetailViewController`:

```
@IBOutlet var drawer: UIView!
var isDrawerOpen = false
var drawerPanStart: CGFloat = 0
```

Also, add an extension to `ContactDetailViewController` that holds an `@IBAction` for the tap action. We use an extension so we can group together the animation code nicely:

```
extension ContactDetailViewController {
    @IBAction func toggleDrawerTapped() {
    }
}
```

Connect the outlet you've created to the drawer view in Interface Builder. Also, connect `@IBAction` to the toggle button's touch up inside action by dragging the connection from the outlet's inspector panel.

Lastly, add the following lines to the end of `viewDidLoad()`:

```
let panRecognizer = UIPanGestureRecognizer(target: self, action:
#selector(didPanOnDrawer(recognizer:)))
drawer.addGestureRecognizer(panRecognizer)
```

The preceding code sets up and attaches a pan gesture recognizer to the drawer view so we can detect when a user starts dragging their finger on the drawer. Gesture recognizers are a great way to respond to several user interactions, such as tapping, double-tapping, pinching, swiping, panning, and more.

Also, add the following `placeholder` method to the extension you created earlier for the `@IBAction`:

```
@objc func didPanOnDrawer(recognizer: UIPanGestureRecognizer) {

}
```

Now that all of the placeholders are there, let's create a simple first version of our animation. When the user taps on the toggle, we open or close the drawer depending on the current state. The following snippet shouldn't contain anything surprising for you:

```
@IBAction func toggleDrawerTapped() {
    animator = UIViewPropertyAnimator(duration: 1, curve: .easeOut) {
[unowned self] in
        if self.isDrawerOpen {
            self.drawer.transform = CGAffineTransform.identity
```

```
        } else {
            self.drawer.transform = CGAffineTransform(translationX: 0,
            y: -305)
        }
    }
    animator.addCompletion { [unowned self] _ in
        self.animator = nil
        self.isDrawerOpen = !(self.drawer.transform ==
CGAffineTransform.identity)
    }
    animator.startAnimation()
}
```

Depending on the current state of the application, an animation is created. Once the animation finishes, the `isDrawerOpen` variable is changed, depending on whether the current transformation of the drawer is the default transformation or not. If the drawer is not transformed, the drawer is closed. Otherwise, the drawer is opened. You can build and run the app now to see this animation in action.

To allow the user to interrupt or start the animation by dragging their finger on the screen, we'll need to create a new animator if one doesn't already exist. If one does exist, but it's not running for any reason, we'll also want to create a new animator. In all other circumstances, it's possible to reuse the existing animator. So let's refactor the animator creation code from `toggleDrawerTapped()` so it reuses the animator if possible or creates a new animator if needed.

Add the following method to the extension and replace all lines except for the line that starts the animation in `toggleDrawerTapped` with a call to this method:

```
func setUpAnimation() {
    guard animator == nil || animator?.isRunning == false
        else { return }
    animator = UIViewPropertyAnimator(duration: 1, curve: .easeOut) {
[unowned self] in
        if self.isDrawerOpen {
            self.drawer.transform = CGAffineTransform.identity
        } else {
            self.drawer.transform = CGAffineTransform(translationX: 0,
            y: -305)
        }
    }

    animator.addCompletion { [unowned self] _ in
        self.animator = nil
        self.isDrawerOpen = !(self.drawer.transform ==
CGAffineTransform.identity)
```

```
        }
    }
```

Now add the following implementation for `didPanOnDrawer(recognizer: UIPanGestureRecognizer)`:

```
    @objc func didPanOnDrawer(recognizer: UIPanGestureRecognizer) {
        switch recognizer.state {
            case .began:
                setUpAnimation()
                animator.pauseAnimation()
                drawerPanStart = animator.fractionComplete
            case .changed:
                if self.isDrawerOpen {
                    animator.fractionComplete = (recognizer.translation(in:
    drawer).y / 305) + drawerPanStart
                } else {
                    animator.fractionComplete = (recognizer.translation(in:
    drawer).y / -305) + drawerPanStart
                }
            default:
                drawerPanStart = 0
                let timing = UICubicTimingParameters(animationCurve:
                .easeOut)
                animator.continueAnimation(withTimingParameters: timing,
                durationFactor: 0)
                let isSwipingDown = recognizer.velocity(in: drawer).y > 0
                if isSwipingDown == !isDrawerOpen {
                    animator.isReversed = true
                }
        }
    }
```

This method is called for any change that occurs in the pan gesture recognizer. When the pan starts, we configure the animation and then `pauseAnimation()` is called on the animator object. This allows us to change the animation progress based on the user's pan behavior. Because the user might begin panning in the middle of the animation, for instance after tapping the toggle button first, the current `fractionComplete` value is stored in the `drawerPanStart` variable.

The value of `fractionComplete` is a value between `0` and `1` and it's decoupled from the time that your animation takes to run. So imagine that you are using an ease-in and ease-out timing parameter to animate a square from an `x` value of `0` to an `x` value of `100`, the `x` value `10` is not at `10%` of the time the animation takes to complete. However, the `fractionComplete` will be `0.1 (10%)`. This is because `UIViewPropertyAnimator` converts the timescale for your animation to linear once you pause it. Usually, this is the best behavior for an interactive animation. However, you can change this behavior by setting the `scrubsLinearly` property on your animator to false. If you do this, `fractionComplete` will take any timing parameters you've applied into account. You can try playing with this to see what it feels like for the drawer animation.

Once the initial animation is configured and paused, the user can move their finger around. When this happens, the `fractionComplete` property is calculated and set on the animator by taking the distance traveled by the user's finger and dividing it by the total distance required. Next, the progress made by the animation before being interrupted is added to this new value.

Finally, if the gesture ends, is canceled, or anything else, the start position is reset. Also, a timing parameter to use for the rest of the animation is configured and the animation is set up to continue. By passing a `durationFactor` of `0`, we tell the animator to use whatever time is left for the animation while taking into account its new timing function. Also, if the user tapped the toggle button to close the drawer, yet they catch it mid-animation and swipe upward, we want the animation to finish in the upward direction. The last couple of lines take care of this logic.

It's strongly recommended you experiment and play around with the code that you just saw. You can do extremely powerful things with interruptible and interactive animations. Let's see how we can add some vibrancy to animations by using springs!

Adding vibrancy to animations

A lot of animations on iOS look bouncy and realistic. For instance, when an object starts moving in the real world, it rarely does so smoothly. Often, something moves because somebody applied an initial force to it, causing it to have an initial momentum. Spring animations help you to apply this real-world dynamism to your animations.

Spring animations usually take an initial speed. This speed is the momentum the object should have when it begins moving. All spring animations require a damping to be set on them. The naming specifies how much an object can overflow its target value. A larger damping will make your animation feel more bouncy.

The easiest way to explore spring animations is by slightly refactoring the animation you just created for the drawer. Instead of using an `easeOut` animation when a user taps the **toggle** button, let's use a `spring` animation instead. The following code shows the changes you need to make to `setUpAnimation()`:

```
func setUpAnimation() {
    guard animator == nil || animator?.isRunning == false
        else { return }
    let spring: UISpringTimingParameters
    if self.isDrawerOpen {
        spring = UISpringTimingParameters(dampingRatio: 0.8,
initialVelocity: CGVector(dx: 0, dy: 10))
    } else {
        spring = UISpringTimingParameters(dampingRatio: 0.8,
initialVelocity: CGVector(dx: 0, dy: -10))
    }

    animator = UIViewPropertyAnimator(duration: 1, timingParameters:
spring)
    animator.addAnimations { [unowned self] in
        if self.isDrawerOpen {
            self.drawer.transform = CGAffineTransform.identity
        } else {
            self.drawer.transform = CGAffineTransform(translationX: 0,
            y: -305)
        }
    }

    // ...
}
```

To add a spring timing function, we need to use a different initializer for `UIViewPropertyAnimator`. Since we can't add our animations to this initializer, we add them by calling `addAnimations(_:)`. We did not change much code, but try running the app and tapping on the toggle button. The drawer will now feel more realistic because its animation curve is not as static as it was before; it behaves more like it would in the real world.

Play around with the values for the spring damping and the velocity; you'll find some interesting results. Keep in mind that the damping should be a value between `0` and `1` and that a value closer to `1` will make your animation bounce less.

We can take our animations one step further by updating the pan gesture handling animation too. When the user ends their pan, we can set the sprint timing's `initialVelocity` based on the actual pan velocity. This will make the animation feel even more realistic!

```
@objc func didPanOnDrawer(recognizer: UIPanGestureRecognizer) {
    switch recognizer.state {
        // ...
        default:
            drawerPanStart = 0
            let currentVelocity = recognizer.velocity(in: drawer)
            let spring = UISpringTimingParameters(dampingRatio: 0.8,
initialVelocity: CGVector(dx: 0, dy: currentVelocity.y))

            animator.continueAnimation(withTimingParameters: spring,
durationFactor: 0)
            let isSwipingDown = currentVelocity.y > 0
            if isSwipingDown == !isDrawerOpen {
                animator.isReversed = true
            }
    }
}
```

As you've just seen, the use of spring animations can really benefit your animations and they are not very hard to add to your apps. While they might not always be the best solution, their ease of implementation makes spring animations a worthy candidate to experiment with in order to determine whether your animation needs a spring or not.

Another effect that your app could benefit from is the usage of real-world physics. To see how this works, let's have a brief look at UIKit Dynamics.

Adding dynamism with UIKit Dynamics

Most apps implement simple animations like the ones we have already seen. However, some animations could benefit from a slightly more dynamic approach. This is what UIKit Dynamics are for. With UIKit Dynamics, you can place one or more view in a scene that emulates physics. For instance, you can apply gravity to a certain object, causing it to fall downward on the screen. You can even have objects bumping in to each other; if you assign a mass to your views, this mass is actually taken into account when two objects bump into each other. Or, for instance, when you apply a certain force to an object with very little mass, it will be displaced more than an object with a lot of mass, just like you would expect in the real world.

To see how this all works, let's take a little break from building our contacts app and let's see if we can build a nice physics experiment! Create a new project and name it `CradleExperiment`. Make sure you configure it so only the landscape orientations are supported. In the `Main.Storyboard` file, make sure to set the preview to landscape and add three square views to the main view. Make each view about 100 x 100 points and give them a background color. Normally, you would set up constraints to position these views. However, since we're just experimenting right now and our code will be simpler if we don't set up constraints, we're going to skip the constraints for now. Your layout should look similar to the following screenshot:

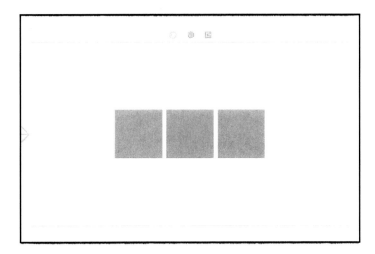

Create `@IBOutlets` in `ViewController.swift` for the views you just added and connect them to the storyboard in the same way you did before. You can name the outlets `square1`, `square2`, and `square3` if you want to follow along with the code samples.

The simplest thing we can do now is to apply some gravity to the views you just added. This will cause them to fall off the screen. Let's see how this works!

First, add the following property to `ViewController.swift`:

```
var animator: UIDynamicAnimator!
```

Then, in `viewDidLoad()`, add the following:

```
override func viewDidLoad() {
    super.viewDidLoad()

    let squares: [UIDynamicItem] = [square1, square2, square3]
    animator = UIDynamicAnimator(referenceView: view)
```

```
        let gravity = UIGravityBehavior(items: squares)
        animator.addBehavior(gravity)
    }
```

If you test your app now, you'll notice that your views start falling immediately. Setting up a simple scene like this is really easy with UIKit Dynamics; however, the current scene is not very interesting (yet). Let's see what would happen if our views were somehow attached to the top of the screen with ropes. This should cause them to fall a little and then bounce and swing around until they eventually come to a standstill.

Add the following code to `viewDidLoad()`:

```
var nextAnchorX = 250

for square in squares {
    let anchorPoint = CGPoint(x: nextAnchorX, y: 0)
    nextAnchorX -= 30
    let attachment = UIAttachmentBehavior(item: square,
    attachedToAnchor: anchorPoint)
    attachment.damping = 0.7
    animator.addBehavior(attachment)
}
```

If you run the app now, you'll note that every square is now attached to an invisible point on the screen that keeps it from falling. We're still missing a few things though; the squares can now simply cross over each other. It would be a lot cooler if they bumped into each other.

All you need to do is add the following two lines to `viewDidLoad()`:

```
let collisions = UICollisionBehavior(items: squares)
animator.addBehavior(collisions)
```

Are you convinced that UIKit Dynamics are cool? I thought so; it's amazing how much you can do with just a little bit of code. Let's add some mass to our squares and make them more elastic to see if this has any effect on how the squares collide.

Update the for loop from before by adding the following code:

```
for square in squares {
    //...
    let dynamicBehavior = UIDynamicItemBehavior()
    dynamicBehavior.addItem(square)
    dynamicBehavior.density = CGFloat(arc4random_uniform(3) + 1)
    dynamicBehavior.elasticity = 0.8
    animator.addBehavior(dynamicBehavior)
}
```

If you build and run now, you won't see a huge difference. However, you can tell that the animation has changed because the variables that go into the physics simulation have changed. Even though this example was very simple, you should be able to implement some interesting behaviors by creating an animator and playing around with the different traits you can add to it.

Even though the UIKit Dynamics physics engine is powerful and performant, you should not use it to build games. If you want to build a game, have a look at SpriteKit. It has a similar, powerful physics engine except the framework is a lot better optimized for building games.

The last stop on our journey through animation-land is view controller transitions! Let's dive right in, shall we?

Customizing view controller transitions

Implementing a custom view controller transition is one of those things that can take a little while to get used to. There are several parts involved that are not always easy to make sense of.

However, once you get the hang of how it all ties together and you are able to implement your own transitions, you have a very powerful tool at your disposal. Proper custom view controllers can entertain and amaze your users. Making your transitions interactive could even ensure that your users will spend some extra time playing around with your app, which is exactly what you want. We'll implement a custom transition for the *HelloContacts* app. First, you'll learn how you can implement a custom modal transition. Once you've implemented that, we'll also explore custom transitions for `UINavigationController`, so we can show and hide the contact details page with a custom transition. We'll make the dismissal of both the modal view controller and the contact detail page interactive, so users can swipe to go back to where they came from.

To reiterate, the following are the steps we will go through:

1. Implement a custom modal presentation transition.
2. Make the transition interactive.
3. Implement a custom `UINavigationController` transition.

Implementing a custom modal presentation transition

A lot of applications implement modally presented view controllers. A modally presented view controller is typically a view controller that is presented on top of the current screen. By default, they animate up from the bottom of the screen and are often used to present forms or other temporary content to the user. In this section, we'll take a look at the default transition and how to customize it to suit your own needs.

The first thing you need to do is create a view controller to be presented modally. Start by creating a new file; pick **Cocoa Touch Class** and name it `CustomPresentedViewController`. Make sure that it subclasses `UIViewController`. Open `Main.storyboard` and drag out a new `UIViewController` from the Object Library and set its class to `CustomPresentedViewController` in the identity inspector panel. Next, drag out a bar button item to the left side of the navigation bar on the contacts overview page. Set the bar button's label text to **Show Modal** and press *Ctrl*, and drag from the bar button item to the new view controller. Select the **Present Modally** segue (refer to the next screenshot). Finally, give the new view controller's view a bright blue background color, so it will be easier to see the transition later. If you run your app now, you can click on the **Show Modal** button and you'll see an empty view controller pop up from the bottom. You can't dismiss this view controller right now. That's okay, we'll get to that later. Let's work on a custom transition to display this view controller first:

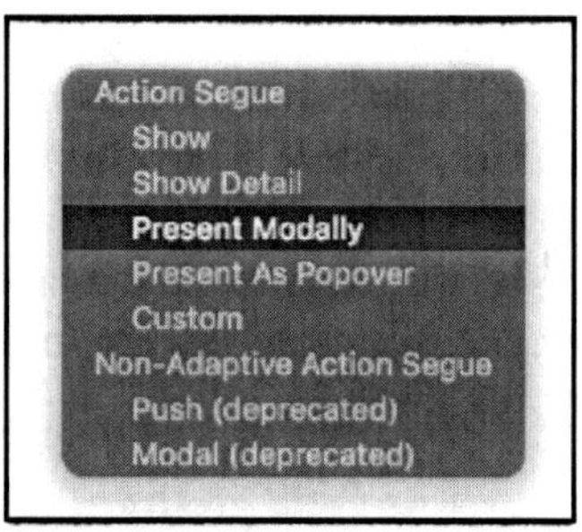

Now that we have a view controller to play with, it's time to explore how to actually implement a custom modal transition. The first object we will look at is the `transitioningDelegate` for `UIViewController`. The `transitioningDelegate` method is responsible for creating an animation controller for the custom transition. Under the hood, the created animation controller makes use of a transitioning context that contains information about the view controllers involved in the transition.

The transitioning flow can be described in the following steps:

1. A transition begins; the target view controller is asked for its `transitioningDelegate`.
2. The `transitioningDelegate` is asked for an animation controller.
3. The animation controller is asked for the animation duration.
4. The animation controller is told to perform the animation.
5. When the animation is complete, the animation controller calls `completeTransition(_:)` on the transitioning context to inform it about the successful transition.

If step 1 or step 2 returns `nil`, or isn't implemented at all, the default animation for the transition is used. The objects involved in a custom transition are displayed in the following figure:

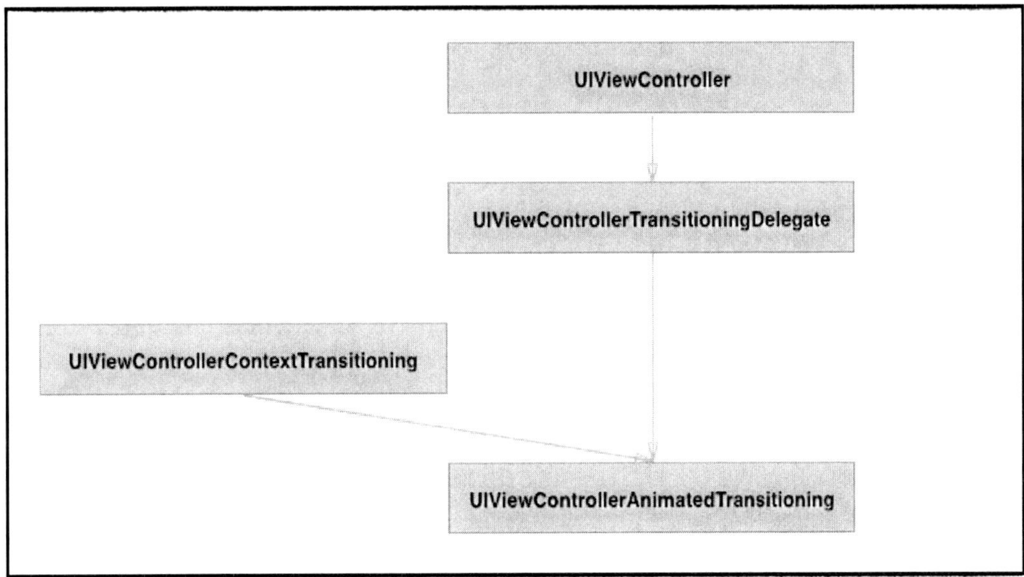

The view controller we're going to present will be its own `transitioningDelegate`. The animation controller will be a separate object that conforms to `UIViewControllerAnimatedTransitioning`, and it will take care of animating the presented view onto the screen. Before we implement this, we'll create the animation controller that's responsible for performing our animation.

Create a new `Cocoa Touch` class and name it `CustomModalShowAnimator`. Pick `NSObject` as its superclass. This class will act as both the transitioning delegate and the animation controller. After creating the new file, open it and change the class declaration as follows:

```
class CustomModalShowAnimator: NSObject,
UIViewControllerAnimatedTransitioning {
}
```

This makes our new class conform to the protocol that's required to be an animation controller. Xcode will show a build error because we haven't implemented all the required methods yet. Let's go over the methods one by one so we end up with a full implementation for our animation controller.

The first method we need to implement for the animation controller is `transitionDuration(using:)`. The implementation for this method is shown below:

```
func transitionDuration(using transitionContext:
UIViewControllerContextTransitioning?) -> TimeInterval {
    return 0.6
}
```

This method returns a `TimeInterval`. This is the time (in seconds) we want the transition to last.

The second method that needs to be implemented is `animateTransition(using:)`. Its purpose is to take care of the actual animation for the custom transition. Our implementation will take the target view controller and its view will be animated from the top down to its final position. It will also do a little bit of scaling, and the opacity for the view will also be animated; to do this, we'll use `UIViewPropertyAnimator`. Add the following implementation to the animator:

```
func animateTransition(using transitionContext:
UIViewControllerContextTransitioning) {
    guard let toViewController = transitionContext.viewController(forKey:
UITransitionContextViewControllerKey.to)
        else { return }

    let transitionContainer = transitionContext.containerView

    var transform = CGAffineTransform.identity
    transform = transform.concatenating(CGAffineTransform(scaleX: 0.6,
    y: 0.6))
    transform = transform.concatenating(CGAffineTransform(translationX:
    0, y: -200))
```

```
    toViewController.view.transform = transform
    toViewController.view.alpha = 0

    transitionContainer.addSubview(toViewController.view)

    let animationTiming = UISpringTimingParameters(
            dampingRatio: 0.8,
            initialVelocity: CGVector(dx: 1, dy: 0))

    let animator = UIViewPropertyAnimator(
            duration: transitionDuration(using: transitionContext),
            timingParameters: animationTiming)

    animator.addAnimations {
        toViewController.view.transform = CGAffineTransform.identity
        toViewController.view.alpha = 1
    }

    animator.addCompletion { finished in
transitionContext.completeTransition(!transitionContext.transitionWasCancel
led)
    }

    animator.startAnimation()
}
```

The implementation above first obtains a reference to the target view controller from the context. Then, the view that will contain the transition is fetched and the final frame for the target view controller is read.

The next step is to set up the initial frame for the target view controller. This is the position at which the animation will start. For this transition, the target view's alpha is set to 0, and a combined transition is used to create an offset on the *Y*-axis and to scale the target view down.

Then, the target view is added to the `transitionContainer` and the actual animation is implemented. Once the animation completes, the `completeTransition(_:)` method is called on the context to inform it that the transition is finished.

Now that the animation controller is complete, we should implement the `UIViewControllerTransitioningDelegate` protocol on `CustomPresentedViewController` and make it its own `transitioningDelegate`. Open the file and add the following implementation code:

```
class CustomPresentedViewController: UIViewController {

    override func viewDidLoad() {
        super.viewDidLoad()
        transitioningDelegate = self
    }
}

extension CustomPresentedViewController:
UIViewControllerTransitioningDelegate {
    func animationController(forPresentedController presented:
UIViewController, presenting: UIViewController, sourceController source:
UIViewController) -> UIViewControllerAnimatedTransitioning? {
        return CustomModalShowAnimator()
    }

    func animationController(forDismissedController dismissed:
UIViewController) -> UIViewControllerAnimatedTransitioning? {
        return nil
    }
}
```

This code adds conformance to the `UIViewControllerTransitioningDelegate` protocol and assigns the view controller as its own transitioning delegate. The `animationController(forPresentedController:presenting:source)` method returns the animation controller you created before. The `animationController(forDismissedController:)` method returns `nil` for now. Go ahead and test your custom transition! This is all the code required to create a custom display transition. Now that we can display our view controller with a custom transition, let's add an interactive dismissal transition.

Making an interactive dismissal transition

Implementing an interactive transition requires a bit more work than the non-interactive version, and the way it works is also somewhat harder to grasp. The non-interactive transition worked by returning the object that took care of the animations in the `animationController(forPresentedController:presenting:source)` method.

For the interactive dismiss transition, two methods should be implemented. These two methods work together to make the interactive animation happen. The first method is `animationController(forDismissedController:)`. This method will return an object that will perform animations, just like its counterpart that is called to present a view controller. However, to make the animation interactive, we must also implement the `interactionController(forDismissal:)` method. This method should return an object that works in conjunction with the object we returned from `animationController(forDismissedController:)`. The way this all ties together can roughly be summed up as follows:

1. A `UIViewControllerAnimatedTransitioning` object is requested by calling `animationController(forDismissedController:)`.
2. A `UIViewControllerInteractiveTransitioning` object is requested by calling `interactionController(forDismissal:)`. The `UIViewControllerAnimatedTransitioning` object that was retrieved earlier is passed to this method. If this method returns `nil`, the transition will be executed without being interactive.
3. If both methods return a valid object, the transition is interactive.

Let's take a look at how this compares to the previous animation flow we looked at earlier in the following diagram:

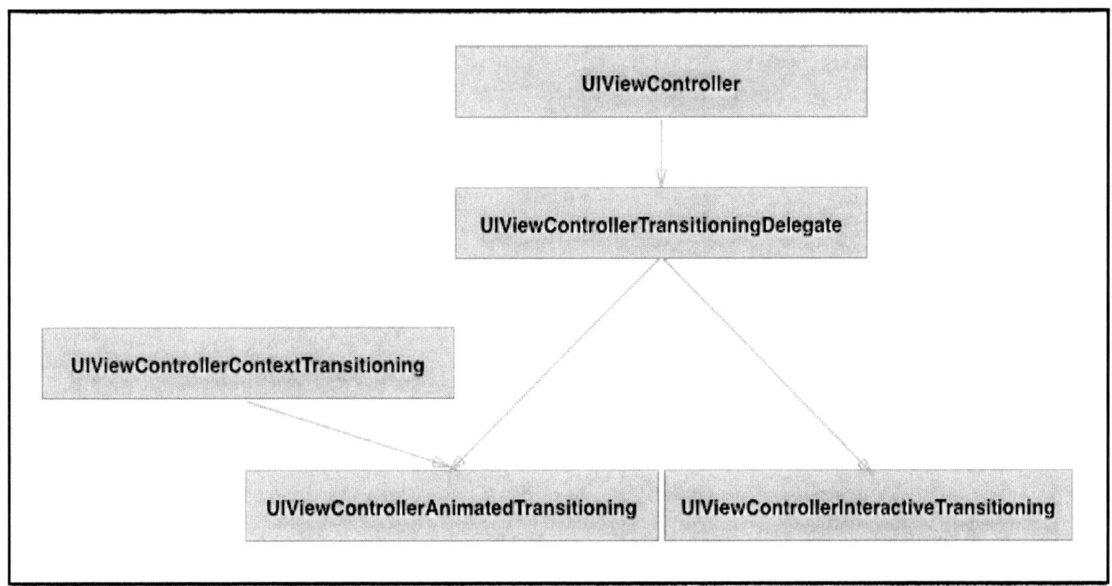

For convenience, we'll implement both `UIViewControllerAnimatedTransitioning` and `UIViewControllerInteractiveTransitioning` in a single class. This will make it a little bit easier to see how everything ties together.

Start off by creating a new `Cocoa Touch` class and name it `CustomModalHideAnimator`. Choose `UIPercentDrivenInteractiveTransition` as its superclass. This class implements convenience methods to easily update the interactive transition. It also conforms to `UIViewControllerInteractiveTransitioning`, so we don't have to add conformance ourselves. However, you should make sure to add conformance to the `UIViewControllerAnimatedTransitioning` to `CustomModalHideAnimator` declaration yourself.

Let's start off by implementing a custom initializer that will tie the `CustomPresentedViewController` instance to `CustomModalHideAnimator`. This enables us to add a gesture recognizer to the modal view and update the animation based on the status of the gesture recognizer. Add the following code to the implementation for `CustomModalHideAnimator`:

```
let viewController: UIViewController

init(withViewController viewController: UIViewController) {
    self.viewController = viewController

    super.init()

    let panGesture = UIScreenEdgePanGestureRecognizer(
            target: self,
            action: #selector(handleEdgePan(gestureRecognizer:)))

    panGesture.edges = .left
    viewController.view.addGestureRecognizer(panGesture)
}

@objc func handleEdgePan(gestureRecognizer:
UIScreenEdgePanGestureRecognizer) {
    let panTranslation = gestureRecognizer.translation(in:
viewController.view)
    let animationProgress = min(max(panTranslation.x / 200, 0.0), 1.0)

    switch gestureRecognizer.state {
    case .began:
        viewController.dismiss(animated: true, completion: nil)
    case .changed:
        update(animationProgress)
        break
    case .ended:
```

```
            if animationProgress < 0.5 {
                cancel()
            } else {
                finish()
            }
            break
        default:
            cancel()
            break
        }
    }
```

This snippet starts off with a custom initializer that immediately ties a `UIViewController` instance to itself. Then it completes initialization by calling the superclass's initializer, and then the pan gesture is added to the view. We're using `UIScreenEdgePanGestureRecognizer` so we can bind it to swiping from the left edge of the screen. This mimics the standard gesture that's normally used to go back a step.

Next, the `handleEdgePan(_:)` method is implemented. This method figures out the distance that is swiped. Then, the state of the gesture is checked. If the user just started the gesture, we tell the view controller to dismiss it. This will trigger the sequence of steps that was outlined before, and it will start the interactive dismissal.

If the gesture just changed, the animation's progress is updated by calling the `update(_:)` method of `UIPercentDrivenInteractiveTransition`. If the gesture ended, we check the progress made so far. If there is enough progress, we finish the transition; otherwise, we cancel it. If we receive any other status for the gesture, we assume it got canceled so we also cancel the transition. If you noticed some similarities between this implementation and the interactive `UIViewPropertyAnimator` example you saw before, you're not wrong! These implementations are pretty similar in terms of tracking a gesture and updating an animation's progress.

Next, we implement the `UIViewControllerAnimatedTransitioning` methods that describe the transition we're executing. This transition basically does the opposite from the transition we used to display our modal view controller. The following snippet implements this:

```
    func transitionDuration(using transitionContext:
    UIViewControllerContextTransitioning?) -> TimeInterval {
        return 0.6
    }

    func animateTransition(using transitionContext:
    UIViewControllerContextTransitioning) {
```

```
    guard let fromViewController = transitionContext.viewController(
            forKey: UITransitionContextViewControllerKey.from),
        let toViewController = transitionContext.viewController(
            forKey: UITransitionContextViewControllerKey.to) else {
                return
    }

    let transitionContainer = transitionContext.containerView

    transitionContainer.addSubview(toViewController.view)
    transitionContainer.addSubview(fromViewController.view)

    let animationTiming = UISpringTimingParameters(
        dampingRatio: 0.8,
        initialVelocity: CGVector(dx: 1, dy: 0))

    let animator = UIViewPropertyAnimator(
        duration: transitionDuration(using: transitionContext),
        timingParameters: animationTiming)

    animator.addAnimations {
        var transform = CGAffineTransform.identity
        transform = transform.concatenating(CGAffineTransform(scaleX:
        0.6, y: 0.6))
        transform = transform.concatenating(CGAffineTransform(translationX:
0, y: -200))

        fromViewController.view.transform = transform
        fromViewController.view.alpha = 0
    }

    animator.addCompletion { finished in
transitionContext.completeTransition(!transitionContext.transitionWasCancel
led)
    }

    animator.startAnimation()
}
```

If you study this code, you'll find that it's not very different from its counterpart responsible for displaying the modal view. All that's left to do now is to make sure that our `CustomPresentedViewController` uses this custom animation to create an instance of our `CustomModalHideAnimator` and implement the `interactionController(forDismissal:)` and `animationController(forDismissedController:)` methods. Replace the current `viewDidLoad` implementation in your `CustomPresentedViewController` with the following code:

```
var hideAnimator: CustomModalHideAnimator?

override func viewDidLoad() {
    super.viewDidLoad()

    transitioningDelegate = self
    hideAnimator = CustomModalHideAnimator(withViewController: self)
}
```

The preceding code creates an instance of `CustomModalHideAnimator` and binds the view controller to it by passing it to the initializer. Next, update the code in `animationController(forDismissedController:)` so it returns `hideAnimator` instead of `nil`, as follows:

```
func animationController(forDismissedController dismissed:
UIViewController) -> UIViewControllerAnimatedTransitioning? {
    return hideAnimator
}
```

Finally, implement the `interactionController(forDismissal:)` method so the transition becomes interactive, as follows:

```
func interactionController(forDismissal animator:
UIViewControllerAnimatedTransitioning) ->
UIViewControllerInteractiveTransitioning? {
    return hideAnimator
}
```

Try to run your app now and swipe from the left edge of the screen once you've presented your custom modal view. You can now interactively make the view go away by performing a gesture. Clever implementations of custom transitions can really make users feel in control of your application and the way it responds to them.

Implementing a custom transition is a task that isn't easy by any means. There are a lot of moving parts involved and the amount of delegation and the number of protocols used can be daunting. Take the time to go over the code you've written a few more times to figure out what exactly is going on if you need to. Again, this isn't an easy topic to understand or grasp.

Implementing a custom UINavigationController transition

The view controller transition technique that we've explored is very nice whenever you want to create a custom modal presentation. However, if you want to customize transitions in `UINavigationController` or `UITabBarController` that persist throughout your app, you will need to implement the transitions in a slightly different way.

Let's take a look at how the setup for animating push animations for a `UINavigationController` differs from the setup we saw before:

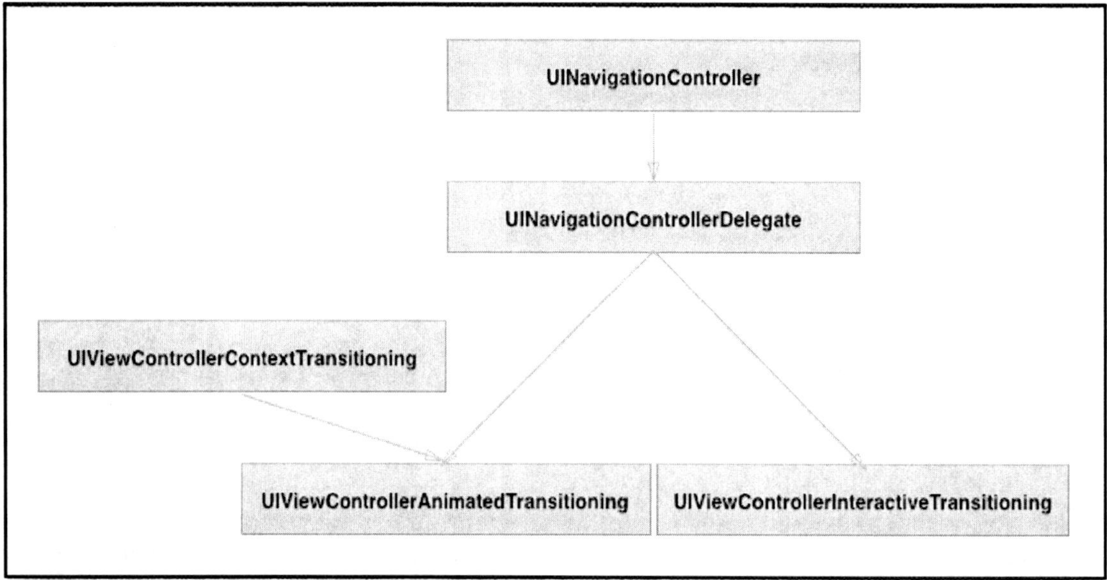

The depicted flow is one for an interactive transition. It's very similar to the way a view controller transition works, except that, this time, `UINavigationControllerDelegate` is the object that provides the `UIViewControllerAnimatedTransitioning` and the `UIViewControllerInteractiveTransitioning` objects that are used to perform the transitions between views.

As the delegate responsible for the transitions is set on the navigation controller instead of on a displayed view controller, every push and pop that is performed by the navigation controller that has a custom delegate will use the same custom transition. This can really come in handy when you want to have consistent behavior throughout your app without manually assigning transitioning delegates all of the time.

To see how exactly a custom navigation controller transition can be implemented, we will create a custom transition that zooms in on a contact. Whenever a user taps a contact, the contact's detail page will expand and grow from the contact's picture until it covers the entire window like it's supposed to. Pressing the Back button will shrink the view back down onto the tapped contact's image. Swiping from the left edge of the screen will interactively shrink the view, using the same animation that is triggered by tapping the back button.

To implement this custom transition, we'll use three classes. A `NavigationDelegate` class will implement the `UINavigationController` delegate and this class will use a `UIPercentDrivenInteractiveTransition` object to manage the interactive back transition. The other two classes are the animator classes; they both implement the `UIViewControllerAnimatedTransitioning` protocol. One is responsible for the hide transition; the other will handle the show transition. Create three files and name them `NavigationDelegate`, `ContactDetailShowAnimator`, and `ContactDetailHideAnimator`. All three should inherit from the `NSObject` class.

Let's begin by implementing `ContactDetailShowAnimator`. The first thing you should do with this class is add conformance to the `UIViewControllerAnimatedTransitioning` protocol by listing it after the `NSObject` superclass declaration. Just like before, we have to implement two methods: one for the duration and one for the animation. In the following implementation, there will be two parts of code that are highlighted; these parts are of interest because they are quite different from what we've seen before, and they play an interesting role in the animation:

```
func transitionDuration(using transitionContext:
UIViewControllerContextTransitioning?) -> TimeInterval {
    return 0.3
}

func animateTransition(using transitionContext:
```

```
UIViewControllerContextTransitioning) {
    guard
        let toViewController = transitionContext.viewController(
                forKey: UITransitionContextViewControllerKey.to),
        let fromViewController = transitionContext.viewController(
                forKey: UITransitionContextViewControllerKey.from),
        let overviewViewController = fromViewController as? ViewController,
        let selectedCell = overviewViewController.collectionView
                .indexPathsForSelectedItems?.first,
        let sourceCell = overviewViewController.collectionView
                .cellForItem(at: selectedCell) as?
ContactCollectionViewCell
    else {
        return
    }

    let transitionContainer = transitionContext.containerView
    let toEndFrame = transitionContext.finalFrame(for: toViewController)

    let imageFrame = sourceCell.contactImage.frame
    let targetFrame = overviewViewController.view.convert(imageFrame,
                          from: sourceCell)

    toViewController.view.frame = targetFrame
    toViewController.view.layer.cornerRadius = sourceCell.frame.height
    / 2

    transitionContainer.addSubview(toViewController.view)

    let animationTiming = UICubicTimingParameters(
                            animationCurve: .easeInOut)

    let animator = UIViewPropertyAnimator(
        duration: transitionDuration(using: transitionContext),
        timingParameters: animationTiming)

    animator.addAnimations {
        toViewController.view.frame = toEndFrame
        toViewController.view.layer.cornerRadius = 0
    }

    animator.addCompletion { finished in
transitionContext.completeTransition(!transitionContext.transitionWasCancel
led)
    }

    animator.startAnimation()
}
```

The first step in the preceding snippet shows how we're extracting information about the tapped cell by casting the `fromViewController` to an instance of `ViewController`, the view controller that contains the overview page. We ask its collection view for the selected index path and use that to extract a cell. All of the work we're doing here returns `Optionals`, which means that the values might not be present according to the compiler. Even though we know these values should always be present, we're safely unwrapping the optional values into variables we can use later in the method.

Then, the detail view controller's initial frame is set up. To determine this frame, the frame for `contactImage` in `sourceCell` is extracted. Then, this frame is converted to the coordinates of `overviewViewController`. If you don't do this, the y position of the frame will be off by about 64 points. That's because the collection view has a content inset of `64` so it can extend beneath the navigation bar.

After converting the image's frame, it's used as the frame for the target view. The target also gets rounded corners so as to aid the zooming-in effect. The animation is set up to remove the rounded corners and to adjust the frame to the planned end frame.

The next step is to implement the back transition. This transition is nearly identical to the show transition. Open the `ContactsDetailHideAnimator.swift` file and add conformance to the `UIViewControllerAnimatedTransitioning` protocol. After doing this, use the code from the show animator to implement the duration delegate method. The following snippet omits the animation setup, the completion handler, and the animation start code. You can use the same implementation for these parts of the method as you did before in the show transition. The optional unwrapping is also omitted; implement this identically to the way you did before except that, this time, `toViewController` should be cast to `ViewController` instead of `fromViewController`:

```
func animateTransition(using transitionContext:
UIViewControllerContextTransitioning) {
    // Optional unwrapping

    let transitionContainer = transitionContext.containerView()

    transitionContainer.addSubview(toViewController.view)
    transitionContainer.addSubview(fromViewController.view)

    let animationTiming = UICubicTimingParameters(animationCure:
.easeInOut)
    // rest of animation setup

    animator.addAnimations {
        let imageFrame = sourceCell.contactImage.frame
```

```
            let targetFrame =
            overviewViewController.view.convert(imageFrame,
                                        from: sourceCell)

            fromViewController.view.frame = targetFrame
            fromViewController.view.layer.cornerRadius =
            sourceCell.contactImage.frame.height / 2
        }

        // animation completion and start
    }
```

Now that we have the animations implemented, its time to implement `UINavigationControllerDelegate`. As discussed before, this delegate is responsible for providing animations and managing interactive back gesture. First, we'll set up the basics for this class. Make sure that `NavigationDelegate` conforms to the `UINavigationControllerDelegate` protocol. Add the following code to the `NavigationDelegate` class:

```
    let navigationController: UINavigationController
    var interactionController: UIPercentDrivenInteractiveTransition?

    init(withNavigationController navigationController: UINavigationController)
    {
        self.navigationController = navigationController

        super.init()

        let panRecognizer = UIPanGestureRecognizer(target: self,
                                 action: #selector(handlePan(gestureRecognizer:)))
        navigationController.view.addGestureRecognizer(panRecognizer)
    }
```

This code allows us to instantiate the `NavigationDelegate` and immediately associate a navigation controller with it. We also add a `UIPanGestureRecognizer` to the view of the navigation controller. This gesture recognizer will drive our interactive transition. Next, let's implement the `handlePan(gestureRecognizer:)` method. This method is called whenever the pan gesture recognizer updates, as follows:

```
    @objc func handlePan(gestureRecognizer: UIPanGestureRecognizer) {
        guard let view = self.navigationController.view
            else { return }

        switch gestureRecognizer.state {
        case .began:
            let location = gestureRecognizer.location(in: view)
```

```
        if location.x < view.bounds.midX &&
            navigationController.viewControllers.count > 1 {

            interactionController = UIPercentDrivenInteractiveTransition()
            navigationController.popViewController(animated: true)
        }
        break
    case .changed:
        let panTranslation = gestureRecognizer.translation(in: view)
        let animationProgress = fabs(panTranslation.x / view.bounds.width)
        interactionController?.update(animationProgress)
        break
    default:
        if gestureRecognizer.velocity(in: view).x > 0 {
            interactionController?.finish()
        } else {
            interactionController?.cancel()
        }

        interactionController = nil
    }
}
```

This method is very similar to the one we saw before for the regular view controller transition. The major difference here is that we're creating the `UIPercentDrivenInteractiveTransition` when the gesture begins. We destroy it when the gesture ends. This way of managing interactive transitions is no better or worse than the other method. It's just a different way of doing the same thing.

There are two methods left to implement. These methods are required in order to conform to `UINavigationControllerDelegate`. Add the following implementation for these methods.

```
func navigationController(_ navigationController: UINavigationController,
animationControllerFor operation: UINavigationControllerOperation,
from fromVC: UIViewController, to toVC: UIViewController) ->
UIViewControllerAnimatedTransitioning? {

    if operation == .pop {
        return ContactsDetailHideAnimator()
    } else {
        return ContactDetailShowAnimator()
    }
}

func navigationController(_ navigationController: UINavigationController,
interactionControllerFor animationController:
```

```
    UIViewControllerAnimatedTransitioning) ->
    UIViewControllerInteractiveTransitioning? {
        return interactionController
    }
```

These two methods are responsible for providing the required objects for the animations. Previously, we had one method that got called whenever a view controller was shown, and one when it was dismissed. The `UINavigationControllerDelegate` has only one method for this. You can check whether the navigation controller is pushing or popping a view controller and, based on that, you can return a different animator.

The final step is to connect the animators to `ViewController`. Declare the following variable in `ViewController.swift`:

```
var navigationDelegate: NavigationDelegate?
```

Next, add the following lines of code to `viewDidLoad()`:

```
if let navigationController = self.navigationController {
    navigationDelegate = NavigationDelegate(withNavigationController:
navigationController)
    navigationController.delegate = navigationDelegate
}
```

You'll notice that the drawer we added to the contact detail view controller earlier is visible outside the boundaries of the detail view controller. Also, the rounded corners we added to the show and hide animations don't seem to be working yet. Set `clipsToBounds` to `true` on the contact detail view controller; this will make the animation look much better!

That's it, we've successfully implemented an interactive transition for a navigation controller. Build and run your app, tap on a cell, and see our freshly created zoom in and out effect in action. Also, try swiping from the left edge of the screen to interactively go back to the overview page.

Summary

In this chapter, you've learned a lot about animation. You are now aware that you can easily animate a view's property using the powerful `UIViewPropertyAnimator` object. You learned what timing functions are and how they affect animations. Also, more importantly, you saw how to make use of springs to make your animations look more lifelike. After learning animation basics, you also learned how to add custom animations to view controller transitions. The complexity for this does not necessarily lie in the animations themselves. The web of collaborating objects makes it quite hard to grasp custom view controller transitions at first. Once you have implemented this a few times, it will get easier to make sense of all the moving parts, and you'll see how all the building blocks fall right into place.

Despite the amount of information already present in this chapter, it does not cover every single aspect of animation. Just the most important parts of animations are covered, so you can utilize them to build better, more engaging apps. If you want to learn more about animation, you should look for resources on Core Animation. This is the framework iOS uses under the hood to drive all of the animations we've created.

With these animations in place, the *HelloContacts* app is complete. Also, with that, the first section of this book is complete. You've learned everything you need to know about creating layouts with Auto Layout, displaying data in lists, and pushing new views to the screen. The next section will focus on Swift and how you can make use of some of Swift's most powerful features, such as protocols and value types.

5
Improving Your Code with Value Types

Now that you have a deeper understanding about layout and user interfaces, it's time to take a step back and take a look at the underlying code you have been writing to build the *HelloContacts* app. If you have prior experience with OOP, nothing we have done so far should have frightened you. You might not have seen protocols used in class declarations before, but apart from that, inheritance in Swift is pretty much the same as you might have seen before.

However, as you have been playing around with Swift and iOS development, you might have noticed two object types you have not seen before: structs and enums. These two object types are what we refer to as value types. What this means and why it matters is covered in this chapter.

You will learn what structs and enums are and how you can use them in your own applications. You will also learn how these object types compare to traditional classes and how to make a choice between using a class, an enum or a struct. First, we'll look into classes and how they manifest themselves throughout apps a bit more, so you have a better understanding of the situation as you've seen it being set up until now. The topics covered in this chapter are the following:

- Understanding classes, also known as reference types
- Value types and how they compare to reference types
- Improving your code with structs
- Containing information in enums
- How to choose between the types

At the end of this chapter, you'll be able to distinguish between different object types and you should be able to use them in your own apps. During this chapter, we'll use a **Playground** to experiment with code. You can check out the Playground for this chapter in the Git repository for this book or you can create a new Playground and follow along.

Understanding reference types

In the previous chapters, you've been creating classes to contain your app's logic and user interface. This works perfectly fine, and to make use of these classes, we didn't need to know anything about how classes behave on the inside and how they manifest themselves in terms of memory and mutability. To understand value types and how they compare to reference types, it's essential that you do have an understanding of what's going on under the hood.

In Swift, there are two types of object that are considered a reference type: **classes** and **closures**. Classes are the only objects in Swift that can inherit from other classes. More on this later, when we discuss structs. Let's examine what it means for an object to be a reference type first.

Whenever you create an instance of a class, you have an object that you can use and pass around. For example, you could use an instance of a class as an argument of a method. This is demonstrated in the following snippet:

```
class Pet {
    var name: String

    init(name: String) {
        self.name = name
    }
}

func printName(forPet pet: Pet) {
    print(pet.name)
}

let cat = Pet(name: "Bubbles")
printName(forPet: cat) // Bubbles
```

The preceding code isn't too exciting. We pass an instance of the `class Pet` to the `printName` function and it prints our pet's name. By passing the instance of `Pet` to a function, we actually passed a reference from our `Pet` instance to the function. This might sound confusing, and before everything becomes clear, let's make things a little bit more confusing. If you change the `printName` function as displayed in the following snippet, you will see some behavior that probably confuses you just a bit more:

```
func printName(forPet pet: Pet) {
    print(pet.name)
    pet.name = "Jeff"
}

let cat = Pet(name: "Bubbles")
printName(forPet: cat) // Bubbles
print(cat.name) // Jeff
```

After calling the `printName` function, our `cat` has a different name. You probably consider this strange; how does setting the name of the pet you received in the function change the name of the `cat` variable? If you've programmed in other languages, you might consider this obvious; after all, didn't we just pass that exact constant to the `printName` function? Also, doesn't it make sense, then, that the name of the original constant also changed? If this is what you thought, then your mindset is in the world of reference types. If this isn't what you thought, you expected our constant to behave more like a value type, which isn't a bad thing at all. However, you still don't really know what exactly is happening with our `Pet` instance.

The snippet we used to change the `Pet`'s name is small, but it shows exactly how reference types work. Whenever you create an instance of a class, some space in memory is allocated to the instance. When you pass the instance as an argument to a function, you don't pass the contents of the instance. Instead, you pass the memory address or, in other words, a reference to the instance. Unless you explicitly copy a reference type, every time you pass your instance around or point another variable to it, the same address in memory is changed. Let's expand our initial example a bit more, so this becomes even more apparent:

```
let cat = Pet(name: "Bubbles")
let dog = cat

printName(forPet: cat) // Bubbles
dog.name = "Benno"

print(cat.name) // Benno
```

Here, we created a `cat` constant, then we created a `dog` constant and set the `cat` constant as its value. Then, we called the `printName` function; this works as before. Next, we changed the name of the `dog`. When we print the name of the `cat` instance, it's not what you might expect at first because the name of the `dog` is printed. This is because we didn't copy anything, we simply pointed the `dog` constant to the same address in memory that the `cat` pointed to.

Reference types are passed around by the address in memory they point to. Unless you explicitly copy an object, multiple variables or constants point to the same instance of the object. As a result of this, mutating one of these variables will mutate them all.

Although this behavior can be convenient at certain times, it could also turn out to pack some nasty surprises if your apps grow to a substantial size. Therefore, it's a good idea to understand value types and know when to use them, because value types can save you quite some debugging time.

Understanding value types

You just saw how passing around a reference type can yield results you might not expect. The idea behind a value type is that this doesn't happen, because instead of passing around references to be addresses in memory, you're passing around actual values. Doing this will often lead to safer and more predictable code. As if this isn't enough of a benefit on its own, value types are also cheaper to instantiate than reference types. More on that later. We'll focus on the most visible differences first.

Differences between values and references in usage

Let's take a look at the `Pet` example again; this time we'll use a `struct` instead of a `class`:

```
struct Pet {
    var name: String

    init(name: String) {
        self.name = name
    }
}

func printName(forPet pet: Pet) {
    print(pet.name)
```

```
}

let cat = Pet(name: "Bubbles")

printName(forPet: cat) // Bubbles
```

The initial example for our value-type exploration looks nearly identical to the reference-type version. The only notable difference is that we're now using a `struct` instead of a `class` in the definition of `Pet`. If we attempt to make the same change to the name of our `pet` instance as we did before, it won't work. Try to alter the `printName` function as follows:

```
func printName(forPet pet: Pet) {
    print(pet.name)
    pet.name = "Jeff"
}
```

You will get an error saying that `pet` is a `let constant`. We didn't declare `pet` anywhere except for the function parameter, and we sure didn't declare it to be a `let constant`. The reason we're seeing this error is because any value type passed to a function is considered to be constant; it's immutable. If we want to mutate the `pet` name anyway, we will need to do the following:

```
func printName(forPet pet: Pet) {
    print(pet.name)
    var mutablePet = pet
    mutablePet.name = "Jeff"
}
```

This will create a `mutablePet` variable, and then the name for this `mutablePet` is changed. If you print the name for the original pet after calling `printName`, what do you think will be printed? If you guessed that it will print `Jeff`, you guessed wrong, because that's referencetype behavior. The name of our pet is still `Bubbles`. This is the case because we never passed around the address in memory for our initial `Pet` instance. We only passed its value around. This means that every time we assign one variable to another, or if we pass a value type to a function, a copy is created instead. Consider the following example that we saw before when using a reference type:

```
let cat = Pet(name: "Bubbles")
var dog = cat

printName(forPet: cat) // Bubbles
dog.name = "Benno"
print(cat.name) // Bubbles
```

You can see that no unexpected mutations were made. You might also notice that the `dog` variable was declared as a variable rather than a constant. Value types are a lot stricter when it comes to mutation. If a value type is declared as a constant, none of its members can be mutated.

Memory differences between values and references

The predictability of value types is great; it can really save you some headaches because values don't change unless you explicitly define them to be changed. Also, they will never be changed at times you don't expect, because you don't pass them around by reference.

Another big plus that value types have is that they are a lot faster to create in memory. This is because value types are typically created on the stack, whereas reference types are created on the heap. Let's take a brief look at what this means and why it matters because it's actually good to be aware that the type of object you pick can influence your application's performance.

Heap allocation

Objects that get allocated on the heap can change their size at any time. A good example of an object that is allocated on the heap is a mutable array. This kind of array can be modified so elements can be added and removed. This means that your app can't allocate a fixed size of memory for this array, and it has to grow and shrink the allocated memory based on the required size.

Classes are also allocated like this; the compiler assumes that a class might have to resize its required memory at any time. One of the reasons for this is that classes aren't as strict about mutability as structs are. In our experiments earlier, you saw that you could change the `name` property of a class instance that was declared with `let`. Because this is possible, the size in memory for our instance could change whenever we assign a new name.

As the memory allocation for reference types is very dynamic, it's also a lot slower to create instances of reference types. The memory overhead is a lot bigger than the overhead caused by value types that are allocated on the stack. Let's take a look at this now.

Stack allocation

As mentioned, value types are allocated on the stack. Stack allocation means that an object has a fixed size in memory that does not change. Sometimes, this fixed size is known at compile time. An example of this is `Int`. The compiler knows how much memory an integer value can use, so it knows how much to allocate ahead of time. This leads to a much faster instantiation process because it's a lot easier to optimize for this scenario.

Value types are also allocated on the stack because, once they are allocated, they typically don't change size anymore. There are some cases where a value type will still need to use the heap; for instance, if a value type contains a constant that is a reference type. You shouldn't worry about these cases too much though. In general, value types are simply faster due to the way they are allocated.

As a side note, it's worth mentioning that stack-allocated objects don't always take up memory. Often, a value type can be kept in the CPU instead of memory, which makes value types even more efficient.

Now that you know more about the way value types and reference types impact your app's memory usage and speed, let's take a look at how structs can improve your code.

Using structs to improve your code

You already saw how value types can benefit your code by being more predictable. What you didn't see is one of the struct's most convenient features: default initializers. You saw that when we declared the `struct Pet`, we provided our own `init` method. For classes, this is required; for structs, it's not. If you create a `struct` without an initializer, it will generate its own. The default initializer for a `struct` is generated based on its members. Let's see what this looks like for the `struct Pet`:

```
struct Pet {
    let name: String
}

let cat = Pet(name: "Bubbles")
```

The default initializer that is generated takes all of the `struct`'s properties that don't have a default value. This is a very convenient way to create your structs. When you're challenged with the task of deciding whether you should use a struct or an enum, there are three basic rules of thumb that you can follow to determine whether you should at least try to use a struct instead of a class.

If you add a custom initializer to one of your structs, the default initializer is not generated anymore. You can keep the generated initializer and have a custom initializer if you declare your custom initializer in an extension for the struct, instead of directly in the struct definition.

Starting your models as structs

One of the most popular things that people declare as structs are models. Models tend to be fairly static; most of their data doesn't have to change, and when it does change, you want that change to be predictable and contained to one instance only, so you can prevent race conditions. Whenever you define a model, try to start off with a struct. If you can't accomplish your goals using a struct, switch to a class.

Using a struct if you don't need inheritance

One thing these structs can't do that classes can is inherit from a superclass. Structs enforce a very flat hierarchy of objects, which is actually a good thing. Less inheritance makes your code easier to reason about due to reduced complexity. Another upside is that you can't accidentally run into conflicts with superclass definitions of properties or methods.

However, if you're creating view controllers or other objects that need to be inherited from the `UIKit` classes, you will need to use a class. Whenever this isn't what you're doing, using a struct might be worth a shot.

A struct cannot inherit from other structs or classes. Note that this does not mean that a struct cannot conform to a protocol. Conforming to protocols is still possible if you use a struct.

Enforcing immutability with structs

If you're creating an object that isn't going to be very likely to change, a struct is a great choice. Due to the stricter nature of structs, as we saw before, declaring an instance of a struct as a constant makes it and its members immutable. This means that you can't accidentally change the value of a struct's property if you didn't explicitly plan to do so. If this is the behavior you desire, you should try using a struct instead of a class because this will greatly improve your ability to manage mutation.

One important note to make here is that whenever a struct has a reference type as one of its properties, the reference type might still mutate. Consider the following example:

```
class Food {
    var name: String

    init(name: String) {
        self.name = name
    }
}

struct Pet {
    let name: String
    let food: Food
}

let cat = Pet(name: "Bubbles", food: Food(name: "Chicken"))
cat.food.name = "Turkey"
print(cat.food.name) // Turkey
```

This example demonstrates that even though `cat` is declared as a constant and the `Food` of the `cat` property is a constant, we can still mutate it. This is due to the fact that `Food` is a reference type, and therefore its properties can be mutated, even if it's contained in a value type.

Final words on structs

The preceding three rules of thumb can be used as a guideline to determine whether or not you should or could use a struct. Of course, there are other reasons why you would or wouldn't use a struct, but it's considered best practice to use one whenever possible. The main reason for this is the way it handles immutability. As you saw, structs are a lot stricter about mutability, and many programmers consider this a good thing because it makes their code more predictable and safer.

Containing information in enums

In Swift, there's a second value type that you can use in your apps. This type is called an enum. Enums are used to store a finite set of options, and they can be used as arguments to functions and methods, and also as properties on structs and classes. Enums are best used when you have property that's, for example, an `Int` or `String`, but it can't take all `String` or `Int` values. Alternatively, an enum can be used to describe a value for which there isn't a suitable type. In that case, the enum is the type.

Whenever you have a predetermined set of possible values, it's probably a wise idea for you to use an enum. Let's take a look at how you can define an `enum` in your own code:

```
enum MessageStatus {
    case sent, delivered, read, unsent
}
```

This `enum` defines a set of statuses a message in a chat app could have. Storing this data in an `enum` allows us to use it as a `status` property on a message struct. Using an `enum`, we know that the `status` can never have an invalid value. Let's take a look at a quick example of using an `enum` as a property on a `struct`:

```
struct Message {
    let contents: String
    let status: MessageStatus
}

let message = Message(contents: "Hello, world", status: .unsent)
```

Whenever you're referring to an `enum` value, you have two options. One is to write out the full enum type and the value you're referring to, for example, `MessageStatus.unsent`. Often, the Swift compiler will already know the type of enum you're accessing. This allows you to use a shorthand notation such as `.unsent`.

Enum values can do more than just provide a set of options that have no type. In Swift, an enum can have a type that describes the type of its values. For example, you could implement an `enum` that has values that are of type `String`, as follows:

```
enum FoodType: String {
    case meat = "Meat"
    case vegetables = "Vegetables"
    case fruit = "Fruit"
    case mixed = "Mixed food"
}
```

This `enum FoodType` specifies four types of food a pet might eat. Associated with the available options is a string value. This value is the enum's `rawValue` and can be accessed through the `rawValue` property.

An enum can't contain any stored properties, but it can contain computed properties. You can use these computed properties to associate even more information with the enum than you can through the `rawValue`. Let's take a look at an example:

```
enum FoodType: String {
    case meat = "Meat"
    case vegetables = "Vegetables"
    case fruit = "Fruit"
    case mixed = "Mixed food"

    var description: String {
        switch self {
        case .meat:
            return "A meaty food type"
        case .vegetables:
            return "Vegetables are good!"
        case .fruit:
            return "Fruity goodness"
        case .mixed:
            return "Just about anything edible"
        }
    }
}
```

The `enum FoodType` now has a `description` property that can be read. Let's take a look at an example of this as well:

```
let food: FoodType = .meat
print(food.description) //A meaty food type
```

The description is computed by a switch construct. This is great if you want to cover all possible values for an enum. Sometimes you might want to have a simpler check in place. For instance, imagine that you want to print some text whenever the food is of type `.meat`. Swift has some extremely powerful patternmatching logic that you can use to implement a simple if statement instead of a switch to check whether an enum has a certain value:

```
if case .meat = food {
    print("Food is meat")
}
```

Using the `if case` syntax, you can check whether `food` equals `.meat`. Performing a check like this is a lot simpler than writing a full-blown `switch` statement to achieve the same.

As you can see, an `enum` behaves a lot like any other type, except you don't need an initializer to use it. You should also know that an `enum` case can act as a box for other values. A great example of this behavior is to look at a simplified version of the `Optional` datatype. Let's look at how an `Optional` containing an `Int` would look:

```
enum Optional {
    case some(Int)
    case none
}
```

This `enum` has two cases. The `some` case has a value associated with it between the braces. Creating and using an `enum` value such as this one is demonstrated in the following code:

```
let optionalInt: Optional = .some(10)
if case let .some(value) = optionalInt {
    print(value) // 10
}
```

To access the associated value, you can unwrap the `enum` value as shown in preceding section. To do so, we use Swift's powerful pattern matching in the form of a `case let` check. The last thing you need to know about enums is that they cannot inherit from other enums or classes. However, you can make enums conform to protocols, just like structs. This means that enums can't just have computed properties, but that they can contain instance and type functions as well. The main thing that sets structs apart from enums, actually, is the fact that enums are used to contain a finite set of possible cases.

Summary

In this chapter, you have looked at value types and reference types. The difference between these two types might seem subtle at first. However, you saw that the memory implications make these types fundamentally different. You saw the most important distinction by examining how they behave. You saw how class instances are passed around by passing the address in memory. This means that mutating one instance mutates everything that points to it. Sometimes, it's not obvious that you're mutating more than one instance. Then, you saw how structs are passed around by value. This meant that all the instances essentially get copied when you pass them around. This ensures that you don't accidentally change values you don't expect to change. Finally, you saw how enums are used to contain a finite set of possible cases.

Picking the right option isn't always easy or straightforward, so if you try to stick to the rules of thumb provided, you should be able to make an informed decision. If you turn out to have picked the wrong option, you can always refactor your code to use a different type. It's recommended that you always try to start off with a value type. In this chapter, it was mentioned that value types don't inherit from other objects. However, they can conform to and implement protocols. This characteristic allows you to use a powerful programming paradigm called protocol-oriented programming. The next chapter will show you exactly what this is and how you can implement it in your own apps.

6

Making Your Code More Flexible with Protocols and Generics

If you've been around a Swift developer long enough, you must have heard them mention protocol-oriented programming at least once. This programming paradigm was introduced by Apple at *WWDC 2015* in a talk that generated a lot of buzz among developers. Suddenly, we learned that thinking in classes and hierarchies leads to code that's hard to maintain, change, and expand. The talk introduced a method of programming that is focused on what an object can do instead of explicitly caring about what an object is.

This chapter will demonstrate to you how you can make use of the powers of POP, and it will show you why it's an important feature of Swift. We'll start off with some simple use cases, and then we'll take a deep dive into its associated types and generic protocols.

Understanding these design patterns and recognizing situations in which a protocol, protocol extension, or a generic protocol can help you improve your code will lead to code that is not only easier to maintain but also a joy to work with. The structure for this chapter is as follows:

- Defining your own protocols
- Checking for traits, not types
- Extending your protocols with default behavior
- Improving your protocols with associated types

By the end of this chapter, you might feel a bit overwhelmed and amazed. Don't worry, shifting your mindset from OOP to a Protocol-Oriented approach isn't easy by any means. It's an entirely different way of thinking about structuring your code that will take some getting used to. It's time to dive right in by defining some of your own protocols.

Defining your own protocols

Throughout `UIKit`, protocols are first-class citizens. You might have noticed this when you were implementing the custom `UIViewController` transitions. When you implemented these transitions, you had to create an object that functioned as a delegate for the transition and conformed it to the `UIViewControllerTransitioningDelegate` protocol. You also implemented an `NSObject` subclass that conformed to `UIViewControllerAnimatedTransitioning`.

It's possible for you to define and use your own protocols. This usage is not confined to delegate behavior only. Defining a protocol is very similar to defining a class, struct, or enum. The main difference is that a protocol does not implement or store any values on its own. It acts as a contract between whoever calls an object that conforms to a protocol and the object that claims to conform to the protocol.

Create a new **Playground (File | New... | Playground)** if you want to follow along, or check out the Playground in the book's Git repository.

Let's implement a simple protocol of our own that establishes a baseline for any object that claims to be a pet. The protocol will be called the `PetType` protocol. Many protocols defined in `UIKit` and the Swift standard library use either `Type`, `Ing`, or `Able` as a suffix to indicate that the protocol defines a behavior rather than a concrete type. We should try to follow this convention as much as possible:

```
protocol PetType {
    var name: String { get }
    var age: Int { get set }

    func sleep()

    static var latinName: String { get }
}
```

The definition for `PetType` states that any object that claims to be `PetType` must have a get-only variable called `name`, an `age` that can be changed because it specifies both `get` and `set`, a method that makes the pet `sleep`, and finally, a static variable that describes the `PetType`'s Latin name.

Whenever you define that a protocol requires a certain variable to be present, you must also specify whether the variable should be gettable, settable, or both. If you specify that a certain method must be implemented, you write the method just as you normally would, but you stop at the first curly brace. You only write down the method signature.

A protocol can also require that the implementer add a static variable or method. This is convenient in the case of `PetType` because the Latin name of a pet does not necessarily belong to a specific pet, but to the entire species of animal that the pet belongs to, so implementing this as a property of the object rather than the instance makes a lot of sense.

To demonstrate how powerful a small protocol such as this can be, we will implement two pets: a cat and a dog. We'll also write a function that takes any pet and then makes them take a nap by calling the `sleep` method.

To do this in OOP, you would create a class called `Pet` and then you'd create two subclasses, `Cat` and `Dog`. The `nap` method would take an instance of `Pet`, and it would look a bit like this:

```
func nap(pet: Pet) {
    pet.sleep()
}
```

The object-oriented approach is not a bad one. Also, on such a small scale, no real problems will occur. However, when the inheritance hierarchy grows, you typically end up with base classes that contain methods that are only relevant to a couple of subclasses. Alternatively, you will find yourself unable to add certain functionalities to a certain class because the inheritance hierarchy simply gets in the way after a while.

Let's improve this simple example using a `PetType` protocol to solve this challenge without using inheritance at all:

```
protocol PetType {
    var name: String { get }
    var age: Int { get set }
    static var latinName: String { get }

    func sleep()
}

struct Cat: PetType {
    let name: String
    var age: Int

    static let latinName: String = "Felis catus"
```

```
    func sleep() {
        print("Cat: ZzzZZ")
    }
}

struct Dog: PetType {
    let name: String
    var age: Int

    static let latinName: String = "Canis familiaris"

    func sleep() {
        print("Dog: ZzzZZ")
    }
}

func nap(pet: PetType) {
    pet.sleep()
}
```

We just managed to implement a single method that can take both our `Cat` and `Dog` and make them take a nap. Instead of checking for a class, we're checking that the pet we're passing in conforms to the `PetType` protocol, and if it does, we can call its `sleep` method because the protocol dictates that any `PetType` must implement this method. This brings us to the next topic of this chapter, *checking for traits instead of types*.

Checking for traits instead of types

In classic OOP, you often create superclasses and subclasses to group together objects with similar capabilities. If you roughly model a group of felines in the animal kingdom with classes, you end up with a diagram that looks like this:

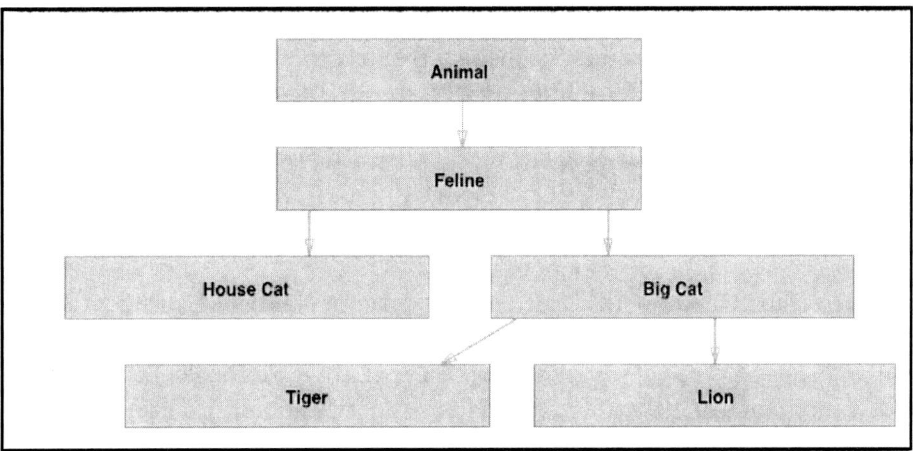

If you tried to model more animals, you would find that it's a really complex task because some animals share a whole bunch of traits, although they are actually quite far apart from each other in the class diagram.

One example would be that both cats and dogs are typically kept as pets. This means that they should optionally have an owner and maybe a home. But cats and dogs aren't the only animals kept as pets because fish, guinea pigs, rabbits, and even snakes are kept as pets. However, it would be really hard to figure out a sensible way to restructure your class hierarchy in such a way that you don't have to redundantly add owners and homes to every pet in the hierarchy, because it would be impossible to selectively add these properties to the right classes.

This problem gets even worse when you write a function or method that prints a pet's home. You would either have to make that function accept any kind of animal or write a separate implementation of the same function for each type that has the properties you're looking for. Both don't really make sense because you don't want to write the same function over and over again with just a different class for the parameter, and passing an instance of `GreatWhiteShark` to a function called `printHomeAddress` doesn't really make a lot of sense either, because sharks typically don't have home addresses. Of course, the solution to this problem is to use protocols.

In the situation described in the previous section, we referred to objects just by what they are, not by what they do. We care about the fact that a certain animal is part of a certain family or type, not about whether it lives on land or not. We can't really differentiate between animals that can fly and animals that can't because not all birds can fly. Inheritance simply isn't compatible with this way of thinking. Imagine a definition for a `Pigeon` struct that looks like this:

```
struct Pigeon: Bird, FlyingType, OmnivoreType, Domesticatable
```

As `Pigeon` is a struct, we know that `Bird` isn't a struct or class; it's a protocol that defines a couple of requirements about what it means to be a bird. The `Pigeon` struct also conforms to the `FlyingType`, `OmnivoreType`, and `Domesticatable` protocols. Each of these protocols tells us something about `Pigeon` in terms of its capabilities or traits. The definition actually shows us what a pigeon is and does instead of simply communicating that it inherits from a certain type of bird. For instance, almost all birds can fly, but there are some exceptions to the rule. You could model this with classes, but this approach is tedious and might be inflexible, depending on your needs. Setting the `Pigeon` struct up with protocols is really powerful; we can refactor the `printHomeAddress` function now and set it up so that it accepts any object that conforms to `Domesticatable`:

```
protocol Domesticatable {
    var homeAddress: String? { get }
}

func printHomeAddress(animal: Domesticatable) {
    if let address = animal.homeAddress {
        print(address)
    }
}
```

The `Domesticatable` protocol has a `homeAddress` property that's optional. Not every animal that can be domesticated actually is. For example, think about the pigeon; some pigeons are kept as pets, but most aren't. This also applies to cats and dogs, as not every cat or dog has a home.

This approach is powerful, but shifting your mind from an object-oriented mindset where you think of an inheritance hierarchy to a protocol-oriented mindset where you focus on traits instead of inheritance isn't easy.

Let's expand our example code a bit more by defining OmnivoreType, HerbivoreType, and CarnivoreType. These types will represent the three main types of eaters in the animal kingdom. We'll actually make use of inheritance inside of our protocols because the OmnivoreType is both a HerbivoreType and a CarnivoreType, so we can make the OmnivoreType inherit from both of these protocols:

```
protocol HerbivoreType {
    var favoritePlant: String { get }
}

protocol CarnivoreType {
    var favoriteMeat: String { get }
}

protocol OmnivoreType: HerbivoreType, CarnivoreType {}
```

Composing two protocols into one as we did in the previous section is really powerful, but be careful when you do this, as you don't want to create a crazy inheritance graph, as you typically end up within OOP. Imagine if we wrote two new functions, one to print a carnivore's favorite meat and one to print a herbivore's favorite plant. Those functions would look like this:

```
func printFavoriteMeat(forAnimal animal: CarnivoreType) {
    print(animal.favoriteMeat)
}

func printFavoritePlant(forAnimal animal: HerbivoreType) {
    print(animal.favoritePlant)
}
```

The preceding code might actually be exactly what you would write yourself. However, neither of these methods accept an OmnivoreType. This is perfectly fine because the OmnivoreType inherits from the HerbivoreType and CarnivoreType. This actually works just in the same way that you're used to in classical object-oriented programming, with the main exception being that our OmnivoreType inherits from multiple protocols instead of just one. This means that the printFavoritePlant function accepts a Pigeon instance as its argument because Pigeon confirms to the OmnivoreType, which inherits from the HerbivoreType.

Using protocols to compose your objects like this can greatly simplify your code. Instead of thinking about complex inheritance structures, you can compose your objects with protocols that define certain traits. The beauty of this is that it makes defining new objects relatively easy.

Imagine that a new type of animal is discovered. One that can fly, swim, and lives on land. This weird new species would be really hard to add to an inheritance-based architecture since it doesn't really fit in with other animals. When using protocols, you could simply add conformance to the `FlyingType`, `LandType`, and `SwimmingType` protocols and you'd be all set. Any methods or functions that take a `LandType` animal as an argument will happily accept your new animal since it conforms to the `LandType` protocol.

Getting the hang of this way of thinking isn't simple, and it will require quite some practice. But anytime you're getting ready to create a superclass or subclass, ask yourself why. If you're actually trying to encapsulate a certain trait in that class, try using a protocol. This will train you to think differently about your objects, and before you know it, your code is cleaner, more readable, and more flexible, using protocols and checking for traits instead of taking action based on what an object is.

As you've seen, a protocol doesn't need to have a lot of requirements; sometimes one or two are enough to convey the right thing. Don't hesitate to create protocols with just a single property or method; as your projects grow larger over time and your requirements change, you will thank yourself for doing so.

Extending your protocols with default behavior

The previous examples have mainly used variables as the requirements for protocols. One slight downside of protocols is that they can result in a bit of code duplication. For example, any object that is a `HerbivoreType` has a `favoriteMeat` variable. This means that you have to duplicate this variable in every object that conforms to the `HerbivoreType`. Usually, you would want as little code repetition as possible, and duplicating a variable like this might seem like a step backward.

Even though it's nice if you don't have to declare the same property over and over again, there's a certain danger in not doing this. If your app grows to a large size, you won't remember each and every class, subclass, and superclass all of the time. This means that changing or removing a certain property can have undesired side effects in other classes.

Declaring the same properties on every object that conforms to a certain protocol isn't that big a deal; it usually takes just a few lines of code to do this. However, protocols can also require certain methods to be present on objects that conform to them. Declaring those over and over again can be cumbersome, especially if the implementation is the same for most objects. Luckily, you can make use of **protocol extensions** to implement a certain degree of default functionality.

To explore protocol extensions, let's move the `printHomeAddress` function into the `Domesticatable` protocol so all `Domesticatable` objects can print their own home addresses. The first approach we can take is to immediately define the method on a protocol extension:

```
extension Domesticatable {
    func printHomeAddress() {
        if let address = homeAddress {
            print(address)
        }
    }
}
```

By defining the `printHomeAddress` method in this protocol extension, every object that conforms to `Domesticatable` has the following method available without having to implement it with the object itself:

```
let myPidgeon = Pigeon(favoriteMeat: "Insects",
                       favoritePlant: "Seeds",
                       homeAddress: "Leidse plein 12, Amsterdam")

myPidgeon.printHomeAddress() // "Leidse plein 12, Amsterdam"
```

This technique is very convenient if you want to implement default behavior that's associated with a protocol. You didn't even have to add the `printHomeAddress` method as a requirement to the protocol. However, this approach will give you some strange results if you're not careful. The following snippet illustrates the problem by adding a custom implementation of `printHomeAddress` to the `Pigeon` struct:

```
struct Pigeon: Bird, FlyingType, OmnivoreType, Domesticatable {
    let favoriteMeat: String
    let favoritePlant: String
    let homeAddress: String?

    func printHomeAddress() {
        if let address = homeAddress {
            print("address: \(address.uppercased())")
        }
    }
}

let myPigeon = Pigeon(favoriteMeat: "Insects",
                      favoritePlant: "Seeds",
                      homeAddress: "Leidse plein 12, Amsterdam")

myPigeon.printHomeAddress() // address: Leidse plein 12, Amsterdam
```

```
func printAddress(animal: Domesticatable) {
    animal.printHomeAddress()
}
printAddress(animal: myPigeon) // Leidse plein 12, Amsterdam
```

When we call `myPigeon.printHomeAddress`, the custom implementation is executed. However, if we define a function, `printAddress`, that takes a `Domesticatable` object as its parameter, the default implementation is used.

This happens because `printHomeAddress` isn't a requirement of the protocol. Therefore, if you call `printHomeAddress` on a `Domesticatable` object, the implementation from the protocol extension is used. If you use the exact same snippet as in the preceding section, but adapt the protocol as shown in the following code, both calls to `printHomeAddress` print the same thing, that is, the custom implementation in the `Pigeon` struct:

```
protocol Domesticatable {
    var homeAddress: String? { get }

    func printHomeAddress()
}
```

This behavior is likely to be unexpected in most cases, so it's usually a good idea to define all methods you use in the protocol requirements unless you're absolutely sure you want the behavior we've just explored.

Protocol extensions can't hold stored properties. This means that you can't add your variables to the protocol in order to provide a default implementation for them. Even though extensions can't hold stored properties, there are situations where you can still add a computed property to a protocol extension in order to avoid duplicating the same variable in multiple places. Let's take a look at an example (the updated code is highlighted):

```
protocol Domesticatable {
    var homeAddress: String? { get }
    var hasHomeAddress: Bool { get }

    func printHomeAddress()
}

extension Domesticatable {
    var hasHomeAddress: Bool {
        return homeAddress != nil
    }

    func printHomeAddress() {
        if let address = homeAddress {
```

```
                print(address)
            }
        }
    }
```

If we want to be able to check whether a `Domesticatable` has a home address, we can add a requirement for a `Bool` value, `hasHomeAddress`. If the `homeAddress` property is set, `hasHomeAddress` should be `true`; otherwise it should be `false`. This property is computed in the protocol extension, so we don't have to add this property to all of our `Domesticatable` objects. In this case, it makes a lot of sense to use a computed property because the way its value is computed should most likely be the same across all `Domesticatable` objects.

Implementing a default behavior in protocol extensions makes the protocol-oriented approach we've seen before even more powerful; we can essentially mimic multiple inheritances this way without all the downsides of subclassing. Simply adding conformance to a protocol can add all kinds of functionality to your objects, and if the extensions allow it, you won't need to add anything else. Let's see how we can make the most of our protocols and extensions by making them generic with associated types.

Improving your protocols with associated types

One more awesome aspect of protocol-oriented programming is the use of associated types. An associated type is a generic, nonexisting type that can be used in your protocol as if it were a type that exists. The real type of this generic is determined by the compiler based on the context it's used in. This description is abstract, and you might not immediately understand why or how an associated type can benefit your protocols. After all, aren't protocols themselves a very flexible way to make several unrelated objects fit a criteria based on the protocols they conform to?

To illustrate and discover the use of associated types, we will expand our animal kingdom a bit. What we'll do is give our herbivores an `eat` method and an array to keep track of the plants they've eaten, as follows:

```
protocol HerbivoreType {
    var plantsEaten: [PlantType] { get set }

    mutating func eat(plant: PlantType)
}

extension HerbivoreType {
    mutating func eat(plant: PlantType) {
```

```
            plantsEaten.append(plant)
        }
    }
```

This code looks fine at first sight. A herbivore eats plants, and this is established by this protocol. The `PlantType` is a protocol defined as follows:

```
protocol PlantType {
    var latinName: String { get }
}
```

Let's define two different plant types and an animal that we'll use to illustrate the problem with the preceding code:

```
struct Grass: PlantType{
    var latinName = "Poaceae"
}

struct Pine: PlantType{
    var latinName = "Pinus"
}

struct Cow: HerbivoreType {
    var plantsEaten = [PlantType]()
}
```

There shouldn't be a big surprise here. Let's continue with creating a `Cow` instance and feed it a `Pine`:

```
var cow = Cow()
let pine = Pine()
cow.eat(plant: pine)
```

This doesn't really make sense. Cows don't eat pines, they eat grass! We need some way to limit this cow's food intake because this approach isn't going to work. Currently, we can feed our `HerbivoreType` animals anything that's considered a plant. We need some way to limit the types of food our cows are given. In this case, we'd like to limit the `FoodType` to `Grass` only, without having to define the `eat(plant:)` method for every plant type we might want to feed a `HerbivoreType`.

The problem we're facing now is that all `HerbivoreType` animals mainly eat one plant type, and not all plant types are a good fit for all herbivores. This is where associated types are a great solution. An associated type for the `HerbivoreType` protocol can constrain the `PlantType` to a single type that is defined by the `HerbivoreType` itself. Let's see what this looks like. First, we'll redefine the protocol:

```
protocol HerbivoreType {
    associatedtype Plant: PlantType

    var plantsEaten: [Plant] { get set }

    mutating func eat(plant: Plant)
}

extension HerbivoreType {
    mutating func eat(plant: Plant) {
        print("eating a \(plant.latinName)")
        plantsEaten.append(plant)
    }
}
```

The first highlighted line associates the generic `Plant` type, which doesn't really exist as a real type, to our protocol. We've added a constraint for the `Plant` to ensure that it's a `PlantType`, so that only a `PlantType` is allowed to be used here.

The second highlighted line demonstrates how the `Plant` associated type is actually used as a `PlantType`. The plant type itself is merely an alias for any type that conforms to `PlantType` and is used as the type of object we use for `plantsEaten` and the `eat` methods. Let's redefine our `Cow` struct to see this associated type in action:

```
struct Cow: HerbivoreType {
    var plantsEaten = [Grass]()
}
```

The changed code is highlighted. Instead of making `plantsEaten` a `PlantType` array, we've now made it a `Grass` array. In the protocol and the definition, the type of plant is now `Grass`. The compiler understands this because we've defined the `plantsEaten` array as an array of `Grass`. Let's define a second `HerbivoreType` that eats a different type of `PlantType`:

```
struct Carrot: PlantType {
    let latinName = "Daucus carota"
}

struct Rabbit: HerbivoreType {
    var plantsEaten = [Carrot]()
}
```

If we try to feed our `Cow` carrots, or if we try to feed the `Rabbit` a `Pine`, the compiler will throw errors. The reason for this is that the associated type constraint allows us to define the type of `Plant` in each struct separately.

One side note about associated types is that it's not always possible for the compiler to properly infer the real type for an associated type. In our current example, this would happen if we didn't have the `plantsEaten` array in the protocol. The solution would be to define a `typealias` on objects that conform to the `HerbivoreType` so that the compiler understands which type `Plant` represents:

```
protocol HerbivoreType {
    associatedtype Plant: PlantType

    mutating func eat(plant: Plant)
}

struct Cow: HerbivoreType {
    typealias Plant = Grass
}
```

Associated types can be really powerful when used correctly, but sometimes using them can also cause you a lot of headaches because of the amount of inferring the compiler has to do. If you forget a few tiny steps, the compiler can easily lose track of what you're trying to do, and the error messages aren't always the clearest messages. Keep this in mind when you're using associated types, and try to make sure that you're as explicit as possible about the type you're looking to be associated. Sometimes, adding a `typealias` to give the compiler a helping hand is better than trying to get the compiler to correctly infer everything on its own.

Summary

This chapter is packed with complex and interesting information that is essential if you want to write beautiful Swift code. Protocols allow you to write extremely flexible code that doesn't rely on inheritance, which makes it a lot easier to understand and reason with your code. In this chapter, you saw how you can leverage the power of protocols to work with an object's traits or capabilities rather than just using its class as the only way of measuring its capabilities.

Next, you saw how protocols can be extended to implement a default functionality. This enables you to compose powerful types simply by adding protocol conformance, instead of creating a subclass. You also saw how protocol extensions behave depending on your protocol requirements, and that it's wise to have anything that's in the protocol extension defined as a requirement. This makes the protocol behavior more predictable. Finally, you learned how associated types work and how they can lift your protocols to the next level by adding generic types to your protocols, that can be tweaked for every type that conforms to your protocol.

The concepts shown in this chapter are pretty advanced, complex, and powerful. To truly master their use, you'll need to exercise yourself to think in terms of traits instead of an inheritance hierarchy. Once you've mastered this, you can experiment with protocol extensions and generic types. It's okay if you don't fully understand these topics right off the bat; they're completely different and new ways of thinking for most programmers with OOP experience. Now that we've explored some of the theory behind protocols and value types, let's see how we can put this new knowledge to use by quickly revisiting the *HelloContacts* app from previous chapters.

7
Refactoring the HelloContacts Application

When we first built *HelloContacts*, we used classes and Object-Oriented Programming techniques. Now that you have seen how value types and protocols can improve your code, it's a good idea to revisit the *HelloContacts* application to see how we can improve it with this newfound knowledge. Even though the app is fairly small, there are a few places where we can improve it and make it more flexible and future-proof.

This chapter is all about making the *HelloContacts* application Swiftier than it is now. We'll do this by implementing elements of the app with protocols and value types. This chapter will cover the following topics:

- Properly separating concerns
- Adding protocols for clarity

Let's get started right away.

Properly separating concerns

Before we can improve our project structure with value types and protocols, it's a good idea to improve upon our general structure. We haven't really thought about the reuse of certain aspects of the *HelloContacts* app, which results in code that's harder to maintain in the long run. If you take a look at the source code for this project in the book's code bundle, you' find that the project was slightly modified.

First, all the different files were put together in sensible groups. Doing so makes it easier for you to navigate your project's files, and it creates a natural place for certain files, as shown in the following screenshot:

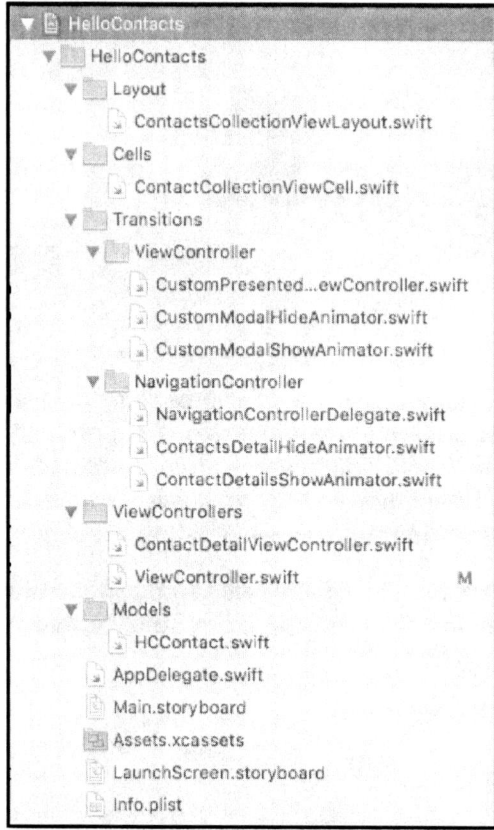

The structure applied in this project is merely a suggestion; if you feel that a different structure will suit you better, go ahead and make the change. The most important part is that you've thought about your project structure and set it up so it makes sense to you and helps you navigate your project.

With this improved folder structure, you may notice that there's some sort of a divide between certain files. There are files that help with transitions, a model file, and among other things we also have view controllers that are grouped together. By doing this, you've given yourself an overview of the file types in your project, and each file belongs to a certain group that describes its place in your app. This makes it easier for other developers (and yourself) to browse the code in your project. Let's get started with refactoring some code.

The file we will refactor first is `ViewController.swift`. This file contains the code for our contacts overview screen. Currently, this view controller fetches contacts, acts as a delegate and data source for the collection view, and takes care of the animations that play when a user taps on a cell.

You may consider this to be fine. However, ideally any given class shouldn't be responsible for that many things at once. What if we would like to create a second kind of overview page; how can we reuse the code that fetches contacts? What if we'd like to add the bouncing cell image animation to another image? These are two scenarios that are pretty likely to happen at some point in the future. Let's extract the contact-fetching code and the animation code and send them out to their own structs.

Extracting the contact-fetching code

Start off by creating a new Swift file called `ContactFetchHelper.swift`. After creating the file, add it to a new folder called `Helpers`. First, we'll extract all the contact-fetching code to our `ContactFetchHelper` struct. Then, we'll refactor `ViewController.swift` so it uses our new helper instead of implementing all the fetching code in the view controller. The following code shows the implementation for `ContactFetchHelper`:

```
import Contacts

struct ContactFetchHelper {
    typealias ContactFetchCallback = ([HCContact]) -> Void

    let store = CNContactStore()

    func fetch(withCallback callback: @escaping
      ContactFetchCallback) {
        if CNContactStore.authorizationStatus(for: .contacts) ==
.notDetermined {
            store.requestAccess(for: .contacts, completionHandler:
              {authorized, error in
                if authorized {
                    self.retrieve(withCallback: callback)
                }
            })
        } else if CNContactStore.authorizationStatus(for: .contacts) ==
.authorized {
            retrieve(withCallback: callback)
        }
    }

    private func retrieve(withCallback callback: ContactFetchCallback) {
```

```
        let containerId = store.defaultContainerIdentifier()

        let keysToFetch =
            [CNContactGivenNameKey as CNKeyDescriptor,
             CNContactFamilyNameKey as CNKeyDescriptor,
             CNContactImageDataKey as CNKeyDescriptor,
             CNContactImageDataAvailableKey as CNKeyDescriptor,
             CNContactEmailAddressesKey as CNKeyDescriptor,
             CNContactPhoneNumbersKey as CNKeyDescriptor,
             CNContactPostalAddressesKey as CNKeyDescriptor]

        let predicate =
CNContact.predicateForContactsInContainer(withIdentifier: containerId)

        guard let retrievedContacts = try? store.unifiedContacts(matching:
          predicate, keysToFetch: keysToFetch) else {
            // call back with an empty array if we fail to retrieve
contacts
            callback([])
            return
        }

        let contacts: [HCContact] = retrievedContacts.map {
          contact in
            return HCContact(contact: contact)
        }

        callback(contacts)
    }
}
```

This simple struct now contains all the required logic to fetch contacts. Let's go through some of the most interesting parts of code in this struct:

```
typealias ContactFetchCallback = ([HCContact]) -> Void
```

This line of code defines an alias, named `ContactFetchCallback`, for a closure that receives an array of `HCContact` instances and returns nothing. This is the closure that is passed to the `fetch` method, and it's called after the fetching is performed.

The `fetch` method is the method we'll call whenever we want to fetch contacts. The only argument it takes is a closure that needs to be called when the contacts are fetched. The fetch method performs the same authorization check we had in the view controller's `viewDidLoad` method.

Next, we have a private method, `retrieve`, that actually retrieves the contacts. The `fetch` method calls this method and passes it the `callback` it received. Once retrieve has retrieved the contacts, it calls the `callback` with the array of fetched contacts.

The `ContactFetchCallback` that `fetch(withCallback:)` receives is marked as `@escaping`. This keyword indicates that the supplied closure will escape the scope of the scope it was passed to. In this example, the `callback` is passed to the scope of `fetch(withCallback:)`, which in turn passed this closure to the scope of `retrieve(withCallback:)`.

In `ViewController.swift`, all you need to do is use the following code to retrieve contacts:

```
let contactFetcher = ContactFetchHelper()
contactFetcher.fetch { [weak self] contacts in
    self?.contacts = contacts
    self?.collectionView.reloadData()
}
```

You can delete the `retrieveContacts` method entirely and the preceding snippet replaces the code that checked for permissions in `viewDidLoad`. Also, because we're not directly using the `Contacts` framework anymore, you can remove its `import` at the top of the file. You have now successfully extracted the contact's fetching code into a struct and you're using a `typealias` to make your code more readable. This is already a big win for maintainability and reusability. Now, let's extract our animation code as well.

Extracting the bounce animation

The process of extracting our bounce animation is a little more complex than the process of extracting the contacts. The purpose of extracting this bounce animation is to make it bounce so that we can make other objects in other sections of our app bounce just as the contact cell's image does.

To figure out what our bounce animation helper should do exactly and how it should work, it's a great idea to think about how you want to use this helper at the call site. The call site is defined as the place where you plan to use your helper. So, in this case, the call site is considered the `ViewController`. Let's write some pseudo code to try and determine what we will program later:

```
let onBounceComplete = { [weak self] finished in
    self?.performSegue(withIdentifier: "contactDetailSegue", sender: self)
}

let bounce = BounceAnimationHelper(targetView: cell.contactImage,
onComplete: onBounceComplete)
```

This looks pretty good already, and in reality, it's very close to the actual code we'll end up with later. All we really want to do is configure a bounce animation by passing it a view to perform the bounce on and to have some control over what should happen after the animation is completed. We should consider the following two things before we can write the `BounceAnimationHelper` implementation:

- We can't set the bounce duration; is this acceptable?
- We have no control over the start time of the animation, so manually starting it would be nice

To address the first point, we could implement two initializers: one that uses a default duration and another where the users of the helper can specify their own duration. Doing this makes use of Swift's powerful method overloading, which enables us to write multiple initializers for the same object. This also enables programmers to write methods with the same name but a different signature because of different parameters.

The second point is valid, and we should write the helper in a way that requires manually starting the animation. Theoretically speaking, we could add a Boolean value to the initializer that enables users of the helper to choose whether the animation should start automatically or not. We won't do this for now because manually starting the animation will make it feel more in line with the `UIViewPropertyAnimator` instance that's used under the hood. The calling code we'll end up with is shown in the following code snippet. You can go ahead and add it to the `ViewController.swift` file in place of the current bounce animation. We'll implement the helper shortly:

```
let onBounceComplete: BounceAnimationHelper.BounceAnimationComplete = {
[unowned self] position in
    self.performSegue(withIdentifier: "contactDetailSegue", sender: self)
}

let bounce = BounceAnimationHelper(targetView: cell.contactImage,
```

```
onComplete: onBounceComplete)
bounce.startAnimation()
```

Note that the preceding snippet explicitly defines the type of the `onBounceComplete` callback. This type will be a `typealias` on the helper we're about to implement, meaning that we need to define the `callback`, as shown in the preceding code snippet.

Now that we have the call site figured out, let's take a look at the implementation of our `BounceAnimationHelper`. Create a new Swift file and add it to the `Helpers` folder. Start off by defining a struct named `BounceAnimationHelper` in the corresponding Swift file. Next, let's define a `typealias` for the completion handler and specify the properties we need in our struct, as follows:

```
import UIKit

struct BounceAnimationHelper {
    typealias BounceAnimationComplete = (UIViewAnimatingPosition) -> Void

    let animator: UIViewPropertyAnimator
}
```

The initial implementation for the struct is pretty bare. We define a `typealias` that passes a `UIViewAnimatingPosition` into a closure that has no return value. We'll also hold on to the `UIViewPropertyAnimator` so we can tell it to start animating whenever the helper's `startAnimation` method is called. Let's add the initializers we came up with earlier:

```
init(targetView: UIView, onComplete: @escaping BounceAnimationComplete) {
    self.init(targetView: targetView, onComplete: onComplete, duration:
0.4)
}

init(targetView: UIView, onComplete: @escaping BounceAnimationComplete,
duration: TimeInterval) {

}
```

These two initializers provide the APIs we're looking for. The first initializer calls out to the second with a default `duration` value of `0.4`. Doing this allows us to write the actual animation in just a single place. There is just one initializer that's responsible for fully configuring our helper: the designated initializer. The following code sample shows the implementation for the designated initializer; it replaces the empty initializer you saw in the previous snippet:

```
init(targetView: UIView, onComplete: @escaping BounceAnimationComplete,
duration: TimeInterval) {
    let downAnimationTiming = UISpringTimingParameters(dampingRatio: 0.9,
initialVelocity: CGVector(dx: 20, dy: 0))

    self.animator = UIViewPropertyAnimator(duration: duration/2,
timingParameters: downAnimationTiming)

    self.animator.addAnimations {
        targetView.transform =CGAffineTransform(scaleX: 0.9, y: 0.9)
    }

    self.animator.addCompletion { position in
        let upAnimationTiming = UISpringTimingParameters(dampingRatio: 0.3,
initialVelocity:CGVector(dx: 20, dy: 0))

        let upAnimator = UIViewPropertyAnimator(duration: duration/2,
timingParameters: upAnimationTiming)

        upAnimator.addAnimations {
            targetView.transform = CGAffineTransform.identity
        }

        upAnimator.addCompletion(onComplete)

        upAnimator.startAnimation()
    }
}
```

This snippet is very similar to the old animation; the main differences are highlighted. Instead of hard-coding a duration, we will use half of the total duration for the downward motion and half for the upward motion. Also, instead of using the cell's image directly, we will use the specified `targetView`.

Finally, instead of passing our own `callback` to the `upAnimator` closure's completion, we will use the `onComplete` closure that was passed to the initializer. Note that the down animation isn't started in the initializer; we'll implement a separate method for that:

```
func startAnimation() {
    animator.startAnimation()
}
```

Add the preceding method to the `BounceAnimationHelper` and run your app. Your animation should bounce just as it did before, except the animation is reusable now and the code in `ViewController.swift` looks a lot cleaner.

With our cleaned up `ViewController` in place, let's see where we could benefit from protocols.

Adding protocols for clarity

We've already seen how protocols can be used to improve code by removing complex inheritance hierarchies. You also know how powerful it is when it comes to checking for protocol conformance instead of checking whether a certain object is of a certain type. Let's see how we can improve and future-proof the *HelloContacts* application by adding some protocols.

We will define two protocols for now: one that specifies the requirements for any object that claims to be able to add a special animation to a view, and one that defines what it means to be able to be displayed as a contact.

Defining the ViewEffectAnimatorType protocol

The first protocol we will define is called `ViewEffectAnimatorType`. This protocol should be applied to any object that implements the required behaviors to animate a view. This protocol does not necessarily give us a direct advantage, but there are a few considerations that make this a very useful protocol.

A protocol is not only used to check whether or not an object can do something: It can also formalize a certain API that you came up with. In this case, we've decided that our `BounceAnimationHelper` needed certain initializers. It also needs to hold on to an animator, and it has a `startAnimation` method.

Adding a protocol to this helper makes sure that any other helpers that conform to the same protocol have the same interface. This helps you, the developer, make sense of what you should minimally implement for your new animation helper. It also makes adding new effects or swapping one effect for an other very easy and straightforward.

Another advantage is that we can move the `startAnimation` method to a protocol extension. Its implementation is simple and straightforward; we typically won't need to customize it, so it's a great candidate to provide a default implementation for. Create a new Swift file named `ViewEffectAnimatorType`, and add it to a new folder called `Protocols`. Now add the following implementation for the protocol:

```
import UIKit

typealias ViewEffectAnimatorComplete = (UIViewAnimatingPosition) -> Void

protocol ViewEffectAnimatorType {

    var animator: UIViewPropertyAnimator { get }

    init(targetView: UIView, onComplete: @escaping
ViewEffectAnimatorComplete)
    init(targetView: UIView, onComplete: @escaping
ViewEffectAnimatorComplete, duration: TimeInterval)

    func startAnimation()
}

extension ViewEffectAnimatorType {
    func startAnimation() {
        animator.startAnimation()
    }
}
```

This protocol defines all of the requirements we discussed before. Note that a globally available `typealias` named `ViewEffectAnimatorComplete` has been defined. This means that you can replace the type declaration for `onBounceComplete` in `ViewController` so it is `ViewEffectAnimatorComplete` instead of `BounceAnimationHelper.BounceAnimationComplete`. This enables us to use the same handler type across our app, which enhances code consistency. To use this protocol, update the initializers for `BounceAnimationHelper` to use the new `typealias` and remove the old one. Also, remove the `startAnimation` method, and finally, add `ViewEffectAnimatorType` to the `BounceAnimationHelper` definition, as shown in the following code:

```
struct BounceAnimationHelper: ViewEffectAnimatorType
```

By adding this conformance, we use the protocol extension's default implementation for `startAnimation`, and we have a predictable, formalized interface for the `BounceAnimationHelper` and any future effects that we may wish to add to our app. Let's add a protocol to our contact object as well.

Defining a contact display protocol

Many apps display lists of contents that are almost the same, but not quite. Imagine displaying a list of contacts: a placeholder for a contact that can be tapped to add a new contact and other cells that could suggest people you may know. Each of these three cells in the collection view could look the same, yet the underlying models can be almost completely different.

You can achieve this with a simple protocol that defines what it means to be displayed in a certain way. It's a perfect example of the situation where you're more interested in an object's capabilities than its concrete type. To determine what it means to be displayed in the contact overview, we should look inside `ViewController.swift`. The following code is used to configure a cell in the contact overview page:

```
let contact = contacts[indexPath.row]

cell.nameLabel.text = "\(contact.givenName) \(contact.familyName)"

contact.fetchImageIfNeeded()
if let image = contact.contactImage {
    cell.contactImage.image = image
}
```

From this, we can extract four things a contact displayable item should contain:

- A `givenName` property
- A `familyName` property
- A `fetchImageIfNeeded` method
- A `contactImage` property

Since `givenName` and `familyName` are pretty specific to a real person, it's wise to combine the two in a new property:
`displayName`: This provides us with a bit more flexibility in terms of what kinds of object can conform to this protocol without having to resort to crazy tricks. Create a new Swift file named `ContactDisplayable` and add it to the `Protocols` folder. Add the following implementation:

```
import UIKit

protocol ContactDisplayable {
    var displayName: String { get }
    var contactImage: UIImage? { get set }

    mutating func fetchImageIfNeeded()
}
```

Now add the following computed property to `HCContact` and make sure that you add conformance to `ContactDisplayable` in its definition. While you're at it, replace the `class` keyword for `HCContact` with `struct`. That's much nicer, since we don't need any of the reference-type semantics that a class has. Also, don't forget to mark `prefetchImageIfNeeded()` as `mutating` in order to conform to the protocol. Changing from a class to a struct will give you some compiler errors. We'll take a look at fixing those soon:

```
var displayName: String {
    return "\(givenName) \(familyName)"
}
```

Next, update the declaration for the contacts array in `ViewController.swift` to look as follows (this will enable us to add any object that can be displayed as a contact to the array):

```
var contacts = [ContactDisplayable]()
```

The final adjustment in `ViewController` we will need to make is in `prepare(for:sender:)`. Because our contacts are now `ContactDisplayable` instead of `HCContact`, we can't assign them to the detail view controller right away. Update the implementation as follows to typecast the `ContactDisplayable` to `HCContact` so it can be set on the detail view controller:

```
override func prepare(for segue: UIStoryboardSegue, sender: AnyObject?) {
    if let contactDetailVC = segue.destination as?
ContactDetailViewController,
        let selectedIndex =
collectionView.indexPathsForSelectedItems?.first,
        let contact = contacts[selectedIndex.row] as? HCContact,
```

```
    segue.identifier == "contactDetailSegue" {

            contactDetailVC.contact = contact
        }
    }
```

We're almost done. Just a few more changes to make sure that our project compiles again. The issues we're seeing are all related to the change from a class to a struct and the addition of the `ContactDisplayable` protocol. In `ViewController.swift`, update the `collectionView(_:cellForItemAt:)` method to look as follows:

```
func collectionView(_ collectionView: UICollectionView,
cellForItemAtindexPath: IndexPath) -> UICollectionViewCell {
    let cell = collectionView.dequeueReusableCell(withReuseIdentifier:
"contactCell", for: indexPath) as! ContactCollectionViewCell
    var contact = contacts[indexPath.row]

    cell.nameLabel.text = contact.displayName

    contact.fetchImageIfNeeded()
    if let image = contact.contactImage {
        cell.contactImage.image = image
    }

    contacts[indexPath.row] = contact

    return cell
}
```

The changes you need to make are highlighted. Because `HCContact` is now a value type, pulling it from the array will create a copy. This means we will need to put it back into the array ourselves. If we don't do this, the prefetching of the image won't persist, which would be a shame. Whenever you need to perform tricks like this to make your value type work properly, it should be a red flag to you. Once you start doing this, you'll often end up with strange contraptions to make value types work throughout your code, and this will lead to all kinds of inconsistencies and bugs. This is a great example of a case where you should seriously consider replacing your value type with a reference type for clarity and simplicity.

Next, open up `ContactDetailViewController.swift`. In this file, we need to change the `contact` property declaration from `let` to `var` because the `prefetchImageIfNeeded` method call will mutate the `contact` property.

Also make sure you update the following line in `previewingContext(_:viewControllerForLocation:)`.

```
viewController.contact = contact as? HCContact
```

Finally, `ContactFetchHelper` needs to be modified. Update the following lines:

```
typealias ContactFetchCallback = ([ContactDisplayable]) -> Void

private func retrieve(withCallback callback: ContactFetchCallback) {
    // current implementation
    let contacts: [ContactDisplayable] = retrievedContacts.map { contact in
        return HCContact(contact: contact)
    }

    callback(contacts)
}
```

The important change here is that the contact array type is now `[ContactDisplayable]` instead of `[HCContact]`. That's it you can now build and run your project without errors!

Summary

This chapter wraps up our exploration of protocol-oriented programming, value types, and reference types. In the previous two chapters, you saw some theoretical situations that explain the power of these features in Swift. This chapter tied it all together by applying your newfound knowledge to the *HelloContacts* app we were working on before. You now know how you can bump up the quality and future-proof an existing application by implementing protocols and switching to using a struct instead of a class. In order to implement protocols, we had to improve our application by making sure that our `ViewController` didn't contain too many functionalities. This in itself was a huge improvement that we were able to take to the next level with a protocol.

Refactoring from classes to structs isn't always easy; the two aren't interchangeable, as we saw when we changed `HCContact` from a class to a struct. The main difference we encountered was due to how structs handle mutability. Adapting our code for this wasn't too complex, and it made our intent clearer than it was when we used classes.

Now that we have explored some of the best practices of Swift and applied them to an existing app, it's time to deep dive Core Data. The next chapters outline how Core Data works and how you can take advantage of it in your own applications. If all this value type and protocol oriented programming talk has made your head reel, don't worry. Take some time to review this chapter and to experiment. The best way to learn these principles is by practicing.

8
Adding Core Data to Your App

Core Data is Apple's data persistence framework. You can utilize this framework whenever your application needs to store data. Simple data can often be stored in `NSUserDefaults`, but when you're handling data that's more complex, has relationship, or needs some form of efficient searching, Core Data is much better suited to your needs.

You don't need to build a very complex app or have vast amounts of data to make Core Data worth your while. Regardless of your app's size, even if it's really small, with only a couple of records, or if you're holding on to thousands of records, Core Data has your back.

In this chapter, you'll learn how to add Core Data to an existing app. The app we will build keeps track of a list of favorite movies for all members of a family. The main interface will be a table view that shows a list of family members. If you tap on a family member, you'll see the tapped his/her favorite movies. Adding family members can be done through the overview screen, and adding movies can be done through the detail screen.

We won't build the screens in this app from scratch. In the repository for this book, a starter project called `FamilyMovies` is included. This starter project contains all of the screens, so we don't have to implement them before we get around to implementing Core Data.

In this chapter, we will cover the following topics:

- Understanding the Core Data stack
- Adding Core Data to an application
- Modeling data in the model editor

We won't store any data yet; this will be covered in `Chapter 9`, *Storing and Querying User Data*. For now, we'll just focus on what Core Data is and how you can add it to your application. Let's take a look at exactly what Core Data is and how it works.

Understanding the Core Data stack

Before we delve into the first project and add Core Data to it, we'll take a look at how Core Data actually works, what it is, and what it isn't. In order to make efficient use of Core Data, it's essential that you know what you're working with.

When you work with Core Data, you're actually utilizing a stack of layers that starts with managed objects and ends with a data store. This is often an SQLite database but there are different storage options you can use with Core Data, depending on your application needs. Let's take a quick look at the layers involved with Core Data and discuss their roles in an application briefly:

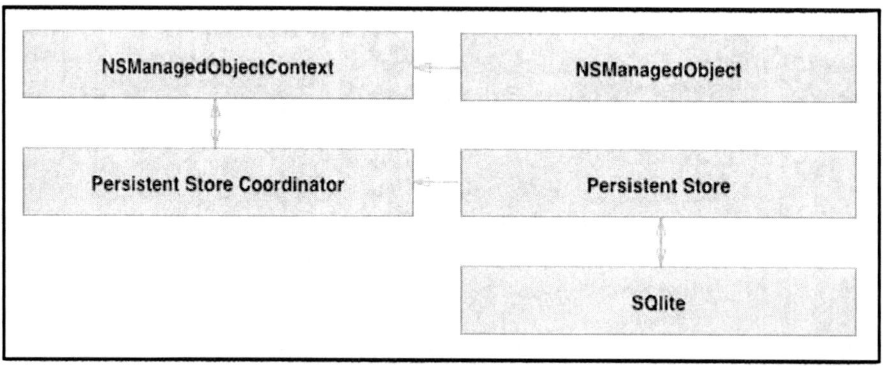

At the top right of this diagram is the `NSManagedObject` class. When you are working with Core Data, this is the object you'll interact with most often since it's the base class for all Core Data models your app contains. For instance, in the app we will build, the family member and movie models are subclasses of `NSManagedObject`.

Each managed object belongs to an `NSManagedObjectContext`. The managed object context is responsible for communicating with the persistent store coordinator. Often, you'll only need a single managed object context and a single **Persistent Store Coordinator**. However, it is possible for you to use multiple persistent store coordinators and multiple managed object contexts. It's even possible to have multiple managed object contexts for the same **Persistent Store Coordinator**.

A setup like this can be particularly useful if you're performing costly operations on your managed objects, for example if you're importing or synchronizing large amounts of data. We'll stick to using a single managed object context and a single **Persistent Store** coordinator because we simply don't have the need for more.

The Persistent Store coordinator is responsible for communicating to the Persistent Store. In most scenarios, the Persistent Store uses SQLite as its underlying storage database. However, you can also use other types of storage, such as an in-memory database. Using an in-memory database is especially useful if you're writing unit tests or if your app has no need for long-term storage. More information on testing can be found in `Chapter 21`, *Ensuring App Quality with Tests*.

If you've worked with MySQL, SQLite, or any other relational database before, it is tempting to think of Core Data as a layer on top of a relational database. Although this isn't entirely false since Core Data can use SQLite as its underlying storage, Core Data does not work the same as using SQLite directly; it's an abstraction on top of this.

One example of a difference between SQLite and Core Data is the concept of primary keys. Core Data doesn't allow you to specify your own primary keys. Also, when you define relationships, you don't use object IDs or other keys; you simply define the relationship and Core Data will figure out how to store this relationship in the underlying database. We will cover more on this subject later. It's important to be aware of the fact that, if you try to translate your SQLite experience to Core Data, you will run into issues, simply because Core Data is not SQLite. It just so happens that SQLite is one of the ways that data can be stored.

Now that you have an overview of the Core Data stack and where all the parts involved with its usage belong, let's add the Core Data stack to the `FamilyMovies` application.

Adding Core Data to an application

When you create a new project in Xcode, Xcode asks whether you want to add Core Data to your application. If you check this checkbox, Xcode will automatically generate some boilerplate code that sets up the Core Data stack. Prior to iOS 10, this boilerplate code spanned a couple of dozen lines because it had to load the data model, connect to the persistent store, and then it also had to set up the managed object context.

In iOS 10, Apple introduced `NSPersistentContainer`. When you initialize an `NSPersistentContainer`, all this boilerplate code is obsolete and the hard work is done by the `NSPersistentContainer`. This results in much less boilerplate code to obtain a managed object context for your application. Let's get started with setting up your Core Data stack. Open `AppDelegate.swift` and add the following `import` statement:

```
import CoreData
```

Next, add the following `lazy` variable to the implementation of `AppDelegate`:

```
private lazy var persistentContainer:
  NSPersistentContainer = {
    let container = NSPersistentContainer(name:
      "FamilyMovies")
container.loadPersistentStores(completionHandler: {
  (storeDescription, error) in
        if let error = error {
fatalError("Unresolved error \(error), \(error.userInfo)")
        }
    })
    return container
}()
```

If you declare a variable as `lazy`, it won't be initialized until it is accessed. This is particularly useful for variables that are expensive to initialize, rely on other objects, or are not always accessed. The fact that the variable is initialized just in time comes with a performance penalty since the variable needs to be set up the first time you access it. In certain cases this is fine, but in other cases it might negatively impact the user experience. When used correctly, `lazy` variables can have great benefits.

The preceding snippet does all the work required to load the data model we'll create shortly. It also connects this data model to a persistent store and initializes our managed object context.

If you let Xcode generate the Core Data code for your app, a method called `saveContext` is added to `AppDelegate` as well. This method is used in `applicationWillTerminate(_:)` to perform a last-minute save of changes and updates when the application is about to terminate. Since we're setting up Core Data manually, we will also add this behavior. However, instead of placing the `saveContext` method in `AppDelegate`, we will add this method as an extension to the `NSPersistentContainer`. This makes easier for other parts of your code to use this method, without relying on `AppDelegate`.

Create a new folder in the **Project navigator** and name it `Extensions`. Also, create a new Swift file and name it `NSPersistentContainer.swift`. Add the following implementation to this file:

```
import CoreData

extension NSPersistentContainer {
    func saveContextIfNeeded() {
        if viewContext.hasChanges {
            do {
                try viewContext.save()
            } catch {
                let nserror = error as NSError
                fatalError("Unresolved error \(nserror),
\(nserror.userInfo)")
            }
        }
    }
}
```

The preceding code adds a custom method to `NSPersistentContainer` so that we can call on instances of the `NSPersistentContainer`. This is really convenient because it decouples this method from `AppDelegate` entirely. Add the following implementation of `applicationWillTerminate(_:)` to `AppDelegate` to save the context right before the app terminates:

```
func applicationWillTerminate(_ application: UIApplication) {
    persistentContainer.saveContextIfNeeded()
}
```

Now, whenever the application terminates, the persistent store will check whether there are any changes to the managed object context that the `viewContext` property points to. If there are any changes, we'll attempt to save them. If this fails, we crash the app using `fatalError`. In your own app, you might want to handle this scenario a bit more gracefully. It could very well be that saving before termination isn't something that you want to crash your app on if it fails. You can modify the error handling implementation of `saveContextIfNeeded` if you think a different behavior is more appropriate for your app.

Now that we have our Core Data stack set up, we need to make it available to the app's view controllers. We will make this happen by using a from of dependency injection. This means that our `AppDelegate` will pass the managed object context to our initial view controller. It will then be this view controller's job to pass the context on to other view controllers that might need the managed object context as well.

First, add a property to `FamilyMembersViewController` that holds the managed object context. Don't forget to import Core Data at the top of this view controller:

```
var managedObjectContext: NSManagedObjectContext?
```

Now, in `AppDelegate`, modify the `application(_:, didFinishLaunchingWithOptions:)` method as follows:

```
func application(_ application: UIApplication,
didFinishLaunchingWithOptions launchOptions: [UIApplicationLaunchOptionsKey
: Any]? = nil) -> Bool {

    if let navVC = window?.rootViewController as?
      UINavigationController,
        var initialVC = navVC.viewControllers[0] as?
          MOCViewControllerType {

        initialVC.managedObjectContext =
          persistentContainer.viewContext
    }

    return true
}
```

Even though this code does exactly what it should, we can still make one major improvement. We know that there will be more view controllers that will hold on to a managed object context, and checking for classes is something we'd rather not do. As an exercise, attempt to fix this issue by adding a protocol called `MOCViewControllerType`. This protocol should add a requirement for an optional `managedObjectContext` property. Make sure that `FamilyMembersViewController` conforms to this protocol and fix the implementation of `application(_:, didFinishLaunchingWithOptions:)` as well.

The implemented code has layed out the base for our application's Core Data stack. We initialized the stack, and the managed object context is injected into the app's main view controller through a protocol. Let's see how we can define and set up our models.

Modeling data in the model editor

So far, we looked at the bottom part of the Core Data stack: the persistence layer. We created an `NSPersistentContainer` to create and manage all of the layers, but there is one key element that we haven't looked at: the models. In Core Data, models are represented by `NSManagedObject` subclasses. The instances of your models are instantiated by the `NSManagedObjectContext` whenever you query them.

The first thing we should do is to create our models. Once the models are defined, you can set up relationships between the models. Relationships are great for our application, so we can have separate entities for our family members and their favorite movies.

Creating the models

In order for Core Data to understand which models your application uses, you define them in Xcode's model editor. Let's create a new model file so we can add our own models to the `FamilyMovies` application. Create a new file, and from the file template selection screen pick **Data Model**. Name your model file `FamilyMovies`. First, we'll create the basic models and then see how we can define a relationship between family members and their favorite movies. Finally, we'll have a look at `NSManagedObject` subclasses:

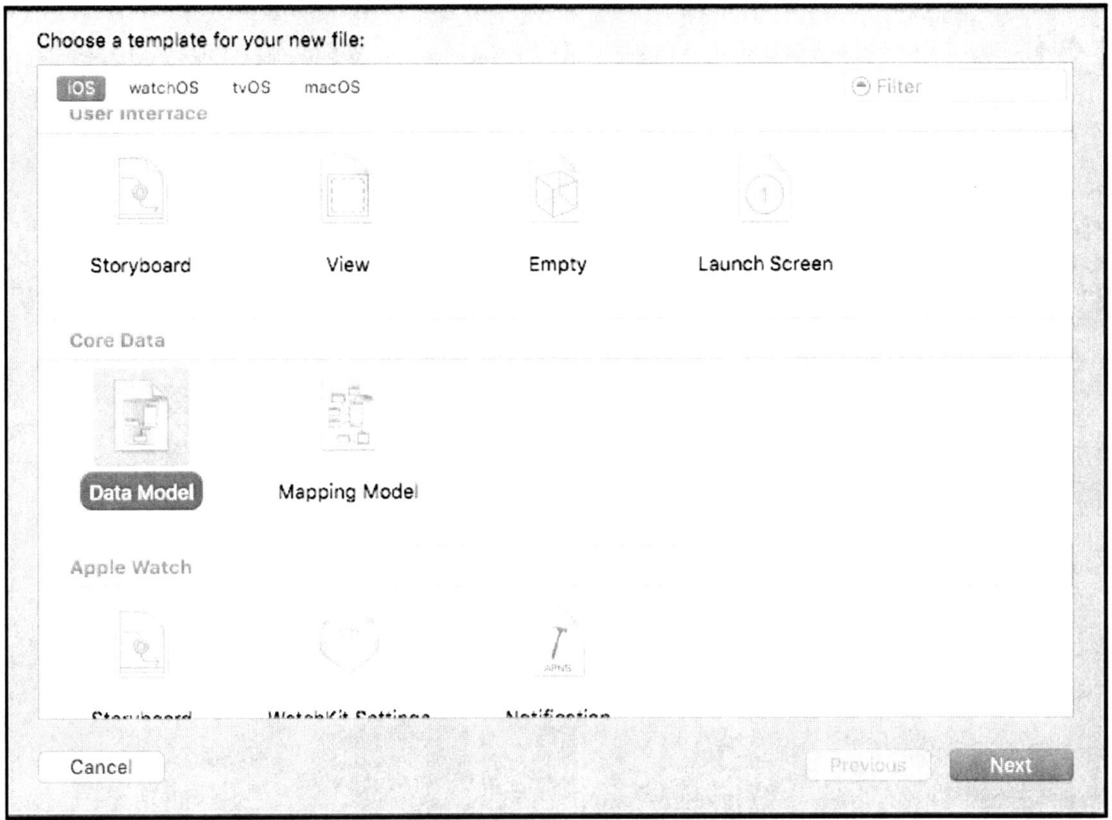

Your project now contains a file called `FamilyMovies.xcdatamodeld`. Open this file to go to the model editor. In the bottom-right corner of the editor, you'll find a button labeled **Add Entity;** clicking on this will create our first model, `FamilyMember`. After doing this, a new entity is added to the list of entities. Rename this new entity to `FamilyMember` and select it.

After selecting an entity, you can see all of its attributes, relationships, and fetched properties. Let's add a **name** property to our family member. Click on the plus (+) icon at the bottom of the empty attributes list and add a new attribute called **name**. Make sure that you select `String` as the type for this attribute:

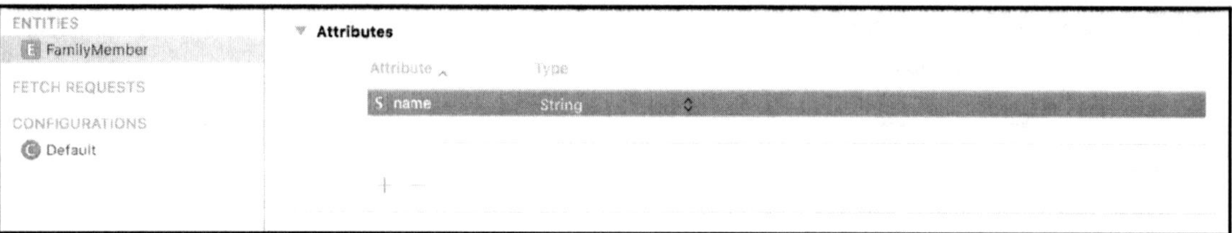

Click on this new property to select it. In the sidebar on the right, select the third tab to open the **Data Model inspector**. This is where you can see more detailed information on this attribute. For instance, you can configure a property to be indexed for faster lookups. You can also choose whether you want the attribute to be optional. For now, we don't care too much about indexing since we're not performing lookups by family members' names and even if we were a family doesn't tend to have hundreds or thousands of members. By default, the **Optional** checkbox is checked. Make sure that you uncheck this box because we don't want to store family members without a name.

Some other options you have for attributes are adding validation, adding a default value, and enabling indexing in Spotlight. For now, leave all options:

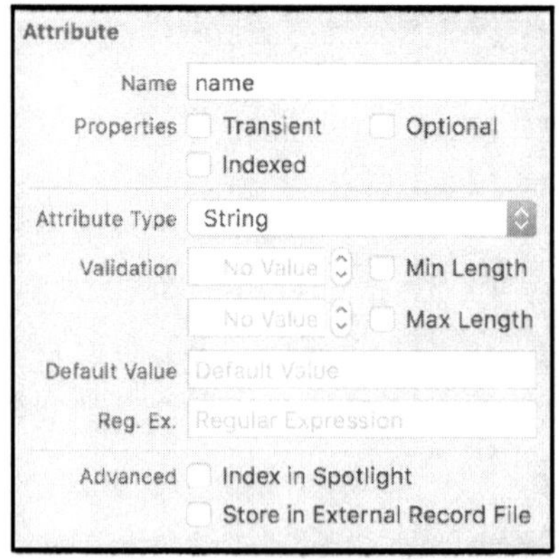

We also need to have a `Movie` entity. Create this entity using the same steps as before and give it a single property: `title`. This property should be a string and it shouldn't be optional. Once you've done this, we can set up a relationship between our family members and their favorite movies.

Defining relationships

A relationship in Core Data adds a related object as a property to another object. In our case, we want to define a relationship between `FamilyMember` and `Movie`. The relationship we're looking for is a one-to-many relationship. This means that every movie will have only one family member associated with it and every family member can have multiple favorite movies.

This setup is not the most efficient one since a many-to-many relationship would allow us to reuse a single movie for multiple family members. By using a one-to-many relationship, we're forcing ourselves to create a duplicate movie instance if multiple family members want to add the same movie. For the sake of keeping our setup simple, this is okay. However, if you're building your own application, it is worth considering a many-to-many relationship since it's more flexible and less wasteful.

Select the `FamilyMember` entity and click on the plus icon at the bottom of the **Relationships** list. Name the relationship `favoriteMovies` and select `Movie` as the destination. Don't select an **Inverse** relationship yet because we haven't defined it yet. The **Inverse** relationship will tell the model that `Movie` has a property that points back to the `FamilyMember`. In the Data Model inspector, make sure you select **To Many** as the **type** for this relationship. Also, select **Cascade** as the value for the **delete rule**.

The **delete rule** is a very important property to be set correctly. Not paying attention to this property could result in a lot of orphaned and even corrupted data in your database. For instance, setting this property to nullify simply sets the **Inverse** of the relationship to nil. This is the behavior we'd like to see when we delete a movie. Deleting a movie shouldn't delete the entire family members who added this movie as their favorite. It should simply be removed from the list of favorites.

However, if we delete a `FamilyMember` and nullify the relationship, we end up with a bunch of movies that don't have a family member associated with them. In our application, these movies are worthless; we won't use them anymore because every movie only belongs to a single `FamilyMember`. For our app, it's desirable that, if we delete a `FamilyMember`, we also delete their favorite movies. This is exactly what the cascade option does; it cascades the deletion over to the relationship's **Inverse**.

After setting the delete rule to cascade, select the `Movie` entity and define a relationship called `FamilyMember`. The destination should be `FamilyMember`, and the **Inverse** for this relationship is `favoriteMovies`. After adding this relationship, the **Inverse** will be automatically set on our `FamilyMember` entity:

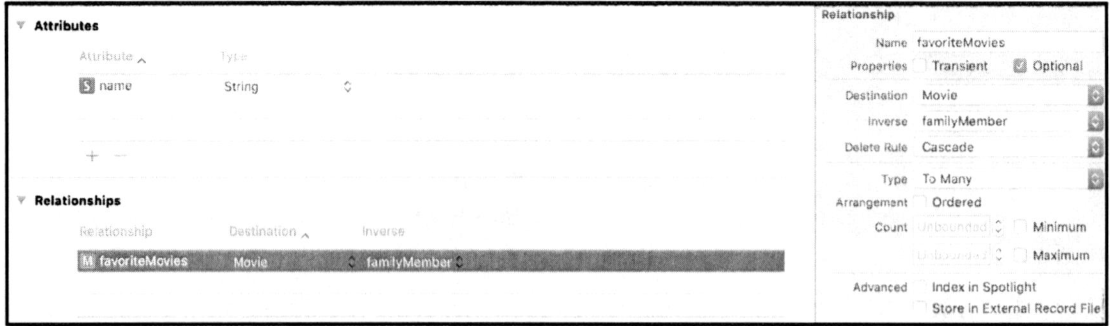

With the data models in place, we can start creating our `NSManagedObject` subclasses.

Creating NSManagedObject subclasses

There are a couple of ways to create or generate `NSManagedObject` subclasses. In the simplest of setups, an `NSManagedObject` subclass contains just the properties for a certain managed object and nothing else. If this is the case, then you can let Xcode generate your model classes for you.

This is actually what Xcode does by default. Build your project and try to write some code, such as the following:

```
let fam = FamilyMember(entity: FamilyMember.entity(),
  insertInto: managedObjectContext)
```

It will work automatically; you don't have to write any code yourself. Don't worry about what the preceding code does just yet, we'll get into that very soon. The point is that you can see that a `FamilyMember` class exists in your project even though you didn't have to create one yourself.

If this default doesn't suit the approach you want to example, if you want to prevent your code from modifying your models by defining your variables as `private(set),`) you may want to create a custom subclass instead of allowing Xcode to generate one for you. A custom `NSManagedObject` subclass for `FamilyMember` would look like this:

```
class FamilyMember: NSManagedObject {
    @NSManaged private(set) var name: String
    @NSManaged private(set) varfavoriteMovies: [Movie]?
}
```

This custom `FamilyMember` subclass makes sure that external code can't modify our instances. Depending on your application, it might be a good idea to implement this since it will ensure that your models can't accidentally change.

One final option you have is to let Xcode generate the properties for your `NSManagedObject` as an extension on a class you will define. This is particularly useful if you have some custom-stored properties that you'd like to define on your model or if you have a customized `NSManagedObject` subclass that you can use as the base for all of your models.

All code that Xcode generates for your Core Data models is added to the `Build` folder in Xcode's Derived Data. You shouldn't modify it, or access it directly. These files will be automatically regenerated by Xcode whenever you perform a build, so any functionality you add inside the generated files will be overwritten.

For our *FamilyMovies* app, we'll have Xcode generating the model definition classes since we don't have any custom properties that we'd like to add. In the model editor, select each entity and make sure that the **Codegen** field is set to **Class Definition**; you can find this field in the Data Model inspector panel:

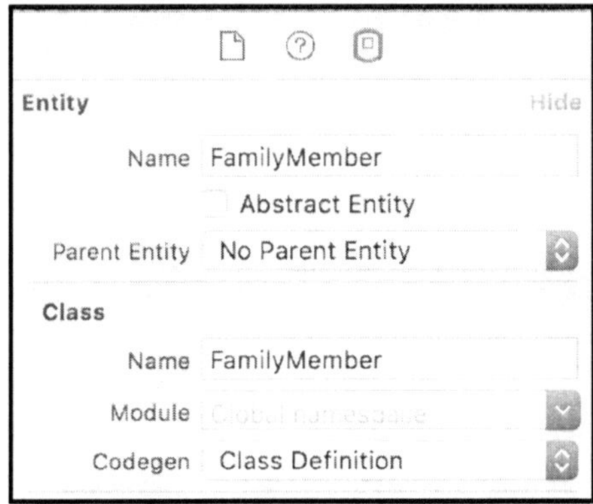

Summary

This chapter was all about getting your feet wet with Core Data. You learned what the Core Data stack looks like and which parts are involved in using Core Data in your application. Even though the `NSPersistentContainer` object abstracts away a great deal of all of the complexity involved in the Core Data stack, it's still good to have a rough understanding of the parts that make up the Core Data stack. After seeing this, you learned how to set up the Core Data stack and how you can use dependency injection to cleanly pass along the managed object context from the `AppDelegate` to the initial view controller.

Then, you saw how to define your Core Data models and how to set up relationships between them. Doing this is made relatively simple in the editor because we can add properties by clicking on a plus icon. You saw that there's a range of options available to you when you add a new property but for a small application, such as the one we're building, most options can be set to their default values. Finally, we took a look at generating our model classes. You saw three ways that Xcode allows us to create classes for our models: manually, automatically, and automatically as an extension.

The next chapter will show you how you can store new objects in the database and how you can fetch them using `NSFetchRequest` and `NSFetchedResultsController`. This will turn our app into a real application that makes use of a database. Let's not waste time and push right through to the next chapter!

9
Storing and Querying Data in Core Data

Now that you know what Core Data is, how it works, and how you can integrate it in your application, the time is right to figure out how to store and query data with it. Adding the Core Data stack wasn't very complex. However, handling actual data in your apps is a bit more complex since you might have to deal with things such as multithreading, or objects that suddenly get updated when you've just read them from the database. Dealing with databases isn't easy, especially if you're trying to ensure data integrity. Luckily for us, Core Data helps tremendously with that.

In this chapter, we will insert some pieces of data into our database and read them. You'll learn how to update the user interface whenever the underlying data changes. You will also learn how you can ensure that you don't accidentally try to read or write objects on the wrong thread and why it matters. To read and filter data, you will use predicates. Finally, you will learn about some of the ways iOS 10 helps in making sure that you always use the correct objects from your database. To wrap everything up, we'll briefly look at what it's like to have an app with multiple `NSManagedObjectContext` instances and how it affects the way you should set up your code.

In this chapter, we will cover the following topics:

- Storing data with Core Data
- Reading data with a simple fetch request
- Filtering data with predicates
- Reacting to database changes
- Understanding the use of multiple `NSManagedObjectContexts`

Storing data with Core Data

The first step to implement data persistence for your app is to make sure that you can store data in the database. The models that we will store were already defined with Xcode's model editor in the previous chapter. First, we'll take a look at what's involved in storing data, and then we'll implement the code that persists our models to the database. Finally, we'll improve our code by refactoring it to be more reusable.

Understanding data persistence

Whenever you want to persist a model with Core Data, you must insert a new `NSManagedObject` into a `NSManagedObjectContext`. Doing this does not immediately persist the model you created. It merely stages your object in the current `NSManagedObjectContext`. If you don't properly manage your managed objects and contexts, this is a potential source of bugs. For example, not persisting your managed objects results in the loss of your data once you refresh the context. Even though this might sound obvious, it could lead to several hours of frustration if you don't carefully manage this.

If you want to properly save managed objects, you will need to tell the managed object context to persist its changes down to the persistent store coordinator. The persistent store coordinator will take care of persisting the data in the underlying SQLite database.

Extra care is required when you use multiple managed object contexts. If you insert an object in one managed object context and persist it, you will manually need to synchronize the changes between managed object contexts. Also, managed objects are not thread-safe. This means that you will need to make sure that you create, access, and store a managed object on the same thread at all times. The managed object context has a helper method called `perform(:_)` to help you with this.

Inserting new objects, updating them, or adding relationships between objects should always be done using this helper method. The reason is that the helper method makes sure that all pieces of code in the closure you want to perform are executed on the same thread that the managed object context is on.

Now that you're aware of how data persistence works in Core Data, it's time to start implementing the code to store our family members and their favorite movies. We'll implement the family member persistence first. Then we'll expand the app so we can safely add movies to family members.

Persisting your models

The first model we will persist is the family member model. The app is already set up with a form that asks for a family member name and a delegate protocol that will inform the `FamilyMembersViewController` whenever we want to store a new family member.

Note that none of the input data is validated; normally, you'd want to add some checks that make sure that we're not trying to insert an empty family member name. For now, we'll skip that because this type of validation isn't Core Data specific. Our persistence code will be added to the `saveFamilyMember(withName:)` method.

Add the following implementation to the `FamilyMembersViewController`; we'll go over it line by line after adding the code:

```
func saveFamilyMember(withName name: String) {
    guard let moc = managedObjectContext
        else { return }

    moc.perform {
        let familyMember = FamilyMember(context: moc)
        familyMember.name = name

        do {
            try moc.save()
        } catch {
            moc.rollback()
        }
    }
}
```

The first thing the preceding code does is to make sure that the `managedObjectContext` is set; if we don't have a managed object context, we can't save our model. Next, the code to store the family member is passed to the `perform(:_)` method in a closure to ensure that the insertion of our model will happen on the correct thread.

Inside the closure that's passed to the `perform(:_)` method, a new instance of the `FamilyMember` class is created. The current `managedObjectContext` is passed to the initializer for this class. This attaches the instance of `FamilyMember` to the correct managed object context. The instance is not persisted yet at this point, as we have only created an instance of `FamilyMember`.

Next, we set the name for our family member to the name we received from the form and then we attempt to save the managed object context. Saving the managed object context will persist any new, changed, or deleted objects down to the persistent store. A `do catch` construct is used for saving the context. We need to do this because it's possible for a save action to fail. In our case, we roll back the changes in the managed object context if saving fails. For this example, rolling back changes in the managed object context means that the newly created `FamilyMember` instance will be discarded.

Now that we are storing family members, let's set up the `MoviesViewController` so it can store movies for a family member. If you build and run the app, this feature won't work right away because we can't tap on any actual family members in the overview yet. We'll implement the required code anyway, and then we'll make it work right after we start reading data from our database.

The code to store movies for a family member is very similar to the code we wrote earlier. Before you implement the following snippets, make sure that you conform `MoviesViewController` to `MOCViewControllerType` and import `CoreData`.

We also need a variable to hold a family member; add the following declaration:

```
var familyMember: FamilyMember?
```

After doing this, add the following implementation for `saveMovie(withName:)`:

```
func saveMovie(withName name: String) {
    guard let moc = managedObjectContext,
        let familyMember = self.familyMember
        else { return }

    moc.perform {
        let movie = Movie(context: moc)
        movie.name = name
        let newFavorites: Set<AnyHashable> =
familyMember.favoriteMovies?.adding(movie) ?? [movie]
        familyMember.favoriteMovies = NSSet(set: newFavorites)

        do {
            try moc.save()
        } catch {
            moc.rollback()
        }
    }
}
```

The most important differences between adding the movie and the family member are highlighted. As you can see, both save methods share about half of the implementation. We can make clever use of extensions and generics in Swift to avoid writing all this duplicated code. Let's refactor our app a bit.

Refactoring the persistence code

Many iOS developers dislike the amount of boilerplate code that is always involved with using Core Data. Simply persisting an object requires you to repeat a lot of code, which can become quite a pain to write and maintain over time. The approach to refactoring the persistence code presented in the following examples is heavily inspired by the approach taken in the *Core Data* book written by Florian Kugler and Daniel Eggert. If you're interested in learning more about Core Data outside of what this book covers, and if you'd like to see more clever ways to reduce the amount of boilerplate code, you should definitely pick up the book.

One pattern you can find in both save methods is the following:

```
moc.perform {
    // persistence code

    do {
        try moc.save()
    } catch {
        moc.rollback()
    }
}
```

It would be great if we could write the following code to persist our data instead:

```
moc.persist {
    // persistence code
}
```

This can be achieved by writing an extension for `NSManagedObjectContext`. Add a file called `NSManagedObjectContext` to the extensions folder, and add the following implementation:

```
import CoreData

extension NSManagedObjectContext {
    func persist(block: @escaping ()->Void) {
        perform {
            block()
```

```
                do {
                    try self.save()
                } catch {
                    self.rollback()
                }
            }
        }
    }
```

The preceding code enables us to reduce the amount of boilerplate code, which is something that we should always try to achieve, regardless of Core Data. Reducing boilerplate code greatly improves your code's readability and maintainability. Update both the family overview and the movie list view controllers to make use of this new persistence method.

Reading data with a simple fetch request

The simplest way to fetch data from your database is to use a fetch request. The managed object context forward fetches requests to the persistent store coordinator. The persistent store coordinator will then forward the request to the persistent store, which will then convert the request to an SQLite query. Once the results are fetched, they are passed back up this chain and converted to `NSManagedObjects`. By default, these objects are called faults. When an object is a fault, it means that the actual properties and values for the object are not fetched yet, but they will be fetched once you access them. This is an example of a good implementation of lazy variables because fetching the values is a pretty fast operation, and fetching everything up front would greatly increase your app's memory footprint because all values must be loaded into memory right away.

Let's take a look at an example of a simple fetch request that retrieves all `FamilyMember` instances that were saved:

```
let request: NSFetchRequest<FamilyMember> = FamilyMember.fetchRequest()

guard let moc = managedObjectContext,
    let results = try? moc.fetch(request)
    else { return }
```

As you can see, it's not particularly hard to fetch all of your family members. Every `NSManagedObject` has a class method that configures a basic fetch request that can be used to retrieve data. If you have large amounts of data, you probably don't want to fetch all of the persisted objects at once. You can configure your fetch request to fetch data in batches by setting the `fetchBatchSize` property. It's recommended that you use this property whenever you use the fetched data in a table view, for example. You should set this property to a value that is just a bit higher than the number of cells you expect to display at a time. This makes sure that Core Data fetches plenty of items to display while avoiding loading everything at once.

As mentioned before, objects are retrieved from the data store as faults. This behavior is usually the behavior you want because it helps to improve your app's memory usage. Prior to iOS 10, faulting could cause some issues if you loaded a faulted object that got deleted from the persistent store before you accessed any of its properties. As you might expect, this causes errors because the framework attempts to load the properties you're accessing, except they don't exist anymore.

In iOS 10, Core Data makes use of snapshots. Whenever you have a set of results, you can always safely access each result and its properties even if they're faults. Once you persist or refresh the managed object context, any changes made after you first fetched your result set will be merged and you get a new snapshot that you can use from that moment on. This is really convenient, and it makes your data safer to use.

Now that you know how to fetch data, let's display some data in the family member's table view. Add a new variable called `familyMembers` to the `FamilyMembersViewController`. Give this property an initial value of `[FamilyMember]()`, so you start off with an empty array of family members. Also, add the example fetch request you saw earlier to `viewDidLoad()`. Next, assign the result of the fetch request to this property as follows:

```
familyMembers = results
```

Finally, update the table view delegate methods so `tableView(_:numberOfRowsInSection:)` returns a number of items in the `familyMembers` array. Also, update the `tableView(_:cellForRowAtIndexPath:)` method by adding the following two lines before returning the cell:

```
let familyMember = familyMembers[indexPath.row]
cell.textLabel?.text = familyMember.name
```

If you build and run your app now, you should see the family members you already saved. New family members won't show up right away. You could manually reload the table view right after you insert a new family member, but this isn't the best approach. We'll get to a better way soon. Let's finish the family member detail view first so we can see some favorite movies and add new ones. Add the following code to the `prepare(for:sender:)` method in the overview view controller:

```
if let moviesVC = segue.destination as? MoviesViewController {
    moviesVC.managedObjectContext = managedObjectContext
    moviesVC.familyMember = familyMembers[selectedIndex.row]
}
```

The preceding lines of code pass the selected family member and the managed object context to the `MoviesViewController` so it can display and store our family member's favorite movies.

All we need to do to make this work now is use the family member's favorite movies in the `MovieViewController` class's table view data source methods, as follows:

```
func tableView(_ tableView: UITableView, numberOfRowsInSection
  section: Int) ->Int {
    return familyMember?.favoriteMovies?.count ?? 0
}

func tableView(_ tableView: UITableView, cellForRowAtindexPath:
  IndexPath) ->UITableViewCell {
    guard let cell = tableView.dequeueReusableCell(withIdentifier:
"MovieCell"),
        let movies = familyMember?.favoriteMovies
        else { fatalError("Wrong cell identifier requested") }

    let moviesArray = Array(movies as! Set<Movie>)
    let movie = moviesArray[indexPath.row]
    cell.textLabel?.text = movie.name

    return cell
}
```

We don't need to use a fetch request here because we can simply traverse the `favoriteMovies` relationship on the family member to get their favorite movies. This isn't just convenient for you as a developer, it's also good for your app's performance. Every time you issue a fetch request, you force a query to the database. If you traverse a relationship, Core Data will attempt to fetch the object from memory instead of asking the database.

Again, adding new data won't immediately trigger the table view to update its contents. We'll get to that after we take a look at how to filter data. If you want to see if your code works, simply build and run the app again so all the latest data is fetched from the database.

Filtering data with predicates

A common operation you'll want to perform on your database is filtering. In Core Data, you make use of predicates to do this. A predicate describes a set of rules that any object that gets fetched has to match.

When you are modeling your data in the model editor, it's wise to think about the types of filtering you need to do. For instance, you may be building a birthday calendar where you'll often sort or filter dates. If this is the case, you should make sure that you have a Core Data index for this property. You can enable this with the checkbox you saw earlier in the model editor. If you ask Core Data to index a property, it will significantly improve performance when filtering and selecting data.

Writing predicates can be confusing, especially if you try to think of them as the `where` clause from SQL. Predicates are very similar, but they're not quite the same. A simple predicate will look as follows:

```
NSPredicate(format: "name CONTAINS[n] %@", "Gu")
```

A predicate has a format; this format always starts with a key. This key represents the property you want to match on. In this example, it would be the name of a family member. Then, you specify the condition, for instance ==, >, <, or `CONTAINS[n]`. There are more conditions available, but the one listed are some examples of conditions you'll commonly use. Finally, you will specify a placeholder that is substituted with the true value. This placeholder is `%@`. If you have written any Objective-C before you picked up this book, the `%@` placeholder might look familiar to you because it's used as a placeholder there as well.

The example predicate is very simple and bare; it could be the template for a search feature you're building. Usually, a simple search doesn't have to be much more complex than this as long as there's an index added to the properties you'll search for.

If you have multiple predicates you want to match on, you can combine them using `NSCompoundPredicate`. This class will combine different predicates using either an `and`, `or`, or `not` clause. A common use case for this approach is when you build a complex filter in your app.

To make use of a predicate, you assign it to the `predicate` property of a fetch request. Every fetch request has a predicate property that you can set. It can handle both a single predicate and a compound predicate. If you set this property before executing the fetch request, the predicate is applied to the request and you will receive a filtered dataset instead of the full dataset.

Predicates are really powerful, and they have many options available. If you're interested in an in-depth overview of predicates and all of the ways in which you can make use of format strings, I recommend that you read *Apple's Predicate Programming Guide at* `http://apple.co/2fF3qHc`. It provides a really well documented overview of predicates and their uses.

Next up, we'll cover how to respond to changes in the managed object context. For instance, when you add new family members and movies.

Reacting to database changes

In its current state, our app doesn't update its interface when a new managed object is persisted. One proposed solution for this is to manually reload the table right after we insert a new family member. Although this might work well for some time, it's not the best solution to this problem. If our application grows, we might add a functionality that enables us to import new family members from the network. Manually refreshing the table view would be problematic because our networking logic should not be aware of the table view. Luckily, there is a better suited solution to react to changes in your data.

First, we'll implement a fetched results controller to update our list of family members. Next, we'll listen to notifications in order to update the list of a family member's favorite movies.

Implementing a NSFetchedResultsController

The `NSFetchedResultsController` class notifies a delegate whenever its fetched data is changed. This means that you won't have to worry about manually reloading the view and you can simply process whatever updates the fetched results controller passes on.

Being a delegate for the fetched results controller involves the following four important methods:

- `controllerWillChangeContent(_:)`
- `controllerDidChangeContent(_:)`

- `controller(_:didChange:at:for:newIndexPath:)`
- `controller(_:didChange:atSectionIndex:for:)`

The first method, `controllerWillChangeContent(_:)`, is called right before the controller passes updates to the delegate. If you're using a table view with a fetched results controller, this is the perfect method to begin updating the table view.

Next, `controller(_:didChange:at:for:newIndexPath:)` and `controller(_:didChange:atSectionIndex:for:)` are called to inform the delegate about updates to the fetched items and sections, respectively. This is where you should handle the updates in the data. For instance, you could insert new rows in a table view.

Finally, `controllerDidChangeContent(_:)` is called. This is the point where you should let the table view know you've finished processing the updates so all the updates can be applied to the table view's interface.

For the `FamilyMovies` application, we will implement just the first three methods because our table view doesn't have any sections. The first thing we should do is create the `NSFetchedResultsController` and assign the `FamilyMembersViewController` as its delegate. Then, we can implement the delegate methods so we get notified about changes to the results we fetched. Remove the `familyMembers` array from the variable declarations and add the following `fetchedResultsController` property:

```
var fetchedResultsController: NSFetchedResultsController<FamilyMember>?
```

The `viewDidLoad` method should be adjusted as follows:

```
override func viewDidLoad() {
    super.viewDidLoad()
    guard let moc = managedObjectContext
        else { return }
    let request = NSFetchRequest<FamilyMember>(entityName: "FamilyMember")
    request.sortDescriptors = [NSSortDescriptor(key: "name", ascending:
true)]
    fetchedResultsController = NSFetchedResultsController(fetchRequest:
request,
managedObjectContext: moc,
sectionNameKeyPath: nil,
                                                               cacheName: nil)
    fetchedResultsController?.delegate = self
    do {
        try fetchedResultsController?.performFetch()
    } catch {
```

```
            print("fetch request failed")
        }
    }
```

This implementation initializes the `NSFetchedResultsController`, assigns the delegate, and tells it to execute the fetch request. Note that we set the `sortDescriptors` property of the fetch request to an array that contains a `NSSortDescriptor`. A fetched request controller requires this property to be set, and for our list of family members, it makes sense to order family members by name.

Now that we have a fetched results controller, we should implement the delegate methods and add conformance to `NSFetchedResultsControllerDelegate`. We'll do this in an extension of the `FamilyMembersViewController`. We're using an extension because it makes our code easier to browse; any code in our extension will relate to the delegate methods we will implement, creating logical groups of code.

Start off by defining an extension inside of the `FamilyMembersViewController.swift` file, as follows:

```
extension FamilyMembersViewController: NSFetchedResultsControllerDelegate {

}
```

We don't have to add any code to set up our delegate, and that's because all delegate methods in the `NSFetchedResultsControllerDelegate` protocol are optional. Let's implement the `controllerWillChangeContent(_:)` and `controllerDidChangeContent(_:)` methods first; these are the simplest methods we will need to implement:

```
func controllerWillChangeContent(_ controller:
NSFetchedResultsController<NSFetchRequestResult>) {
  tableView.beginUpdates()
}

func controllerDidChangeContent(_ controller:
NSFetchedResultsController<NSFetchRequestResult>) {
  tableView.endUpdates()
}
```

These implementations are fairly straightforward. We will simply notify the table view whenever updates will occur and when we're done updating. The bulk of our work needs to be done in `controller(_:didChange:at:for:newIndexPath)`. This method is responsible for receiving and processing updates. In our app, we simply want to update a table view, but you could also update a collection view or store all of the updates in a list and do something else with them.

Let's take a look at how we can process these changes in the following method:

```
func controller(_ controller:
NSFetchedResultsController<NSFetchRequestResult>, didChange anObject: Any,
at indexPath: IndexPath?, for type: NSFetchedResultsChangeType,
newIndexPath: IndexPath?) {
    switch type {
    case .insert:
        guard let insertIndex = newIndexPath
            else { return }
        tableView.insertRows(at: [insertIndex], with: .automatic)
    case .delete:
        guard let deleteIndex = indexPath
            else { return }
        tableView.deleteRows(at: [deleteIndex], with: .automatic)
    case .move:
        guard let fromIndex = indexPath,
            let toIndex = newIndexPath
            else { return }
        tableView.moveRow(at: fromIndex, to: toIndex)
    case .update:
        guard let updateIndex = indexPath
            else { return }
        tableView.reloadRows(at: [updateIndex], with: .automatic)
    }
}
```

This method contains quite a lot of code, but it's actually not that complex. The preceding method receives a `type` parameter. This parameter is a `NSFetchedResultsChangeType` that contains information about the kind of update we received. The following are the four types of updates available for objects:

- `Insert`
- `Delete`
- `Move`
- `Update`

Each of these change types corresponds to a database action. If an object was inserted, we'll receive an `insert` change type. The proper way to handle these updates for our app is to simply pass them on to the table view. Once all updates are received, the table view will apply all of these updates at once.

Had we implemented the `controller(_:didChange:atSectionIndex:for:)` method, we would also have received a change type; however, the sections only deal with the following two types of changes:

- `Insert`
- `Delete`

Sections don't update or move, so if you implement this method, you don't have to account for all cases because you won't encounter any other than the two listed types of changes.

If you take a close look at the implementation for `controller(_:didChange:at:for:newIndexPath)`, you'll notice that we receive two index paths: one is named `indexPath` and the other is named `newIndexPath`. They're both optional, so you will need to make sure that you safely unwrap them if you use them. For new objects, only the `newIndexPath` property will be present. For deletion and updates, the `indexPath` property will be set. When an object is moved around, both properties will contain a value.

The last thing we need to do is update our app so it uses the fetched results controller instead of the `familyMembers` array we used earlier. First, update the `prepare(for:sender:)` method as follows:

```
if let moviesVC = segue.destination as? MoviesViewController,
    let familyMember = fetchedResultsController?.object(at: selectedIndex)
{
        moviesVC.managedObjectContext = managedObjectContext
        moviesVC.familyMember = familyMember
}
```

This makes sure that we're passing a valid family member to the movies view controller. Update the table view data source methods as shown in the next code. A fetched results controller can retrieve objects based on an index path. This makes it even more compatible to use in combination with table views and collection views.

Finally, update the table view data source methods as follows; the important changes are highlighted and should speak for themselves:

```
func tableView(_ tableView: UITableView, numberOfRowsInSection section:
Int) ->Int {
    return fetchedResultsController?.fetchedObjects?.count ?? 0
}

func tableView(_ tableView: UITableView, cellForRowAtindexPath: IndexPath)
->UITableViewCell {
    guard let cell = tableView.dequeueReusableCell(withIdentifier:
"FamilyMemberCell")
        else { fatalError("Wrong cell identifier requested") }

    guard let familyMember = fetchedResultsController?.object(at:
indexPath)
        else { return cell }

    cell.textLabel?.text = familyMember.name

    return cell
}
```

If you run your app now, the interface updates automatically whenever you add a new family member to the database. However, the movie listing doesn't update yet. Also, since we're not using a fetched results controller here, we'll need to figure out some other way to update the interface if we're inserting new movies.

The reason you shouldn't use a fetched results controller for the movie list is that fetched result controllers will always need to drop down all the way to your persistent store (SQLite in this app). As mentioned before, querying the database has a large memory overhead compared to traversing the relationship between family members and their movies; it's much faster to read the `favoriteMovies` property rather than fetching them from the database.

Whenever a managed object context changes, a notification is posted to the default `NotificationCenter`. The `NotificationCenter` is used to fire events inside of your app, that different parts of your code can listen to.

It can be very tempting to use notifications instead of delegates, especially if you're coming from a background that makes heavy use of events such as JavaScript. Don't do this; delegation is far more suited for many cases and it will make your code much more maintainable.

Only use notifications if you don't really care about who's listening to your notifications or if setting up a delegate relationship between objects would mean you'd create very complex relationships between unrelated objects just to set up the delegation.

Let's subscribe the `MoviesViewController` to the `NSManagedObjectContextDidChangeNotification` so it can respond to data changes if needed. Before we add the actual subscription, we will implement the method that handles the updates we receive:

```
extension MoviesViewController {
  @objc func mangedObjectContextDidChange(notification: NSNotification) {
        guard let userInfo = notification.userInfo,
            let updatedObjects = userInfo[NSUpdatedObjectsKey] as?
Set<FamilyMember>,
let familyMember = self.familyMember
            else { return }

        if updatedObjects.contains(familyMember) {
tableView.reloadData()
        }
    }
}
```

This method reads the notification's `userInfo` dictionary to access the information that's relevant to the current list. We're interested in changes to the current `familyMember` because whenever this object changes we can be pretty sure that a new movie was just inserted. The `userInfo` dictionary contains keys for the inserted, deleted, and updated objects. In our case, we will need to look for the updated objects because we can't delete or insert new family members on this view. If our family member was updated, we reload the table view in order to display the newly added movie.

Let's subscribe to the managed object context which changed the notification so we can see this in action. Add the following implementations to `MoviesViewController`:

```
override func viewDidLoad() {
    super.viewDidLoad()
    let center = NotificationCenter.default
    center.addObserver(self, selector:
#selector(self.mangedObjectContextDidChange(notification:)), name:
.NSManagedObjectContextObjectsDidChange,
                       object: nil)
}

deinit {
    let center = NotificationCenter.default
    center.removeObserver(self, name:
.NSManagedObjectContextObjectsDidChange, object: nil)
}
```

When the view loads, we add ourselves as an observer to the `NSManagedObjectContextObjectsDidChange` notification and tell it to execute the change handler we just implemented. When this view controller is destroyed, we have to make sure that we remove ourselves as observers from the notification center to avoid a retain cycle.

Go ahead and build your app; you should now see the user interface update whenever you add new data to your database.

Understanding the use of multiple NSManagedObjectContexts

It has been mentioned several times throughout the past two chapters that you can use multiple managed object contexts. In many cases, you will only need a single managed object context. Using a single managed object context means that all of the code related to the managed object context is executed on the main thread. If you're performing small operations, that's fine. However, imagine importing large amounts of data. An operation like that could take a while. Executing code that runs for a while on the main thread will cause the user interface to become unresponsive. This is not good, as the user will think your app has crashed. So how do you work around this? The answer is using multiple managed object contexts.

In the past, using several managed object contexts was not easy to manage, you had to create instances of `NSManagedObjectContext` using the correct queues yourself. Luckily, the `NSPersistentContainer` helps us manage more complex setups. If you want to import data on a background task, you can either obtain a managed object context by calling `newBackgroundContext()` on the persistent container, or you can use this context to perform tasks, for instance a data import, in the background. If you don't need a reference to the background context, you could call `performBackgroundTask` and pass it a closure with the processing you want to do in the background.

One important thing to understand about core data, background tasks, and multithreading is that you must always use a managed object context on the same thread it was created on. Imagine the following example:

```
let backgroundQueue = DispatchQueue(label: "backgroundQueue")
let backgroundContext = persistentContainer.newBackgroundContext()
backgroundQueue.async {
   let results = try? backgroundContext.fetch(someRequest)

   for result in results {
       // use result
   }
}
```

The preceding behavior of the code can cause you a couple of headaches. The background context was created on a different queue than the one we're using it on. It's always best to make sure to use the context on the same queue it was created on by using the `NSManagedObject`'s `perform(_:)` method. More importantly, you must also make sure to use the managed objects you retrieve on the same queue that the managed object context belongs to.

Often, you'll find that it's best to fetch data on the main queue using the managed object context that lives in the main thread. Storing data can be delegated to background contexts if needed. If you do this, you must make sure that the background context is a child context of the main context. When this relationship is defined between the two contexts, your main context will automatically receive updates when the background context is persisted. This is quite convenient because it removes a lot of manual maintenance which keeps your contexts in sync.

When you find that your app requires a setup with multiple managed object contexts, it's important to keep the rules mentioned in this section in mind. Bugs related to using managed objects or managed object contexts in the wrong places are often tedious to debug and hard to discover. Your code can run fine for weeks and suddenly start crashing or behaving unreliably. Therefore, if you don't need multiple contexts, it might be better to avoid them for a while until you have a solid understanding of Core Data. Learning Core Data and debugging concurrency troubles are not somethings that you're going to want to learn at the same time.

Summary

This chapter focused on inserting and retrieving data with Core Data. You saw how you can make use of fetch requests, predicates, fetched result controllers, and notifications to fetch data. The examples started out simple, by inserting a new object by writing all the boilerplate code that's involved with this. Then you saw how you can refactor this kind of boilerplate code by using extensions; this makes your code more readable and maintainable. It's highly encouraged that you create your own extensions whenever you encounter the same kind of patterns as we did in this chapter. Once you saw how to insert data, you learned about fetch requests and predicates. Even though these two objects aren't very complex, they are very powerful and you'll often use them when you work with Core Data.

Next, you learned how to react to database changes with `NSFetchedResultsController` and `NotificationCenter`. A fetched results controller gives you a very powerful way to subscribe to changes for a set of results. Notifications are more of a general purpose solution, but our implementation makes sure that we are actually only observing a single object. To wrap up this chapter, you gained some insights into using multiple managed object contexts and how not to use them. In the next chapter, *Fetching and Displaying Data from the Network*, we will deep dive into retrieving data from the network so we can fetch ratings for our family member's favorite movies. You'll learn how to make a network request and add its results to your database.

10
Fetching and Displaying Data from the Network

Most modern applications communicate with a web service. Some apps rely on them heavily, acting as a layer that simply reads data from the web and displays it in app form. Other apps use the web to retrieve and sync data to make it locally available, and some others only use the web as backup storage. Of course, there are a lot more reasons to use data from the internet other than the ones mentioned.

In this chapter, we will expand the `FamilyMovies` application so that it uses a web service to retrieve popularity ratings for the movies our family members have added as their favorites. We'll store these popularity ratings in a Core Data database and display them together with the names of the movies.

In this chapter, you'll learn about the following topics:

- URLSession
- Working with JSON in Swift
- Updating Core Data objects with fetched data

Let's see how you can fetch data from the web first, shall we?

Fetching data from the web

Retrieving data from the web is something that you will do often as an iOS professional. You won't just fetch data from a web service; you'll also send data back to it. For example, you might make an HTTP `POST` request to log in a user or to update their information. Over time, iOS has evolved quite a bit in the web requests department, making it easier, simpler, and more consistent to use the web in apps, and we're currently in a pretty good spot with the `URLSession` class.

HTTP (or HTTPS) is a protocol that almost all web traffic uses for communication between a client, like an app, and a server. The HTTP protocol supports several methods that signal the request's intent. `GET` is used to retrieve information from a server. A `POST` request signals the intent to push new content to a server. For instance, submitting a form.

The `URLSession` class makes asynchronous web requests on your behalf. This means that iOS loads data from the internet on a background thread, ensuring that the user interface remains responsive throughout the duration of the entire request. If the request is performed synchronously, the user interface will be unresponsive for the duration of the network request because a thread can only do one thing at a time, so if it's waiting for a response from the network, it can't respond to touches or other user input.

If your user has a slow internet connection, a request could take several seconds. You don't want your interface to freeze for several seconds. Even a couple of milliseconds will create a noticeable drop in its responsiveness and frame rate. This can be easily avoided using `URLSession` to perform asynchronous network requests.

First, we will look at basic network requests in a playground. You can create a new playground or use the one provided in this book's code bundle. After you've seen the basics of `URLSession`, we'll implement a way to fetch movies from an open source movie database and finally put this implementation to use in the FamilyMovies app.

Understanding URLSession basics

Let's look at a basic network request that simply loads the `https://google.com` homepage:

```
let url = URL(string: "https://www.google.com")!
let task = URLSession.shared.dataTask(with: url)
{
    data, response, error in
    print(data)
    print(response)
```

```
        print(error)
    }

    task.resume()
```

This is a very basic example: A URL is created and then the shared `URLSession` instance is used to create a new `dataTask`. This `dataTask` is an instance of `URLSessionDataTask` and allows us to load data from a remote server. Alternatively, we could use a download task if we're downloading a file, or an upload task if we're uploading files to a web server. After creating the task, we need to call resume on the task, because new tasks are always created in the suspended state.

If you run this sample in an empty playground, you'll find that the sample doesn't work. Because our network request is made asynchronously, the playground finishes its execution before the network request is complete. To fix this, we need to make sure that the playground runs indefinitely. Doing so will allow the network request to finish. Add the following lines to the top of the playground source file to enable this behavior:

```
import XCPlayground
XCPlaygroundPage.currentPage.needsIndefiniteExecution = true
```

Now that the playground runs indefinitely, you'll find that there isn't a lot of useful data printed to the console. We're not really interested in the raw data, HTTP headers, or the fact that the error is `nil`. When you load data from a URL, you're often most interested in the response's body. The body of a response usually contains the data you requested. In the case of the example we're studying now, the body is the HTML that makes up Google's homepage. Let's see how we can extract this HTML from the response. Replace the data task's completion callback with the following:

```
{ data, response, error in
    guard let data = data, error == nil
        else { return }

    let responseString = String(data: data, encoding: String.Encoding.utf8)
    print(responseString)
}
```

The preceding callback closure makes sure that there are no errors returned by the web service and that there is data present. Then, we convert the raw data to a string and that string is printed to the console. If you use this callback instead of the old one, you'll see the HTML for the Google homepage printed. Simple requests to a web server like the one we just examined are relatively simple to implement.

You can take more control over the request that's executed by creating your own `URLRequest` instance. The example you saw before is one where you let the `URLSession` create the `URLRequest` on your behalf. This is fine if you want to perform a simple HTTP `GET` request with no custom headers, but if you want to post data or include certain headers, you will need to have more control over the request that's used. Let's take a look at what a `GET` request with some parameters and a custom header looks like.

The following code uses an API key from `https://www.themoviedb.org/`. If you want to try this code example, create an account on their website and request an API key on your account page. Setting this up should only take a couple of minutes, and if you want to follow along with this chapter, you will need to have your own API key:

```
let api_key = "YOUR_API_KEY_HERE"
var urlString = "https://api.themoviedb.org/3/search/movie/"
urlString = urlString.appending("?api_key=\(api_key)")
urlString = urlString.appending("&query=Swift")

let movieURL = URL(string: urlString)!

var urlRequest = URLRequest(url: movieURL)
urlRequest.httpMethod = "GET"
urlRequest.setValue("application/json", forHTTPHeaderField: "Accept")

let movieTask = URLSession.shared().dataTask(with: urlRequest) { data,
response, error in
   print(response)
}

movieTask.resume()
```

The preceding code is a bit more complex than the example you saw before. In this example, we have set up a more complex URL that includes some HTTP `GET` parameters. We also specified the `httpMethod` for the `URLRequest` and a custom header that informs the receiver of our request about the type of response we're willing to accept.

The flow for executing this URL request is the same as the one you saw earlier. However, the URL that is loaded responds with a JSON string instead of an HTML document. JSON is used by many APIs as the preferred format to pass data around on the web. In order to use this response, we'll need to convert the raw data to a dictionary. We'll continue under the assumption that you are familiar with JSON as a format for data. If you haven't seen or worked with JSON before, it's a good idea to take a step back and read up on the JSON data format.

Working with JSON in Swift

The following snippet shows how you can convert raw data to a JSON dictionary. Working with JSON in Swift can be a little tedious at times, but overall, it's an all right experience. Let's look at an example:

```
guard let data = data,
    let json = try? JSONSerialization.jsonObject(with: data, options: [])
    else { return }

print(json)
```

The preceding snippet converts the raw data that is returned by a URL request to a JSON object. The print statement prints a readable version of the response data, but it's not quite ready to be used. Let's see how you gain access to the first available movie in the response.

If you look at the type of object returned by the `jsonObject(with:options:)` method, you'll see that it returns `Any`. This means that we need to typecast the returned object to something we can work with, such as an array or a dictionary. When you inspect the JSON response we received from the API, for instance by using print to make it appear in the console, like you did before with Google's homepage HTML, you'll notice that there's a dictionary that has a key called `results`. The `results` object is an array of movies. In other words, it's an array of `[String: AnyObject]`, because every movie is a dictionary, where strings are the keys and the value can be a couple of different things, such as `Strings`, `Int`, or `Booleans`. With this information, we can access the first movie's title in the JSON response, as shown in the following:

```
guard let jsonDict = json as? [String: AnyObject],
    let resultsArray = jsonDict["results"] as? [[String: AnyObject]]
    else { return }

let firstMovie = resultsArray[0]
let movieTitle = firstMovie["title"] as! String
print(movieTitle)
```

As mentioned before, working with JSON in Swift isn't the most convenient thing to do. Because the JSON object is of the `AnyObject` type and we need to typecast anything we access, there's a lot of boilerplate code you will need to add. Luckily, Swift 4 enables us to easily create instances of objects from JSON. The following example shows how you can quickly create an instance of a `Movie` struct without having to cast all the keys in the JSON dictionary to the correct types for the `Movie` struct.

First, let's define two structs, one for the `Movie` itself, and one for the response that contains the array of `Movie` instances:

```
struct MoviesResponse: Codable {
    let results: [Movie]
}

struct Movie: Codable {
    let id: Int
    let title: String
    let popularity: Float
}
```

Next, you can use the following snippet to quickly convert the raw data from a URL request to an instance of `MoviesResponse`, where all movies are converted to instances of the `Movie` struct:

```
let decoder = JSONDecoder()
guard let data = data,
    let movies = try? decoder.decode(MoviesResponse.self, from: data)
    else { return }

print(movies.results[0].title)
```

You might notice that both `MoviesResponse` and `Movie` conform to the `Codable` protocol. The `Codable` protocol is new in Swift 4, and it enables you to easily encode and decode objects. The only requirement is that all properties of a `Codable` object conform to the `Codable` protocol. A lot of built-in types like `Array`, `String`, `Int`, `Float`, `Dictionary`, and more conform to `Codable`. Because of this, you can easily convert an encoded JSON object into a `MoviesResponse` instance that holds `Movie` instances.

By default, each property name should correspond to the key of the JSON response it is mapped to. However, sometimes you might want to customize this mapping. For instance, the `poster_path` property in the response we've been working with so far would be best mapped to a `posterPath` property on the `Movie` struct. The following example shows how you would tackle these circumstances:

```
struct Movie: Codable {

    enum CodingKeys: String, CodingKey {
        case id, title, popularity
        case posterPath = "poster_path"
    }

    let id: Int
    let title: String
```

```
        let popularity: Float
        let posterPath: String?
    }
```

By specifying a `CodingKeys` enum, you can override certain mappings. You must cover all keys that are mapped, including the ones you don't want to change. As you've seen, the `Codable` protocol provides powerful tools for working with data from the network. Custom key mapping makes this protocol even more powerful because it allows you to shape your objects exactly how you want them instead of having the URL responses dictate the structure to you.

Now let's move on to storing fetched data in the Core Data database.

Updating Core Data objects with fetched data

So far, the only thing we have stored in Core Data is movie names. We will expand this functionality by performing a lookup for a certain movie name through the movie database API. We will use the fetched information to display and store a popularity rating for the movies in our database.

A task such as this seems straightforward at first; you could come up with a flow such as the one shown in the following steps:

1. The users fill out their favorite movie.
2. It fetches popularity.
3. It stores the movie and its popularity.
4. The interface updates with the new movie.

At first sight, this is a fine strategy; insert the data when you have it. However, it's important to consider that API calls are typically done asynchronously, so the interface stays responsive. Also, more importantly, API calls can be really slow if your user doesn't have a good internet connection. This means that you would be updating the interface with noticeable lag if the preceding steps are executed one by one.

The following would be a much better approach to implement the feature at hand:

1. The users fill out their favorite movie.
2. The users store the movie.
3. Update the interface with the new movie.

4. Begin popularity fetching.
5. Update the movie in the database.
6. Update the interface with popularity.

This approach is somewhat more complex, but it will give the user a very snappy and responsive experience. The interface will respond to new movies immediately, and the interface automatically updates as soon as new data is retrieved. Before we can fetch the data and update our models, we will update our Core Data model in order to store the movie popularity rating.

Open the Core Data model editor and select the `Movie` entity. All you have to do is add a new property and name it **popularity**. Select the `Double` type for this property because the **popularity** is stored as a decimal value. You have to make sure that this property is optional since you won't be able to provide a value for it straight away:

If you've worked with Core Data before iOS 10 was released, this is the part where you expect to read about migrations and how you can orchestrate them. However, for simple changes like this, we don't need to manage migrations. All you need to do is simply build and run your application to regenerate your model definitions, and for a simple change, such as the one we performed just now, Core Data will automatically manage the migration on its own.

If you want to support iOS versions earlier than 10, make sure that you read up on Core Data migrations. Whenever you update your models, you have to make sure that your database can properly migrate from one model version to another. During development, this isn't extremely important: you just reinstall the app whenever your models change. However, app updates will crash on launch if the Core Data model isn't compatible with the previous model.

Now that the model is updated, we can figure out how to implement the flow that was described earlier.

Implementing the fetch logic

The asynchronous nature of network requests makes certain tasks, such as the one we're about to implement, quite complex. Usually, when you write code, its execution is very predictable. Your app typically runs line by line, so any line that comes after the previous one can assume that the previous line has finished executing. This isn't the case with asynchronous code. Asynchronous code is taken off the main thread and runs separately from the rest of your code. This means that your asynchronous code might run in parallel with other code. In the case of a network request, the asynchronous code might execute seconds after the function in which the request started.

This means that you need to figure out a way to update and save the movie as soon as its data has been retrieved. What's interesting about this is that once you see the code that implements this feature, it will feel natural to you that this is how it works. However, it's important that you're aware of the fact that it's not as straightforward as it may seem at first.

It's also important that you're aware of the fact that the code we will look at in a moment is executed across threads. This means that even though all pieces of the code are defined in the same place, they are not executed on the same thread. The callback for the network request is executed on a different thread than the code that initiated the network request. We discussed earlier that Core Data is not thread-safe. This means that you can't safely access a Core Data object on a different thread other than the thread it was created on.

If this confuses you, that's okay. You're supposed to be a bit confused right now. Asynchronous programming is not easy, and fooling you into thinking it is will cause you frustration once you run into concurrency related troubles (and you will). Whenever you work with callbacks, closures, and multiple threads, you should be aware that you're doing complex work that isn't straightforward.

Now that we've established an understanding about the complexity of the asynchronous code, let's take a more concrete look at what we're dealing with. It's time to start implementing the network request that fetched popularity ratings for movies. We will abstract the fetching logic into a helper named `MovieDBHelper`. Go ahead and create a new helper folder in Xcode and add a new Swift file called `MovieDBHelper.swift` to it.

Abstracting this logic into a helper has multiple advantages. One of them is simplicity; it will keep our view controller code nice and clean. Another advantage is flexibility. Let's say that you want to combine multiple rating websites, or a different API, or compute popularity based on the number of family members who added this same title to their list; it will be easier to implement since all logic for ratings is in a single place.

Add the following skeleton implementation to the `MovieDBHelper` file:

```
import Foundation

struct MovieDBHelper {
    typealias MovieDBCallback = (Double?) -> Void
    let apiKey = "YOUR_API_KEY_HERE"

    func fetchRating(forMovie movie: String, callback: @escaping
MovieDBCallback) {

    }

    private func url(forMovie movie: String) -> URL? {
        var urlString = "https://api.themoviedb.org/3/search/movie/"
        urlString = urlString.appending("?api_key=\(apiKey)")
        urlString = urlString.appending("&query=\(movie)")

        return URL(string: urlString)
    }
}
```

The preceding code starts off with an interesting line:

```
typealias MovieDBCallback = (Double?) -> Void
```

This line specifies the type we will use for the callback closure that's called when the rating is fetched. This means that our view controller is only concerned with whether a rating is found. If it can't find a rating, the `Double?` will be `nil`. If it did find a rating, this argument will contain the rating. This supplements the flexibility mentioned earlier.

Next, we have a dummy method that performs the fetch; we will implement this method soon. Finally, we have a method that builds a URL. This method is private because it's only supposed to be used inside of the helper struct. Before we implement `fetchRating(forMovie:callback)`, add a new file named `MovieDBResponse.swift` to the helper folder. We will use this file to define a struct that represents the response we expect to receive from the `Moviedb` API. Add the following implementation to this file:

```
struct MovieDBLookupResponse: Codable {

    struct MovieDBMovie: Codable {
        let popularity: Double?
    }

    let results: [MovieDBMovie]
}
```

The preceding code uses a nested struct to represent the movie objects that we're interested in. This is similar to what you have already seen earlier, in the playground example. Structuring the response this way makes it very obvious what our intent is, which usually makes code easier to reason with. With this struct in place, let's see what the implementation of `fetchRating(forMovie:callback)` looks like in the following code:

```
func fetchRating(forMovie movie: String, callback: @escaping
MovieDBCallback) {
    guard let searchUrl = url(forMovie: movie) else {
        callback(nil)
        return
    }

    let task = URLSession.shared.dataTask(with: searchUrl) { data,
response, error in
        var rating: Double? = nil

        defer {
            callback(rating)
        }

        let decoder = JSONDecoder()
        guard error == nil, let data = data,
            let lookupResponse = try?
decoder.decode(MovieDBLookupResponse.self, from: data),
            let popularity = lookupResponse.results.first?.popularity
            else { return }
        rating = popularity
    }

    task.resume()
}
```

This implementation looks very similar to what we experimented with earlier in our playground. The URL building method is used to create a valid URL. If this fails, we can't continue the retrieval of the rating, so the callback is called with a `nil` argument. This will inform the caller of this method that the execution is done and we didn't find a result.

Next, a new data task is created, as shown before, and `resume` is called on this task to kick it off. There is an interesting aspect of how the callback for this data task is called, though. Let's take a look at the following lines of code:

```
var rating: Double? = nil

defer {
    callback(rating)
}
```

A `rating` double is created here, and it is given an initial value of `nil`. Then there's a `defer` block. The code inside of the `defer` block is called right before exiting the scope. In other words, it's executed right before we return from a function or closure.

Since this defer block is defined inside the callback for the data task, the callback for the `fetchRating(forMovie:callback:)` method is always called just before we exit the data task callback. This is convenient because all we must do is set the value for our rating to a double, and we don't have to manually invoke the callback for each possible way we exit the scope. This also applies when we're returning because of unmet requirements. For instance, if there is an error while calling the API, we don't need to invoke the callback. We can simply return from the closure, and the callback is called automatically. This strategy can also be applied if you instantiate or configure objects temporarily and you want to perform some clean-up when the method, function, or closure is done.

The rest of the code should be fairly straightforward since most of it is nearly identical to the code used in the playground. Now that we have the networking logic down, let's take a look at how to actually update our movie object with a popularity rating.

Updating a movie with a popularity rating

To update our movie, we will implement the final step of the approach that was outlined earlier. We need to asynchronously fetch a rating from the movie database and then use that rating to update the movie. The following code should be added to `MoviesViewController.swift`, right after adding a new movie to a family member, inside of the `persist` block, at approximately line 40 (depending on how you have formatted your code):

```
let helper = MovieDBHelper()
helper.fetchRating(forMovie: name) { rating in
    guard let rating = rating
        else { return }

    moc.persist {
        movie.popularity = rating
    }
}
```

You can see that the helper abstraction provides a nice interface for our view controller. We can simply use the helper and provide it a movie to fetch the rating for with a callback and we're all set. Abstracting code like this can make maintaining your code a lot more fun in the long run.

The most surprising thing in the preceding snippet is that `moc.persist` is called again inside of the helper callback. We need to do this because this callback is actually executed long after the initial persist has finished. Actually, this callback isn't even executed on the same thread as the code it's surrounded by.

To see how your code fails if you don't properly persist your model, try replacing the `moc.persist` block with the following code:

```
movie.popularity = rating
do {
    try moc.save()
} catch {
    moc.rollback()
}
```

If you add a new movie now, the rating will still be fetched well enough. However, you will suddenly run into issues when reloading your table view. This is because the managed object context was saved on a background thread. This means that the notification that informs the table view about updates is also sent on a background thread. You could resolve the issue by pushing the `reloadData()` call onto the main thread like we've done before, but in this case, we're simply making our problem bigger. Your app might work fine for a while, but once your app grows in complexity, using the same managed object context in multiple threads will most certainly cause crashes. Therefore, it's important to always make sure that you access managed objects and their contexts on the correct thread by using a construct such as the `persist` method we implemented for this app.

Now that we have looked at all the code involved, let's see what all this threading talk means in a more visual way.

Visualizing multiple threads

The following figure will help you understand multiple threads:

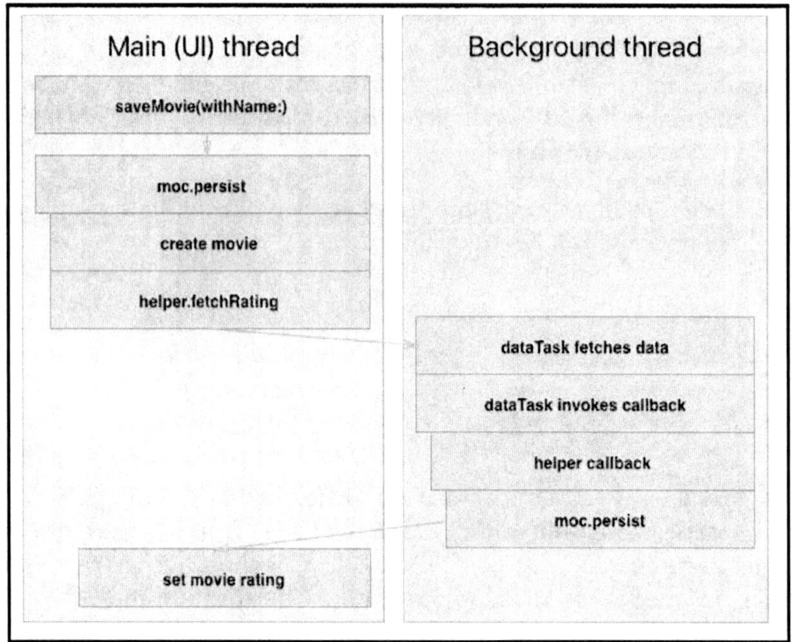

When `saveMovie(withName:)` is called, we're still on the main thread. The persistence block is opened, the movie is created, its name is set, a helper is created, and then `fetchRating(forMovie:callback:)` is called on the helper. This call itself is still on the main thread. However, the fetching of data is pushed to a background thread. This was discussed earlier when you experimented with fetching data in a playground.

The callback that's invoked by our `dataTask` is called on the same thread that the task itself is fetching data on the background thread. We will do what we need to do with the JSON and finally call the callback that was passed to `fetchRating(forMovie:callback:)`. The code inside of this callback is pulled into the background thread and executed there.

You can see that the set movie rating step in the update flow is somehow pushed back to the main thread. This is because of the `persist` method we added as an extension to the managed object context. The context uses the `perform` method internally to ensure that any code we execute inside of the `persist` block is executed on the thread the managed object context is on. Also, since we created the managed object context on the main thread, the movie rating will be set on the main thread.

If we didn't set the movie rating on the same thread that the managed object belongs to, we'd get errors and undefined behavior. Always make sure that you manipulate Core Data objects on the same thread as their managed object context.

Threading is a complex subject, but it's essential for building responsive applications. Network logic is a great example of why multithreading is important. If we didn't perform the networking on a separate thread, the interface would be unresponsive for the duration of the request. If you have other operations that might take a while in your app, consider moving them onto a background thread so they don't block the user interface.

Wrapping the features up

All of the code is in place, and now you understand multithreading and how callbacks can be used in a multithread environment. You learned about the defer statement and how it can be used to execute a block of code at the end of a scope. Yet, if you build and run your app and add a new movie, the rating won't be displayed yet.

The following are the three reasons why this is happening:

- We aren't setting the movie's rating on the table view cell
- The network request doesn't succeed because of App Transport Security
- We're not observing the update

We'll solve these issues in order, starting with the table view cell.

Adding the rating to the movie cell

Currently, the movie table view displays cells that just have a title. `UITableViewCell` has a built-in option to display a title and a subtitle for a cell. Open the `Main.storyboard` and select the prototype cell for the movies. In the `Attributes Inspector` field, change the cell's style from basic to subtitle. This will enable us to use the `detailTextLabel` on our table view cell. This is where we'll display the movie rating.

In `MoviesViewController`, add the following line to `tableView(_:cellForRow:AtIndexPath:)`, right after you set the cell's title:

```
cell.detailTextLabel?.text = "Rating: \(movie.popularity)"
```

This line will put the movie's popularity rating in a string and assign it as a text for the detail text label.

If you build and run your app now, all movies should have a popularity of 0.0. Let's fix this by resolving our networking issue.

Understanding App Transport Security

With iOS 9, Apple introduced **App Transport Security** (**ATS**). ATS makes applications safer and more secure by prohibiting the use of non-HTTPS resources. This is a great security feature, as it protects your users from a wide range of attacks that can be executed on regular HTTP connections.

If you paid close attention to the URL we were using to fetch movies, you would have noticed that we attempted to use an HTTPS resource, so we should be fine. However, our network requests are still blocked by ATS. Why is this?

Well, Apple has strict requirements. At the time of writing this book, the movie database used the SHA-1 signing of certificates, whereas Apple required SHA-2. Because of this, we will need to circumvent ATS for now. Our users should be safe regardless, since the movie database supports HTTPS, just not the version Apple considers to be secure enough.

To do this, open the `Info.plist` file and add a new dictionary key named **App Transport Security Settings**. In this dictionary, you will need an **Exception Domains** dictionary. Add a new dictionary key named **themoviedb.org** to this dictionary and add two Booleans to this dictionary. Both should have **YES** as their values, and they should be named **NSIncludesSubdomains** and **NSTemporaryExceptionAllowsInsecureHTTPLoads**. Refer to the following screenshot to make sure that you've set this up correctly:

▼ App Transport Security Settings	Dictionary	(1 item)
▼ Exception Domains	Dictionary	(1 item)
▼ themoviedb.org	Dictionary	(2 items)
NSIncludesSubdomains	Boolean	YES
NSTemporaryExceptionAllow...	Boolean	YES

If you add a new movie to a family member now, nothing updates yet. However, if you go back to the family overview and then back to the family member, you'll see that the rating for the most recent movie is updated. Great! Now all we need to do is make sure that we observe the managed object context for updates to the movies so we can reload them if their rating changes.

Observing changes to movie ratings

We're already observing the managed object context for changes, but we're only processing them if the family member we're looking at has updated. We should replace this logic so that it will reload the table view if either the family member, or their favorite movies change. Update the `managedObjectContextDidChange(_:)` method in `MoviesViewController.swift` as follows:

```
func managedObjectContextDidChange(notification: NSNotification) {
    guard let userInfo = notification.userInfo
        else { return }

    if let updatedObjects = userInfo[NSUpdatedObjectsKey] as?
Set<FamilyMember>,
        let familyMember = self.familyMember,
          updatedObjects.contains(familyMember) {

        tableView.reloadData()
    }

    if let updatedObjects = userInfo[NSUpdatedObjectsKey] as? Set<Movie> {
        for object in updatedObjects {
            if object.familyMember == familyMember {
                tableView.reloadData()
                break
            }
        }
    }
}
```

The logic for observing the family member hasn't changed; its conditions simply moved from the guard statement to an if statement. Another if the statement was also added for the movies. If the updated object set is a list of movies, we loop through the movies and check whether one of the movies has the current family member as its family member. If so, we refresh the table immediately and break out of the loop.

It's important that we set the loop in the second if statement up like this because we could have just added a movie for family member A and then switched to family member B while the new movie for family member A was still loading its rating. Also, breaking out of the loop early ensures that we won't loop over way more objects than needed. All we want to do is refresh the table view if one of the current family member's favorite movies is updated.

Okay, build and run your app to take it for a spin! You'll notice that everything works as you'd want it to right now. Adding new movies triggers a network request; as soon as it finishes, the UI is updated with the new rating. Sometimes, this update will be done in an instant, while it could take a short while if you have a slow internet connection. Great! That's it for this feature.

Summary

This chapter was all about adding a small, simple feature to an existing app. We added the ability to load real data from an API. You saw that networking is made pretty straightforward by Apple with `URLSession` and data tasks. You also learned that this class abstracts away some very complex behavior regarding multithreading, so your apps remain responsive while data is loaded from the network. Next, you implemented a helper struct for networking and updated the Core Data model to store ratings for movies. Once all this was done, you could finally see how multithreading worked in the context of this app. This wasn't everything we needed to do, though. You learned about ATS and how it keeps your users secure. You also learned that you sometimes need to circumvent ATS, and we covered how you can achieve this.

Even though the feature itself wasn't very complex or big, the concepts and theory involved can be quite overwhelming. You suddenly had to deal with code that would be executed asynchronously, in the future. And not just that. The code even used multiple threads to make sure that its performance was optimal. The concepts of multithreading and asynchronous programming are arguably two of the more complex aspects of programming. Practice them a lot and try to remember that any time you're passing around a closure, you could be writing some asynchronous code that gets executed on a different thread.

Now that our list of movies is updated with data from the web, let's take it one step further in the next chapter. We can use background fetching to make sure that we always fetch the most up-to-date information for our movies and update them without the user even noticing.

11
Being Proactive with Background Fetch

So far, the `FamilyMovies` application is shaping up to be quite nice. You can add family members and associate movies with them, and these movies are automatically enriched with the first rating we can find from the movie database API. There are still some movies we added earlier that don't have a rating, and although the ratings for the existing movies might be correct for now, we don't know whether they will still be accurate after a couple of days, weeks, or months. We could update the ratings whenever the user accesses them, but it's not very efficient to do this. We would potentially reload the same movie a couple of times in a single session.

Ideally, we'd update the movies in the background, when the user isn't using the app. We can do this relatively easily with background fetching. This chapter is all about fetching data on behalf of the user while the app isn't active in the foreground. Implementing this feature can greatly benefit your users because your app will have fresh content every time the user opens up the app. No pull to refresh is needed, and users love these little touches of magic in the apps they use.

In this chapter, we'll cover the following topics:

- Understanding how background fetching works
- Implementing the prerequisites for background fetch
- Updating movies in the background

Besides implementing the background fetch feature, we will also do a lot of refactoring. It's important to understand how and when to refactor your code because it's highly unlikely that you'll be able to exactly nail a flexible setup for your app that can adapt to any requirement that is thrown at it. Being able to refactor your code whenever you see duplication or readability issues is an extremely important skill that you will utilize almost every day as your understanding of your code base, the requirements, and the iOS platform grows.

Understanding how background fetch works

Any application that provides users with some form of data that updates over time is able to implement background fetch. An application that implements background fetch is woken up by iOS periodically, and it's given a small window of time to fetch and process new data that has become available. The OS expects applications to call a callback when they're done with fetching and processing the data. The application uses this callback to inform the OS about whether or not new data was fetched. We'll take a look at a broad overview of background fetch first and then we'll highlight each of the moving parts in more detail before implementing background fetch in the `FamilyMovies` application.

Looking at background fetch from a distance

Background fetch allows apps to download new content in the background without draining the battery because iOS manages the wake-up intervals as efficiently as possible. Since iOS will not allow your application to stay active for a very long time, you must keep in mind that your app might not be able to perform all the tasks you would like it to perform. If this is the case, you're probably implementing background fetch for the wrong reasons. Sometimes, it's a better idea to split the work between your background fetch and application launch.

One example of this would be to download a large amount of data and perform some expensive processing with the downloaded data. If your app takes too long to process the data, it won't be able to finish. It may be a good idea to continue processing as the app launches. An even better idea would be to download only the data and perform all of the expensive processing once the app launches. Background fetch is intended to pull in quick, small updates and not to process large amounts of data.

The time intervals that iOS uses to wake your app up aren't entirely transparent. You can specify the desired time interval for your application if you want to, but ultimately the OS itself decides whether or not your app is woken up and how much time it has to perform its tasks.

A neat feature of background fetch is that iOS learns how often your app actually has updated data, because you have to report this to the `callback`, and also the time your users are most likely to use your app. If a user tends to open your app every morning around 10:00 A.M., chances are that your app will be awakened from the background sometime before 10:00 A.M. This feature makes sure that your users will see recent content for your application. Similarly, if iOS notices that your app rarely has new content within a certain time interval, it's likely that your app isn't awoken as often as you'd like.

Leaving this interval in the hands of the OS might seem a bit scary at first; you often want as much control over these things as possible. What if you know that once a month, at a certain time, you will publish a bunch of new content and you want your app to fetch this in the background? How will you know that all users will receive this new content in time? The answer to this is simple: You don't. Background fetch is a service that makes an attempt to help your users to receive content in the background. There are no guarantees made.

You should always be aware that your app might have to update content in the foreground, since users can turn off background fetching entirely. One more important aspect of background fetch is that it will only work if your app isn't completely killed. If a user opens the multitasking window and swipes your app upward to close it, it won't be awakened for a background refresh, and your app will have to refresh when the user launches it the next time.

A nice way to facilitate this in your code is to implement your background fetch logic in a separate method or a helper you can call. You could invoke a method that's responsible for fetching a new content whenever your application is freshly launched, or when it's awakened, to perform a background fetch. This strategy will make sure that your users always receive the latest content whenever they open your app.

This is really all you will need to know about background fetching; on the surface, it's simply a feature that periodically wakes up your application so it can perform a task for a short time. You don't exactly have control over when and how your app is awakened, which is okay because iOS learns how often your app should be awoken, and more importantly, iOS learns the best time to wake your app up. All you have to do is make sure that iOS knows that your app wants to be woken up.

Looking at background fetch in more depth

Now that you have a broad understanding of background fetch, let's investigate what your app needs to do in order to be compatible with background fetch. First of all, you will need to let iOS know that your app wants to be woken up periodically. To do this, you will need to turn on the **Background Modes** capability for your app. Within this capability, you can opt into for background fetch. Enabling this mode will automatically add a key for this service to your app's `Info.plist`.

When this capability is enabled, iOS will allow your app to be woken up periodically. However, it won't magically work right away. In the `AppDelegate`'s `application(_:didFinishLaunchingWithOptions:)` method, we must inform the system that we actually want our app to become active every once in a while and also specify the interval we desire.

Then, once this is done, your application will be awoken in the background, and the `application(_:performFetchWithCompletionHandler:)` method is called whenever we're allowed to do work. This method should be implemented in `AppDelegate`, and it's expected to call the provided completion handler once the work is completed. If you fail to call this method in time, iOS will make a note of this, and missing the window to call this completion handler could result in your app not being woken up as often as you'd like.

Once the completion handler is called, your app will be put back to sleep until the user opens the app or until the next time your app is allowed to perform a background fetch. Calling the completion handler shouldn't be done until all of the work that you intended to do is done because once the completion handler is called, there are no guarantees about how and when your app will make a transition to the background, except that it will happen soon.

Implementing the prerequisites for background fetch

In order to implement background fetch, you will need to take the following three steps:

1. Add the background fetch capability to your app.
2. Ask iOS to wake your app up.
3. Implement `application(_:performFetchWithCompletionHandler:)` in `AppDelegate`.

We'll implement step 1 and 2 right now; step 3 will be implemented separately because this step will involve writing the code to fetch and update the movies using a helper struct.

Adding the background fetch capabilities

Every application has a list of capabilities they can opt in for. Some examples of these capabilities are Maps, Home Kit, and Background Modes. You can find the **Capabilities** tab in your project settings. If you select your project in the file navigator, you can see the **Capabilities** tab right next to your app's Delete settings.

If you select this tab, you will see a list of all the capabilities your app can implement. If you expand one of these capabilities, you're informed about what the capability does and what happens automatically if you enable it. If you expand the **Background Modes** capability, you'll see the following information:

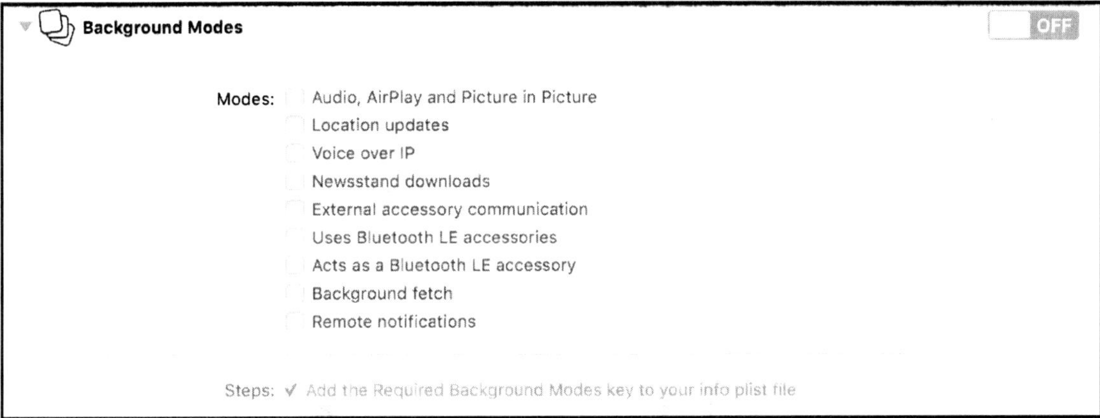

There are several modes available to our app, but we're only interested in one at this time. We want to implement **Background fetch**. Click on the on/off checkbox to enable this capability for our application, and check the **Background fetch** option.

Enabling **Background fetch** isn't something that magically changes some invisible settings for your application. You can actually enable background fetch manually if you'd like to do so.

Open up the `Info.plist` file and search for the **Required background modes** key. You can see that it contains a single item with a value of **App downloads content from the network**. This entry in the `Info.plist` file enables your app to request iOS to wake it up periodically:

▼ Required background modes	Array	(1 item)
Item 0	String	App downloads content from the network

However, just because we can do this manually does not mean we should. The *capabilities* tab is a very convenient place in which you can manage capabilities, and manually adding the right key to the `Info.plist` file is tedious and error-prone. It's interesting to know that there's no magic involved in this process, and it makes the entire feature feel more transparent.

Asking iOS to wake our app up

We're halfway there in terms of enabling background fetching for our app. All that's left to do is inform iOS about our desire to be woken up every once in a while. We will implement this behavior in AppDelegate's `application(_:didFinishLaunchingWithOptions:)`. We will need to implement our request in the preceding method because we would have to ask iOS to wake us every time the app launches. Once the app is launched, it can make the transition from the foreground to the background, which is when our app should be woken up. However, if the app is killed entirely, iOS won't be able to wake our app up again, so we will need to ask it to do so the next time the app launches.

There isn't much code involved to enable background fetching for your app. Add the following line to `application(_:didFinishLaunchingWithOptions:)`:

```
application.setMinimumBackgroundFetchInterval(UIApplicationBackgroundFetchI
ntervalMinimum)
```

This line will ask iOS to wake the app up at a minimum interval. This means that the app is woken up as often as iOS will allow it to be woken up. It's impossible to predict how often this will be since iOS throttles this interval as it sees fit. If your app often has new data available or is used many times throughout the day, odds are that your app will be woken up more often than it would be if you rarely have new data available or if the user opens your app once every couple of days.

Alternatively, you could set the fetch interval to `UIApplicationBackgroundFetchIntervalNever` if you want to prevent your app from being woken up, or you can use a custom value. If you provide a custom value, iOS will attempt to honor your custom interval, but again, there are no guarantees with background fetch, as the system remains in charge with respect to the intervals that are actually used.

The only thing iOS does guarantee is that your app is not woken up more often than when you specified. So, let's say you specify a custom interval for your app to be awoken once every 3 hours iOS won't wake your app up more often than that, but it's possible that your app is awoken only once every 8 hours. This depends on several factors that are not transparent to you as a developer.

Your app is now ready for fetching data in the background. Let's go ahead and implement the fetching of data.

Updating movies in the background

The final step in enabling background fetch for our application is to add the `application(_:performFetchWithCompletionHandler:)` method. As explained before, this method is called by iOS whenever the app is awoken from the background and it allows us to perform an arbitrary amount of work. Once the app is done performing its task, it must call the completion handler that iOS has passed into this method.

Upon calling the completion handler, we will inform iOS about the results of the operation. It's important to correctly report this status because background fetch is intended to improve user experience. If you falsely report to iOS that you have new data all the time so your app is woken up more often, you're actually degrading user experience. You should trust the system to judge when your app is woken up. It's in the best interest of your users, their battery life, and ultimately your app to not abuse background fetch.

In order to efficiently implement background fetch, we will take the following steps:

1. Updating the data model so we can query the movie database more efficiently.
2. Refactoring the existing code to use the improved data model.
3. Implementing background fetch with the existing helper struct.

The first two steps are not directly tied to implementing background fetch, but they do illustrate that an efficient background fetch strategy may involve refactoring some of your app's existing code. Remember, there is nothing wrong with refactoring old code to implement a new feature. Both the new feature and the old code will benefit from refactoring your app.

Updating the data model

The data model we currently have associates movies with a single family member. This means that the app potentially stores the same movie over and over again. When we were only storing data, this wasn't that big of a deal. However, now that we will query the movie database in a background fetch task, we need this task to be as fast as we possibly can make it. This means that we don't want to ask the server for the same movie twice. Also, we most certainly don't want to use the search API as we did before; we want to be as specific about a movie as we can.

To facilitate this, we must change the relationship between movies and family members to a many-to-many relationship. We'll also add a new field to the movie entity: `remoteId`. This `remoteId` will hold the identifier the movie database uses for the particular movie so we can use it directly in later API calls.

Open the model editor in Xcode and add the new property to **Movie**. Make sure that it's a 64-bit integer and that it's optional. Also, select the **familyMember** relationship and change it to a **To Many** relationship in the sidebar. It's also a good idea to rename the relationship to **familyMembers** since we're now relating it to more than one family member as shown in the following screenshot:

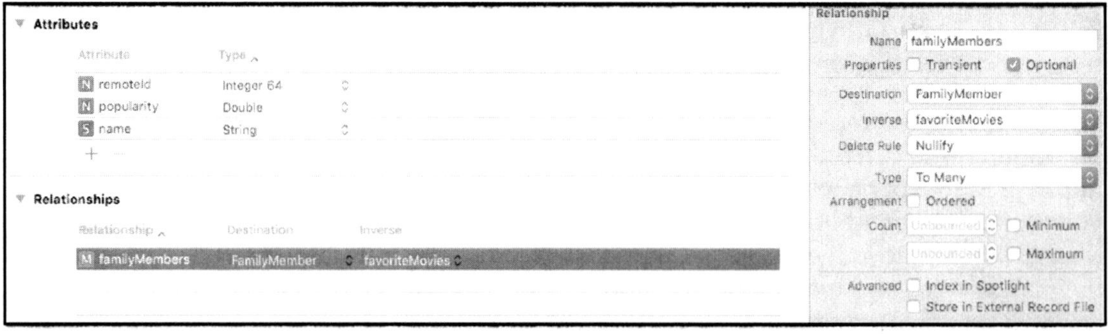

Great, the model has been updated. We still need to perform a bit of work though. Because we changed the name and nature of the family member relationship, our code won't compile. Make the following modifications to the `managedObjectContextDidChange(_:)` method in `MoviesViewController.swift`; the modified lines are highlighted:

```
if let updatedObjects = userInfo[NSUpdatedObjectsKey] as? Set<Movie> {
    for object in updatedObjects {
        if let familyMember = self.familyMember,
            let familyMembers = object.familyMembers,
            familyMembers.contains(familyMember) {
```

```
                tableView.reloadData()
                break
            }
        }
    }
```

There is just one more model-related change that we will need to incorporate. In order to efficiently search for an existing movie or create a new one, we will add an extension to the `Movie` model. Create a new group called **Models** and add a new Swift file named `Movie.swift` to it. Finally, add the following implementation to the file:

```
import CoreData

extension Movie {
    static func find(byName name: String, orCreateIn moc:
NSManagedObjectContext) -> Movie {
        let predicate = NSPredicate(format: "name ==[dc] %@", name)
        let request: NSFetchRequest<Movie> = Movie.fetchRequest()
        request.predicate = predicate

        guard let result = try? moc.fetch(request)
            else { return Movie(context: moc) }

        return result.first ?? Movie(context: moc)
    }
}
```

The preceding code queries `CoreData` for an existing movie with the same name. The movies are matched case-insensitive by passing `[dc]` to the == operator. This lookup is efficient because people might write the same movie name with different capitalization. If we aren't able to find a result, or if the results come back empty, a new movie is created. Otherwise, we return the first and presumably the only result `CoreData` has for our query. This wraps up the changes we need to make to the app's data layer.

Refactoring the existing code

The existing code compiles, but it's not optimal yet. The `MovieDBHelper` doesn't pass the movie's remote ID to its callback, and the movie insertion code doesn't use this remote ID yet. When the user wants to save a new movie, the app still defaults to creating a new movie even though we just wrote our helper method to either find or create a movie to avoid data duplication. We should update our code so the callback is called with the fetched remote ID.

Let's update the `MovieDBHelper` first. Replace the following lines in the `fetchRating(forMovie:callback:)` method; changes are highlighted:

```
typealias MovieDBCallback = (Int?, Double?) -> Void
let apiKey = "YOUR_API_KEY_HERE"

func fetchRating(forMovie movie: String, callback: MovieDBCallback) {
    guard let searchUrl = url(forMovie: movie) else {
        callback(nil, nil)
        return
    }

    let task = URLSession.shared().dataTask(with: searchUrl) { data,
response, error in
        var rating: Double? = nil
        var remoteId: Int? = nil

        defer {
            callback(remoteId, rating)
        }

        let decoder = JSONDecoder()
        guard error == nil, let data = data,
            let lookupResponse = try?
decoder.decode(MovieDBLookupResponse.self, from: data),
            let movie = lookupResponse.results.first
            else { return }
        rating = movie.popularity
        remoteId = movie.id
    }

     task.resume()
}
```

These updates change the callback handler so it takes both the remote ID and the rating as parameters. We also add a variable to hold the remote ID, and we incorporate this variable into the callback. With this code, the `MovieDBHelper` is fully up to date.

You should also update the response struct so the `MovieDBMovie` struct includes the ID from the API response:

```
struct MovieDBMovie: Codable {
    let popularity: Double?
    let id: Int?
}
```

Let's update the movie creation code to wrap up the refactoring step. Update the following lines in the `MoviesViewController`'s `saveMovie(withName:)` method; changes are once again highlighted:

```
moc.persist {
    let movie = Movie.find(byName: name, orCreateIn: moc)
    if movie.name == nil || movie.name?.isEmpty == true {
        movie.name = name
    }

    let newFavorites: Set<AnyHashable> =
familyMember.favoriteMovies?.adding(movie) ?? [movie]
    familyMember.favoriteMovies = NSSet(set: newFavorites)

    let helper = MovieDBHelper()
    helper.fetchRating(forMovie: name) { remoteId, rating in
        guard let rating = rating,
            let remoteId = remoteId
            else { return }

        moc.persist {
            movie.popularity = rating
            movie.remoteId = Int64(remoteId)
        }
    }
}
```

First, the preceding code either fetches an existing movie or creates a new one with the `find(byName:orCreateIn:)` method we just created. Next, it checks whether or not the returned movie already has a name. If it doesn't have a name yet, we will set it. Also, if it does have a name, we can safely assume we were handed an existing movie object so we don't need to set the name. Next, the rating and ID are fetched and we set the corresponding properties on the movie object to the correct values in the callback.

This is all the code we needed to refactor to prepare our app for background fetch. Let's implement this feature now.

Updating movies in the background

We have almost all of the building blocks required to update movies in the background in place. All we need now is a way to fetch movies from the movie database using their remote ID instead of using the movie database search API.

In order to enable this way of querying movies, another fetch method is required. The simplest way to do this would be to copy and paste both the fetch and URL building methods and adjust them to enable fetching movies by ID. This isn't the best idea; if we add another fetch method or require more flexibility later, we will be in trouble. It's much better to refactor this into a more flexible format right away.

Preparing the helper struct

In order to maintain a clear overview of the available API endpoints, we will add a nested enum to the `MovieDBHelper`. Doing this will make other parts of our code more readable, and we can avoid errors and abstract away duplication with this enum. We'll make use of an associated value on the enum to hold on to the ID of a movie; this is convenient because the movie ID is part of the API endpoint.

Add the following code inside of the `MovieDBHelper` struct:

```
static let apiKey = "YOUR_API_KEY_HERE"

enum Endpoint {
    case search
    case movieById(Int64)

    var urlString: String {
        let baseUrl = "https://api.themoviedb.org/3/"

        switch self {
        case .search:
            var urlString = "\(baseUrl)search/movie/"
            urlString =
urlString.appending("?api_key=\(MovieDBHelper.apiKey)")
            return urlString
        case let .movieById(movieId):
            var urlString = "\(baseUrl)movie/\(movieId)"
            urlString =
urlString.appending("?api_key=\(MovieDBHelper.apiKey)")
            return urlString
        }
    }
}
```

The line that defines the `apiKey` constant is highlighted because it's been changed from an instance property to a static property. Making it a static property enables us to use it inside of the nested `Endpoint` enum. Note that the value associated with the `movieById` case in the switch is `Int64` instead of `Int`. This is required because the movie ID is a 64-bit integer type in `CoreData`.

With this new `Endpoint` enum in place, we can refactor the way we build the URLs as follows:

```
private func url(forMovie movie: String) -> URL? {
    guard let escapedMovie =
movie.addingPercentEncoding(withAllowedCharacters:
      .urlHostAllowed)
        else { return nil }

    var urlString = Endpoint.search.urlString
    urlString = urlString.appending("&query=\(escapedMovie)")

    return URL(string: urlString)
}

private func url(forMovieId id: Int64) -> URL? {
    let urlString = Endpoint.movieById(id).urlString
    return URL(string: urlString)
}
```

The `url(forMovie:)` method was updated to make use of the `Endpoint` enum. The `url(forMovieId:)` method is new and uses the `Endpoint` enum to easily obtain a movie-specific URL.

Fetching the rating without writing a lot of duplicate code requires us to abstract away all of the code that we will have to write regardless of the URL we will use to fetch the movie data. The parts of the current fetch method that qualify for this are as follows:

- Checking whether we're working with a valid URL
- Creating the data task
- Extracting the JSON
- Calling the callback

If you think about it, the only real difference is the API response that is used. In the search results, this information is stored in the first item inside of a result's array. In the single movie API call, it's inside of the root object.

With this in mind, our refactored code should be able to retrieve the desired data using just a URL, a data extraction strategy, and a callback. Based on this, we can write the following code:

```
typealias IdAndRating = (id: Int?, rating: Double?)
typealias DataExtractionCallback = (Data) -> IdAndRating

private func fetchRating(fromUrl url: URL?, extractData: @escaping
DataExtractionCallback, callback: @escaping MovieDBCallback) {
    guard let url = url else {
        callback(nil, nil)
        return
    }

    let task = URLSession.shared.dataTask(with: url) { data, response,
error in
        var rating: Double? = nil
        var remoteId: Int? = nil

        defer {
            callback(remoteId, rating)
        }

        guard error == nil
            else { return }

        guard let data = data
            else { return }

        let resultingData = extractData(data)
        rating = resultingData.rating
        remoteId = resultingData.id
    }

    task.resume()
}
```

There is quite a lot going on in the preceding snippet. Most of the code will look familiar, but the type aliases created at the beginning of the code might throw you off a bit. These aliases are intended to make our code a bit more readable. After all, `DataExtractionCallback` is much easier to read than `(Data) -> (id: Int?, rating: Double?)`. Whenever you create a callback or a tuple, it's often a good idea to use a `typealias`. This will improve your code's readability tremendously.

The following section in the `fetchRating(fromUrl:extractData:callback:)` method is where the `DataExtractionCallback` is used:

```
guard let data = data
    else { return }

let resultingData = extractData(data)
rating = resultingData.rating
remoteId = resultingData.id
```

What's interesting here is that regardless of what we're doing, we will need to extract the `data` object. This object is then passed to the `extractData` closure, which returns a tuple containing the data we're interested in.

Let's use this method to implement both the old way of fetching a movie through the search API and the new way that uses the movie ID to request the resource directly, as follows:

```
func fetchRating(forMovie movie: String, callback: @escaping
MovieDBCallback) {
    let searchUrl = url(forMovie: movie)
    let extractData: DataExtractionCallback = { data in
        let decoder = JSONDecoder()
        guard let response = try?
decoder.decode(MovieDBLookupResponse.self, from: data),
            let movie = response.results.first
            else { return (nil, nil) }
        return (movie.id, movie.popularity)
    }
    fetchRating(fromUrl: searchUrl, extractData: extractData, callback:
callback)
}

func fetchRating(forMovieId id: Int64, callback: @escaping MovieDBCallback)
{
    let movieUrl = url(forMovieId: id)
    let extractData: DataExtractionCallback = { data in
        let decoder = JSONDecoder()
        guard let movie = try?
decoder.decode(MovieDBLookupResponse.MovieDBMovie.self, from: data)
            else { return (nil, nil) }
        return (movie.id, movie.popularity)
    }
    fetchRating(fromUrl: movieUrl, extractData: extractData, callback:
callback)
}
```

The code duplication is minimal in these methods, which means that this refactor action is a success. If we add new ways to fetch movies, all we need to do is obtain a URL, explain how to retrieve the data we're looking for from the `data` object, and finally, we need to kick off the fetching.

We're now finally able to fetch movies through their ID without duplicating a lot of code. The final step in implementing our background update feature is to implement the code that updates movies. Let's go!

Updating the movies

The process of updating movies is a strange process. As we saw earlier, network requests are performed asynchronously, which means that you can't rely on the network request being finished by the time a function is finished executing. Because of this, a callback is used, which enables us to know when a request is done.

But what happens if we need to wait for multiple requests? How do we know that we have finished making all of the requests to update movies? Since the movie database doesn't allow us to fetch all of our movies at once, we'll need to make a bunch of requests. When all of these requests are complete, we'll need to invoke the background fetch `completionHandler` with the result of our operation.

To achieve this, we will need to make use of grand central dispatch. More specifically, we will use a dispatch group. A dispatch group keeps track of an arbitrary number of tasks, and it won't consider itself as completed until all of the tasks that are added to the group have finished executing.

This behavior is exactly what we need. Whenever we fetch a movie from the network, we can add a new task that we'll complete once the underlying movie is updated. Finally, when all of the movies are updated, we can report back to the `completionHandler` to inform it about our results. Let's take a step-by-step look at how to achieve this behavior using the following code:

```
func application(_ application: UIApplication,
performFetchWithCompletionHandler completionHandler: @escaping
(UIBackgroundFetchResult) -> Void) {

    let fetchRequest: NSFetchRequest<Movie> = Movie.fetchRequest()
    let managedObjectContext = persistentContainer.viewContext
    guard let allMovies = try? managedObjectContext.fetch(fetchRequest)
else {
        completionHandler(.failed)
        return
```

```
        }
    }
```

This first part of the implementation is fairly straightforward. We obtain a fetch request and a managed object context. Then, we query the managed object context for all of its movies, and if we are unable to fetch any, we'll notify the completion handler that we failed to fetch new data and exit the method.

All the following code snippets should be added to the `application(_:performFetchWithCompletionHandler:)` method inside of `AppDelegate` in the same order as they are presented. A full overview of the implementation will be provided at the end:

```
let queue = DispatchQueue(label: "movieDBQueue")
let group = DispatchGroup()
let helper = MovieDBHelper()
var dataChanged = false
```

These lines create a dispatch queue and a dispatch group. We'll use the dispatch queue as a mechanism to execute the tasks inside of our group. We'll also create an instance of our helper struct; a variable is created to keep track of whether we received updates to our data or not:

```
for movie in allMovies {
    queue.async(group: group) {
        group.enter()
        helper.fetchRating(forMovieId: movie.remoteId) { id, popularity in
            guard let popularity = popularity,
                popularity != movie.popularity else {
                group.leave()
                return
            }

            dataChanged = true

            managedObjectContext.persist {
                movie.popularity = popularity
                group.leave()
            }
        }
    }

}
```

Next, we loop through the fetched movies. We add the code we want to execute to the dispatch queue and call `group.enter()`. This informs the dispatch group that we just added a task to it. Then, we perform our fetch for the rating and check whether or not a popularity was fetched and whether it's different to the one we currently have in the movie. If either of these isn't the case, we call `group.leave()` to tell the group this task is complete and return from the callback.

If our `guard` passes, we are dealing with updated data, so we set `dataChanged` to `true`. We also persist the new popularity to `CoreData` and then leave the group. Once again, the `persist` method is very convenient because it makes sure that we're executing the code inside of the persist block on the right thread.

The following final snippet we will need to add will execute when all the tasks in the queue are performed; at this point, we want to check whether we've fetched new data by reading the `dataChanged` property, and based on this property, we will call the `callbackHandler`:

```
group.notify(queue: DispatchQueue.main) {
    if dataChanged {
        completionHandler(.newData)
    } else {
        completionHandler(.noData)
    }
}
```

The `group.notify` method takes a queue and a block of code that we want to execute. The queue is set to the main queue, which means that the code inside of the block is executed on the main queue. Then, we read the `dataChanged` variable and inform the `completionHandler` about the results of the fetch operation.

As promised, the full implementation for `application(_:performFetchWithCompletionHandler:)` is as follows:

```
func application(_ application: UIApplication,
performFetchWithCompletionHandler completionHandler: @escaping
(UIBackgroundFetchResult) -> Void) {

    let fetchRequest: NSFetchRequest<Movie> = Movie.fetchRequest()
    let managedObjectContext = persistentContainer.viewContext
    guard let allMovies = try? managedObjectContext.fetch(fetchRequest)
else {
        completionHandler(.failed)
        return
    }

    let queue = DispatchQueue(label: "movieDBQueue")
```

```
        let group = DispatchGroup()
        let helper = MovieDBHelper()
        var dataChanged = false

        for movie in allMovies {
            queue.async(group: group) {
                group.enter()
                helper.fetchRating(forMovieId: movie.remoteId) { id, popularity
    in
                    guard let popularity = popularity,
                        popularity != movie.popularity else {
                        group.leave()
                        return
                    }

                    dataChanged = true

                    managedObjectContext.persist {
                        movie.popularity = popularity
                        group.leave()
                    }
                }
            }
        }

        group.notify(queue: DispatchQueue.main) {
            if dataChanged {
                completionHandler(.newData)
            } else {
                completionHandler(.noData)
            }
        }
    }
```

In order to test whether background fetching is working well, you can build and run your app. Then, add a new movie so you have a movie for which the ID is stored. Finally, you can use the debug menu item in Xcode that's at the top of your screen to simulate a background refresh. This will trigger a background refresh.

Summary

We started this chapter with an overview of background fetch, how it works, and how it benefits your users. You learned about the prerequisites and best practices with regards to this feature. After establishing this basic understanding, you learned how background fetch works in concert with your application. Then, we continued to implement the required permissions and asked iOS to wake up the FamilyMovies application periodically so we could update the movies' ratings.

Once we did this, we needed to refactor a good portion of our application to accommodate the new feature. It's important to be able to recognize scenarios where refactoring is a good idea, especially if it enables smooth implementation of a feature later on. It also demonstrates that you don't have to think about every possible scenario for your code every time you implement a feature. After refactoring our application, we were finally able to implement background fetching behavior. In order to do this, we glanced over dispatch groups and how they allow you to group an arbitrary amount of asynchronous work together in order to be notified when all of the tasks in a group are completed.

This chapter wraps up the Core Data section. In the following chapters, we will focus on app extensions and how they are used to create a richer user experience. The first extension we will look at is `Spotlight`. We'll use this extension to index the data from the `FamilyMovies` application so we can find our family members and their favorite movies through the `Spotlight`.

12
Enriching Apps with the Camera, Motion, and Location

Your iPhone is a device that is capable of many things. So far, you've seen how the iPhone does networking and data management. You also know that the iPhone is really good at displaying content to your users with the help of components such as the collection view. However, the iPhone can do much more. It's a device that people carry with them every day, and it contains all kinds of sensors that provide unique opportunities to build apps that make use of these sensors for fun or even to truly improve people's lives.

People use their phones to navigate through traffic or to figure out where they're heading using maps and compass apps. The iPhone is also used to track workouts or even runs. Also, let's not forget that both the iPhone and iPad are used by people to take pictures and shoot videos. When we build apps, we should be aware that the iPhone's sensors can be used to create a rich and interactive experience.

In this chapter, we'll take a look at the following three sensors that are part of the iPhone. We'll have a look at some simple use cases for these sensors and how they can be used in a real application:

- The camera
- The motion sensor
- GPS

Accessing and using the camera the simple way

We will focus on building a nice login screen for a fictional app named ArtApp. This application is an **Augmented Reality** (**AR**) application that focuses on art. The login form fields will be positioned at the center of the screen. The camera will provide a background, and as the user moves their phone, we'll make the login field move around a bit. This effect will look similar to the iOS wallpaper parallax effect you might have noticed while using your iPhone. We'll use location data to provide a fictional indication of how many pieces of Augmented Reality art are near the user's current location. Before you get started, create a new single page app named ArtApp; you don't have to include Core Data or unit tests for this application.

The application we will build in this chapter requires you to test it on a real device. The iOS simulator has limited support for GPS, but it doesn't have a camera or motion sensor access. Make sure that you have a device that runs iOS 11 nearby.

There are different ways to access the camera in iOS. A lot of applications don't need direct access to the camera. An example of a situation where you don't need this direct access is when a user uploads a profile picture. Your end goal in this case is to obtain a photo. This photo can be provided either from the camera roll or from the camera itself. In these situations, the `UIImagePickerController` class is ideal.

This class is the easiest way for developers to access the camera as all of the controls and interface elements are already implemented. The `UIImagePickerController` enables users to take a photo, switch to the front-facing camera, and more. In short, it provides access to all controls a user may expect from the default camera app. Once a photo has been taken, it is passed on to your application so you can process it as desired.

If you simply want to enable your user to take a picture or shoot a video that is used in your app, `UIImagePickerController` is very likely to be the tool you need. Let's take a quick look at how to use this class in your app. Note that the following code does not work as you might want it to in the iOS simulator because it does not have access to the camera:

```
let imagePicker = UIImagePickerController()

if UIImagePickerController.isSourceTypeAvailable(.camera) {
    imagePicker.sourceType = .camera
    imagePicker.cameraCaptureMode = .photo
} else {
    imagePicker.sourceType = .photoLibrary
```

```
}

present(imagePicker, animated: true, completion: nil)
```

The preceding code will present the user with a camera interface, if possible. If the camera is not available, the users are presented with an image picker that shows their photo library.

This example isn't very useful because it does not yet obtain a reference to the selected photo. Once a user has selected a photo, the `UIImagePickerController` notifies its delegate about the selection the user has made. This means that in order to be notified about the user's choice, you must implement and assign a delegate for `UIImagePickerController`. The method you should implement to receive the selected photo is `imagePickerController(_:didFinishPickingMediaWithInfo:)`.

The chosen image is available in the `info` dictionary that's passed to the delegate method. An implementation of this delegate method could be the following:

```
extension ViewController: UIImagePickerControllerDelegate {
    func imagePickerController(_ picker: UIImagePickerController,
didFinishPickingMediaWithInfo info: [String : Any]) {

        guard let image = info[UIImagePickerControllerOriginalImage]
            else { return }

        anImageView.image = image
    }
}
```

The preceding snippet extracts the selected image from the info dictionary and sets it as the image for an image view. You can configure `UIImagePickerController` to allow the user to crop an image they selected. To do this, you will need to set the image picker controller's `allowsEditing` property to `true`. If you do this, the cropped image is available through the `UIImagePickerControllerCroppedImage` key in the `info` dictionary that is passed to `imagePickerController(_:didFinishPickingMediaWithInfo:)`. For an exhaustive list of keys that are passed to the info dictionary, refer to the `UIImagePickerController` page on *Editing Information Keys* in Apple's documentation.

Although the preceding approach is very convenient if all you need to do is access an image from the user's library, or if you want them to supply an image through the camera, it's not the way to go if you need to read input from the camera in real time. The login screen we're going to build for ArtApp should show a real-time camera feed as a background. This means we need direct access to the camera.

Exploring the AVFoundation framework

Obtaining direct access to the iPhone's camera is possible through the `AVFoundation` framework. The `AVFoundation` framework is used to record, edit, and play back audio and video. If you look up the documentation for `AVFoundation`, you'll find that it's a huge framework that contains a whole range of audio- and video-related classes. In order to build the login screen for our app, we will focus on the classes that are related to reading the camera data and displaying images from the camera on the screen in real time.

The range of possibilities that `AVFoundation` offers is large enough to cover multiple chapters, so we will focus on a small section of capabilities of `AVFoundation`. However, this book wouldn't be complete if we didn't at least skim over some of its other classes and capabilities.

We'll take a look at two relatively simple use cases for `AVFoundation` before we move on to implementing the video feed background for ArtApp. First, we will take a look at `AVPlayer` and how it can be used to play back a list of audio streams. Next, we'll take a look at video playback and how picture-in-picture works for the iPad.

Playing audio with AVFoundation

Playing audio with `AVFoundation` is fairly straightforward. For the most basic use cases, all you need is an `AVPlayer`, or `AVQueuePlayer` if you have multiple items you want to play. Each resource that you play should be wrapped in an `AVPlayerItem` instance. An `AVPlayerItem` provides an interface to the media it contains. For instance, it enables you to play or pause media and change the playback speed.

As we'll see in a moment, `AVPlayer` itself can also be directly addressed to manipulate the play back of an item that is currently playing. Let's dive right into a basic example of audio playback with `AVFoundation`. For this and the following snippets regarding `AVFoundation`, you can refer to the `AVFoundationExploration` project in this book's accompanying source code:

```
import UIKit
import AVFoundation

class AudioViewController: UIViewController {

    let streamUrls = [
        URL(string: "link/to/audio/resource"),
        URL(string: "link/to/audio/resource")]
```

```
        var audioPlayer: AVQueuePlayer!

        override func viewDidLoad() {
            super.viewDidLoad()

            var playerItems = [AVPlayerItem]()
            for url in streamUrls {
                playerItems.append(AVPlayerItem(url: url!))
            }

            audioPlayer = AVQueuePlayer(items: playerItems)
        }

        @IBAction func startStopTapped() {
            if audioPlayer.rate == 0.0 {
                audioPlayer.play()
            } else {
                audioPlayer.pause()
            }
        }
    }
```

The preceding example plays audio files from a URL. This example shows how simple it can be to stream media from the network with `AVQueuePlayer`. To play with this yourself, you could turn to Spotify's free-to-use API. This API enables you to play 30 second previews for songs. Paste a couple of these URLs into the `streamUrls` array, and you're good to go.

This example is very basic, of course, and if you plan to build a full-blown audio player, you'll still have a lot of work to do in order to enable seeking, skipping songs, and more. All of these playback-related manipulations can be done through `AVPlayer` and `AVPlayerItem`. If you plan on building an audio player, rest assured that the available tools allow you to focus on building an amazing user experience instead of focusing on the nitty-gritty details of audio playback.

One final remark on audio playback is that Apple recommends that you use `AVAudioPlayer` instead of `AVPlayer` if you play audio files that are locally available on the device. If your media is locally available, `AVAudioPlayer` provides several convenient properties that you can use, such as `isPlaying`, `volume`, and `pan`. These properties are not available on `AVPlayer`, and you'll need to resort to implementing these properties yourself if you find yourself needing these features. So, if possible, use `AVAudioPlayer` instead of `AVPlayer` to play back audio files.

Playing video with AVFoundation

Playing video with `AVFoundation` is pretty similar to playing audio. We can use an `AVPlayer` instance and pass it an instance of `AVPlayerItem` that points to a video on the web. This approach requires us to create an `AVPlayerLayer` that uses the `AVPlayer` as an input for its visual contents, as shown in the following code:

```
import UIKit
import AVFoundation

class VideoViewController: UIViewController {

    let url = URL(string: "path/to/video/file")
    var videoPlayer: AVPlayer!
    var playerLayer: AVPlayerLayer!

    override func viewDidLoad() {
        super.viewDidLoad()

        let videoItem = AVPlayerItem(url: url!)
        videoPlayer = AVPlayer(playerItem: videoItem)
        playerLayer = AVPlayerLayer(player: videoPlayer)

        playerLayer.backgroundColor = UIColor.black.cgColor
        playerLayer.videoGravity = AVLayerVideoGravityResizeAspectFill

        view.layer.addSublayer(playerLayer)

        videoPlayer.play()
    }

    override func viewDidLayoutSubviews() {
        let playerWidth = view.bounds.width - 20
        let playerHeight = playerWidth / (16/9)
        let yPos = (view.bounds.height - playerHeight) / 2

        playerLayer.frame = CGRect(x: 10,
                                   y: yPos,
                                   width: playerWidth,
                                   height: playerHeight)
    }
}
```

The preceding code speaks for itself. You'll notice the similarities to playing audio and how we manually set up a player layer that uses the player instance to drive its visual contents. If you test this example, you'll notice that there are no controls available for the video. Users typically expect to be able to have some control over video play back, for instance, pausing the video or scrubbing through it to move the video playback forward or backward.

For this purpose, Apple has created the `AVPlayerViewController`. This view controller provides all the native interaction controls your users expect from iOS, and it's often a great idea to use this view controller instead of manually programming controls for your media playback. Let's take a look at a quick example:

```
playerController = AVPlayerViewController()
playerController.willMove(toParentViewController: self)
addChildViewController(playerController)
playerController.didMove(toParentViewController: self)

playerController.player = videoPlayer
view.addSubview(playerController.view)
playerController.view.translatesAutoresizingMaskIntoConstraints = false

NSLayoutConstraint.activate([
    playerController.view.widthAnchor.constraint(equalTo: view.widthAnchor,
      multiplier: 1, constant: -20),
    playerController.view.heightAnchor.constraint(equalTo:
      playerController.view.widthAnchor, multiplier: 9/16),
    playerController.view.centerXAnchor.constraint(equalTo:
view.centerXAnchor),
    playerController.view.bottomAnchor.constraint(equalTo:
view.safeAreaLayoutGuide.bottomAnchor, constant: -70)
])
```

You'll notice that there are a couple of lines at the beginning of this code snippet that you haven't seen before, and that aren't even related to `AVFoundation`. When you use a component such as `AVPlayerViewController`, you can embed the component in another view controller by adding it as a child view controller.

This means that we create an instance of a view controller, such as `AVPlayerViewController`, and add its view to the container view controller's view. We need to call `willMove(toParentViewController:)` and `didMove(toParentViewController:)` so that the child and parent view controllers can perform some internal work. Once a view controller is another view controller's child, the parent will pass several life cycle methods to its child, such as trait collection changes or orientation changes. It's important that you properly take care of adding a child view controller, otherwise the child will never receive life cycle updates that could be important to it.

After we create the player view controller, we associate a player with it, and we're good to go. All that's left to do is to add the player controller's view and set up some constraints for it so it has a good-looking layout. It's interesting to note that if you have multiple players that use the same player item, both players will play the media item back in sync. Go ahead and take a look at the sample code to see this in action.

With this video primer done, it's time to move on to using the camera. We didn't cover all of `AVFoundation` since there's simply too much to cover, and most of it is very specialized and only useful if you're building a video or audio editing app. If you're interested in more information about `AVFoundation`, I highly recommend browsing Apple's documentation and example code. There is a lot of great information there.

Rendering the camera feed

Now that you know about `AVFoundation` and what it does, we can zoom in on the area we're most interested in; the camera. First, we'll have a look at the `AVFoundation` classes that are needed to implement the video feed that will act as the background for our screen. Once the classes and their usage are clear, we'll implement the login screen.

Understanding the building blocks of a video feed

Whenever you capture a video feed with `AVFoundation`, there are several classes involved. This is in contrast with the extremely easy-to-use `UIImagePickerController`, which enables the user to take a picture, crop it, and pass it back to its delegate.

The foundation for our login screen is `AVCaptureDevice`. This class is responsible for providing access to the camera hardware. On an iPhone, this is either the front or back camera. `AVCaptureDevice` also provides access to camera hardware settings, such as the flash or camera brightness.

The `AVCaptureDevice` works in conjunction with `AVCaptureDeviceInput`. `AVCaptureDeviceInput` is responsible for reading video data from the camera and making this data available. The available data is never read directly; it is made available through a subclass of `AVCaptureOutput`.

`AVCaptureOutput` is an abstract base class. This means that you never use this class directly, but instead you make use of one of its subclasses. There are subclasses available for photos, such as `AVCaptureStillImageOutput`, which is used for capturing photos. There's also `AVCaptureVideoOutput`. This class provides access to raw video frames that can be used, for example, to create a live video preview. This is exactly what we will use later.

The input and output class instances are managed by `AVCaptureSession`. `AVCaptureSession` ties the input and output together and ensures that everything works. If either the input or the output generates an error, `AVCaptureSession` will raise the error.

To recap, these are the four classes that are involved when you work with the camera directly:

- `AVCaptureDevice`
- `AVCaptureDeviceInput`
- `AVCaptureOutput`
- `AVCaptureSession`

The capture device works together with the device input. The output provides access to the output of the capture input and the session ties it all together. The following diagram illustrates these relationships:

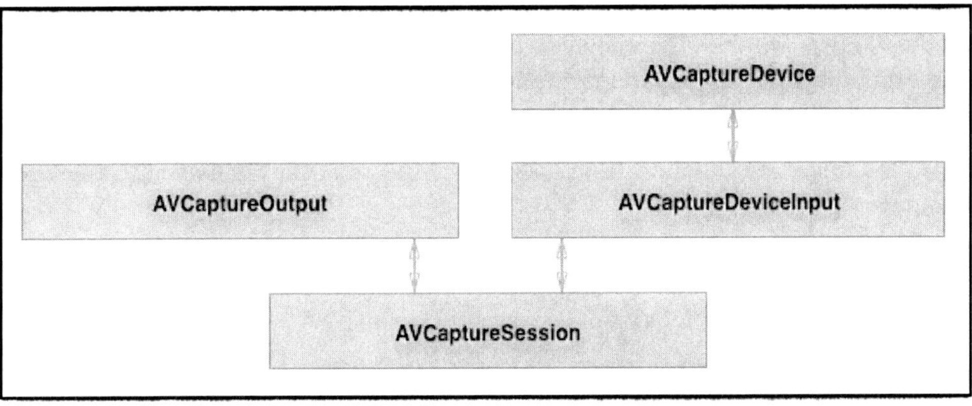

Let's implement our live video preview.

Implementing the video feed

If you have used an app that accesses the camera before, you know that an app must ask permission before it can access the camera. In iOS 10, asking permission became a bit stricter. If you want to access the camera, you will need to specify this in your app's `Info.plist`. Similar to how you obtained access to the user's contacts, this involves adding a key and a description to the `Info.plist`. Let's do this. Create a new single view application named ArtApp, open its `Info.plist` and add a key named `NSCameraUsageDescription` and a short description; refer to the following screenshot to make sure that you added the key correctly:

Information Property List	Dictionary	(14 items)
Privacy - Camera Usage Description	String	Provides a live camera view on the login page

After adding this key, we're ready to start implementing the camera feed. First, we'll prepare our storyboard so it can display the video feed in a way that allows us to add the login view later. In `ViewController.swift`, we will need a `@IBOutlet` for the video view:

```
@IBOutlet var videoView: UIView!
```

In `Main.storyboard`, place a `UIView` and use constraints to make it cover the view controller's view. Also, add constraints to center it inside of the view horizontally and vertically. This will properly position the video view. Now, use the Outlet Inspector to connect the `videoView` with the view you just added. Lastly, go to the project settings and make sure that the only supported orientation is portrait, since we will not make our camera view adaptive.

Add the following empty method to `ViewController.swift`. We'll use this method to implement the camera view soon:

```
func displayCamera() {

}
```

Next, add the following implementation for `viewDidLoad`:

```
override func viewDidLoad() {
    super.viewDidLoad()

    let authStatus = AVCaptureDevice.authorizationStatus(forMediaType:
      AVMediaTypeVideo)
    switch authStatus {
    case .notDetermined:
```

```
            AVCaptureDevice.requestAccess(forMediaType: AVMediaTypeVideo) {
              authorized in
                if authorized {
                    DispatchQueue.main.async {
                        self.displayCamera()
                    }
                } else {
                    print("Did not authorize")
                }
            }
        case .authorized:
            displayCamera()
        case .denied, .restricted:
            print("No access granted")
        }
    }
```

The code in this implementation should look somewhat similar to when you asked permission to access the user's contacts. Depending on the current authorization status, we either ask the user for permission or call the `displayCamera` method. If the access is denied or the user doesn't accept the authorization request, you could implement a method that instructs the user to open the *Settings* app and allow access in order to display the live feed.

The next step for our app is to actually display the camera feed. Start off with adding the following constant to `ViewController`:

```
let captureSession = AVCaptureSession()
```

The capture session can be instantiated right away because it doesn't need any configuration. We'll set it up to suit our needs in the `displayCamera` method.

The simplest way to get the live camera feed to show is by using the following `displayCamera` implementation:

```
func displayCamera() {
    let discoverySession = AVCaptureDevice.DiscoverySession(deviceTypes:
[.builtInWideAngleCamera], mediaType: .video, position: .back)
    let availableCameras = discoverySession.devices

    guard let backCamera = availableCameras.first,
        let input = try? AVCaptureDeviceInput(device: backCamera)
        else { return }

    if captureSession.canAddInput(input) {
        captureSession.addInput(input)
    }
```

```
        let preview = AVCaptureVideoPreviewLayer(session: captureSession)

        preview.frame = view.bounds
        videoView.layer.addSublayer(preview)

        captureSession.startRunning()
    }
```

The preceding code uses an `AVCaptureDeviceDiscoverySession` to find all camera devices we're interested in. In this case, we only want the regular back-facing camera. The standard camera that all devices have is a wide-angle camera. You could also look for a specific camera, for instance, the telephoto lens that the iPhone 7+ and iPhone X contain.

If we find a camera, we attempt to create `AVCaptureDeviceInput` with this device. Then, we check whether our session is able to receive our input. If so, we add it. Finally, we use a class that wasn't discussed before. We use an `AVCaptureVideoPreviewLayer` instance to display the raw output from the camera. This preview layer wraps the required classes we discussed previously in a convenient way. In order to start capturing and displaying the video output, we must manually call `startRunning` on the capture session.

If you build and run your app with this code in place, you'll see a live preview of whatever is visible to the camera at that time. The next step is to add the login fields and use the motion sensors to make it move as we move the device.

Implementing CoreMotion

The `CoreMotion` framework implements many motion-related classes. The functionality for these classes varies, from counting steps with `CMStepCounter`, to figuring out the user's altitude with `CMAltimeter`, to accessing gyroscope data with `CMGyroData`, or even to reading whether a user is walking, running, or driving with `CMMotionActivityManager`. Reading the hardware sensors, such as the gyroscope, is done through an instance of `CMMotionManager`. The motion manager class provides an interface that enables developers to read data from the accelerometer, gyroscope, and more.

Our application will use a combination of sensors to function properly. However, before we get to that, we'll explore the available sensors a bit more because there are a lot of interesting features present in `CoreMotion`. We'll cover the pedometer first, and then we'll take a look at reading other sensors, such as altitude, accelerometer, and gyroscope.

If you use `CoreMotion` in your application, the new privacy restrictions in iOS 10 dictate that you must include the `NSMotionUsageDescription` key in your app's `Info.plist`. This key is similar to the one we used for the camera, except it should describe why we want to access motion data.

Tracking walks with the pedometer

The first sensor we will explore is the pedometer. The pedometer is generally used to track the number of steps a user takes and to measure the distance a user has walked. This information is exposed to your application through the `CMPedometer` class. The pedometer data you retrieve from this class should be consistent regardless of the way the user holds their phone. Apple even stated in a *WWDC 2015* session that the pedometer adapts to its user in order to become more accurate over time.

If you're looking to build an application that tracks a user's running or walking activity, `CMPedometer` is perfect for calculating the distance your user has traveled over a given time. There's more than one way to read information about the user's traveled distance. One is to rely on real-time updates. These kinds of updates can be listened to using the `startUpdates(from:withHandler:)` method that is implemented on `CMPedometer`. If you call this method, you have to supply a start date and a handler.

The start date tells the method the point from which you want to accumulate the data. You could use a date in the past, if you like, and your handler will be called with the number of steps and the distance traveled since the date you specified.

The handler you supply to `startUpdates(from:withHandler:)` is called with two arguments: an instance of `CMPedometerData` and an instance of `Error`. Both of the arguments are optional, so if there's no error or no data, the corresponding argument will be passed in as `nil`. The following code serves as an example of how you'd call this method in your own application; the example assumes that you imported the `CoreMotion` framework at the top of your file:

```
let pedometer = CMPedometer()
pedometer.startUpdates(from: Date(), withHandler: { data, error in
    print(data)
    print(error)
})
```

A snippet as simple as this is all you need to start receiving updates about the pedometer data. This data isn't provided to your application in real time. You will receive updates as they become available through the framework. Usually, this is very close to real time, but you should be aware that there are no guarantees with the timing.

If you're building an application that tracks runs, you could have the users start and stop their workout. If you want to get the number of steps and distance traveled for that run, you can use the `queryPedometerData(from:to:handler:)` method. This method allows you to query the pedometer up to one week in the past. The following example assumes that your users have started and stopped their workout; the start and end dates for the workout are stored in the `workoutStart` and `workoutEnd` properties:

```
let pedometer = CMPedometer()
pedometer.queryPedometerData(from: workoutStart, to: workoutEnd, handler: {
data, error in
    print(data)
    print(error)
})
```

This snippet looks very similar to the previous snippet. They work pretty differently from each other, though, because the latter example's handler is only called once, when the query data becomes available.

The pedometer provides a nice interface that makes it easy to track walks and runs. However, there is one issue with this. If somebody is running, they might take a short break, meaning that there will be no steps taken for a short while. If your app is not aware of these breaks, you might come up with a very skewed calculation for average running speeds. Luckily, the pedometer can detect these breaks, and you can listen to start and stop events in your app.

To listen to these start and stop events, you use `CMPedometerEvent`. To obtain these events, you ask the pedometer for event updates, and, just as we did before, we implement a handler that is called whenever an update becomes available, as shown in the following code snippet:

```
if CMPedometer.isPedometerEventTrackingAvailable() {
    pedometer.startEventUpdates(handler: { update, error in
        print(update)
        print(error)
    })
}
```

One important thing to note in this snippet is the use of `CMPedometer.isPedometerEventTrackingAvailable()`. We must check whether event tracking is available because this feature is only available on iPhone 6s, iPhone SE, and newer versions because of the motion coprocessor that is present in these devices.

The updates we receive in the update handler are `CMPedometerEvent` objects. These objects have a `date` and a `type` property. The `date` tells you when the event occurred. The `type` property informs you whether the user stopped walking or started walking.

Storing these events for the duration of a workout enables you to compute a better workout result because temporary stops don't count towards the total activity time if you subtract the pause time from the total time.

One last thing you should know about the pedometer is that its distance calculations are more accurate if your app has access to the device's GPS coordinates. How you obtain access to GPS is discussed later in this chapter.

If your app has access to GPS, the pedometer will combine its own readings and estimations with the GPS data. If the GPS data is accurate enough, the pedometer performs almost no calculations on its own for the distance traveled. However, if the GPS is drifting, the pedometer will use its own readings to calculate the traveled distance. Combining the GPS and the pedometer's own readings ensures that the distance reported by `CMPedometer` is as accurate as possible.

Reading sensor data with CoreMotion

The `CoreMotion` framework provides access to several device motion-related sensors. In order to access these sensors, you make use of `CMMotionManager`. This class enables you to read data from the following sensors:

- Gyroscope
- Accelerometer
- Magnetometer

The **gyroscope** sensor provides information about the device's current rotation rate in 3D space. The rotation of the device is measured in relation to a variable frame. This means that you can't make any assumptions about the orientation the device is actually in. If you lie the device flat on a table and raise it, the gyroscope will show an increasing value on the X-axis if we pick the phone up in portrait mode. Once we stop rotating the device, the value will be close to zero again.

The accelerometer also measures rotation in 3D space, just like the gyroscope. This makes it very easy to get confused about the differences between the accelerometer and the gyroscope. Both sensors respond to movement, but while the gyroscope measures rotation, the accelerometer measures acceleration. So if we pick up our phone from a table and the gyroscope measures an *X*-axis rotation, the accelerometer will measure more movement on the *Y*-axis. This is because the phone is accelerating upward, along the *Y*-axis. This distinction is very important. The gyroscope measures rotation around an axis and the accelerometer measures movement along an axis.

The last sensor we can individually target is the magnetometer. This sensor uses the earth's magnetic field to determine a device's orientation in the physical world. The `CoreLocation` framework uses this sensor to determine which direction a user is headed. The ratings you get from this sensor are fairly abstract, and if you're looking to determine the exact device orientation, it's a lot easier to use the `CMAttitude` class. We'll cover this class soon.

All three of the preceding sensors can be monitored individually with `CMMotionManager`. The following example shows how you can read the data you receive from the gyroscope; the APIs for reading the accelerometer or the magnetometer follow the same pattern, so for brevity, there is just a single version shown:

```
let motionManager = CMMotionManager()

func startTracking() {
    motionManager.gyroUpdateInterval = 1
    motionManager.startGyroUpdates(to: OperationQueue.main, withHandler: {
data, error in
        guard let gyroData = data
            else { return }

        print("gyro data: \(gyroData)")
    })
}
```

Note how the `motionManager` is defined outside of the `startTracking` method. This is important because if we declare the manager inside of the function, the manager will be de-allocated after the function is executed. We need to make sure that there is something referencing, or holding on to, the manager for as long as we use it. Defining it inside of a function means that by the time the function is executed, nothing holds on to the manager, so the system will clean it up by removing it. If our class is holding onto it, the manager will exist until the instance of the class stops existing.

Also note that we specify an operation queue that we want to use for our motion updates. Depending on your use case, your app might do some in-depth analysis on the received data, or maybe you're storing it somewhere in a database instead of directly displaying it. If this is the case, you might want to handle the incoming motion data on a background queue to prevent the interface from locking up. In the preceding snippet, the main operation queue is used, so the data readings can be passed to the user interface directly without dispatching the UI changes to the main queue explicitly.

If your app needs a more refined output than what the raw sensor data gives you, the `CMDeviceMotion` class is probably what you're looking for. This class contains processed and ready-to-use information about a device's orientation, rotation, magnetic field, and acceleration. A great use case for this class is to figure out whether a device is currently laid out flat on a table or mounted in a dock. To do this, you use the attitude property of `CMDeviceMotion`. The attitude provides information about a device's yaw, pitch, and roll. The yaw is the rotation along the *Y*-axis, the pitch is the rotation along the *X*-axis, and roll is the rotation on the *Z*-axis. The following example shows how you can read the device rotation through `CMDeviceMotion`:

```
motionManager.startDeviceMotionUpdates(to: OperationQueue.main,
withHandler: {
  data, _ in
    self.xLabel.text = "pitch: \(data?.attitude.pitch ?? 0.0)"
    self.yLabel.text = "roll: \(data?.attitude.roll ?? 0.0)"
    self.zLabel.text = "yaw: \(data?.attitude.yaw ?? 0.0)"
})
```

The API for device motion is similar to the raw sensor APIs. We tell the motion manager to start updating, provide an operation queue, and process the incoming data as it's pushed to the app.

Creating the login interface

Just like before, we'll implement the required code and set up the outlets we need before we implement the interface in the Interface Builder. Apple recommends that apps that make use of a `CMMotionManager` only use a single motion manager throughout their app. To make this manageable, and to follow the best practices for dependency injection, we will make `AppDelegate` responsible for injecting a motion manager into our view controller. You saw this approach before when we injected a managed object context into a view controller.

Add the following code to your `AppDelegate`'s `application(_:didFinishLaunchingWithOptions:)` method:

```
if let viewController = window?.rootViewController as? ViewController {
    viewController.motionManager = CMMotionManager()
}
```

Even though this code isn't spectacularly complex, it follows the best practices that make the code more maintainable in the long run.

Next, add the following properties to `ViewController.swift`:

```
@IBOutlet var hConstraint: NSLayoutConstraint!
@IBOutlet var vConstraint: NSLayoutConstraint!

var motionManager: CMMotionManager!
var startRoll: Int?
var startPitch: Int?
```

The properties you just added will aid us in the following three areas:

1. We can manipulate constraints to move the login fields across the screen.
2. There is an implicitly unwrapped motion manager instance. Normally, implicitly unwrapping variables should be considered a red flag. In this case, however, it's not a big problem because if the motion manager is not set, this is considered a programming error and it needs to be fixed.
3. There are start values for the device attitude. These values will help us determine how much the device has moved.

The final step we need to take is to begin listening for device motion updates and handle them to make the login interface move across the screen. Add the following code to `viewDidLoad`:

```
motionManager.startDeviceMotionUpdates(to: OperationQueue.main) { data, _
in
    guard let motionData = data
        else { return }

    let roll = Int(motionData.attitude.roll * 180 / .pi)
    let pitch = Int(motionData.attitude.pitch * 180 / .pi)

    if self.startRoll == nil { self.startRoll = roll }
    if self.startPitch == nil { self.startPitch = pitch }

    guard let startRoll = self.startRoll,
        let startPitch = self.startPitch
```

```
        else { return }

    self.vConstraint.constant = CGFloat(pitch - startPitch)
    self.hConstraint.constant = -CGFloat(roll - startRoll)
}
```

The preceding code starts the motion updates, just like before. It then makes sure that the data is set, and the `roll` and `pitch` values are read from the `attitude`. Because these values are in radians, they need to be converted to degrees, which is done by multiplying them by `180` and then dividing by `.pi`.

Then, we set the start values if they aren't set already, and after this we safely unwrap the values using a guard. This is just a double safety measure, and force unwrapping `startPitch` and `startRoll` shouldn't hurt much because we actually set these values a few lines earlier. However, it's typically better to be safe than sorry, so it's always recommended to properly unwrap values whenever possible.

Finally, the horizontal and vertical constraints are adjusted to suit the new positions on screen, and that wraps up the processing we want to do on the motion data.

All that's left to do now is to add the login interface. A `UIStackView` is very suited to stack up an input for the email, password, and a login button. Open the `Main.storyboard` file and start by dragging out a `UIStackView`. Now, drag out two `UITextField` instances and a `UIButton`, and add them to the stack view. Make sure that your view hierarchy looks exactly as shown in the following screenshot so that the **Stack View** and the **Video View** are siblings and the **Video View** is positioned below the **Stack View**:

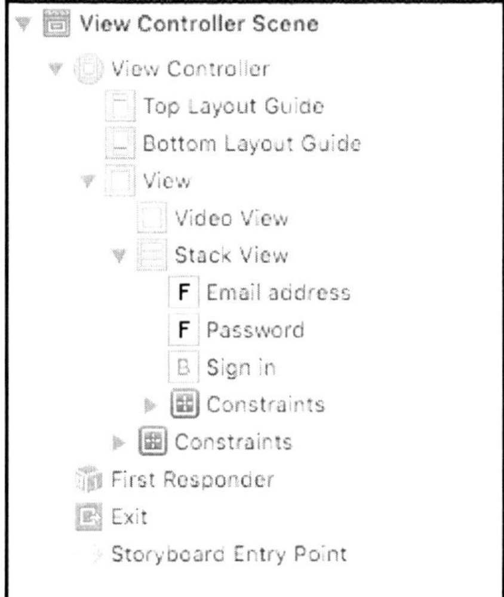

Now that the views are in place, let's make sure that they're laid out properly. Add a width constraint to the stack view and set the width to 250. Do this by holding *Ctrl* and dragging your cursor inside of the stack view in a horizontal direction and letting go. Go to the **Size Inspector** panel to change the constant for the constraint.

Also, add constraints to center the stack view horizontally and vertically so it's positioned nicely, and finally, change the spacing inside of the stack view to `8`. Use the **Attributes Inspector** in the stack view to do this.

Lastly, select the entire view controller and connect the **vConstraint** outlet to the **center.y** constraint for the stack view. Do this by dragging from the **Outlets Inspector** to the Document Outline. Also, connect the **hConstraint** to the **center.x** constraint on the stack view.

You can build and run your app now, and you should see the login interface displayed on top of the camera preview. If you move your phone around a bit, you'll notice that the login fields respond to this movement by moving it to the opposite direction of your phone.

The effect you've implemented here uses a lot of sensors under the hood, but `CoreMotion` has made it fairly simple to read the sensor data and use it to create a simple, effective, user-driven animation. Keep in mind that you could also implement this by directly reading data from the gyroscope, magnetometer, and accelerometer, but the calculations to properly determine the roll or pitch are very complex, and it's almost always better to have `CoreMotion` analyze and combine sensor values instead.

Our final task is to fetch the GPS location of the users so we can inform them about the number of AR art pieces that are available near their current location. Let's do this.

Using CoreLocation to locate your users

The final feature that needs to be added to the login screen of the ArtApp application is a label that shows where a user is currently located. Devices such as the iPhone contain a GPS chip that can accurately determine a user's location. Incorporating this into your apps can greatly improve the user experience. However, implementing location services poorly can and will frustrate your users, and could even drain their battery if you're not careful.

Before we add location services to ArtApp, we should explore the `CoreLocation` framework to see what features it has and how we can efficiently implement it into ArtApp and other applications. Some of the features and examples you will be familiar with are the following:

- Obtaining a user's location
- Geofencing
- Tracking a user while they're moving

Let's dive right in with the basics.

Obtaining a user's location

The documentation for `CoreLocation` states the following as a one-line definition of what `CoreLocation` does.

> *Determine the current latitude and longitude of a device. Configure and schedule the delivery of location-related events.*

In other words, figuring out a user's location is one of the two core features in the `CoreLocation` framework. For now, we will focus on determining the user's current latitude and longitude since that's the simplest and most basic thing we can do.

Before an app is allowed access to a user's location, it must ask permission to do so. Similar to how permission is asked for camera and motion access, you are required to specify in `Info.plist` that you want to query your user's location, and also the reason for doing so. The key that you must add to the `Info.plist` is `NSLocationWhenInUseUsageDescription`. The description should be short and concise, as usual, for example: *Provides information about the nearby artwork.* If you add this key and value pair, you are allowed to access the user's location while they're using the app. If you want to have access to the user's location while your app is in the background, you will need to add the `Privacy - Location Always Usage Description` key to your app.

Once you add the appropriate key to your `plist` file, you can use the `CoreLocation` framework in your app. Just as with the camera, adding the correct key to the `plist` file isn't enough. The user needs to manually allow your app to access their location. The steps to ask permission for the location are similar to the steps for the camera, but not quite the same.

When you ask permission to access the camera, a callback is used to communicate the result of this authorization to your application. For location services, a delegate method is called instead of a callback handler. This means that you must set a delegate on an instance of `CLLocationManager` that conforms to `CLLocationManagerDelegate` in order to be notified when the authorization status changes.

The `CLLocationManager` class acts as a gateway for the location services of the user's device. The location manager is not only used for location updates but also to determine heading, scheduling events, and more. We'll get to that later; for now, we will use the location manager to simply figure out the user's location.

To get started, import `CoreLocation` in `ViewController.swift` and make the `ViewController` class conform to `CLLocationManagerDelegate` by adding it to the class declaration. You should also add a property to `ViewController` that holds onto the location manager, as follows:

```
import CoreLocation

class ViewController: UIViewController, CLLocationManagerDelegate{
  let locationManager = CLLocationManager()
```

Next, add the following method to the class and make sure that you call it in `viewDidLoad`:

```
func setupLocationUpdates() {
    locationManager.delegate = self

    let authStatus = CLLocationManager.authorizationStatus()
    switch authStatus {
    case .notDetermined:
        locationManager.requestWhenInUseAuthorization()
    case .authorizedWhenInUse:
        startLocationTracking()
    default:
        break
    }
}
```

This method adds the view controller as the delegate for the location manager and verifies its authorization status. If the status is undetermined, we ask for permission, and if permission is already given, `startLocationTracking` is called immediately. This is a method we'll implement soon.

Whenever the permission status regarding the location changes, the location manager informs its delegate about this change. We must implement the following method to be notified of authorization changes:

```
func locationManager(_ manager: CLLocationManager, didChangeAuthorization
status:
  CLAuthorizationStatus) {
    if status == .authorizedWhenInUse {
        startLocationTracking()
    }
}
```

In this method, we check the authorization status, and if the app is authorized to access the user's location, the `startLocationTracking` method is called. The implementation for this method is really short since we just want to tell the location manager to start sending us updates regarding the user's location. Before your app begins listening for location updates, you should make sure that location services are enabled, as shown in the following code snippet; you must do this because the user can disable location services entirely in the settings app:

```
func startLocationTracking() {
    if CLLocationManager.locationServicesEnabled() {
        locationManager.startUpdatingLocation()
    }
}
```

Now that the location manager has activated the GPS chip and started to process the user's location, you just need to implement a delegate method that is called whenever the location is updated. The method we should implement is `locationManager(_:didUpdateLocations:)`.

The location manager supplies itself and an array of `CLLocation` instances to `locationManager(_:didUpdateLocations:)`. The location array contains at least one `CLLocation` instance, but it could also contain multiple locations. This occurs if the location manager receives location updates faster than it can supply them to its delegate. All location updates are added in the order in which they occur. If you're just interested in the most recent location update, this means that you should use the last location in the array.

For our app, we will use the following implementation for `locationManager(_:didUpdateLocations:)`:

```
func locationManager(_ manager: CLLocationManager, didUpdateLocations
locations:
  [CLLocation]) {
    guard let location = locations.last
```

```
        else { return }

    print(location)
    manager.stopUpdatingLocation()
}
```

This implementation is perfect for ArtApp. We listen for location updates and pick the last one from the locations array. Then, we use the location, and after that, we stop listening for location updates. We do this for two reasons. The first is good manners; our app shouldn't listen for location updates longer than it has to. We just want to know where the user is at that moment in time, and we don't need continuous updates.

The second reason is to conserve battery life. If our app keeps listening for location updates all the time, the user's battery will empty faster than it needs to. As a developer, it's your job to make sure that your app does not needlessly drain the user's battery.

If you take a look at the printed output from the preceding method, you should see something similar to the following line:

```
<+52.30202835,+4.69597776> +/- 5.00m (speed 0.00 mps / course -1.00) @
30-08-16 21:52:55 Midden-Europese zomertijd
```

This output is a summary of some of the information that's available in the `CLLocation` class. Every instance has the GPS coordinates, the accuracy, the speed, the direction the user is traveling in, and a timestamp.

This is plenty of information for our app since the latitude and longitude are the only things needed to look up nearby pieces of art. If ArtApp was a real application, we could send the GPS coordinates to the backend, and it could respond with the number of available art pieces. However, we also want to have a readable location to display to the user, such as Amsterdam or New York.

The act of translating coordinates to a location or vice versa is called geocoding. To convert GPS coordinates to a human-friendly location, you will make use of the `CLGeocoder` class. This class has a single purpose: Geocoding locations. If you convert from coordinates to a human-readable location, you call the `reverseGeocode(_:completionHandler:)` method. If you already have an address and the coordinates for it, you call one of the address geocoding methods that are available.

If you're using the `CLGeocoder` class, it's important that your user has access to the internet, since `CLGeocoder` uses the network to geocode your requests. This is why you provide a callback to the geocoding methods; they don't return a value immediately. It's also important to be aware that geocoding is rate limited. Your app cannot make an infinite amount of geocoding requests, so it's important that you attempt to cache results locally to prevent unnecessary geocoding lookups.

A simple example of using the `CLGeocoder` is shown in the following code snippet:

```
func locationManager(_ manager: CLLocationManager, didUpdateLocations
locations:
   [CLLocation]) {
    guard let location = locations.last
        else { return }

    let geocoder = CLGeocoder()
    geocoder.reverseGeocodeLocation(location, completionHandler: {
      placemarks, _ in
        guard let placemark = placemarks?.first
            else { return }

        print(placemark)
    })

    locationManager.stopUpdatingLocation()
}
```

This example uses the last location received from the location manager and reverse geocodes it into a `CLPlacemark` instance. The completion handler for geocoding receives an array of possible `CLPlacemarks` that match the request, and an `NSError`. Both are optional, and only have a non-nil value if there is a real value available.

We'll get to displaying the address in a human-friendly form when we finish our login screen for ArtApp. Let's take a look at geofencing first.

Providing location-based updates with geofencing

In addition to just listening for location updates, we can monitor the user's location with regards to a certain area. This is called geofencing, and it allows us to notify the user whenever they enter or exit an area. We can use `CoreLocation` to define a region that is of interest to our user. For instance, iOS itself uses geofencing to provide location-based reminders to people.

Monitoring a region is done by configuring a `CLLocationManager` instance to monitor changes to either a `CLCircularRegion` or a `CLBeaconRegion`. If you're monitoring GPS coordinates, you will need a circular region. If you're monitoring a user's proximity to an iBeacon, you will use the beacon region.

Once you configure the area you'd like to monitor, you should use the location manager's `startMonitoring(for:)` method to begin monitoring exit and enter events for your region. The location manager will call its delegate whenever one of these events occurs.

If your app is in the background or not running, iOS will continue monitoring enter and exit events for your region. If one of these events occurs, your app is either woken up or launched in order to handle the region event. The options passed to `application(_:didFinishLaunchingWithOptions:)` in your app delegate will contain a key named `UIApplicationLaunchOptionsLocationKey` to indicate that your app was launched because of a location-related event. It's your responsibility to create a location manager object and assign it a delegate that can handle the received region event.

After you create your location manager and set its delegate, the delegate method is automatically called. If you have other regions set up, they will be available in the location manager you created. Whenever you create a location manager object, it will have access to all of the monitored regions. The monitored regions will persist between app launches, so your app doesn't have to keep track of the regions it wants to monitor.

Let's take a look at an example of monitoring a region. We'll build upon the example shown in the previous segment, so all of the location permissions are already taken care of:

```
func locationManager(_ manager: CLLocationManager, didUpdateLocations
locations:
  [CLLocation]) {
    guard let location = locations.last
        else { return }

    let region = CLCircularRegion(center: location.coordinate, radius: 100,
      identifier: "HomeArea")
    if !locationManager.monitoredRegions.contains(region) {
        locationManager.startMonitoring(for: region)
    }
}

func locationManager(_ manager: CLLocationManager, didEnterRegion region:
  CLRegion) {
    print("user entered region with identifier: \(region.identifier)")
    manager.stopMonitoring(for: region)
}
```

The preceding snippet uses the `locationManager(_:didUpdateLocations:)` method to obtain the user's current location and sets up a region around this location. If the location manager is not already monitoring this location, we begin to monitor it.

The `locationManager(_:didEnterRegion:)` method is implemented, so it will be called whenever the users enter this location again. Also, when they do, we stop monitoring the location because we don't need to monitor it any longer. If you try running the app, then quit it and run it again, you could inspect the `monitoredRegions` property for your location manager and note that the region is still there. Pretty convenient, right? Let's take a look at what we can do with the user's location data while they are moving.

Tracking the user's location while they're on the move

If you're tracking user movement, there are a couple of methods that `CLLocationManager` calls. As with the other `CoreLocation` features, `CLLocationManager` is at the center of movement-related events.

One of the methods is already covered: `locationManager(_:didUpdateLocations:)`. This is the method you're interested in if you want to track the user's location throughout, for example, a run, or a bicycle ride. If you're not interested in your user's exact location, but you want to be notified if the user changes the direction they're heading in, you can use the `locationManager(_:didUpdateHeading:)` method.

The `locationManager(_:didUpdateHeading:)` is called with a `CLHeading` instance. This instance contains information about the heading of your user in relation to the magnetic north, but also in relation to true north. To access the heading in relation to true north, you should use the `trueHeading` property. This property has a value that represents the heading in degrees.

A value of 90 degrees means the user is heading east. A value of 180 means the user is heading south and a value of 270 represents west. If the value of `trueHeading` is a negative value, the true heading could not be determined. The following snippet provides an example for listening to heading changes:

```
func startLocationTracking() {
    if CLLocationManager.headingAvailable() {
        locationManager.startUpdatingHeading()
    }
}
```

```
func locationManager(_ manager: CLLocationManager, didUpdateHeading
newHeading:
  CLHeading) {
    print("user is now facing \(newHeading.trueHeading) degrees away from
north")
}
```

In order to be notified about heading updates, we need to inform the location manager to start updating the heading. Also, we should make sure that the heading information is available. If it is, the `startUpdatingHeading` method is called to actually start updating the heading.

If the user changes their heading, the `locationManager(_:didUpdateHeading:)` method is called and we can obtain the new heading through the `trueHeading` property. This is all actually pretty straightforward if you consider that all of the delegate methods and location updates are available through the `CLLocationManager` and `CLLocationManagerDelegate` classes.

If your app continuously tracks your user's location, you probably shouldn't be using the methods described in the preceding section. Apps that really benefit from constantly tracking updates about the user's location are mostly workout apps. It's very likely that you're not interested in a user's location all of the time. You probably want to know whether they enter or leave a certain region or whether they have traveled a significant distance. Geofencing has already been discussed, and should be used if you're monitoring a user's proximity to a point of interest. Again, the exact location of the user isn't relevant to your application until they are right where you want them to be. It's not only best practice in regards to a user's privacy but it also saves battery life if you use geofencing over continuous tracking.

If you are interested in your user's movement but don't need to know every tiny move they make, you should use the significant location changes API. If you use this method of tracking your users, you will only receive notifications if the user has moved 500 meters or more, and only once every 5 minutes at most. Using this API instead of listening for all location changes can greatly improve battery performance.

If you use the significant location changes API and your app is allowed to use the user's location in the background, your app will be woken up or restarted whenever a significant location change event occurs. The steps to handle the location change are similar to the steps you take to handle geofencing. If your app launches due to a significant location change, the `UIApplicationLaunchOptionsLocationKey` key will be set in the launch options dictionary. It's up to your application to create a location manager and set a delegate to receive the available events.

The delegate method that's called whenever a significant location change occurs is the `locationManager(_:didUpdateLocations:)` method. This is the same delegate method that's called when you listen for all location changes.

One last mechanism that `CoreLocation` provides to track the movement of the users is the visits service. Visits work similar to significant location changes, except they aren't created while a user is moving. A visit occurs when a user is in a single location for a longer period of time. Visits are a lower power alternative for apps that don't need regular updates or don't need to be aware of the user's movements; for example, this API is not suitable for building navigation apps. A great use case for this API is the way Apple predicts travel times based on locations you often visit. If you regularly travel between your home and work, iOS will suggest a good time to leave your house while taking travel times into account. This is possible by monitoring visits and analyzing the times when the visits occur.

If you start listening for visits, you will only be notified about events that occur after you've begun listening. This means that if the user is already visiting a location when you call `startMonitoringVisits()`, the visit data will be inaccurate because the start time will be a time after you start listening for visits.

Whenever a visit occurs, the location manager calls `locationManager(_:didVisit:)` on its delegate. This method receives a `CLVisit` instance that contains information about the visit. Every visit contains an arrival and departure time, coordinates, and a horizontal accuracy value for the coordinates.

If you use this service, events are usually only delivered if your app is in the foreground. However, if you have requested that you always have access to the user's location and your app is in the location background mode, your app will be awoken or relaunched whenever a visit occurs. This is signified by the same `UIApplicationLaunchOptionsLocationKey` key in the launch options that are used for other location events.

All location services work in a similar way through a `CLLocationManager` instance. This makes working with `CoreLocation` a pleasant experience, and it allows you to master the classes and services that are made available without too much effort. Studying the documentation will often give you answers to any questions you might have regarding location services on iOS. Remember that most APIs require you to check their availability before you use them because not all devices support the same location services.

Now that you're up to date with everything `CoreLocation` has to offer, let's add the final touches to the ArtApp login screen. We'll push the user's location to the screen and display a fictional number of nearby pieces of art for our user. In reality, you would probably set up a backend call that returns the actual number of nearby art pieces.

Finishing the ArtApp login screen

In order to finish the login screen, you'll need to make sure that you have the correct prerequisites present from the `CoreLocation` examples. First and foremost, you'll need to make sure that the correct privacy keys are present in the app's `Info.plist`. Once you've done this, it's time to write the code that will query the user's location and update the user interface. After implementing the code, we'll get to implement the interface and hook up the outlets. Most of the code we need to add is already covered in the section on `CoreLocation`, so most of the code presented now won't be covered in depth.

Add the following two properties to the `ViewController` class:

```
@IBOutlet var nearbyArtLabel: UILabel!
let locationManager: CLLocationManager = CLLocationManager()
```

The need for these properties should speak for itself. We need a label in order to display the information we want to communicate to our user, and the location manager should be implemented so that the app can query the user's location. We don't need a property for the location because we will use the location updates we receive from the location manager right away.

The following method should also be present in your `ViewController`; it's unchanged from the `CoreLocation` section:

```
func setupLocationUpdates() {
    locationManager.delegate = self

    let authStatus = CLLocationManager.authorizationStatus()
    switch authStatus {
    case .notDetermined:
        locationManager.requestWhenInUseAuthorization()
    case .authorizedWhenInUse:
        startLocationTracking()
    default:
        break
    }
}
```

Finally, the following three methods should be in your `ViewController`:

```
func locationManager(_ manager: CLLocationManager, didChangeAuthorization
status:
  CLAuthorizationStatus) {
    if status == .authorizedWhenInUse {
        startLocationTracking()
    }
}

func startLocationTracking() {
    if CLLocationManager.locationServicesEnabled() {
        locationManager.startUpdatingLocation()
    }
}

func locationManager(_ manager: CLLocationManager, didUpdateLocations
locations:
  [CLLocation]) {
    guard let location = locations.last
        else { return }

    let geocoder = CLGeocoder()
    geocoder.reverseGeocodeLocation(location, completionHandler: { [weak
self]
      placemarks, _ in
        guard let placemark = placemarks?.first,
            let city = placemark.locality
            else { return }

        self?.nearbyArtLabel.text = "Explore 17 pieces of art in \(city)"
    })

    manager.stopUpdatingLocation()
}
```

Again, the preceding code is not much different from the code you have already seen. The implementation of `locationManager(_:didUpdateLocations:)` has been updated to change the `nearbyArtLabel`'s text when a location is retrieved. Apart from that, there should be no surprises here. Let's implement the layout.

Drag a `UILabel` from the **Object Library** into the login form stack view; add it above the login fields, and use the Attributes Inspector to align the text in the center and adjust the font size to `19`. Since some city names won't fit on the screen, we should make sure that we set the number of lines for the label to `0` so it will automatically resize to accommodate the city name on the next line if needed:

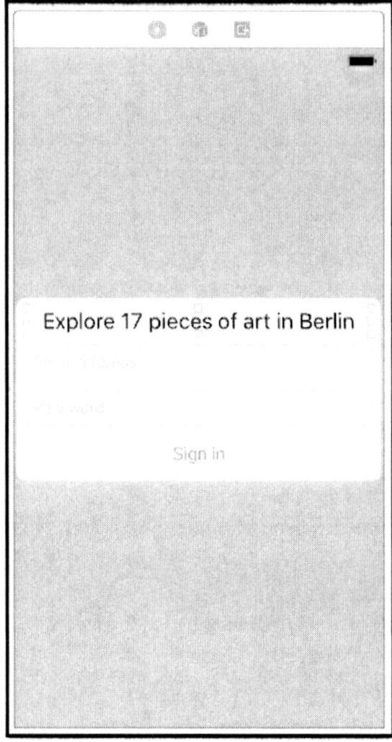

Refer to the preceding screenshot to verify your work. All you need to do now is to hook up the new `UILabel` to the `ViewController` through the Outlet Inspector. Once you've done this, you can build and run your app to see all the pieces of the puzzle put together.

Summary

This chapter covered several of sensors that are available in iOS devices. First, you learned about each of the frameworks in isolation. We covered `AVFoundation`, `CoreMotion`, and `CoreLocation`. Piece by piece, you set up a login screen for an AR app. To properly do this, you had to learn a lot about all the motion sensors, the camera, and location services.

The sensors that modern devices contain are impressive, and they enable you to build great apps that truly immerse users. However, we should be honest with each other right now. The login screen we built might be nice, but it's not truly AR. The next chapter will show you how to build an application using ARKit, Apple's new framework that makes implementing AR a breeze.

13
Extending the World with ARKit

When Apple announced iOS 11 at *WWDC 2017*, one of the new features that had many developers excited was ARKit. ARKit is Apple's new framework that enables developers to create great Augmented Reality experience using techniques that are already familiar to them.

This chapter will focus on teaching you how ARKit works and which techniques you can use to create a great experience for your users. In the previous chapter, you built a login screen for an Augmented Reality art gallery.

In this chapter, we will cover the following topics:

- Understanding how ARKit works
- Exploring SpriteKit
- Implementing an Augmented Reality gallery

Understanding how ARKit works

For quite some time now, **Augmented Reality** (**AR**) has been a topic that many people and app creators have been interested in. Implementing AR has never been easy, and most AR applications have not quite lived up to the hype. Small details such as object placement and lighting have always made creating a proper AR experience extremely complex.

In the previous chapter, you explored a very basic and rudimental example of what an AR app should do. When you think about an AR app, you're thinking of an app that does at least the following:

- Show a camera view
- An overlay of content on top of the camera
- The content responds to movements from the device
- The content is attached to a certain point in the real world

Even though these four bullet points are relatively simple to come up with, they are really hard to implement on your own. Reading movement from the sensors in an iOS device is not very complex, we've already established that. However, making sense of this data and putting it to good use in an AR application is a very different story.

To help developers create great AR experiences, Apple has released a new framework called ARKit for iOS 11. ARKit is one of the few frameworks that Apple has created over the years that does not only have a software requirement, but also a hardware requirement. ARKit requires that the device it runs on has at least an A9 chip. This means that anything from an iPhone 6s and iPad Pro supports ARKit. This also includes the iPhone SE. All iPad Air models and iPhone 6 and lower are excluded from making use of AR using ARKit.

The ARKit framework makes use of existing rendering technologies to make it as easy and straightforward as possible to get started with building your own AR experiences. To make AR content appear on screen, ARKit uses a rendering engine. The rendering engines you can use are the following:

- SpriteKit
- SceneKit
- Metal

Third-party support for ARKit will be provided by the creators of the Unreal Engine and Unity. This means that, if you are familiar with any of these five rendering engines, you already have the basic knowledge for working with ARKit in your toolkit! When we get around to implementing our own AR experience, we will make use of the SpriteKit engine because, out of the five options we have, SpriteKit is the simplest to get started with.

In addition to a rendering engine, ARKit needs a way to make sense of the world surrounding it. After all, the content you show on screen must appear as if it is part of the world. Every ARKit session uses an instance of `ARSession`. This session uses an instance of `ARSessionConfiguration` to describe how it should track the user's surroundings. The following diagram illustrates the basic relationships between the objects that make up an ARKit experience:

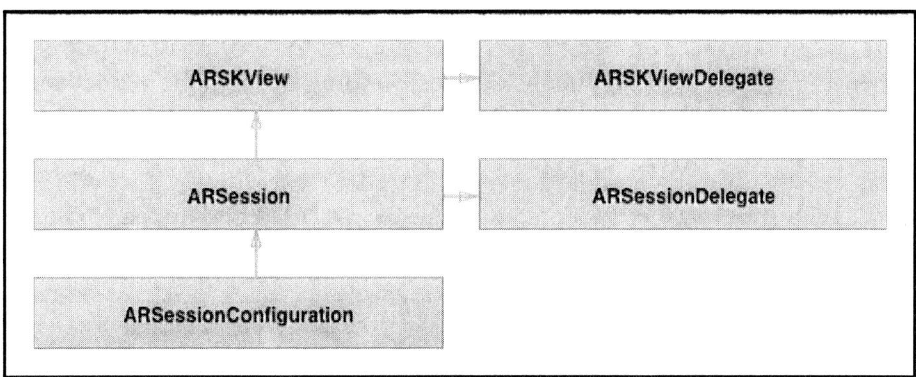

You can see in the preceding figure that a configuration is assigned to the session. The session is then passed to the view that renders the scene. In the case of SpriteKit, this is an `ARSKView`. Both the session and the view can have a delegate assigned to them. Implementing these delegate protocols allows you to customize parts of the experience and to observe certain changes in the state of the session. You will learn more about these delegate protocols later in the chapter. Let's take a closer look at the session configuration first to see how it helps the session make sense of the world surrounding the user.

Making sense of the world

As mentioned before, one of the hard parts of building an AR experience is the amount of work you have to perform in order to make sense of all the sensor data your app receives. This becomes especially hard if you try to make content that you add to the AR world behave as if it's part of the real world. Even if you successfully interpret device motion, acceleration, and orientation, it still would not be enough to create a proper AR experience because your implementation would be unaware of what the user's surroundings look like. Simply knowing what the user is doing with their device is not enough information to create a convincing AR illusion. Apple has solved this problem in ARKit by comparing all images coming in from the camera with each other.

By comparing all images, ARKit can detect and analyze different aspects of the user's surroundings. By doing this, ARKit can detect that one object is closer to the user than another object. It might also detect that there is a large flat square (plane) in the camera's view. It can then even go so far as recognizing that a certain plane is a floor. Or maybe that two seemingly different planes are in fact a single larger plane. Apple calls this feature detection. Feature detection is one of the key aspects of how ARKit is able to make sense of a scene and the contents in it.

An `ARSessionConfiguration` determines how much of the world surrounding the user is tracked. In order to track all three dimensions surrounding the user, you must enable world tracking on the configuration. When world tracking is enabled, the entire world surrounding the user is tracked. For instance, if the user rotates their device or moves it, ARKit will notice this and the rendered scene will update accordingly. This will make sure that any nodes that you have added to your scene are rendered and appear to be pinned in the real world as you would expect. The following screenshots illustrate this:

These screenshots show the end result of the gallery you'll have built by the end of the chapter. As you can see, the picture is placed at a certain location in the physical world and when you pan the camera around this object its position does not appear to change. It's as if the object is pinned to the real world.

In order to get the best results from world tracking, you will want to make sure that the image your user is looking at is as static as possible. A living room with some furniture in it will work far better than trying to use AR in a crowded shopping mall. If your user uses your AR app in a sub-optimal environment, tracking of the scene might be limited. If this happens, ARKit will call the `session(_:cameraDidChangeTrackingState:)` delegate method from the `ARSessionObserver` protocol. The `ARSessionDelegate` and `ARSKViewDelegate` protocols both extend `ARSessionObserver`. This means that you can implement `ARSessionObserver` methods if you conform to any of the protocols that extend it. You can access a `trackingState` property on the `ARCamera` instance that this method receives to figure out what happened, whether tracking is limited, and why. It's a good idea to implement this delegate method so you can inform your user if their experience might not be as good as it can be.

Now that you are aware that ARKit tracks the user's environment by reading data from sensors and comparing camera images, let's see how ARKit knows what to do with all the information it receives. After all, ARKit is supposed to make implementing AR as simple as possible and, to do this, it must be quite clever!

Understanding scenes

Every ARKit experience takes place in a so-called scene. This scene contains many interesting features that we have already mentioned before. One example of such a feature is a plane. Planes are flat squares in a three-dimensional environment. A table, the floor, or a piece of paper might all be detected as planes. ARKit can only detect planes that are horizontal with respect to gravity. This means that ARKit will be able to detect flat squares, such as a book that's on a table. It will not be able to detect walls or paintings that are hanging on a wall since these planes will be positioned vertically with respect to gravity.

In order to find planes, you must make use of a tracking configuration called `ARWorldTrackingSessionConfiguration`. If you don't use world tracking, ARKit will only measure basic device motion. As mentioned before, ARKit uses the camera to compare many images in order to make sense of the world. If ARKit does not track the device's full range of motion, it will not be possible to properly analyze all the incoming data and therefore planes will not be detected. In addition to using world tracking, you must enable plane detection for your session configuration by setting the `planeDetection` property to `.horizontal`. If you decide to enable or disable plane detection while your `ARSession` is already running, you can simply adjust the configuration and run the session again to make it use the latest configuration.

In order to place objects in the scene, ARKit uses instances of the `ARAnchor` class. These anchors contain all information about the positioning, rotation, and transformations for an object. When ARKit detects a plane, a special type of anchor is added to the scene. This anchor is an instance of `ARPlaneAnchor` and it contains information about the plane that ARKit has found. If your app makes use of these planes, it's probably a good idea to implement the `session(_:didUpdate:)` method from `ARSessionDelegate`. This method is called whenever ARKit finds new planes, removes them from the scene, or if they get updated.

For instance, ARKit might detect a large plane. When you move the camera around, it might find a second plane and when you move the camera some more, ARKit might learn that these two planes it has detected are in fact just a large single plane. If this happens, `session(_:didUpdate:)` is called and your app can respond to it as needed. If your app visualizes the found planes, you could remove the two planes that seemed separate at first and replace them with the single, larger plane that has been discovered.

Part of the magic of AR is that you can place objects on top of a table, a couch, the floor, or any other horizontal plane. To enable this behavior in ARKit, Apple has implemented some very sophisticated hit testing that makes use of all the features it has already detected in a scene. ARKit uses a virtual ray that intersects planes in a given order to figure out whether the user is directly looking at a plane or to see if one plane should be on top of the other.

If you make use of hit testing in your app you can call `hitTest(_:types:)` on your scene's view. This method will return an array of results that are ordered by distance. This means that the closest hit object is the first in the returned array. If you have obtained hit test results, you can use the `ARHitTestResult`'s `worldTransform` property to get the transformation matrix for the result. This transformation matrix contains all information about the hit object's position in the scene. ARKit's hit testing is pretty powerful and it works extremely well. Because of this, you can place objects in a scene pretty realistically since you have a lot of information about the environment you're working with.

One last scene understanding feature that deserves to be highlighted is light estimation. Objects won't truly blend in with their environment unless they are properly lighted. ARKit measures ambient lighting to make sure that you know how bright the environment around the user is. You can then use this information to make your content look darker or brighter, depending on the environment. Light estimation is enabled on `ARSessionConfiguration` by default.

Whenever ARKit renders a new frame, it calls the `session(_:didUpdate:)` method on its `ARSessionDelegate`. Inside this method, you can read the `lightEstimate` property to obtain a reference to an `ARLightEstimate` instance. This instance contains the current intensity of the ambient light. Making good use of this property will greatly benefit the realism of the AR experience you are creating because it makes your objects blend in that much better.

Now that you know a lot of theory about how ARKit works, let's take a quick look at two of the plug-and-play rendering engines Apple provides: SceneKit and SpriteKit.

Rendering a scene

One of ARKit's most appealing aspects is that Apple has figured out a way to use existing, well-known, and well-documented rendering techniques in ARKit. Because of this, anybody who has used SceneKit or SpriteKit before won't have to learn everything all over again from scratch. The only truly new features are all ARKit-related. And since ARKit allows developers to bring in their own rendering engines as well, it's possible for existing gaming engines such as Unreal and Unity to port their renderers to ARKit. This ease of use makes sure that the barrier of entry for experimenting with ARKit is as low as possible.

In this section, we will explore two rendering engines: SceneKit and SpriteKit. Both engines are gaming engines created by Apple. Their biggest difference is that SceneKit uses 3D rendering and SpriteKit is used for two-dimensional games. First, we will explore both engines to see how they incorporate ARKit. Once you have a very basic understanding of both engines, we will take a closer look at SpriteKit since this is the engine that we will use to build our gallery.

Using ARKit with SceneKit

As mentioned before, SceneKit is a rendering engine that is used to build three-dimensional games. SceneKit uses the Metal rendering engine under the hood, which means that it has great performance and it can be used to build truly sophisticated games. It makes a lot of sense that Apple chose to augment SceneKit in order to be compatible with ARKit. They both operate in all three dimensions to create an immersive experience.

When you create a three-dimensional scene, you often use a camera object that is used as the window through which the user looks at the scene. In a game, the camera is often positioned from the perspective of the player. As the player moves around, the camera moves through the scene and this updates the view.

Think about this for a second. A 3D game is a three-dimensional world in which the player controls the camera. Why wouldn't you replace this fictional camera with a real camera? And instead of pressing buttons to make the camera move, you could actually move the physical camera. When this idea clicks, the combination of ARKit and SceneKit seems to be almost obvious; AR is simply another way of controlling the virtual camera.

To make SceneKit compatible with ARKit, Apple has created a subclass of one of SceneKit's core components. This component is `SCNView`. The `SCNView` class is used to render a scene with SceneKit. When combining SceneKit with ARKit, you are expected to use `ARSCNView`. This subclass of `SCNView` is configured so it uses an `ARSession` to help to render the scene. It also helps with controlling the camera and it automatically estimates lighting. This means that it will make sure that your 3D models are always incorporated into the world as well as possible.

When you render content in SceneKit, you make use of `SCNNode` instances to represent the contents in your scene. When using an `ARSCNView`, all `SCNNodes` are automatically mapped to `ARAnchor` instances so you don't have to manually convert them. This makes combining SceneKit and ARKit pretty simple and straightforward so you can focus on creating a great AR experience. However, if you do want to manually convert certain nodes, you can implement the `ARSCNDelegate` protocol to provide some custom node mapping if needed.

If you don't have a need for 3D models, or if you're looking for a quicker and simpler way to get started with ARKit, the next rendering engine just might be what you're looking for. Let's take a look at SpriteKit.

Using ARKit with SpriteKit

If you're not looking for a full-blown 3D rendering engine, SpriteKit can help you create a cool AR experience without having to understand the complexities of rendering a 3D world. SpriteKit is Apple's two-dimensional game rendering engine. Some of the biggest game titles on iOS are actually SpriteKit apps, so even though it's not a full 3D rendering engine, it's still a really powerful framework that you can use to build great games and AR experiences.

Similar to how ARKit and SceneKit work together, Apple has created some classes that you can use to replace regular SpriteKit classes. In the case of SpriteKit, a scene is normally rendered in a `SKView`. If you use SpriteKit to create an AR experience, you replace `SKView` with an instance of `ARSKView`. An `ARSKView` is tied to an `ARSession` and can render `ARAnchors` similarly to how SceneKit does. You can provide normal `SKNode` instances and they will automatically be rendered in the scene.

One major difference between SceneKit and SpriteKit is that SpriteKit is a 2D rendering engine. This means that any objects that you place in a SpriteKit scene are only rendered in two dimensions. In practice, this means that you can't view a rendered `SKNodes` from all sides like you would be able to do for a 3D model. A `SKNode` will always face towards the user, but event though SpiteKit is two-dimensional, all nodes are placed in the three-dimensional world. Because of this, you can place an object before or behind another object or behind the user. This behavior enables you to create an immersive experience, even if you aren't using 3D models.

Since we'll be using SpriteKit to build our AR gallery, let's take a closer look at SpriteKit to get you up to speed with the information you need to make use of SpriteKit in your own applications.

Exploring SpriteKit

As mentioned before, SpriteKit's main usage is to build two-dimensional games. The SpriteKit framework has been around for quite some time already and it has enabled developers to build many successful games over the years. SpriteKit contains a full-blown physics simulation engine and it is able to render many sprites at a time. A sprite represents a graphic in a game. It could be an image for the player, but also a coin, an enemy, or even the floor that a player walks on. When we mention sprites in the context of SpriteKit, it means that we refer to a node that is visible on the screen.

Because SpriteKit has a physics engine, it can also detect collisions between objects, apply forces to them, and more. This is pretty similar to what UIKit Dynamics is capable of. If you're a bit rusty on what UIKit Dynamics are and how they work, truncated

To render content, SpriteKit uses scenes. These scenes can be considered levels or major building parts of a game. In the context of AR, you will find that you typically only need a single scene. A SpriteKit scene is responsible for updating the position and state of the scene. As a developer, you can hook into this rendering through the `SKScene`'s `update(_:)` method. This method is called every time SpriteKit is about to render a new frame for your game or ARKit scene. It is important that this method's execution time is as short as possible because a slow implementation of `update(_:)` method will cause frames to drop, which is considered bad. You should always aim for maintaining a steady 60 frames per second. This means that the `update(_:)` method should always return in 1/60th of a second.

To begin our exploration of SpriteKit, create a new project in XCode and choose the Game template. Pick SpriteKit as the underlying game technology and give your project a name. For instance, `HelloSpriteKit`.

When Xcode generates this project for you, you are given some files that you haven't seen before. These are the following:

- `GameScene.sks`
- `Actions.sks`

These two files are pretty much what storyboards are to regular apps. You can use these to set up all nodes for your game scene or to set up reusable actions that you can attach to your nodes. We will not go into these files for now as they are pretty specific to game development. If you are interested in learning all the ins and outs of SpriteKit, I recommend that you pick up *Swift 3 Game Development - Second Edition*, by *Stephen Haney*. This book goes in-depth about game development on iOS with SpriteKit.

If you build and run the sample project that Xcode provides, you can tap the screen to make new sprite nodes appear on the screen. Each node performs a little animation before it disappears. This isn't very special in itself, but it does contain a lot of valuable information. For instance, it shows you how to add something to a scene and how to animate it. Let's see exactly how this project is set up so you can apply this knowledge when you build the AR gallery later.

Setting up a SpriteKit scene

In order to render a SpriteKit scene, the first thing you need is a view to render the scene in. The view that you should use for this is an instance of `SKView`. If you're using ARKit, this view is substituted with an instance of `ARSKView` in order to add support for AR. The view itself does not directly manage or contain any of the presented nodes. This is all done by a `SKScene` instance. Typically, every scene you present is a subclass of `SKScene`. This is similar to how almost every view controller you present in an app is a subclass of `UIViewController`.

When you have created a scene, you can tell a `SKView` to present the scene. From this moment on, your game is running. In the sample code for the game project you created earlier, the following lines take care of loading and presenting the scene:

```
if let scene = SKScene(fileNamed: "GameScene") {
    scene.scaleMode = .aspectFill
    view.presentScene(scene)
}
```

When you create your own scenes, you can choose whether you want to use `.sks` files or if you want to create scenes programmatically. For the augmented reality gallery, we're going to create a `SKScene` instance programmatically since we won't have much content to display initially anyway. This is one of the rare occasions where you don't need to create your own subclass of `SKScene`.

When you open the `GameScene.swift` file that Xcode created for you, most of the code should be pretty self-explanatory. When the scene is added to a view, a couple of `SKNodes` are created and configured. The most interesting lines of code in this file are the following:

```
spinnyNode.run(SKAction.repeatForever(SKAction.rotate(byAngle:
CGFloat(Double.pi), duration: 1)))
spinnyNode.run(SKAction.sequence([SKAction.wait(forDuration: 0.5),
                                  SKAction.fadeOut(withDuration: 0.5),
                                  SKAction.removeFromParent()]))
```

These lines set up an animation sequence for the spinning squares that get added when you tap the screen. In SpriteKit, actions are the preferred way to set up animations. You can group, chain, and combine actions in order to achieve pretty complicated effects. This is one of the many powerful tools that SpriteKit contains.

If you examine the code a little bit more, you'll find that copies of the `spinnyNode` are created every time the user taps on the screen, moves their finger, or lifts their finger. Each interaction produces a slightly different copy of `spinnyNode` so you can distinguish between the reasons for making the `spinnyNode` appear.

Go ahead and study this code, play around with it, and try to make sure that you grasp what it does. You don't have to become a SpriteKit expert by any means because all you really need to understand in order to implement our augmented reality gallery is how you can add new nodes to a SpriteKit scene. With this knowledge of SpriteKit at hand, it's time to get down and dirty with augmented reality!

Implementing an Augmented Reality gallery

So far, most of our focus has been on exploring the theory and background of ARKit, but we haven't really seen it in action yet! To get a very basic idea of ARKit and what it can do, all you need to do is create a new AR project in Xcode and choose either SceneKit or SpriteKit as the rendering engine. If you choose SceneKit, you are given a starter project that positions a model of an airplane in the room. You can walk around this plane and view it from all angles. Have a look at the code that is required to set up this scene.

You might be amazed how little code is used! Earlier you learned how a SceneKit augmented reality experience essentially means that a 3D environment is created and the user's physical camera is the viewport into this 3D environment. The SceneKit starter project does a pretty good job of demonstrating this since you can immediately see how you are viewing the 3D scene through the device's camera.

If you start a new AR project in Xcode and you pick SpriteKit as the rendering engine, you are given the ability to add an emoji to the scene every time you tap the screen. The SpriteKit example behaves pretty similarly to the SceneKit example if you move the camera around. The biggest visible differences are that the added sprites are two-dimensional and they always face towards you when you move around. Apart from this, all sprites are positioned in a true 3D environment, so if you move closer to them, they will get bigger and if you move away, they get smaller. This experience is pretty cool, right?

The SpriteKit emoji example is very similar to what we are going to build in this chapter, except that, instead of repeating the same emoji over and over, the user will be able to select pieces of art from a gallery and to place them in their own AR museum. Instead of creating a new AR project in Xcode, you are advised to pick up the started project from the code bundle that comes with this book. In the starter proect, a collection view that contains several pieces of art has been prepared so we can truly focus on building the AR experience in this section of the chapter.

Enabling ARKit in an existing project

In order to truly focus on implementing the AR experience, this chapter comes with a pre-configured project to get you started. The project contains a couple of pitcures that are shown in a horizontally scrolling collection view. Whenever the user taps on one of these images, we are going to add this image to the ARKit scene, similar to what the SpriteKit sample project did with an emoji.

Examine the existing code and try running the project to make sure you understand what's going on before moving on to implementing ARKit. The starter project should not contain anything surprising; if you're unclear on any of the details about the starter project, everything has been covered in the preceding chapters, so make sure to reference back so you understand everything that is going on.

An app that uses ARKit isn't different from a normal app, so we can add ARKit from scratch instead of using Xcode's predefined template. Implementing a feature like this from scratch helps you to get a feeling for what goes on under the hood and it often leads to a better understanding of the subject matter. To get started with implementing our AR experience, open `ViewController.swift` and add an `@IBOutlet` that will hold the `ARSKView` that we're going to use for rendering the AR gallery as follows:

```
@IBOutlet var arView: ARSKView!
```

Don't forget to add `import ARKit` at the top of the file as well since Xcode won't be able to find the `ARSKView` class otherwise. Next, open `Main.storyboard` and set the class for the orange view to `ARSKView`, and connect the outlet you just created to the orange view using the outlet inspector, just like you have done before. This is all we need to do to set up the view for augmented reality. All the remaining work will be done in code.

Because ARKit wants access to the user's camera, we must add the `NSCameraUsageDescription` key to our app's `Info.plist`. If we don't do this, the app will crash on launch, so go ahead and do this now. In addition to adding the `NSCameraUsageDescription`, you should also add a required device capability to the `Info.plist`. Your plist should already contain a **Required device capabilities** field. Add a new item to this field with the value `arkit`. This will ensure that your app is not available for devices that do not support ARKit.

Your project is now set up to support ARKit! The next step is to set up the ARKit session and render the camera on screen. Once this is up and running, we will implement the functionality to add art to your personal augmented reality art gallery.

Open `ViewController.swift` and add the following implementations for `viewDidLoad()`, `viewWillAppear(_:)`, and `viewWillDissappear(_:)`:

```
override func viewDidLoad() {
    super.viewDidLoad()
    collectionView.delegate = self
    collectionView.dataSource = self
    let scene = SKScene(size: CGSize(width: 375, height: 500))
    arView.presentScene(scene)
}

override func viewWillAppear(_ animated: Bool) {
    super.viewWillAppear(animated)
    let configuration = ARWorldTrackingSessionConfiguration()
    arView.session.run(configuration)
}

override func viewWillDisappear(_ animated: Bool) {
```

```
        super.viewWillDisappear(animated)
        arView.session.pause()
    }
```

In `viewDidLoad()`, we create and present the scene. When the view appears, a session configuration is created and the `run(_:)` method of `ARSession` is called. Once the `run(_:)` method is called, the scene will begin rendering the camera output. To preserve resources, the session is paused whenever the view is about to dissappear. It is always good practice to free up any resources your app doesn't need and ARKit is no exception to this rule. If you were expecting that setting your app up for augmented reality would be more complex, I'm sorry but this is all there is to it.

However, this experience is quite boring since we only show the raw camera output. Let's allow the user to tap on one of the images in the collection view on the bottom of the screen. When they do, we will place the selected image in the AR world so the user can physically walk through their own art gallery.

In order to do this, we'll need to have a list of all pieces of art a user has added. We must also know where the art was added exactly so we can provide the correct `SKNode` for each `ARAnchor`. When adding contents to our `ARSKView`, we make use of anchors. Each anchor contains all the required information about the anchor's size and placement. Every anchor also has a `UUID` identifier that can be used to uniquely identify each anchor in a scene. We will create a dictionary that uses these identifiers as a key, and a `UIImage` as a value. This way, we always know which image belongs to which anchor. Add the following property to `ViewController`:

```
var nodes = [UUID: UIImage]()
```

Next, implement `collectionView(_:didSelectItemAt:)` as follows:

```
func collectionView(_ collectionView: UICollectionView, didSelectItemAt
indexPath: IndexPath) {
    guard let camera = arView.session.currentFrame?.camera
        else { return }
    var translation = matrix_identity_float4x4
    translation.columns.3.z = -1
    let transform = simd_mul(camera.transform, translation)
    let anchor = ARAnchor(transform: transform)
    nodes[anchor.identifier] = images[indexPath.row]
    arView.session.add(anchor: anchor)
}
```

This code reads the camera from the current frame in the `ARSession`. Next, it computes a transform matrix that places the new node one meter in front of the camera. Then, an anchor is created and the identifier/image pair is stored in the `nodes` dictionary. The final step is to add this newly created anchor to the current session.

Note that the anchor does not contain any information about the image or what we want to display at the position of the anchor. An `ARAnchor` is merely a point of interest for our `ARSession`. To add our image to the view, we must set ourselves as the delegate for the `arView` and implement a method from the `ARSKViewDelegate` protocol. First, add the following extension for `ViewController`:

```
extension ViewController: ARSKViewDelegate {
    func view(_ view: ARSKView, nodeFor anchor: ARAnchor) -> SKNode? {
        guard let image = nodes[anchor.identifier]
            else { return nil }
        let texture = SKTexture(image: image)
        let scale = min(100 / image.size.width, 100 / image.size.height)
        let sprite = SKSpriteNode(texture: texture, size: CGSize(width:
image.size.width * scale, height: image.size.height * scale))
        return sprite
    }
}
```

This code implements the `view(_:nodeFor:)` method. It is responsible for creating an `SKNode` instance that can be placed at the anchor's position. In this case, we create an `SKSpriteNode` that uses the selected image as a texture. The node is scaled so all images are the same size and finally the `SKSpriteNode` is returned so the view can render it.

Before you build and run your app, make sure to add the following line of code to `viewDidLoad()`:

```
arView.delegate = self
```

This wil set `ViewController` as the delegate for `arView`. Now go ahead and test your gallery. Whenever you tap on one of the images in the collection view, this image is added to the view. If you walk around, you'll notice that it truly appears as if the images are fixed in the real world. Pretty cool, right?

Summary

This chapter served as a primer in augmented reality. You even got to play with it a little bit by implementing your own basic AR experience. Of course there is much more to learn about augmented reality and with SceneKit you can create extremely immersive and mind-boggling experiences. Building an experience like this is, unfortunately, a slightly beyond the of scope of this book since it requires very specific knowledge about 3D modelling and 3D game design. If you are experienced with game development in a 3D world, transferring this knowledge to ARKit should be possible using the information in this chapter. And if you are not experienced in this area at all, at least you have a clear idea of where to start building great experiences right now.

I personally believe that augmented reality will thrive on iOS thanks to the introduction of ARKit. In the first weeks after the iOS 11 beta shipped, amazing demos have started popping up on the internet and I believe these demos are only the beginning. If you want to delve into AR and want some inspiration or if you're curious what others are doing with ARKit, make sure to check out the website `http://www.madewitharkit.com` as it features many cool demos.

The next chapter will expand the AR experience you have built in this chapter by incorporating drag and drop capabilities and a little bit of machine learning. Let's go!

14
Exchanging Data with Drag and Drop

If you have ever wanted to move a couple of photos from one app on your iPad to another, chances are that you had to copy and paste each photo individually. If you compare this experience with the desktop, where you can grab one or multiple items and simply drag those items from one place to the other, iOS has a pretty subpar drag and drop experience. Actually, the drag and drop experience on iOS has essentially been non-existent up until iOS 11.

With iOS 11, users can finally enjoy a full drag and drop experience. Implementing drag and drop in your own apps has been made surprisingly simple since all you need to do is implement a couple of required methods from a handful of protocols. This chapter is aimed at showing you how to handle drag and drop in the augmented reality gallery you have built before with ARKit. The gallery app will be expanded so that users can add photos from their own photo library, the internet, or any other source to their art library.

This chapter is focused on the following topics:

- Understanding the drag and drop experience
- Implementing basic drag and drop functionality
- Customizing the drag and drop experience.

Understanding the drag and drop experience

The drag and drop experience is quite simple to use; pick up an item on the screen, drag it somewhere else, and let it go to make the dragged item appear in the new place. However, iOS hasn't had this behavior until iOS 11. And even now, its full range of capabilities is only available on the iPad. Despite this limitation, the drag and drop experience is really powerful on both the iPhone and iPad.

Users can pick up an item from any app, and move it over to any other app that implements drag and drop, as they please. And dragging items is not even limited to just a single item, it's possible for users to pick up multiple items in a single drag session. The items that a user adds to their drag session don't even have to be of the same type; this makes the drag and drop experience extremely flexible and fluid. Imagine selecting some text and a picture in Safari and dragging them over to a note you're making. Both the image and the text can be added to a note in just a single gesture.

Unfortunately, apps are not able to handle drag and drop out of the box; you'll need to do a little bit of work yourself in order to support this feature. At the heart of the drag and drop experience are two protocols and two new interaction classes. Let's briefly go over the protocols and classes before going more in-depth and implementing drag and drop for your augmented reality museum.

The first requirement for a drag and drop session is the ability of a view to receive or start a drag session. This ability is added to a view through either a `UIDropInteraction` or a `UIDragInteraction`. Both interactions are subclasses of the `UIInteraction` base class. A `UIInteraction` manifests itself similarly to a `UIGestureRecognizer` in the sense that you create an instance of it and attach it to a view. The following figure shows this relationship:

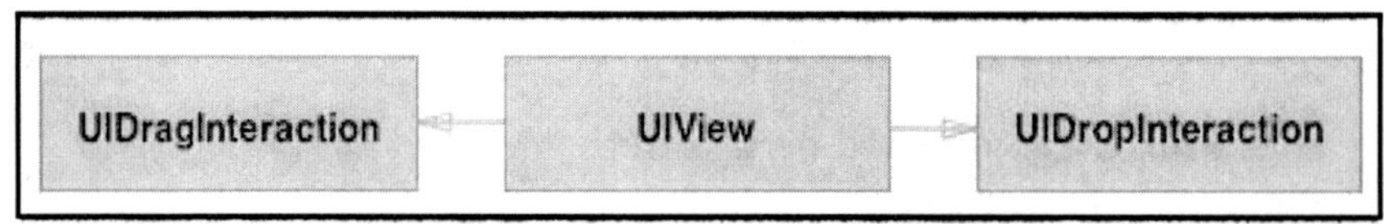

When adding either a `UIDragInteraction` or a `UIDropInteraction` to a `UIView`, you must also set up a delegate for the interaction you're adding. When you're adding a `UIDropInteraction`, you must set a `UIDropInteractionDelegate` on it. When adding a `UIDragInteraction`, you must set a `UIDragInteractionDelegate`. The following figure illustrates this relationship:

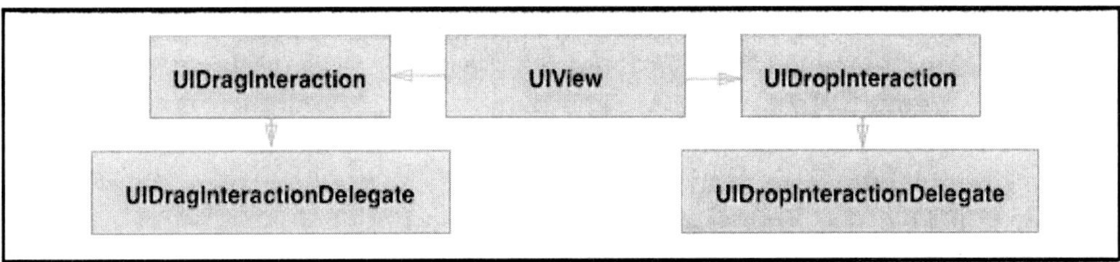

Each protocol has a different set of responsibilities, as is suggested by their names. Let's have a look at `UIDragInteractionDelegate` first.

Understanding UIDragInteractionDelegate

Any time the user long-presses an item that has a `UIDragInteraction` associated with it, a new drag session is started. This drag session uses the interaction's `UIDragInteractionDelegate` to obtain the data for the item that is being dragged, a drag preview, and more.

The `UIDragInteractionDelegate` only has a single required method: `dragInteraction(_:itemsForBeginning:)`. If you implement this method, your app can start supplying data to other apps. The return type for `dragInteraction(_:itemsForBeginning:)` is `[UIDragItem]`. A `UIDragItem` is a container for an `NSItemProvider`. The drag item is also responsible for providing a preview of the dragged item while it's being dragged. Normally, the selected view will be used, but sometimes you might want to provide a custom view for the preview. If this is the case, you can provide your own preview through the `UIDragItem`.

A very simple example of `dragInteraction(_:itemsForBeginning:)` looks as follows:

```
func dragInteraction(_ interaction: UIDragInteraction, itemsForBeginning
session: UIDragSession) -> [UIDragItem] {
    let text = "Hello, world"
    let provider = NSItemProvider(object: text as NSString)
    let item = UIDragItem(itemProvider: provider)
    return [item]
}
```

It has been mentioned before that users can add multiple objects to an existing drag session by tapping on them. Whenever the user taps on a draggable item while a session is in progress, `dragInteraction(_:itemsForAddingTo:withTouchAt:)` is called on the `UIDragInteractionDelegate`. If you return an empty array in this method, the tapped item will be ignored. But if you return one or more `UIDragItem` instances, those items will be appended to the existing drag session.

A drag session can be roughly divided into three stages:

1. The *lift* stage: This is the stage where the first drag item is requested and the view that is about to be dragged is animated so the user sees that they have started a drag session.
2. The *dragging* stage: The user is now moving the drag item around.
3. The *end* stage: Either a drop has been performed or the drag session got canceled. If a session is canceled, the dragged item is animated back to its starting position.

You can monitor and respond to each of the stages through `UIDragInteractionDelegate`. To customize the lift animation, you could implement `dragInteraction(_:willAnimateLiftWith:session:)`, for instance. For a full overview of available drag customization, you should take a look at the documentation for `UIDragInteractionDelegate`; there are quite a bunch of methods available for you to implement!

Now that you know how to set up your app for dragging, let's see how dropping works.

Understanding UIDropInteractionDelegate

Similarly to how `UIDragInteractionDelegate` works, `UIDropInteractionDelegate` is used to respond to different stages in the drag and drop life-cycle. Even though `UIDropInteractionDelegate` has no required methods, there are at least two methods that you should implement to support drag and drop. The first method is `dropInteraction(_:sessionDidUpdate:)`.

As soon as the user moves their finger on top of a drop target, the drop target is asked whether it can handle a drop with the contents from the current drop session. Assuming the data can be handled, `dropInteraction(_:sessionDidUpdate:)` is called. You must return an instance of `UIDropProposal` from this method. A drop proposal simply lets the session know what you'd like to happen if the drop is executed at some point. For instance, you can make a copy proposal or a move proposal. The UI surrounding the contents that are being dragged will update accordingly to let the user know what will happen if they perform the drop.

Now let's say your app can only handle objects of a certain type: You should implement `dropInteraction(_:canHandle:)`. You can use this method to inspect whether the drop session contains items that your app is interested in. An example of this looks as follows:

```
func dropInteraction(_ interaction: UIDropInteraction, canHandle session:
UIDropSession) -> Bool {
    for item in session.items {
        if item.itemProvider.canLoadObject(ofClass: UIImage.self) {
            return true
        }
    }
    return false
}
```

This example looks for at least one image in the current drop session. You can use `canLoadObject(ofClass:)` on `NSItemProvider` to figure out whether the item provider contains an instance of a certain class, in this case, a `UIImage`. If your app restricts drag and drop to the same application, you might not need to implement this method even though it is recommended that you always make sure the session can be handled by the drop target.

The second method you should always implement is `dropInteraction(_:performDrop:)`. If you don't implement this method, your app doesn't really have a proper implementation of the drop interaction. Once the user drops an item onto a drop target, they expect something to happen. `dropInteraction(_:performDrop:)` is the perfect place to do so.

An example implementation of `dropInteraction(_:performDrop:)` could look as follows:

```
func dropInteraction(_ interaction: UIDropInteraction, performDrop session:
UIDropSession) {
    for item in session.items {
        if item.itemProvider.canLoadObject(ofClass: UIImage.self) {
            item.itemProvider.loadObject(ofClass: UIImage.self) { [weak
self] item, error in
                // handle the item
            }
        }
    }
}
```

We loop through all items in the drop session. If an item can provide an image, the image is loaded. Note that `loadObject(ofClass:)` uses a callback. This means that the data is loaded asynchronously. The dropped data could be huge and, if it was loaded and processed on the main thread by default, it would make your app freeze for a while. By making `loadObject(ofClass:)` asynchronous, your app's responsiveness is guaranteed and your users won't notice any freezes or lagging.

Just like a drag session, a drop session typically has three stages:

1. The session starts when a user drags content onto a drop target.
2. Performing the drop, this is when the user lifts their finger while it's on a drop target.
3. Ending the drop, the user has either dragged their finger away from the drop target or the drop has been performed successfully.

Apple has not defined stages as they were mentioned here. The life cycle stages that you just learned are merely intended to help you to grasp the life cycle of drag and drop. If you want to learn everything about the drag and drop life cycle, make sure to check out the documentation for both `UIDropInteractionDelegate` and `UIDragInteractionDelegate`.

All right, now that you know what drag and drop looks like in theory, let's see what it looks like in practice!

Implementing basic drag and drop functionality

The previous section explained how drag and drop works from a theoretical point of view. This section focuses on implementing drag and drop in a sample app. First, we'll explore how a simple, regular implementation of drag and drop might work. Next, you'll see how Apple has implemented drag and drop for `UICollectionView` and `UITableView`. These two components have received special treatment, making it even easier to implement drag and drop in certain apps.

Adding drag and drop to a plain UIView

Before we implement drag and drop in the Augmented Reality gallery, let's see how we can implement a simple version of drag and drop with a simple view and an image. In the code bundle for this book, you'll find a sample project named `PlainDragDrop`. Open the starting version for this project and run it on an iPad simulator. You'll see the user interface shown in the following screenshot:

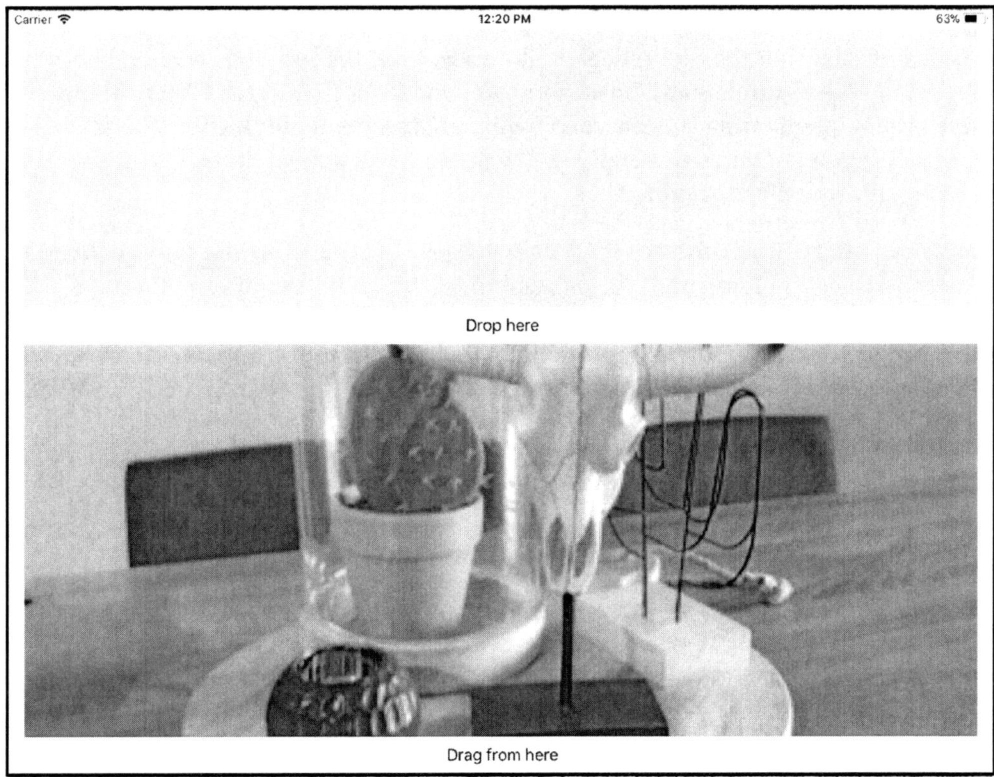

The goal for this example is to allow users to perform the following actions:

1. Drag the image to the drop area.
2. Drag an external image to the drop area.
3. Drag the bottom image to an external app.

While this might sound like we're going to have to do a lot of work, it's actually quite simple to implement all three features at once. Simply implementing the first feature enables the other two! Quite convenient, right? We'll implement drag and drop for this example in just three simple steps:

1. Making `ViewController` conform to `UIDragInteractionDelegate`.
2. Making `ViewController` conform to `UIDropInteractionDelegate`.
3. Adding interactions to the image and drop area.

If you feel confident that the theoretical exploration from the previous section left you with enough knowledge to implement these steps on your own, that's great! You should definitely give implementing this on your own a go and then refer back to the following code snippets if you get stuck or simply to check the work you've done. If you prefer to follow along instead, that's great too.

Making `ViewController` conform to `UIDragInteractionDelegate` only requires a single method to be implemented. As shown before, the only required method on `UIDragInteractionDelegate` makes sure that we provide a `UIDragItem` for the drag session. Since we don't support dragging multiple items from the app, we don't have to implement any extra delegate methods for this.

Add the following extension to `ViewController.swift`:

```
extension ViewController: UIDragInteractionDelegate {
    func dragInteraction(_ interaction: UIDragInteraction,
itemsForBeginning session: UIDragSession) -> [UIDragItem] {
        guard let image = imageView.image
            else { return [] }
        let itemProvider = NSItemProvider(object: image)
        return [UIDragItem(itemProvider: itemProvider)]
    }
}
```

This code should look familiar to you since it closely resembles the example code from the previous section. Now that we conform to `UIDragInteractionDelegate`, let's conform to `UIDropInteractionDelegate` as well. Add the following extension to `ViewController.swift`:

```
extension ViewController: UIDropInteractionDelegate {
    func dropInteraction(_ interaction: UIDropInteraction, sessionDidUpdate
session: UIDropSession) -> UIDropProposal {
        return UIDropProposal(operation: .copy)
    }
    func dropInteraction(_ interaction: UIDropInteraction, performDrop
```

```
session: UIDropSession) {
        guard let itemProvider = session.items.first?.itemProvider,
            itemProvider.canLoadObject(ofClass: UIImage.self)
            else { return }
        itemProvider.loadObject(ofClass: UIImage.self) { [weak self]
loadedItem, error in
            guard let image = loadedItem as? UIImage
                else { return }
            DispatchQueue.main.async {
                self?.dropArea.image = image
            }
        }
    }
}
```

Again, this implementation should look familiar to you. The first method, `dropInteraction(_:sessionDidUpdate:)`, returns a copy proposal since we don't want to move data around. The second method is `dropInteraction(_:performDrop:)`. This method retrieves the image from the `itemProvider` that has been created in the `UIDragInteractionDelegate` and sets the loaded image as the image for the `dropArea`.

Now for the third step: Adding the interactions to the correct views as follows:

```
override func viewDidLoad() {
    super.viewDidLoad()
    let dragInteraction = UIDragInteraction(delegate: self)
    imageView.addInteraction(dragInteraction)
    let dropInteraction = UIDropInteraction(delegate: self)
    dropArea.addInteraction(dropInteraction)
}
```

Now that all interactions are set up, go ahead and run the app on an iPad. You'll be able to drag the bottom image to the top section and the image will appear in the top section. If you run the photos app alongside `PlainDragDrop`, you can drag the bottom image to the photos app and it will be added to photos. If you drag an image from the *Photos* app to the top section, the image from *Photos* will be set as the image for the drop area. Pretty cool stuff! And it was pretty simple to cover all these cases.

Even though the iPhone does not have full drag and drop support, you can enable the first use case we mentioned. It is possible to drag items around within an iPhone app by explicitly enabling a drag interaction. Try running the app on an iPhone right now. You can't drag the bottom image to the top section yet. Let's enable this by adding the following line to `viewDidLoad`:

```
dragInteraction.isEnabled = true
```

The iPhone disables all drag interactions by default. Enabling the drag interaction manually allows you to perform a drag interaction within an iPhone app. Go ahead and give it a go! Once you're done playing with your first drag and drop implementation, we'll have a look at adding drag and drop to the `UICollectionView` in the `AugmentedRealityGallery` app.

Adding drag and drop to a UICollectionView

A lot of iOS apps make extensive use of collections and tables. Therefore, it makes a lot of sense that, whenever Apple introduces a huge feature such as drag and drop, they take a step back and evaluate how the feature should work for collections or tables. Luckily, drag and drop was no exception and Apple truly put some thought into making drag and drop work great.

In this section, you'll implement drag and drop for the collection of images that is at the bottom of the screen for `AugmentedRealityGallery`. We will implement the following features using drag and drop for `UICollectionView`:

1. Dragging photos from the collection onto the AR viewport.
2. Reordering items in the collection view.
3. Adding items from external sources to the collection view.

As a bonus, we'll make sure that the first two features also work on an iPhone since these features are only used inside the app which is supported by iPhone. Since Apple has tailored drag and drop to work perfectly with `UICollectionView`, the basic concepts for drag and drop still apply; we simply have to use slightly different protocols. For instance, instead of implementing a `UIDragInteractionDelegate`, you implement a `UICollectionViewDragDelegate`.

The first feature, dragging photos from the collection of images to the AR gallery, is implemented in a similar fashion to what we did before. We'll implement the protocols first, and then we'll enable the interactions. The code bundle for this chapter contains a slightly modified version of `AugmentedRealityGallery` in comparison to the version you built in the previous chapter. The modifications allow us to focus on implementing drag and drop instead of having to make minor adjustments to the existing code as well.

Since you should be familiar with the dropping implementation already, add the following extension to `ViewController.swift` in the `AugmentedRealityGallery`:

```
extension ViewController: UIDropInteractionDelegate {
    func dropInteraction(_ interaction: UIDropInteraction, sessionDidUpdate
```

```
session: UIDropSession) -> UIDropProposal {
        return UIDropProposal(operation: .copy)
    }
    func dropInteraction(_ interaction: UIDropInteraction, performDrop
session: UIDropSession) {
        guard let itemProvider = session.items.first?.itemProvider,
            itemProvider.canLoadObject(ofClass: UIImage.self)
            else { return }
        itemProvider.loadObject(ofClass: UIImage.self) { [weak self] item
,error in
            guard let image = item as? UIImage
                else { return }
            DispatchQueue.main.async {
                self?.addImageToARView(image)
            }
        }
    }
}
```

Nothing crazy happens in this snippet. In fact, it's so similarly to the code you have seen already that we'll move on to implementing the `UICollectionViewDragDelegate` protocol since that implementation should look a little less familiar. Implement `UICollectionViewDragDelegate` as follows:

```
extension ViewController: UICollectionViewDragDelegate {
    func collectionView(_ collectionView: UICollectionView,
itemsForBeginning session: UIDragSession, at indexPath: IndexPath) ->
[UIDragItem] {
        let image = images[indexPath.row]
        let itemProvider = NSItemProvider(object: image)
        return [UIDragItem(itemProvider: itemProvider)]
    }
}
```

This implementation serves the same purpose as a `UIDragInteractionDelegate`. The main difference is that you have access to the `IndexPath` of the item that was selected for dragging. You can use this `IndexPath` to obtain the dragged image and create a `UIDragItem` for it. Let's set up the interactions for this part of the app now. Add the following lines of code to `viewDidLoad()`:

```
collectionView.dragDelegate = self
collectionView.dragInteractionEnabled = true

let dropInteraction = UIDropInteraction(delegate: self)
arView.addInteraction(dropInteraction)
```

If you build and run the app now, you can drag photos into the AR gallery from the collection view at the bottom. If you run the app on an iPad, you are even able to drag images from external apps into the gallery! This is quite awesome, but we're not done yet. Let's allow users to drag items from external apps into the collection so they have easy access to it. And while we're at it, let's implement reordering of the collection using drag and drop as well.

To implement reordering and to allow users to add external images to their collection, you must implement `UICollectionViewDropDelegate`. As you will see soon, we can distinguish between a drop session that originated from within the app or outside the app. This information can be used to determine whether we should reorder the collection or add an item to it. Add the following extension for `ViewController`; all the following snippets should also be added to this extension. This is done to nicely group together our drop-related functionality:

```
extension ViewController: UICollectionViewDropDelegate {
    func collectionView(_ collectionView: UICollectionView,
dropSessionDidUpdate session: UIDropSession, withDestinationIndexPath
destinationIndexPath: IndexPath?) -> UICollectionViewDropProposal {
        if session.localDragSession != nil {
            return UICollectionViewDropProposal(operation: .move, intent:
.insertAtDestinationIndexPath)
        }
        return UICollectionViewDropProposal(operation: .copy, intent:
.insertAtDestinationIndexPath)
    }
}
```

This snippet implements `collectionView(_:dropSessionDidUpdate:withDestinationIndexPath:)`. This delegate method is pretty similarly to `dropInteraction(_:sessionDidUpdate:)` except you also have access to the destination index path in case the user lifts their finger to perform the drop. By checking whether there is a `localDragSession` on a `UIDropSession`, you are able to detect whether we should reorder the collection or whether we should add an item. By specifying an intent on the drop proposal, the `CollectionView` knows how it should update its interface to visualize the action that is taken when the user performs the drop. Speaking of performing drops, let's implement `collectionView(_:performDropWith:)` as follows:

```
func collectionView(_ collectionView: UICollectionView, performDropWith
coordinator: UICollectionViewDropCoordinator) {
    switch coordinator.proposal.operation {
    case .copy:
        performCopy(forCollectionView: collectionView, with: coordinator)
```

```
        case .move:
            performMove(forCollectionView: collectionView, with: coordinator)
        default:
            return
        }
    }
```

This method is relatively simple; depending on the proposal used, a different method is called. We'll implement the copy and move methods soon, but first let's talk a little bit about the `UICollectionViewDropCoordinator`. A `UICollectionViewDropCoordinator` contains information about the items that are being dragged, the animations that should be performed, the drop proposal, and of course the drop session. When performing a drop, you make use of the coordinator to request the drag items, but also to make sure the collection view properly updates its view.

The first method you'll implement is `performMove(forCollectionView:with:)` since it's the simpler method of the two remaining methods to implement. Add the following snippet to the extension on `ViewController`:

```
    func performMove(forCollectionView collectionView: UICollectionView, with
    coordinator: UICollectionViewDropCoordinator) {
        let destinationIndexPath = coordinator.destinationIndexPath ??
    IndexPath(item: 0, section: 0)
        guard let item = coordinator.items.first,
            let sourceIndexPath = item.sourceIndexPath
            else { return }
        let image = images.remove(at: sourceIndexPath.row)
        images.insert(image, at: destinationIndexPath.row)
        collectionView.performBatchUpdates({
            collectionView.deleteItems(at: [sourceIndexPath])
            collectionView.insertItems(at: [destinationIndexPath])
        })
        coordinator.drop(item.dragItem, toItemAt: destinationIndexPath)
    }
```

The preceding snippet makes use of the coordinator to retrieve the first item in the drag session. We don't support moving multiple items at once so this is alright. Next, the item's source index path is used to remove the image that should be moved from the array of images. The destination index path is then used to add the image back into the array of images at its new location. We do this because the data source must be updated before updating the collection view. After the collection view is updated, `drop(_:toItemAt:)` is called on the coordinator to animate the drop action.

The final method you need to implement is `performCopy(forCollectionView:with:)`. Add the following code to your extension of `ViewController`:

```
func performCopy(forCollectionView collectionView: UICollectionView, with
coordinator: UICollectionViewDropCoordinator) {
    let destinationIndexPath = coordinator.destinationIndexPath ??
IndexPath(item: 0, section: 0)
    for item in coordinator.items {
        let dragItem = item.dragItem
        guard dragItem.itemProvider.canLoadObject(ofClass: UIImage.self)
else { continue }
        let placeholder =
UICollectionViewDropPlaceholder(insertionIndexPath: destinationIndexPath,
reuseIdentifier: "GalleryCollectionItem")
        let placeholderContext = coordinator.drop(dragItem, to:
placeholder)
        dragItem.itemProvider.loadObject(ofClass: UIImage.self) { [weak
self] item, error in
            DispatchQueue.main.async {
                guard let image = item as? UIImage else {
                    placeholderContext.deletePlaceholder()
                    return
                }
                placeholderContext.commitInsertion { indexPath in
                    self?.images.insert(image, at: indexPath.row)
                }
            }
        }
    }
}
```

Take a close look at the `UICollectionViewDropPlaceholder` in this snippet. This class is new in iOS 11 and it is used to add temporary items to a `CollectionView`. Because it might take a little while to load data from an item provider, you need a mechanism to update the UI while you're loading data. This is the goal of using a placeholder. When you call `drop(_:to:)` on the `coordinator`, you receive a placeholder context. You use this context to either remove the placeholder, if loading data from the item provider failed, or to commit the insertion if it succeeds. Once it has succeeded and you commit the insertion, you must make sure to update the collection's data source by adding the image to the image array. Otherwise, your app could crash due to data source inconsistencies.

Since a placeholder is not part of your `CollectionView`'s data source, it is essential that you proceed with caution if you have a placeholder present in your `CollectionView`. For instance, your placeholder will be gone if you reload the `CollectionView` before committing or removing the placeholder.

Lastly, add the following line to `ViewController`'s `viewDidLoad`:

```
collectionView.dropDelegate = self
```

With this information, you should already be able to create a very good implementation of drag and drop in your apps. However, there is more to learn on the topic since you can customize many aspects of how drag and drop works for your app.

Customizing the drag and drop experience

Sometimes you will find yourself working on an app where the default implementations simply don't work for you. For instance, any application's drop delegate can propose a move action instead of a copy action. However, it's possible that you don't want to support this. You can restrict the allowed proposals by implementing `dragInteraction(_:sessionAllowsMoveOperation:)`. If you only want to allow copy operations, you can return `false` from this method. Another restriction you can enable through a delegate method is `dragInteraction(_:sessionIsRestrictedToDraggingApplication:)`. If you return true from this method, users won't be able to drag content from your app to another app.

Other methods on both the drag and the drop delegates are related to monitoring the state of the drag or drop session. Imagine that your app supports move proposals. When the user decides to move one or more objects from your app to another, you'll need to update the user interface accordingly once the drop is finished. You can implement `dragInteraction(_:sessionDidTransferItems:)` to implement this or perform any other cleanup that you might want to do after a successful drop session. For instance, you could show an alert to let the user know that data was transferred successfully.

In addition to logic, you can also provide custom previews and perform animations alongside the animations performed by the drag and drop sessions. All methods for this are defined in the `UIDropInteractionDelegate` and `UIDragInteractionDelegate` protocols as optional methods. In many cases, you won't need to implement many customization for drag and drop. If you do find yourself wanting to customize part of the drag and drop experience, chances are that a quick glance at the available methods on the delegate protocols will guide you in the right direction.

Summary

This chapter showed you how to implement a smooth drag and drop experience for your users. Drag and drop has limited functionality on the iPhone but this doesn't stop it from being a powerful feature that can be used to support the dragging of contents within an application or to reorder a `CollectionView`. Collections and tables have received special treatment because they have their own delegate methods and enable you to easily access the cell that is selected by the user for dragging.

While drag and drop might seem complex at first glance, Apple did a great job of containing this complexity in a couple of relatively simple delegate methods that you can implement. A basic drag and drop implementation only requires you to implement fewer than a handful of methods, which is quite impressive for such a powerful feature! Now that your AR gallery supports drag and drop, let's make it a little bit smarter by adding some machine learning to it, shall we?

15
Making Smarter Apps with CoreML

Over the past few years machine learning has gained popularity. For the past couple of iOS releases, Apple has mentioned how they used advanced machine learning to improve Siri, make smart suggestions for the Apple Keyboard on iOS, and improve Spotlight and many more features. While this is all great, machine learning has never been easy to implement on a mobile device. And if you do succeed in implementing machine learning, chances are that your implementation is not the most performant and energy efficient implementation possible.

Apple aims to solve this problem in iOS 11 with the **CoreML** framework. CoreML is Apple's solution to all problems they have run into themselves while implementing machine learning for iOS. As a result, CoreML should have the fastest, most efficient implementations for working with complex machine learning models through an interface that is as simple and flexible as possible.

In this chapter you will learn what machine learning is, how it works, and how you can use trained models in your own apps. We'll also have a brief look at the new vision framework that works beautifully with CoreML to perform complex analysis on images. This chapter covers the following topics:

- Understanding what machine learning is
- Understanding CoreML
- Combining CoreML and computer vision

By the end of the chapter you will have updated the augment reality application from the preceding chapters with automated content analysis for the images in your user's art gallery.

Understanding what machine learning is

A lot of developers sooner or later hear about the topic of machine learning, deep learning, or neural networks. You might have already heard about these topics. If you have, you know that machine learning is a pretty complex field that requires very specific domain knowledge. However, machine learning is becoming bigger and more popular every single day and it is used to improve many different types of applications.

For instance, machine learning can be used to predict what type of content a certain user might like to see in a music app based on music that they already have in their library, or to automatically tag faces in photos, connecting them to people in the user's contact list. It can even be used to predict costs for certain products or services based on past data. While this seems like magic, the flow for creating machine learning experiences like these can be split roughly in two phases:

1. Training a model.
2. Using inference to obtain a result from the model.

In order to perform the first step, large amounts of high quality data must be collected. If you're going to train a model that should recognize cats, you will need large amounts of pictures of cats. You must also collect images that do not contain cats. Each image must then be properly tagged to indicate whether the image contains a cat or not.

If your dataset only contains images of cats that face towards the camera, chances are that your model will not be able to recognize cats from a sideways point of view. If your dataset does contain cats from many different sides, but you only collected images for a single breed or with a solid white background, your model might still have a really hard time recognizing all cats. Obtaining quality training data is not easy, yet it's essential.

During the training phase of a model, it is extremely important that you provide a set of inputs that are of the highest quality possible. The smallest mistake could render your entire dataset worthless. It's in part due to the process of collecting data that training a model is a tedious task. One more reason is that training a model takes a lot of time. Certain complex models could take a couple of hours to crunch all the data and train themselves.

A trained model comes in several types. Each type of model is good for a different type of task. For instance, if you are working on a model that can classify certain email messages as spam, your model might be a so-called **Support Vector Machine**. If you're training a model that recognizes cats in pictures, you are likely training a Neural Network.

Each flavor of model comes with its own pros and cons and each model is created and used differently. Understanding all these different models, their implications, and how to train them is extremely hard and you could likely write a book on each different type of model.

In part, this is why CoreML is so great. CoreML enables you to make use of pre-trained models in your own apps. On top of this, CoreML standardizes the interface that you use in your own code. This means that you can use complex models without even realizing it. Let's learn more about CoreML, shall we?

Understanding CoreML

Due to the complex nature of machine learning and using trained models, Apple has built CoreML to make incorporating a trained model as simple as possible. On top of making CoreML as simple as possible, another goal was to ensure that whenever you implement machine learning using CoreML, your implementation is as fast as possible, and energy efficient. Since Apple has been enhancing iOS with machine learning for a couple of years now, they have loads of experience implementing complex models in apps.

If you have ever done research into machine learning, you might have come across cloud based solutions. Typically, you send a bunch of data to such a cloud based solution and the result is passed back as a response to your request. CoreML is very different since the model lives on the device instead of in the cloud. This means that your user's data never has to leave the device, which is very good for your user's privacy. Also, having your trained model on the device means that no internet connection is required to use CoreML which saves both time and precious data. And since there is no potential bottleneck in terms of response latency, CoreML is capable of calculating results in real time.

In the previous section you learned that there are several types of trained models. Each type of model is used slightly differently, so if you were to manually implement machine learning in your app, you would have to write different wrappers around each of the different models your app uses. CoreML makes sure that you can use each type of model without even being aware of this in your app; they all share the same programming interface. A CoreML model is domain agnostic.

In order to be domain agnostic, all trained models that you use with CoreML must be in a special format. Since machine learning already has a vibrant community with several popular formats, Apple has made sure that the most popular models can be easily converted to Apple's own `.mlmodel` format. Let's see how to obtain `.mlmodel` files for you to use in your apps.

Obtaining CoreML models

The are two ways to obtain a model for you to use in your apps. The simplest way is to find an existing `.mlmodel` file. You can find several ready to use `.mlmodel` files on Apple's machine learning website: `https://developer.apple.com/machine-learning/`. This website contains several popular models that are interesting for a large group of people. At the time of writing, most of these models are focused on recognizing dominant objects in an image, so chances are that you have different needs for your app.

If you're looking for something that isn't already converted by Apple, you can try to look in several places online for a pre-converted `.mlmodel` file or you can convert an existing model you have found online. Apple has created converters for several popular machine learning formats such as *caffe*. The conversion tools for converting an existing model to a `.mlmodel` file are written in Python and they ship as part of Xcode 9. If your needs do not fit the converters that Apple provides, you can easily extend the **toolchain** since the conversion tools are open source. This means that everybody can easily add their own converters or tweak existing converters.

Once you have obtained a CoreML model for your app by either converting one or using an existing one, you're ready to add it to your project and begin using it. Let's see how to do this next.

Using a CoreML model

Applications can utilize CoreML for many different purposes. One of these purposes is text analysis. You can use a trained model to detect whether a certain piece of text has a positive or negative sentiment. To implement a feature like this, you can use a trained and converted CoreML model.

In the code bundle for this chapter, a project named `RateMyText` is included. If you open the starter version of this project, you'll find a project that has a simple layout implemented and a button that is hooked up to an `IBAction` named `analyze()`. We'll use the `.mlmodel` file that is in the project folder to rate the sentiment for the text that the user writes in the `UITextView`. First of all, let's add the `.mlmodel` file to Xcode by dragging it to the project navigator from the **Finder**.

Once the `.mlmodel` is added to your project, you can click on it to see more information about the model as illustrated in the following screenshot:

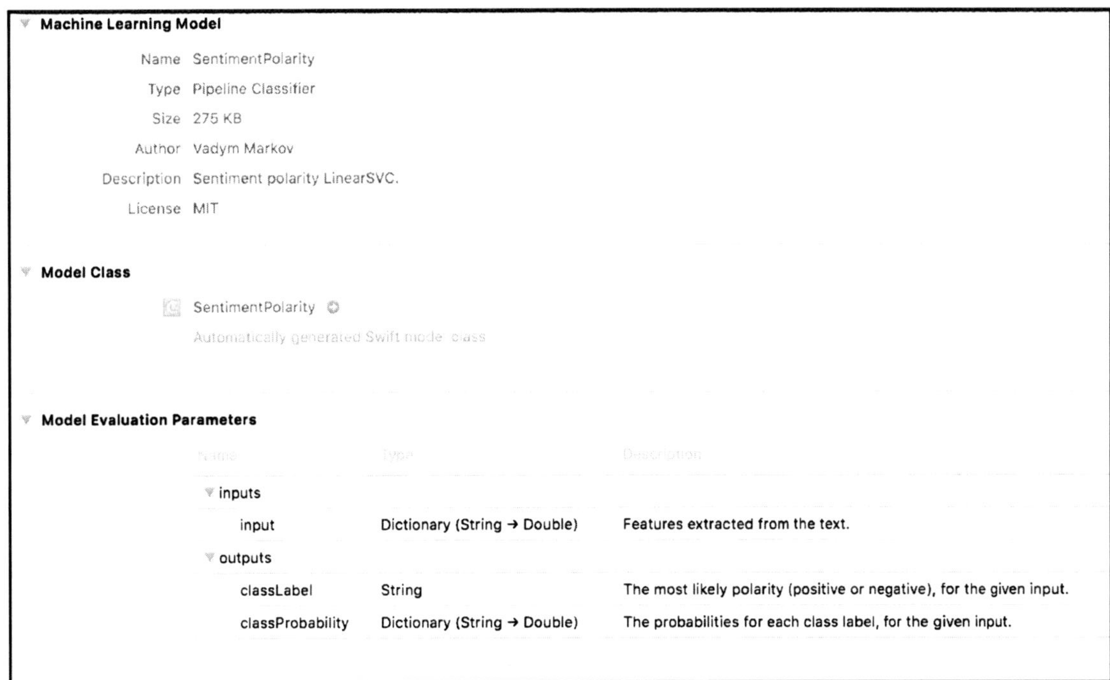

You can see that this model is provided by Vadym Markov under the **MIT** license. You can also see in the bottom section which **inputs** and **outputs** you can expect this model to work with. In this case the **inputs** is a dictionary of type `[String: Double]`. This means that we should feed this model a dictionary of word counts. If you just add this model to Xcode, the center section that lists the **Model Class** notifies you that the model isn't part of any targets yet. Fix this, as you have done before, by adding this model to your app target in the **Utilities** sidebar on the right side of the window.

Now that your model is implemented, it's time to make use of it. First, let's implement a method that extracts the word count from any given string. We can implement this using `NSLinguisticTagger`. The `NSLinguisticTagger` is a powerful text analysis class that can detect words, sentences, names, and more. You can use this class to perform pretty complex text analysis. In this example we'll set up the `NSLinguisticTagger` so it detects individual words, and we'll tell it to omit white-space and punctuation since we're not interested in any of that. Implement the word count method as follows:

```
func getWordCounts(fromString string: String) -> [String: Double] {
    var wordCount = [String: Double]()
    let tagger = NSLinguisticTagger(tagSchemes: [.tokenType], options: 0)
    tagger.string = string
    typealias TagEnumerating = (NSLinguisticTag?, NSRange, NSRange,
```

```
UnsafeMutablePointer<ObjCBool>) -> Void
    let enumerateTag: TagEnumerating = { tag, token, sentence, stop in
        let word = (string as NSString).substring(with: token)
        wordCount[word] = (wordCount[word] ?? 0) + 1
    }
    tagger.enumerateTags(in: NSRange(location: 0, length: string.count),
scheme: .tokenType, options: [.omitPunctuation, .omitWhitespace,
.omitOther], using: enumerateTag)
    return wordCount
}
```

The preceding method uses a `typealias` to make the method a bit more readable. It also sets up an `NSLinguisticTagger` and a dictionary of type `[String: Double]` so it can be easily used with the `SentimentPolarity` model. We enumerate of all the words that are found by the `NSLinguisticTagger` and add them to the count dictionary.

Let's see how we can combine this method and the `NSLinguisticTagger` to find out the sentiment score. Add the following implementation for the `analyze()` method:

```
@IBAction func analyze() {
    guard let text = textView.text
        else { return }
    let wordCount = getWordCounts(fromString: text)
    let model = SentimentPolarity()
    guard let prediction = try? model.prediction(input: wordCount)
        else { return }
    let alert = UIAlertController(title: nil, message: "Your text is rated:
\(prediction.classLabel)", preferredStyle: .alert)
    let okayAction = UIAlertAction(title: "Okay", style: .default, handler:
nil)
    alert.addAction(okayAction)
    present(alert, animated: true, completion: nil)
}
```

You might be surprised that this method is so short, but that's how simple CoreML is! First, we retrieve the `wordCount` using the method we implemented earlier. Then, an instance of the CoreML model is created. When you added the `SentimentPolarity` model to the app target, Xcode generated a class interface that abstracted away all complexities involving the model. Because the model is now a simple class, we can obtain a prediction for the sentiment of the text by calling `prediction(input:)` on the model instance.

The `prediction` method returns an object that contains the processed prediction (`classLabel`) as well as an overview (`classProbability`) of all options and how certain the model is about each option. You can use this property if you want to be a bit more transparent to the user about the different options that the model suggested and how certain it was about these options.

This example was simple enough. Now let's see if we can make the Augmented Reality app you've been working on a bit cooler by detecting the contents in each image that a user adds to their gallery.

Combining CoreML and computer vision

When you work on an app that works with photos or live camera footage, there are several things you might like to do. For instance, it could be desirable to detect faces in an image. Or maybe you would like to detect rectangular areas such as traffic signs. You could also be looking for something more sophisticated like detecting the dominant object in a picture.

In order to work with computer vision in your apps, Apple has created the Vision framework. You can combine the Vision framework and CoreML to perform some pretty sophisticated image recognition. Before we get to implementing the detection of dominant objects in our user's Augmented Reality galleries, let's take a quick look at the Vision framework so you have an idea of what it's capable of and when you might like to use it.

Understanding the Vision framework

The Vision framework is capable of many different tasks that revolve around computer vision. The Vision framework is built upon several powerful deep learning techniques in order to enable state of the art facial recognition, text recognition, barcode detection, and more. When using Vision for facial recognition, you get much more than just a location of a face. The framework can recognize several facial landmarks such as eyes, a nose, or a mouth. All this is possible due to the extensive use of deep learning behind the scenes.

For most tasks, using Vision consists of three stages:

1. You create a request that specifies what you want. For instance, an `VNDetectFaceLandmarksRequest`.
2. You set up a handler that can analyze the images.
3. The resulting observation contains the information you need.

The following code sample illustrates how you might find facial landmarks in an image:

```
let handler = VNImageRequestHandler(cgImage: image, options: [:])
let request = VNDetectFaceLandmarksRequest(completionHandler: { request,
error in
    guard let results = request.results as? [VNFaceObservation]
        else { return }
    for result in results where result.landmarks != nil {
        let landmarks = result.landmarks!
        if let faceContour = landmarks.faceContour {
            print(faceContour.normalizedPoints)
        }
        if let leftEye = landmarks.leftEye {
            print(leftEye.normalizedPoints)
        }
        // etc
    }
})

try? handler.perform([request])
```

For something as complex as detecting the contour of a face or the exact location of an eye, the code is quite simple. You set up a `handler` and a `request`. Next, the `handler` is asked to perform one or more `requests`. This means that you can run several `requests` on a single image.

In addition to enabling computer vision tasks like this, the Vision framework also tightly integrates with CoreML. Let's see just how tight this integration is by adding an image classifier to the Augmented Reality gallery app you have been working on!

Implementing an image classifier

In order to add an image classifier, we're going to need a CoreML model. On Apple's machine learning website (`https://developer.apple.com/machine-learning`) there are several models available. A nice lightweight model you can use is the `MobileNet()` model; go ahead and download it from the machine learning page. Once you have downloaded the model, open the `AugmentedRealityGallery` project and drag the model into Xcode. Make sure to add it to your app target so the class interface for the model is generated.

Once the model is generated, the implementation for using the model is very similar to the facial landmark detection sample. The major difference is that the request portion of the Vision request is a special `VNCoreMLRequest`. This type of request takes the CoreML model you want to use in addition to a completion handler.

When combining CoreML and Vision, Vision will take care of image scaling and converting the image to a type that is compatible with CoreML. You should make sure that the input image has the correct orientation. If your image is rotated in an unexpected orientation, CoreML might not be able to analyze it correctly.

Add the following method to `ViewController.swift`:

```
func classifyImage(_ image: UIImage) {
    guard let cgImage = image.cgImage,
        let classifier = try? VNCoreMLModel(for: MobileNet().model)
        else { return }
    let request = VNCoreMLRequest(model: classifier, completionHandler: {
[weak self] request, erorr in
        guard let classifications = request.results as?
[VNClassificationObservation],
            let prediction = classifications.first
            else { return }
        let alertController = UIAlertController(title: nil, message:
"Added: \(prediction.identifier) (\(round(prediction.confidence * 100))%
confidence)", preferredStyle: .alert)
        let okayAction = UIAlertAction(title: "Okay", style: .default,
handler: nil)
        alertController.addAction(okayAction)
        DispatchQueue.main.async {
            self?.present(alertController, animated: true, completion: nil)
        }
    })
    let handler = VNImageRequestHandler(cgImage: cgImage, options: [:])
    try? handler.perform([request])
}
```

The preceding method implementation takes a `UIImage` and converts it to a `CGImage`. Also, a `VNCoreMLModel` is created based on the `MobileNet()` model. This special model class wraps the CoreML model so it works seamlessly with Vision. The request is very similar to the request you have seen before. In the `completionHandler`, the results array and first prediction of the image contents are extracted and shown to the user. Note that the presentation of the alert is explicitly casted to the main thread to avoid crashes.

Now, all you need to do is add the following line to `addImageToARView(_:)` as follows:

```
func addImageToARView(_ image: UIImage) {
    classifyImage(image)
    // existing implementation...
}
```

This makes sure that we always show an alert as soon as the user attempts to add an image to their gallery.

Summary

This chapter wraps up the work we'll do on the Augmented Reality app. By now you have built an app that implements some of iOS 11's most exiting new technologies. In this chapter we focused on CoreML, Apple's machine learning framework. You saw that adding a machine learning model to your app is extremely simple since you only have to drag it to Xcode and add it to your target app. You also learned how you can obtain models and where to look in order to convert existing models to CoreML models. Creating a machine learning model is not simple so it's great that Apple has made it so simple to implement machine learning by embedding trained models in your apps.

In addition to CoreML, we also looked at the Vision framework. Vision combines the power of CoreML and smart image analysis to create an extremely powerful framework that can perform a huge amount of work on images. Convenient requests like facial landmark detection, text detection, and barcode detection are available out of the box without adding any machine learning models to your app. If you're looking for custom analysis, you can always add your own CoreML model just like we did for the Augmented Reality gallery app. The next chapter introduces you to entirely different aspects of iOS that are partially backed by machine learning: Spotlight and Universal Links.

16

Increasing Your App's Discoverability with Spotlight and Universal Links

Many users of macOS and iOS love one feature in particular: Spotlight search. Spotlight keeps an index of all files, contacts, contents, and more on your Mac, and it's been in iOS too for a while now. With iOS 9, Apple made it possible for developers to index the contents of their own apps, enabling users to discover app contents right from the Spotlight search they know and love. Ever since opening up Spotlight on iOS to developers, Apple has been pushing to make Spotlight better, more relevant, more impactful and more helpful to users. In this chapter, we'll explore what Spotlight can do for your apps and how you can make use of the `CoreSpotlight` APIs to provide your users with an amazing search experience that helps them find and navigate your app.

In this chapter, the following topics are covered:

- Understanding Spotlight search
- Adding your app contents to the Spotlight index
- Handling search result selection
- Adhering to Spotlight best practices
- Increasing your app's visibility with Universal Links

Let's not waste any time and jump right in to Spotlight!

Understanding Spotlight search

If you have a Mac, which you most likely do, you have probably used the blazingly fast Spotlight search feature on it. Furthermore, if you love this feature on your Mac, you have probably used it on iOS as well. Spotlight is a highly optimized search engine that enables you to find content throughout your device.

If you haven't used Spotlight, try swiping down on your home screen on iOS and use the search box. This is Spotlight. Or, on your Mac, press *command* + space to open the Spotlight search dialog.

Spotlight has been around since iOS 3. However, it wasn't until iOS 9 that Apple opened up Spotlight to developers. This means that, starting with iOS 9, Spotlight indexes everything from web results, apps, app store results, and any content you add to the Spotlight index yourself. Results are presented with an image, a title, and some extra information, and sometimes extra buttons are added to make a phone call or to start turn-by-turn navigation to an address.

The results that are displayed by Spotlight are a mix of public or online contents and private results. If your app has indexed items that are publicly available, Apple will make them visible to all users who have your app installed for as long as enough people actually interact with this particular searchable item.

A great example of public content for almost any app is the main navigation items in your app. Imagine you have an app that has a couple of tabs in a `UITabBar`. Any user that downloads your app and opens it can immediately access each tab if they want to. This means that these tabs are public; any user of your app can access these tabs.

Your app can index these tabs using `CoreSpotlight` and mark them as publicly available. When you mark an item as public, it will not be globally visible right away. What happens behind the scenes is that `CoreSpotlight` actually indexes this item as it normally would when indexing a private item. Whenever a user selects this particular item from a list of Spotlight search results, an irreversible hash of the item is sent to Apple's servers. If Apple receives the same hash over and over again, a certain threshold will be reached. Once this threshold is reached, the indexed item is pushed to all people who have your app installed. If your indexed item has a public web resource associated with it, your public searchable item will even be shown to people who don't have your app installed because the content is available on the web. If a user selects this item but doesn't have your app installed, they will be taken to your website instead in order to view the requested content there.

The fact that public results in Spotlight are kept private for a while helps to make sure that everything your users see when they use Spotlight is relevant. Imagine that any app developer could mark any piece of content as public and every time a developer does this, the item is immediately pushed to all users. This would pollute Spotlight, and the entire feature would become essentially worthless. Spotlight's goal is to provide relevant and interesting results. The threshold for interactions makes sure that enough people consider the displayed item to be appropriate for their search query, which means that bad indexing or spam doesn't have a chance to thrive.

Another reason this threshold exists is to protect your user's data. It's perfectly fine to add personal and private data to Spotlight. The standard mail app does this so users can search their email messages using Spotlight. Obviously, these email messages should not be publicly indexed so they shouldn't be marked as such. Mistakes happen though, and in event you do end up marking private data as public by accident, there is no way this specific item will show up for other users because the public result threshold for the item will never be reached, since only one user has interacted with the Spotlight search result.

It goes without saying that great Spotlight visibility can really boost usage of your apps, especially since users don't even need to have your app installed to see results for your app as long as there is a web resource available for your indexed contents. Apple has worked really hard to ensure that Spotlight is fast and provides a seamless experience to your users. This means that users won't notice whether a result comes straight from their own device or if a result is shown because it was publicly indexed.

You might have noticed that Safari sometimes shows results for in-app content. These results come from Spotlight. Whenever you add a web resource to an item you index, Safari will show this resource if it matches a user's query in the search bar. In this chapter, you will learn all about optimally indexing your app's contents; so, if you have an app that has a website that mirrors its contents, you'll know how to maximize your presence in search results for both Spotlight and Safari.

Adding your app contents to the Spotlight index

If you have ever worked on a website, you must have heard something about SEO (Search Engine Optimization). More importantly, you will know that any website you create and publish is indexed by several search engines. All you have to do is make sure that you write semantic and structured HTML markup and any web spider will understand what your website is about and what parts of it are more important. Search engines, such as Google, have indexed billions of web pages based on their contents and semantic markup.

Apps tend to be a little less neatly structured, and crawling them is a lot harder if not impossible. There is no structured way to figure out what content is on screen and what this content means. Also, more importantly, a lot of content you'd want to index is only available to users who have logged in or created content of their own.

This is why Apple decided that the developers themselves probably know their app's contents best and should be in charge about how, when, and why a particular content is indexed. Even though this does put a little bit of manual burden on the developers, it gives them a huge advantage over the automatic indexing that's done on the web. Since developers are in control, they can decide precisely which content matters most to specific users. As you'll soon see, you can index content based on the screens your user visits, which means that you will just index those pages that your user may want to visit again.

Even more important than being in control is the ability to safely index private contents. The web is limited to indexing public contents. If you use online email software to check your inbox or if you have an online project management tool, you must rely on the internal search functions inside the web page for these tools. You won't find your emails or projects through a regular search query. With Spotlight indexing, your users can do just that: Search through their own content. Indexing private contents is secure because the data is not made available to other apps and you can't accidentally make one user's private data visible to other users due to the public indexing threshold mentioned earlier.

So how exactly do developers take control then? That's the question that will be answered next. We'll take a look at the following three different methods that Apple came up with to index app contents:

- `NSUserActivity`
- `CSSearchableItem`
- Universal Links

Indexing your app through user activity

As part of a feature set called **Continuity**, Apple launched Handoff in iOS 8. Handoff allows users to start an activity on one device and then continue it on another. In iOS 9, Apple introduced the ability to index these user activities in Spotlight. There are several advantages to this because apps that support Handoff hardly need to do anything to support Spotlight indexing and vice versa. So, even though this chapter is all about search and Spotlight, you've already learned something about enabling Handoff for your app.

The philosophy behind user activities is that, whenever your user interacts with your app, you create an instance of `NSUserActivity`. For Spotlight, these activities revolve solely around viewing content. Any time your user looks at a piece of content in your app is a good time to create a user activity and have Spotlight index it. After the user activity is added to the index, the user will be able to find it through Spotlight; when they tap on it, your app can take the user straight to the relevant section of the app, allowing the user to resume their activity.

In the previous chapters, we worked on an app called `familymovies`. In this app, we collected data about `Family Members` and their favorite movies. We also had a rating for each of the movies. This content is great to index in Spotlight, so let's add some indexing to it.

Since the last time you worked on this app, a few additions were made. The app now contains a tab bar. There is a tab for the `Family Members` list, and there is one that lists all of the movies that are added to the app. Selecting a movie will display a list of `Family Members` who have added this movie to their favorites.

An app such as `familymovies` is a great candidate for indexing. We can add the separate `Family Members`, the tabs from the navigation bar, and the movies to Spotlight to make them searchable from anywhere within iOS. We'll start off simple; we'll index the `Family Members` and Movie tabs in Spotlight when the user visits them.

We will use user activities for this, so we should create an activity whenever our user opens one of the two tabs. At first sight, there isn't much use in repeatedly pushing the same activity over and over again if we know that we already pushed it once. The following are two of the available options we have for tracking the opening of a tab:

- Pushing the activity in `viewDidAppear`
- Pushing the activity in `viewDidLoad`

If we create the user activity in `viewDidAppear`, we push a user activity every time the user switches tabs or navigates back to our view controller from another view controller. Even though it doesn't cost much to index a user activity, it seems like it's something of an overkill to index our tab every single time a user sees it.

Event though this train of thought isn't wrong, the best way to go about this is to actually create the activity in the `viewDidAppear` method. If you put this logic in `viewDidLoad`, it will only be executed once even though the idea of user activities is that they describe each activity a user performs. In this case, repeatedly inserting the same activity over and over again is actually the desired behavior because it accurately reflects what the user is doing inside your app.

Let's take a look at some code that indexes the `Family Members` tab; it should be added in the `FamilyMembersViewController`:

```
override func viewDidAppear(_ animated: Bool) {
    super.viewDidAppear(animated)
    let userActivity = NSUserActivity(activityType:
"com.familymovies.openTab")
    userActivity.title = "Family Members"
    userActivity.isEligibleForSearch = true
    userActivity.isEligibleForPublicIndexing = true
    self.userActivity = userActivity
    self.userActivity?.becomeCurrent()
}
```

The preceding code shows how to create a very simple user activity. The activity we just created only has a title because there isn't much involved with it. Note that we added a string that looks similar to the app's bundle identifier as the `activityType` parameter for the `NSUserActivity` initializer. This identifier will help us distinguish the intent for the activity later on.

The most important thing to note in this method of indexing content is the `isEligibleForSearch` property. This property tells the system that the user activity that we're about to set as the current activity can be indexed for searching. Other, similar, properties are `isEligibleForHandoff` and `isEligibleForPublicIndexing`. It's actually a great idea for our activity to make it eligible for public indexing, so go ahead and set that property to `true`. Doing this will make our activity show up in the search results of a lot more people, if enough people interact with it. Making an activity eligible for handoff enables us to continue the activity on another device. Since our app only works on iOS and we don't really need to take multiple users with multiple devices into account, we don't have to set this property to true.

Finally, the user activity we just created is made the current activity. This makes sure that the OS registers our activity and adds it to the Spotlight index. It won't be made available publicly right away because, as discussed, there is a threshold of people (that interact with this activity) that we need to reach before Apple will push it to all users. Even though it won't be indexed publicly, it will appear in search results locally for the current user.

If you build and run your application, the `Family Members` tab should be the first tab to appear. This means that a user activity for that view is to be created and indexed immediately. After opening the app, go ahead and open Spotlight by swiping down on the home screen and perform a search for **family**.

You'll notice that the activity we just added is listed under the `familymovies` header in the Spotlight search results, as shown in the following screenshot:

Pretty neat, right? You were able to add a simple entry in Spotlight's search index with very minimal effort. You should be able to add a similar implementation to the `familymovies` app to have it index the `Movies` page. Go ahead and add a modified version of the earlier snippet to `MoviesListViewController`.

Now that both tabs show up in Spotlight, how do you make sure that the correct tab is opened when the user selects a result from Spotlight? The answer lies in one of the `AppDelegate` methods. Whenever your app is brought to the foreground because a user selected your app as a Spotlight search result, the `application(_:continueUserActivity:restorationHandler:)` method is called.

This method receives the activity that we are supposed to resume, and it's up to the application to resume this activity as soon as possible. Apple actually has algorithms in place that measure how long it takes for your app to resume the activity to make sure that it can either reward or punish your app in Spotlight's rating system based on how fast the app is up-and-running.

We'll discuss this a bit more when we get to best practices and ranking, but regardless of Apple's ranking algorithms you should show the users what they're looking for as fast as you possibly can. In our case, it's quite simple for us to resume the activities we receive. There are only two possible scenarios that we need to handle right now. Either the users want to look at the `Family Members` tab or they want to see the Movies tab. Let's take a look at how this behavior can be implemented in `AppDelegate`.

The implementation of `application(_:continueUserActivity:restorationHandler:)` should inspect the user activity we passed to determine which tab should be displayed. Once we know this, we should obtain a reference to the `UITabBar` that holds the tabs and set its active view controller to the tab we need to select. Finally, we should bring the navigation controller that's displayed to its root view controller. We should do this because, otherwise if our user looked at a detail page before going into Spotlight, we would show them the detail page instead of the page they expect to see: The overview page. Popping to the root view controller ensures we show the user the overview page:

```
func application(_ application: UIApplication, continue userActivity:
NSUserActivity, restorationHandler: @escaping ([Any]?) -> Void) -> Bool {
    guard let tabBar = window?.rootViewController as? UITabBarController
        else { return false }

    let tabIndex: Int?
    if userActivity.title == "Family Members" {
        tabIndex = 0
    } else if userActivity.title == "Movies" {
```

```
        tabIndex = 1
    } else {
        tabIndex = nil
    }

    guard let index = tabIndex
        else { return false }

    guard let navVC = tabBar.viewControllers?[index] as?
UINavigationController
        else { return false }

    navVC.popToRootViewController(animated: false)
    tabBar.selectedIndex = index

    return true
}
```

In this basic implementation of `application(_:continueUserActivity:restorationHandler:)`, we only take care of the two activities that were indexed. First, we make sure that we actually have a `UITabBarController` to work with in the app. If this isn't the case, the activity can't be handled and we return false. Next, we set the `tabIndex` if possible and extract the corresponding navigation controller from the tab bar controller. Again, if this fails, we can't handle the activity and we return false. Finally, when all the requirements are met, we pop the navigation controller to its root and set the selected index on the tab bar to the correct value for the activity that is being handled.

We're currently at a point where we've managed to index the two main screens for the app. However, there are a couple more screens that we can index. This will make our implementation for `application(_:continueUserActivity:restorationHandler:)` much more complex.

Manually creating and resuming user activities for each screen in our app is tedious and involves quite a lot of boilerplate code. We'll solve this by utilizing an activity factory. A common pattern in apps is to use a specific helper object called a **Factory** . The sole purpose of a factory is to have a central place in which to create instances of a certain type. This greatly reduces boilerplate code and increases maintainability. Create a new file called `IndexingFactory.swift` in the `Helpers` folder and add the following implementation:

```
import Foundation

struct IndexingFactory {
    enum ActivityType: String {
        case openTab = "com.familymovies.openTab"
```

```
        case familyMemberDetailView =
"com.familymovies.familyMemberDetailView"
        case movieDetailView = "com.familymovies.movieDetailView"
    }

    static func activity(withType type: ActivityType, name: String,
makePublic: Bool) -> NSUserActivity {
        let userActivity = NSUserActivity(activityType: type.rawValue)
        userActivity.title = name
        userActivity.isEligibleForSearch = true
        userActivity.isEligibleForPublicIndexing = makePublic

        return userActivity
    }
}
```

An `enum` is used to abstract away the activity types we will use, and we have a single static method in the `IndexingFactory` struct. This method takes a couple of configuration arguments and uses these to create and return a new user activity instance. Let's take a look at a usage example for the family member details screen:

```
override func viewDidAppear(_ animated: Bool) {
    super.viewDidAppear(animated)

    guard let familyMemberName = familyMember?.name
        else { return }

    self.userActivity = IndexingFactory.activity(withType:
.familyMemberDetailView, name: familyMemberName, makePublic: false)
    self.userActivity?.becomeCurrent()
}
```

The preceding implementation is a lot smaller than creating a user activity from scratch in every `viewDidAppear`. Also, if we decide to make changes to the way we create user activities, it will be easier to refactor our code because we can simply change a single method.

This wraps up simple indexing with `NSUserActivity`. Next up, we'll take a look at `CSSearchableItem` and how we can use this class to index content the user hasn't seen yet. You'll also see how you can associate more sophisticated data with your searchable items and how Spotlight handles updating and re-indexing contents.

An exercise for you, the reader. We haven't implemented any code to open details pages for `Family Members` and movies when a user selects one in their Spotlight search results. We'll get to this soon, but it's a pretty good exercise to try and add this functionality on your own. If you get stuck, don't hesitate to take a look at the source code for this chapter because a full implementation can be found there. For a proper implementation, you'll need to add a new find method to **Movie** and **FamilyMember** and you'll have to instantiate view controllers straight from a storyboard.

Indexing with CSSearchableItem

Currently, our indexing works and we can find any content we saw before. We can even select results from the Spotlight index and have our app open on the correct page. If you've taken on the challenge of implementing the handling of detail pages, your app should be able to handle continuation of any activity that has been indexed. Wouldn't it be cool if we could be a bit more proactive about indexing though? Ideally, we would index any new `Family Members` or movies as soon as the user adds them.

This is exactly what `CSSearchableItem` is good at. The `CSSearchableItem` class enables you to index content the user might not have seen before. Indexing `CSSearchableItem` instances is pretty straightforward. The steps involved are similar to how we indexed user activities. To index a searchable item, we will create an instance of `CSSearchableItem` and provide it with collection attributes that describe the item we will index. These attributes are encapsulated in an instance of `CSSearchableItemAttributeSet`.

Containing information in CSSearchableItemAttributeSet

The attributes set are populated correctly since they describe almost all of the important information for Spotlight. You can set a title, content description, a thumbnail image, keywords, even ratings or phone numbers, GPS information, and much, much more. For a full overview of what's possible, refer to the `CSSearchableItemAttributeSet` documentation. Every time you are about to create a new item that can be indexed, you should take a look at the documentation to make sure you don't miss any attributes.

The better use you make of the available attributes, the more effectively your content can be indexed and the higher your app will rank. Therefore, it's worth putting slightly more time and effort into your search attributes because getting it wrong can be a costly mistake, especially considering the available documentation. At a minimum, you should always try to set `title`, `contentDescription`, `thumbnailData`, `rating`, and `keywords`. This isn't always relevant or even possible for the items you're indexing, but whenever possible make sure that you set these attributes.

You may have noticed that the `NSUserActivity` instances we indexed in our app didn't receive any special attributes. We just set a name and some other basic information, but we never added a description or a rating to any of the indexed objects. If you're indexing user activities in your own applications, it's worth noting that user activities can and should have attributes associated with them. All you need to do is set the `contentAttributeSet` property on the user activity. After we implement indexing through `CSSearchableItem`, we'll shortly revisit user activity indexing to make the indexed item richer and also to make sure that `CoreSpotlight` understands that the user activities and searchable items point to the same underlying index in Spotlight.

Whenever we index items through multiple methods, it's inevitable that we'll run into data duplication. The application we're working on right now indexes every visited screen. So, if a user visits the details page of a movie, we will index a user activity that points to that specific movie. However, we also want to index movies as they are created by the user. To avoid duplicate results in Spotlight search, we should add a `relatedUniqueIdentifier` to the attributes set. Setting this attribute on a user activity makes sure that Spotlight doesn't add duplicate entries for items with the same identifier.

Let's expand the `IndexingFactory` with two methods that can generate attribute sets for searchable items. Putting this functionality in the `IndexingFactory` as a separate method is a good idea because, if it is set up correctly, these methods can be used to generate attributes for both user activities and searchable items. This avoids code duplication and makes it a lot easier to add or remove properties in the future. Add the following methods to the `IndexingFactory` struct:

```
static func searchableAttributes(forMovie movie: Movie) ->
CSSearchableItemAttributeSet {
    do {
        try movie.managedObjectContext?.obtainPermanentIDs(for: [movie])
    } catch {
        print("could not obtain permanent movie id")
    }

    let attributes = CSSearchableItemAttributeSet(itemContentType:
ActivityType.movieDetailView.rawValue)
```

```
    attributes.title = movie.name
    attributes.contentDescription = "A movie that is favorited by
\(movie.familyMembers?.count ?? 0) family members"
    attributes.rating = NSNumber(value: movie.popularity)
    attributes.identifier =
"\(movie.objectID.uriRepresentation().absoluteString)"
    attributes.relatedUniqueIdentifier =
"\(movie.objectID.uriRepresentation().absoluteString)"

    return attributes
}

static func searchableAttributes(forFamilyMember familyMember:
FamilyMember) -> CSSearchableItemAttributeSet {
    do {
        try familyMember.managedObjectContext?.obtainPermanentIDs(for:
[familyMember])
    } catch {
        print("could not obtain permanent family member id")
    }

    let attributes = CSSearchableItemAttributeSet(itemContentType:
ActivityType.familyMemberDetailView.rawValue)
    attributes.title = familyMember.name
    attributes.identifier =
"\(familyMember.objectID.uriRepresentation().absoluteString)"
    attributes.contentDescription = "Family Member with
\(familyMember.favoriteMovies?.count ?? 0) listed movies"
    attributes.relatedUniqueIdentifier =
"\(familyMember.objectID.uriRepresentation().absoluteString)"

    return attributes
}
```

For both objects, a set of attributes is created. This set meets Apple's recommendations as closely as possible. We don't have any thumbnail images or keywords that we can add besides the movie name or the name of a family member. Adding these to the keywords is kind of pointless because the title in itself is essentially a keyword that our item will match on.

Note that we use the `objectID` property as a means of uniquely identifying objects. Because the factory methods is called before the objects are assigned a permanent ID, we could be in trouble. Objects are assigned a permanent ID when they are saved or if we explicitly tell the managed object context to obtain permanent IDs.

We need to do this to ensure that the `objectID` does not change at a later time. The `objectID` property is available on all managed objects and is the most reliable and convenient way for us to make sure that we have a unique identifier available.

To create an attribute set, all we have to do now is call the method that matches the object we want to index and we're good to go. Nice, convenient, and simple.

Adding CSSearchableItem instances to the search index

In the `familymovies` application, we want to add `family members` and movies to the search index as soon as they are added by the user. We already have a factory method in place that creates the `CSSearchableItemAttributeSet` instance that describes the item we want to index. However, we can't directly add these to the index. To add information to the search index manually, as we want to, we need instances of `CSSearchableItem`. To create such an instance, we need the following two further pieces of information: a unique identifier and a domain identifier.

The unique identifier is used to uniquely identify an indexed item. It's important that you set this value to something that is actually unique because otherwise Spotlight will overwrite the entry with something else that has the same identifier or you'll get duplicate entries if you combine user activities and search items like we're doing for `familymovies`.

The domain identifier functions as a namespace. Within any given namespace, all entries must be unique and are identified through their own unique identifier. These identifiers, must only be unique within their own namespace. Think of this as streets and addresses. In a certain area, every street name is unique (domain, namespace). Inside each street the house number is unique (unique identifier), but the same number can occur in different streets. The domain identifier for your Spotlight entry is not only used to uniquely identify entries, it's also used to perform certain batch actions on the index, such as deleting all indexed items from a certain domain.

The domain identifier, unique identifier, and the attributes together make up a searchable item. The following code adds factory methods to `IndexingFactory` that will make it simple for our app to add items to the search index:

```
enum DomainIdentifier: String {
    case familyMember = "FamilyMember"
    case movie = "Movie"
}

static func searchableItem(forMovie movie: Movie) -> CSSearchableItem {
```

```
    let attributes = searchableAttributes(forMovie: movie)

    return searachbleItem(withIdentifier:
"\(movie.objectID.uriRepresentation().absoluteString)", domain: .movie,
attributes: attributes)
}

static func searchableItem(forFamilyMember familyMember: FamilyMember) ->
CSSearchableItem {
    let attributes = searchableAttributes(forFamilyMember: familyMember)

    return searachbleItem(withIdentifier: "\(familyMember.objectID)",
domain: .familyMember, attributes: attributes)
}

private static func searachbleItem(withIdentifier identifier: String,
domain: DomainIdentifier, attributes: CSSearchableItemAttributeSet) ->
CSSearchableItem {
    let item = CSSearchableItem(uniqueIdentifier: identifier,
domainIdentifier: domain.rawValue, attributeSet: attributes)

    return item
}
```

The preceding code defines an enum that contains the domains that we want to add items for. Note that `searchableItem(withIdentifier:domain:attributes:)` is marked as private. This is done to make sure anybody using our code has to use `searchableItem(forFamilyMember:)` and `searchableItem(forMovie:)` instead. These methods are simpler to use because they only take a family member or a movie and if we use only these methods, we can rest assured that we're inserting consistently set up-searchable items to our index.

Now that everything is set up for indexing new data, let's begin with indexing `family members` as soon as they are created. Update `FamilyMembersViewController`'s implementation of `controller(_:didChange:at:for:newIndexPath:)` as follows; the updated lines are highlighted. Make sure that you import `CoreSpotlight` at the top of your file:

```
func controller(_ controller:
NSFetchedResultsController<NSFetchRequestResult>,
                didChange anObject: Any,
                at indexPath: IndexPath?,
                for type: NSFetchedResultsChangeType,
                newIndexPath: IndexPath?) {

    switch type {
```

```
    case .insert:
        guard let insertIndex = newIndexPath,
            let familyMember = fetchedResultsController?.object(at:
insertIndex)
            else { return }

        let item = IndexingFactory.searchableItem(forFamilyMember:
familyMember)
        CSSearchableIndex.default().indexSearchableItems([item],
completionHandler: nil)
        tableView.insertRows(at: [insertIndex], with: .automatic)
        // existing implementation
    }
}
```

Because of the factory methods you set up before, new items can be added to the search index with just a few lines of code. To insert an item into the search index, we obtain an instance of `CSSearchableIndex` and tell it to index the searchable items. If needed, a completion handler can be passed to the index method. This handler is called with an optional error. If the indexing has failed, the error should tell us a bit about why Spotlight couldn't index the item and we could retry or take a different action. In our app, we'll assume that the indexing succeeded and we don't want to handle potential errors.

Update the `mangedObjectContextDidChange(notification:)` method in `MoviesViewController` as follows; updated parts of the code are highlighted:

```
func mangedObjectContextDidChange(notification: NSNotification) {
    guard let userInfo = notification.userInfo
        else { return }

    if let updatedObjects = userInfo[NSUpdatedObjectsKey] as?
Set<FamilyMember>,
        let familyMember = self.familyMember ,
updatedObjects.contains(familyMember) {
            let item = IndexingFactory.searchableItem(forFamilyMember:
familyMember)
            CSSearchableIndex.default().indexSearchableItems([item],
completionHandler: nil)
            tableView.reloadData()
    }

    if let updatedObjects = userInfo[NSUpdatedObjectsKey] as? Set<Movie> {
        for object in updatedObjects {
            let item = IndexingFactory.searchableItem(forMovie: object)
            CSSearchableIndex.default().indexSearchableItems([item],
completionHandler: nil)
```

```
            if let familyMember = self.familyMember,
                let familyMembers = object.familyMembers,
                familyMembers.contains(familyMember) {
                    tableView.reloadData()
                    break
            }
        }
    }
}
```

Right after we add the movie to the current family member, we add it to the Spotlight index. You might argue that we're adding the item too early because we haven't fetched a rating for the movie yet at that point. This is OK because, when the context is saved the second time with the ratings attached, we automatically add the item to the index again due to the save notification we're observing.

If you run the app now, you should be able to go into Spotlight right after you add a family member or movie, and you should immediately be able to find the freshly added content in Spotlight. If you search for a movie you just added, you'll notice that you can see how many `family members` have added a certain movie to their favorites list and the rating a movie has. More importantly, there should be only a single entry for each movie because we're using a proper unique identifier.

One final update we should add to our `saveMovie(withName:)` method is that it should also take care of updating the family member's entry so we get a correct reading of the number of added favorite movies in Spotlight.

Update your code as follows:

```
familyMember.favoriteMovies = familyMember.favoriteMovies?.adding(movie) as
NSSet?
let item = IndexingFactory.searchableItem(forMovie: movie)
CSSearchableIndex.default().indexSearchableItems([item], completionHandler:
nil)

let familyMemberItem = IndexingFactory.searchableItem(forMovie: movie)
CSSearchableIndex.default().indexSearchableItems([familyMemberItem],
completionHandler: nil)
```

The amendment to the code should speak for itself; after we create the movie, we re-index the family member item. One final adjustment we will need to make is to make sure that `CoreSpotlight` does not mix up our activities and searchable items. We'll update our factory methods for user activities and set them up similar to how we set up the factory methods for searchable items.

Safely combining indexing methods

Since we're not associating any unique information with our user activities, Spotlight can't figure out that a family member that's indexed through a user activity is actually the same item we already inserted as a searchable item. To ensure that Spotlight understands this, we'll add two more factory methods that will create an activity item for either a family member or a movie with the correct information associated with them. Add the following methods to the `IndexingFactory`:

```
static func activity(forMovie movie: Movie) -> NSUserActivity {
    let activityItem = activity(withType: .movieDetailView, name:
movie.name!, makePublic: false)
    let attributes = searchableAttributes(forMovie: movie)
    attributes.domainIdentifier = DomainIdentifier.movie.rawValue
    activityItem.contentAttributeSet = attributes

    return activityItem
}

static func activity(forFamilyMember familyMember: FamilyMember) ->
NSUserActivity {
    let activityItem = activity(withType: .movieDetailView, name:
familyMember.name!, makePublic: false)
    let attributes = searchableAttributes(forFamilyMember: familyMember)
    attributes.domainIdentifier = DomainIdentifier.familyMember.rawValue
    activityItem.contentAttributeSet = attributes

    return activityItem
}
```

The most important lines to take note of are the ones where a `domainIdentifier` is set on the attributes constant. Since iOS 10, developers have been able to associate a `domainIdentifier` with user activities through the `contentAttributeSet`. By adding a `domainIdentifier` to the indexed item, searchable items and user activities are unified even more. Update the `viewDidAppear` implementation for `MovieDetailViewController` as follows:

```
override func viewDidAppear(_ animated: Bool) {
    super.viewDidAppear(animated)

    guard let movie = self.movie
        else { return }

    self.userActivity = IndexingFactory.activity(forMovie: movie)
    self.userActivity?.becomeCurrent()
}
```

We also need to update the `viewDidAppear` method in `MoviesViewController`. You should be able to do this on your own; the code will look similar to the preceding snippet, except you're indexing a family member instead of a movie.

Now that all of your app contents are indexed in Spotlight, it's time to discuss some of the methods Spotlight uses to rate your content and the best practices you should keep in mind when you add your app's contents to Spotlight.

Handling searchable item selection

If a user taps on a search result for one of the items you indexed manually, the `application(_:continue:restorationHandler:)` method is called on the `AppDelegate`. This is the same method that's used for user activities, but the internal handling is not quite the same.

For user activity items, we relied on the user activity's title. We can't do the same for our searchable items. Luckily, the user activity instance we get of a user selects one of our searchable items as a special activity type: `CSSearchableItemActivityIdentifier`. This identifier tells us that we're dealing with an item that's different from our regular user activities, and we can adjust our course of action based on this information. Update your code in `AppDelegate` as follows:

```
func application(_ application: UIApplication, continue userActivity:
NSUserActivity, restorationHandler: @escaping ([Any]?) -> Void) -> Bool {
    if let identifier =
userActivity.userInfo?[CSSearchableItemActivityIdentifier] as? String,
userActivity.activityType == CSSearchableItemActionType {
        return handleCoreSpotlightActivity(withIdentifier: identifier)
    }
    // existing implementation..
}

func handleCoreSpotlightActivity(withIdentifier identifier: String) -> Bool
{
    guard let url = URL(string: identifier),
        let objectID =
persistentContainer.persistentStoreCoordinator.managedObjectID(forURIRepres
entation: url),
        let object = try?
persistentContainer.viewContext.existingObject(with: objectID)
        else { return false }

    if let movie = object as? Movie {
        return handleOpenMovieDetail(withName: movie.name!)
```

```
        }

        if let familyMember = object as? FamilyMember {
            return handleOpenFamilyMemberDetail(withName: familyMember.name!)
        }
        return false
    }
```

The updated version of `application(_:continue:restorationHandler:)` checks whether it received a searchable item or not. If it did, a special method is called. This method uses the persistent store to convert the string identifier to a managed object ID which is then used to ask the managed object context for the corresponding object. If all of this succeeds, we attempt to cast the fetched object to either a movie or a family member and if this succeeds, one of the existing handlers is called. If none of the casts succeed, we have failed to continue the activity so we return false.

Understanding Spotlight best practices and rating

If you implement Spotlight indexing in your app, it's beneficial for both you and your users if you adhere to the best practices for doing so. Sticking with the best practices will positively affect your ratings and can ultimately drive more users to your app.

We'll cover two best practices that you should always implement if you're able to. Doing so will give your app great advantages over other apps. The following are the two aspects we'll cover:

- Adding metadata to your web links
- Registering as an indexing delegate

Adding metadata to your web links

In the next section about Universal Links, we'll cover Universal Links and how you should implement them in your application. Enabling Universal Links benefits your Spotlight search ranking and visibility because Spotlight can associate web resources that Apple's bot can crawl with the items you add to the Spotlight index. To associate Universal Links and your locally indexed items with each other, you should set the contentUrl that matches the web resource for a local item on your search attributes objects.

Doing so enables Apple to easily display your search results as public and it can even display your Universal Links in Safari's search results. This means that it will be even easier for your users to discover your app. More importantly, if you associate a contentUrl with an indexed item, your app is shown even to people who don't have your app installed. That aspect alone should persuade you to make sure that your app has online resources that mirror the public content in your app.

Once you've decided to add content URLs to your content, it's important that you add proper, structured metadata to your web pages. If your web page has well-formatted metadata available, Spotlight will index your app's contents even if you don't manually add it. This is because Apple continuously crawls the marketing and support URLs you advertise with in the App Store.

In order for Apple's bot to be able to discover the URLs your app can handle, it checks whether there is a Smart App Banner implemented in your app. The Smart App Banner is visible to people who visit your website. If they already have your app installed, the banner will prompt the user to view this content in your app. If you've added a URL to the banner that your app can handle, Apple's bot is able to discover this link and associates it with your app.

The second thing you should do is add metadata about the content. When we manually index content, you can set properties on your attributes set to represent your data. On the web, you can't create an attribute set, so you need to embed the metadata in your page's HTML markup. If you're implementing Open Graph metadata, Apple is able to understand that. However, Apple recommends that you implement richer and more fine-grained data for your app.

To do this, it's recommended implement metadata as specified in the schema.org standards. These standards provide definitions for a wide range of different entities. For instance, you can express a product rating, pricing, or a business address through `schema.org` definitions of these entities.

If you've implemented metadata for your app, or if you want to make sure that Spotlight is able to index your contents, you can use Apple's verification tools for searching. Go to `https://search.developer.apple.com` to paste in your website's URL and verify that everything can be indexed as you expected.

Having a complete set of metadata positively impacts your rating. An obvious reason is that it's better because more information means more matches for a search query. However, a different reason is that, if a user sees a search result that provides a lot of information at a glance, it's easier for them to decide whether or not a specific result is relevant to them.

This quick assessment of relevancy up front makes sure that whenever a user selects a result for your app, they know for sure that they want to interact with that item. Apple measures this form of engagement to ensure that results that are tapped often and longer engagements are pushed to the top.

Directly related to this is the concept of keyword stuffing. When optimizing for a search, it can be tempting to stuff a lot of keywords into your contents. Doing this will not positively impact your ratings in Spotlight. The reasoning behind this is that keyword-stuffed results will often simply look like spam. The preview won't be a coherent preview of contents, but it will look as if somebody tried to put as many relevant words together as they could. A result that looks poor is less likely to be tapped by a user and will be pushed down in the rankings eventually.

If the users do end up tapping a keyword-stuffed item, it's unlikely that they will actually find what they were looking for. Often, this means that the user exits your app after just a couple of seconds, and this negatively impacts your result rating.

In other words, add as much metadata as you reasonably can, but ensure that any data you add is relevant, true, and actually exists in your app. A good preview in Spotlight and a matching experience in your app is the best way to rank highly for Spotlight.

Registering as an indexing delegate

An item you index today might change over time. Some items you add to Spotlight could even have an expiration date if you've set the `endDate` property on the item attributes. Therefore, it's important that you register your app as an indexing delegate.

The indexing delegate is used for a single purpose: re-indexing contents. If you've added items that expire over time, Spotlight will ask you to index them again to make sure that the expiration date is still correct. The indexing delegate is also called if something goes wrong with the index itself; for example, if all pieces of data are lost or if the search index becomes corrupted.

The indexing delegate has two required methods: `searchableIndex(_:reindexAllSearchableItemsWithAcknowledgementHandler:)` and `searchableIndex(_:reindexSearchableItemsWithIdentifiers:acknowledgementHandler:)`.

The first method is called if the index has been lost and everything should be indexed. It's up to you to figure out how to index your entire app. In the `familymovies` app, this would probably mean fetching all `family members` and indexing them. You could use the `favoriteMovies` relationship to loop over all of the movies we have in the database and index them. Alternatively, you could query both entities separately and index them separately. The second method receives an array of identifiers that need to be indexed.

After you index the required items, you should call the `acknowledgementHandler` that your `delegate` method has received. This will make sure that Spotlight understands that you have successfully executed the tasks you needed to perform. To set the indexing delegate, you set the `indexDelegate` of the search index. For most apps, this is `CSSearchableIndex.default()`.

Now that you know everything about properly implementing Spotlight indexing, let's see how you can step up your indexing game a little bit more by implementing Universal Links.

Increasing your app's visibility with Universal Links

A Universal Link is very similar to a deep link. Deep links allow apps to link users straight into a certain section of an application. Before Universal Links, developers had to use a custom URL scheme to create their deep links.

You might have seen a URL with a custom scheme in the past. These URLs are easily recognized and look as follows:

```
familymovies://FamilyMember/jack
```

It's obvious that this isn't a regular web URL because web URLs start with a scheme of either `http://` or `https://`. An application can register itself as capable of opening URLs with a certain scheme. So, the `familymovies` app we've been working on could manifest itself as a handler of `familymovies:// urls`.

However, there are a couple of downsides to this approach. First and foremost, this URL isn't sharable at all. You can't send this URL to any friends that don't have the same app installed. If you were to send this URL to somebody and they didn't have the corresponding app installed, they wouldn't be able to open this URL. This is inconvenient because, in order for others to access the same content, assuming it's publicly available on the web, we would have to share a different URL that points to the website. But sharing a link to the website usually means that the content is shown in Safari instead of the app, even if it's installed.

The solution to this problem before iOS 9 came out was to use JavaScript on a web page to attempt to redirect a user to a link that the app could handle. If this failed, the user stayed on the website and they would be redirected into the app that the link originally came from. This approach is tedious and error-prone. It's simply not as convenient as sharing a link to a website.

There is also a huge privacy concern regarding this approach. Any website can try to redirect a user to a certain URL scheme. This means that websites can attempt to redirect you to a banking app, dating app, or any other app that could give away information you don't want to share with everybody. Once a redirect succeeds or fails, the website knows that you have a certain app installed even though this information should remain private.

The third problem with custom URL schemes is that any app can register as being capable of opening a certain URL scheme. This means that you could create an application that registers as being capable of opening URLs with any scheme you can come up with and unfortunately iOS offers the users no control over which application opens what URL scheme.

Universal Links were introduced in iOS 9 to solve all of the problems that exist with custom URL schemes and more. First of all, a Universal Link looks identical to a regular web link. In fact, a Universal Link is identical to a regular web link. If you've found a great news article on the web and you share it with somebody who has installed the app that belongs to the news website the link is from, the link will redirect straight to the corresponding app. Safari does not open intermediately, no attempts are made to redirect you from a web page to a custom URL scheme. The user is simply taken from the place where they tap the link, right to the app.

This is much more secure because in this scenario it's impossible to sniff for installed apps. It's also more convenient because users can share the same link; it doesn't matter if the receiver of the link does't have the corresponding app installed because iOS will know whether the link should be opened in an app or if Safari should handle the URL.

Also, not every app can register as capable of opening a Universal Link. Any app that claims to be able to open a certain Universal Link must be accompanied by the server that hosts the website. This means that, if your app claims to be able to open links from a certain domain, you must own that domain. Apple uses a verification file that you must host on the same domain that your app wants to handle links for, to make sure that your app does not try to open links on behalf of another app or website.

Apart from security benefits, Universal Links also provide a more unified, seamless experience to your users. With Universal Links, Apple didn't just open the door to a better, easier way to link to content inside your app, it also opened up an API that makes it really easy for your app and website to share login information securely. Just like tieing the links for your app and website together, you can also tie your app to the login credentials stored in Safari for your app. Any user that logs in to your website through Safari can automatically be logged in to your app.

Now that you're aware of the great features and possibilities of Universal Links, let's see how this all works on the server side.

Preparing your server for Universal Links

Setting up Universal Links on the server side has been made as straightforward as possible by Apple. All you have to do is host a file on your own server that can prove the connection between your app and your server. This is done through a file called the `apple-app-site-association` file.

The `apple-app-site-association` file contains a dictionary of information that describes exactly how your app is tied to your site. Let's have a look at an example of an `apple-app-site-association` file. The example describes the implementation for a recipe app where users can simply browse and search recipes for food:

```
{
    "applinks": {
        "apps": [],
        "details": {
            "6QA73RGQR2.com.donny.recipes": {
                "paths": [
                    "/recipes/*/",
                    "/search/"
                ]
            }
        }
    }
}
```

Let's go over this configuration file bit by bit. Firstly, we need to create some mandatory dictionary keys. The `applinks` key tells Apple that this part of our association applies to Universal Links. Inside this key, we define an empty `apps` array that we don't need to put anything in and then we have the `details` key. The `details` key is a dictionary that contains our configuration.

First of all, your app identifier should be added as a key for the `details` dictionary. The prefix you see in front of the app identifier is your team identifier. You can find your team identifier in the Apple Developer portal.

Finally, there is a `paths` array inside the dictionary that's associated to our bundle identifier key. This array specifies all the paths on our website that we want to handle. Imagine that our website's base URL is `https://www.donnysrecipes.com/`. For this URL, `https://` is the scheme, `www.donnysrecipes.com` is the domain, and anything after the trailing / is called the path.

The example configuration handles the `/recipes/*/` and the `/search/` paths. The `*` in `/recipes/*/` means that we're matching on a wildcard. In other words, we specify that our app is able to open URLs such as `https://www.donnysrecipes.com/recipes/10/`, `https://www.donnysrecipes.com/recipes/20/`, or any other URL that looks similar.

The `/search/` path is a bit more interesting. We didn't specify a wildcard anywhere, yet our app will be able to handle URLs such as `https://www.donnysrecipes.com/search/?q=macaroni`. That final segment, `?q=macaroni`, is called the query string and we don't need to specify that we match on that because it's not part of the path.

Once you have created and configured your `apple-app-site-association` file you need to upload it to your server. It's important that you host the association file in a way that makes it accessible on a URL similar to `https://www.donnysrecipes.com/apple-app-site-association`. In other words, the path to this verification file on your server should be `/apple-app-site-association`.

Now that the server is ready to communicate to Apple that your app can open links for your site, it's time to see how you can set up your app to handle Universal Links.

Handling Universal Links in your app

With all parts in place you can now enable your app to handle Universal Links. In the previous sections of this chapter, we put in a lot of work in order to handle continuing user activities. The implementation that is shown uses the `application(_:continue:restorationHandler:)` method to inspect and dissect user activities and it serves as a handoff point for us to call other methods from. This setup now becomes very beneficial because we could use a similar setup to handle Universal Links.

Whenever our application is expected to open a Universal Link, the `application(_:open:options:)` method is called on the `AppDelegate`. This method receives the URL it's expected to open. If we're not able to open the URL for whatever reason, this method is expected to return `false`. If this method does manage to handle the URL, it's expected to return `true`.

Any application that handles Universal Links is expected to have the **Associated Domains** capability set up. To do this, go to the **Capabilities** tab in your project settings and enable **Associated Domains**. For every domain that you want to handle Universal Links for, you need to create a new `applinks:` entry. The following screenshot shows an example implementation:

We've already established that our application receives a URL and that we're supposed to handle opening it. In other words, we need to map the URL we receive to a view in our application and take the user to that specific view. This process is called routing and it's a well-known technique throughout programming languages and platforms.

Let's assume that our application received the following URL:

```
https://www.familymoviesapp.com/familymember/dylan/
```

Just by looking at this URL you probably have a vague idea of what should happen if an application is asked to open this URL. We should be taken to a family member screen that shows the detail page for Dylan.

Whenever we're passed a URL like this in `AppDelegate`, there are three properties of the URL that we can distinguish. One is the `scheme`; this property tells us which URL scheme, for example, `https://`, was used to navigate to the app. Usually the scheme isn't very relevant to your app unless you're handling multiple custom URL schemes. Second, there is the host, for example `example.com`. This property describes the domain that belongs to the URL. Again, this is usually not relevant unless your app handles links from multiple hosts. Finally, there is the `pathComponents` property. The `pathComponents` is an array of components that are found in the path for the URL. Printing the `pathComponents` for the example URL gives the following output:

```
["/", "familymember", "dylan"]
```

The first component can be ignored, usually because it's just a `/`. The second and third components are a lot more interesting. They tell you more about the route that we need to resolve. Going back to the `familymovies` example, we could handle URLs in that app easily with the methods present in `AppDelegate`. Let's see how:

```
func application(_ app: UIApplication, open URL: URL, options:
  [UIApplicationOpenURLOptionsKey : Any] = [:]) -> Bool {
    let pathComponents = URL.pathComponents
    guard pathComponents.count == 3
        else { return false }

    switch(pathComponents[1], pathComponents[2]) {
    case ("familymember", let name):
        return handleOpenFamilyMemberDetail(withName: name)
    case ("movie", let name):
        return handleOpenMovieDetail(withName: name)
    default:
        return false
    }
}
```

We're using a switch with powerful pattern matching to check whether the second component in the URL points to a family member or a movie and we parse the third component into a variable called `name`. If one of these matches, we call the existing methods; if nothing matches, we return `false` to indicate the fact that we couldn't open the URL.

Earlier, you saw this URL: `https://www.donnysrecipes.com/search/?q=macaroni`. With `pathComponents` you can easily gain access to the search portion of the URL. But how do you get the final part of the URL? Well, that's a little harder. We can get the query property for a URL, but then we get a single string in the form of `q=macaroni`. What we really want is a dictionary with `q` as a key and `macaroni` as a value. The following extension on `URL` implements a `naive` method to make this happen:

```
extension URL {
    var queryDict: [String: String]? {
        guard let pairs = query?.components(separatedBy: "&")
            else { return nil }

        var dict = [String: String]()

        for pair in pairs {
            let components = pair.components(separatedBy: "=")
            dict[components[0]] = components[1]
        }

        return dict
    }
}
```

First, we obtain the query string. Then we separate the string by the `&` character because multiple key value pairs in the query string are expected to be separated with that character. We loop over the resulting array and we separate each string on the `=` character. The first item in the resulting array is expected to be the key and the second is the value. We add each key and value to a dictionary and finally that dictionary is returned. This enables us to get the value for `q` shown as follows:

```
URL.queryDict!["q"]
```

Great job! This is all that's needed to implement Universal Links in your app and to enhance discover ability for your users.

Summary

This chapter focused on getting your app indexed with the powerful `CoreSpotlight` framework. You saw how you can use user activities to index items that the user has already seen and how you can use searchable items to index content that the user might not have seen. You also learned how to make use of unique identifiers to ensure that you don't end up with duplicate entries in the search index. We also took a look at continuing user activities from either a user activity or a searchable item.

After you knew everything about how `CoreSpotlight` can index your items, you learned about Universal Links and web content. It's important to think about publishing content on the web because it helps your Spotlight indexing tremendously and it enables Apple to show your Spotlight results in Safari. We also covered the metadata that you should add to your web pages and Smart App Banners.

In the next chapter, we'll make our app visible in one more place on the user's device by creating a widget for the notification center.

17

Instant Information with a Notification Center Widget

When Apple added the Notification Center to iOS in iOS 6, they also added some stock widgets to a section called the **Today View**. These widgets had limited functionality and, as developers, we had no ability to add our own widgets to this view. Users were stuck with a weather widget, one for stocks, one for the calendar, and a few more.

It wasn't until iOS 8 that Apple decided that developers should be able to create extensions for the Notification Center in the form of widgets. Together with that addition, Apple has added the ability for developers to create several extensions that integrate apps with iOS. This chapter will focus mainly on creating a **Today Extension:** A widget.

You'll learn what the life cycle of an extension looks like and how extensions integrate with the OS and your app. The basis for this extension will be a small, simple app that has content that varies throughout the day.

We will cover the following topics in this chapter:

- Understanding the anatomy of a Today Extension
- Adding a Today Extension to your app

Even though we only have two bullet points to cover, there will be plenty of information for you to take in. Let's dive right in.

Understanding the anatomy of a Today Extension

The terms **Today Extension** and widget can be used interchangeably; they both refer to a component that is present in iOS's Notification Center. In this chapter, we'll mostly stick to the term widget, unless we're talking more broadly in the context of extensions.

If you swipe down from the top of the screen to open Spotlight and swipe right after that, you're presented with the Today View. On the simulator, this view tends to look rather empty, but on your device, there's probably a lot more going on. The following screenshot shows the Today View on the simulator with a couple of widgets added to it:

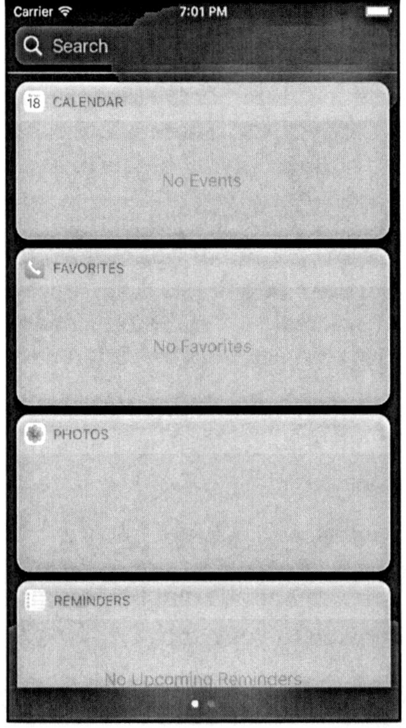

Users can scroll to the bottom of this view and manage their widgets from there. They can add new widgets and remove existing ones. All these widgets have one thing in common: They provide relevant information for the current moment or day. For the **CALENDAR**, this means showing events that are planned for today or tomorrow. The **FAVORITES** widget in the screenshot usually shows contacts that the user interacts with often.

Any widget that you add to your app should aim to provide your users with relevant, easy-to-scan information. Doing this makes your widget more useful and more likely to be added to a user's Today View.

How do these widgets work though? And how do they relate to their corresponding apps since a widget cannot exist without a host application? To answer these questions, we'll have a broad look at extensions in general. Once you understand app extension fundamentals, we'll move on to specifics about widgets.

Understanding app extensions

Ever since iOS 8, developers have acquired more and more opportunities to add extensions to their applications. In iOS 11, there are 24(!) different ways for you to integrate with iOS. Not every app can or should integrate on all 24 extension points, but it's good to be aware of the fact that there are many ways for your app to stand out from the crowd and blend in with iOS:

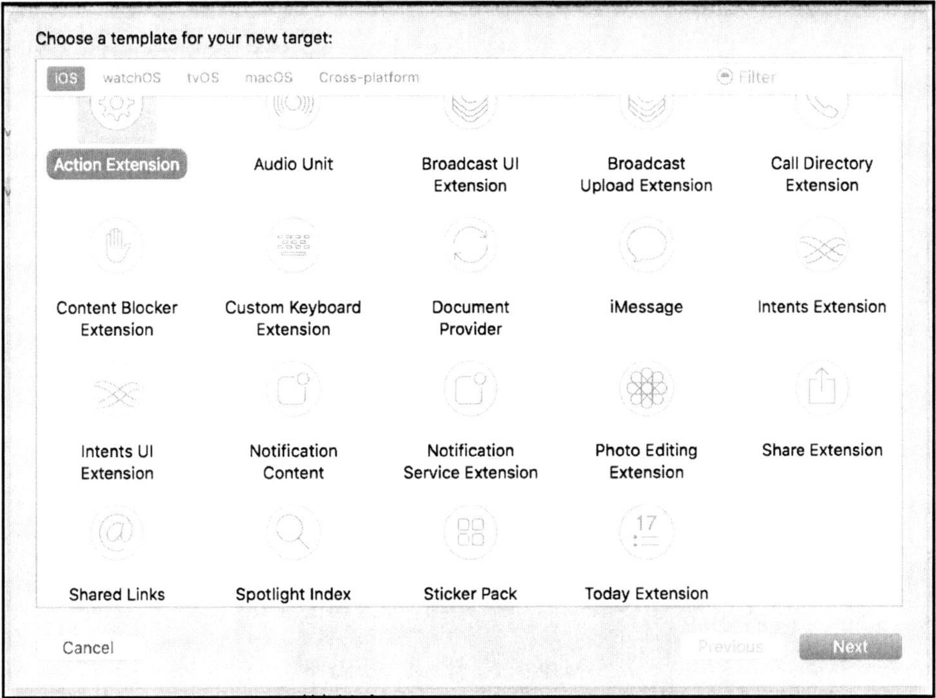

The preceding screenshot captures several names for the 24 extensions that you can integrate into your apps. You'll notice that there's a **Spotlight index** extension. If you're indexing your app in Spotlight and you want to make sure that Spotlight can re-index items even if your app isn't running, this extension is definitely worth checking out and shouldn't be too hard to implement, since its behavior is similar to the indexing delegate you've already seen in the previous chapter.

The extension you're going to implement in this chapter is the **Today Extension**. If you examine the list of extensions closely, you'll notice that all the extensions are very different from one another. Some extensions have a lot of UI associated with them, like the **Today Extension**. Others involve a lot less UI, like the **Share Extension** or the **Shared Links**. Other extensions don't involve any UI at all, such as the **Spotlight index** extension.

Whenever an extension is opened or instantiated, this is done through the extension framework itself. For instance, when you open a photo in the *Photos* app and you tap the share option, there will be a couple of apps on the list that you can share the photo to. If you select one of these apps, you'll be presented with an UI, that allows you to pick a contact you want to share this with. Alternatively, you can write a status update or whatever else the target extension supports:

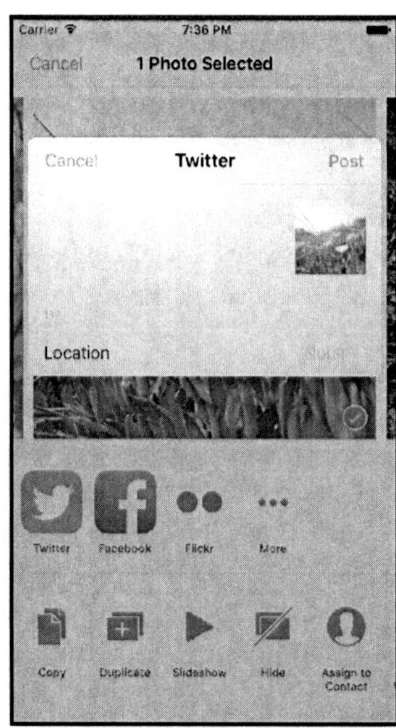

When the extension's UI appears, the host application does not directly create an instance of this UI. Its actually the extension framework that takes care of this. At the same time, the extension is not inherently related to your application. So, when the *Photos* app asks the **Share Extensions** framework for a certain **Share Extension**, the associated application could potentially not be running at all. In other words, extensions function completely independently of their corresponding apps.

Even though extensions run separately from apps, they aren't apps themselves. Most extensions you create are essentially view controllers that are added in the context of a different app. For instance, this means that extensions don't have access to an `AppDelegate`, not even the `AppDelegate` of their app counterparts. All of your initialization code and any life cycle implementation details you wish to integrate will have to be performed based on `UIViewController` life cycle methods.

At first, it may seem counterintuitive because you're used to creating an app that has its own lifetime and life cycle, and in that app, you add view controllers. As a sort of central hub or beating heart of the application, there's your trusty `AppDelegate`. Neither of these things is true in the case of extensions. A different app will load your app extension's view controller and it will add it to its own view hierarchy. So, an app extension isn't just a plain view controller because it has its own build target and even its own `Info.plist` file, but it's also not a full-blown app because it's always instantiated in the context of another app.

What this means exactly will become more clear in a moment when we discuss **Today Extensions**. The most important takeaway for you at this moment is that app extensions are neither a plain view controller nor an application; they're something in between.

Understanding Today Extensions

A **Today Extension** is an extension that adheres to all the rules mentioned before. Most importantly, a **Today Extension** isn't much more than a view controller that is embedded inside the notification center's Today View.

This means that, whenever your **Today Extension** is initialized, there is no `AppDelegate` involved at all. The extension does not have any application life cycle methods such as `application(_:didFinishLaunchingWithOptions:)`. The contents of your widget are added to the Today View through a technique called view controller containment. The concept of view controller containment means that view controllers are embedded in other view controllers. This technique isn't limited to the Today View; you can also use it in your own applications, and its a great way to compose a complex view hierarchy.

If you're using `viewcontroller` containment, the parent view controller notifies its child view controllers of certain important events. For example, the parent will tell the child when the viewport or trait collection changes.

Because the Today View renders and contains your widget, you can't set the frame for the widget's view yourself. Chances are you're already used to this. Normally, when you're putting a view controller onscreen inside a navigation controller, tab bar, or simply as the only view controller in a single-view application, you generally don't set the frame for a view controller's view.

However, **Today Extension**s are somewhat different from an ordinary view controller. Usually, when you present a view controller, you want it to fill all the available space. And usually the available space is just about the entire viewport. **Today Extension**s are a bit more complex because they don't tend to take up an entire screen. They don't take up a set amount of space, and some widgets in the Today View even grow and shrink.

Before iOS 10, a widget would resize itself based on its contents or the size that the widget would set as its `preferredContentSize`. Since iOS 10, this behavior has changed and widgets have a user-defined compact mode and an expanded mode. The compact mode should normally be about 110 points in height, but in reality this height varies based on the user's text-size preferences.

Because there are no real guarantees regarding the height your widget has available, it's important that you only show the most important information in your widget and it's a good idea to adopt dynamic type in your widget. This makes your widget more accessible by scaling the text inside your widget based on the user's preferences. You'll learn how to do this once we get to implement the widget.

If your widget supports it, your user can switch to the expanded state for your widget. In this state, you have a bit more freedom to set the size of the widget yourself. We'll explore supporting this a bit more when we implement our own widget.

One more key principle of **Today Extension**s is that the widget never communicates with its host app directly. If you have a widget that the user can tap to go into a detail view, the widget doesn't directly instruct the app to do this. Instead, URLs are used. You can use a custom URL scheme or a Universal Link to achieve this. In several snippets of example code, Apple uses custom URL schemes to achieve this effect. The app we're going to extend in this chapter will work in a similar fashion.

Now that you're completely up-to speed about app extensions, and **Today Extensions** in particular, it's time to introduce you to the app we're going to extend in this chapter: *The Daily Quote*. The name of the app probably gives away the entire concept. It's an app that randomly displays a new quote to the user every day. Because this application has new content every day, it's a great candidate for a **Today Extension**. Let's dive right in.

Adding a Today Extension to your app

In this book's code bundle, you can find an app named *The Daily Quote*. If you want to follow along with this section of the chapter, its a great idea to go ahead and check out the starter code for this app. If you look at **Main.storyboard** and the `ViewController.swift` file, you'll find that there isn't too much going on there. The interface just contains two labels, and the `ViewController` grabs a `Quote` and displays it.

Even though it doesn't look like much, each file contains something cool. If you select one of the labels in the **Storyboard** and examine its attributes, you'll find that the font for the quote itself is actually **Title 1** and the font for the quote created is **Caption 1**. This is different from the default system font that we normally use. Selecting one of the predefined styles enables the text in our app to dynamically adjust to the user's preferences. This is great from an accessibility standpoint and it costs us very little effort.

If your interface allows it, its recommended that you make use of accessible type, simply because it will make your app easier to use for all your users.

If you look at the `ViewController` class, there are only a couple of lines involved in displaying the quote. This code is simple and concise due to a great deal of preparation work that's been done in the `Quote` model file. Go ahead and open that file to see what's going on.

The `Quotes` struct is set up in such a way that it can be used as a very simple and basic database. The struct contains several static properties and methods to generate quotes based on a predetermined list of quotes. If you were to build this app and put it in the App Store, you'd probably want to download these quotes from a server somehow, because pushing an update every time you want to add or remove a couple of quotes is quite a lot of effort for a simple change. There are only a couple of constant instance properties present on the `Quote` struct:

```
let text: String
let creator: String
```

These properties are the ones that `ViewController` reads and displays to the user. Furthermore, `UserDefaults` is used to store which quote is shown for a given day. `UserDefaults` is a simple data store that holds on to app-related settings. It's essentially a lightweight persistence layer that you can use to store simple objects. For *The Daily Quote*, `UserDefaults` is used to store the date on which the current quote was set as well as the index in the list of `Quote` instances that points to the current quote:

```
static var current: Quote {
    if let lastQuoteDate = userDefaults.object(forKey: "lastQuoteDate") as?
Date {
        if NSCalendar.current.compare(Date(), to: lastQuoteDate,
toGranularity: .day) == .orderedDescending {
            setNewQuote()
        }
    } else {
        setNewQuote()
    }

    guard let quoteIndex = userDefaults.object(forKey: "quoteIndex") as?
Int,
        let quote = Quote.quote(atIndex: quoteIndex)
        else { fatalError("Could not create a quote..") }

    return quote
}

static func setNewQuote() {
    let quoteIndex = Quote.randomIndex
    let date = Date()

    userDefaults.set(date, forKey: "lastQuoteDate")
    userDefaults.set(quoteIndex, forKey: "quoteIndex")
}
```

The preceding snippet illustrates the process of retrieving and storing the current `quote`. First, the code checks if a `quote` has already been set before and if so, it makes sure that the `quote` is at least a day old before generating a new one. Next, the current `quoteIndex` is retrieved from the `UserDefaults` and returned as the current `quote`.

Setting and retrieving objects in `UserDefaults` is fairly straightforward. It's a simple key-value store that easily stores simple objects. We don't have to do anything special; we don't even have to manually save the `UserDefaults` like we would if this was Core Data. This makes `UserDefaults` a great candidate to store this type of non-sensitive, simple data.

Don't use `UserDefaults` to store privacy-sensitive data. It's not considered secure; the keychain should be used for this purpose. Also, make sure that you're not storing complex or repetitive data in `UserDefaults`. It's not a database, nor is it optimized for reading and writing a large number of times. Stick to simple, application-specific settings only.

The rest of the `Quotes` struct should speak for itself. To add a **Today Extension** to your app, open your project settings and make sure the sidebar button is enabled and you can see your **PROJECT** and **TARGETS**:

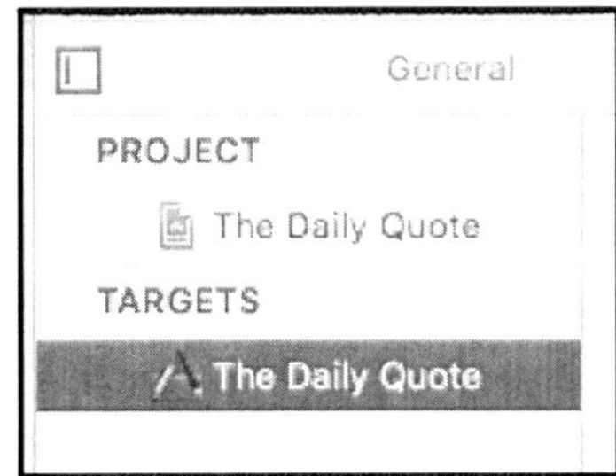

In the bottom-left corner of this sidebar, there's a plus button. If you click this, you can add additional targets to your app. You should see all the available iOS App Extensions; click on **Today Extension** and then click **Next**. Give your extension a name, for example, *The Daily Quote Widget*, and click **Finish**.

Xcode will ask you if you want to activate a scheme with the name of your widget. Click **Activate**. This enables you to build and run your extension. Next to the **Play** and **Stop** buttons in the top-right corner, you can now choose between the scheme for the app and the widget. Make sure to select the widget and then build and run your application:

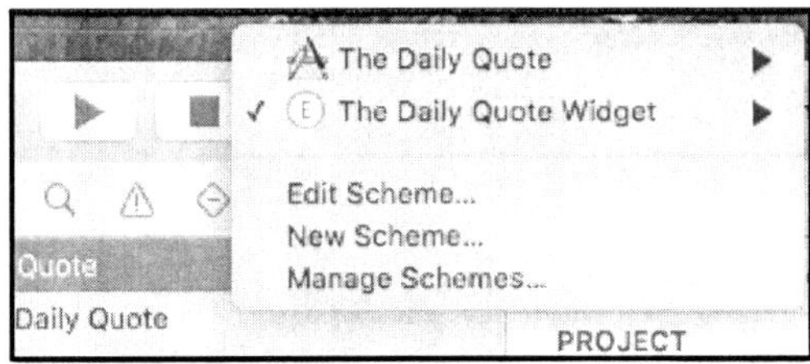

The first time you do this, your widget might not show up immediately. Don't worry if this is the case, just build and run again and your app should show up as a widget in the Today View.

Congratulations! You have just enabled your very first app extension. Let's see what kind of files and boilerplate code Xcode has added for us. In the **PROJECT** navigator, you'll find a new group. This group is named after your widget and it contains an `Info.plist` file, a view controller, and a Storyboard. This looks very similar to a fresh app project, except there is no assets folder and no launch screen. If you open the Storyboard in Interface Builder, you'll notice that there's a tiny view controller instead of one that looks like a device.

You can actually change the display size for the view controller if you like, but note that the display size for the widget was taller than the visible size in the storyboard. This is due to the standard compact widget height iOS 10 uses. We can't influence this, but we know that we're constrained for space, so it's good to make sure that your widget is flexible enough to look good at the compact size the Today View imposes on our widget.

To give our labels a little bit of breathing room, select the view controller (not the view itself) and click on the **Size** inspector. Here you'll see that the simulated size for the view controller is set to free-form and you can set a custom width and height. Leave the width as it is for now and set the height to *110*. This size should be the smallest size at which our widget displays and it gives us plenty of room to lay out our interface. Also, delete the default label that has been added to the interface automatically.

Drag a `UILabel` into the view and set its font to **Headline**. Click the **Font** icon in the **Attributes** inspector to change the font and select the **Font** drop-down to find the dynamic text styles. Position the label in the top-left corner using the blue helper lines and then add the following constraints to the label:

- Leading space to superview margin
- Top space to vertical layout guide
- Trailing space to superview margin

Finally, set the number of lines to 3 so the quote doesn't take up more than three lines. Now, drag out another label and position it right below the first label. Set its font style to **Caption 1**. Also, add the following constraints to this view:

- Leading space to superview margin
- Vertical spacing between this label and the label above it

Go ahead and run your extension again. Your layout should look similar to the one shown in the following screenshot:

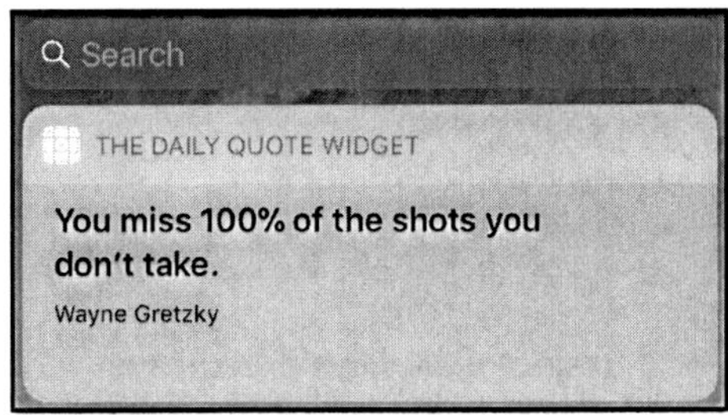

OK, great! You have customized the layout for your first extension. Let's add some outlets to the widget view controller so we can display the quotes to our users:

```
@IBOutlet var quoteLabel: UILabel!
@IBOutlet var quoteCreator: UILabel!
```

Open the widget's Storyboard file and connect the outlets as you've done before. Select the view controller, go to the Outlet Inspector, and drag from the Outlet Inspector to the corresponding views to connect the outlets to the view.

The next step to built this widget is to display the `quotes` to our users. This is a problem, though, because the app itself is already grabbing and storing the `quote` for the day and we've already established that extensions do not communicate directly with their host apps.

For us, this means that we're stuck right now. We can't ask the app for a `quote` to display. We did store the `quoteIndex` in `UserDefaults`, but unfortunately the app and the extension don't share this store. We could settle for different quotes in each and just have the widget set and display its own quote. This isn't ideal, but if this is the best we can get we should live with it, right? Update the following code in the `TodayViewController` file:

```
override func viewDidLoad() {
    super.viewDidLoad()

    updateWidget()
}

func updateWidget() {
    let quote = Quote.current
    quoteLabel.text = quote.text
    quoteCreator.text = quote.creator
}
```

If you try to build and run your project now, you'll be presented with the following error:

```
Use of unresolved identifier `Quote`
```

This is bad. Our extension and app don't share anything. They don't share code, they don't share data, and they can't communicate with each other. However, if you look at some of Apple's stock widgets, there seems to be some data sharing going on. And you can imagine that copying the `Quote` struct into your widget's code isn't maintainable for any serious application.

Luckily, there is a solution available. If you select the `Quotes.swift` file and look at the file inspector on the right-hand side of the window, you'll see a small header called `Target Membership`. Below this header, you can see your app target and your extension target. If you check the checkbox next to your extension target, your app is suddenly able to build and run. Awesome! Refer to the following screenshot:

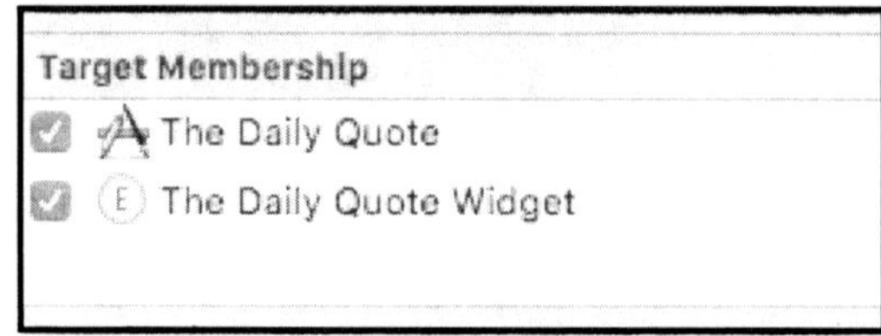

To avoid confusion down the line, it's probably a good idea to create a new group at the root of the project, call it shared, and move `Quotes.swift` into this group. This should make it clear to you and any future developer that `Quotes.swift` is used in both targets.

Before we move on, there is just one more addition we need to make to the widget. Currently, we update the widget only when its view loads. The boilerplate code Xcode generated for us shows a method named `widgetPerformUpdate(completionHandler:)`. We should use this method to update our widget, if needed, and then inform the callback about the result of the update action. Add the following implementation for this method:

```
func widgetPerformUpdate(completionHandler: @escaping (NCUpdateResult) ->
Void) {
    let currentText = quoteLabel.text
    updateWidget()
    let newText = quoteLabel.text

    if currentText == newText {
        completionHandler(NCUpdateResult.noData)
    } else {
        completionHandler(NCUpdateResult.newData)
    }
}
```

This method updates the widget by calling `updateWidget()`, just like `viewDidLoad` does. Before doing this, we grab the current text for the quote. After doing that, we grab the new text for the quote. Based on the comparison of these two strings, we inform the callback about the result of the update request.

This wraps up our widget implementation for now. Let's explore the several ways users can discover and use your widget in iOS 10. So far, we've seen the Today View that Xcode automatically sends us to, but there are more ways for people to interact with your widget.

Discovering your widget

In iOS, there are several places where people can see and use your widget. Most places where your widget is displayed look similar. They're basically all the same Today View, except they have minor modifications. The first place where your widget is shown is on the lock screen. If a user swipes right on the lock screen, they are presented with their widgets. Secondly, a user can swipe down from the top of the screen to see the Notification Center. Swiping right on this screen will present the same Today View that's presented on the lock screen. Finally, the Today View is available if the user swipes to the leftmost screen on their home screen.

There are quite a lot of places where users can discover and view your widget, but possibly the most interesting use case for your app is that users have been able to view the widget directly on the home screen ever since iOS 10. All they need to do is force-touch on your app's icon and the widget will pop right up:

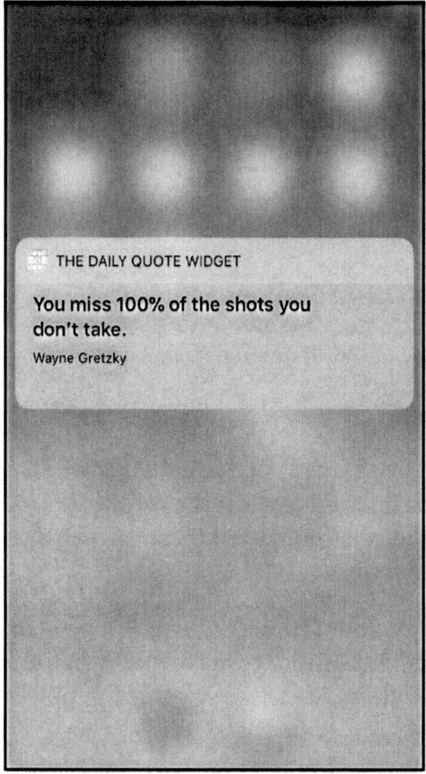

The project runs fine, and we can find our widget in several parts of iOS, but doesn't it feel a bit silly to show a different quote for each of our targets? Other apps seem to be able to synchronize data in the extension and app just fine and it's safe to assume that they don't use some kind of web API to retrieve information.

If you were expecting a solution to this problem by now, you are absolutely correct to do so. We can fix this. We can share data between our application and our extension using a feature called *App Groups*.

Sharing data with App Groups

When you're developing an application or extension that's part of a suite of apps, extensions, or a combination of both, you're probably going to want to share some code and data. You already saw how to share code by including a file in multiple targets. This doesn't immediately allow for data sharing, though.

To share data between apps, you make use of **App Groups**. An **App Group** is a group of applications that have the **App Groups** entitlement enabled in their capabilities. More importantly, the applications in an **App Group** must specify that they want to share information with a certain group.

An **App Group** is specified as a unique string. Every app or extension that is part of an **App Group** must have this same unique string added to the list of groups the target belongs to. A single target can be part of several **App Groups**. To enable **App Groups**, select your target and go to its Capabilities tab. Next, enable the **App Groups** capability and specify a unique identifier for your group.

Let's do this for the *The Daily Quote* and its **Today Extension** right away. Refer to the following screenshot to make sure that you've enabled the capability correctly. Don't forget to repeat the steps for both the app and the extension. Every target that should be part of an **App Group** should specify this separately:

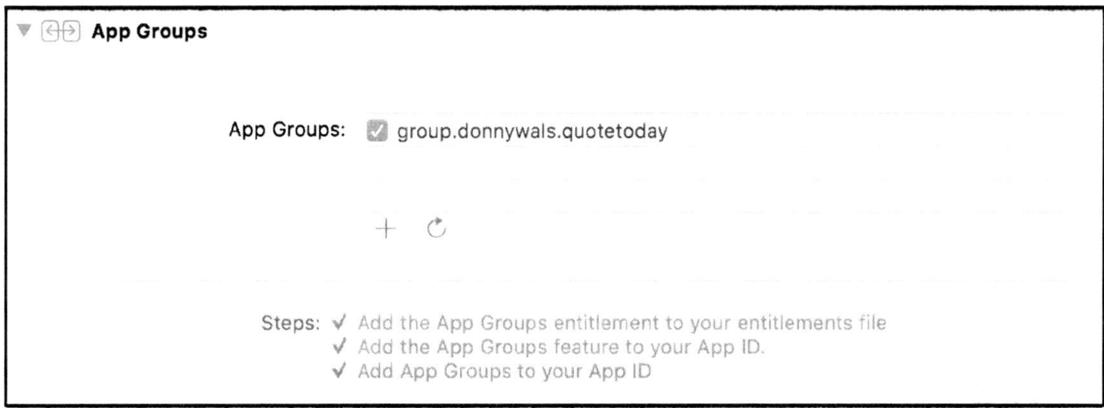

Now that the **App Groups** is enabled, we have gained several capabilities. First and foremost, we've gained the ability to share `UserDefaults` between our app and our extension. You'll see how to do this soon.

Another powerful feature we've gained is the ability to read and write data to a shared folder. This means that we could share an entire Core Data database between multiple targets through **App Groups**. Doing this comes with a couple of risks that we won't go into too much.

The most important takeaway is that you should always make sure that you use appropriate locking mechanisms if you're reading or writing data from a shared container. Even though it's unlikely, it's possible that two apps read or write data from the same file at the same time. This could cause data corruption and Apple has made it the responsibility of the developers themselves to ensure that you perform your read and write operations safely and responsibly.

Let's get back to *The Daily Quote*. This app uses `UserDefaults` to store the date on which the most recent `quote` was created and it's also responsible for picking and storing a new `quote`. In the current setup, the app and the widget both use their own `UserDefaults` instance. We just saw that it's possible to improve on this with **App Group**s. Doing this is probably a lot simpler than you would expect. This line of code is what we currently use to obtain an instance of `UserDefaults`:

```
private static var userDefaults = UserDefaults.standard
```

To use our shared `UserDefaults` instead of the standard one we only need to update that single line of code by creating our own instance of `UserDefaults` and initializing it with a `suiteName` parameter:

```
private static var userDefaults = UserDefaults(suiteName:
"group.donnywals.quotetoday")!
```

Because the initializer for `UserDefaults` can fail, it returns an optional instance. This would happen if we were to try to initialize the `UserDefaults` with a group that we don't have access to. In this example, we're pretty sure that we have set everything up correctly so the instance is for unwrapped. Note that this is not always the best idea, and you might want to stick with the optional instance in your application instead.

Running the app and widget now will result in your widget and app always using the exact same `quote`. The reason they use the same `quote` is that they now use a shared `UserDefaults` store, and because they already share the `Quote` struct, we only had to make sure that this struct uses the shared store instead of the target-specific store. Now that our app and widget share their `UserDefaults`, we have successfully implemented out **Today Extension** and widget.

Summary

This chapter was all about app extensions, and more specifically **Today Extension**. We started by exploring the basic anatomy of an extension in iOS. You learned that extensions are mostly view controllers that live separately from your main application. You learned how you can add an extension target to your project and how to run it in the Simulator. After getting the extension up-and-running, you learned how to share pieces of code and functionality between your application and the extension by adding a file to both targets.

This left the app and widget in a state where they were unable to share data. We implemented data sharing by enabling **App Group**s so that our app and its extension use a shared `UserDefaults` store. With this powerful tool and knowledge under your belt, we're going to delve even more deeply into the iOS Notification Center. We're going to implement the new notification features that iOS 10 implements through Notification Extensions.

18
Implementing Rich Notifications

The previous chapter introduced you to App Extensions. You learned that App Extensions enables you to tightly integrate your app with iOS. In iOS 10, Apple added extension possibilities for notifications while also completely revamping how notifications work. In this chapter, we're going to explore how notifications work and how you can implement extensions that will have a tremendous positive impact on the user experience of receiving notifications.

First, we will look at notifications from a broad perspective and how they manifest throughout iOS. Even though we won't go into a lot of detail straight away, you'll gain a deep understanding of notifications by looking at the different types of notification and the different ways of scheduling notifications that are available. Next, we'll have a detailed look at how your app can schedule and handle notifications. Finally, we'll look at the extension points that have been added by Apple in order to implement richer and more engaging notifications.

By the end of this chapter you'll know everything there is to know about notifications and how they can be used to create a unique, engaging user experience. People receive lots of notifications throughout the day, so providing a great experience that stands out will ensure that people don't get annoyed with your notifications to the point of wanting to disable them entirely.

This chapter is divided into the following topics:

- Gaining a deep understanding of notifications
- Scheduling and handling notifications
- Implementing notification extensions

Ready? Let's take dive head-first into notifications.

Gaining a deep understanding of notifications

Since you're planning to become a master at iOS development, you've probably used an iPhone or iPad more than a couple of times. It's also very likely that you've had applications sending you notifications while you were using the device, or maybe while the device was sitting idle on your desk, in your pocket, or somewhere else.

Notifications are a perfect way to inform users about information in your app that is of interest to them. New messages in a messaging app, breaking news events, or friend requests in social apps are just a few examples of great scenarios for notifications. From the get-go, it's important that you're aware of the fact that a lot of apps are fighting for the user's attention at all times. Notifications are a great way to gain the user's attention, but if you send too many notifications, or only use notifications as a marketing tool instead of a way to provide meaningful information, it's very likely that the user is going to disable push notifications for your app.

There are four forms of notification that you can send to your users:

- Sounds
- Vibrations
- Visual notifications (banner, alert)
- Badges

Most apps use a combination of these, and we'll go into these in depth using a real-world scenario soon. To send notifications to your users, there are two mechanisms available:

Local notifications and push notifications. Local notifications are scheduled inside your app and kept on the device. To trigger these notifications, you use either a location, calendar, or time-based trigger.

Push notifications are pushed to a device through a server and the **Apple Push Notification Service** (**APNS**). Push notifications are always delivered by APNS using best-effort delivery. This means that a notification will be sent to the user and if this fails, APNS may or may not try again. There are no guarantees made about this, so you should never assume that your notification did or did not end up on the user's device.

Push notifications can send either a user-facing notification or a silent notification. A user-facing notification will actively notify the user about what happened, often in the shape of a banner or badge icon. A silent notification signals the app that it should be woken up to perform a background fetch. This is a great way to complement the background fetch features you read about in `Chapter 11`, *Being Proactive with Background Fetch*.

Prior to iOS 10, local and push notifications were hardly related to each other. You had to do a lot of duplicate work and it simply wasn't straightforward to work with notifications. When iOS 10 came along, the UserNotifications framework was introduced. This framework unified the registration, delegation, and handling of notifications. An added benefit of this approach is that the framework doesn't just work with iOS, but also with watchOS and tvOS. Not all platforms support the same functionality, so if you plan to add notifications to a watch or TV app you should make sure that everything will function as you expect.

In order to complement the notifications you send to your user, you can implement Notification Extensions. These extensions add a whole new dimension to notifications, especially for devices that support 3D Touch. There are two types of extension we can add: Service Extensions and Content Extensions. Service Extensions enable you to modify or augment the contents of a notification before its displayed to the user. Content Extensions enable you to display a custom interface when the user 3D Touches a notification.

More on these extensions later. Now that you have a basic understanding of notifications and how they work in iOS, let's start with the basics of implementing notifications: Scheduling and handling them.

Scheduling and handling notifications

Every notification you see on iOS has been scheduled or pushed to the user in one way or an other. But before an app is even allowed to send notifications, we actually have to go through a few steps. The steps you need to follow can be roughly divided as follows:

1. Registering for notifications.
2. Creating notification contents.
3. Scheduling your notification.
4. Handling incoming notifications.

Not every step is identical for push and local notifications, so whenever relevant, the difference will be described. Because of the UserNotifications framework, these differences will be minimal, but they're there. We'll expand the quotes app from the previous chapter with a daily notification as a way to showcase and test notifications.

Registering for notifications

The first step you must go through if you're planning on showing notifications to your user is asking permission to do so. We call this registering for notifications. It's important that you make sure your user understands why they're being prompted for this permission. After all, you're interrupting your user while they're trying to achieve something in your app and the permission alert prevents them from doing so. It's often a great idea to hold off on asking permission for notifications until the user does something that can be improved if they turn on notifications.

When you ask permission for notifications, you have the option to specify the kinds of notification that you want to send the user. You can pick the following types:

- Alerts
- Badges
- Car Play
- Sounds

The user can go into your app's page in the *Settings* app at any time to change these settings themselves. With the UserNotifications framework, you can read these settings, use them to inform your users about the current notification status, and ask them to turn notifications on if needed.

In `The Daily Quote`, we're going to add a small piece of UI that informs the user about the benefits of enabling notifications for this app. We'll display a button below the text that the user can tap in order to make the notification permissions dialog appear. This strategy is common in many apps because we only ask permission to send notifications if the user is likely to say yes. They initiated the prompt voluntarily after all.

If the user has denied notifications or disabled them at a later stage, we'll still inform the user about the benefits of notifications, but the button below the text will link to the app's settings instead of opening the initial prompt.

Add the following outlets and action to `ViewController.swift`:

```
@IBOutlet var notificationSugestionLabel: UILabel!
@IBOutlet var enableNotificationsButton: UIButton!

@IBAction func enableNotificationsTapped() {
}
```

Also, add a button and a label in the app's **Main.storyboard**. The button should stick to the bottom margin of the screen and the label is added above. Make sure you center everything and use the blue lines in Interface Builder to help you position the views. Refer to the following screenshot to make sure that you've set up the layout correctly:

Enable notifications to receive a daily notification containing the latest quote

Enable notifications

Don't forget to connect the outlets and actions to the interface in your Storyboard by dragging from the Outlets inspector for `ViewController` to the UI elements. Touch Up inside should be used as the trigger for the button-tap action.

Reading the current notification settings and asking permission to send notifications is always done through an `UNNotificationCenter` instance. We can obtain such an instance through the static `current()` method on `UNNotificationCenter`.

`UNNotificationCenter` is not to be confused with `NotificationCenter`. `UNNotificationCenter` is responsible for user notifications, while `NotificationCenter` is used to send notifications internally inside your app: The user never sees or notices these notifications.

Since we'll be using the `UNNotificationCenter` in more than one place, add the following property to `ViewController.swift`:

```
let notificationCenter = UNUserNotificationCenter.current()
```

Every time the view appears, we'll want to update the user interface to reflect the current state of notification permissions. We can override the `viewWillAppear` method to make this happen. Add the following implementation:

```
override func viewWillAppear(_ animated: Bool) {
    super.viewWillAppear(animated)
    notificationCenter.getNotificationSettings {[weak self] settings in
        let authorizationStatus = settings.authorizationStatus
        switch(authorizationStatus) {
        case .authorized:
            self?.hideNotificationsUI()
        case .denied:
            self?.showNotificationsUI()
        default: return
```

```
            }
        }
    }

    func hideNotificationsUI() {
        DispatchQueue.main.async { [weak self] in
            self?.notificationSugestionLabel.isHidden = true
            self?.enableNotificationsButton.isHidden = true
        }
    }

    func showNotificationsUI() {
        DispatchQueue.main.async { [weak self] in
            self?.notificationSugestionLabel.isHidden = false
            self?.enableNotificationsButton.isHidden = false
        }
    }
```

This code retrieves the current notification settings from the `notificationCenter` and reads these settings in order to determine the current authorization status. Once the current status has been determined, we can figure out whether we should `show` or `hide` the notifications UI. Because the `show` and `hide` methods are called from a handler that's not necessarily executed on the main thread, we manually dispatch all UI-related code on the main thread.

There are a total of three possible authorization statuses: `authorized`, `denied`, and `notDetermined`. Here is a list for each status and what the status means:

- `notDetermined` means that we haven't asked for permissions before
- `authorized` means that we have asked for permissions and we're allowed to send notifications to the user
- `notAuthorized` means that we have asked for permissions and we're not allowed to send notifications to the user because they either declined the permissions prompt or they turned off notifications in their settings

We don't need to check for `notDetermined` in `viewWillAppear` because it's the default status and the notifications UI will always be visible if we're in this state.

Add the following implementation for the `enableNotificationsTapped` action:

```
    @IBAction func enableNotificationsTapped() {
        notificationCenter.getNotificationSettings { [weak self] settings in
            let authorizationStatus = settings.authorizationStatus
            switch(authorizationStatus) {
            case .notDetermined:
```

```
            self?.notificationCenter.requestAuthorization(options: [.alert,
.sound]) { [weak self] granted, error in
                guard error == nil, granted == true
                    else { return }
                self?.hideNotificationsUI()
            }
        case .denied:
            let settingsUrl = URL(string:
UIApplicationOpenSettingsURLString)
            UIApplication.shared.open(settingsUrl!, options: [:],
completionHandler: nil)
        default:
            return
        }
    }
}
```

If the notification status hasn't been determined before, permission will be asked. If the user grants permission for notifications, we hide the notifications interface. If the user taps the **Enable** button and the current status is denied, we open the *Settings* app on the section for our app so the user can enable notifications.

If we want to register for push notifications, this capability must be enabled in the app's Capabilities tab. Note that this feature is available only if you're on the paid developer program. Free developer accounts cannot enable this capability.

After enabling the push notifications capability, we need to add a couple of lines of code to make sure that we properly register the current device with APNS. To do this, we call a method on `UIApplication` that will register the device on APNS. Then a delegate method in `AppDelegate` is called with the current device token that we should upload to our server so we can send messages to the device through the `device token`.

Because the token could change at any time, you should always register for remote notifications whenever the app launches. For our app, we should register both in `viewWillAppear` and `enableNotificationsTapped`, right after we hide the notifications UI. Add the following line right after both `hideNotificationsUI` calls in `ViewController`:

```
UIApplication.shared.registerForRemoteNotifications()
```

In `AppDelegate`, add the following method:

```
func application(_ application: UIApplication,
didRegisterForRemoteNotificationsWithDeviceToken deviceToken: Data) {
    print("received device token: \(deviceToken.hexString)")
}
```

If you want to support push notifications, you should upload the `device token` to your server instead of printing to the console. You're all set to send notifications to your user now. Let's look at creating content for our notifications.

Creating notification contents

Notifications typically consist of a few pieces of content. First of all, every notification has a title, a subtitle, and a message body. Not all fields have to be present, but you'll often want to provide a little bit more information than just a bit of body text. You can also add media attachments to notifications. These attachments provide a preview of a photo, video, or audio file that is stored locally on the device, and are great for providing better-looking, richer notifications to your user.

Creating content for notifications is where the biggest gap between push and local notifications is present. Push notifications are always created on the server and are pushed to the device in the JSON format, while local notifications are created on the device. Let's look at each notification type separately.

Creating push notifications

If you ignore the complexities of setting up and hosting your own server, push notifications are actually pretty simple to create. Push notifications are always delivered using a JSON payload that your own server sends to APNS. APNS will then take care of sending your notification through to the device that's intended to receive the notification. Let's look at a simple example of a JSON payload that could be used to inform users about a new quote in `The Daily Quote`:

```
{
    "aps" : {
        "alert" : {
            "title" : "A new quote is available",
            "body" : "Stay hungry, stay foolish"
        },
        "badge" : 1
    },
    "quote_id" : "10"
}
```

This notification only contains a title and a body. We also add the number 1 to the app icon to indicate the number of quotes available. You'll notice that this content is inside the `aps` dictionary. This `aps` dictionary contains the push notification's content. The `quote_id` is not part of this content on purpose; it's a custom property that can be read in the app so we can find data for this quote from a local database or fetch it from a backend using the ID.

If you want to send a silent push notification to trigger a background data refresh action, you should add the `content-available` key to the `aps` dictionary with a value of `1`. If you want to use a custom sound for your notification, you can add a `sound` key to `aps`. The value of this key should point to an audio file that's embedded in your app. Finally, a notification can be part of a category of notifications. If this is the case, add a `category` key to the `aps` dictionary where the value is the category identifier. We'll go in-depth on categories later.

Creating local notifications

Local notifications are created and stored locally on the device. They are very similar to push notifications in terms of the contents they can contain. The way these contents are set up is slightly different though, because we can't schedule notifications locally for content that is not available yet.

In the context of `The Daily Quote`, this means that a server could push a quote to the application every 24 hours. If we create the notification locally, we don't know what tomorrow's quote should be, so we can't schedule a notification with content for this new quote yet. This is actually an important distinction between local and push notifications that you should keep in mind when choosing whether you should create a notification locally or if you should leave it up to a server to create the notification.

Let's have a look at how we would recreate a notification similar to the one we've created before in JSON. While you're looking at this method, you should add it to `ViewController.swift` in `The Daily Quote` so it can be used later when scheduling local notifications:

```
func createNotification() -> UNNotificationContent {
    let content = UNMutableNotificationContent()
    content.title = "New quote available"
    content.body = "A new quote is waiting for you in The Daily Quote"
    content.badge = 1
    return content
}
```

This code looks somewhat similar to the JSON we looked at earlier. The main difference is that we have to create an instance of `UNMutableNotificationContent` and assign values to it. A lot of the options we had for push notifications are present on this class as well. We can add custom properties such as the `quote_id` to the `userInfo` dictionary. We can assign a value to the `sound` property, or we can assign a notification category through the `categoryIdentifier` property. We can even add media attachments through the `attachments` property.

Now that you know how to create notification contents, let's see how you can schedule them.

Scheduling your notification

In order to deliver local notifications to your users, you'll need to schedule them somehow. Scheduling remote notifications is not needed; they are pushed through the server and delivered as soon as possible. When you schedule a local notification, you make use of a notification trigger. As discussed previously, there are multiple triggers for a local notification: Location-based, calendar-based, or timed.

We'll look at scheduling a very simple notification first. We'll schedule it to be timed so it fires in a couple of seconds. Then we'll look at repeating this notification with a time interval. Next, we're going to use a calendar to schedule a notification, and finally we'll look at location-based triggers.

Scheduling a timed notification

A timed notification is the simplest notification to schedule, which makes it a great candidate to explore first. Before we start, you should add the following method call after both calls to `hideNotificationsUI` in `ViewController.swift`:

```
self?.scheduleNotification()
```

This method will provide a nice spot to implement the scheduling of different notifications. Add the following implementation for this method to the `ViewController` class:

```
func scheduleNotification () {
    let trigger = UNTimeIntervalNotificationTrigger(timeInterval: 10,
repeats: false)
    let request = UNNotificationRequest(identifier: "new-quote", content:
createNotification(), trigger: trigger)
    notificationCenter.add(request, withCompletionHandler: nil)
}
```

First, a `trigger` is created for the notification. In this case, we're creating a notification that is set up to fire after a certain amount of time has passed, in this case `10` seconds, so we create an instance of `UNTimeIntervalNotificationTrigger`. Next, we create a notification request and pass it an `identifier`, the `trigger` we just created, and the content we want to display. Finally, we ask the notification center to add our notification request.

The `identifier` attribute for a notification should be unique for the content of your notification. The system uses this identifier to avoid sending multiple notifications with the same content. For our app, we wouldn't want the user to have multiple unread notifications, because the content will always be the same. If you do want to display multiple entries in the Notification Center you should make sure that every notification you schedule has a unique identifier.

If you want to send a repeating notification to a user, you must set the `repeats` property of the time interval trigger to `true`.

The minimum time interval for repeating notification is 60 seconds. Scheduling a repeating `trigger` with an interval under 60 seconds will crash your application.

Scheduling a calendar-based notification

Calendar-based notifications make use of `DateComponents()` to determine when they should be fired. The only difference with time-interval-based scheduling is in the `trigger` we use to determine when the notification should be displayed.

Let's dive right in and look at an example of how a calendar-based trigger can be set up:

```
var components = DateComponents()
components.day = 1
components.hour = 8

let trigger = UNCalendarNotificationTrigger(dateMatching: components,
repeats: false)
```

The preceding code sets up a `trigger` that fires on the first day of the month at 08:00 AM. If we want this notification to trigger every month, we just need to set the `repeats` property to `true`. Setting the notification as shown in the code will fire the notification the very next time it's 08:00 AM on the first day of a month. `Date()` components are very powerful because you could even use them to schedule a notification that fires next week on the current day. The following example shows how you would set up the `dateComponents` for this.

```
let cal = Calendar.current
var components = cal.dateComponents([.year, .weekOfYear, .day], from:
Date())
let scheduleWeek = components.weekOfYear! + 1
components.weekOfYear = scheduleWeek > 52 ? 1 : scheduleWeek
let trigger = UNCalendarNotificationTrigger(dateMatching: components,
repeats: false)
```

We fetch the user's current calendar and use it to extract the year, day, and the week of the year from the current date. Then we increment the week of the year by `1` and that's all we have to do. A ternary operator is used to do a quick check to make sure that we don't schedule notifications in a non-existing week.

Calendar-based notifications provide a powerful way for you to schedule both recurring and one-time-only notifications that are tied to being fired at a certain offset in time that's easier to express in days, hours, weeks, or months than it in a time interval.

The `The Daily Quote` app is a great candidate for calendar-based notifications. Try to implement a notification that fires every day at 08:00 AM so your users have a fresh quote to read every morning.

Scheduling a location-based notification

The last type of notification you're allowed to schedule is a location-based notification. To set up a location-based `trigger`, you'll need to make use of `CoreLocation` to set up a region to which the `trigger` applies. So, if you're following along, don't forget to import `CoreLocation` at the top of your file.

A location-based trigger is actually a lot like geo-fencing. The main difference is that, if a geo-fence triggers, the user is not necessarily informed about this. If a location-based notification triggers, its intent is to inform the user about it. Let's look at an example:

```
let coords = CLLocationCoordinate2D(latitude: 52.373095, longitude:
4.8909129)
let region = CLCircularRegion(center: coords, radius: 1000, identifier:
"quote-notification-region")
region.notifyOnExit = false
region.notifyOnEntry = true
let trigger = UNLocationNotificationTrigger(region: region, repeats: false)
```

This snippet sets up a location-based notification using a circular region with a radius of `1000` meters. The `notifyOnExit` and `notifyOnEntry` properties are used to specify whether we want to be notified when the user enters or exits the `region` or both.

Just like before, we have the option to choose whether we want this notification to repeat or if we just want to fire it once.

We've covered all the ways for you to schedule notifications. Let's explore the last piece of the notifications puzzle: Handling incoming notifications and notification actions.

Handling notifications

Once a user receives a notification, it's typically displayed on the lock screen and in the Notification Center. The user can see the contents of the notification and they can tap it. For a while now, Apple has been working to make notifications on iOS more useful and more interactive.

People can swipe on a notification to make special actions appear that enable them to take quick actions, such as accepting a calendar invite or quickly replying to a message. It wasn't until iOS 9 that Apple opened up the APIs so developers could implement these quick interactions in their own apps. In this section, we'll cover the following features of notification handling:

- Handling notifications in your app
- Managing pending and delivered notifications
- Adding actions to notifications

These three aspects of handling notifications will provide you with enough knowledge to provide a great notification experience to your users.

Handling notifications in your app

Incoming notifications are most often received when the user is not using your app. This means that your app is not directly aware of the incoming notification and doesn't get to handle it until the user actually taps the notification to enter your application.

When this happens, the `UNUserNotificationCenterDelegate` of the `UNUserNotificationCenter` is called. This delegate is responsible for handling the incoming notification whether the app is currently in the foreground, background, or not active at all because it's been killed by the system or force-closed by the user.

The `UNUserNotificationCenterDelegate` must be set before the app has finished launching. This means that you should set this delegate as soon as possible, and `application(_:didFinishLaunchingWithOptions:)` is a great candidate for this.

When the user has tapped a notification or selects one of the custom actions we will add later, the `userNotificationCenter(_:didReceive:withCompletionHandler:)` method is called. If the app is in the foreground and a notification is received, the `userNotificationCenter(_:willPresent:withCompletionHandler:)` method is called. Prior to iOS 10 it was not possible for apps to display the native notification interface if the receiving app was already in the foreground. This delegate method enables us to do that.

Let's have a look at what these delegate methods look like when we implement them. Update `AppDelegate` with the following code. Don't forget to import the `UserNotification` framework at the top of the file and add `UNUserNotificationCenterDelegate` to the declaration of `AppDelegate` to make it conform to the protocol:

```
func application(_ application: UIApplication,
didFinishLaunchingWithOptions launchOptions:
[UIApplicationLaunchOptionsKey: Any]?) -> Bool {
    UNUserNotificationCenter.current().delegate = self
    return true
}

func userNotificationCenter(_ center: UNUserNotificationCenter, didReceive
response: UNNotificationResponse, withCompletionHandler completionHandler:
@escaping () -> Void) {
    let notification = response.notification
    let action = response.actionIdentifier
    let notificationTitle = notification.request.content.title
    let customAttributes = notification.request.content.userInfo
    completionHandler()
}
```

```
func userNotificationCenter(_ center: UNUserNotificationCenter, willPresent
notification: UNNotification, withCompletionHandler completionHandler:
@escaping (UNNotificationPresentationOptions) -> Void) {
    completionHandler([.alert, .sound])
}
```

Both delegate methods provide access to the original notifications and their contents. You can use this information to determine exactly which actions should be taken by your app to properly handle the notification. When a notification is tapped, `userNotificationCenter(_:didReceive:withCompletionHandler:)` is called. This method receives a `UNNotificationResponse`, which provides information about the selected action in addition to the notification information.

If your app receives a notification and it's in the foreground, `userNotificationCenter(_:willPresent:withCompletionHandler:)` allows you to determine what should happen with the notification. This method is passed a `callback` that you need to call to inform iOS about what should happen with the notification. If you want to handle the notification yourself, you can simply call the `callback` without any display options. In the preceding snippet, the desired behavior is to display all notification alerts to the user and play the corresponding sounds.

You have full access to the notification, so it's entirely up to you to decide what to do with it. You could check the notification category, content, or `userInfo` dictionary to determine the desired behavior on a per-notification basis. This is really powerful, because you are now in full control of the notification characteristics of your application.

Managing pending and delivered notifications

While looking at scheduling notifications, we saw that we needed to provide a unique identifier to each notification that is scheduled. If a new notification is added with an existing identifier, the new notification will overwrite the existing notification, limiting the amount of similar and duplicate notifications in the Notification Center.

The preceding example describes what happens if a notification has already been delivered. However, this overwrite behavior is not limited to notifications that have already been delivered. You can also manipulate pending notifications in the same fashion. Imagine that we've scheduled a recurring notification notifying the user about a certain event every morning. A silly example might be to notify the user about the number of times they opened your app the day before.

To do this, all you need to do is schedule the same recurring notification over and over again with a different number associated to it. As long as the notification uses the same identifier, the pending notification will simply be replaced with the new one.

You can also remove delivered notifications by calling `removeDeliveredNotifications(withIdentifiers:)` on the notification center in your app. If your app allows the user to select the types of notification they want to receive, you could use this feature to remove all notifications of a certain type. That way, the user won't see the notifications anymore.

To update notifications that have been sent by your server, you simply push a new notification with the `apns-collapse-id` header set on the request that your server sends to APNS. If this header is present, the new notification will overwrite any existing notifications that have been pushed with the same `apns-collapse-id`.

Updating your notifications instead of pushing new ones all the time is a great alternative, that will avoid clutter in the Notification Center; more importantly, there won't be any duplicate, redundant, or outdated messages fighting for the user's attention.

Let's see how we can further improve the notification experience through custom actions.

Adding actions to notifications

When we covered the different ways for you to handle notifications in your app, you briefly saw that the notification response that is passed to `userNotificationCenter(_:didReceive:withCompletionHandler:)` contains information about the action the user chose for the notification. By default, every notification has a single action, which is triggered when the user taps or swipes your notification, depending on where it appeared, to open your app.

This default action isn't the only type of action that can be associated with a notification. There are three main kinds of actions that notification support. The first is a background action. Background actions dismiss the notification and wake the app in the background so it can take appropriate measures for the selected action. An example of this is accepting a calendar invite through an action. If a user accepts or declines an invite inside the notification, we don't really need to take them to the app. We can handle their response in the background.

The second type of action is a foreground action. A foreground action will take the user right into your app. It's up to your app to handle the selected action in a way that makes sense. Finally, you can add test input actions to your notifications. These types of action are basically background actions, except they take user input. A text input action is great if you're building a messaging app, for example. In addition to these standard actions, the user can 3D-touch a notification to make custom actions appear. Let's see how you can add these custom actions to our notifications.

All notification actions are associated with a notification category. These categories must be registered with the Notification Center at app launch. Again, the perfect place to set this up is `application(_:didFinishLaunchingWithOptions:)`. Add the following implementation to this method:

```
let favoriteAction = UNNotificationAction(identifier: "addfavorite", title:
"Favorite", options: [])
let viewAction = UNNotificationAction(identifier: "view", title: "View in
app", options: [.foreground])

let quoteCategory = UNNotificationCategory(identifier: "quote", actions:
[favoriteAction, viewAction], intentIdentifiers: [], options: [])
UNUserNotificationCenter.current().setNotificationCategories([quoteCategory
])
```

The preceding snippet adds two custom actions to a category we've named `quote`. One action is used to mark a `quote` as favorite and is handled in the background. The other allows the user to view the `quote` in the app and is marked explicitly to run in the foreground. If we hadn't done this, the action would have been handled in the background. Finally, the category is added to the notification center, allowing us to associate this category with new notifications.

Associating a category with a notification is done through the `categoryIdentifier` property of `UNNotificationContent`. Add the following line of code to the `createNotification` method in `ViewController` to add the quote category to the notifications we're scheduling:

```
content.categoryIdentifier = "quote"
```

If you 3D-touch the received notification now, you're presented with two custom actions:

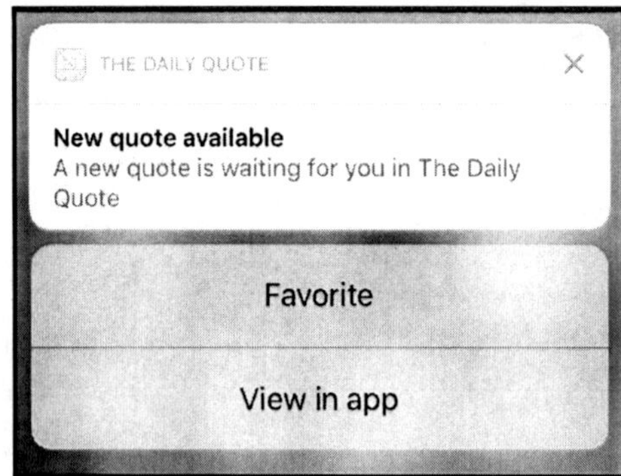

Notification actions are a great way to add quick interactions to your notifications, and they are already a huge improvement over simply sending a plain notification. There is one more feature that greatly improves notifications and their usefulness: Notification Extensions.

Implementing Notification Extensions

The most exciting new feature in the realm of notifications is Notification Extensions. Apple has added two extension points to notifications, which enables you to take the notification experience up a notch from custom actions. The available extensions are Service Extensions and Content Extensions. These extensions are both very powerful and relatively simple to implement. We'll have a look at Service Extensions first.

Adding a Service Extension to your app

Service Extensions are intended to act as middleware for push notifications. The Service Extension receives the notification before it's displayed to the user. This allows you to manipulate or enrich the content before it's displayed.

A Service Extension is perfect if you're implementing end-to-end encryption, for example. Before this extension was introduced in iOS 10, notifications had to be sent in plain text. This means that any app that implements end-to-end encryption still wasn't completely secure because push notifications were not encrypted. Since iOS 10, you can push the encrypted message from your server to the device and decrypt the message in the Service Extension before showing it to the user.

Another great use for a Service Extension is to download media attachments from a push notification, save it locally, and add it as a media attachment to the notification contents. Remember that all media attachments for notifications must be stored locally on the device. This means that a push notification can't really have media attachments unless a Service Extension is used to download and store the media locally.

To allow a Service Extension to handle a push notification, you must add the `mutable-content` property to the aps dictionary on the notification:

```
{
    aps: {
        alert: "You have a new message!",
        badge: 1,
        mutable-content: 1
    },
    custom-encrypted-message: "MyEncryptedMessage"
}
```

When the `mutable-content` property is detected by iOS, your Service Extension is activated and receives the notification before it's displayed to the user. A service extension is created in the same way as other extensions. You go to the project settings in Xcode and, in the sidebar that shows all targets, you click the plus icon. In the dialog that appears, you select the Notification Service Extension, you give it a name, and Xcode will provide you with the required boilerplate code. When you add a Service Extension, a sample extension is added to `The Daily Quote` to illustrate what a Service Extension that updates the notification's body text looks like.

To apply this service extension to `The Daily Quote`, the service extension must receive access to the app group we created earlier and the `Quote.swift` file should be added to the extension target. This enables the extension to read quotes from the shared `UserDefaults`.

The boilerplate code that Xcode generates for a Service Extension is rather interesting. Two properties are created, a `contentHandler` and `bestAttemptContent`. The properties are initially given a value in `didReceive(_:withContentHandler:)`. This method is called as soon as we're expected to handle the notification.

If we fail to call the `callback` handler in a timely manner, the system calls `serviceExtensionTimeWillExpire()`. This is essentially our last chance to quickly come up with content for the notification. If we still fail to call the `callback`, the message is displayed to the user in its original form. Xcode generated a version of this method for us that uses the stored `callback` and the current state that our notification is in, and the `callback` is called immediately.

Let's look at a simple implementation of `didReceive(_:withContentHandler:)`:

```
override func didReceive(_ request: UNNotificationRequest,
withContentHandler contentHandler: @escaping (UNNotificationContent) ->
Void) {
    self.contentHandler = contentHandler
    bestAttemptContent = (request.content.mutableCopy() as?
UNMutableNotificationContent)

    if let bestAttemptContent = bestAttemptContent {
        let todayQuote = Quote.current
        bestAttemptContent.subtitle = "Quote by \(todayQuote.creator)"
        bestAttemptContent.body = todayQuote.text
        contentHandler(bestAttemptContent)
    }
}
```

In this snippet, we grab the incoming notification contents and we add a subtitle and a body to them. The quote struct is used to obtain the current quote from `UserDefaults`. This approach enables us to push a fresh quote to users every day, even if the server has no idea which quote should be displayed today. Pretty awesome, right?

Adding a Content Extension to your app

The last notifications feature that we'll explore is arguably the most awesome, exciting feature that has been added to notifications in iOS. Content Extensions enable developers to take custom notification actions to a whole new level. We've already seen that 3D-Touching a notification will make custom actions pop up. However, the notification remains the same and possibly doesn't provide as much context as we would like.

Consider receiving an invite for an event. The notification allows you to accept the invite or decline it. Wouldn't it be great if your calendar popped up inside that notification as well, allowing you to actually check your calendar before responding to the invite? This is what Content Extensions are for. When implemented correctly, they can provide users with essential information relevant to the notification that's currently on display.

Content Extensions are limited in terms of interaction. A Content Extension itself does not receive any touches; it can only display contents. It can, however, respond to the actions that are associated with the notification. This means that you can update the user interface based on the selected action. A great example of this is the Content Extension that Apple created for the *Messages* app. You can almost have the full messages experience right inside a notification. You can see new messages appear as they come in and you can respond to them right inside the Content Extension.

To demonstrate the possibilities for Content Extensions, we'll take the simple notification we created for `The Daily Quote` to the next level. Earlier, we scheduled a local notification that simply notified the user about the presence of a new `quote`. The notification didn't specify what the contents of the `quote` are or even who the creator of the `quote` is.

Let's implement a Content Extension that will reveal the `quote` and its creator to the user when they 3D-Touch on the notification. To do this, we need to add a new extension to our project. This time, you should pick the Notification Content Extension.

Again, Xcode gives you some generated boiler code when you add this extension, just like it always does. Before you do anything, you should add the App Groups capability to the Content Extension and make sure you include the `Quote.swift` file in the extension target. Doing this allows you to use the shared `UserDefaults` and fetch the currently active quote.

Next, replace the single existing outlet in the `NotificationViewController` class that was added to your extension with the following outlets:

```
@IBOutlet var quoteLabel: UILabel!
@IBOutlet var quoteCreator: UILabel!
```

Then, remove the existing implementation for `viewDidLoad()` and add the following implementation for `didReceive(_:)`:

```
func didReceive(_ notification: UNNotification) {
    let quote = Quote.current
    quoteLabel.text = quote.text
    quoteCreator.text = quote.creator
}
```

Whenever the Content Extension is activated to handle an incoming notification, we simply want to grab the `quote` for today and show it to the user. In your own application, you probably want to examine the contents of the actual notification to provide more context about the notification. In this case we don't need that; we already know what we're supposed to display.

In the storyboard, remove the existing label and add two new labels, one for the quote itself and one for its creator. Give the quote the Title 1 styling and the creator label should have the Caption 1 style. Add constraints so the quote label is constrained to the view's top, left, and right-hand sides. Constrain the creator label to the bottom and the sides. You should end up with a view that looks likes what is shown in the following screenshot. Giving the view controller a height of ±100 points will help you position the labels more easily:

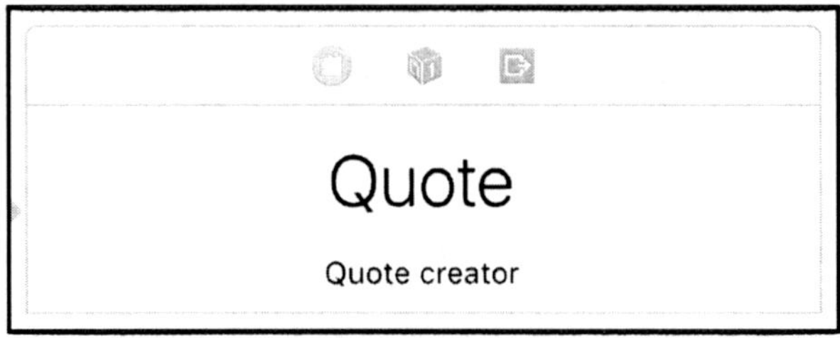

Finally, open the Content Extension's `Info.plist` file. As mentioned before, Content Extensions are associated to notifications through categories. We use the `Info.plist` to specify the category that the current extension should be associated with. Expand the `NSExtension` and `NSExtensionAttributes` properties to find the `UNNotificationExtensionCategory` property. Give this field a value of `quote`.

In the main app's `ViewController` class, use the following trigger to schedule a notification we can use to test our Content Extension:

```
let trigger = UNTimeIntervalNotificationTrigger(timeInterval: 10, repeats:
false)
```

We're ready to take our extension for a spin. Select your extension in the drop-down menu next to the run and stop controls in the top-left corner of Xcode and run your project. Xcode will ask you for an app to run; pick `The Daily Quote`. After opening the app, a notification will trigger after 10 seconds. Once the notification comes in, 3D-Touch it to see your extension in action:

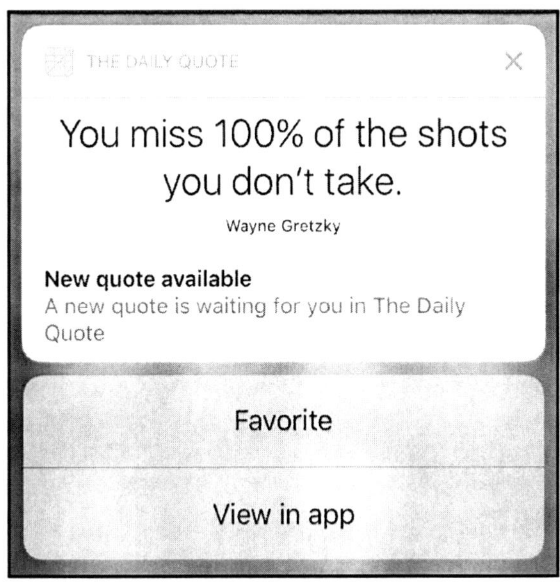

If you've tested this example yourself, you may have noticed that the notification's custom view was displayed too high initially, and that animated to the correct size for properly fitting your notification's contents. The correct size was determined by auto layout because we've added a constraint to the top and bottom of our view. However, we would probably like to make sure the amount of animating we need to do is minimal, because it just doesn't look very good.

In the extension's `Info.plist` there is a property called `UNNotificationExtensionInitialContentSizeRatio` that's right below the notification category property. The default value for this property is `1`, but our app could probably use a value that's a lot smaller. Try setting this value to **0.3** and run your extension again. It doesn't have to animate nearly as much because the initial height is now just 30% of the extension's width. Much better.

You probably also noticed that the original notification contents are visible below our custom view. We can hide this default content by adding the `UNNotificationExtensionDefaultContentHidden` property to the extensions `Info.plist` file. All properties you add for your extension should be added at the same level as `UNNotificationExtensionInitialContentSizeRatio` and `UNNotificationExtensionCategory`.

Key	Type	Value
▼ NSExtension	Dictionary	(3 items)
▼ NSExtensionAttributes	Dictionary	(3 items)
UNNotificationExtensionDefaultContentHidden	Boolean	YES
UNNotificationExtensionCategory	String	quote
UNNotificationExtensionInitialContentSizeRatio	Number	0.3
NSExtensionMainStoryboard	String	MainInterface
NSExtensionPointIdentifier	String	com.apple.usernotifications.content-extension

This wraps up the interface part of the Content Extension. In addition to showing a custom UI for a notification, Content Extensions can respond to actions that the user selects right inside the Content Extension itself. To do this, we need to implement the `didReceive(_:completionHandler:)` delegate method in the extension. Once this method is implemented, the extension becomes responsible for all actions that are chosen by the user. This means that the extension should either handle all the actions, or that it should explicitly pass them on to the host app if the selection action can't be handled within the Service Extension.

After handling the incoming action, the notification extension determines what should happen next. We do this by calling the completion handler with a `UNNotificationContentExtensionResponseOption`. There are three options to choose from. The first is to simply dismiss the notification. The second is to dismiss the notification and forward the chosen action to the host app. The final option is to keep the extension active so the user can pick more actions or, using Apple's *Messages* app as an example, so that the user can carry on the conversation inside the Content Extension.

The following snippet demonstrates a very plain and simple example that prints the action a user chose and forwards it to the app:

```
func didReceive(_ response: UNNotificationResponse, completionHandler
completion: @escaping (UNNotificationContentExtensionResponseOption) ->
Void) {
    print(response.actionIdentifier)
    completion(.dismissAndForwardAction)
}
```

As you've seen just now, Content Extensions are not complex to implement, yet they are amazingly powerful. You can add an entire new layer of interaction and increase the relevance of notifications by implementing a Content Extension, and it is strongly recommended that you always consider ways to implement extensions for your notifications to provide the user with rich information about their notification as quickly as possible.

Summary

In this chapter, we've explored the amazing world of notifications. Even though notifications are simple in nature and short-lived, they are a vital part of the iOS ecosystem and users rely on them to provide timely, interesting, and relevant updates about subjects that matter to them, right then and there. You saw how to go from the basics, simply scheduling a notification, to more advanced subjects such as custom actions. You saw that Service Extensions allow you to implement great new features, such as true end-to-end encryption, or enrich push notifications with content that is stored on the device.

Finally, we explored Content Extensions and you saw how a Content Extension can take a simple, plain notification, and make it interesting, rich, and more relevant. The example of a calendar that appears with event invites comes to mind immediately, but the possibilities are endless. Proper usage of Notification Extensions will truly make your app stand out in a positive and engaging way.

The next chapter focuses on another extension; the iMessage extension!

19
Extending iMessage

As part of Apple's effort to introduce more and more extension points into the iOS ecosystem, iMessage extensions have been introduced in iOS 10. These extensions allow your users to access and share content from your app with their friends right inside the Messages app. This chapter will show you exactly how to tap into these extensions points and build your own iMessage extensions.

We'll go over two types of extension: Sticker packs and iMessage apps. Note that we call these extensions apps and not just extensions. This is because iMessage extensions behave a lot like apps even though they're not apps. Also, iMessage apps are distributed through their own iMessage App Store. More on this later.

As with other extensions we've covered so far, the first step is to gain a broad understanding of iMessage apps and what possibilities they give you as a developer. Once we've established this basic understanding, we'll dive into several aspects of iMessage apps in more detail. To be more specific, the following are the topics that we'll cover in this chapter:

- Creating a sticker pack for iMessage
- Implementing custom, interactive iMessage apps
- Understanding sessions, messages, and conversations

By the end of this chapter, you'll understand how iMessage apps work and how you can create an experience for your users that is fun and engaging. More importantly, you'll be able to launch an amazing sticker pack that features cats, dogs, or any other type of sticker you'd like to slap on messages you send and receive.

Understanding iMessage apps

An iMessage app is really an app extension that lives inside iMessage. It's kind of a weird type of extension because it behaves like a hybrid between an extension and an application. Extensions typically contain a single view controller and, more importantly, they can't be distributed through the iOS ecosystem without containing an application.

This rule does not apply to iMessage apps. An iMessage app can be distributed directly through the iMessage app store without a containing application. This means that you can build an iMessage app, for example, a sticker pack, and distribute it without associating any other app to it. Also, you can add in-app purchases to an iMessage app. In-app purchases are normally unavailable to extensions, which makes iMessage apps behave more like an app than an extension.

Apart from distribution and in-app purchases, iMessage apps behave just like other extensions. They are created on behalf of a host application, Messages in this case, and they have a relatively short lifespan. An iMessage app specializes in sending messages from one user to another. These messages are shaped and created inside your extension and added to the conversation by sending them. An iMessage app can contain or send three different types of message:

- Interactive messages
- Stickers
- Media content

An interactive message is intended to be tapped by the receiving user so they can interact with it somehow. Stickers are a special kind of image that the user can place right on top of other messages or send as a single image. Media content can be distributed in the form of photos, videos, links, and basically any other type of content that iMessage natively supports. iMessage apps are built using the **Messages** framework. This framework has been specifically created for iMessage extensions and it functions as a gateway from your app into the conversation that your user is currently having.

As mentioned before, iMessage apps can be distributed without a host application. This means that you can distribute your iMessage app independently of any other app. You must still provide an app icon that is square and would otherwise be used on the user's home screen by a containing app. This image is required for display in the settings app and other places in iOS where a square app icon is required.

If you do have a containing app for your iMessage app, users can directly add the iMessage app to their list of available apps through the iMessage App Store without having to download it separately from the containing application. The simplest app we can build for iMessage is a sticker pack. Let's go ahead and create one so we can start exploring iMessage apps in the simulator.

Creating an iMessage sticker pack

Stickers in iMessage are a fun way to share images with your friends. Stickers can be slapped onto a message as a response to a message you've received or just for fun with no particular reason at all.

To create a sticker pack, open Xcode and create a new project. One of the available project templates is the **Sticker Pack App**; select it and click **Next**. Give your sticker pack a name and click **Next** again to create your project:

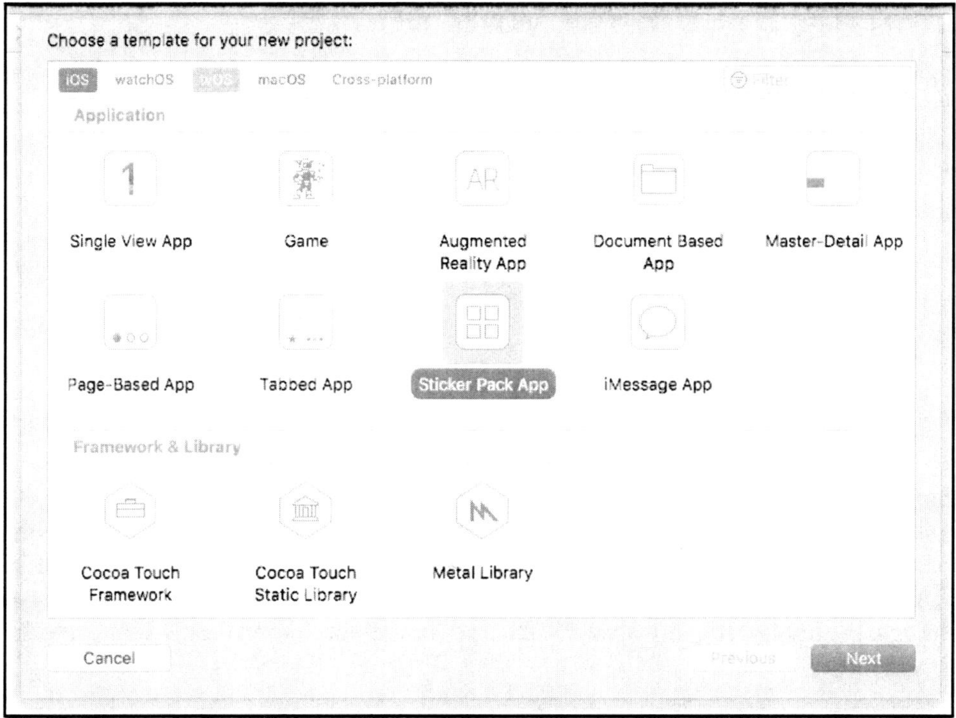

In the generated project, you'll find two folders. One is named `Stickers.xcstickers` and the other is named `Products`. We're only interested in the `stickers` folder. If you open it, you'll find an app icon template and a folder named `Sticker Pack`.

All you need to do to create your sticker pack is to drag images into this `Sticker Pack` folder. After doing this, you can build and run your extension and try it out in the simulator. You'll find that the simulator comes with two active conversations in the Messages app. These are dummy conversations and you use them to test your iMessage app.

The simulator cannot send messages outside the simulator so you must use these predefined conversations while testing. Tapping a sticker or dragging it onto an existing speech bubble will send it from one conversation to the other. Go ahead and give that a shot. You can also send text messages and any other type of message you would normally send in the dummy conversation.

Optimizing assets for your stickers

Creating a sticker pack is really easy and to make the best sticker packs, you should make sure that you properly optimize your image assets. Stickers can be displayed to the user in three sizes; small, medium, and large. To change the size of stickers in your sticker pack, simply click the `Sticker Pack` folder and open the attributes inspector. You can pick the sticker size there.

You should optimize the size of the stickers you provide according to the display size you choose. The following is a list of sticker sizes and their recommended asset sizes:

- Small: 100x100@3x
- Medium: 136x136@3x
- Large: 206x206@3x

Note that all sizes have a @3x annotation. This means that the exported dimension of your images should be three times larger than the size listed to accommodate screens with a 3x resolution, such as the plus-sized iPhones. So, a small sticker should be exported at 300x300 pixels. Unlike other image assets on iOS, you only supply a single image for each resource; the 3x image. Normally you supply a 1x, 2x, and 3x version of each asset you provide.

Sticker packs can contain PNG images, animated PNG images, GIFs, and JPEGs. All images you supply must be smaller than 500kb. It's recommended that you provide all of your assets as either PNG or animated PNG because this image format has superior image quality and supports transparency. Transparent stickers are recommended because they look a lot better when placed on top of other stickers or messages.

Now that you're familiar with sticker packs and testing them in the simulator, let's see how we make our sticker pack a bit more special by customizing the sticker picking interface a bit.

Creating a custom sticker app

The sticker app you created before doesn't contain a lot of user interface elements. Your app shows stickers on a white background and that's about it. Sticker apps shouldn't be more complex than this, but wouldn't it be great if we could at least change the background color for our sticker app? This isn't possible if you're using the simple sticker pack template. You can, however, create your own sticker pack app and customize the background. Figuring out how to do this will allow you to familiarize yourself with the code that's involved in creating an iMessage app, so let's create a custom sticker pack.

In the source code repository for this book, you'll find a project named `CustomStickers`. This project already contains the stickers we're going to display. The images for these stickers are made available through `openclipart.org` by a user named bocian. Note that the images have not been added to the `Assets.xcassets` folder, but to the `Stickers` folder in the `MessagesExtension`. The project was set up like this because the `Assets.xcassets` folder belongs to the containing app that we don't have.

In the `MessagesExtension` folder, you'll find a view controller file and a storyboard file. Open the storyboard and remove the default `UILabel` that was placed in the interface. We're not going to add any interface elements through Interface Builder because our interface elements aren't directly available in Interface Builder.

In the `MessagesViewController`, you'll find several boilerplate methods. We'll get into them soon; you can ignore them for now. We're going to use `viewDidLoad` to set up a `MSStickerBrowserViewController` to display stickers in. The `MSStickerBrowserView` instance that is contained inside the `MSStickerBrowserViewController` behaves somewhat like a `UITableView` does because it requires a data source to determine how many and which stickers to display.

The first step in implementing our own sticker app is to add a property for an instance of `MSStickerBrowserViewController` to `MessagesViewController`:

```
var stickerBrowser = MSStickerBrowserViewController(stickerSize: .regular)
```

Next, add the following implementation for `viewDidLoad`:

```
override func viewDidLoad() {
    super.viewDidLoad()
    stickerBrowser.willMove(toParentViewController: self)
    addChildViewController(stickerBrowser)
    stickerBrowser.didMove(toParentViewController: self)
    view.addSubview(stickerBrowser.view)
    stickerBrowser.stickerBrowserView.dataSource = self
    stickerBrowser.stickerBrowserView.reloadData()
    stickerBrowser.stickerBrowserView.backgroundColor = UIColor.red
}
```

This snippet should not contain any surprises for you. First, the `stickerBrowser` is added as a child view controller of the messages view controller. Then we add the view of `stickerBrowser` as a subview of the messages view controller's view. Next, we set a `dataSource` on the `stickerBrowserView` and we tell it to reload its data. And finally, we set the background color for the `stickerBrowserView`; the whole reason why we implemented a custom sticker app. Again, nothing strange or surprising.

If you build your app now, Xcode will complain about the fact that `MessagesViewController` does not conform to `MSStickerBrowserViewDataSource`. Add this protocol to the declaration of `MSMessagesViewController` and implement the following two methods to conform to `MSStickerBrowserViewDataSource`:

```
func stickerBrowserView(_ stickerBrowserView: MSStickerBrowserView,
stickerAt index: Int) -> MSSticker {
    return OwlStickerFactory.sticker(forIndex: index)
}

func numberOfStickers(in stickerBrowserView: MSStickerBrowserView) -> Int {
    return OwlStickerFactory.numberOfStickers
}
```

The first method is expected to return a sticker for a certain index and the second returns the number of stickers in our app. The logic for this has been abstracted into a sticker factory. This is done in order to keep the code in the view controller nice, compact, and to the point. Add a Swift file to the project and name it `OwlStickerFactory`. Add the following implementation to this file:

```
import Foundation
import Messages

struct OwlStickerFactory {
    static private let stickerNames = [
        "bike", "books", "bowler", "drunk", "ebook",
        "family", "grill", "normal", "notebook", "party",
        "punk", "rose", "santa", "spring"
    ]
    static var numberOfStickers: Int { return stickerNames.count }
    static func sticker(forIndex index: Int) -> MSSticker {
        let stickerName = stickerNames[index]
        guard let stickerPath = Bundle.main.path(forResource: stickerName,
ofType: "PNG")
            else { fatalError("Missing sicker with name: \(stickerName)") }
        let stickerUrl = URL(fileURLWithPath: stickerPath)
        guard let sticker = try? MSSticker(contentsOfFileURL: stickerUrl,
localizedDescription: "\(stickerName) owl")
            else { fatalError("Failed to retrieve sticker: \(stickerName)")
}
        return sticker
    }
}
```

Most of this code should speak for itself. There is an array of sticker names and a computed variable that returns the number of stickers for the app. The interesting part of this code is the `sticker(forIndex:)` method. This method retrieves a sticker name from our array of names. Then it retrieves the file path that can be used to retrieve the image file from the application bundle. Finally, it creates a URL with this path in order to create a sticker.

Note that the `MSSticker` initializer can throw errors so we prefix our initialization call with `try?` since we're not interested in handling the error. Also, note that the sticker initializer takes a `localizedDescription`. This description is used by screen readers to read back the sticker to users that have certain accessibility features enabled.

Any time we add an `MSSticker` to the view, regardless of whether we're using a sticker browser or not, the Messages framework takes care of the sticker peel, drag, and drop actions for us. This means that you can create a completely different, custom interface for your stickers if you'd like. Keep in mind that most sticker apps will make use of the standard layout and your users might not be too pleased if your app presents them with an unexpected sticker sheet layout.

However, apps that aren't about stickers do require a special layer of design and interaction. This is the next topic we'll cover.

Implementing custom, interactive iMessage apps

Sticker apps are nice, but they're not particularly useful for every use case. We can build far more interesting and interactive applications for iMessage through the Messages framework. Some of the larger, well-known apps on iOS have been able to implement iMessage applications that make sharing content from their apps easier. There are people that have built games in iMessage already. The Messages framework enables developers to build a wide range of extensions straight into the Messages app.

We've just seen how you can build sticker packs and how you can create a somewhat customized sticker pack by picking the app template instead of the sticker pack template in Xcode. We haven't gone in-depth into the different life cycle methods that Xcode generates for us when we create a new iMessage app.

Let's do this while we build an iMessage app for `The Daily Quote`, the app you've already built a notification extension and a widget for. First, we'll look at the life cycle of an iMessage app. Then we'll implement the compact view for our app. Finally, we'll implement the expanded view for our app. Exactly what the compact and expanded views are will be made clear when we cover the life cycle of iMessage apps.

Understanding the iMessage app life cycle

An iMessage app lives inside the Messages app, just like you would expect from an extension. As mentioned before, iMessage apps are a special kind of extension, which makes them behave a lot like apps at times even though they are still extensions at their core.

The main view controller for an iMessage app must always be a subclass of `MSMessagesAppViewController`. You can't have a primary view controller that is not a subclass of this class. When the user navigates to your extension through the iMessage apps drawer, this view controller is added in the compact mode. You've already seen this mode in action when you created your sticker pack.

When the Messages framework instantiates your extension, the `willBecomeActive(with:)` method is called, followed by `didBecomeActive(with:)`. These messages are called after `viewDidLoad` in the view controller life cycle, but before `viewWillAppear`. When it's time to dismiss your extension, the `viewWillDisappear` and `viewDidDisappear` life cycle methods are called. Next, `willResignActive(with:)` and `didResignActive(with:)` are called.

Once the resignation methods are called, the process for your iMessage app is killed shortly thereafter. You do not get any time to do work in the background, just like with other extensions. Again, even though Messages extensions behave a lot like apps, they're not.

There are two more methods you should know about for now. These methods are called whenever we're transitioning from one display mode to another. The display mode is changed whenever the user taps the upward chevron in the bottom right part of the iMessage interface. Take a look at the following screenshot:

You can also trigger this transition from your code by calling `requestPresentationStyle(_:)`. The delegate methods that get called are `willTransition(to:)` and `didTransition(to:)`. The first is called right before the transition occurs, the second is called right after. This just like their names suggest.

Implementing the custom compact view

To start implementing our iMessage app, a new extension should be added to The Daily Quote. Pick the iMessage extension and name it `The Daily Quote Messages`. Enable the **App Groups** capability for this extension and include `Quotes.swift` in the extension target just like you've done before.

We're going to use the same view controller containment technique we used before when we built our custom sticker pack. This time we're going to need to add the view controller we want to display to `Main.storyboard` without connecting it to the `MessagesViewController`. Before we create the interface, let's implement the code for our compact view. The compact view will feature a quote, the creator of the quote, and a **Share** button.

Create a new `UIViewController` subclass and name it `CompactViewController`. Make sure to add it to The Daily Quote target by selecting its group before creating the new file. The setup for this view controller will be really similar to all of the other view controllers we've created for The Daily Quote and its extensions. We'll need two outlets, one for the quote and one for its creator. In `viewDidLoad`, the current quote must be fetched and the labels should be populated with their corresponding values. I trust you to be able to do this on your own. When in doubt, check the other projects. Alternatively, check the source code in this book's `git` repository.

When the Share button is tapped, we want to share the message into the conversation. This means that we're going to have to notify `MessagesViewController` of the button tap inside `CompactViewController` somehow. To do this, we'll create a `QuoteSelectionDelegate` protocol that `MessagesViewController` can conform to.

The delegate and the share action should be implemented in `CompactViewController` as shown in the following code snippet:

```
var delegate: QuoteSelectionDelegate?
@IBAction func shareTapped() {
    delegate?.shareQuote(Quote.current)
}
```

The delegate is optional because we can't set it before we have initialized the view controller elsewhere. The tap action simply calls a method on the delegate and passes the current quote along with it. Create a new file to define the protocol and name it `QuoteSelectionDelegate`. The protocol should be implemented as follows:

```
protocol QuoteSelectionDelegate {
    func shareQuote(_ quote: Quote)
}
```

This is a simple protocol with just a single method requirement. Now, let's write all the required code in `MessagesViewController` before we implement the interface for `CompactViewController`. First of all, add the property shown in the following snippet to the message view controller so we can hold onto the compact view controller. Also, update your `viewDidLoad` implementation as follows:

```
var compactViewController: CompactViewController?

override func viewDidLoad() {
    super.viewDidLoad()
    compactViewController =
storyboard?.instantiateViewController(withIdentifier:
"CompactViewController") as? CompactViewController
    compactViewController?.delegate = self
}
```

We're using the `instantiateViewController(withIdentifier:)` method from `UIStoryboard` to obtain an instance of `CompactViewController` from the storyboard.

Make sure to add `QuoteSelectionDelegate` to the declaration of `MessagesViewController` and add an empty implementation for `shareQuote(_:)`. We'll implement the share functionality later. We'll use a separate method to display the compact view. This will make our code a bit more readable once we add the expanded view and we need to remove views:

```
func showCompactView() {
    guard let compactViewController = self.compactViewController
        else { return }
    compactViewController.willMove(toParentViewController: self)
    self.addChildViewController(compactViewController)
    compactViewController.didMove(toParentViewController: self)
    view.addSubview(compactViewController.view)
    compactViewController.view.frame = view.frame
}
```

This code is very similar to what you've seen before when we implemented the sticker pack. Finally, let's implement `willBecomeActive(with:)`. This is where we'll call `showCompactView()` from:

```
override func willBecomeActive(with conversation: MSConversation) {
     if self.presentationStyle == .compact {
         showCompactView()
     }
 }
```

Lastly, open `MainInterface.storyboard` and drag out a view controller. Add two labels and a button to this view controller. Lay them out as shown as shown in the following screenshot:

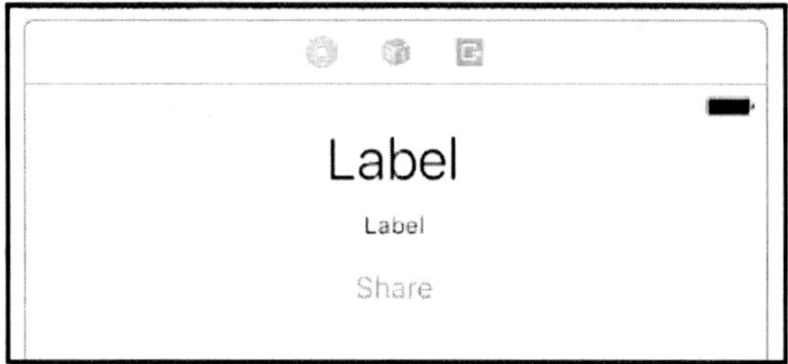

The quote is styled as a `title` and its maximum number of lines is set to `0` lines so it automatically expands to fit the content. The creator is styled as a `caption one` and it's positioned below the title. The button should be laid out below the caption. Make sure to set `CompactViewController` as both the subclass and the storyboard ID for the view controller you just dragged out. And to wrap it up, connect the outlets to the views. Make sure to select **touch up inside** as the trigger action for `shareTapped()`. Take a look at the following screenshot:

Add the following implementation for `viewDidLoad()` to the `CompactViewController` in order to populate the labels that you just set up:

```
override func viewDidLoad() {
    super.viewDidLoad()
    let quote = Quote.current
    quoteLabel.text = quote.text
    creatorLabel.text = quote.creator
}
```

If you build and run your application now, the quote for today should pop up right inside iMessage. This is all we have to do for the compact view. Now let's go ahead and implement an expanded view for our iMessage app.

Implementing the expanded view

The expanded view for our iMessage app will be a table view that lists all of the quotes in the `Quote` struct. We'll use a similar setup to what we used before by creating a new view controller file and using the delegate protocol that was defined earlier to communicate the selection of a quote back to the `MessagesViewController`.

First, create a new `UITableViewController` subclass and name it `QuotesTableViewController`. You can remove most of the commented template code; the only methods you should keep are `tableView(_:cellForRowAt:)`, `tableView(_:numberOfRowsInSection:)`, and `numberOfSections(in:)`. In addition to the commented delegate methods, you can remove the `viewDidLoad()` and `didReceiveMemoryWarning()` methods; we don't need them.

For starters, we're going to need to implement the methods shown in the following code snippet. These methods provide the table view with its data:

```
override func numberOfSections(in tableView: UITableView) -> Int {
    return 1
}

override func tableView(_ tableView: UITableView, numberOfRowsInSection
section: Int) -> Int {
    return Quote.numberOfQuotes
}

override func tableView(_ tableView: UITableView, cellForRowAt indexPath:
IndexPath) -> UITableViewCell {
    let cell = tableView.dequeueReusableCell(withIdentifier:
"QuoteTableViewCell", for: indexPath)
    let quote = Quote.quote(atIndex: indexPath.row)
    cell.textLabel?.text = quote?.text
    cell.detailTextLabel?.text = quote?.creator
    return cell
}
```

The preceding snippet uses a `numberOfQuotes` property on the `Quote` struct. However, this property is not defined yet. Add it to the `Quote` struct as shown in the following code snippet:

```
static var numberOfQuotes: Int { return quotes.count }
```

The last thing you should take care of before creating and connecting the interface is the quote selection delegate and implementing cell selection in the `QuotesTableViewController`. The code to do this is pretty straightforward:

```
var delegate: QuoteSelectionDelegate?

override func tableView(_ tableView: UITableView, didSelectRowAt indexPath:
IndexPath) {
    guard let quote = Quote.quote(atIndex: indexPath.row)
        else { return }
    delegate?.shareQuote(quote)
}
```

This leaves us with a complete implementation of the table view in code. Let's create the interface in Interface Builder. Open `MainInterface.storyboard` and drag out a table view controller. Assign `QuotesTableViewController` as its class and Storyboard ID. Also, click the prototype cell and set its style to **Subtitle**. The Identifier for the cell should be set to `QuoteTableViewCell`. That's all we need to do for now. Let's make sure that we display this view controller when our iMessage app is in the expanded presentation mode.

In `MessagesViewController`, update `willBecomeActive(with:)` so it can display both the expanded and compact mode as the initial view, depending on the `presentationStyle`:

```
override func willBecomeActive(with conversation: MSConversation) {
    if self.presentationStyle == .compact {
        showCompactView()
    } else if self.presentationStyle == .expanded {
        showExpandedView()
    }
}
```

Also, we should take into account that the view can transition from one display mode to the other. Add the following implementation for `willTransition(to:)`:

```
override func willTransition(to presentationStyle:
MSMessagesAppPresentationStyle) {
    if presentationStyle == .compact {
        showCompactView()
    } else if presentationStyle == .expanded {
```

```
        showExpandedView()
    }
}
```

Finally, we should take care of showing the correct view. We should always remove any existing view controllers before we show a new one. We also haven't implemented `showExpandedView()` yet, but if you think about this method's contents for a second, it should look very similar to what we've already done for `showCompactView()`. We'll implement a special cleanup method and we'll refactor `showCompactView()` so we can reuse it for `showExpandedView()`. First, add the following method that will be used to clean up our view controllers when needed:

```
func cleanupChildViewControllers() {
    for viewController in childViewControllers {
        viewController.willMove(toParentViewController: nil)
        viewController.removeFromParentViewController()
        viewController.didMove(toParentViewController: nil)
        viewController.view.removeFromSuperview()
    }
}
```

One last thing that needs to be done before implementing the presentation of the expanded view controller is adding a property for this expanded view controller in the `MessagesViewController` and updating `viewDidLoad()` so it creates a new instance of the `QuotesTableViewController` that will be used as the expanded view controller. The updated lines have been highlighted in bold:

```
var expandedViewController: QuotesTableViewController?

override func viewDidLoad() {
    super.viewDidLoad()
    compactViewController =
storyboard?.instantiateViewController(withIdentifier:
"CompactViewController") as? CompactViewController
    compactViewController?.delegate = self
    expandedViewController =
storyboard?.instantiateViewController(withIdentifier:
"QuotesTableViewController") as? QuotesTableViewController
    expandedViewController?.delegate = self
}
```

Next, let's implement the refactored view controller presentation methods:

```
func showCompactView() {
    guard let compactViewController = self.compactViewController
        else { return }
    showViewController(compactViewController)
```

```
}

func showExpandedView() {
    guard let expandedViewController = self.expandedViewController
        else { return }
    showViewController(expandedViewController)
}

func showViewController(_ viewController: UIViewController) {
    cleanupChildViewControllers()
    viewController.willMove(toParentViewController: self)
    self.addChildViewController(viewController)
    viewController.didMove(toParentViewController: self)
    view.addSubview(viewController.view)
    viewController.view.frame = view.frame
}
```

After doing this, build and run the app to see your extension in action. It flawlessly switches between showing the list of quotes and the single daily quote. The simulator might seem a bit jumpy, unfortunately; this seems to be an issue with messages in the simulator that we can't really work around.

The final step in implementing our iMessage app is to implement the `shareQuote(_:)` method. This method will compose a message that can be shared. Let's have a look at message composing and everything related to it.

Understanding sessions, messages, and conversations

So far we have been looking at user interface-related aspects of iMessage apps only. When you're creating an iMessage app, your app will sooner or later have to send a message. To do this, we make use of `MSMessage` and `MSSession`. In addition to messages and sessions, there is the `MSConversation` class. These three classes together enable you to send messages, identify recipients in conversations, and even update or collapse existing messages in the messages transcript.

When an iMessage extension is activated, `willBecomeActive(with:)` is called in the `MessagesViewController`. This method receives a `MSConversation` instance that you can use to send messages, stickers, and even attachments. More importantly, the conversation contains unique identifiers for participants in the conversation and the currently selected message.

The `localParticipantIdentifier` and `remoteParticipantIdentifier` properties respectively, identify the current user of your app, the person who is sending messages with your app, and the recipients of these messages. Note that these identifiers are unique to your app so you can't use this identifier to identify users across different iMessage apps. Also, these identifiers can change if the user uninstalls and then reinstalls your app. These identifiers are mostly meant to identify users in a group conversation for example.

The `selectedMessage` property is only set if your extension was launched due to a user tapping on a message that was sent by your extension. This is especially useful if you're building an app that sends multiple messages that build upon each other. In Apple's 2016 WWDC talk , *iMessage Apps and Stickers, Part 2,* they demonstrated an ice cream designer app. Each user designs a part of the ice cream and the `selectedMessage` is used in combination with the `MSSession` to collapse old messages so the history does not get polluted with old pictures of ice creams. We'll see how to use this session in a bit. First, we'll have a look at `MSMessage` so we can compose messages.

Composing a message

The `MSMessage` class encapsulates all the information that is contained inside a message. When you initialize a message, you can initialize it with or without a session. If you instantiate a message with a session, other messages that are attached to this session will be collapsed to only show the message's `summaryText`. The summary is supposed to be a short, clear description of the message so that, even when it's collapsed, the message still makes sense.

If possible, you should always aim to attach an `url` and `accessibilityLabel` to your messages, depending on the types of message your app will send. If you're sending plain text messages like we'll do with The Daily Quote, you don't need an accessibility label since iOS can simply read the text message out loud for users with accessibility needs. The `url` property is mainly used by platforms that don't support iMessage extensions, such as macOS. Attaching a `url` makes sure that users can still navigate to your content online. When you're sending plain text, this isn't really an issue.

Finally, if you're sending a message that has media attached to it, you should make use of the `MSMessageTemplateLayout` class. `MSMessage` has a layout property that can be set to an instance of `MSMessageTemplateLayout`. This layout template is highly configurable. You can assign an image or media to it, set a caption, an image title, a sub-caption, and more. Messages will make sure that your layout looks good and is laid out nicely depending on the information you set.

If you set both a media URL and an image on your message layout, the image will be used and the other media are ignored. Any images you add should be 300x300 @3x. Avoid rendering text on the image as the scaling on different devices might degrade the quality of your image and render the text illegible. Instead, use the image title and image subtitle properties of the message layout.

An `MSMessage` instance is always intended to either have some form of media associated with it or to be interactive.

Sending a message

Once you have composed a message, you need to attach it to a conversation. To do so, you can use the `activeConversation` property, which is already present on your `MSMessagesAppViewController`. There are several methods on `MSConversation` that will insert a message. You can insert an instance of `MSMessage` if you have composed one. Alternatively, you can insert a sticker or you can simply insert some text.

In `MessagesViewController`, add the following:

```
func shareQuote(_ quote: Quote) {
    guard let conversation = activeConversation
        else { return }
    conversation.insertText("\(quote.text) - \(quote.creator)",
completionHandler: nil)
}
```

If you run this code, you'll notice two things. First of all, if you have the app in expanded mode, the presentation mode does not change to compact after sending the message, so we don't see the quote appear at all. Second of all, we don't actually send the quote. The user is always in control of which messages are sent and when they are sent. To fix the problem with quotes not appearing if we're in expanded mode, we need to add a single line of code to `shareQuote(_:)`. After inserting the quote, add the following line:

```
dismiss()
```

This will dismiss the extension entirely, allowing the user to focus on the quote and send it to the recipient. Once the user decides that they want to send the message you've composed on their behalf, they must manually send the messages. Once this happens, `didStartSending(_:conversation:)` is called on your messages view controller. You won't be notified when this message is actually sent, though, so you can't make any assumptions in your app about whether the message was delivered to the recipient or not.

If the user decided to not send your `MSMessage` instance, `didCancelSending(_:)` is called. You can use this method to clean up or respond to the cancel action in another, appropriate manner. Note that both the start and cancel methods are only called when you're working with `MSMessage` instances. If you're sending simple text like The Daily Quote does, you won't be notified about these events at all.

Summary

In this chapter, you've learned everything about iMessage apps. This new type of extension, which is very similar to an app, is an exciting, powerful new way for you to integrate your apps further into the iOS ecosystem. You now know how you can create a sticker pack to provide your users with a fun, refreshing way to share imagery from your app. You saw how to create a standard and custom sticker pack and you even learned how to create interactive experiences that allow your users to compose stickers together by using a messages session and conversation objects.

Most importantly, you learned that, even though iMessage apps can be very complex, they can also be simple. Some iMessage apps will make heavy use of interactive messages, others are simply standard sticker packs, or somewhere in between, like The Daily Quote. The possibilities are endless and you can have a lot of fun with iMessage extensions. Just be aware that during testing you'll only be able to use your extension in the simulator so, unfortunately, you can't surprise your friends by suddenly sending them stickers from a sticker pack you're still developing.

Once you're done creating an awesome sticker pack, skip ahead to the next chapter in which we'll cover Siri and how you can integrate your app with Apple's powerful, voice-activated personal assistant.

20
Integrating Your App with Siri

At the *WWDC* conference in 2016, Apple announced a new framework named **SiriKit**. SiriKit enables developers to integrate their apps with Apple's digital assistant. This chapter will teach you all the ins and outs of SiriKit, the framework that's used to build extensions for Siri. Similar to iMessage apps, widgets, and notifications, Siri makes use of extensions to integrate with other apps. This is convenient because a lot of the knowledge we've already gained from studying extensions in iOS carries over to Siri extensions.

Even though SiriKit is built upon familiar ideas and concepts, it also introduces a whole new set of terminologies and implementation details. One example of this is that Siri extensions use intents and a specialized vocabulary to integrate with your app. These concepts have been introduced especially for Siri extensions, so you'll need to learn about them before you can implement a Siri extension.

The topics covered in this chapter show the entire flow that your extension goes through when a user uses Siri to make a request for your app. In this chapter, we won't be working on a specific app. Instead, we'll explore the different types of requests that Siri can handle through a series of very small apps that only receive requests from Siri. We won't implement a lot of code to handle these requests.

In this chapter, we're going to cover the following topics:

- Understanding intents and vocabularies
- Handling intents in your extension
- Adding a custom UI to Siri

You'll see why this is an effective approach to learning about SiriKit soon. Let's dive into intents and vocabularies.

Understanding intents and vocabularies

Siri is a powerful, smart, and ever-learning personal assistant that aims to give natural responses to natural speech input. This means that there is often more than one way to say something to Siri. Some users like to be extremely polite to Siri, saying please and thank you whenever they ask for something. Other users like to be short and to the point; they simply tell Siri what they want and that's it.

This means that Siri has to be really smart about how it interprets language and how it converts the user's requests to actionable items. Not only does Siri take into account the language used, it's also aware of how a user is using Siri. If user activates Siri by saying *Hey Siri*, Siri will be more vocal and verbose than when a user activates Siri by pressing and holding the home button, because it's likely that the user is not looking at their device if they didn't press the home button.

To convert a user's spoken requests into actions, Siri uses intents. An intent is a way to describe an action. These intents are supported by app-specific vocabularies; this allows you to make sure that your users can use terms that are familiar to them because they are also used in your app.

Siri does not handle an unlimited amount of intents. All of the intents that Siri can handle belong to a predefined set of domains. If you plan to create a Siri extension for your own app, it must fit into one of the predefined domains that Siri understands. Currently, Siri handles a handful of domains:

- Messaging ("Send a message to Donny that says Hello, World")
- Calling ("Call my sister")
- Payments ("Transfer 5 euros to Jeff")
- Workouts ("Start an outdoor run")
- Ride booking ("Get me a taxi to the airport")
- Photo search ("Find me photos from Paris")
- Notes ("Create a note that says 'Don't forget the dishes')
- Reminders ("Remind me to do the dishes when I get home")
- Visual codes ("Show me my ticket for tonight's concert")

If your app is not in one of these domains, Siri won't be able to integrate with your app very well and your app might even be rejected during review for the App Store if your integration does not implement the appropriate handling for certain intents. In order to integrate Siri with your app, your app must ask the user for permission for it to be used with Siri. It's recommended that you do this as soon as your user first opens your app, because this ensures that your app is available to Siri as soon as possible. Make sure that you ask for permission appropriately though, you don't want to unpleasantly surprise your user with a permission request. You also need to add the `NSSiriUsageDescription` key to your `Info.plist` file and you need to enable the Siri capability in your main app's capabilities tab.

You can only enable the Siri capability for your app if you are a paying member of Apple's Developer Program. Unfortunately, you can't enable or test Siri if you haven't got such a membership.

In order for Siri to work with your app, it's important that a user mentions your app's name to Siri when asking it something related to your app. This is to make sure that apps don't hijack certain words or verbs, which would result in a confusing experience. It doesn't matter exactly how or when the user does this. Siri is all about natural language and it will even understand if your app name is used as a verb. For example, *MyBankApp some money to John Doe* would be interpreted as a money transfer action from an app named *MyBankApp* to a person named *John Doe*.

However, if a user were to ask Siri to perform this task, it would not have all of the information needed to send money to John Doe yet. To handle incomplete requests like this one, intents are used. Let's see what these intents are and how they work.

Adding intents to your extension

Any time a user asks Siri for something, the user's query is resolved to an intent. Every intent has a number of parameters or variables associated with it. Siri will always attempt to fill in these parameters to the best of its ability. Every app that integrates with Siri should have an extension. This extension is used by Siri to make sure that all the parts of an intent are present and valid.

You might expect intents to be a part of SiriKit. In reality, they're not. Intents have their own framework in iOS, enabling other applications, such as Maps, to make use of intents as well. This means that any knowledge regarding intents that you will obtain in this chapter translates over to other extensions that make use of intents.

To enable Siri handles certain intents with your applications, you must specifically register for these intents in your extension's `Info.plist` file. In this book's repository, you'll find a project named `SiriKitMessaging`. We'll add extensions to this application in order to create a fake messaging app.

Before we explore the project, let's set it up so that it is able to integrate with Siri. First, make sure that the signing identity for the project is set to your own paid developer team. You can find and change your team on the **General** tab for your application target. Next, go to the **Capabilities** tab and enable Siri. Also, open the `Info.plist` file and add the `NSSiriUsageDescription` key to it. Provide a short description about what Siri is being used for in this app.

Finally, open `ViewController.swift` and add the following implementation for `viewDidLoad`:

```
override func viewDidLoad() {
    super.viewDidLoad()

    INPreferences.requestSiriAuthorization { status in
        print(status)
    }
}
```

This snippet asks for permission to use Siri as soon as possible in this app, just such as Apple recommends. If permission is already granted, the permissions dialog won't be displayed, so we don't have to check for the current status prior to asking permission. Now that you're all set up to integrate your app with Siri, let's go ahead and explore the example project .

In the project, you'll find two extensions: `MessagingExtension` and `MessagingExtensionUI`. Whenever you add a new Intents Extension to your project, you're offered the option to add a UI extension as well. We'll look into these UI extensions later. Currently, we're only interested in registering our extension to be used for certain intents.

If you open the `MessagingExtension` folder, there are two files in there. A file named `IntentHandler.swift` and the extension's `Info.plist`. The `IntentHandler` class is responsible for communicating with Siri to resolve, confirm, and handle the intents we're registered for. The `Info.plist` is used to determine which intents can be handled by our extension.

Open the `Info.plist` file and expand the `NSExtension` key. You'll notice that there are two intent-related keys in the file: `IntentsRestrictedWhileLocked` and `IntentsSupported`. The second key contains all of the intents our extension can handle. The `IntentsRestrictedWhileLocked` key specifies which of these supported keys can or can't be used without unlocking the device. SiriKit itself will lock certain intents by default. Money transfers, for example, can't be done without unlocking the device, regardless of your extension settings:

Key	Type	Value
NSExtension	Dictionary	(3 items)
NSExtensionAttributes	Dictionary	(2 items)
IntentsRestrictedWhileLocked	Array	(0 items)
IntentsSupported	Array	(3 items)
Item 0	String	INSendMessageIntent
Item 1	String	INSearchForMessagesIntent
Item 2	String	INSetMessageAttributeIntent

The list of intents in **IntentsSupported** is a list of intent class names that your extension is able to handle. Xcode has added a couple of example intents, but this list is not even close to being an exhaustive list of available intents. For a complete list of available intents, you should have a look at the documentation for the Intents framework.

The available intents range from starting a workout to booking a restaurant reservation or requesting that another person transfer money into your account. Each of these intents has their own corresponding class that holds all of the properties that are used to describe the intent.

For our demonstration of integrating Siri into your app, only the `INSendMessageIntent` is required, so you can remove the other two intents. If you want to experiment with multiple intents from the get-go, go ahead and keep any intents you want to play around with. Or add more if you like.

Even though Siri is quite clever when it comes to resolving intents, some apps have their own terminology for certain actions. Custom terminology like this will make resolving certain intents a lot harder for Siri. Luckily, we can help Siri out by adding vocabulary information to Siri. The next section explains how you can do this.

Adding vocabularies to your app

Siri always makes an effort to understand what a user is trying to do with an app, and is usually quite good at this. However, sometimes it's really hard for Siri to figure out what's going on or what a user is trying to do. To help Siri figure out what a user might mean, you can provide vocabularies. A vocabulary is a set of strings that map to intents or parameters.

There are two ways for you to teach Siri the vocabulary for your app. One way is through a `.plist` file. This approach is mostly used for when your app has a global vocabulary that applies to all users. If your app can't supply all custom vocabularies in a static file, you can provide them dynamically. This is particularly useful if, for instance, you want to teach Siri about contacts in a messaging app.

Adding vocabularies through a .plist file

We've already covered that Siri understands when a user wants to do something with your application, even if your user uses your app name as a verb. However, your app name might not be the only thing that's specific to your app. Let's look at an example for a workout app.

If a user were to tell Siri, *Hey Siri, start an Ultimate Run using RunPotato,* Siri would be able to figure out what RunPotato is -- it's the app that is expected to handle the intent. What it won't be able to understand instantly is what it means to *start an Ultimate Run*. This is where a custom vocabulary entry in a `.plist` makes a lot of sense.

Custom vocabularies are always provided through the app itself, never through the corresponding extension. To add vocabulary in the form of app-specific words, like the workout name above, an extra `.plist` file must be added to the app. To add a new `.plist` file, add a new file to your project and select the **Property List** file type under the **Resource** header:

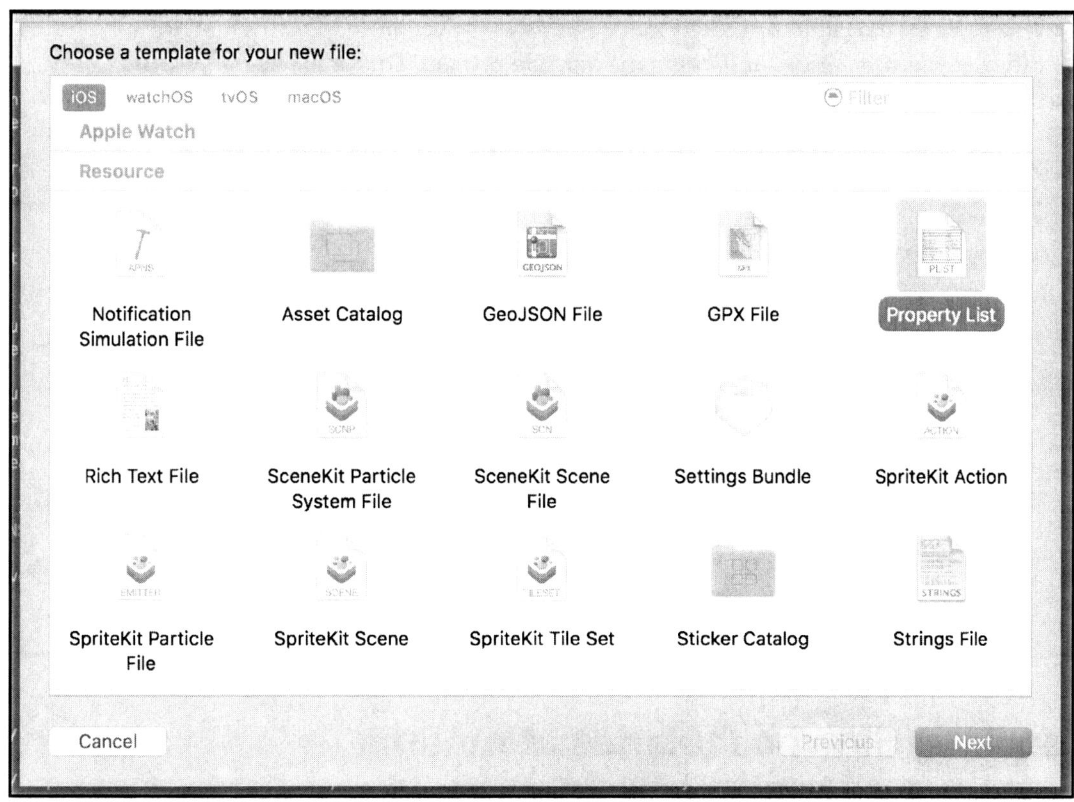

The file you create must be named `AppIntentVocabulary`. This file contains all of the information about an app's custom vocabulary. The example phrase, *Hey Siri, start an Ultimate Run using RunPotato*, contains a workout type that Siri can't understand straight away, so we'll need to add this workout to our `.plist` somehow.

The vocabulary `.plist` is rather specific and verbose. This is important though, because its purpose is to provide a clear window into the vocabulary our app uses. When we created our `AppIntentVocabulary.plist` file, Xcode added a dictionary at the top level of our file. This file is a dictionary that will contain all of our custom vocabulary.

For our example phrase, we're going to need a `Parameter Vocabularies` array. This array will contain `Parameter Vocabulary` items that specify the vocabulary our app uses for workout names. The first item we should specify is a `Parameter Names` array. For our app, it contains a single entry: `INStartWorkoutIntent.workoutName`. We also must add a `Parameter Vocabulary` dictionary to our entry in the `Parameter Vocabularies` array.

The `Parameter Vocabulary` dictionary has keys for the item identifier, synonyms for this identifier, a pronunciation, and even an example phrase. This is all really verbose, but it provides Siri with all of the information it could ever need to resolve user input for your app. The following screenshot shows an example of the entry we'd create for the ultimate run workout:

Key	Type	Value
▼ App Intent Vocabulary Property List	Dictionary	(1 item)
▼ Parameter Vocabularies	Array	(1 item)
▼ Item 0 (Parameter Vocabulary)	Dictionary	(2 items)
▼ Parameter Names	Array	(1 item)
Item 0 (Parameter Name)	String	INStartWorkoutIntent.workoutName
▼ Parameter Vocabulary	Array	(1 item)
▼ Item 0 (Parameter Vocabulary)	Dictionary	(2 items)
Vocabulary Item Identifier	String	ultimate run
▼ Vocabulary Item Synonyms	Array	(1 item)
▼ Item 0 (Vocabulary Item Synonym)	Dictionary	(3 items)
▼ Vocabulary Item Examples	Array	(1 item)
Item 0 (Vocabulary Item Example)	String	Start an Ultimate Run with RunPotato
Vocabulary Item Phrase	String	Ultimate Run
Vocabulary Item Pronunciation	String	ultemit run

Teaching Siri vocabularies at runtime

The second way you can teach Siri about specific content in your app is through the `INVocabulary` class. The `INVocabulary` class is used to teach Siri about information that is specific to the user or changes over time.

A great example of user-specific vocabulary is a workout program that your user manually creates inside of your app. Or maybe the user's friends in a messaging app if those friends don't match the people your user has in their list of contacts on their device.

Updating the vocabularies for your app always occurs in batches. You don't add or remove individual words or phrases for a specific string type. For example, if your user adds a new workout type to a workout application, or if they add new content in a messaging application, you must update the entire vocabulary for this type of string. Let's look at an example:

```
let workoutNames = Workout.orderedNames
INVocabulary.shared().setVocabularyStrings(workoutNames, of:
.workoutActivityName)
```

This snippet uses a computed property on a `Workout` model to retrieve an ordered set of `Workout` names. These names are then added to the shared `INVocabulary` instance so Siri can learn all about them. The ordering of these names is important. You should always order the set you're adding by their likeliness of being used by your user. If your user adds or removes a workout, you must simply repeat the two preceding lines. You must always overwrite your custom vocabulary for a specific string type if you change or update it.

If your user logs out or does something else that makes their custom vocabulary redundant or invalid, you need to make sure you delete the entire user-specific vocabulary by calling `removeAllVocabularyStrings()` on the shared `INVocabulary`. This method of teaching vocabulary to Siri is not intended for vocabularies that are common to all users. If a vocabulary is the same for all users of your app, you should provide this vocabulary through the `.plist` file that was mentioned earlier.

Now that you're completely up to speed regarding intents and vocabularies, let's see how we can start handling the intents Siri sends your way.

Handling intents in your extension

Handling intents can be divided into three stages. The first stage is the resolving stage. In this stage, your extension will go back and forth with Siri to figure out the correct parameters for the given intent. In this step, Siri could ask your app to verify that a certain username exists. Your extension will then have to figure out if the given input is valid and you'll provide Siri with a response code that tells it whether the parameter is resolved or maybe requires a little bit more clarification on the user's end.

The second stage is expected to confirm that everything is set up correctly and all requirements for executing the action are met. The final step is to actually act on the intent and perform the desired action. Let's go through these stages one by one.

Resolving the user's input

When you create an Intents Extension, Xcode creates the main class for your extension, named `IntentsExtension`. This is the class that serves as an entry point for your Intents Extension. It contains a `handler(for:)` method that returns an instance of `Any`. The `Any` type indicates that this method can return virtually anything and the compiler will consider it valid. Whenever you see a method signature like this, you should consider yourself on your own. Being on your own means that the Swift compiler will not help you to validate that you return the correct instance from this method.

The reason the `handler(for:)` method returns `Any` is because this method is supposed to return a handler for every intent that your app supports. If you're handling a send message intent, the handler is expected to conform to the `INSendMessageIntentHandling` protocol. Xcode's default implementation returns `self` and the `IntentHandler` class conforms to all of the intents the extension handles by default.

This default approach is not inherently bad, but if we add an intent to our extension and we forget to implement a handler method, we could return an invalid object from the `handler(for:)` method. A cleaner approach is to check the type of intent we're expected to handle and return an instance of a class that's specialized to handle the intent. This is more maintainable and will allow for a cleaner implementation of both the intent handler itself and the `IntentHandler` class.

Replacing Xcode's default implementation with the following implementation ensures that we always return the correct object for every intent:

```
override func handler(for intent: INIntent) -> Any? {
    if intent is INSendMessageIntent {
        return SendMessageIntentHandler()
    }

    return nil
}
```

The `SendMessageIntentHandler` is a class we'll define and implement to handle the sending of messages. Create a new `NSObject` subclass named `SendMessageIntentHandler` and make it conform to `INSendMessageIntentHandling`. Every intent handler has different required and recommended methods. `INSendMessageIntentHandling` has just one required method: `handle(sendMessage:completion:)`. Other methods are used to confirm and resolve the intent. We'll look at a single resolve method, because they all work similarly; they are just used for different parts of the intent.

Imagine you're building a messaging app that uses groups to send a message to multiple contacts at once. These groups are defined in our app and Siri wants us to resolve a group name. The `resolveGroupName(forSendMessage:with:)` method is called on the intent handler. This method is now expected to resolve the group name and inform Siri about the result by calling the callback it's been passed. Let's see how:

```
let supportedGroups = ["neighbors", "coworkers", "developers"]

func resolveGroupName(forSendMessage intent: INSendMessageIntent, with
completion: @escaping (INStringResolutionResult) -> Void) {
```

```
        guard let givenGroupName = intent.groupName else {
            completion(.needsValue())
            return
        }

        let matchingGroups = supportedGroups.filter{ group in
            return group.contains(givenGroupName)
        }

        switch matchingGroups.count {
        case 0:
            completion(.needsValue())
        case 1:
            completion(.success(with: matchingGroups.first!))
        default:
            completion(.disambiguation(with: matchingGroups))
        }
    }
```

In order to simplify the example a bit, the supported groups are defined as an array. In reality, you would use the given group name as input for a search query in Core Data, your server, or any other place where you might have stored the information about contact groups.

The method itself first makes sure that a group name is present on the intent. If it's not, we'll tell Siri that a group name is required for our app. Note that this might not be desirable for all messaging apps. Actually, most messaging apps will allow users to omit the group name altogether. If this is the case, you'd call the completion handler with a successful result.

If a group name is given, we look for matches in the `supportedGroups` array. Again, most apps would query an actual database at this point. If we don't find any results, we tell Siri that we need a value. If we find a single result, we're done. We can tell Siri that we successfully managed to match the intent's group with a group in our database. If we have more than one result, we tell Siri that we need to disambiguate the results found. Siri will then take care of asking the user to specify which one of the provided inputs should be used to send the message to. This could happen if you ask Siri to send a message to a person named Jeff and you have multiple Jeffs in your contact list.

Confirming the intent status

After you've made sure that everything you need to eventually handle the intent is in place, you must confirm this to Siri. Every intent handler has a `confirm` method. The signature might vary, but there is always some form of confirmation in place. Refer to the documentation for the intent you're handling to confirm which method you're expected to implement. When you're sending messages, the confirmation method is `confirm(sendMessage:completion:)`.

We can make this confirmation step as complex as we desire. For example, we could check whether a message is too long, contains forbidden content, or virtually anything else. Most commonly, you'll want to make sure that the user is authenticated and allowed to send a message to the recipient.

Again, it's completely up to your best judgment to determine which preconditions apply to your extension. The important takeaway for the confirm method is that you're expected to make sure that everything is in place to smoothly perform the action later.

Let's look at an example of a confirmation implementation to see some of the possible outcomes of the confirmation step:

```
func confirm(sendMessage intent: INSendMessageIntent, completion: @escaping
(INSendMessageIntentResponse) -> Void) {
    guard let user = User.current(), user.isLoggedIn else {
        completion(INSendMessageIntentResponse(code:
.failureRequiringAppLaunch, userActivity: nil))
        return
    }


    guard MessagingApi.isAvailable else {
        completion(INSendMessageIntentResponse(code:
.failureMessageServiceNotAvailable, userActivity: nil))
        return
    }


    completion(INSendMessageIntentResponse(code: .ready, userActivity:
nil))
}
```

The preceding implementation checks whether a current user is available, and whether they are logged in or not. Also, the availability of the API that will eventually handle the message sending is checked. Note that these two classes don't exist in the example project and they should be defined by you if you decide to go with this confirmation approach. These classes simply serve as placeholder examples to demonstrate how confirmation of an intent works.

If we don't have a logged in user, we launch the app. If we don't have a messaging API available, we return an error message that reflects the fact that the service is not available. Every intent has their own set of response codes. Refer to the documentation for the intent you're handling to find the relevant response code and decide which ones are appropriate to handle in your extension.

If a user must be taken to your app in order to log in, for example, Siri will automatically create a user activity that's passed to `AppDelegate` in your application. You must implement `application(_:continue:restorationHandler:)` to catch and continue the user activity. Just as when we used user activities with Spotlight, it's important that you take the shortest path possible to resume and handle the user activity.

A user activity that's created by Siri has its `interaction` property set. This property contains an `INInteraction` object that reflects the action the user attempts to complete using Siri. A good implementation will fulfill this interaction as soon as possible inside of the app. It's also possible to create your own user activity if you want to add custom information that Siri doesn't pass on. If you want to do this, you should pass your custom user activity to the `INSendMessageIntentResponse` initializer.

After confirming that everything is in place, it's time to perform the action for the user.

Performing the desired action

Once Siri knows exactly what the user wants to do and which parameters to use, and once your app has confirmed that everything is in place to handle the user's request, the time has finally come to execute the requested action. Once this time has come, Siri calls the `handle` method on your intent handler.

Just like the `confirm` method, every intent has their own version of this method, but they all follow a similar pattern. For sending messages, the method signature is `handle(sendMessage:completion:)`. The parameters for this method are identical to the ones in the confirmation step. The major difference is that you're now expected to handle the intent instead of only confirming that the intent is valid.

Once you're done handling the intent, you must call the completion handler with an `INSendMessageIntentResponse`. If everything goes well, you're expected to use a success response code. If you're unable to process the intent quickly, you're expected to call the completion handler with an `inProgress` status code. Using the `inProgress` informs Siri that you're handling the intent but it's taking a while. An example of a handle method is shown in the following code snippet:

```
func handle(sendMessage intent: INSendMessageIntent, completion: @escaping
(INSendMessageIntentResponse) -> Void) {
    guard let groupName = intent.groupName,
        let message = intent.content else {
            completion(INSendMessageIntentResponse(code: .failure,
userActivity: nil))
    }


    MessagingApi.sendMessage(message, toGroup: groupName) { success in
        if success {
            completion(INSendMessageIntentResponse(code: .success,
userActivity: nil)
        } else {
            completion(INSendMessageIntentResponse(code: .failure,
userActivity: nil)
        }
    }
}
```

Just like before, we're using non-existing dummy classes, so copying and pasting this code won't work in the example app. The purpose of this snippet is to show you what an implementation of sending a message could look like. First, we confirm that we can extract all of the required information to send a message with. If this fails, we tell Siri that we couldn't send the message. Then a `MessagingApi` class method is used to send the message to the selected group. Finally, we inform Siri about how we handled the intent based on the response from the API.

The final aspect of the Siri experience we need to take into account is the user interface. Siri will provide us with a default interface for every intent, but it's often desirable to customize this interface to match your app's look and feel. Let's see how we can achieve this.

Adding a custom UI to Siri

When your user is using Siri, they aren't always looking at their device. But when they are, it's desirable that the experience a user has when using your app through Siri looks and feels a lot like when they're directly interacting with your app. One of the tools you've already seen is custom vocabularies. You can use a vocabulary to map user and app-specific terms to Siri's vocabulary.

Another way we can customize the Siri experience is through an **Intents UI Extension**. Whenever you add an **Intents Extension** to your project, Xcode asks you if you also want to add an interface extension. If you select this checkbox, you don't have to do anything to add the UI extension since it's already there. However, if you didn't check the checkbox, you should add a new **Intents UI Extension** through the targets menu, as you do for all extensions.

A custom user interface for an intent works a lot like other UI extensions. When you create the extension, you're given a storyboard, a view controller, and a `.plist` file. The `.plist` file is expected to specify all of the intents that this specific UI extension can handle. In the case of the example app, this is just a single intent: `INSendMessageIntent`.

If you intend to support multiple intents, it's often a good idea to split your extension up in multiple extensions, grouping intents together based on how similar they are. This will make it easier to maintain your code in the long run and it's easier to reason about the way your code and extensions work.

If you open the `IntentViewController` file, you'll discover a method named `configure(with:context:completion:)`. We're expected to use this method to configure our view. We need to display the recipient group and the message contents for our extension, so add the following two `@IBOutlets` in the `IntentViewController`:

```
@IBOutlet var recipientGroupLabel: UILabel!
@IBOutlet var messageContentLabel: UILabel!
```

Next, add the following implementation for `configure(with:context:completion:)`:

```
func configure(with interaction: INInteraction!, context:
INUIHostedViewContext, completion: ((CGSize) -> Void)!) {
    // Do configuration here, including preparing views and calculating a
desired size for presentation.


    guard let messageIntent = interaction.intent as? INSendMessageIntent
        else { return }


    recipientGroupLabel.text = messageIntent.groupName
    messageContentLabel.text = messageIntent.content


    let viewWidth = extensionContext?.hostedViewMaximumAllowedSize.width ??
0
    completion(CGSize(width: viewWidth, height: 100))
}
```

This implementation verifies that we're dealing with a message sending intent and then populates the receiving group and the message accordingly. We also determine at which width our UI should be displayed. Finally, we call the completion handler and pass in the size that we want to use for our interface. A value of 100 should be plenty of room to accommodate our message for now.

Add two labels to your Storyboard and lay them out as shown in the following screenshot. Don't forget to hook up the outlets for these labels as well. The message content has a **body** style and the recipient group uses a **Caption 1** style.

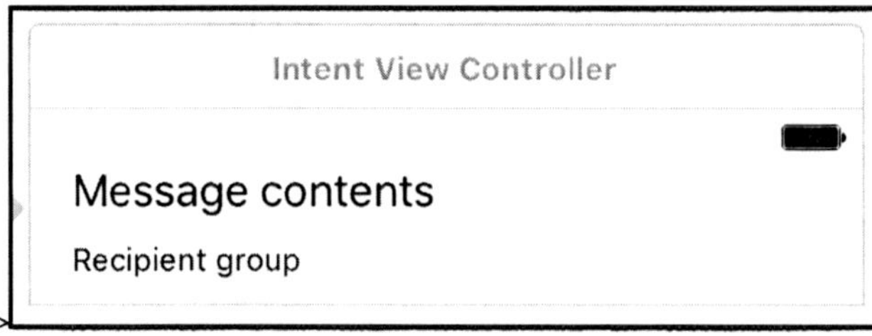

After hooking this up, you can try to send a message to one of the predefined groups and you'll see that your custom layout is now added into the conversation with Siri:

There is one problem though. The message transcript is now shown twice: Once through our extension and once through Siri itself. To prevent this from happening, all we need to do is make our view controller conform to `INUIHostedViewSiriProviding`. Add this protocol to `IntentViewController`'s declaration and add the following property:

```
var displaysMessage = true
```

By doing this, Siri is now aware that we render our own version of the message transcript, so we don't need Siri to show the message for us.

Just like the notifications UI extension, Intent UI Extensions are not interactive. They can only provide a static interface. Your custom interface should be simple and to the point. Siri is often used as a quick way to perform certain tasks and you should keep this in mind when you're designing your custom Siri interface elements.

Summary

In this chapter, you've seen everything you need to know about integrating your app with Siri. You know everything about intents and the Intents framework. We've implemented a Siri extension that fakes sending messages to groups of users. We saw that there are methods that can be implemented to help Siri resolve a user's query and fill in the missing parameters that Siri needs to build an intent. You also learned that you can add custom vocabularies to Siri, meaning that your Siri extension can make use of user and app-specific terms. These custom vocabularies allow your users to communicate with Siri in terms that fit in with terminology that you might use in your app. Finally, you saw how to create a custom user interface for your Siri extensions, enabling a maximum amount of app recognition to the user.

A good integration with Siri can improve your app tremendously, but only if it fits into one of the predefined domains. Even though you can stretch the meaning of certain intents slightly, it's recommended to only attempt to integrate with Siri if it truly makes sense to do so. A bad implementation will frustrate users because they'll feel like Siri simply isn't listening to them. You don't want this to happen. Siri was the last extension we'll cover in this series of chapters on extensions. The next couple of chapters will mainly focus on improving and maintaining the quality of your applications through testing, measuring performance, and improving performance before you submit your app to the App Store.

21
Ensuring App Quality with Tests

In all chapters up to this one, we've mostly focused on writing code that's used in our apps. The apps we've built are small and can be tested manually, quite quickly. However, this approach doesn't scale well if your apps become larger. This approach also doesn't scale if you want to verify lots of different user input, lots of screens, complex logic, or even if you want to run tests on many different devices.

Xcode comes with built-in testing tools. These tools allow you to write tests so you can make sure that all of the business logic for your app works as expected. More importantly, you can test that your user interface works and behaves as intended in many different automated scenarios.

Many developers tend to shy away from testing, postpone it until the end of the project, or simply don't do it at all. The reason for this is often that it's pretty hard to figure out how to write proper tests if you just start out. For instance, many developers feel like large parts of testing are so obvious that writing tests feels silly. However, if not approached properly, tests can be more of a burden than a relief by being high-maintenance and not testing important areas.

This chapter aims to be an introduction to writing both logic and interface tests using Xcode and its built-in tools. By the end of this chapter, you should be able to set up a solid, basic suite of tests and understand how you can make use of the tools provided by both Xcode and Swift to write better code that is testable and reliable.

This chapter covers the following two topics:

- Testing logic with XCTest
- Testing the user interface with XCUITest

Let's not waste any time and dive straight into the wonderful world of testing your app logic.

Testing logic with XCTest

If you're just starting out with testing your app logic, there are a couple of thoughts you might already have on the subject, or maybe none at all. To start testing your code, you don't need to have a computer science degree or spend days studying the absolute best way to test your code. In fact, chances are that you're already sort of testing your code and you don't even know it.

So, what does it really mean to test your code? That's exactly what we'll cover in this section. First, we'll look at testing code and the different types of test you might want to write. Then we'll dive into `XCTest` and setting up a test suite for an app. Finally, we're going to see how we can optimally test some real code and how we should refactor it to improve testability.

Understanding what it means to test code

When you test your code, you're essentially making sure that certain inputs produce the desired outputs. A very basic example of a test would be to make sure that calling a method that increments its input by a given value does, in fact, produce the output we expect.

Whenever you launch your application in a simulator or on a device and test whether you can perform certain actions, you are testing your code. Any time you print something to the console to manually verify that the expected value is printed, you are also testing your code. Once you think about testing this way, a concept that might have sounded hard before actually does not seem as foreign as it once was. This probably raises a new question for you; if it doesn't, let me raise it for you. What exactly should you be testing?

Determining what to test

When you start testing, it's often hard to decide what logic you want to test and what logic you don't want to test. Reasons for this could include certain logic being too trivial, too hard, or just not important enough to test. This implies that you do not have to test absolutely everything your app does, and that is intentional. Sometimes it's simply not reasonable to write tests for a certain part of your code. For instance, you don't have to test that `UIKit` behaves as it should; it's Apple's job to make sure that `UIKit` is bug-free.

Determining what to test is important, and the longer you defer deciding whether you will add tests for a certain piece of logic, the harder it will become to write tests for it. A simple rule of thumb is that you don't need to test Apple's frameworks. It's safe to assume that Apple makes sure that any code they ship is tested and if it contains bugs, there's not much you can do to fix it anyway. Moreover, you don't want your own tests to fail where Apple's tests should have.

What you should at least test is the *call-site* of your methods, structs, and classes. The call-site is defined here as the methods that other objects use to perform tasks. It's actually good practice to make anything that's not on the call-site of your objects private, meaning that outside code can't access that part of the code. We'll look more into that later when we refactor code to be more testable.

You should also test code that you might consider too trivial to write tests for. These parts of your code are likely to receive the *too trivial* approach in other aspects of the process as well. This leads to you and your coworkers paying less and less attention to this trivial piece of code and before you know it, a bug is introduced that you might not catch until your app is in the *App Store*. Writing trivial tests for trivial code takes very little time and saves you from minor oversights leading to large complications.

So, to sum up, a few simple guidelines that you might want to follow when you're writing tests are:

- Test trivial code; minimal effort is involved
- Test the call-site of your objects; they will make sure that your public APIs are consistent and work as expected
- Don't test Apple's frameworks or any other dependencies; doing this is the responsibility of the framework vendor

Once you've determined what you're going to test, it's time to start writing the actual tests. However, if you've heard about testing before, you might have heard of terms such as integration tests, unit tests, sanity tests, and a couple of others. The next segment will focus on a couple of the most important and well-known types of testing.

Choosing the correct test type

Whenever you're writing tests, it's often a good idea to ask yourself what type of test you're writing. The type of testing you want to do will typically guide you towards the way your test should be structured and scoped. Having tests that are well-scoped, structured, and focused will ensure that you're building a stable test suite that properly tests your code without unintended side-effects that influence the quality of your tests.

Unit tests

Probably the most well-known type of test is the unit test. A lot of people call virtually any test they write to test their code a unit test, which is probably why this is such a well-known term for testing. Another reason for the unit test being so popular is that it's a very sensible test type.

A unit test is intended to make sure that a unit of code works as intended. A unit of code is often an entire object such as a class or struct, but it could just as well be a standalone method. It's important that unit tests do not rely on the cooperation of any other test or object. It's OK to set up an environment where certain preconditions are met as we'll see later, but it's extremely important that a unit test does not accidentally test other objects, or even worse, depends on other tests being executed first.

When you're writing unit tests, it's not uncommon to create instances of models that are stored in an array to represent a dummy database or fake REST APIs. This is all done to ensure that a unit test does not fail due to, for example, a network error. When you're testing a unit, you should test that specific unit and eliminate as many outside influences as possible.

Integration tests

An integration test ensures that a certain piece of code is able to integrate with other parts of the system. Similar to unit tests, an integration test should never rely on other tests. This is important for any test you write. Whenever a test depends on a certain precondition, the test must set this up on its own. Not doing this will create implicit dependencies between your tests, meaning that your tests must execute in a certain order. This type of implicit dependency can cause tests to fail in unexpected ways and it makes your test suite unreliable.

If you can't depend on other tests, an integration test requires a little more setup than a unit test. For example, you might want to set up an API helper, fetch some data from the API, and feed it into a database. A test like this verifies that the API helper can cooperate with the database layer. Both layers should have their own unit tests to ensure they work in isolation while the integration test ensures that the database and API can work together as well. There are many other types of test that you can write or learn about, but for now, we'll stick to these two definitions. Sticking to just two definitions of testing will prevent you from getting lost in the world of testing before you even get started. Also, it's important to not pretend that testing is more than it really is: Writing code that tests other code.

We mentioned earlier that tests should never rely on other tests. Let's expand on that a little bit more before we start setting up our test suite in Xcode.

Isolating tests

Assumptions are a huge risk when you're testing. Any time you assume anything about the environment you're testing in, your test is not reliable. If you're just getting into writing tests, it's tempting to make assumptions such as *I'm testing on the simulator and my test user is always logged in so my tests can be written under the assumption that a logged in user exists*. This assumption makes a lot of sense to a lot of people, but what if something happened that made the user log out? ne example is a test that makes sure your user can log out, which would leave the simulator without a logged in user.

When this happens, a lot of your tests will fail due to assumptions that were made about the test environment. More importantly, these tests might fail even if the code they're testing works flawlessly.

As mentioned before, tests should test a single thing in your app. They should rely on as little outside code as possible and they should be properly focused. A common pattern that people use to structure their tests and improve reliability is the 3-As or AAA approach. This name of this pattern is short for Arrange, Act, and Assert. The following is an explanation for each of the As.

Arrange

The arrange step is all about preparation. Make sure a logged in user exists, populate the (in memory) database, create instances of your fake API or other helpers. You essentially arrange everything to be in place for your testing environment. Note that this step should not involve too much setup. If you find yourself writing a lot of code in the arrange step, your test might be too broad. Or the code you're testing relies on too many other pieces of code. This can't always be avoided, but if it happens, make sure you consider refactoring your code and test to keep the quality on-par with what you're trying to achieve.

Act

During the act stage, you set everything for your test in motion. You call methods on the object you're testing, you feed it data, and you manipulate it. This is essentially where you take your code for a proverbial spin. Don't perform too many actions in succession though; too much acting will lead to problems during the next step, assert.

Assert

The final A in the 3-As approach is assert. During the assert step, you make sure that the state of the object you're testing is as you'd expect. Act and assert can be used multiple times in a single test. For instance, you might want to assert that doing something once places the object in a certain state and that doing it again places the object in another state. Or possibly that the state stays the same. Just as with the other two steps, if you're asserting a lot of things, or if you're acting and asserting over and over again in a test, chances are that your test is too broad. This can't always be avoided, but long tests with a lot of acting and asserting are often an indication of testing too much at once.

Reading about testing can be quite boring and it tends to get rather abstract quickly, so let's leave the theory for now. We'll set up a test suite for an existing project in Xcode and we'll start writing some tests so all of the information you've been taking in so far becomes a bit more tangible.

Setting up a test suite with XCTest

In this section, we're going to add a test suite for a new app: `MovieTrivia` You'll find the basic setup for this project in the Git repository. If you open the project, there are some view controllers, an `Info.plist`, and all the other files you would normally expect to exist in a regular project. There's also a JSON file in the project named `TriviaQuestions.json`. This file contains a couple of dummy questions that you can load by uncommenting a couple of lines in `LoadTriviaViewController.swift`.

By default, `LoadTriviaViewController.swift` attempts to load questions from a non-existing web server. This is intentional, to demonstrate how one would normally set up a project like this. Since we don't have a web server at our disposal right now, you can swap out the dummy networking code for the JSON file to test this app.

Before we write tests or perform any optimization, we should add a test target to the project. A test target is added similarly to how you added extensions before. You just select a different type of target: The **iOS Unit Testing Bundle**. The following screenshot illustrates the correct template you should select:

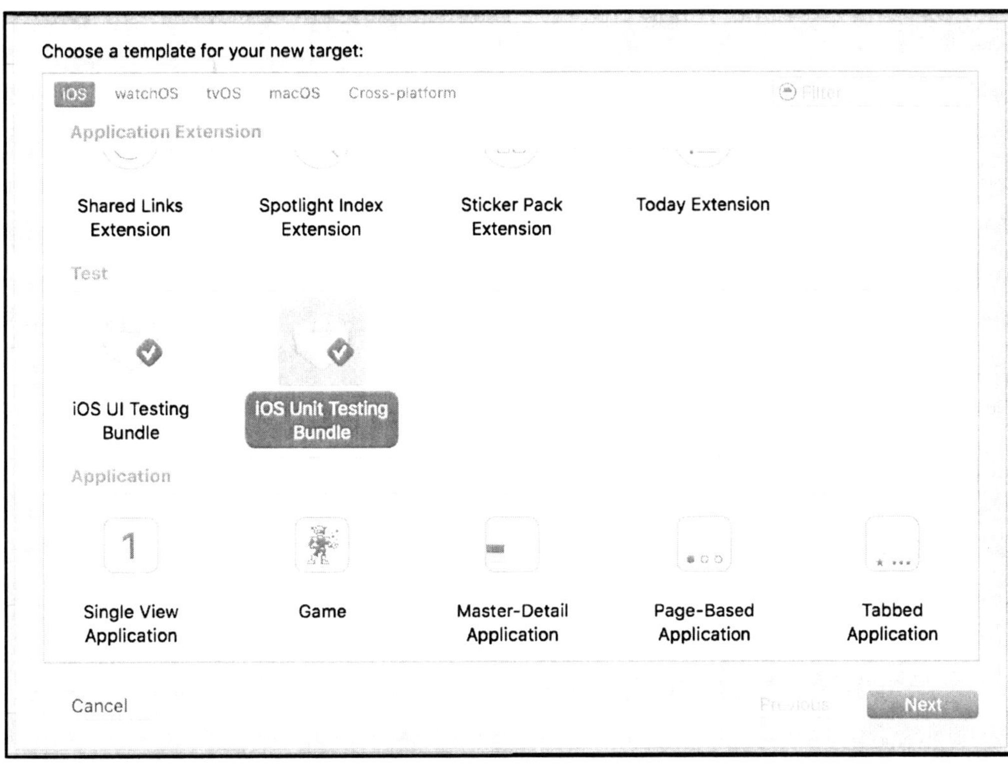

After adding the target, a new folder is added to your project. If you choose the default name for the test target, it's called `MovieTriviaTests`. In this target, we'll write all of our tests.

If you think about when we used files in multiple targets with extensions, you might expect that we're going to need to add all of the files we want to test to both of our targets. Fortunately, this isn't the case. When we write tests, we can import our entire app, enabling us to write tests for all of the code we have in the app target.

If you look inside the `MovieTriviaTests` folder, you'll find a single file; `MovieTriviaTests.swift`. This file contains a couple of hints about what tests should look like for your test suite. First of all, note that the test class inherits from `XCTestCase`. All of your test classes should inherit from this superclass to be discovered as a test.

First of all, you'll find a `setUp()` method in the test class. This method is used mainly for you to fulfill the first stage of the AAA pattern in testing: Arrange. You use this method to ensure that all of the preconditions for your test are met. You could make sure that your user is logged in or that your database is populated with test data. Note that the nature of this setup forces you to do something interesting. You can't write all of your tests in the same class because not every test has the same preconditions.

Separating tests into several classes is a good thing. You should create a test class for every unit of code that you're testing. One test class should typically not test more than a single class or struct in your app. If you're writing an integration test there might be more than one class involved in the test, but you should still make sure that you're only testing a single thing: The integration between the classes involved in the integration you're testing.

Also, note that there are two methods prefixed with `test` in the test class. These methods are executed as tests and they are expected to perform the act and assert steps. The majority of work should be performed in these `test` methods. Do note that it's often better to have multiple short test methods rather than a single test method that tests everything. The larger the methods, the harder it will be to maintain and debug your tests.

Finally, you'll find a `tearDown()` method. This method is intended to give you an opportunity to clean up after yourself. When you have inserted dummy data into your database, it's often desirable to remove this data when your tests are done. This will ensure a clean slate for the next test that runs and it minimizes the chances that your first test accidentally influences the second test that runs. As mentioned before, we don't want our tests to depend on other tests. This means that we also don't want to pollute other tests by leaving traces of previous tests.

Now that you have a test suite in place, let's see how we can write tests for our existing code and how it can be refactored to be properly tested.

Optimizing code for testability

Now that the project has a test target, it's time to start adding some tests to it. Before we do this, we should determine what to test. Take some time to look at the app and the code and try to think of things to test. Assume that the app is finished and that we're loading trivia questions from a server.

Some of the things you might have thought of to test are:

- Making sure that we can display the data we load from the network
- Testing that selecting the correct answer triggers the expected code
- Testing that selecting a wrong answer triggers the expected code
- Ensuring that the first question is displayed after we show the last one
- Testing that the question index increments

If you came up with most of the tests on this list, good job. You've successfully identified a lot of valid test cases. But how do we test these cases? The project has been made hard to test intentionally, but let's see how far we can get with the current architecture.

Remove the test class that Xcode has generated for you and create a new one called `LoadQuestionsTest` Use the following bit of boilerplate code in this file's implementation so we have a starting point to write our test:

```
import XCTest
@testable import MovieTrivia

typealias JSON = [String: Any]

class LoadQuestionsTest: XCTestCase {
    override func setUp() {
        super.setUp()
    }
    func testLoadQuestions() {
    }
}
```

Note the `@testable import MovieTrivia` line at the top of the file. This line imports the entire app target so you can access it in your tests. Before the implementation for `testLoadQuestions` is added, it's wise to think about what this method should test. If you look at the code in the app target, the trivia questions are loaded in the `LoadTriviaViewController`'s `viewDidAppear(_:)` method. Once the questions are loaded, we segue to the next screen. An important detail is that the `triviaJSON` property on `LoadTriviaViewController` is set once the questions are loaded.

Based on this information, our test should create an instance of our view controller, make it appear, then the questions will load and we'll have to wait until `triviaJSON` has a value. Writing this test involves many moving parts, way more than we should be comfortable with. For instance, because this app uses a storyboard, we would have to involve a storyboard in our test to make sure that we can instantiate our view controller. This means that any changes or mistakes in the user interface would cause our logic test to fail. This is not desirable because we're testing whether we can load data from the network, not if the user interface updates once the data is loaded.

This is a great moment to start refactoring our code and making it more testable. The first piece of code that we'll revamp for testability is the question loading code.

Introducing the question loader

To make our code more testable we'll create a special helper that can load questions for our view controller. The helper will go to the network and fetch the questions. Once the data is loaded, a callback is called to notify the object that initiated the request about the loaded questions. Because we already know that we're going to be testing this code, we'll need to think of a way to make sure that the helper works with both an offline and an online implementation. We wouldn't want the test to fail due to a broken internet connection.

Because tests should rely on as few outside factors as possible, removing the networking layer from this test would be great. This means that we're going to need to split our helper up in two parts; the actual helper and a fetcher. The fetcher will implement a protocol that defines the interface that a question fetcher must have, which will allow us to inject either an online or offline fetcher into the helper.

If the preceding seems a little bit abstract and confusing to you, that's OK. We're going to slowly work our way to the nicely abstracted, testable implementation that we want to end up with. First, let's create the helper struct. Add a new Swift file named `QuestionsLoader.swift` and add the following implementation to it:

```
struct QuestionsLoader {
    typealias QuestionsLoadedCallback = (JSON) -> Void
    func loadQuestions(callback: @escaping QuestionsLoadedCallback) {
        guard let url = URL(string: "http://questions.movietrivia.json")
            else { return }
        URLSession.shared.dataTask(with: url) { data, response, error in
            guard let data = data,
                let jsonObject = try? JSONSerialization.jsonObject(with:
data, options: []),
                let json = jsonObject as? JSON
                else { return }
```

```
                callback(json)
            }
        }
    }
```

This struct defines a method to load questions with a callback. This is already nice and a lot more testable than before. We can now isolate the question loader and test it separated from the rest of our app. A test for the helper in its current state would look like the test shown in the following code snippet:

```
func testLoadQuestions() {
    let questionsLoader = QuestionsLoader()
    let questionsLoadedExpectation = expectation(description: "Expected the
questions to be loaded")
    questionsLoader.loadQuestions { _ in
        questionsLoadedExpectation.fulfill()
    }
    waitForExpectations(timeout: 5, handler: nil)
}
```

First, an instance of the `QuestionsLoader` is created. Next, we create an `expectation`. An expectation is used when you expect something to eventually happen. In our case, we're loading the trivia questions asynchronously. This means that we can't expect the questions to be loaded by the time our test method is finished executing. The callback that's called when the questions are loaded has a single purpose in our tests: It must fulfill the expectation. In order to make sure that the test waits for us to fulfill the expectation, `waitForExpectations(timeout:handler:)` is called after `loadQuestions(callback:)`. If we don't fulfill the expectation within the five-second timeout that is specified, the test fails.

Examine this test closely; you should be able to see all of the A's that you read about earlier. The first A, arrange, is where we create the loader and set up the expectation. The second A, act, is when we call `loadQuestions(callback:)` and make sure that our tests wait for any unfulfilled expectations. The final A, assert, is inside the callback. We're currently not validating anything inside the callback, we'll get to that later.

One issue that we still have with the loader is the reliance on an active connection to the internet. We also assume that the server we're calling is up and that the data it returns is valid. These are all assumptions that influence the reliability of our test. If we don't have an internet connection or if the server is down, our test fails even though our code might be fine. That is not an ideal situation to find yourself in. Tests should be able to run without relying on any external factors.

We can improve this by utilizing some protocol-oriented programming and the dependency injection pattern. This means that we should define a protocol that defines the public API for a networking layer. Then we'll implement a networking struct in the main project that conforms to the protocol and we'll create a property on the `QuestionsLoader` that holds anything that implements the networking logic. We'll also add a struct in our test target that implements the networking protocol.

By setting the test up like this, we can take the entire networking logic out of the equation and arrange our test in such a way that the networking doesn't matter. Our mock networking layer will respond with valid, reliable responses that we can test.

Mocking API responses

It's common practice to mock API responses when you're testing. In this segment, we're going to implement the mock API that was described before in order to improve the quality and reliability of our test. First, let's define our protocol. Create a new file in the app target and name it `TriviaAPIProviding`:

```
typealias QuestionsLoadedCallback = (JSON) -> Void

protocol TriviaAPIProviding {
    func loadTriviaQuestions(callback: @escaping QuestionsLoadedCallback)
}
```

The protocol only requires a single method right now. If you want to expand this app later, everything related to the Trivia API must be added to the protocol in order to make sure that you can create both an online version for your app and an offline version for your tests. Next, create a file named `TriviaAPI` and add the following implementation to it:

```
import Foundation

struct TriviaAPI: TriviaAPIProviding {
    func loadTriviaQuestions(callback: @escaping QuestionsLoadedCallback) {
        guard let url = URL(string: "http://quesions.movietrivia.json")
            else { return }
        URLSession.shared.dataTask(with: url) { data, response, error in
            guard let data = data,
                let jsonObject = try? JSONSerialization.jsonObject(with:
data, options: []),
                let json = jsonObject as? JSON
                else { return }
            callback(json)
        }
    }
}
```

Lastly, update the `QuestionsLoader` struct with the following implementation:

```
struct QuestionsLoader {
    let apiProvider: TriviaAPIProviding
    func loadQuestions(callback: @escaping QuestionsLoadedCallback) {
        apiProvider.loadTriviaQuestions(callback: callback)
    }
}
```

The question loader now has an `apiProvider` that it uses to load questions. Currently, it simply delegates any load call over to its API provider, but we'll update this code soon to make sure that we convert the raw JSON data that the API returns to us to question models. First, update our view controller and we'll implement the mock API struct in our test so we can create our first passing test.

Update the `viewDidAppear(_:)` method of the `LoadTriviaViewController` as shown in the following code snippet. This implementation uses the loader struct instead of directly loading the data inside the view controller:

```
override func viewDidAppear(_ animated: Bool) {
    super.viewDidAppear(animated)
    let apiProvider = TriviaAPI()
    let questionsLoader = QuestionsLoader(apiProvider: apiProvider)
    questionsLoader.loadQuestions { [weak self] json in
        self?.triviaJSON = json
        self?.performSegue(withIdentifier: "TriviaLoadedSegue", sender:
self)
    }
}
```

The preceding code is not only more testable, it's also a lot cleaner. Next up, we'll create the mock API inside our test target.

First of all, the JSON file in the app target should be removed from the app target and added to the test target. Drag it into the correct folder and make sure you update the **Target Membership** so the JSON file is only available in the test target. Now add a new Swift file named `MockTriviaAPI` to the test target and add the following code to it:

```
import Foundation
@testable import MovieTrivia

struct MockTriviaAPI: TriviaAPIProviding {
    func loadTriviaQuestions(callback: @escaping QuestionsLoadedCallback) {
        guard let filename = Bundle(for:
LoadQuestionsTest.self).path(forResource: "TriviaQuestions", ofType:
"json"),
```

```
            let triviaString = try? String(contentsOfFile: filename),
            let triviaData = triviaString.data(using: .utf8),
            let jsonObject = try? JSONSerialization.jsonObject(with:
triviaData, options: []),
            let triviaJSON = jsonObject as? JSON
            else { return }
        callback(triviaJSON)
    }
}
```

This code fetches the locally stored JSON file from the test bundle. In order to determine the exact path to load, we use one of the test classes to retrieve the current bundle. This is not the absolute best way to retrieve a bundle because we rely on an external factor being in our test target. However, we can't use structs to look up the current bundle. Should we remove the class we rely on, the compiler will throw an error and we can easily fix our mistake. Once the file is loaded, we call the callback and we have successfully handled the request.

Mocking APIs is often done with external frameworks. This is mostly because not all APIs are as straightforward as the ones we've just mocked. A lot of apps have way more complex interactions than we've just tested. The main ideas surrounding your testing architecture remain the same, regardless of application complexity. Protocols can help you to define a common interface for certain objects. Combining this with dependency injection like we just did for the `QuestionsLoader` helps to isolate the pieces of your code that you're testing, and it enables you to switch out pieces of code to make sure that you don't rely on external factors if you don't have to.

So far, our test is not particularly useful. We only test if the `QuestionsLoader` passes our request on to the `TriviaAPIProviding` object and if the callbacks are called as expected. Even though this technically qualifies as a test, wouldn't it be better to test whether we can covert the JSON from the API into question objects that our app can display? And when doing so, wouldn't it be nice if we did so by creating instances of a model class instead of JSON?

Testing whether our `QuestionsLoader` can convert JSON into a `Question` model is a test that's a lot more interesting than solely testing whether the callback is called. We're now confronted with the question of whether we should add a new test, or modify the existing test. If we create a new test, we're saying that we want to test whether the callback is called and we also want to test whether the loader converted the JSON response to valid models.

If we choose to modify the existing test, we're essentially saying that we assume that the callback will be called. It's been established before that assumptions are bad and we shouldn't make them. But testing if the `callback` is called and testing whether the `callback` is called with the correct information could be considered testing the same thing twice. If the `callback` isn't called, it also won't be called with the correct information.

We'll write a single test with one expectation and multiple assertions. Doing this makes sure that we fulfill our expectation of the `callback` being called and at the same time we can use assertions to ensure that the data that's passed to the `callback` is valid and correct. Using the `QuestionsLoader` to create instances of a model rather than using it like we do now has the added benefit of improving our app's code as well.

Right now, the app uses raw JSON to display questions. If the JSON changes, we are forced to update the view controller. If the app grows, this process becomes more painful because you'd have to search in multiple view controllers. The more manual labor we have to perform in that kind of situation, the bigger the chance that we'll forget or overlook something. This is why it's a much better idea to use the new `Codable` protocol to encapsulate API responses. Using Codable objects also enables us to get rid of directly accessing JSON in view controllers. It's much cleaner to have direct access to models than having access to raw and dirty JSON.

Using models for consistency

Adding a question model involves quite some refactoring. First, we must define the `Question` model. Create a new Swift file named `Question` and add the following implementation to it:

```
import Foundation

struct Question: Codable {
    enum CodingKeys: String, CodingKey {
        case title
        case answerA = "answer_a"
        case answerB = "answer_b"
        case answerC = "answer_c"
        case correctAnswer = "correct_answer"
    }
    let title: String
    let answerA: String
    let answerB: String
    let answerC: String
    let correctAnswer: Int
}
```

If you followed along with `Chapter 10`, *Fetching and Displaying Data From the Network*, this model should look somewhat familiar. The `Question` struct conforms to the `Codable` protocol. Since not all property names match the JSON data, a custom mapping is provided. This is all that needs to be done in order to convert the JSON to a `Question` struct. In order to properly use this model with the dummy JSON data, a `QuestionsFetchResponse` will be added as well. This struct also conforms to the `Codable` protocol and encapsulates the questions as follows:

```
import Foundation

struct QuestionsFetchResponse: Codable {
    let questions: [Question]
}
```

Now that the `Question` model and the response container are in place, a couple of changes must be made to the existing code. First of all, the typealias in the `TriviaApiLoading` protocol should be modified as follows:

```
typealias QuestionsFetchedCallback = (Data) -> Void
```

Next, update the implementation of the TriviaAPI for the `URLSession` callback in `loadTriviaQuestions(callback:)` as follows:

```
URLSession.shared.dataTask(with: url) { data, response, error in
    guard let data = data
        else { return }
    callback(data)
}
```

The `QuestionsLoadedCallback` `typealias` should be updated to the following definition:

```
typealias QuestionsLoadedCallback = ([Question]) -> Void
```

And lastly, the implementation for `loadQuestions(callback:)` should be updated as follows:

```
func loadQuestions(callback: @escaping QuestionsLoadedCallback) {
    apiProvider.loadTriviaQuestions { data in
        let decoder = JSONDecoder()
        guard let questionResponse = try?
decoder.decode(QuestionsFetchResponse.self, from: data)
            else { return }
        callback(questionResponse.questions)
    }
}
```

This wraps up the changes for the API. However, there still is some refactoring we must do in the view controllers. Rename the `triviaJSON` property on `LoadTriviaViewController` to the following:

```
var questionsArray: [Question]?
```

Make sure you replace all occurrences of `triviaJSON` to the new questions array. Also, make sure you change the following line in `prepare(for:sender:)`:

```
questionViewController.triviaJSON = triviaJSON
```

Change this line to:

```
questionViewController.questionsArray = questionsArray
```

In `QuestionViewController` change the type of `questionsArray` to `[Question]` and remove the `triviaJSON` property. At this point, you can clear all of the JSON-related code from the guards in this class. You should be able to do this on your own since the compiler should guide you with errors. If you get stuck, look at the finished project in the Git repository.

By now, you should be able to run the tests and they should pass. To run your tests, click the Product menu item and select Test. Alternatively, press Cmd + *U* to run your tests. The tests run fine, but currently we haven't made sure that all of our questions in the JSON data have been converted to Question models. To make sure this worked, we'll load the JSON file in our test case, count the number of questions in the JSON file, and assert that it matches the number of questions in the callback.

Update the `testLoadQuestions()` method as shown in the following code snippet:

```
func testLoadQuestions() {
    let apiProvider = MockTriviaAPI()
    let questionsLoader = QuestionsLoader(apiProvider: apiProvider)
    let questionsLoadedExpectation = expectation(description: "Expected the
questions to be loaded")
    questionsLoader.loadQuestions { questions in
        guard let filename = Bundle(for:
LoadQuestionsTest.self).path(forResource: "TriviaQuestions", ofType:
"json"),
            let triviaString = try? String(contentsOfFile: filename),
            let triviaData = triviaString.data(using: .utf8),
            let jsonObject = try? JSONSerialization.jsonObject(with:
triviaData, options: []),
            let triviaJSON = jsonObject as? JSON,
            let jsonQuestions = triviaJSON["questions"] as? [JSON]
            else { return }
```

```
        XCTAssert(questions.count > 0, "More than 0 questions should be
passed to the callback")
        XCTAssert(jsonQuestions.count == questions.count, "Number of
questions in json must match the number of questions in the callback.")
        questionsLoadedExpectation.fulfill()
    }
    waitForExpectations(timeout: 5, handler: nil)
}
```

We use the same code as the code that was used before in the fake API to load the JSON file. Once the JSON is loaded, we use XCTAssert to make sure that more than zero questions were passed to the callback and that the number of questions in the JSON file matches the number of questions that were loaded.

`XCTAssert` takes a Boolean expression and a description. If the assertion fails, the description is shown. Adding good descriptions will help you to easily figure out which assertion in your test has made your test fail.

This new `test` method is a small addition to our test but has huge consequences. By improving our test, we have improved the quality of our app because we are now sure that our question loader correctly transforms JSON into model objects. By adding model objects, we have improved the code in our view controllers because, instead of reading raw JSON, we're reading properties from a model. And the final improvement that this modification gives us is that our view controllers are a lot cleaner.

One more metric that has improved by refactoring our code is the amount of code that is covered by our tests. We can measure this metric with Xcode's built-in code coverage tracking. We'll look at how to use this tool next.

Gaining insights through code coverage.

With the introduction of Xcode 7, Apple has greatly improved its testing tools. One of the tools newly introduced with Xcode 7 is Code Coverage. The Code Coverage tool aims to provide us with insights about how thorough our tests are. Not only that, it also informs us about which parts of our code are tested in our unit tests and which parts of our code aren't.

To enable **Code Coverage**, first open the scheme editor through the **Product | Scheme** menu as shown in the following screenshot:

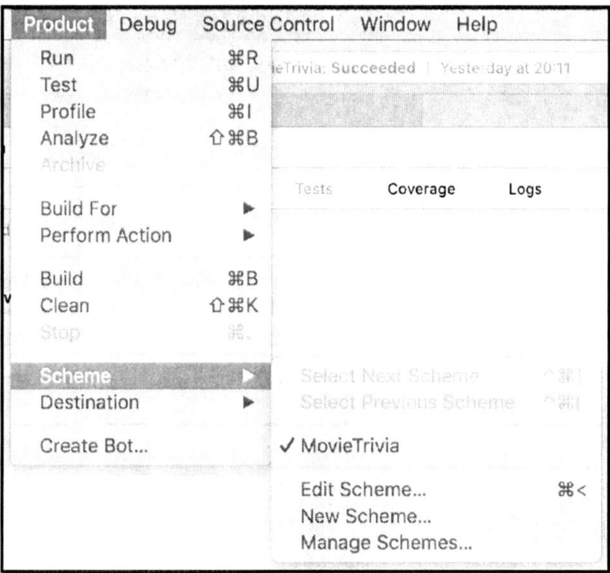

Select the testing action and make sure the **Gather coverage** data checkbox is checked as shown in the following screenshot:

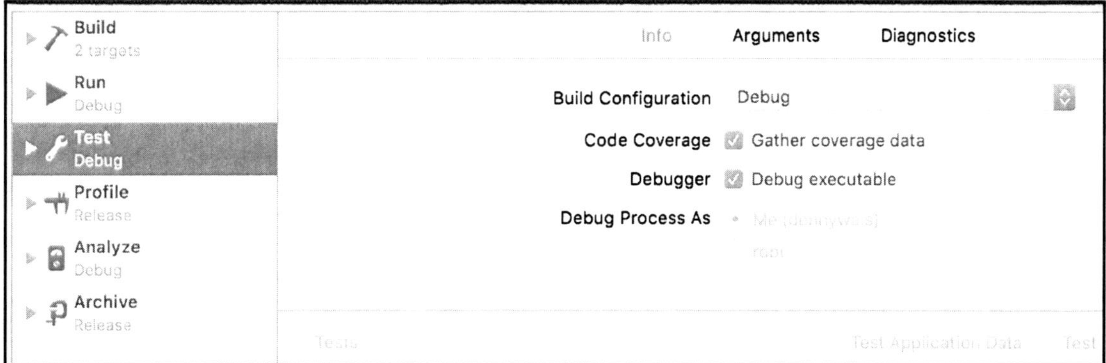

You can also press Cmd + < to quickly open the scheme editor.

After doing this, close the scheme editor and run your tests. This time, Xcode will monitor which parts of your code have been executed during this tests, and which parts haven't. This information can give you some good insights about which parts of your code could use some more testing. To see the coverage data, open the Report navigator in the leftmost sidebar in Xcode. The rightmost icon in this sidebar represents the Report navigator as shown in the following screenshot:

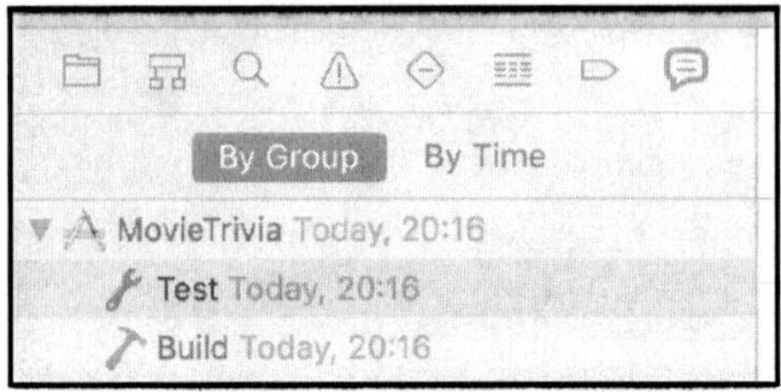

If you expand the controls for your app, you can select the test report. This report will open in the Editor area of Xcode and you'll be presented with three tabs: Tests, Coverage, and Logs. We're only interested in the Coverage tab right now. If you select this tab, you're presented with several bars that are filled to indicate the amount of code tested in the corresponding file. The following screenshot shows Coverage for the `MovieTrivia` app:

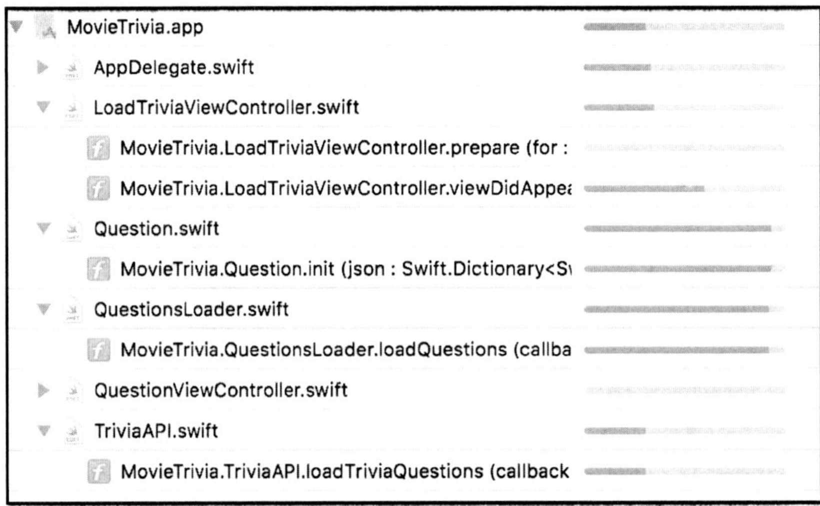

The more a bar is filled, the more lines of code in that file or method were executed during your test. You'll notice that our `AppDelegate.swift` file is covered under the tests even though we haven't written any tests for it. The reason this happens is that the app must launch during the test to act as a host for our tests. This means that parts of the code in `AppDelegate.swift` are actually executed during the test and therefore Xcode considers it covered in the tests.

If you expand the `AppDelegate.swift` file you'll see that a lot of methods are not tested at all. If you open up the `AppDelegate.swift` file, you can see that these untested methods are, in fact, empty methods. To improve your test coverage and to avoid accidental bugs, you should remove these empty implementations.

One last feature of Code Coverage that's worth mentioning is inline Code coverage. Inline Code coverage will show you how often a certain block of code has been executed during testing. This will give you insights into your code coverage inline, in your files, without having to navigate to the Reports navigator. To enable this feature, open up your Xcode preferences and navigate to the *Text Editing* tab. Check the Show iteration counts checkbox at the bottom of the tab. If you open a file now, you'll see the iteration count for your code on the right side of the editor window. The following screenshot shows the iteration count for the `loadQuestions(callback:)` method:

```
func loadQuestions(callback: @escaping QuestionsLoadedCallback) {
    apiProvider.loadTriviaQuestions { json in
        guard let jsonQuestions = json["questions"] as? [JSON]
            else { return }

        let questions = jsonQuestions.map { jsonQuestion in
            return Question(json: jsonQuestion)
        }.flatMap { $0 }

        callback(questions)
    }
}
```

Even though Code Coverage is a great tool for gaining insights into your tests, you shouldn't let it influence you too much. Regularly check the Code Coverage for your app and look for methods that are untested and are either easy to write tests for or should be tested because they contain important logic. Code Coverage is also great for discovering parts of your code that should be tested but are hard to test because they're nested deep inside a view controller, for example.

What you should not do is aim for a full 100% coverage. Doing this will make you jump through crazy hoops and you'll invest way more time in testing than you should. Not all paths in your code have to be tested. However, don't shy away from doing some refactoring like we've done before. Proper testing helps you to avoid bugs and structure your code better. Code Coverage is just one extra tool in your tool belt to help identify which parts of your code could benefit from some tests.

If we look at the current state of the coverage in the MovieTrivia app, we're actually doing quite well. Most of the logic in the app is tested. The only part of our app that's not tested thoroughly is the view controllers. If you're using storyboards, like we are, it's not necessarily easy to test view controllers. Even if you opt for an all-code approach where you omit storyboards and write all of your layout purely in code, it can be tedious to test your view controllers.

Luckily, there is one last testing tool that we'll discuss in this chapter; `XCUITest`.

Testing the user interface with XCUITest

Knowing that most of your app logic is covered with tests is great. What's not so great, however, is adding your view controllers to your logic test. Before Xcode 7 came out, you had to put quite some effort into testing view controllers. This led to people simply not testing a lot of view controller code, which would ultimately lead to bugs in the user interface that could have been prevented with tests. We were able to perform some degree of tests using UI Automation in Instruments, but it simply wasn't great.

In Xcode 7, Apple introduced interface testing and the `XCUITest` framework. With this feature, we suddenly gained a great framework to write interface tests in; we also gained a tool that allows us to record these tests as we go through them manually.

To top it all off, `XCUITest` uses the accessibility features in iOS to gain access to the interface. This means that implementing user interface tests forces you to put at least a little bit of effort into accessibility for your applications. Apps that are hard to navigate through accessibility features will be harder to test than apps that are accessible.

So `XCUITest` has two really great features that we should look at in greater detail. First of all, it helps us to enhance accessibility for our app. Secondly, it's easy to get started with UI testing and it allows us to test different paths in the view layer, which drives up the amount of code that's covered by tests.

Before we start recording our first UI test, let's have a quick look at accessibility.

Making your app accessible to your tests

One of the lesser-known features in iOS is accessibility. The design teams at Apple work really hard to ensure that iOS is accessible for everybody. This includes blind people and people with other disabilities that could somehow affect the user's ability to operate their iOS device.

Just looking at the accessibility settings in the iOS settings app makes it evident that this is a subject that Apple invests a lot of time in. If you're working on an app, Apple expects you to put in the same kind of effort. Doing this will be rewarded by more app downloads and if you're lucky even a couple of reviews. In their talk on iOS Accessibility from WWDC 2015, Apple has even mentioned that implementing accessibility features can be helpful if you ever want to be featured in the *App Store*. Only the best apps get featured by Apple and if your app is accessible to all people, that really boosts your app's quality.

A common myth surrounding accessibility is that it's hard to implement or that it takes a lot of time. Some people even go as far as saying that it looks ugly or gets in the way of beautiful design. None of this is entirely true. Sure, making your app accessible requires some effort, but the UIKit framework is very helpful in terms of accessibility. Using standard components and keeping your user in mind while you design your app will make sure that your app is both accessible and looks good.

So, how does accessibility work on iOS? And how can we make sure our app is accessible? A fun way to experiment with this is to turn on **VoiceOver** on your device. To enable **VoiceOver**, go to the **Accessibility** menu. You'll find several vision-related accessibility settings; **VoiceOver** should be the topmost one. To quickly enable and disable **VoiceOver**, scroll all the way to the bottom of the settings page and select **VoiceOver** as your accessibility shortcut.

This will allow you to toggle **VoiceOver** off and on by triple-clicking the home button as shown in the following screenshot:

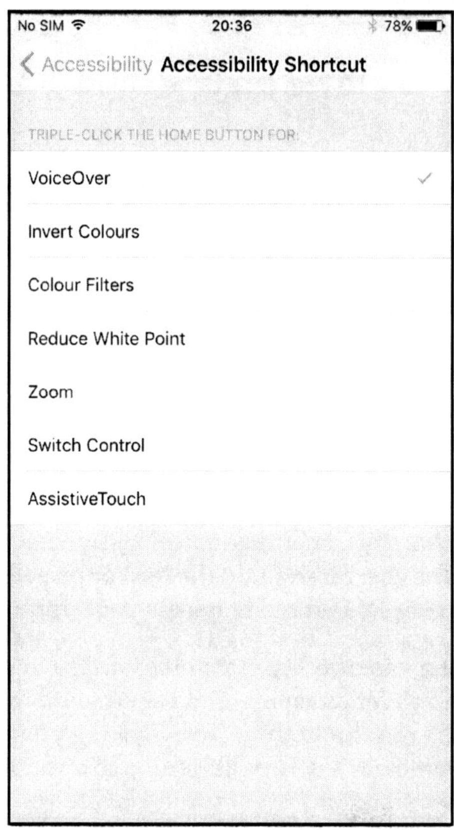

After enabling this, go ahead and run the `MovieTrivia` app on your device and triple-click your home button to enable **VoiceOver**. Swipe around and try to use the app. This is how a person with a vision impairment uses your app. You won't get past the loading screen because we're not loading dummy questions, but the splash screen is actually pretty accessible, especially considering we haven't done anything to make this happen. UIKit helps us a great deal in the accessibility realm because most labels and button titles are used as accessibility labels.

You can set your own accessibility information through the Identity Inspector in Interface Builder. You can add custom labels, hints, identifiers, and traits to your interface to aid accessibility and, coincidentally, your UI tests. The following screenshot shows the accessibility panel:

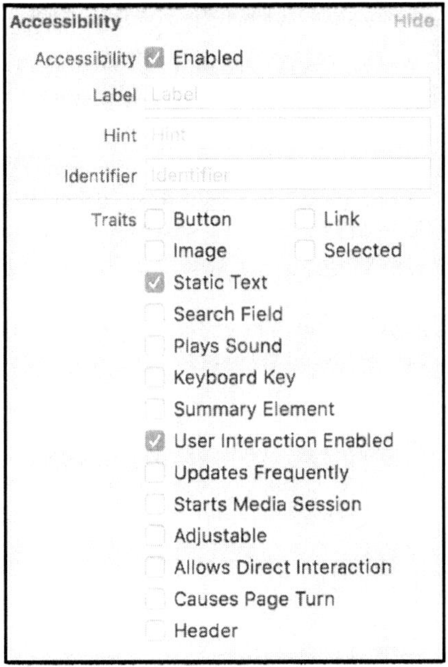

For most UIKit interface elements you won't have to touch these settings yourself. UIKit will make sure that your objects have sensible defaults that automatically make your app accessible. Now that you have a little bit of background information about accessibility, let's have a look at testing our (accessible) UI.

Recording UI tests

Before we can record our UI tests, we need to add a UI testing target to our project. Follow the same steps as before to add a new testing target, but pick the iOS UI Testing Bundle this time around. If you look inside the newly-created group in your project, the structure for your UI tests looks very similar to the structure for Unit tests.

One very important difference between UI test targets and Unit test targets is that your UI tests do not gain access to any code that's inside your app. A UI test can purely test the interface of your app and make assertions based on that.

If you open the `MovieTriviaUITest.swift` file, you'll notice the `setUp()` and `tearDown()` methods present. Also, all of the tests that must be executed are methods with the test prefix. This is all similar to what you've already seen.

One big difference is that we must manually launch the app in the setup stage. This is due to the fact that the UI test target is essentially just a different app that can interact with your main app's interface. This limitation is very interesting and it's also the reason why it's important to make your app accessible.

To start recording a UI test in Xcode, you must start a recording session. If you're editing code in a UI test target, a new interface element is visible in the bottom-left corner of your code editor area: A red dot:

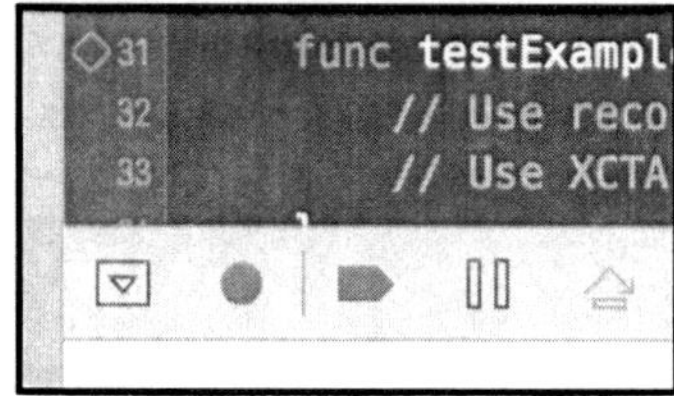

Place your typing cursor inside the `testExample()` method and click the red dot. Your app will be launched and anything you do is recorded as a UI test and played back when you run your tests. If you tap on the label and the activity indicator, Xcode will produce the following Swift code in the testing method:

```
let app = XCUIApplication()
app.staticTexts["Loading trivia questions..."].tap()
app.otherElements.containing(.activityIndicator, identifier:"In
progress").element.tap()
```

The UI test we recorded is a set of instructions that get sent to the app. We look for a certain element in the app's UI and we `tap()` it. This test doesn't do a lot so it's not particularly useful. To make our test more useful, we should let the app know that it should run in a special test mode so we can load questions from the JSON file instead of loading it from the network, making the test more reliable. To do this, we will use so-called launch arguments. Launch arguments can be used by the app to enable or disable certain functionality. You can think of them as variables that you can insert into your app dynamically.

Passing launch arguments to your app

In order to switch the loading of questions from the network to a local file for testing, we can pass a launch argument. This launch argument is then read by the app so it can load questions from the JSON file like we did before in the unit tests, rather than attempting to load trivia questions from the server.

To prepare for the launch argument and loading the JSON file, create a folder named `Shared` in your project and move the `TriviaQuestions.json` file to it. Make sure you add it to the test target, the app target, and the UI test target. We won't need it in the UI test target just yet, but we will later, so you might just as well add it to the UI test target while you're at it.

In order to pass launch arguments to the app, we should modify the `setUp()` method in the UI test class:

```
override func setUp() {
    super.setUp()
    continueAfterFailure = false
    let app = XCUIApplication()
    app.launchArguments.append("isUITesting")
    app.launch()
}
```

The `XCUIApplication` instance that represents the app has a `launchArguments` property, which is an array of strings. You can add strings to this array prior to launching the app. We can then extract this launch argument in our app. Modify the `loadTriviaQuestions(callback:)` method in `TriviaAPI.swift` as shown in the following code snippet:

```
func loadTriviaQuestions(callback: @escaping QuestionsFetchedCallback) {
    if ProcessInfo.processInfo.arguments.contains("isUITesting") {
        loadQuestionsFromFile(callback: callback)
        return
    }
    // existing implementation...
}
```

The code highlighted in bold should be inserted above the existing implementation of this method. The snippet checks whether we're UI testing by reading the app's launch arguments. If the UI testing argument is present, we call the `loadQuesionsFromFile(callback:)` method to load the questions from the JSON file instead of loading it from the network.

Note that it's not ideal to perform checks such as the preceding one in your production code. It's often better to wrap configuration like this in a struct that can be modified easily. You can then use this struct throughout your app instead of directly accessing process info throughout your app. An example of such a configuration could look like this:

```
struct AppConfig {
    var isUITesting: Bool {
        ProcessInfo.processInfo.arguments.contains("isUITesting")
    }
}
```

We won't use this configuration class in this app since it's not needed for our small app. But for your own apps you might want to implement a configuration object regardless of app size since it leads to more maintainable code.

If you build the app right now, you should get a compiler error because `loadQuesionsFromFile(callback:)` is not implemented in the API class yet. Add the following implementation for this method:

```
func loadQuestionsFromFile(callback: @escaping QuestionsFetchedCallback) {
    guard let filename = Bundle.main.path(forResource: "TriviaQuestions",
ofType: "json"),
        let triviaString = try? String(contentsOfFile: filename),
        let triviaData = triviaString.data(using: .utf8)
        else { return }
    callback(triviaData)
}
```

It's very similar to the question loading method we wrote for the unit tests; the only difference is that we're using a different way to obtain the bundle from which we're loading the questions.

If you run your UI tests now, they will fail. The reason for this is that, when the test framework starts looking for the elements we tapped before, they don't exist. This results in a test failure because we can't tap elements that don't exist.

We should adjust our tests a bit because tapping loaders are not the most useful UI test. It's a lot more useful for us to make sure that we can tap buttons and that the UI updates according to the result of tapping a button. To do this, we're going to write a UI test that waits for the question and buttons to appear, taps them, and checks whether the UI has updated accordingly. We'll also load the questions file so we can check that tapping a wrong or right answer works as intended.

Making sure the UI updates as expected

We're going to write two tests to make sure that our trivia game works as expected. The first test will test that the question and answer buttons appear and that they have the correct labels. The second test will make sure that we can tap the answers and that the UI updates accordingly.

Instead of recording the tests, we're going to write them manually. Writing tests manually gives you a bit more control and allows you to do much more than just tapping on elements. Before we do this, you should open the `Main.storyboard` file and give accessibility identifiers to the UI elements. Select the question title and give the `UILabel` an identifier of `QuestionTitle`. Select each of the answers and give them the identifiers `AnswerA`, `AnswerB`, and `AnswerC`, respectively. Make sure your layout looks as shown in the following screenshot:

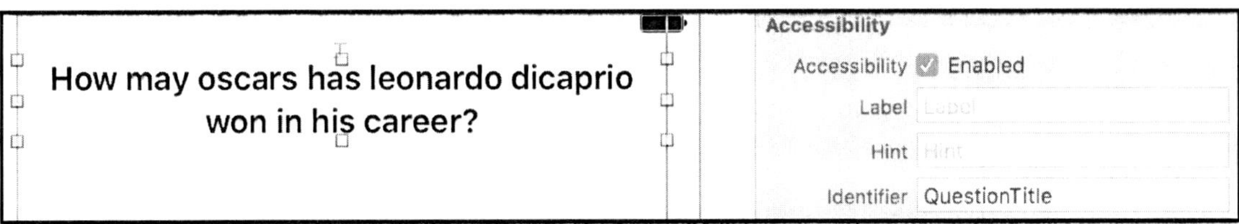

Remove the existing UI test from the `MovieTriviaUITests` class and add the one shown in the following code snippet:

```
func testQuestionAppears() {
    let app = XCUIApplication()
    let buttonIdentifiers = ["AnswerA", "AnswerB", "AnswerC"]
    for identifier in buttonIdentifiers {
        let button = app.buttons.matching(identifier: identifier).element
        let predicate = NSPredicate(format: "exists == true")
        _ = expectation(for: predicate, evaluatedWith: button, handler:
nil)
    }
    let questionTitle = app.staticTexts.matching(identifier:
"QuestionTitle").element
    let predicate = NSPredicate(format: "exists == true")
    _ = expectation(for: predicate, evaluatedWith: questionTitle, handler:
nil)
    waitForExpectations(timeout: 5, handler: nil)
}
```

Each element is selected through its accessibility identifier. We can easily do this because the `XCUIApplication` instance we create provides easy access to our elements. Next, we create a predicate that will check whether the exists property of our element is true. Then we create an expectation that will evaluate the predicate for the UI element. Lastly, we wait for these expectations to fulfill. Our expectations are considered fulfilled whenever the predicate we pass to it is true. If this never happens, our tests fail and we'll know that something's wrong.

To make sure that our questions are loaded correctly, we'll need to load the JSON file like we did before. Add the following property to the test so we have a place to store the trivia questions:

```
var questions: [JSON]?
```

Next, add the following code to the `setUp()` method right after calling `super.setUp()`:

```
guard let filename = Bundle(for: MovieTriviaUITests.self).path(forResource:
"TriviaQuestions", ofType: "json"),
    let triviaString = try? String(contentsOfFile: filename),
    let triviaData = triviaString.data(using: .utf8),
    let jsonObject = try? JSONSerialization.jsonObject(with: triviaData,
options: []),
    let triviaJSON = jsonObject as? JSON,
    let jsonQuestions = triviaJSON["questions"] as? [JSON]
    else { return }

questions = jsonQuestions
This code should look familiar to you because it's similar to the code
we've already used to load json before. To make sure that the correct
question is displayed, update the test method as shown below:
func testQuestionAppears() {
    // existing implementation...
    waitForExpectations(timeout: 5, handler: nil)
    guard let question = questions?.first
        else { fatalError("Can't continue testing without question
data...") }
    validateQuestionIsDisplayed(question)
}

func validateQuestionIsDisplayed(_ question: JSON) {
    let app = XCUIApplication()
    let questionTitle = app.staticTexts.matching(identifier:
"QuestionTitle").element
    guard let title = question["title"] as? String,
        let answerA = question["answer_a"] as? String,
        let answerB = question["answer_b"] as? String,
        let answerC = question["answer_c"] as? String
```

```
        else { fatalError("Can't continue testing without question
data...") }
    XCTAssert(questionTitle.label == title, "Expected question title to
match json data")
    let buttonA = app.buttons.matching(identifier: "AnswerA").element
    XCTAssert(buttonA.label == answerA, "Expected AnswerA title to match
json data")
    let buttonB = app.buttons.matching(identifier: "AnswerB").element
    XCTAssert(buttonB.label == answerB, "Expected AnswerB title to match
json data")
    let buttonC = app.buttons.matching(identifier: "AnswerC").element
    XCTAssert(buttonC.label == answerC, "Expected AnswerC title to match
json data")
}
```

This code is run after we know for sure that our UI elements exist because it's executing after waiting for the expectations we created. The first question is extracted from the JSON data and all of the relevant labels are then compared to the question data using a method that we can reuse to validate that a certain question is currently shown.

The second test we should add is intended to check whether the game UI responds as expected. We'll load a question, tap the wrong answers, and make sure that the UI doesn't show the button to go to the next question. Then we'll tap the correct answer and tap the next question button. Finally, we'll validate that the second question is properly displayed and that the next question button is hidden again:

```
 func testAnswerValidation() {
    let app = XCUIApplication()
    let button = app.buttons.matching(identifier: "AnswerA").element
    let predicate = NSPredicate(format: "exists == true")
    _ = expectation(for: predicate, evaluatedWith: button, handler: nil)
    waitForExpectations(timeout: 5, handler: nil)
    let nextQuestionButton = app.buttons.matching(identifier:
"NextQuestion").element
    guard let question = questions?.first,
        let correctAnswer = question["correct_answer"] as? Int
        else { fatalError("Can't continue testing without question
data...") }
    let buttonIdentifiers = ["AnswerA", "AnswerB", "AnswerC"]
    for (i, identifier) in buttonIdentifiers.enumerated() {
        guard i != correctAnswer
            else { continue }
        app.buttons.matching(identifier: identifier).element.tap()
        XCTAssert(nextQuestionButton.exists == false, "Next question button
should be hidden")
    }
    app.buttons.matching(identifier:
```

```
buttonIdentifiers[correctAnswer]).element.tap()
    XCTAssert(nextQuestionButton.exists == true, "Next question button
should be visible")
    nextQuestionButton.tap()
    guard let nextQuestion = questions?[1]
        else { fatalError("Can't continue testing without question
data...") }
    validateQuestionIsDisplayed(nextQuestion)
    XCTAssert(nextQuestionButton.exists == false, "Next question button
should be hidden")
}
```

The preceding code depicts the entire test that validates that our UI responds properly to good and bad answers. Tests like these are quite verbose, but they save you a lot of manual testing; tests like these are absolutely worth writing.

When you test your UI like this, you can rest assured that your app will at least be somewhat accessible. The beauty in this is that both UI testing and accessibility can greatly improve your app quality and each strongly aids the other.

Testing your UI is mostly a matter of looking for elements in the UI, checking their state or availability, and making assertions based on that. In the two tests we've written for MovieTrivia, we've combined expectations and assertions to test both existing UI elements and elements that might not be on screen yet. Note that your UI tests will always attempt to wait for any animations to complete before the next command is executed. This will make sure that you don't have to write expectations for any new UI that gets pushed using a transition.

Summary

Congratulations! You've made it to the end of this lengthy, information-packed chapter. You should know enough about testing and accessibility right now to begin exploring testing in greater depth than we have in this chapter. No matter how small or big your app is, writing automated tests will ensure that your app is of high-quality. More importantly, instead of assuming that something works because it worked before, your automated tests will guarantee that it works because your tests don't pass if you broke your code.

You also learned that writing testable code sometimes requires you to refactor large portions of code. More often than not, these refactoring sessions leave your code in a much better state than it was before. Code that is easy to test is often cleaner and more robust than code that is hard to test. If you're interested in learning more about the topic of testing, you could have a look at *Test-Driven iOS Development with Swift 3,* written by Dr. Dominik Hauser. This book takes a practical approach to developing an iOS application using TDD principles. Now that you know how to cover your app with tests, let's see how you can measure your app's performance using some of the great tools Xcode provides in the next chapter.

22
Discovering Bottlenecks with Instruments

In order to debug and improve your apps, you need to understand which tools are available to you. One of these tools is called **Instruments**. **Instruments** is a collection of measurement tools that help you to profile and analyze your app in order to debug and detect complex problems or performance bottlenecks. For example, Instruments can help you figure out if your app is suffering from memory leaks. Tracking a memory leak blindly is tedious and nearly impossible. A good tool such as Instruments helps you track down several possible causes for a memory leak, saving both your time and your sanity.

In this chapter, we're going to look at an app named *Instrumental*. This app is a very plain app and it's not even close to a real app, but it has some issues. The app is very slow, and the longer it's used and the more the user interacts with the app, the worse the problems seem to get. We're going to use **Instruments** to measure and analyze this app so we can make improvements where needed and hopefully, we'll end up with a fast app that works well.

This chapter is divided into the following segments:

- Exploring the Instruments suite
- Discovering slow code
- Closing memory leaks

By the end of this chapter, you'll be able to deeply analyze your apps to find potential issues and solve them before they really become a problem. Let's get going, shall we?

Exploring the Instruments suite

In this book's Git repository, you'll find a project named *Instrumental*. The app is still in its early stages of development, so there is plenty of work that needs to be done to improve the app. Some implementations are not ideal and the app contains some placeholders that might not make a lot of sense.

Even though the app isn't finished and the code isn't perfect, the app should be working fine, especially in the performance department. If you launch the app and click around, you'll notice that the app isn't working fine. It's actually really slow! Let's see if we can find the issue that's making the app slow.

If you dig through the source code, you'll immediately see that the app has three main screens: a table view, a collection view, and a detail view. The table view displays a list of 50 items, each of which links to an infinitely scrolling collection view with a custom layout. The layout for the `collectionview` is custom because we needed to have exactly one pixel of spacing between items, and this layout can be achieved with a reusable layout that can be used in other collections or apps. Finally, the detail view just shows an image and a label on top of the image.

Based on knowledge from earlier chapters, you should know that a simple app such as this should be able to run smoothly on virtually any iOS device. Collection views and table views are optimized to display huge datasets, so an endless scrolling collection view that keeps adding fifty new rows whenever we almost reach the end of the list should not be too much of a problem. In other words, this app should be able to run at 60 frames per second with no trouble at all.

However, if you start scrolling through the collection view and move back and forth between screens and then scroll more and more, you'll find that some collections will stop scrolling smoothly. They will randomly freeze for a little while and then continue scrolling. And the more we scroll through the collections, the bigger this issue seems to become.

When we look at the memory usage in Xcode's Debug navigator (the sixth icon in the left sidebar), we can tell that something is wrong because memory usage just keeps on going up when we navigate through screens. This in itself is nothing to worry about, temporary memory spikes are normal. When the used memory never gets freed even though you might have expected it to, that's when you should start worrying. Take a look at the following graph:

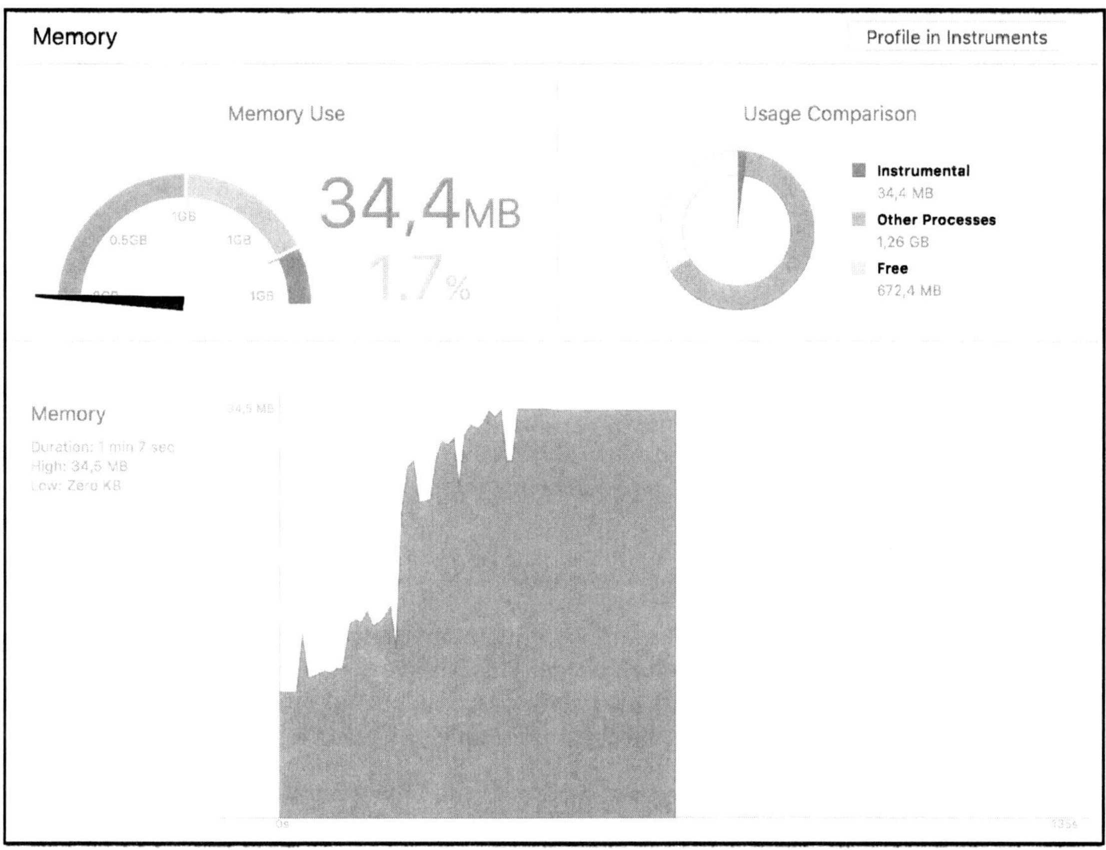

Whenever you debug performance issues or if you're trying to measure performance, make sure to measure on a real device. If you measure using the simulator, your app might run fine even though it might not run fine on a device. This is due to the way the simulator works. It mimics an iOS device, but it's backed up by all the power your Mac has to offer. So, the processor and available memory are those of your Mac, resulting in performance that's often much better than it would be on a device.

For now, we'll make a mental note of our app's rising memory usage and shift our attention towards the *Instruments* app. To profile your app with **Instruments**, you can either select **Product | Profile** from the toolbar or hit Cmd + *I* on your keyboard. Xcode will then build your project and launch **Instruments** so you can select a profiling template:

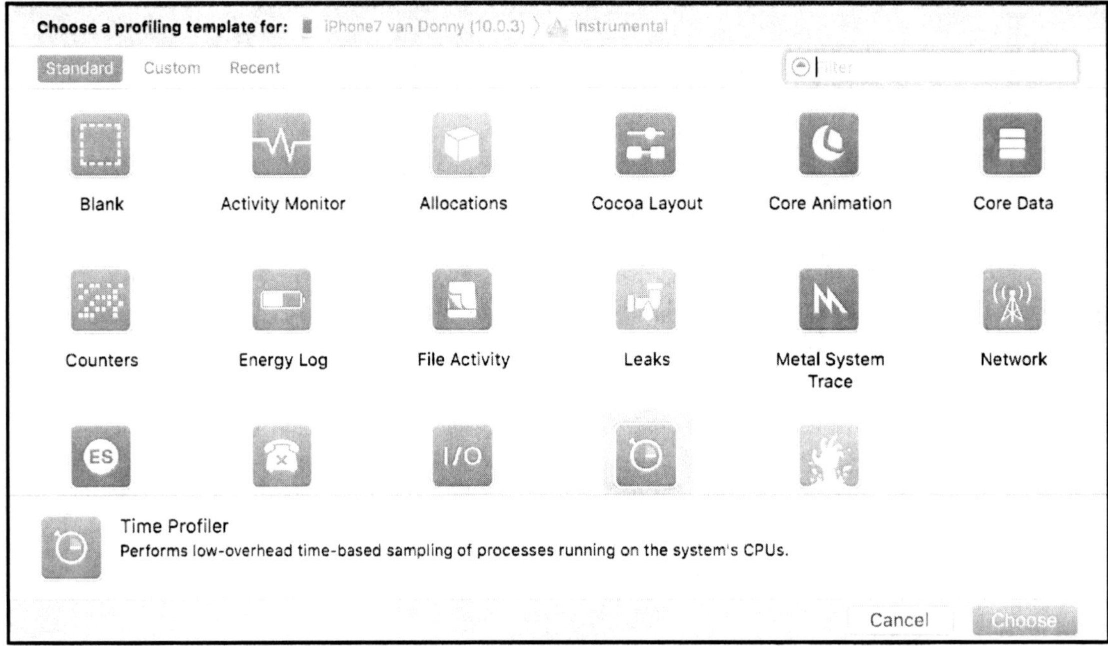

There are many available templates and most of them are pretty specific. For instance, the **Network** template will measure network usage. This isn't very relevant if you're not trying to debug networking issues. There are also templates available to profile animations, database operations, layout, Metal graphics performance, and more.

If you select a blank template, you're presented with the **Instruments** interface. The interface features a record button that we can use to start or stop profiling for our app. If you look further to the right side of the top toolbar, there's a plus icon. You can use this icon to add profiling for certain metrics yourself. You could use this to create a profiling suite that fits your needs without having to switch between the default templates all of the time. The center of the **Instruments** interface is the timeline. This is where graphs are drawn, depicting the measurements that were made for your app. The bottom section of the screen shows detail about the currently selected metric, as we'll see soon:

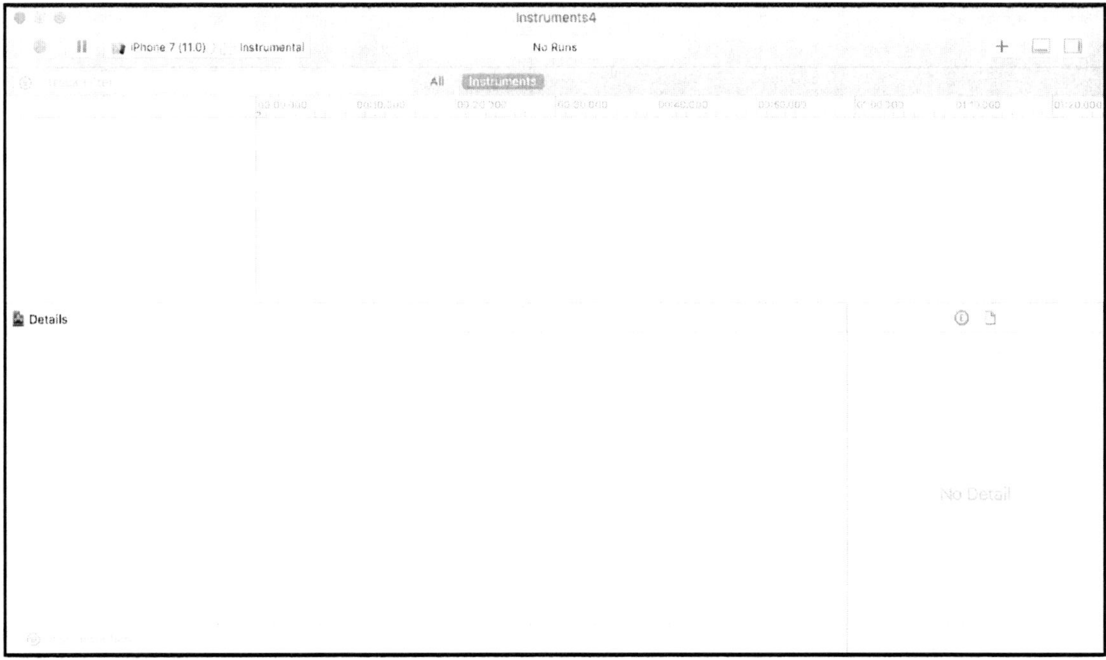

Now that you know a little bit about how the **Instruments** app is laid out, let's make an attempt at profiling the *Instrumental* app. The biggest issue in the app is the choppy scrolling. We know that the app has a memory issue, but choppy scrolling occurs even if the app's memory usage is low. This should be a flag that a memory leak probably isn't the problem that is causing the collection views to scroll badly. Something in the code is likely to be slow and **Instruments** can help us figure out which parts of the app's code are taking a long time to complete.

Discovering slow code

Whenever you find that your app is slow or choppy, chances are that something in your code is taking longer than it should, especially if your memory usage appears to be within reasonable range. For instance, if your app uses less than 50 MB, memory is not likely to be an issue for you, so seeking the problem in your code makes a lot of sense.

To discover slow code, you should profile the app by either selecting **Product** | **Profile** in the toolbar of Xcode or by pressing Cmd+ *I*. To figure out what the code is doing, you need to select the **Time Profiler** template once **Instruments** asks you which template you want to use. This template measures how long certain blocks of code run.

To record a profiling session of our app, make sure that a device is connected to your Mac and make sure that it's selected as the device that your app will run on by selecting your iOS device from the list of devices and simulators in the scheme toolbar menu in Xcode. Once you've selected your device, start profiling the app. When **Instruments** launches, pick the **Time Profiler** template and hit record. Now use the app to navigate to a collection and begin scrolling until the app starts feeling choppy and scroll some more. After seeing the app stutter a couple of times, there should be enough data to start filtering out what's going on. Press the stop button to stop the recording session.

If you take a first look at the data we've recorded, you'll notice a graph that has a bunch of peaks. This part of the timeline is marked CPU, and if you hit Cmd + *a* couple of times to zoom in on this timeline, you'll note that these spikes seem to last longer and longer as the scrolling becomes choppier and choppier. We must be on to something here; it looks like something is going on that makes these peaks last longer every time they occur.

In the bottom section of the window, you'll find an overview of the code in the app that has been executed while the recording session was active. The code is separated by a thread and since we're seeing the user interface lagging, we can be pretty sure that something on the main thread is slow. If you drill down a couple of levels, though, you won't find much useful information. It doesn't even look like most of the executed code is code that we wrote! Take a look at the following screenshot:

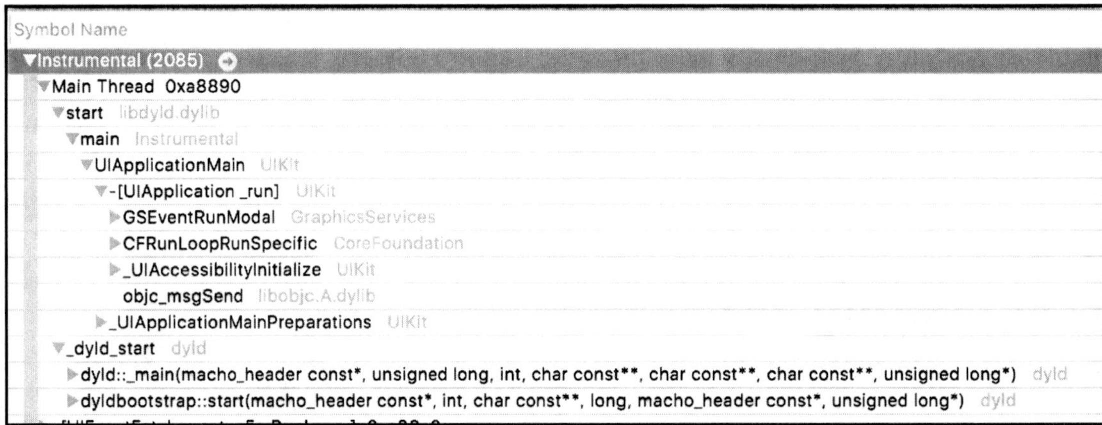

This is fine, though. We should apply a couple of filtering options to clean up this list, and it will soon become clear which part of our code is misbehaving. If you click on the **Call Tree** button in the bottom of the window, you can invert the call tree and hide system libraries, in addition to separating code by thread:

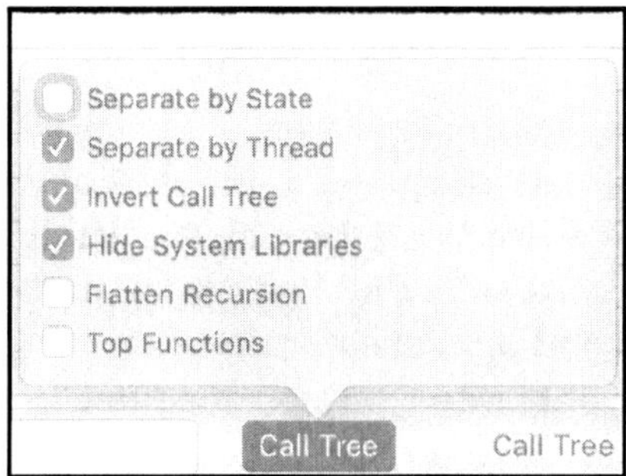

Doing this makes sure that you will only see code that you wrote and instead of drilling our way down from `UIApplicationMain`, we get to directly see the methods that have been tracked in our profiling session:

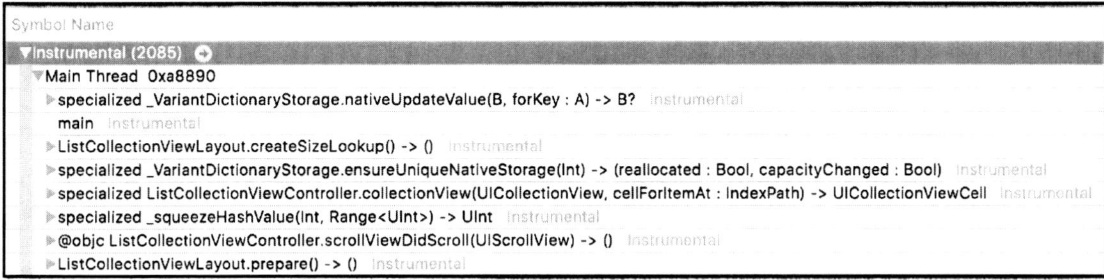

Upon examining the output, it's immediately clear that our issue is in the collection view layout. On the left side of the detail area, the percentage of time spent in a certain method is outlined and we can see that a huge percentage of time is spent in a method we don't know, nor did we write it. It's got something to do with a dictionary, but it's not entirely clear right away. The first candidate that does make sense, because it's code that is actually written inside of the project, is `ListCollectionViewLayout.createSizeLookup()`. This method is way too slow for our liking. Let's see if we can figure out why we're spending so much time in that specific method.

It's probably tempting to immediately point at the `createSizeLookup()` method and call it slow. It would be hard to blame you if you did, that method is a pretty rough one because we're actually computing an entire layout there. However, this layout is being computed pretty efficiently. Unfortunately, we can't really prove this with our current data in **Instruments**. If we could see the time each individual method call takes, we would be able to prove the claim that `createSizeLookup()` is not slow.

What we can prove, though, is that `createSizeLookup()` is called way more often than it should be called. If we add a `print` statement at the start of this method, you'll see that we get literally hundreds of prints as we scroll through the list. If we dig deeper and figure out when we call `createSizeLookup`, we'll find two places; in the `prepare()` method where `createSizeLookup` is called, and it is called again in `rectForThumbAtIndex(_:)`. This is strange because `rectForThumbAtIndex(_:)` is called in a loop inside of the `prepare` method after we've already generated the size lookup.

More importantly, as the number of items in the collection grows, the number of items we loop over grows too. It looks like we've found our bug. We should be able to safely remove the call to `createSizeLookup()` from `rectForThumbAtIndex(_:)` because the lookup is already created before we loop over the items, so it's safe to assume that the lookup exists whenever we call `rectForThumbsAtIndex(_:)`. Go ahead and remove the call to `createSizeLookup()` and run your app on the device. Much smoother now, right?

To make sure that everything is fixed, we should use **Instruments** again to see what the Time Profiler report looks like now. Start a new Time Profiler session in **Instruments** and repeat the steps you did before. Navigate to a collection and scroll down for a while so we load lots of new pages.

Looking at the result of our tests now, the percentage of time spent in `createSizeLookup()` has dramatically decreased. It has decreased so much that it's not even visible as one of the heaviest methods anymore. The app performs way better now and we have the measurements to prove it. Refer to the following screenshot:

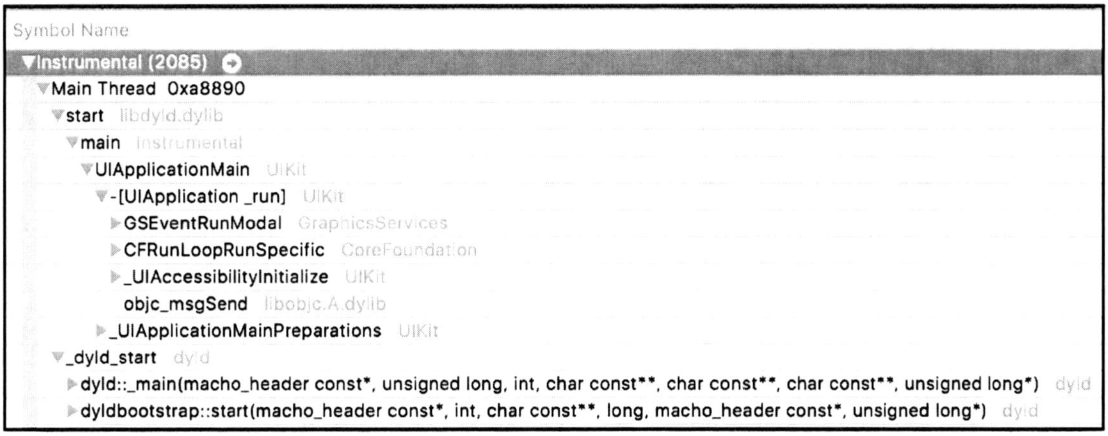

```
Symbol Name
▼Instrumental (2085)
  ▼Main Thread 0xa8890
    ▼start libdyld.dylib
      ▼main Instrumental
        ▼UIApplicationMain UIKit
          ▼-[UIApplication _run] UIKit
            ▶GSEventRunModal GraphicsServices
            ▶CFRunLoopRunSpecific CoreFoundation
            ▶_UIAccessibilityInitialize UIKit
             objc_msgSend libobjc.A.dylib
          ▶_UIApplicationMainPreparations UIKit
    ▼_dyld_start dyld
      ▶dyld::_main(macho_header const*, unsigned long, int, char const**, char const**, char const**, unsigned long*) dyld
      ▶dyldbootstrap::start(macho_header const*, int, char const**, long, macho_header const*, unsigned long*) dyld
```

Now that the visual performance issue is solved, you can navigate through the app it and everything is working smoothly, but if you take a look at the memory usage in **Instruments**, the memory usage still goes up all the time. This means that the app might have another problem in the form of a memory leak. Let's see how to discover and fix this leak with **Instruments**.

Closing memory leaks

Usually, if you navigate around in your app, it's normal to see memory usage spike a little. More view controllers on a navigation controller's stack mean that more memory will be consumed by your app. This makes sense. When you navigate back, popping the current view controller off the navigation controller's stack, you would expect the view controller to be deallocated and the memory to be freed up.

The preceding scenario is exactly how *Instrumental* should work. It's OK if we use some more memory if we're deeper in the navigation stack, but we expect the memory to be freed back up after the back button is tapped.

In the *Instrumental* app, the memory just keeps growing. It doesn't really matter if you drill deep into the navigation stack, hit back, or scroll a lot, once memory has been allocated it never seems to be deallocated. This is a problem, and we can use **Instruments** to dig into our app to look for the issue. Before we do this, though, let's have a deeper look at memory leaks, how they occur, and what the common causes are.

Understanding what a memory leak is

When your app contains a memory leak, this means that it's using more memory than it should. More specifically, the app fails to release memory that is no longer needed. We can essentially differentiate between different scenarios where this could occur. Once you're aware of them, they could be quite easy to spot. If you haven't seen them before or have never even heard of them, it's easy to fall into the trap of having a memory leak in your app.

Preventing objects from using infinite memory

The first type of memory leak we can identify is one where an object is allowed to take up an infinite amount of memory without any restrictions. A common example for this is caching data. When you implement a cache that holds on to certain model objects, API responses, or other data that was expensive to obtain in the first place, it's easy to overlook the fact that you essentially just built yourself a memory leak.

If your user is using your app and your cache object just keeps on caching more and more data, the device will eventually run out of memory. This is a problem because if we don't free the memory in time, your app will be terminated by iOS to make sure that essential processes and other apps don't suffer because of your app's out of control memory usage.

Luckily, it's easy to solve issues such as these. The operating system will notify your app through the `NotificationCenter` whenever it needs you to free up memory. Listening to this notification and purging any cached data you can recreate or reload will prevent your app from hogging memory and, ultimately, it prevents your app from being terminated due to memory reasons.

A very simple example of an image cache class that purges its cache when memory is tight is shown in the following code:

```
class ImageCache: NSObject {
    var cache = [UIImage]()
    override init() {
        super.init()
        NotificationCenter.default.addObserver(self, selector:
#selector(purgeCache), name: .UIApplicationDidReceiveMemoryWarning, object:
nil)
    }
    deinit {
        NotificationCenter.default.removeObserver(self, name:
.UIApplicationDidReceiveMemoryWarning, object: nil)
    }
    @objc func purgeCache() {
```

```
            cache.removeAll()
        }
    }
```

All you need to do is listen for the `.UIApplicationDidReceiveMemoryWarning` notification and purge any data that you can recreate when needed. Always make sure to unsubscribe from the notification when your class is deinitialized. If you don't do this correctly, chances are that you're creating a reference cycle, which is coincidentally the next type of memory leak that we'll discuss.

Avoiding reference cycles

When an object contains references to other objects, you should always be careful to avoid situations where both objects continuously hold a reference to each other. For example, a relationship between a table view and its delegate or data source could become a reference cycle if the relationship isn't managed properly. Objects can only be deallocated and the memory they use can only be freed if there are no objects referencing them anymore:

The preceding figure illustrates this. The view controller holds onto to the `tableView` and the `tableView` holds on to its delegate, which is the view controller. This means that neither object can ever be deallocated because for both the view controller and the `tableView` there is always at least one object referencing each at any given time. Of course, Apple has made sure that this doesn't occur in your apps by making sure that a `tableView` does not hold on to its delegate forever. You'll see how in just a second.

Another situation where a reference cycle could be created is in a closure. When you implicitly reference `self` in a closure, the compiler complains that you must explicitly refer to `self`. Doing this creates a reference to `self` inside of the closure, potentially resulting in a reference cycle. Throughout this book, you've seen a bunch of closures and we've always used a capture list when we referred to `self` inside of the closure:

```
api.fetchData { [weak self]
    self?.tableView.reloadData()
}
```

The preceding example shows an example of using a capture list, it's the part right before the in a keyword. The list captures a `weak` reference to `self`, which means that we don't create a reference cycle between the closure and `self`. If our `api` object somehow stores the closure in a variable and we haven't used a weak reference to `self`, we potentially have a reference cycle. If the `api` object itself is held onto by another object, we can be pretty sure that a reference cycle is created.

Making the reference `weak` tells the app that the reference to `self` does not add up to the reference count of `self`. This means that if there are only weak references left to an object, it's OK to deallocate it and free the memory. Memory management, and more specifically reference counts, isn't a simple subject. One way to think about this subject is that your app has an internal count of the number of objects that point to another object. For instance, if you create an instance of a `UIView` inside of a `UIViewController`, the reference count for the `UIView` is one. When the `UIViewController` is deallocated, the reference count for the `UIView` is zero, meaning that it can be deallocated safely.

If the `UIView` has a reference to the `UIViewController` as well, both objects will keep each other around because the reference count for each instance won't ever reach zero. This is called a reference cycle. This cycle can be resolved by making at least one of the references involved a `weak` reference. Since `weak` references don't contribute to the reference count, they prevent reference cycles from happening. This is how Apple has made sure that a `tableView` does not create a reference cycle with its delegate or data source; the references are marked as `weak`.

As an alternative to making a reference `weak`, you can also mark it as `unowned`. While weak is essentially a safe optional value, unowned makes the object implicitly unwrapped. It's often best to take the safe route and mark a captured reference as weak because your app won't crash if the `weak` referenced instance has been deallocated somehow, while it would crash if the reference is `unowned`.

Reference cycles aren't easy to grasp, especially if you consider weak references and reference counting. It's really easy to find yourself confused and frustrated. Luckily, the *Instrumental* app contains a couple of issues with references and retain cycles, so we can try and understand them better by discovering them in our app.

Discovering memory leaks

To figure out why the memory usage of *Instrumental* increases every time a new screen is loaded in the app, we're going to profile our app using the Allocations template. When you've started a new Allocations profiling session, navigate through the app and you'll see the memory usage graph rise consistently. This behavior is typical for a memory leak, so it's time to dig in deeper to figure out what we're doing exactly that causes this to happen. Take a look at the following screenshot:

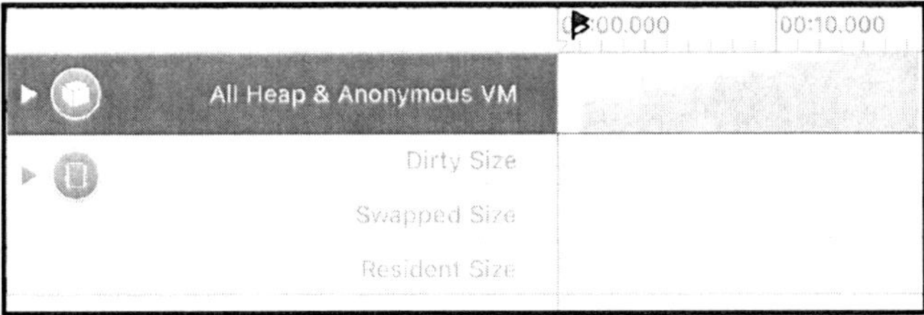

If you look at the detail area in **Instruments**, there is a lot of information there that does not make a lot of sense. A lot of the objects that are created are not objects created or managed by us, which makes it really hard to figure out what's causing our problem. It's not very likely to be an issue with UIKit, for instance, and even if it is, we can't really fix that. Luckily, you can use the search dialog in the top-right corner of the detail area to look for objects that do belong to us, giving us insight into what's happening with the objects we create.

If you look for the word *Instrumental* you'll find a couple of objects, and they should all look familiar to you. In the detail area, you can now see the number of instances of a certain object that is in memory. Refer to the following screenshot:

Graph	Category	Persistent B...	# Persistent
	Instrumental.ListCollectionViewCell	50,62 KiB	90
	Instrumental.ListCollectionViewController	4,97 KiB	6
	Instrumental.ListCollectionViewLayout	1,97 KiB	6
	Instrumental.ListViewController	800 Bytes	1
	Instrumental.AppDelegate	32 Bytes	1

If you look closely, you'll find that there are way more collection view cells, collection view controllers, and collection view layouts present than we'd expect. We can only show one collection view at a time, and when we navigate back to the list view controller, we expect the collection view controller to be deallocated since nothing should be referencing it anymore.

When we segue to one of the collection view controllers, it's added to the `viewControllers` array on the navigation controller. This means that the navigation controller keeps a reference to the `viewControllers`, which means that it should not be deallocated; the reference count for the view controller is **1** at this point.

When we pop back to the list view controller, the navigation controller removes the collection view controller from its `viewControllers` array. The result of this is that the reference count for the collection view controller is now decremented since the navigation controller is not referencing it anymore. This puts the reference count at 0, meaning that the collection view controller should be deallocated and the memory should be freed up.

However, something is preventing this from happening, because the collection view controller remains allocated according to our observations in **Instruments**. Unfortunately, **Instruments** does not tell us much more than we just saw. Objects are sticking around for too long, which means that we've created a retain cycle somehow. This probably means that something is referencing the collection view controller and the collection view controller is referencing something else in turn.

To figure out what's going on, we should probably start searching for the collection view controller. The collection view controller has a delegate relationship with an object conforming to `ListCollectionDelegate`. It also acts as a delegate for the list collection view cells it displays, and it's also a delegate for the detail view. All the delegate relationships are references to other objects. These delegates could very well be the source of our trouble. We can use Xcode to visualize all the objects in memory and see how they relate to each other. This means that it's possible to capture the state of the app's memory once we've seen a couple of collections, and we can actually see which objects are holding references to other objects. This enables us to visually look for reference cycles instead of blindly guessing.

To visualize your app's memory usage, build and run the app and navigate to a couple of screens. Then open the memory view in the Debug navigator in Xcode and finally click the **Debug Memory Graph** button in the bottom toolbar of the screen:

After clicking this button, Xcode will show you a visual representation of all memory that your app is using. In the toolbar on the left side of the screen, look for the `ListCollectionViewCell` and click it. Xcode will show you the relationship between the `CollectionViewCell` and other objects. At first glance, nothing special is happening. There is a list view controller, which holds a reference to a collection view, then there are a couple of other objects, and finally, there's the collection view cell:

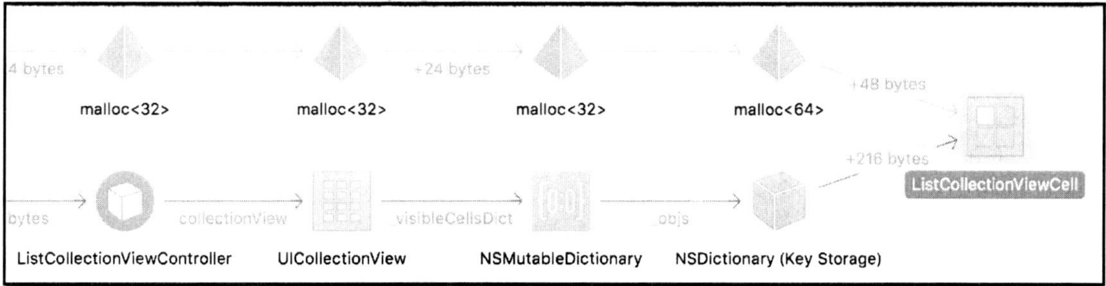

Next, click on the collection view controller. When you click this, a couple of different views could be shown to you. One shows that there's a navigation controller that points to an array, which eventually points to the collection view controller. This is the graph you would expect to see; it's exactly the relationship between navigation controllers and view controllers that we've discussed before:

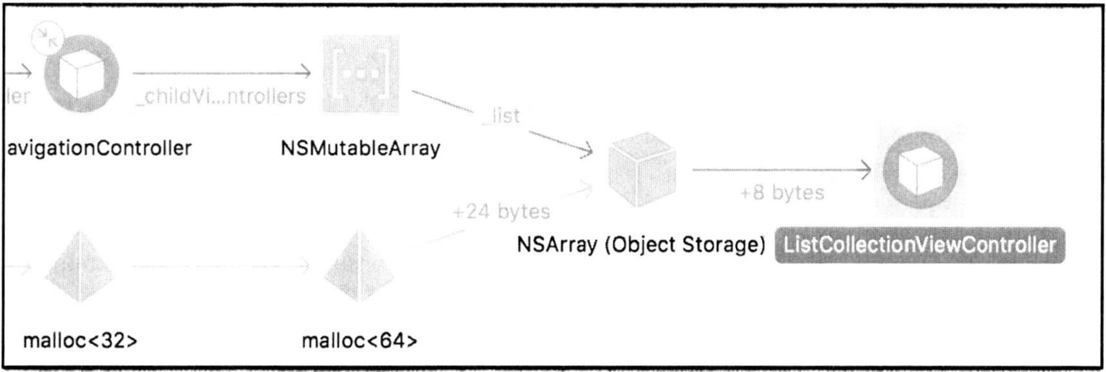

The other situations you might see are not like this at all. They show collection view cells that directly point to the collection view controller. If you compare this to what you've seen before, there is no way to make sense of it. The first collection view controller we looked at is the one that's currently displayed. That's why the navigation controller is there. The second one, however, is not tied to a navigation controller. It's not currently displayed and it seems that the only reason for it to stick around is the collection view cells pointing to it:

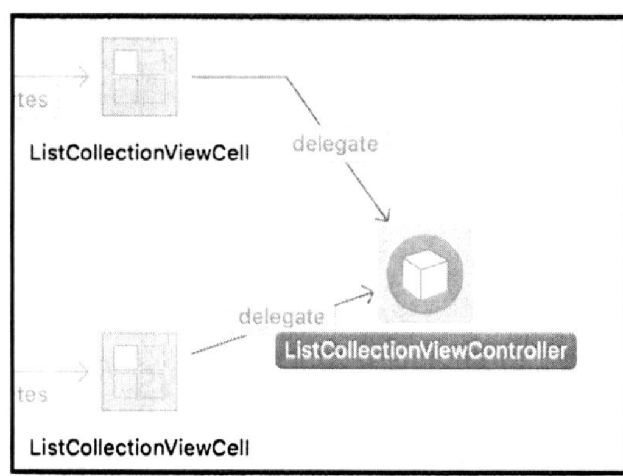

This is pretty typical for a reference cycle. Objects that should be long gone stick around because somewhere, somehow, they are keeping references to each other. Now that we suspect that the delegate relationship between the collection view controller and the collection view cells is causing our problems, we can begin fixing them.

In this case, the fix is pretty simple. We need to make the delegate relationship between the cell and the controller `weak`. Do this by opening `ListCollectionViewCell.swift` and changing the delegate declaration as shown. `weak var delegate: CollectionItemDelegate?`

Marking the delegate as weak breaks the reference cycle because the references aren't strong anymore. This essentially tells our app that it's OK if the referenced object is deallocated. One final adjustment we must make is to constrain the `CollectionItemDelegate` to class instances only. Due to the nature of value types such as structs, we can't mark references to them as `weak`, and since a protocol can be adopted by both value and reference types, we must constrain the protocol to class instances only. Update the declaration for the `CollectionItemDelegate` protocol as shown:

```
protocol CollectionItemDelegate: class
```

If you run the app now, you can safely navigate around and both the memory debugger and **Instruments** will prove that you no longer have any reference cycles in your app. It's possible that **Instruments** still tells you that your memory usage is growing. Don't worry about this too much, you did your job making sure that your code is safe and that all memory that you don't use any more can be freed up.

The example of a reference cycle you just saw is a very common one. A common way to avoid reference cycles through delegate is to try and make all of your delegates weak by default. This prevents you from making mistakes that you might not catch right away and it's often the safest route to go. Do note that there are many ways in which a reference cycle can occur, and you should always use the appropriate tools to try and troubleshoot your memory issues.

Summary

You've learned a lot about measuring your app's performance in this chapter. You've also learned how to find common issues and how to use **Instruments** to figure out what's going on behind the scenes for your app. In your day-to-day development cycle, you won't use **Instruments** or Xcode's memory debugger very often. However, familiarizing yourself with these tools can literally save you hours of debugging. It can even help you to discover memory leaks or slow code before you ship your app.

Try to audit and measure several aspects of your app while you're developing it, and you can see how the performance of certain aspects of your app improves or degrades over time. This will help you to avoid shipping an app that's full of slow code or memory leaks. However, don't go overboard with optimizing until you encounter actual problems in your app. Prematurely optimizing your code often leads to code that is hard to maintain. The fixes we applied in this chapter are pretty simple; we had a few small bugs that could be fixed in just a few lines of code. Unfortunately, fixing issues in your app aren't always this easy. Sometimes, your code is as fast as it can be, yet it still takes too long and it makes scrolling your tables or collections choppy.

In the next chapter, we'll see how to fix this using asynchronous code and operations.

23
Offloading Tasks with Operations and GCD

The previous chapter showed you how to use instruments to measure your code's performance. This is a vital skill in discovering slow functions or memory leaks. You saw that sometimes it's easy to fix slow code and increase performance by simply fixing a programming error. However, the fix isn't always that easy. Some code simply can't be written to be fast.

An example of this that you've already seen in this book is networking. Whenever you fetch data from the network, you do so asynchronously. If you don't make networking code asynchronous, execution of your app would halt until the network request is finished. This means that your app could freeze for a couple of seconds in bad circumstances.

Another example of slow code is loading an image from the app bundle and decoding the raw data into an image. For small images, this task shouldn't take as long as a networking request, but imagine loading a couple of larger images. This would take longer than we'd want to and it would significantly damage your scrolling performance, or render the interface unresponsive for longer than you should be comfortable with.

Luckily, we can easily make our code run asynchronously through dispatch queues. In Objective-C and early versions of Swift, this was mostly known as GCD. In Swift 3, the `DispatchQueue` class was introduced, improving both the APIs related to dispatch queues and simplifying their naming a bit.

This chapter will teach you how to make use of dispatch queues to write asynchronous code which can perform slow operations away from the main thread, meaning that they don't block the interface while they're running. Once you've got the hang of using dispatch queues, we'll look for reusable pieces of code, and we're going to abstract them into Operations.

We'll cover the following topics in this chapter:

- Writing asynchronous code with dispatch queues
- Creating reusable tasks with Operations

By the end of this chapter, you'll be able to enhance your apps by optimizing your code for asynchronous programming. You'll also be able to abstract certain tasks into Operations in order to make your app easier to understand and maintain.

Writing asynchronous code

In `Chapter 10`, *Fetching and Displaying Data from the Network*, you had your first encounter with asynchronous code and multithreading. We didn't go into too much detail regarding multithreading and asynchronous code because the subject of threading is rather complex, and it's much more suited for a thorough discussion in this chapter.

If you're unclear on what has already been explained, feel free to skip back to `Chapter 10`, *Fetching and Displaying Data from the Network*, to review the information presented there. The biggest takeaway for this chapter is that networking is performed on a background thread to avoid blocking the main thread. Once a network request is done, a `callback` function is executed, which allows you to use the main thread to update the user interface.

In iOS, the main thread is arguably the most important thread you need to keep in mind. Let's see why.

Understanding threads

You've seen the term thread a couple of times now, but you never learned explored any of the details about threads. For instance, you never really learned what a thread is, or how a thread works. This section aims to make the subject of threading a lot clearer to you so you can fully understand what a thread is, and why they are such a vital part of building apps.

A good way to mentally think of a thread is a stack of instructions. In iOS, your app typically starts off with a single thread: The main thread. This thread is also known as the UI thread. It's called the UI thread because the main thread is where all of the user interface elements are drawn, rendered, and pushed to the screen. Anything that is related to the user interface must be executed on the main thread, so if you consider a thread as a stack of instructions, it becomes easy to see why it's important that the main thread doesn't become stuck performing a very slow instruction:

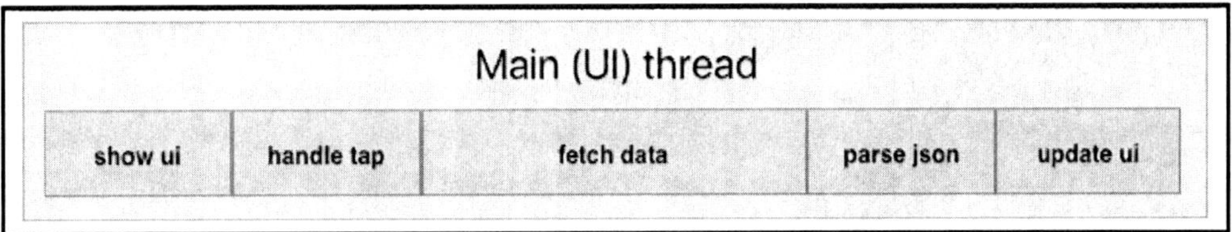

The preceding figure depicts a timeline where all code is executed on the main thread. Notice how we can't update the interface until the fetch data and parse json instructions are completed. Also note that fetching data takes a lot longer than displaying the interface or handling a tap. During the fetch data instruction, the app will not be able to update any user interface elements, or process any gestures or taps. This means that the app is practically frozen until the data is fetched and parsed.

Obviously, a good, responsive application can't afford to wait for slow instructions. The interface should always respond to user input; if this isn't the case, the app will feel slow, buggy, choppy, and just all-round bad. This is where multithreading becomes interesting.

We can run multiple instruction stacks at the same time. Each stack is called a thread, and we can execute certain instructions on a different thread to ensure that the interface remains responsive:

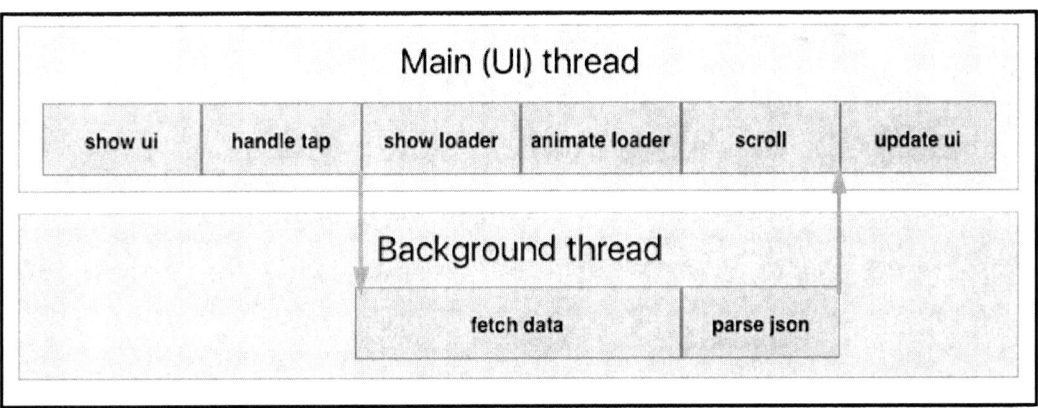

This second figure depicts a more desirable scenario. The main thread only handles user-interface-related tasks such as handling taps, animating loaders, and scrolling. The background thread takes care of the tasks that don't relate to the user interface and could potentially take a while to finish. By removing these instructions from the main thread and placing them on a different thread like iOS does by default for networking, we ensure that our app remains responsive, even if the network requests take several seconds to finish or never finish at all.

Your app can utilize a large number of threads for different tasks.

The number of threads isn't infinite, so even if you use threading like you should, you should still make sure that you optimize your code as much as possible to avoid locking up several threads with slow code.

In `Chapter 22`, *Discovering Bottlenecks with Instruments,* we used instruments to locate a piece of code that was slow. This resulted in an instruction on the main thread that took a very long time to complete, resulting in a frozen interface. Threading would not have solved this issue. The code that was slow was tightly related to the user interface because the collection view can't be rendered without calculating the layout first. This is a scenario where it's extremely important to make sure that you write optimized code, instead of simply relying on threads for anything that's slow.

Now that we've established an understanding of threads and how they can be utilized in your apps, let's have a look at how to manually offload tasks to different threads.

Using dispatch queues in your application

A basic understanding of threads is good enough for you to start using them in your applications. However, once you start using them, chances are that they suddenly become confusing again. If this happens to you, don't worry; threading is not easy. Now, let's go ahead, dive deep, and look at an example of threaded code:

```
var someBoolean = false

DispatchQueue(label: "MutateSomeBoolean").async {
    // perform some work here
    for i in 0..<100 {
        continue
    }
    someBoolean = true
}

print(someBoolean)
```

The preceding snippet demonstrates how you could mutate a global variable after performing a task that is too slow to execute on the main thread. We create an instance of a `DispatchQueue` and give it a label. This will create a new thread on which we can execute instructions. This queue represents the background thread from the visualization we looked at earlier.

Then, we call the `async` method on the `DispatchQueue`, and we pass it the closure that we want to execute on the queue we just created. The loop inside of this block is executed on the background thread; in the visualization, this would roughly compare to the fetch data and parse JSON instructions. Once the task is done, we mutate `someBoolean`.

The last line in the snippet prints the value of `someBoolean`. What do you think the value of `someBoolean` is at that point? If your answer is `false`, good job! If you thought `true`, you're not alone. A lot of people who start writing multithreaded, asynchronous code don't immediately grasp how it works exactly. Let's visualize the preceding snippet like we did with the networking example. Then, it will start to become clear what happened and why the value for `someBoolean` is `false`:

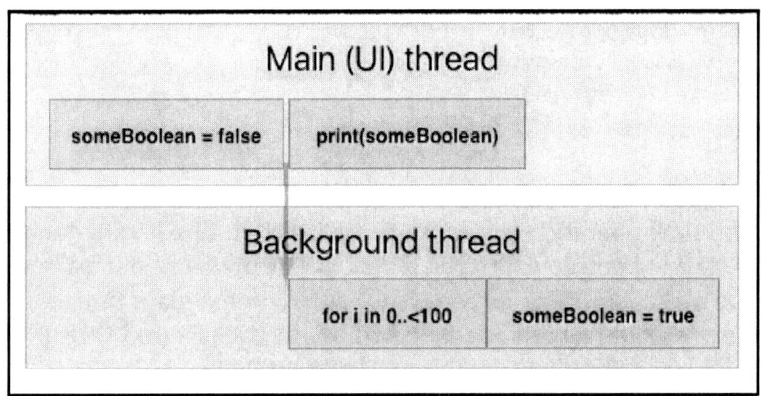

Because we're using a background thread, the main thread can immediately move to the next instruction. This means that the for loop and the print run simultaneously. In other words, we print `someBoolean` before it's mutated on the background thread. This is both the beauty and a caveat of using threads. When everything starts running simultaneously, it is hard to keep track of when something is completed.

The preceding visualization also exposed a potential problem in our code. We create a variable on the main thread and then we capture it in the background thread and mutate it there. Doing this is not recommended; your code could suffer from unintended side effects such as race conditions, where both the main thread and the background thread mutate a value, or worse, you could accidentally try to access a `CoreData` object on a different thread than the one it was created on. The `CoreData` objects do not support this, so you should always try to make sure that you avoid mutating or accessing objects that are not on the same thread as the one where you access them.

So, how can we mutate `someBoolean` safely and print its value after mutating it? Well, we could use a `callback` closure of our own. Let's see what this would look like:

```
func executeSlowOperation(withCallback callback: @escaping ((Bool)
- > Void)) {
    DispatchQueue(label: "MutateSomeBoolean").async {
        // perform some work here
        for i in 0..<100 {
            continue
        }
        callback(true)
    }
}

executeSlowOperation { result in
    DispatchQueue.main.async {
        someBoolean = result
        print(someBoolean)
    }
}
```

In this snippet, the slow operation is wrapped in a function that is called with a **callback closure**. Once the task is complete, the `callback` is executed and it is passed the resulting value. The closure makes sure that its code is executed on the main thread. If we don't do this, the closure itself would have been executed on the background thread. It's important to keep this in mind when calling your own asynchronous code.

The `callback`-based approach is great if your `callback` should be executed when a single task is finished. However, there are scenarios where you want to finish a number of tasks before moving over to the next task. We have already used this approach in `Chapter 11`, *Being Proactive with Background Fetch*. Let's review the heart of the background fetch logic that was used in that chapter:

```
func application(_ application: UIApplication,
performFetchWithCompletionHandler completionHandler: @escaping
(UIBackgroundFetchResult) -> Void) {
    let fetchRequest: NSFetchRequest<Movie> = Movie.fetchRequest()
    let managedObjectContext = persistentContainer.viewContext
    guard let allMovies = try?
managedObjectContext.fetch(fetchRequest) else {
        completionHandler(.failed)
        return
    }
    let queue = DispatchQueue(label: "movieDBQueue")
    let group = DispatchGroup()
    let helper = MovieDBHelper()
```

```
        var dataChanged = false
        for movie in allMovies {
            queue.async(group: group) {
                group.enter()
                helper.fetchRating(forMovieId: movie.remoteId) { id,
                 popularity in
                    guard let popularity = popularity, popularity !=
                       movie.popularity else {
                        group.leave()
                        return
                    }
                    dataChanged = true
                    managedObjectContext.persist {
                        movie.popularity = popularity
                        group.leave()
                    }
                }
            }
        }
        group.notify(queue: DispatchQueue.main) {
            if dataChanged {
                completionHandler(.newData)
            } else {
                completionHandler(.noData)
            }
        }
    }
```

When you first saw this code, you were probably able to follow along, but it's unlikely that you were completely aware of how complex this method really is. Multiple dispatch queues are used in this snippet. To give you an idea, this code begins on the main thread. Then, for each movie, a background queue is used to fetch its rating. Once the fetch is complete, the managed object context's dispatch queue is used to update the movie. Think about all this switching between dispatch queues that is going on for a second. Quite complex, isn't it?

The background fetch method needs to call a completion handler when it is done fetching all the data. However, we're using a lot of different queues, and it's kind of hard to tell when we're done with fetching everything. This is where dispatch groups come in. A dispatch group can hold on to a set of tasks that are executed either serially, or in parallel.

When you call `enter()` on a dispatch group, you are also expected to call `leave()` on the group. The enter call tells the group that there is unfinished work in the dispatch group. When you call `leave()`, the task is marked as completed. Once all tasks are completed, the group executes a closure on any thread you desire. In the example, the `notify(queue:)` is the method used to execute the completion handler on the main queue.

It's okay if this is a bit daunting or confusing right now. As mentioned before, asynchronous programming and threads are pretty complex topics, and dispatch groups are no different.

The most important takeaways regarding dispatch groups are that you call `enter()` on a group to submit an unfinished task. You call `leave()` to mark the task finished and, lastly, you use `notify(queue:)` to execute a closure on the queue passed to this method once all tasks are marked completed.

The approach you've seen so far makes direct use of closures to perform tasks. This causes your methods to become long and fairly complex since everything is written in line with the rest of your code. You already saw how mixing code that exists on different threads can lead to confusion because it's not very obvious which code belongs on which queue. Also, all this inline code is not particularly reusable. We can't pick up a certain task and execute it on a different queue, for instance, because our code is already sort of tightly coupled to a certain dispatch queue.

In order to improve this situation, we should make use of `Operations`.

Creating reusable tasks with Operations

We just explored `DispatchQueues` and how we can use them to schedule tasks that need to be performed on a different thread. You saw how this speeds up code and how it avoids blocking the main thread. In this section, we're going to take this all one step further. The first reason for this is because our asynchronous work would be better organized if we had an object that we could schedule for execution rather than a closure. Closures pollute code and they are much harder to reuse.

The solution to this is using an `Operation` instead of a closure. And instead of queueing everything in a dispatch queue, we should queue `Operation` instances on an `OperationQueue`. The `OperationQueue` and the `DispatchQueue` are similar, but not quite the same. An `OperationQueue` can schedule `Operations` on one or more `DispatchQueue`. This is important because of the way in which `Operations` work.

Using an `OperationQueue`, you can execute `Operations` in parallel or serially. It is also possible to specify dependencies for `Operations`. This means that we can make sure that certain `Operations` are completed before the next operation is executed. The `OperationQueue` will manage the `DispatchQueues` needed to make everything happen, and it will execute the `Operations` in the order in which they become ready to execute.

The next section will briefly cover some of the basic concepts of `Operations`.

If you're looking to learn more about using `Operations` in interesting and advanced ways, make sure to check out *Apple's Advanced NSOperations talk* from *WWDC 2015*. All code for this talk is presented in Swift 2.0, so you'll need to make an attempt to translate this code to Swift 4.0 somehow, but it's definitely worth a watch.

Using Operations in your apps

Let's take a deep dive into `Operations` and refactor the background fetch code from the `FamilyMovies` app so it uses `Operations`. To do this, we're going to create two `operation` subclasses: One that fetches data and updates the `movie` object, and one that calls the completion handler.

Our setup will use a single `OperationQueue` onto which we push all of the instances of our fetch `operation` subclass, and one operation that calls the background fetch completion handler. The completion operation will have all of the fetch operations as its dependencies.

Whenever you create an `OperationQueue` instance, you can specify the amount of concurrent `Operations` that can be executed on the queue. If you set this to zero, the `Operations` will be executed in the order in which they become ready. An operation is considered ready when all preconditions for the operation are met. A great example of this is dependencies. An operation with dependencies is not ready to execute until all of the `Operations` that it depends on are completed. Another example is exclusivity. You can set an operation up in such a way that you make sure that only one operation of the current type is running at any given time. An operation like that is not ready unless there is no operation with the same type running.

If you set the maximum number of concurrent `Operations` to a higher number, it's not guaranteed that this amount is actually used. Imagine setting the maximum amount to 1,000, and you place 2,000 `Operations` on the queue. It's not likely that you will actually see 1,000 `Operations` being executed in parallel. The system ultimately decides how many `Operations` will run at the same time, but it's never more than your maximum value. Apart from the fact that a parallel queue will execute more tasks at the same time, no `Operations` are started before they are ready to execute, just like on a serial queue.

The first thing we'll do is simply create an `OperationQueue` that we can use to push our `Operations` onto. Replace the implementation of `application(_:performBackgroundFetchWithCompletionHandler:)` in the `AppDelegate` with the following:

```
func application(_ application: UIApplication,
performFetchWithCompletionHandler completionHandler: @escaping
(UIBackgroundFetchResult) -> Void) {
    let queue = OperationQueue()
    let fetchRequest: NSFetchRequest<Movie> = Movie.fetchRequest()
    let managedObjectContext = persistentContainer.viewContext
    guard let allMovies = try?
managedObjectContext.fetch(fetchRequest) else {
        completionHandler(.failed)
        return
    }
}
```

This implementation creates a queue for us to push our `Operations` onto. We also fetch the movies like we did before because, ultimately, we'll create an update operation for each movie. Let's create an implementation for this operation now. Create a new group in the project navigator and name it `Operations`. In it, you should add a file called `UpdateMovieOperation.swift`.

Every custom operation you create should subclass the `Operation` base class. The `Operation` class implements most of the glue and boilerplate code involved in managing and executing `Operations` and `queues`. In this file, we'll need to implement a few mandatory, read-only variables that indicate the state of our operation. To update other objects about state changes, we must use the iOS **key value observing (KVO)** pattern. This pattern enables other objects to receive updates when a certain key in an object changes. You'll see how to fire the KVO notifications from your operation soon. Let's define our variables and initializer first. Add the following basic implementation for `UpdateMovieOperation`:

```
import Foundation

class UpdateMovieOperation: Operation {
    override var isAsynchronous: Bool { return true }
    override var isExecuting: Bool { return _isExecuting }
    override var isFinished: Bool { return _isFinished }
    private var _isExecuting = false
    private var _isFinished = false
    var didLoadNewData = false
    let movie: Movie
    init(movie: Movie) {
```

```
            self.movie = movie
        }
    }
```

You'll immediately notice that we override a couple of variables. These are the read-only variables that were mentioned earlier. The `isExecuting` and `isFinished` variables simply return the value of two private variables that we'll mutate appropriately later. Furthermore, we keep track of whether new data was loaded, and we have a property and initializer to attach a `movie` to our operation. So far, this operation isn't very exciting; let's look at the actual heart of the operation. Add these methods to your `operation` class:

```
override func start() {
    super.start()
    willChangeValue(forKey: #keyPath(isExecuting))
    _isExecuting = true
    didChangeValue(forKey: #keyPath(isExecuting))
    let helper = MovieDBHelper()
    helper.fetchRating(forMovieId: movie.remoteId) { [weak self]
id,
      popularity in
        defer {
            self?.finish()
        }
        guard let popularity = popularity,
            let movie = self?.movie,
            popularity != movie.popularity
            else { return }
        self?.didLoadNewData = true
        movie.managedObjectContext?.persist {
            movie.popularity = popularity
        }
    }
}

func finish() {
    willChangeValue(forKey: #keyPath(isFinished))
    _isFinished = true
    didChangeValue(forKey: #keyPath(isFinished))
}
```

Apple's guidelines state that we should override the `start()` method and initiate our operation from there. You'll note that we call the superclass implementation first; this is because the superclass takes care of several under-the-hood tasks that must be performed in order to make `Operations` work well. Next, we use `willChangeValue(forKey:)` and `didChangeValue(forKey:)` to fire the KVO notifications mentioned earlier.

We don't actually change the value for the key, but rather the private property that reflects the value of the key we've changed.

Next, we use our code from before to fetch and update the `movie`. A `defer` block is used to call the `finish()` method, regardless of how our network request went. By using `defer` instead of manually calling `finish()` when appropriate, we can't forget to call `finish()` if our code changes. The `finish()` method makes sure that the operation queue is notified about the operation's completion by firing the corresponding KVO notifications.

We should create another operation that calls the background fetch completion handler. This operation should loop through all of its dependencies, check whether it's a `movie` update operation, and if it is, it should check whether new data was loaded. After doing this, the completion handler should be called with the corresponding result and, finally, the operation should finish itself. Create a new file in the `Operations` folder and name it `BackgroundFetchCompletionOperation`. Add the following implementation:

```
import UIKit class BackgroundFetchCompletionOperation: Operation { override
var isAsynchronous: Bool { return true } override var isExecuting: Bool {
return _isExecuting } override var isFinished: Bool { return _isFinished }
var _isExecuting = false var _isFinished = false let completionHandler:
(UIBackgroundFetchResult) -> Void init(completionHandler: @escaping
(UIBackgroundFetchResult) -> Void) { self.completionHandler =
completionHandler } override func start() { super.start()
willChangeValue(forKey: #keyPath(isExecuting)) _isExecuting = true
didChangeValue(forKey: #keyPath(isExecuting)) var didLoadNewData = false
for operation in dependencies { guard let updateOperation = operation as?
UpdateMovieOperation else { continue } if updateOperation.didLoadNewData {
didLoadNewData = true break } } if didLoadNewData {
completionHandler(.newData) } else { completionHandler(.noData) }
willChangeValue(forKey: #keyPath(isFinished)) _isFinished = true
didChangeValue(forKey: #keyPath(isFinished)) } }
```

The implementation for this operation is pretty similarly constructed to the `movie` update operation. We initialize the operation with the completion handler that was passed to the background fetch method in `AppDelegate`, and we call it once we've determined whether new data was fetched. Let's see how all this comes together by updating the background fetch logic in `AppDelegate`. Add the following code to the `application(_:performFetchWithCompletionHandler:)` method, right after fetching the `movies`:

```
let completionOperation =
BackgroundFetchCompletionOperation(completionHandler:
completionHandler)

for movie in allMovies {
    let updateOperation = UpdateMovieOperation(movie: movie)
    completionOperation.addDependency(updateOperation)
    queue.addOperation(updateOperation)
}

queue.addOperation(completionOperation)
```

This code is a lot more readable than what was in its place before. First, we create the completion operation. Next, we create an update operation for each `movie` and we add this operation as a dependency for the completion operation. We also add the update operation to the queue. Finally, we add the completion operation itself to the queue as well, and that's all we need to do. All of the `movie` update `Operations` will automatically start executing simultaneously and once they're all done, the completion operation becomes ready to execute. Once this happens, the completion operation will start running and the completion handler will be called.

Even though `Operations` involve a bit more boilerplate code in terms of managing execution state, you do end up with code that makes use of your `Operations` cleanly. We've only explored dependencies for now, but if you study *Apple's Advanced NSOperations* video that was mentioned earlier, you'll find that you can do really powerful, complex, and amazing things with `Operations`. However, even in a basic form, `Operations` can greatly improve your code and reduce complexity.

Summary

This chapter showed you that asynchronous code can be hard to understand and reason with, especially when a lot of code is running at the same time; it can be easy to lose track of what you're doing. You also learned that `Operations` can be a convenient way to reduce complexity in your application, resulting in code that is easier to read, change, and maintain. When an operation depends on multiple other `Operations` to be completed, it can be extremely convenient to use an `OperationQueue`, as it greatly reduces the complexity of the code you write.

It's been mentioned before, but if you intend to make use of `Operations` in your app, do make sure to check out *Apple's Demonstration of Advanced Operations* from *WWDC 2015*. The `Operations` are capable of far more than we've just seen, and it's strongly recommended to see how Apple uses `Operations` in order to create rock-solid apps. Once your app is covered by tests, measured with instruments, and improved with asynchronous code and `Operations`, it's probably time that you go and share your app with others. The next and final chapter of this book will show you how to set yourself up for deploying your app through *TestFlight* and the *App Store*.

24

Wrapping Up the Development Cycle and Submitting to the App Store

Possibly the most exciting part of the development cycle is getting your app out to some real-world users. The first step in doing so is usually to send out a beta version of your app so you can get some feedback and gather some real data about how your app is performing, before you submit to the App Store and release your app to the world. Once you're satisfied with the results of your beta test, you must submit your app to Apple so they can review it before your app is released to the App Store.

In this chapter, you'll learn everything about packing up your app and submitting it to iTunes Connect. From iTunes Connect, you can start beta testing your app and you can also submit it to Apple for review. The iTunes Connect portal is also used to manage your app's App Store description, keywords, imagery, and more. We'll cover how to properly fill everything out as well. We'll go through the following steps over the course of this chapter:

1. Adding your application to iTunes Connect.
2. Packaging and uploading your app for beta testing.
3. Preparing your app for launch.

These steps closely resemble the process you'll go through when you're ready to launch your own app. Let's get right to it, shall we?

Adding your application to iTunes Connect

The first thing you're going to want to do when you're gearing up to release your app is to register your app with **iTunes Connect**. To do so, you must be enrolled in the Apple Developer program. You can do this through Apple's developer portal at `https://developer.apple.com`. After purchasing your membership, you can log in to your **iTunes Connect** account on `https://itunesconnect.apple.com` using your **Apple ID**.

After logging into your **iTunes Connect** account, you are presented with a screen that has a couple of icons on it:

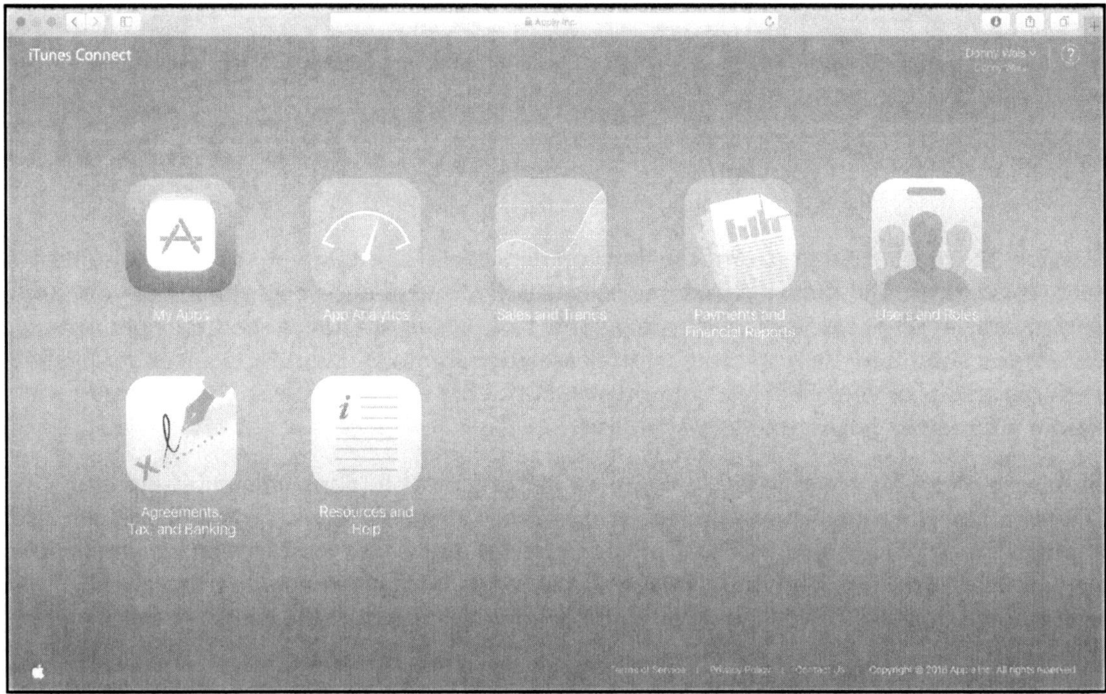

This screen is your portal to manage your App Store presence. From here, you can manage test users, track your app's downloads, track usage, and more. But most importantly, it's where you create, upload, and publish your apps to Apple's beta distribution program called **TestFlight** and to the App Store. Go ahead and peek around a bit; there won't be much to see yet but it's good to familiarize yourself with the **iTunes Connect** portal.

The first step in getting your app out to your users is to navigate to the **My Apps** section. Once you're inside of the **My Apps** area, you'll see all the apps you have currently created and you're able to add new apps. To add your app, click the **+** icon in the top left and click **New App**:

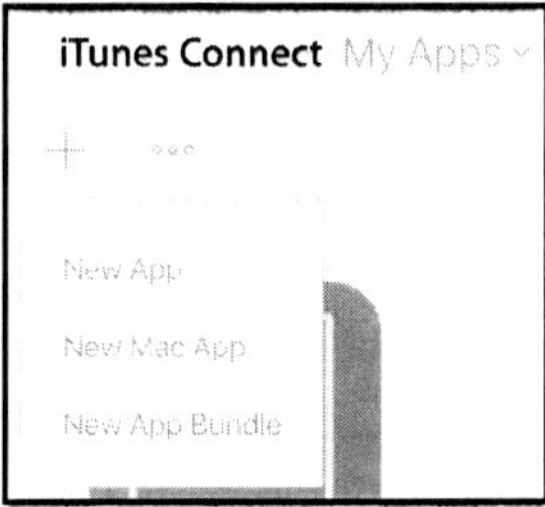

After clicking this, you're presented with a window in which you can fill out all the basic information about your app. This is where you reserve your app's name, select the platform on which it will be released, and more:

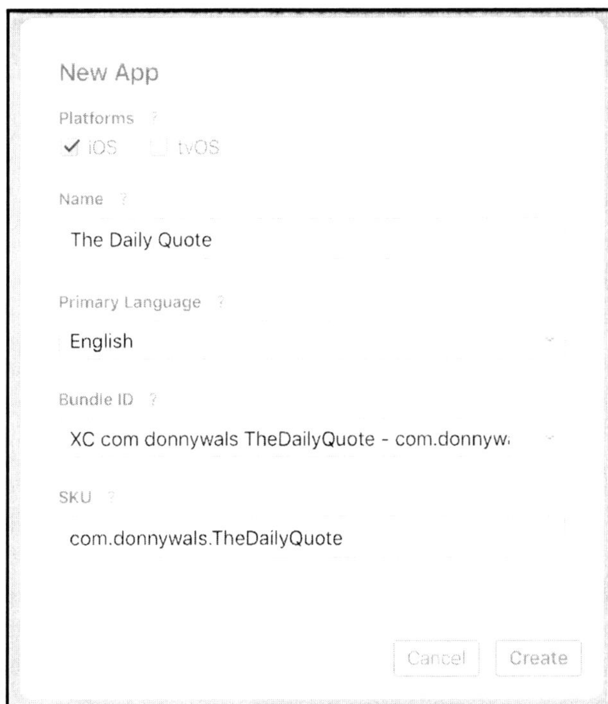

The **Bundle ID** field is a drop-down menu that contains all of the app IDs that you have registered for your team in Apple's developer portal. If you've been developing with the free-tier developer account up until the last minute, or you haven't used any special features such as push notifications or App Groups, chances are that your app's **Bundle ID** is not in the drop-down menu.

If this is the case, you can manually register your **Bundle ID** in the developer portal. Navigate to `https://developer.apple.com/` in your browser and click the **Account menu** item. From this page, you can manage certificates, Bundle IDs, devices, and more. A lot of this is automatically taken care of by Xcode but you'll occasionally find yourself in this portal, for instance, to manually register your app's **Bundle ID**:

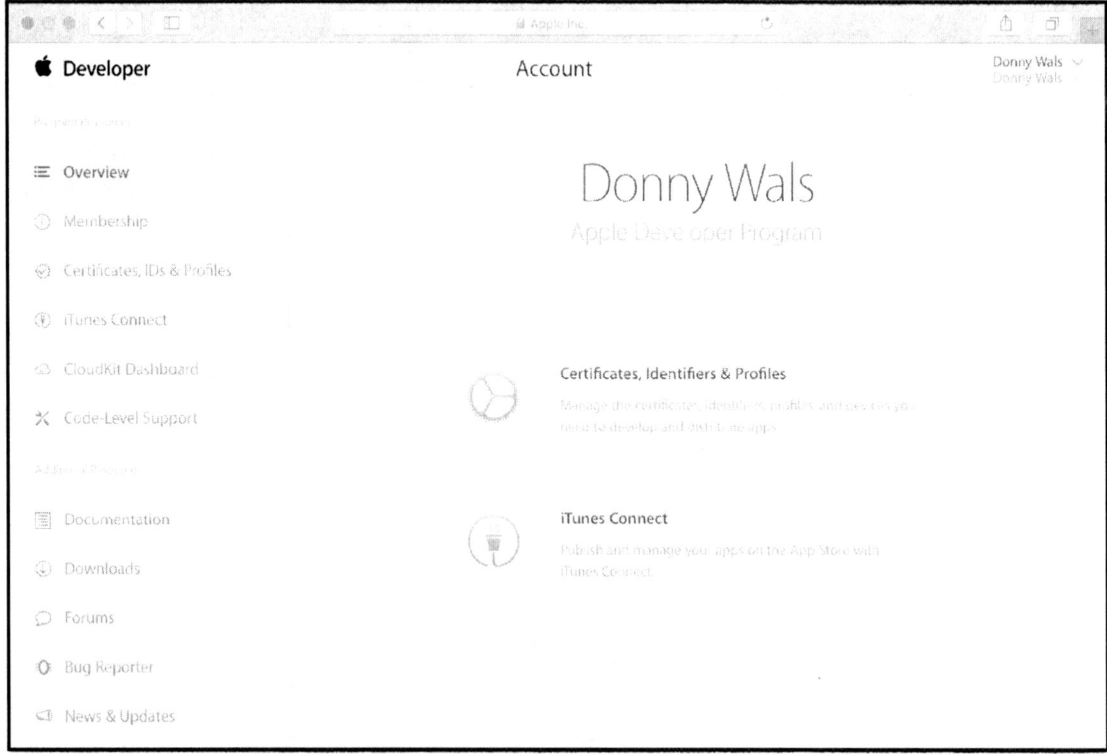

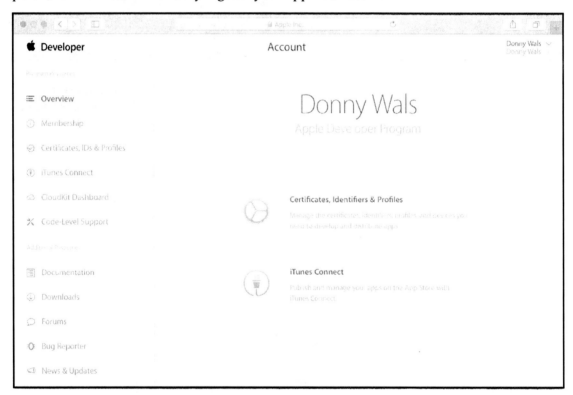

To register your **Bundle ID**, click on the **Certificates, IDs & Profiles** item on the left-hand side. On the page you're taken to, click **App IDs** in the menu on the left-hand side. This will present you with a list of currently registered apps. In the top-right corner, there's a **+** icon. Click this to **add a new ID to your profile**:

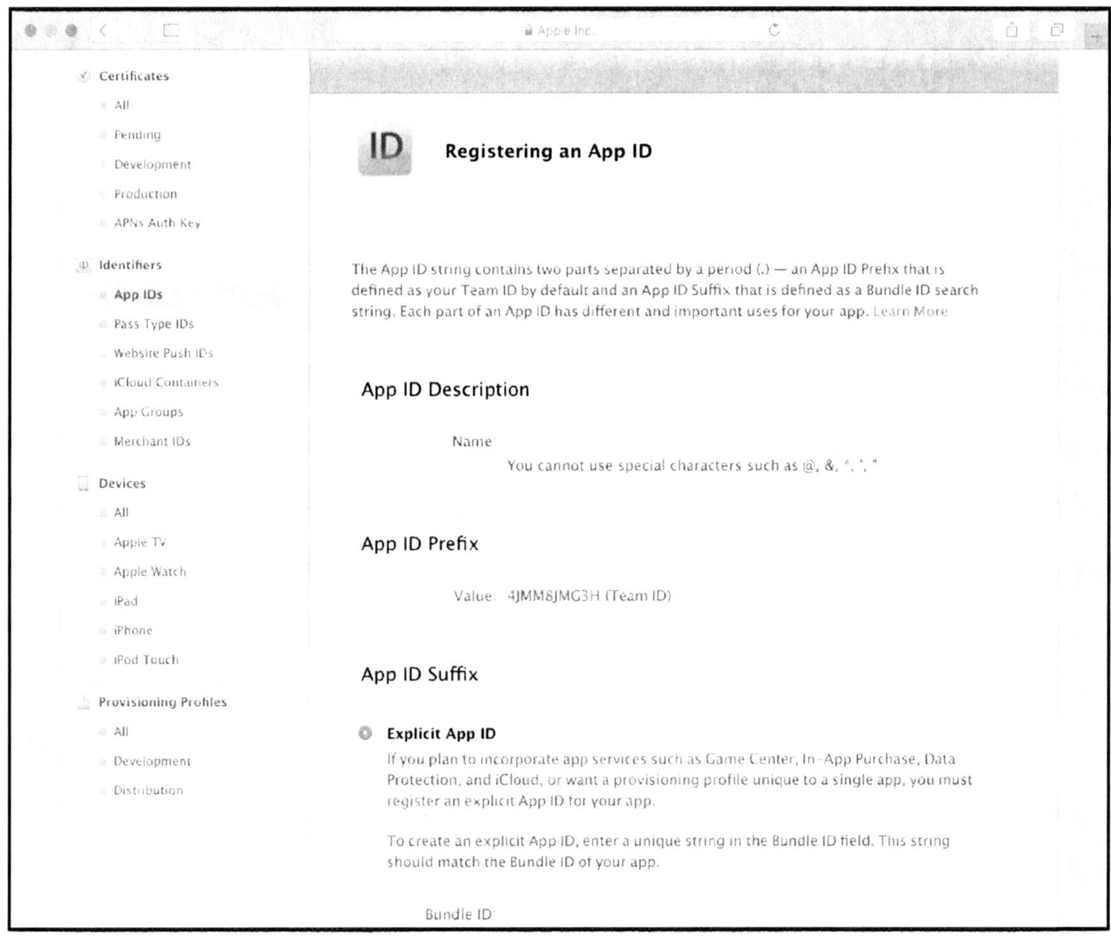

To add your **Bundle ID**, simply fill out the form fields. You'll want to use a descriptive name for your app's name. It can be the same as the name you have set for your app in Xcode but it can also be a different name; it doesn't have to match. Make sure to select the **Explicit App ID** field and copy the **Bundle ID** from your Xcode project. It's important that you perfectly match this. If you don't do this, you'll run into issues later because your app can't be identified.

Once you've done this, you can scroll all the way down and save your new ID. You don't have to select any capabilities since Xcode will automatically manage this for you when you enable or disable them in the **Capabilities** tab.

After manually registering your **Bundle ID**, you should be able to move back to **iTunes Connect**, add a new app, and select your app's **Bundle ID**. After you've done this and you've created your app in the **iTunes Connect** portal, have a look around in your app's settings. There are a lot of form fields that you can fill out. The first screen you'll see is your **App Information** screen. This is where you fill out basic information about your app, assign it a localized name that appears in the App Store, and you can assign categories to your app:

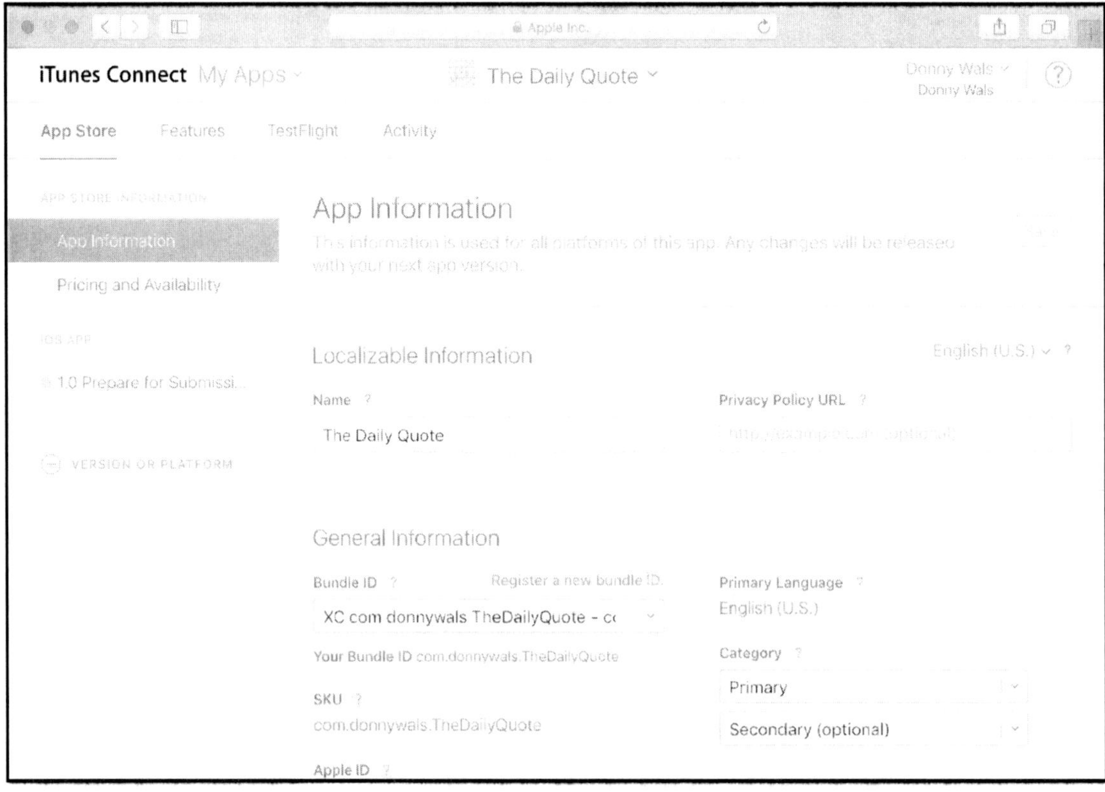

Next, there's the **Pricing and Availability** screen. This is where you decide in which countries your app can be downloaded and also how much it costs. Lastly, there is the **Prepare for Submission** menu item.

Whenever you add a new version of your app, you should fill out the form fields on this screen and there are quite a lot of them. The **Prepare for Submission** form is used to provide screenshots and add keywords, a description for your app, privacy policies, and more. Go ahead and have a look at what's in there. Luckily, everything you have to fill out is pretty straightforward.

Now that our app is registered and ready to be uploaded, let's go back to Xcode, package up the app, and send out some sweet beta invites to our testers!

Packaging and uploading your app for beta testing

To send your app out to both beta testers and real users, you must first archive your app using Xcode. Archiving your app will package up all contents, code, and assets. To archive your app, you must select **Generic iOS Device** from the list of devices your app can run on:

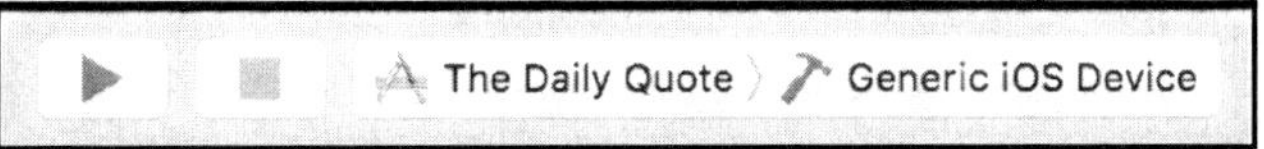

With this build device selected, select **Product** -> **Archive** from the top menu of Xcode. When you do this, a build will start that's a lot slower than usual. That's because Xcode is building your app in a way that enables it to run on all iOS devices. Once the archive is created, Xcode will automatically open the organizer panel for you. In this panel, you get an overview of all apps and archives that you have created:

Before you archive your app, you should make sure that your app is ready to release. This means that you must add all of the required app icon assets to the `Images.xcassets` resource. If your app icon set is incomplete, your app will be rejected upon upload to **iTunes Connect** and you'll have to generate your archive all over again.

When you're ready to upload your build to **iTunes Connect** and make it available for your beta testers and eventually for your users through the *App Store*, you should select your latest build and click the **Upload to App Store** button. A popup will appear to guide you through a couple of settings. You should typically use the default settings and click **Next**. Finally, your app will be verified based on metadata and uploaded to **iTunes Connect**. If there are errors in your archive, such as missing assets or unsigned code, you'll learn about it through error messages in the upload popup window. When your upload succeeds, you'll also be notified through the popup.

Once you've uploaded your build, you can go to the activity panel for your app in **iTunes Connect**. This is where you'll see your build's current status. Right after uploading, it will take a little while to process your app:

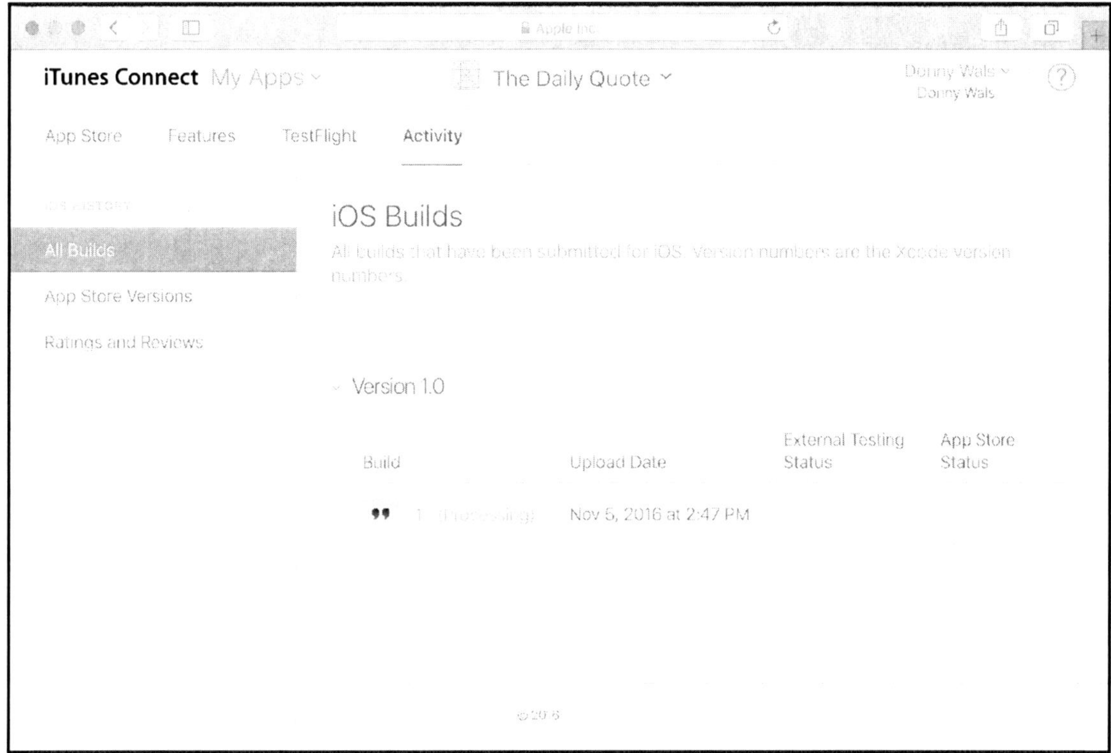

While the app is processing, you can start to prepare your **TestFlight** settings. Select the **TestFlight** menu item and fill out the Test Information form. If you're rolling out your beta test internationally, you might want to provide information in multiple languages, but you don't have to.

Next, select the **Internal Testing** menu item in the sidebar on the right. In this panel, you can select users that are added to your account for beta testing. This type of testing is often the first type of testing you do and it's mostly intended for testing apps inside of your team or with close friends and family. You can add more internal users to your account through the **Users and Roles** section in **iTunes Connect**.

Once your app is done processing, you'll receive an email and you can select which version of your app should be used for internal testing:

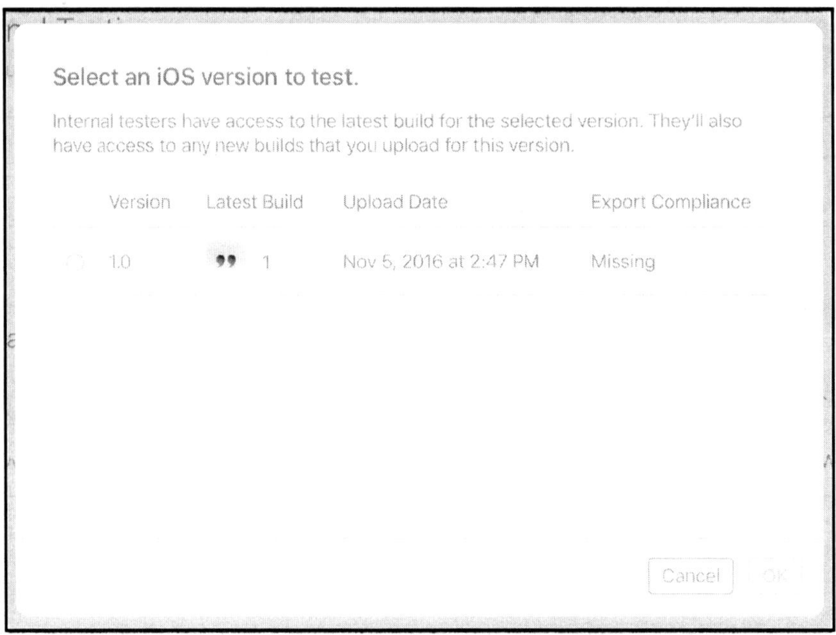

Once you've added testers and you've selected a build to test, you can click the **Start Testing** button to send out a beta invite to your selected testers. They will receive an email that enables them to download your app through the **TestFlight** app for iOS.

Once your internal testers are happy with your app, you can select some external beta testers for your app. External testers are typically people that aren't in your team or organization, for example, existing users of your app or a selection of people from your app's target audience.

Setting up an external beta test is done identically to how you've set up the internal test. You can even use the same build that you used for internal testing for external testing. However, external tests typically require a quick review by Apple before invites can be sent out. These reviews don't take long and passing the beta test review does not mean you'll also pass the *App Store* review.

This is all you need to know about setting up a beta test through **TestFlight**. When you're happy with the results of your beta test and your app has passed the real-world test, it's time for you to prepare to release your app into the wild through the *App Store*.

Preparing your app for launch

Moving from beta testing to releasing your app does not require much effort. You use the exact same version of your app as you've already exported and tested with your users. In order to be able to submit your app for review by Apple, you simply have to add more information about your app and you should set up your *App Store* presence. The first thing you should do is create a couple of screenshots of your app. You add these screenshots to your *App Store* page and they should look as good as possible because potential users will use screenshots to determine whether they want to buy or download your app or not. The simplest way to create screenshots is to take them on a 5.5-inch iPhone and a 12.9-inch iPad. Doing this will allow you to use the **Media Manager** feature in **iTunes Connect**, right under the screenshot area, to upload the large-sized media and have it scale down for smaller devices:

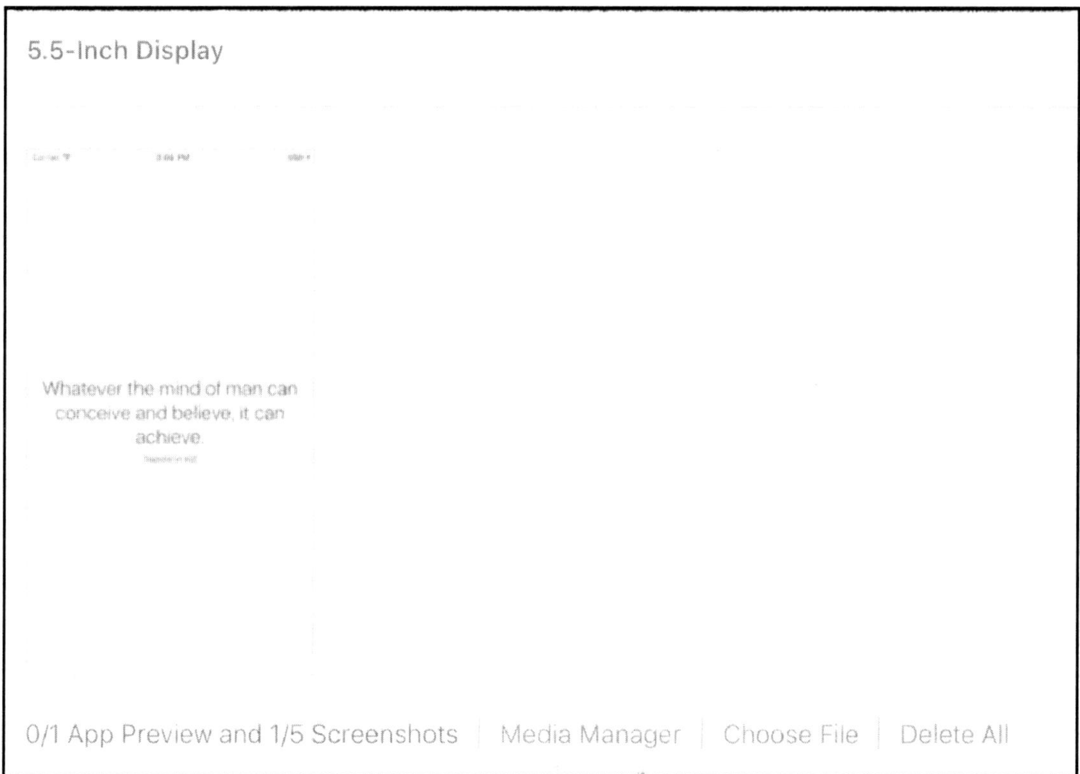

After submitting screenshots, you should also fill out a description and keywords for your application. Make sure that your description is clear, concise, and convincing. Your keywords should be used as much as you can; it's what Apple uses to match people's search queries with. Try to come up with synonyms or words you would look for when you'd search for an app that does what your app does.

If your app features an iMessage or Watch app, you should also upload screenshots for these apps as well. You can't provide separate keywords or descriptions for these extensions, but they will have their own image galleries in the *App Store*.

The next step in the submission form is to select your app binary and provide some general information about the app and the person responsible for publishing the app. Often, you'll want to select the version of the app you've been beta testing up to the point of release.

Lastly, you must provide some information to Apple about how your app should be reviewed. If your app required a demo account, provide credentials to the reviewer. If your app has been rejected before due to something being unclear, it's usually a good idea to clarify the past misunderstanding in the notes section. This has proven to help for some apps, resulting in accepted reviews at the first try rather than being rejected and providing explanations afterward. When everything is filled out, hit the **Save** button to store all of the information you just entered. Then, if you're satisfied with everything and ready to take the final leap toward releasing your app, press **Submit for Review** to initiate the review process.

Getting your app reviewed by Apple can take from a couple of days to a week or longer, so at this point, it's important that you simply patiently wait until you hear from Apple. Sending them inquiries about reviewing your app faster or asking them about the current status often yields no results so you shouldn't do that.

If you do need to get your app reviewed and released really fast and you have a legitimate reason, you can always apply for expedited review. If Apple agrees that a faster review will benefit not just you but also your users, your app could be reviewed in a matter of hours. Note that you should not abuse this. The more often you apply for an expedited review, the less likely Apple is to grant you an exception. Expedited reviews should only be requested in exceptional cases.

Well, time to get some cocoa, coffee, tea, or whatever you prefer to drink. It's time to sit back for a while and wait while Apple reviews your app so you can release it to the *App Store*.

Summary

This final chapter covered preparing to release your app. You learned how to archive and export your app. You saw how to upload it to **iTunes Connect** and how to distribute your app as a beta release. To wrap everything up, you saw how to submit your app for review by Apple in order to release it to the *App Store*. Releasing an app is exciting; you simply don't know how well your app will perform or if people will enjoy using it. A good beta test will help a lot, you'll be able to spot bugs or usability issues, but there's nothing like having your app in the hands of actual users.

A lot of developers invest a lot of time and effort into building their apps and you are one of them. You picked up this book and went from an iOS enthusiast to an iOS master who knows exactly how to build great apps that make use of iOS 10's new, awesome features. When you're ready to launch your own app into the *App Store*, you'll learn how exciting and nerve-racking it can be to wait for Apple to review and hopefully approve your app. Maybe you get rejected on your first try; that's possible. Don't worry too much about it, even the biggest names get rejected sometimes and often fixing the reason isn't too complex. Do make sure to read the *App Store* review guidelines before you submit; these guidelines give a pretty good indication about what you can and can't do in your apps.

Since this is the last chapter in this book, I would like to sincerely thank you for picking up this book and using it as one of the stepping stones toward becoming a master of iOS programming. I hope to have left you with the skills required to venture out on your own, read Apple's documentation, and build amazing applications. Thanks again and if you've built something cool using this book, please feel free to reach out to me. I would love to see your application.

Index

D

E

F

G

H

I

J

K

L

M

N

O

P

V

W

X

CPSIA information can be obtained
at www.ICGtesting.com
Printed in the USA
LVOW09s0734310118
564720LV00010B/419/P

Published in 2025 by
Unicorn, an imprint of Unicorn Publishing Group
Charleston Studio
Meadow Business Centre
Lewes BN8 5RW
www.unicornpublishing.org

ISBN 978 1 916846 08 1
10 9 8 7 6 5 4 3 2 1

Design by newtonworks.uk
Cover design by **Sukhi Kaur Chauhan**
Printed in Malta by Gutenberg Press

THE PERCEPTIVE INVESTOR

THE ART, SCIENCE & TEMPERAMENT OF SUCCESSFUL VALUE INVESTING

Ardal Gronager